Louisiana
Sojourns

Louisiana Sojourns

TRAVELERS' TALES AND LITERARY JOURNEYS

As Recounted by

John James Audubon, Kate Chopin,

Simone de Beauvoir, William Faulkner,

C. C. Lockwood, Frederick Law Olmsted,

Theodore Roosevelt, Frances Trollope,

Mark Twain, Charles Dudley Warner,

and Others . . .

FRANK DE CARO, EDITOR
ROSAN AUGUSTA JORDAN, ASSOCIATE EDITOR

LOUISIANA STATE UNIVERSITY PRESS   *Baton Rouge*

Designer: Michele Myatt Quinn
Typeface: Adobe Garamond
Typesetter: Wilsted & Taylor Publishing Services
Printer and binder: Thomson-Shore, Inc.

The research for this book was supported by the Louisiana Sea Grant College Program, a part of the National Sea Grant College Program maintained by the National Oceanic and Atmospheric Administration, U.S. Department of Commerce. Louisiana Sea Grant is also supported by the State of Louisiana.

Research for this book was also funded under a grant from the Louisiana Endowment for the Humanities, the state affiliate of the National Endowment for the Humanities.

Library of Congress Cataloging-in-Publication Data
Louisiana sojourns : travelers' tales and literacy journeys /
    as recounted by John James Audubon . . . [et al.] ;
    Frank de Caro, editor ; Rosan Augusta Jordan, associate editor.
        p. cm.
    Includes index.
    ISBN 0-8071-2239-4 (cloth : alk. paper).—ISBN 0-8071-2240-8 (pbk. : alk. paper)
        1. Louisiana—Description and travel. 2. Louisiana—Social life and customs.
    3. Travelers' writings, American. I. Audubon, John James, 1785–1851.
    II. De Caro, F.A. III. Jordan, R. A. (Rosan A.)
    F369.L896   1998
    917.6304—dc21   97-50292
                                                                                       CIP

CONTENTS

Preface to the Second Printing

As this second printing was in preparation, I happened to be progressing through a move from Baton Rouge to New Orleans, settling into a small but very pleasant house in the Garden District. Though serenely residential, my new neighborhood seems always to be full of people who are evidently tourists. Some clump in groups with tour guides, others consult maps or guidebooks. Some arrive in chauffeured cars that pull up to the celebrated Commander's Palace restaurant on Washington Avenue, others seem drawn to the gate of Lafayette Cemetery No. 1 across the street from Commander's. Cameras are in evidence. Anne Rice, the fantastically popular "vampire" novelist, has just moved from the neighborhood to a more suburban compound, but I hear visitors still asking for her also-departed shop in the little local retail center called The Rink. Into that same Rink's coffee shop come still others, looking for a toilet, looking for bottled water, looking to get out of a quick rain shower, sometimes even looking for coffee.

I assume that these people are drawn by the lure of the Garden District itself as the non–French Quarter, as that other historic pole of New Orleans: the one where the Americans "had" to settle because the Creoles refused to sell them property in the Vieux Carré (a good story, though history is more complex), and where those Americans built gracious mansions with rambling gardens. Perhaps recent celebrations of the bicentennial of the Louisiana Purchase, an event which brought about great influxes of Americans, has called additional attention to this neighborhood which they so shaped.

Why ever exactly they come, I hope that my tourists are having a good time here in my new neighborhood. Certainly they have made me think about what it means to live in a city and a state that have become increasingly dependent upon a tourism economy but even more so about what it means to travel in the twenty-first century. It is no secret that we live in an age of mass tourism, when vast numbers of people file on to planes or settle into cruise ships, are bused to sites of astonishing cultural importance, or are taken—sometimes by gondola, by mule cart, even by elephant—to see a great array of things that are thought to be worth seeing. What impressions and thoughts such experiences give us varies a great deal from person to person. For some of us the very experience of newness savored in places not our own is sufficient, or the pleasures of fun in the sun or the change of pace suffices. Some of us want to learn through travel about something, and tour-guide anecdotes, however disconnected, may fill the bill.

Others, however, are made uneasy at best by what they see as the superficiality of mass travel and may pause to wonder what it all means, why they travel, what, in the long run, their travels tell them about life and the human condition. Such folk may avoid tours (or find intimate, more specialized ones), shun what some of my British friends call triperies (those obvious destinations where the gangs of holiday-goers almost congeal), or somehow find their ways off the beaten track. Or they may simply attempt to better understand the places they go, to sample local ideas and aesthetics and history along with the local cuisine. Personally, I think that a knowledge of the past of a place visited is an important key to coming to deeper understandings of that place. A purpose of compiling *Louisiana Sojourns* was to provide one entrée into Louisiana by making available to those who might travel here some first-hand accounts of what this place was like in the past (and not necessarily the distant past) as their predecessor visitors and travelers saw it. I hoped that the selections in the book would provide some historical points of reference that might aid present-day visitors/readers to put themselves into a larger picture of travel and thus to appreciate Louisiana the more. I hoped that the selections would help them to slow down a little from the fast pace of postmodern tourists in order to better connect both intellectually and emotionally with what has been here in the Bayou State and what, in many ways, still is here. I continue to hope that the book will do that for some readers who have come or will come to Louisiana. Though I cannot say that I have seen any neighborhood tourists clutching *Louisiana Sojourns,* I like to imagine that my hopes already have been a little bit fulfilled and that some Louisiana travelers have had their travels enriched by this book.

More locally, an eminent humanist has been kind enough to tell me that he considers *Louisiana Sojourns* a "classic." It has been especially gratifying to know that this book has found some favor with Louisianians, who have enjoyed having a convenient source for some writings about their home, themselves, and their predecessors. In recent years Louisiana sometimes has received negative press. I hope that the writings collected in *Louisiana Sojourns* have helped us to remember that, whatever problems we may have, we also have a very fascinating and wonderful place in which to live, one that has attracted much attention over the years. I hope that we can preserve what is best and most interesting about Louisiana, and that *Louisiana Sojourns* can continue to remind us a little about what that is.

FRANK DE CARO
New Orleans, Louisiana
Memorial Day, 2004

PREFACE

This book is in part the result of an accident in my personal history, the fact that in 1970 I accepted a position in the English Department of Louisiana State University. Although academics often manage to largely ignore the places in which they end up living, I was a folklorist, and folklorists ignore what is around them at their peril. Though I had no particular previous interest in Louisiana culture or in Louisiana as a place, I immediately opened my eyes to what was here, frequently marveling, and gradually expanding my experience of the Bayou State over the years.

Of course, I was hardly the first to take a good look, and for many years I was struck by how popular Louisiana was as a destination or stopping point for tourists, travelers, itinerant writers, roving artists, and other visitors, whether prominent or obscure, whether reputable or less than respectable. As a sometime student of the state I developed an interest in how the place presented itself to outsiders and how it was presented by those outsiders who dropped by. From time to time I vaguely thought that a book which drew together some of the work of those who had come to Louisiana and recorded their adventures and impressions would produce a readable and informative volume. Nothing might ever have come out of that vague idea but for the encouragement of LSU Sea Grant Development. Though America's Sea Grant programs have been mostly concerned with such issues as the capacity of fisheries, wetlands loss, and beach erosion, the program at LSU was expanding its interest into tourism development and other areas. The program was therefore willing to support the research to actually produce a book such as I had envisioned, a book that could reflect the travelers of the past but also stimulate the visitors—as well as the residents—of the present by showing what was most of interest here and how it had been encountered by those who had already been here, whether recently or many years ago.

To that end, this book contains a selection of insightful and intriguing accounts of Louisiana travels and sojourns, but in addition each chapter is followed by a travel update (those for Chapters 8 and 9 are combined after Chapter 9). These updates provide additional information on the things and places noted in that section: cultural background, useful readings, and the present status of the locations visited by various traveler writers. Is the place still there? Has it changed? How? How can it be found today (or how can something similar be encountered)? Thus the updates give some helpful details to today's reader and traveler, but they are not meant to be exhaustive nor are they a guidebook. Those traveling in Louisiana today will find a number of useful guidebooks, such as *The Pelican Guide to Louisiana,* by Mary Ann Sternberg (Gretna, La., 1993); *Louisiana Off the Beaten Path,* by Gay Martin (Old Saybrook, Conn., 1993); *Louisiana Dayrides,* by Shelley N. C. Holl (Jackson, Miss., 1995); and *Country Roads of Louisiana,* by Glen Pitre and Michelle Benoit (Oaks, Pa., 1996). The major publishers of travel guides, such as Fodor and Frommer, frequently update their volumes on Louisiana and are particularly strong on accommodations and dining. *Louisiana Yesterday and Today: A Historical Guide to the State* (Baton Rouge, 1996), by John Wilds, Charles L. Dufour, and Walter G. Cowan, offers capsule information on a variety of topics from a historical perspective and also contains sightseeing sections on the various Louisiana regions, emphasizing historical sights.

I have had the help of numerous people, institutions, and organizations in putting this book together. Jack Van Lopik and Mike Liffmann at LSU Sea Grant Development were particularly encouraging. Faye Phillips, Elaine Smyth, and their staff at LSU Libraries Special Collections provided their usual helpful service in giving me access to the premier library holdings for Louisiana materials. My colleague Robin Roberts offered valuable advice at several phases of the project. Several anonymous commentators on my proposal for grant funding provided insightful perspectives on my plans to carry the project out. The anonymous outside reader for Louisiana State University Press presented me with many useful suggestions. Kay Metelka at the Louisiana Endowment for the Humanities gave me helpful advice on grant applications to her agency. At the LSU Press Maureen Hewitt encouraged the book and shepherded it along through various stages; John Easterly provided much help, particularly in the very laborious matter of obtaining permissions to reprint; and Catherine Landry capably oversaw many of the details of editing, illustration, and design decisions. Sarah Richards Doerries edited the manuscript with insight, care, and tact. And I owe thanks to a number of other individuals, notably Germain Bienvenu, Preston Collins, Richard Condrey, Christie David, Irene DiMaio, Jon Donlon, Brent Duet, Jesse Gellrich, H. F. Gregory, Shelley Holl, Jerry Kennedy, Beverly Knox, Jane Landry, Margaret Marshall, Jack May, Bruce Morgan, Elizabeth Oliver, Maida Owens, Susan Roach and Peter Jones, Harold Schexnayder, Harry Schexnayder, Mark Schexnayder, and Patti Young.

I wish to thank Louisiana State University Libraries, Special Collections, for permission to use the WPA transcript in their holdings of *Nouveaux Voyages dans l'Amérique Septentrionale*, by Jean Bernard Bossu, translated by Olivia Blanchard.

I and my publisher are also grateful to those who have granted permission to reprint previously published material. They are individually acknowledged elsewhere. We have made every attempt to locate the authors of copyrighted material or their heirs or assigns and would be grateful for information that would allow us to correct any errors or omissions for subsequent editions.

I am especially grateful to Rosan Jordan, who agreed to act as associate editor for the book, playing a significant role particularly in the planning and shaping of the travel updates and the chapter introductions, and in the final selection of material to be included.

Original titles for selections have been retained where possible, but I have provided titles for a number of selections.

FRANK DE CARO
Baton Rouge, Louisiana
All Saints' Day, 1997

Louisiana
Sojourns

The Importance of Passing Through: Traveler Writers in Louisiana

All travel has its advantages," Samuel Johnson comments. "If the passenger visits better countries, he may learn to improve his own, and if fortune carries him to worse, he may learn to enjoy it." Yet Johnson goes on to profess to his reader, "You have often heard me complain of finding myself disappointed by books of travel." The reason for this, he says, is that places are very much like one another. When there are differences "not unworthy of curiosity," the traveler writer "seldom stays long enough to investigate and compare."[1]

One of the traveler writers[2] included in the present volume, Frederick Turner, had a similar doubt expressed to him one evening in Louisiana. While journeying along the Gulf Coast for material for a travel book, Turner had sought out Barry Ancelet, Cajun folklorist, commentator, and radio personality, for insights into French Louisiana. Ancelet, rocking sagely in his own

1. Quotations from Samuel Johnson are from *A Book of Travellers' Tales,* ed. Eric Newby (New York, 1987), 15.

2. I use the term *traveler writer* rather than the more common *travel writer* because the latter is most used to refer to professional journalists who cover travel and because the former seems more inclusive—taking in those who were primarily travelers and whose writings may have been almost incidental, as well as those who *were* writers but whose accounts included here were not necessarily intended to be primarily about travel.

Tourists, by Caroline Durieux, for a guide-book produced by the Louisiana Writers' Project

From *New Orleans City Guide* (Boston, 1938), by permission of Charles W. Durieux

kitchen, first criticized another travel book—William Least Heat Moon's popular *Blue Highways*—as superficial.[3] Then he queried Turner, "How long are you going to be in this part of the country?" When Turner replied that he had been in the vicinity for two weeks and planned on moving into Texas shortly, Ancelet—"mourning the evident folly of the enterprise"—asked, "Do you think you can get to know a country in a couple of days?" In reflecting on the incident Turner was to wonder, "What, after all, could I say to the thrust of his question? What *were* a traveler's impressions worth?"

3. William Least Heat Moon, *Blue Highways: A Journey into America* (Boston, 1982).

That is, indeed, a key question about travel writing.

Of course, natives have a knowledge of place that transcends that of the visitor, and to understand a place we need to read what local observers have to say—about history, about mores, about the pace of life. Yet often enough the traveler has a distinct advantage in writing about place. For one thing, locals simply may not write about their own environment and lives. In the past particularly, often they were not even able to do so. The "natives" encountered by Western voyagers to Africa or the South Pacific and the European peasantry or urban masses seen by travelers of the nineteenth century, for example, were by and large not literate, and travelers' accounts may be the only written impressions we have of such people's lives and situations. In Louisiana, for instance, we turn to early French travel accounts for colonial impressions of Native Americans, and traveler writers also provide much of the descriptive material on the Acadians well into the twentieth century.

Even when locals are able to write about themselves and their land, they may not be interested in communicating what outsiders would like to know. They may leave much unspoken—for it is too familiar to comment upon— or fail to notice things that are too ingrained to consciously conceive. Thus traveler writers, often persons motivated by an abiding curiosity about places not their own, become important interpreters, able to mediate between what outsiders might like to know about a place and what can be perceived by visiting there.

Furthermore, the traveler writer is able to tell us about not only place but the experience of travel in that place, so as potential travelers we can empathize with his experience and understand something of what we might see from our own outsider's perspective. Traveler writers may enjoy singular adventures, or they may come to have acute insights into a place because of their lively minds or their backgrounds (what Dr. Johnson means when he says, "Books of travel will be good in proportion to what a man has previously in his mind; his knowing what to observe; his power of contrasting one mode of life with another").

Traveler writers may come with stereotypes of place that can result in simplified pictures or can prevent them from seeing some of the subtle realities of the lands wherein they journey. Certainly some of the writers included in this book—Lyle Saxon, William Least Heat Moon, even the sophisticated Simone de Beauvoir—seem to play upon stereotype. Yet, despite this, travel writing often can offer insightful visions of a place, records of often otherwise

Coachmen vie for a visitor's custom. Various nineteenth-century visitors to New Orleans commented upon the aggressive manner in which drivers of the horse-drawn cabs solicited business.

From George A. Sala, *America Revisited* (London, 1883)

unrecorded modes of living, and accounts of personal experiences with landscapes and communities not our own—accounts that put us readers as fellow travelers into indirect but potentially intense communication with other places and the very flow of travel itself.

This book is a collection of accounts of travel in Louisiana, a place that has long been a magnet for visitors. The term *travel* has been interpreted broadly, however, to include what we call *sojourns*—extended stays (for who can say how long travels should last, and many famous travelers have stopped for long periods at particular destinations). Although most of the authors included here traveled from elsewhere into Louisiana, Louisianians have also traveled within their own state and left informative accounts of these journeys (hence we include, for example, Alcée Fortier, the sophisticated Creole, seeking out his Cajun country cousins, and Lyle Saxon boating above the landscape during the great flood of 1927). We also include one or two accounts from fictional works when they have seemed to catch something of the experience of Louisiana travel.

We believe that the writings in the book work as a collection to effect several ends. They provide a broad view of Louisiana over the course of five centuries, calling attention to many facets of the landscape, culture, society, and natural environment of one of the most fascinating of states. We hope the collection thus will be of use to those interested in the literary, cultural, and historical backgrounds of the Bayou State as observed by our varied group of authors. But, insofar as travel to Louisiana is an ongoing endeavor, these authors can also provide specific focus for current explorations. A visit to a particular place is enriched when we share that place with those who have been there before us and left their impressions. The writings included in the book are offered as impressions to be shared in this way. Many were set down in times very different from our own and give us the resonance of the past. All, we think, are by writers whose observations are interesting and evocative, whether they are skilled literary figures like Sherwood Anderson and Kate Chopin, historically important travelers like Frederick Law Olmsted, or obscure ones like James K. Hosmer and Carolyn Ramsey. As such, they provide a dimension that can direct or enrich travel today, providing points for comparison, insights into things that have vanished from places that nonetheless remain, and new perspectives with which to view places familiar and well-known. ("Travel Update" sections are provided to facilitate traveling to places mentioned by our writers or to similar ones.)

Archaeological evidence from the prehistoric settlement at Poverty Point, which indicates it was a trade hub to which people came from many distant regions thousands of years ago, suggests that Louisiana has long been an important destination. Non-Native Americans have voyaged in Louisiana since the sixteenth century, for various reasons and with varied experiences. Early Spanish and French travelers came as conquistadors, explorers, and colonizers. Later travelers often came on business of one sort or another, but certainly

Tourists in the
French Quarter,
by Mircea Vasiliu

From Emily Kimbrough,
So Near and Yet So Far,
copyright © 1955 by
Emily Kimbrough
Wrench, renewed 1983
by Emily Kimbrough.
Reproduced by
permission of Harper-
Collins Publishers, Inc.

by the nineteenth century many who passed through or sojourned were traveling for the sake of traveling—had set out simply to see what they could of this part of the world. As the terminus for Mississippi River steamboats as well as a port for seagoing vessels, New Orleans was often a key destination for world travelers who wanted to include a Mississippi voyage as an essential part of their itineraries. As early as 1817 the frontier geographer William Darby was saying of New Orleans: "There are few places where human life can be enjoyed with more pleasure." Not much later, visitors were coming to be impressed by the bustle of the levee, the foreign flavor, and the vital if sometimes sinful air of the city. By the end of the nineteenth century, large numbers of tourists were being attracted to New Orleans by Mardi Gras (in fact, the first book devoted entirely to the celebration was published in 1882 by a railroad trying to draw visitors), and tourists could be found wandering around the French Quarter clutching copies of George Washington Cable's books, looking for the locations of his stories about the Creoles. So well established was the "myth" of New Orleans by the 1930s that Dorothy Childs Hogner—recounting a journey from New York to the Texas Gulf Coast with her artist husband—could write that New Orleans had "*always meant* gaiety, old worldliness, Mardi Gras festivities, old French houses, history and 'atmosphere.'"[4] These qualities have kept people coming, making New Orleans at the end of the twentieth century one of the most visited of American cities.

Traveler writers did not so readily get out into the rest of Louisiana, which the popular imagination tended to see as an impenetrable swamp. However, while visiting in the 1850s Charlotte Matilda Houstoun arranged to leave New Orleans and go through remote marshes and inlets to get to coastal plantations along Barataria Bay; Lafcadio Hearn, incurably romantic, found his way later in the century to the marsh stilt village of St. Malo on Lake Borgne, inhabited by exotic "Orientals"; and plantations, which were conveniently located along the Mississippi and other rivers and bayous, often welcomed visitors into their self-contained and sometimes monotonous worlds. But many parts of Louisiana were hard to reach, even well into the twentieth century— today Interstate 10 will take anyone with a car through the heart of the vast Atchafalaya Basin, but it did not open until the early 1970s. Traveler writers like Amos Parker—who blithely set out from New England because he was curious to see "some portion of the unknown and unsettled regions of the West and the South" and in 1834 crossed Louisiana on horseback from the Mississippi to the Texas border on the Sabine—were few and far between. Though Longfellow (who never actually set foot in Louisiana) put the Cajuns on the map of the American consciousness in 1847 with his long narrative poem *Evangeline,* and though today Acadiana is undergoing a tourist boom, comparatively few outsiders actually traveled in Cajun country before the 1920s and 1930s. Those who encountered the Acadians at all—like Frederick Law Olmsted and the German writer Charles Sealsfield—tended to view them as marginal: Olmsted as on the peripheries of the plantation world,

4. Dorothy Childs Hogner, *South to Padre* (Boston, 1936), 35. Emphasis added.

Sealsfield almost as dangerous primitives occasionally encountered on the wild prairies.[5]

Where exactly they went in the state, why precisely they came, traveler writers often were looking for and frequently found—whatever their expectations—a different America, a different South in Louisiana. In contradiction to Samuel Johnson's statement that "one town, one country, is very like another," most people travel, when they do so for pleasure and diversion, precisely to see things that are somehow unfamiliar to them. But Louisiana—particularly South Louisiana, which has been the focus of attention far more than the northern part of the state—has often delivered to travelers a singular sense of being in an unusual part of America. Though obviously part of the South, it has often seemed nonetheless foreign—Catholic, populated by an odd ethnic mix predominantly but not exclusively French, governed by interracial relations not found elsewhere. Thus Olmsted could note the multilinguistic signage in New Orleans, and an English traveler might say that the city showed "more than any city in the Union . . . so many foreign features."[6] Barry Ancelet could tell Frederick Turner that south Louisiana was America's Caribbean coast, a place that was "south of the South." Calvin Trillin could write of a place obsessed with its unique culinary traditions, A. J. Liebling of a place bound up in the most byzantine politics. But this sense of difference extends to the very landscape visitors have encountered—not only the cultural landscape of Creole and Cajun houses, dugout canoes, and French Quarter wrought iron, but moreso the physical landscape of swamp and marshland. Though Louisiana may be even more watery in the popular mind than in reality, much of the state is indeed a great wetland—millions of acres despite erosion—that impresses travelers by its immensity and otherworldly mien.

Beyond noting their being struck by a particular sense of difference, it is difficult to generalize about traveler writers' Louisiana experiences. In the selections in this volume, they speak of seeing political rallies, voodoo ceremonies and musical performances, showboats, slave markets and black bears, war and alligator hunting, and a diversity of other things not easily categorized. Nonetheless, we have divided our travelers' accounts into eleven sections: the

5. Charles Sealsfield ["Francis Hardman"], *Frontier Life, or Scenes and Adventures in the South West* (New York, 1856), 16–19.

6. "A Rugbean," *Transatlantic Rambles; or, A Record of Twelve Months' Travel in the United States, Cuba, and the Brazils* (London, 1851), 70.

River, to recognize the impact the Mississippi and other streams had on the consciousness of visitors; New Orleans, because that metropolis has played so important a role in attracting travel; Cajun country, devoted to a region long recognized as ethnically distinctive; central and north Louisiana, incorporating accounts of a large area less visited than others; plantation realms, because of the historical centrality of this economic institution whose way of life intrigued many travelers; the African American presence, because black Louisianians were a focus for much attention from traveler writers; the Civil War, to bring together writings about travels under highly unusual circumstances; bayou, marsh, and coast, to mark the significance of wetlands in the popular image of Louisiana and in the reality of traveling there; wildlife and the natural environment, because the state has attracted many hunters and hikers, fishermen and birders; festivals, feasting, and other diversions, to take note of a famous propensity to celebrate; and the world of the spirits, because diverse spiritual traditions have blended here uniquely.

These section dividers result, of course, from a subjective decision as to what constitutes the most fundamental, broadly conceived subjects commented on by visitors to Louisiana. Others might prefer other classifications. (Florence Brink divided nineteenth-century Louisiana travel writing into accounts of overland travel, river travel, classes of people [along racial lines], and New Orleans hotels.[7]) No doubt there are traveler writers whose experiences fall into none of our categories. (Paul Binding wrote of his literary journey to visit Louisiana writers, for example.[8]) Few who have come here seem to have set out to see only the Mississippi River or African Americans. Yet we hope our categories call attention to those aspects of Louisiana that have most interested travelers and sojourners, that have most occupied their attention and imagination.

We hope also—whatever our chapter divisions—that the individual pieces presented here provide varied and engaging pictures of the fascinating state that folklorist and ethnomusicologist Alan Lomax said was culturally "the richest of all the American states."[9] Certainly our traveler writers found a di-

7. Florence Roos Brink, "Literary Travellers in Louisiana Between 1803 and 1860," *Louisiana Historical Quarterly,* XXXI (1948), 394–424.

8. Paul Binding, *Separate Country: A Literary Journey Through the American South* (Jackson, Miss., 1988).

9. Nicholas R. Spitzer, ed., *Louisiana Folklife: A Guide to the State* (Baton Rouge, 1985), back cover.

versity of things, people, events, and places to comment on: rattlesnakes underfoot, bonfires in the crisp night, sublimely baked duck in the oven, demagogues on the podium, pastoral landscapes in the midst of war, hard work and beautiful light on the water, babies sleeping under tables at the dance hall, giant freighters bobbing in the river, rows of sugarcane receding into the distance, an artist coping with his ancestral past, a grand seigneur entertaining on his plantation, a president of the United States chasing game through the canebrakes. If no one journey or encounter does—or could—define Louisiana for the traveler, collectively these accounts make up a patchwork of definitions, characterizing the state as rugged, cosmopolitan, welcoming, remote, urban, multicultural, harsh, romantic, religious, sensual, and other things as well, but certainly infinitely worth seeing.

1

AMERICAN NILE: THE RIVER

For any traveler to Louisiana, from early exploration to the late nineteenth century, the waterways were the pathways from place to place. Trails and roads developed slowly—in fact, few were paved until the 1920s—and railways were not extensively developed until the last quarter of the nineteenth century. People and goods were moved by river.

Early travelers were so struck by these rivers, their vastness, their beauty, the incredible potential they offered as a system, that those who wrote about experiencing them could only reach out for old-world certainties to express their tenuous grasp of what was still an American unknown. In 1784, for example, Thomas Hutchins compared the Mississippi River to the Nile, while geographer William Darby was later to declare that it was the connecting Red River that was "the true North American Nile." That other connecting stream, the Atchafalaya, he called "the Hoogly of Louisiana."[1]

1. Thomas Hutchins, *An Historical Narrative and Topographical Description of Louisiana and West Florida* (facsimile ed.;

If they were little known at first, these rivers would become the great highways of travel in Louisiana, especially the mighty Mississippi. The early French explorers and colonizers sailed down the Mississippi and up it (though, given the location of the French colony at Biloxi and the difficulties of sailing up the powerful current, passage along the coast and into Lake Pontchartrain was also favored). Later American flatboatmen could simply drift their cargoes down to New Orleans. And once Nicholas Roosevelt introduced steam power to the Father of Waters in 1811, the Mississippi steamboat became the great conveyor of the passengers, crops, and other freight that moved through the American heartland down to Louisiana.

Steamboat and river became American symbols. Perhaps they were commonplace for the people who signaled the boats to pick up produce from their plantations or who were themselves deposited on the teeming levee at New Orleans. But the river journey was clearly a powerful experience for many who wrote about traveling to and in Louisiana. Often the river was the first great fact of life they encountered there. And as their journeys progressed, the river continued to be a key presence. It was a roadway, a commercial lifeline, a way of life. Visitors noted its traffic. They noted its dangers. They noted, with some distraction, how its waters were sometimes higher than the lands on the other side of the protective levees. They noted, with much pleasure, showboats, verdant cane fields, and wildlife along its banks.

The river presents traveler writers with many impressions over a period of centuries. For Cabeza de Vaca and his companions in 1528 it is a powerful "torrent" that prevented their entry and expelled them to sea. For Jacques de la Metairie and the rest of La Salle's expedition over 150 years later, reaching the Mississippi's mouth is a triumph for France and King Louis. For Jean Bernard Bossu in the eighteenth century, the river is already a highway—though not always a safe one—as he and his companions paddle up it, avoiding an Indian ambush upon the warning of their own Indian guides. In the nineteenth century Frances Trollope sees it as "desolate" but finally softened by "bright tints of Southern vegetation," and Frederick Law Olmsted records the worksongs of the slave crewmen who got the steamboats underway and kept their decks piled with cargo. In the late twentieth century Eddy Harris discovers

---

Gainesville, 1968), 27; William Darby, "Navigating the Mississippi, Red, and Atchafalaya Rivers," in *Travels in the Old South, Selected from the Periodicals of the Time,* ed. Eugene L. Schwaab and Jacqueline Bull (2 vols.; Lexington, 1973), I, 70, 72.

the giant tankers and grain boats that dominate the Louisiana river today while floating among them in his tiny canoe. In 1930 Kent and Margaret Lighty find one of the last of the showboats that periodically brought music and drama into the lives of those who lived riverside.

Among other writers in this section, Mark Twain uses the river to poke fun at southern notions of medieval chivalry and at bamboozled tourists; men as diverse as gambler George Devol and naturalist Sir Charles Lyell give us a sense of the vagaries of traveling the steamboat highway, whether it was crooked card games at the Baton Rouge landing or discovering a clerk on a boat below Bayou Sara who wanted to know about Macaulay; while B. C. Hall and C. T. Wood try to fathom the strange mixture of plantation past and chemical-plant present that is the river today.

In the 1930s, two Soviet journalists who had come to New Orleans, Il'ia I'lf and Evgenii Petrov, declared that the river was "dead" because it seemed no longer to have the central role it once enjoyed, had no more Huck Finns.[2] Yet, though it is no longer the traveler's great highway it was, it carries today more cargo than ever, and no visitor to Louisiana who would truly know this place can ignore it, for it resonates with a history and a physical power that demand attention. Today's visitor might well heed what the Irish novelist Sean O'Faolain wrote in 1961: "The Mississippi has affected the nature of many . . . states and cities. It has affected none so profoundly as . . . its most exotic and final settlement," New Orleans, which, he said, "has thrived on its river as London has on the Thames." And he advised: "The first thing a visitor to New Orleans should look at is the river . . . the French Quarter can wait."[3]

2. Il'ia I'lf and Evgenii Petrov, *Little Golden America: Two Famous Soviet Humorists Survey the United States* (London, 1936), 273.

3. Sean O'Faolain, "New Orleans," *Holiday*, XXIX (November, 1961), 50.

Discovering the Mississippi's Mouth

ÁLVAR NÚÑEZ CABEZA DE VACA

Cabeza de Vaca (*ca.*1490–*ca.*1560) was part of an ill-fated Spanish expedition led by Panfilo de Narvaez (the "Governor" of Cabeza de Vaca's narrative), whose members were sailing west in 1528, desperately trying to reach Mexico after disasters in Florida; he was the first European who saw the Mississippi known to have written about it (though it appears on earlier Spanish maps), years before De Soto "discovered" it.

As this section opens, the Spaniards are floating about, uncertain of their location, having had two of their men ("Christians") previously captured by local Indians and having secured Indian hostages themselves. Their conflict with the inhabitants marks an important aspect of many early accounts of travel in Louisiana: contact with the Native Americans who occupied the region.

When morning came, many Indians in canoes came to us asking us to give them the two men they had left as hostages. The Governor said he would hand them over when they brought back the two Christians they had taken. Five or six chiefs came with these people and they seemed to us to be the handsomest people, and with the most authority and composure we had yet seen, although they were not as tall as the others we had described. They wore their hair loose and long and wore sable mantles like those we had already obtained. Some of them were made in a very strange fashion with laces made from tawny skins and they appeared very attractive. They en-

From *The Account: Álvar Núñez Cabeza de Vaca's "Relación,"* by Álvar Núñez Cabeza de Vaca, trans. Martin A. Favata and José B. Fernandez. Copyright © 1993 by Arte Público Press. Reprinted by permission of Arte Público Press, University of Houston.

treated us to go with them, saying that they would hand over the Christians and give us water and many other things. All the while many canoes were approaching us, trying to secure the mouth of the inlet. Because of this and because the country was too dangerous for us to remain, we put out to sea, where we remained with them until midday. As they would not return our Christians, and for this reason neither would we hand over the Indians, they began to throw sticks and sling rocks at us. They gave signs of wanting to shoot arrows at us, but we saw only three or four bows among all of them. While we were engaged in this skirmish, a chilly wind came up and they turned away and left us.

We sailed that day until the hour of vespers, when my boat, which was in the lead, saw a point of land on the other side of which could be seen a very large river. I put up at an islet at the tip of the land to wait for the other boats. The Governor did not want to approach, and instead entered a bay very close-by in which there were many islets. We gathered there and in the sea took on fresh water, because the river emptied out into the sea in a torrent. We landed on that island because we wanted to toast some of the corn we were carrying, since we had been eating it raw for two days. Since we found no firewood, we decided to enter the river which was behind the point one league away. We could not go in because the very strong current totally prevented us and carried us away from the shore despite our effort and determination. The north wind blowing from the land increased so much that it carried us out to sea and we could do nothing. Half a league out we took a sounding and found that we could not reach bottom with more than thirty fathoms. We did not know if the current was the reason we could not take a sounding. We sailed under those conditions for two days, struggling all the time to reach land. At the end of the two days, a little before sunrise, we saw many clouds of smoke along the coast. Struggling to reach them, we found ourselves in three fathoms of water. Since it was night, we did not dare to land. Having seen so many clouds of smoke, we believed that we could be placing ourselves in some sort of danger again, and that we would not be able to determine what to do because of the great darkness. Therefore we decided to wait until morning. At dawn each boat had lost sight of the others.

Vive le Roi: La Salle Reaches the Mississippi's Mouth

Jacques de la Metairie

> Jacques de la Metairie was the notary of La Salle's epic expedition of exploration down the Mississippi (which the French initially called the Colbert) in 1682, but this account—translated from an original manuscript in French archives—was also signed by La Salle and other key members of the party, indicating that it is a sort of collective narrative of their endeavor. Here we read of their finally attaining the lower reaches of the river; they had left present-day Illinois several months before. From *Historical Collections of Louisiana and Florida,* ed. B. F. French (1875).

We continued our voyage until the 6th [of April], when we discovered three channels, by which the River Colbert discharges itself into the sea. We landed on the bank of the most western channel, about three leagues from its mouth. On the 7th M. de la Salle went to reconnoiter the shores of the neighboring sea . . . and M. de Tonty likewise examined the great middle channel. They found these three outlets beautiful, large, and deep.

On the 8th we reascended the river, a little above its confluence with the sea, to find a dry place beyond the reach of inundation. . . . Here we prepared a column and a cross, and to the said column were affixed the arms of France with this inscription:

Louis Le Grand, Roi de France et de
Navarre, Regne; Le Neuvieme
Avril, 1682.

The whole party under arms chanted the *Te Deum,* the *Exaudiat,* the *Domine Salvum fac Regem;* and then, after a salute of fire-arms and cries of *Vive le Roi,* the column was erected by M. de la Salle, who, standing near it, said with a loud voice, in French: "In the name of the most high, mighty, invincible, and victorious Prince, LOUIS THE GREAT, by the grace of God, King of France and Navarre, fourteenth of that name, this ninth day of April, one thousand six hundred and eighty-two, I, in virtue of the commission of his Majesty . . . which I hold in my hand, and which may be seen by all whom it may concern, have taken and do now take in the name of his Majesty and of his successors to the crown, possession of this country of Louisiana, the seas, harbors, ports, bays, adjacent straits; and all the nations, people, provinces, cities, towns, villages, mines, minerals, fisheries, streams, and rivers comprised in the extent of Louisiana, from the mouth of the great River St. Louis on the eastern side, otherwise called Ohio, Alighinsipou (Alleghany) or Chickagoua, and this with the consent of the Chouanons (Shawanoes), Chichacas (Chickasaws), and other people dwelling therein, with whom we have made alliance; as also along the River Colbert or Mississippi, and rivers which discharge themselves therein, from its source; beyond the country of the Kious (Sioux) or Nadouessions, and this with their consent, and with the consent of the Motantees, Illinois, Mesigameas (Metchigamias), Akansas, Natches, and Koroas, which are the most considerable nations dwelling therein, with whom we have also made alliance either by ourselves or by others in our behalf; as far as the mouth of the sea or Gulf of Mexico, about the 27th degree of the elevation of the north pole, and also to the north of the river of Palms . . . upon the assurance that we have received from all these nations that we are the first Europeans who have descended the River Colbert, hereby protesting against all those who may in future undertake to invade any or all of these countries, people, or lands above described to the prejudice of the right of his Majesty acquired by the consent of the nations herein named, of which and all that can be needed, I hereby take to witness those who hear me. . . . "[4]

To which the whole assembly responded with shouts of *Vive le Roi* and with salutes of fire-arms. Moreover, the said Sieur de la Salle caused to be buried at the foot of the tree to which the cross was attached a leaden plate, on one side of which were engraved the arms of France and the following Latin inscription:

4. The writer may be emphasizing that La Salle was here speaking in French—whereas we might simply assume he was doing so—because the party of voyagers has just been chanting in Latin or because French explorers of this period were often accompanied by Native Americans and frequently conversed in Indian languages on these expeditions.

LUDOVICVS MAGNVS REGNAT.

NONO APRILIS CIƆ IƆC LXXXII.

ROBERTVS CAVELIER, CVM DOMINO DE TONTY, LEGATO R.P. ZENOBIO

MEMBRE, RECOLLECTO, ET VIGINTI GALLIS, PRIMVS HOC FLVMEN, INDE AB

ILINEORVM PAGO, ENAVIGAVIT, EJVSQUE OSTIVM FECIT PERVIVM, NONO

APRILIS ANNI

CIƆ IƆC LXXXII.[5]

After which the Sieur de la Salle said that his Majesty, as eldest Son of the Church, would annex no country to his crown without making it his chief care to establish the Christian religion therein, and that its symbol must now be planted, which was accordingly done at once by erecting a cross, before which the *Vexilla* and the *Domine Salvum fac Regem* were sung, whereupon the ceremony was concluded with cries of *Vive le Roi*.

5. "Louis the Great reigns. The Ninth of April, 1682. Robert Cavelier [*i.e.,* La Salle], with the Lord of Tonty, accompanied by the reverend father Zenobe Membre, of the Recollect Order, and twenty Frenchmen, first on this river, sailed from the starting point of the village of the Illinois and made his way to the mouth, the Ninth of April, the Year 1682."

A Near Ambush

JEAN BERNARD BOSSU

Little is known about Bossu (1720–1792), but his career as a French naval officer brought him to Louisiana, where he spent a number of years accompanying various colonial expeditions. Bossu's account calls attention to Louisiana's Native Americans, who were a regular presence in colonial-era travel accounts and, indeed, continue to appear in those of later times, though in a more peripheral way. By "the Natchez country" Bossu means the region occupied at one time by the Natchez tribe, along the Mississippi upriver from the Florida Parishes. Translated by Olivia Blanchard from *Nouveaux Voyages dans l'Amérique septentrionale* (1777) for the Works Progress Administration and Louisiana State University, 1940.

You must know . . . that in passing through the Natchez country, especially when the waters are low, one frequently meets herds of wild buffalo who come to the river to drink. . . .

On the 27th, about eight o'clock in the morning, we were crossing the Mississippi; a few moments later we saw on a bature [the land between river and levee], one hundred feet from where there was a dense woods, deer, bears, and wild buffalo cows with their calves who seemed like they wanted to suck their mother. We thought we saw heifers and young bulls jumping and playing together. The owner of the boat, who was the first to see them, said to us: "Slowly; raise the oars, my friends. Good catch, Good Lord! Wild buffalos! To arms!" We were all excited as would be travellers eager at the sight of this pastoral herd. . . . A former soldier of my company of the Garonne, whose *nom de Guerre* was *Sans-peur* [without Fear], and since the disbanding of the troops, was a *boucanier,* that is, *coureur de bois* or *chasseur* [woodsman or hunter] by profession, was anticipating the pleasure of giving me some fine morsels of these animals. He was thinking of offering me a bear skin in which he was afraid to make a hole because it seemed to be a lovely black, and large enough to hold on my travelling mattress. Another said that he would shoot only the cows (because he said the flesh of the bulls is tough) because when they have calves, their flesh becomes very tender.

Our two Indians were listening in silence. Then they burst out laughing; asked what was the matter, they answered, that they could not help laughing, seeing that we were about to fall into the snare the Chickasaws, our enemies, had set for us. They were ambushed in the woods, near the place we expected to land. They knew how fond the French were of chasing the wild buffalo. Some of them had put on the skins of these animals to draw us to the forest; their plan being to take our scalps or make us prisoners; if we did not hasten to depart, we would receive a shower of arrows. At these words, we were struck with astonishment, and fear; we watched the movements of these pretended bears, cows, calves, and deer, and saw, by their movements, that they were men masked as animals. . . .

The two Indians were rewarded, and we hastened to cross to the other side of the river. Our men never rowed with greater courage.

Entrance of the Mississippi

FRANCES TROLLOPE

> Englishwoman Frances Trollope's *Domestic Manners of the Americans* (1832) appeared to both great success and great controversy because of her wittily acerbic observations of American society. Trollope (1780–1863) had come to America in 1827 to join an experimental settlement run by a friend in Tennessee and begins her book with this account of arriving at the mouth of the Mississippi. Unlike Cabeza de Vaca, she was able to get upstream, but even in 1827 sailing upriver from the Gulf could be a tricky proposition for a ship.

The first indication of our approach to land was the appearance of this mighty river pouring forth its muddy mass of waters, and mingling with the deep blue of the Mexican Gulf. The shores of this river are so utterly flat, that no object upon them is perceptible at sea, and we gazed with pleasure on the muddy ocean that met us, for it told us we were arrived, and seven weeks of sailing had wearied us; yet it was not without a feeling like regret that we passed from the bright blue waves, whose varying aspect had so long furnished our chief amusement, into the murky stream which now received us.

Large flights of pelicans were seen standing upon the long masses of mud which rose above the surface of the waters, and a pilot came to guide us over the bar, long before any other indication of land was visible.

I never beheld a scene so utterly desolate as this entrance of the Mississippi. Had Dante seen it, he might have drawn images of another Bolgia from its horrors.[6] One only object rears itself above the eddying waters; this is the mast

6. A place in canto XVIII of the *Inferno* that has ten circular chasms (*bolgia* in Italian), each with a different kind of sinner.

The Balize, watercolor by Benjamin Latrobe, 1819

From *Latrobe's Views of America, 1795–1820: Selections from the Watercolors and Sketches,* ed. Edward C. Carter II, John C. Van Horne, and Charles E. Brownell (New Haven, 1985), by permission of the Maryland Historical Society

of a vessel long since wrecked in attempting to cross the bar, and it still stands, a dismal witness of the destruction that has been, and a boding prophet of that which is to come.

By degrees bulrushes of enormous growth become visible, and a few more miles of mud brought us within sight of a cluster of huts called the Balize, by far the most miserable station that I ever saw made the dwelling of man, but I was told that many families of pilots and fishermen lived there.[7]

For several miles above its mouths the Mississippi presents no objects more

---

7. The Balize was a beacon set at the mouth of the Mississippi by the French in the 1770s; the name also refers to the settlement that grew up around it from which river pilots operated. It was located on the northeast pass of the river; after the construction of the Eads jetties in the nineteenth century, the south pass became the main entrance to the river. Piloting operations were moved farther upstream to Pilot Town, today still accessible only by boat.

interesting than mud banks, monstrous bulrushes, and now and then a huge crocodile luxuriating in the slime.[8] Another circumstance that gives to this dreary scene an aspect of desolation, is the incessant appearance of vast quantities of drift wood, which is ever finding its way to the different mouths of the Mississippi. Trees of enormous length, sometimes still bearing their branches, and still oftener their uptorn roots entire, the victims of the frequent hurricane, come floating down the stream. Sometimes several of these, entangled together, collect among their boughs a quantity of floating rubbish, that gives the mass the appearance of a moving island, bearing a forest, with its roots mocking the heavens; while the dishonoured branches lash the tide in idle vengeance: this, as it approaches the vessel, and glides swiftly past, looks like the fragment of a world in ruins.

As we advanced, however, we were cheered, notwithstanding the season, by the bright tints of southern vegetation. The banks continue invariably flat, but a succession of planless villas, sometimes merely a residence, and sometimes surrounded by their sugar grounds and negro huts, varied the scene. At no one point was there an inch of what painters call a second distance; and for the length of one hundred and twenty miles, from the Balize to New Orleans, and one hundred miles above the town, the land is defended from the encroachments of the river by a high embankment, which is called the Levée; without which the dwellings would speedily disappear, as the river is evidently higher than the banks would be without it.

8. What Trollope had seen was not a crocodile but its relative, the anatomically different American alligator. In the United States crocodiles are found only in parts of Florida.

Waiting for a Boat

SIR CHARLES LYELL

The noted British scientist Sir Charles Lyell (1797–1895), often called "the father of geology," was in Louisiana in March of 1846 while on a tour of the United States. He was particularly interested in observing the geology and topography, the flora and the fossils of the area. He had explored a swampy habitat just before hailing a boat upriver, an event he describes in this excerpt from *A Second Visit to the United States of North America* (1849).

In order that I might not spend an indefinite time on the Mississippi, I determined to be prepared for a start in the first chance steamer which might be bound for Natchez, 140 miles distant, whenever an opportunity should offer, whether by day or night. I was told by my host that a trusty black servant had been already appointed to look out for a steamer, which was to convey some farm produce to a proprietor far off on the Red River. He proposed, therefore, to give orders to this negro to wake me if any boat bound for Natchez should appear in sight before morning. Accordingly, about an hour after midnight, I was roused from my slumbers, and went down over a sloping lawn to the steam-boat landing on the river's bank. The sky was clear, and it was bright moonlight, and the distant cries of the owls, and other night birds . . . were distinctly heard, mingled with the chirping of myriads of frogs. On the low bank my watchman had lighted a signal fire, and I heard the puffing of a steamer in the distance ascending the stream. She soon neared us, and, on being hailed, answered, "La Belle Creole, bound for Bayou Sara." This port was far short of my destination, and when we shouted "Natchez," the captain first asked if we had any wood to sell, and on learning there was none, sailed away. I returned to the house, and took another nap of several hours, when I received a second summons from my faithful sentinel.

The scene was entirely changed; it was nearly day-break, and the fogs rising from the marshes had begun to cover the river. I was in despair, fearing that our signal fire would not be discerned through the mist. Soon, however, we heard the loud gasping of the two steam-pipes sounding nearer and nearer, and a large steamer coming suddenly close to the landing, was announced as the "Talma of Cincinnati." In a few minutes I was crossing the narrow plank which led from the steep bank to the vessel, which was actually in motion as I walked over it, so that I was glad to find myself safe on deck. They told me I must register my name at the office. The clerk asked me if I was the author of a work on geology, and being answered in the affirmative, wished to know if I was acquainted with Mr. Macaulay. On my saying yes, he took out a late number of the Edinburgh Review, and begged me to tell him whether the article on Addison was written by my friend, for he had been discussing this matter with a passenger that evening. When I had confirmed this opinion he thanked me, expressing much regret that he should not see me again, since I was to land next day at Natchez before he should be up.

Steamboat Accommodations

FREDERICK LAW OLMSTED

Olmsted (1822–1903), the famed designer of Central Park, traveled south to write a book proving slavery uneconomical, thus convincing the South to voluntarily abandon the "peculiar institution," peacefully reconciling the slave and free states. He makes many observant comments about Louisiana in *A Journey in the Seaboard Slave States* (1856), from which this account of a steamboat voyage in 1853 is taken. He presents the steamboat in a manner that modern readers may find exotic, but—in contrast to our historical stereotype—hardly glamorous. If he writes of some of the inconveniences of steamboat travel, others wrote of their fear of actual steamboat explosions, which were not uncommon.

We backed out, winded round head up, and as we began to breast the current, a dozen of the negro boat-hands, standing on the freight, piled up on the low forecastle, began to sing, waving hats and handkerchiefs, and shirts lashed to poles, towards the people who stood on the sterns of the steam-boats at the levee.

"Ye see dem boat way dah ahead.
    CHORUS.—Oahoiohieu.
De San Charles is arter 'em, dey mus go behine.
    CHO.—Oahoiohieu.
    .   .   .   .

After the conclusion of this song, and after the negroes had left the bows, and were coming aft along the guards, we passed two or three colored nurses, walking with children on the river bank; as we did so the singers jumped on some cotton bales, bowed very low to them, took off their hats, and swung and waved them, and renewed their song. . . .

As soon as the song was ended, I went into the cabin to remind the clerk to obtain a berth for me. I found two brilliant supper tables reaching the whole length of the long cabin, and a file of men standing on each side of both of them, ready to take seats as soon as the signal was given. The clerk was in his room, with two other men, and appeared to be more occupied than ever. His manner was, I thought, now rather cool, not to say rude; and he very distinctly informed me that every berth was occupied, and he didn't know where I was to sleep. He judged I was able to take care of myself; and if I was not, he was quite sure that he had too much to do to give all his time to my surveillance. I then went to the captain, and told him that I thought myself entitled to a berth. I had paid for one, and should not have taken passage in the boat, if it had not been promised me. I was not disposed to fight for it, particularly as the gentleman occupying the berth engaged to me was a good deal bigger fellow than I, and also carried a bigger knife; but I thought the clerk was accountable to me for a berth, and I begged that he would inform him so. He replied that the clerk probably knew his business; he had nothing to do with it; and walked away from me. I then addressed myself to a second clerk, or subofficer of some denomination, who more good-naturedly informed me that half the company were in the same condition as myself, and I needn't be alarmed, cots would be provided for us.

As I saw that the supper-table was likely to be crowded, I asked if there would be a second table. "Yes, they'll keep on eatin' till they all get through." I walked the deck till I saw those who had been first seated at the table coming out; then going in, I found the table still crowded, while many stood waiting to take seats as fast as any were vacated. I obtained one for myself at length, and had no sooner occupied it than two half-intoxicated and garrulous men took the adjoining stools.

It was near nine o'clock before the tables were cleared away, and immediately afterwards the waiters began to rig a framework for sleeping-cots in their place. These cots were simply canvas shelves, five feet and a half long, two wide, and less than two feet apart, perpendicularly. A waiter, whose good will I had purchased at the supper-table, gave me a hint to secure one of them for myself, as soon as they were erected by putting my hat in it. I did so, and saw that others did the same. I chose a cot as near as possible to the midship doors of the cabin, perceiving that there was not likely to be the best possible air, after all the passengers were laid up for the night, in this compact manner.

Nearly as fast as the cots were ready they were occupied. To make sure that mine was not stolen from me, I also, without much undressing, laid myself away. A single blanket was the only bed-clothing provided. I had not lain long, before I was driven, by an exceedingly offensive smell, to search for a cleaner neighborhood; but I found all the cots fore and aft, were either occupied or engaged. I immediately returned, and that I might have a dernier resort, left my shawl in that I had first obtained.

In the forward part of the cabin there was a bar, a stove, a table, and a placard of rules, forbidding smoking, gambling, and swearing in the cabin, and a close company of drinkers, smokers, card-players, and constant swearers. I went out, and stepped down to the boiler deck. . . .

As I explored further aft, I found negroes lying asleep in all postures, upon the freight. . . . A few white people—men, women and children—were lying here and there, among the negroes. Altogether, I heard we had two hundred of these deck passengers, black and white. A stove, by which they could fry bacon, was the only furniture provided for them by the boat. They carried

A Mississippi steamer

From Henry A. Murray, *Lands of the Slave and the Free; or, Cuba, the United States, and Canada* (London, 1857)

with them their provisions for the voyage, and had their choice of the freight for beds.

As I came to the bows again, and was about to ascend to the cabin, two men came down, one of whom I recognized to have been my cot neighbor. "Where's a bucket?" said he; "by thunder! this fellow was so strong I could not sleep by him, so I stumped him to come down and wash his feet." "I am much obliged to you," said I, and I was, very much; the man had been lying in the cot beneath mine, which I now returned to, and soon fell asleep.

I awoke about midnight. There was an unusual jar in the boat, and an evident excitement among people talking on deck. I rolled out of my cot, and stepped out on to the gallery. The steamboat "Kimball" was running head-and-head with us, and so close that one might have jumped easily from our paddle-box on to her guards. A few other passengers had turned out beside myself, and most of the waiters were leaning on the rail of the gallery. Occasionally a few words of banter passed between them and the waiters of the Kimball; below, the firemen were shouting as they crowded the furnaces, and some one could be heard cheering them: "Shove her up, boys! Shove her up! Give her hell!" "She's got to hold a conversation with us before she gets by, anyhow," said one of the negroes. "Ye har' that ar' whistlin'," said a white man, "tell ye thar an't any too much water in her bilers when ye har that." I laughed silently, but was not without a slight expectant sensation, which Mr. Burke would have called sublime. At length the Kimball slowly drew ahead, crossed our bow, and the contest was given up. "De ole lady too heavy," said a waiter; "if I could pitch a few ton of dat freight off her bow, I'd bet de Kimball would be askin' her to show de way, mighty quick."

At half-past four o'clock a hand-bell was rung in the cabin, and soon afterwards I was informed that I must get up, that the servants might remove the cot arrangement, and clear the cabin for the breakfast-table.

Breakfast was not ready till half-past seven. In the mean time, having washed in the barber's shop, I walked on the hurricane deck, where I got very damp and faint. The passengers, one set after another, and then the pilots, clerks, mates, and engineers, and then the free-colored people, and then the waiters, chambermaids, and passengers' body servants, having breakfasted, the tables were cleared, and the cabin was swept. The tables were then again laid for dinner. Thus the greater part of the cabin was constantly occupied, and the passengers who had not state-rooms to retreat to were driven to herd in the vicinity of the card-tables and the bar, the lobby (Social Hall, I believe it's called), in which most of the passengers' baggage was deposited, or to go outside. Every part of the boat, except the bleak hurricane deck, was crowded; and so large a number of equally uncomfortable and disagreeable people I think I never saw elsewhere together. We made very slow progress, landing, it seems to me, after we entered Red River, at every "bend," "bottom," "bayou," "point," and "plantation" that came in sight; often for no other object than to roll out a barrel of flour, or a keg of nails; sometimes merely to furnish newspapers to a wealthy planter, who had much cotton to send to market, and whom it was therefore desirable to please.

Gambling on the River

George Devol

George Devol (1829–?) was well known among river-boat gamblers, both before and after the Civil War. He traveled frequently in Louisiana waters and in and out of New Orleans and other Louisiana towns. From *Forty Years a Gambler on the Mississippi* (1887), his anecdotal memoirs, which provide amusing pictures of the seamier side of life along the river.

The Black Deck-Hand

Charlie Clark and I left New Orleans one night on the steamer *Duke of Orleans.* There were ten or twelve rough looking fellows on board, who did their drinking out of private bottles. Charlie opened up shop [gambling] in the cabin, and soon had a great crowd around him. I saw that the devils had been drinking too much, so I gave Charlie the wink, and he soon closed up, claiming to be broke. Then we arranged that I should do the playing, and he would be on the lookout. I soon got about all the money and some watches out of the roughs, besides I beat seven or eight of the other passengers. They all appeared to take it good naturedly at the time; but it was not long before their loss, and the bad whisky, began to work on them. I saw there was going to be trouble, so I made a sneak for my room, changed my clothes, and then slipped down the back stairs into the kitchen. I sent word for Clark to come down. I then blackened my face and hands, and made myself look like a deck-hand. I had hardly finished my disguise, when a terrible rumpus up stairs warned me that the ball was open. The whisky was beginning to do its work. They searched everywhere; kicked in the state-room doors, turned everything upside down, and raised h——l generally. If they could have caught me then, it would have been good bye George. They came down on deck, walked past, and inquired of a roustabout who stood by me if he had seen a well-dressed man on deck. He told them "he had not seen any gemman down on deck afore they came down." They had their guns out, and were swearing vengeance. The boat was plowing her way along up the river; the stevedores were hurrying the darkies to get up some freight, as a landing was soon to be made. The whistle blew, and the boat was headed for shore. Those devils knew I would attempt to leave the boat, so as soon as the plank was put out they ran over on the bank, and closely scanned the face of every one who got off. There was a lot of plows to be discharged, so I watched my chance, shouldered a plow, followed a long line of coons, and I fairly flew past the mob. I kept on up the high bank and threw my plow on to the pile, and then I made for the cotton fields. I lay down on my back until the boat was out of sight, and then I came out, washed myself white, and took a boat for Vicksburg, where I met Clark the next day, and we divided the boodle that he had brought with him. He told me that after I had left the boat they got lights and went down into the hold, looking for me, as they were sure I was still on the boat. It was a pretty close call, but they were looking for a well-dressed man, and not a black deck-hand.

Signal Service

Before the war they had an old steamer fitted up as a wharf-boat and lodging-house at Baton Rouge, to accommodate people that landed late at night, or would be waiting for a boat. This old boat was headquarters for the gamblers that ran the river. Many a night we have played cards in the old cabin until morning, or until our boat would arrive. When thoroughbred gamblers meet around the table at a game of cards, then comes the tug of war. We would have some very hard games at times, and we found it pretty hard to hold our own. My partner proposed that we fix up some plan to down the gamblers that played with us on the old boat, so we finally hit upon a scheme. We bored a hole under one of the tables, and another under one of the beds in a stateroom opposite. Then we fixed a nail into a spring, and fastened the spring on the under side of the floor, so that the nail would come up through the floor under the table. Next we attached a fine wire to the spring, and ran it up into the state-room. Then we bored a hole in the bulkhead of the state-room, just over the top berth, so that a person could lie in the berth and look out into the cabin. Now we were ready for the thoroughbreds. When we would get one of our smart friends, we would seat him at our table in his chair, which was always on the side of our state-room. We called it ours, for we had fitted it up just to suit us; and for fear some one would use it when we were out traveling for our health, we paid for it all the time. We had a good boy that liked to lie down and make money, so we would put him in the upper berth while the game was in progress. He would look through the peep-hole, and if our friend had one pair he would pull the wire once; if two pair, twice; if threes, three times; if fours, four times, etc. We would kick off one boot and put our foot over the nail, and then we would be able to tell what hand our friend held. One day I was playing a friend at our table, and he was seated in his chair. I got the signals all right for some time, and then the under-current seemed to be broken. I waited for the signals until I could not wait any longer, for I was a little behind (time), so I picked up a spittoon and let fly at our room. That restored communications, and I received the signals all right. My friend wanted to know what I threw the spittoon for. I told him the cards were running so bad that I got mad; and that an old nigger had told me once it was a good sign to kick over a spittoon when playing cards; so I thought I would not only kick it over, but would break the d——d thing all to pieces. He replied, "I noticed that your luck changed just after you threw her, and I will try it the next time I play in bad luck."

Lost His Wife's Diamonds

I was playing poker with a gentleman on board the steamer *John Simonds* bound for Louisville, late one night, and had won a few hundred dollars from him, when he got up without saying a word, and went to the ladies' cabin. In a short time he came back with a small velvet covered box in his hand, and said to me, "Come, let us finish our game." He opened the box, and I saw it was full of ladies' diamond jewelry. I said: "What are you going to do with those?" Said he, "I will put them up as money." "Oh, no; I have no use for ladies' jewelry." "Well," says he, "if I lose I will redeem them when we get to Louisville." I told him I was not going above Vicksburg. "Well," says he, "if you win, leave them with the clerk and I will pay him." I then loaned him $1,500 on the jewelry, and we sat down to play. It was about 3 A.M. when we commenced, and before they wanted the tables for breakfast I had won the $1,500 back. We drank a champagne cocktail, and he went to his room. The barber was at work on me, so that I was a little late for breakfast, and the steward had to take me into the ladies' cabin to get me a seat. There was a gentleman, a very beautiful lady, and a sweet little child at the same table; the lady's eyes were red, as if she had been crying. I looked at the gentleman, and saw it was the same person who had lost the diamonds. Somehow, my breakfast did not suit me; and the more I looked at that young wife and mother, the less I felt like eating. So at last I got up and left the table. I went to my room, got the little velvet box, wrapped it up, and carried it back. They were just leaving the table when I returned. I called the chambermaid, and told her the lady had left a package, and for her to take it to her room. After it was gone I felt better, and I eat a square meal. The gentleman came and thanked me, and wanted my address; but as I never had any one to send me money lost at gambling, I told him not to mind the address; for I knew if I did not give it, I would not expect anything, and therefore would not be disappointed.

Castles and Plantations

Mark Twain

Twain (1835–1910) wrote *Life on the Mississippi* (1883), the classic of American travel from which this is taken, after an 1882 trip on the river; in part he based the book on earlier articles and on recollections and journals from his own days as a river pilot. He makes much sport of the Louisiana State Capitol, a medieval castle–like structure.

Baton Rouge was clothed in flowers, like a bride—no, much more so; like a greenhouse. For we were in the absolute South now—no modifications, no compromises, no half-way measures. The magnolia trees in the Capitol grounds were lovely and fragrant, with their dense rich foliage and huge snowball blossoms. The scent of the flower is very sweet, but you want distance on it, because it is so powerful. They are not good bedroom blossoms—they might suffocate one in his sleep. We were certainly in the South at last; for here the sugar region begins, and the plantations—vast green levels, with sugar-mill and negro quarters clustered together in the middle distance—were in view. And there was a tropical sun overhead and a tropical swelter in the air.

And at this point, also, begins the pilot's paradise: a wide river hence to New Orleans, abundance of water from shore to shore, and no bars, snags, sawyers, or wrecks in his road.

Sir Walter Scott is probably responsible for the Capitol building; for it is not inconceivable that this little sham castle would ever have been built if he had not run the people mad, a couple of generations ago, with his medieval romances. The South has not yet recovered from the debilitating influence of his books. Admiration of his fantastic heroes and their grotesque "chivalry" doings and romantic juvenilities still survives here, in an atmosphere in which is already perceptible the wholesome and practical nineteenth-century smell of cotton factories and locomotives; and traces of its inflated language and other windy humbuggeries survive along with it. It is pathetic enough that a whitewashed castle, with turrets and things—materials all ungenuine within and without, pretending to be what they are not—should ever have been built in this otherwise honorable place; but it is much more pathetic to see this architectural falsehood undergoing restoration and perpetuation in our day, when it would have been so easy to let dynamite finish what a charitable fire began, and then devote this restoration money to the building of something genuine. . . .

From Baton Rouge to New Orleans, the great sugar-plantations border both sides of the river all the way, and stretch their league-wide levels back to the dim forest walls of bearded cypress in the rear. Shores lonely no longer. Plenty of dwellings all the way, on both banks—standing so close together, for long distances, that the broad river lying between the two rows becomes a sort of spacious street. A most homelike and happy region. And now and then you see the pillared and porticoed great manor-house, embowered in trees. Here is testimony of one or two of the procession of foreign tourists that filed along here half a century ago. Mrs. Trollope says:

> The unbroken flatness of the banks of the Mississippi continued unvaried for many miles above New Orleans; but the graceful and luxuriant palmetto, the dark and noble ilex, and the bright orange were everywhere to be seen, and it was many days before we were weary of looking at them.

Captain Basil Hall:

> The district of country which lies adjacent to the Mississippi, in the lower parts of Louisiana, is everywhere thickly peopled by sugar-planters, whose showy houses, gray piazzas, trig gardens, and numerous slave villages, all clean and neat, gave an exceedingly thriving air to the river scenery.

All the procession paint the attractive picture in the same way. The descriptions of fifty years ago do not need to have a word changed in order to exactly describe the same region as it appears to-day—except as to the "trigness" of the houses. The whitewash is gone from the negro cabins now; and many, possibly most, of the big mansions, once so shining white, have worn out their paint and have a decayed, neglected look. It is the blight of the war. Twenty-one years ago everything was trim and trig and bright along the "coast," just as it had been in 1827, as described by those tourists.

Unfortunate tourists! People humbugged them with stupid and silly lies, and then laughed at them for believing and printing the same. They told Mrs. Trollope that the alligators—or crocodiles, as she calls them—were terrible creatures; and backed up the statement with a blood-curdling account of how one of these slandered reptiles crept into a squatter cabin one night, and ate up a woman and five children. The woman, by herself, would have satisfied any ordinarily impossible alligator; but no, these liars must make him gorge the five children besides.

The 1927 Flood

LYLE SAXON

Lyle Saxon (1891–1946), who grew up in Baton Rouge and lived much of his life in New Orleans, was well known in his day for his many writings on Louisiana. He traveled into the terrain inundated by the great flood of 1927—which had received tremendous national attention—while researching his book *Father Mississippi,* from which this account is taken. Crevasses—openings in the river's levees that caused land areas to be flooded and even washed away—were a constant fear for those who lived along the Mississippi. In 1927 New Orleans was saved when a crevasse was deliberately opened to divert rising waters, but vast areas of land were inundated all along the river—as Saxon's sailing over distances that were normally dry land makes clear. His piece highlights another face of the river, that which was destructive of human habitation.

Anchored in Old River, between the Mississippi and Red River, the rescue boats were waiting, in charge of Red Cross officials. It was with four men from the coast guard—a rescue squad—that I got into the heart of the flooded area. Our squad was one of a hundred operating there. Bronzed and blistered men are these, working at this grim business of life-saving for many weeks, moving farther and farther down the Mississippi, following the crest of the flood. Here are large river steamboats, picturesque vessels of another and happier age than ours; here are submarine chasers, manned by sailors; here are the stanch river tugs and smaller river boats; here are hun-

From *Father Mississippi,* by Lyle Saxon. Copyright © 1927 by The Century Co. Used by permission of the publisher, Pelican Publishing Company, Inc.

High water on the Mississippi levee, from a book by Willard Glazier. Glazier traveled the Mississippi by canoe, claiming to have discovered the river's true source.

From Willard Glazier, *Down the Great River* (Philadelphia, 1889)

dreds of motor-driven surf-boats, small enough to ride through the holes in the broken levees and cruise about the inundated country where hundreds of men, women, and children are marooned, helpless and hungry, on levee-tops, in trees, and in water-swept houses.

For days I went with the coast guard men in these surf-boats into the back country of the Bayou des Glaises section. The hours dragged on under the burning sun, brighter still reflected from the water. The flood is vast and terrible. Picture to yourself this great inland sea, mile upon mile of muddy water, with never a bit of dry land anywhere; houses askew, roofs fallen in, and the water filled with dead animals. On ridge-poles of houses are roosting chickens, marooned and left to starve. Abandoned dogs bark pitifully from housetops—hunting dogs mostly, pointers and setters, left behind in the mad rush to escape.

And everywhere, rising above the water, are half-submerged trees, pink crepe-myrtles, blossoming magnolias, the creamy blossoms beginning to turn brown already from the surrounding water. Floating here and there, the household treasures are seen, prized possessions which were carried to the levee-tops, only to be abandoned there in the mad rush for safety as the water rose higher and higher. Beds and bedding, chairs and sofas, objects having a mute and tragic quality of their own.

What is the story of this red and blue patchwork quilt, lying in the mud of the levee-top? Where is the miserable and terror-stricken woman who has dropped it here in her flight? To what child did this doll belong, a doll dressed as a baby, wearing a knitted jacket of light blue—some child's prized possession, now lying half in, half out of the water? Where is the girl who dropped the mirror which lies face upturned in the sunlight, sending out blinding radiance into our eyes as we come chugging beside the levee in our motorboat?

As we go farther along Bayou des Glaises—farther from the Mississippi—we find more and more refugees, negroes mostly, living in rough board shacks which they have constructed on the levee-top. Here, surrounded by their chickens, their hogs, and their meager household treasures, they wait for the rescue boats to come for them, preferring to remain near their possessions rather than go to safety:

"No, suh . . . Ah's rather wait till de big boat come fo' us. . . . Den Ah can tek muh mule wid me . . . muh mule and muh dawg. . . . Dat's all Ah got lef'." Then, after a pause: "But, boss, Ah shore is hungry. . . . Ain't yo' got nuthin' tuh eat in dat boat?"

Who can blame the negro, or the white man, for refusing to leave the little that he has? Born and bred in this quiet, peaceful country, he fears the unknown—and what assurance can we give that his possessions will be restored to him?

We press on, farther and farther into the flooded country. Now we have left even Bayou des Glaises far behind and are in the inner country. Chickens, pigs, dogs upon housetops, starving. Chickens in trees—sometimes in close proximity to snakes which coil among the branches, seeking safety from the water. There are squirrels, opossums, 'coons, other small animals, high in the branches above us. And over all this desolation comes the clear, high call of the mocking-bird, winging its way from tree to tree. Cardinals fly low over the water, their crimson feathers glinting in the sunlight. Herons, white and blue, swoop down, undismayed by the flood. And high in the air, black buzzards, circling lower.

Upon a housetop we find an aged negro, crying out to be rescued, but when we come close and urge him to enter our boat, he refuses to leave his beehives—six of them—over which the bees, disturbed, are buzzing angrily. The bronzed and blistered sailor beside me, throws up his hands in exasperation: "And how the hell," he asks, "can we take your beehives into our lifeboat?" The old negro is stubborn. "Ah'll wait fo' de big boat," he says.

We have crossed the "big bend" now and are back in Bayou des Glaises once more. A clear hail comes across the water toward us. A man in a rowboat is calling. We come close. Near-by is his house, the roof projecting above the rushing water which washes about the eaves. Upon this roof is a strange gathering: two half-grown boys, four dogs, a cat and kittens, and perhaps thirty chickens. Red roosters stand like living weather-cocks upon the chimneys.

The man's name is Ambrose Lemoine: "An' I tell you, my frien', this is one hell of a mess to happen to a man. *Mon Dieu!* I assu' you, I was workin' on the levee when she break under me! *Sacre!* How my wife scream! I look behind' me and I see my l'il children flopping like fish in the water! Ah, I tell you, my frien', I work like the devil to get my l'il children on the roof! But what I wan' know is: where my wife an' chile got to?" All this delivered so rapidly that we can hardly understand.

His wife, we learn, along with the smaller children, has been picked up by a rescue boat and taken out to safety aboard one of the large river steamboats anchored in the Mississippi. We tell him that he will find his wife safe in the refugee camp in Baton Rouge, but he is dubious.

"Ha! You don't know my wife! You never can tell what that woman going to do! She got sister in New Iberia. She got brother in Houma. She got cousin in Natchez. God knows where she gone!"

When we try to get him to come with us into the life-boat, he refuses: "What! Me leave my cow and my mule and my dog and cat? I tell you no!" We point out that it is extremely difficult to get food to him in this remote spot, and that he may go hungry many days, but he is determined to stick it out. He has been able to find food for his cows and horses by breaking off leaves from half submerged trees; a little canned food was left for himself, his sons, the cat, and dogs.

Fastened to the eaves of the house is a hastily constructed raft of logs, and upon this are the cow and calf, the mule, and two horses. The raft rises and falls in the rushing water.

The household treasures which he has taken to the roof make an incongruous picture in the blinding sunlight: a photograph album bound in red plush, a patent rocking-chair, quilts and blankets, a water-cooler, trunks, a bicycle, and—oddly enough—half a dozen potted plants, red geraniums, a gay splash of color. A hen and a brood of young chickens are pecking about on the shingles. In the shadow of the chimney a cat lies, regarding us with mild yellow eyes, her paws folded under her.

As we chug on our way he calls after us: "Hey! If you see my wife, tell her we're all right, and we'll stay here till she come home again!"

With my inner eye I see that sad homecoming—ruined crops, ruined houses—the savings of a lifetime destroyed. But Ambrose Lemoine is making the best of it. . . .

Late in the afternoon, when our surf-boat has taken as many refugees as it will hold, we go back through the flood to the *Kankakee,* a large steamboat which is anchored at the mouth of Red River. Here our refugees are put aboard, here they are fed, here they remain until the river steamer *King* comes by to pick them up and bring them down the river to Baton Rouge.

It is twilight, and the big boat is crowded. Men and women stand mute, looking out over the rushing river. Children, blistered from the sun, cry in their mothers' arms. It is like some horror of war—only this time the enemy is the Mississippi.

And yet there is always a glamour about the river, even in this tragic time. Twilight deepens, blotting out the distant line of trees which marks the place where land had been a few weeks ago. All about us is movement—motorboats go chugging by; submarine chasers lie alongside, their decks filled with sailors; other river steamboats are seen, the red and green lights upon the twin smokestacks bright in the gathering dusk. The air becomes cooler since the sun has set, and the breeze is filled with the scent of crushed, wet willow-trees.

Out of the darkness comes a large steamboat—the U.S.S. *William R. King* of St. Louis. All the refugees—286 of us—are put aboard. We swarm over the decks. The *King* pushes three large barges before her, abreast. The center barge is filled with negroes, under a tent, all their worldly goods piled around them. To the left is a barge packed tight with cows which low incessantly. The barge on the right is similarly loaded with a mixed cargo of horses and mules, cows and calves. The animals are crowded with no regard to their torture—this through direct necessity. So tight-packed are they, that they rise one above the other. The horses whinny; the cows low. Their torture is like some dream of hell.

The women and children are crowded together inside the cabin and upon the rear decks of the steamboat; the white men are on the forward deck above the negroes, the mules, and the cattle. Other barges are towed alongside the

King, and the whole presents the picture of a floating island—an island loaded with as miserable a freight as can be imagined.

The searchlight, playing from the upper deck, lights up the barges before us, showing the milling animals, the crouching negroes, the whole miserable scene. Acadians, thin and bronzed, go about the edges of the cattle barges trying to do what they can for the animals there. One tall thin boy wearing a tattered red sweater stands watching a calf being trampled beneath the hoofs of frightened cows.

The animals kick and bite each other, showing the whites of their eyes. And always the pitiful cries of distress, of thirst, of hunger, of fright. I go forward upon the barge and speak to the boy in the red sweater—one refugee to another. I speak of the plight of the animals, and he says: "Po' things . . . they've been there since yesterday." Then he forgets me, watching again the black and white calf which is now flecked with blood from the crushing hoofs of the larger animals.

I go back to the steamer again. Here the decks are filled with sprawling figures, men and boys, making a pretense of sleeping. The breeze is cool, but the deck is hot, for beneath us are the boilers.

A whisper is in circulation. Something is wrong. Fear of the unknown stalks among us. There is a rumor, the captain says, of a crevasse in the river below us. If this is true, he must tie the *King* up for the night—for, should this heavily laden boat come within the area of a crevasse, we might be carried through to death.

The searchlight plays along the distant banks, picking out the levee-tops, standing a scant two feet above the rushing water. Between us and the levees are fringes of willows—growing on the batture, or that part of the bank which extends beyond the levee in low-water time, but which is now completely flooded. The pilot has found trees large enough to offer secure anchorage, and the *King,* with its barges before it, is headed for the bank. The boat and barges nose into the willows, crashing down the smaller trees before us. How green the leaves appear in the glare of the searchlight! How unreal it all seems—the barges of animals, the crouching negroes, the white men, leaning forward, watching anxiously.

The smaller trees crack off like match-stems. Large trees fall before the weight of the cattle barges; then, after a long moment, there is a jolt, a cry. Men run along the edge of the barges, throwing out ropes. We are made fast, and swing about with the current. We find ourselves against a gigantic tree, which stands half out of the water. The green leaves are all about us, reaching to the upper decks. The boat seems to be in a wood—were it not for the rushing water below decks.

The crowded cattle grasp hungrily at the leaves which are just out of their reach. A brown and white spotted cow falls and is trampled upon. The little black and white calf is dead now, flecked with blood. Frenzied mules kick each other with fiendish force.

Above, on the deck, we talk: "Yes, sir! Four thousand acres I had under cultivation. There's not one acre above water. It was the richest land in the State. My hay alone would have brought $10,000 this year." The man sits huddled up, figuring on a scrap of paper by the reflection from the searchlight. He talks to any one who will listen.

Near-by a man of middle age, an Acadian, mumbles excitedly to himself: "A day laborer . . . that's what I'll be. . . . Not a thing left. All I had was two hundred hogs. I didn't get one of them out. Yessir! All of 'em drowned. I'm too old to begin again. . . . I can't." And he wanders off into the darkness.

A crevasse, that is, a break in the levee, by A. R. Waud

From *Harper's Weekly,* May 26, 1866, reproduction courtesy Special Collections, LSU Libraries

Another man: "I'll never go back. No, not me! I never want to see that country again. All my life I live there—and now!"

Still another: "*Sacre,* man! Sure you'll go back! We'll all go back! What I say is this: 'If you haven't got, you can't lose!' Ain't that the truth?" He laughs.

A little boy, round-eyed, holding his father's hand, says: "When will it be mawnin', Papa? Is it nearly mawnin', Papa?" And the man says: "Sh-sh! Let the poor people sleep!"

" . . . And out at Bayou Choupique where I come from, we go on the roof. . . . But what you know? The house capsize . . . like that! I tell you; man, I see trouble this year!"

A woman is walking up and down the deck, moaning. Nobody knows what the trouble is, and she will not answer when spoken to. She has been walking so for an hour. Another woman comes and leads her away.

A boy of perhaps fourteen years comes close to me in the darkness: "Mister, for God's sake, tell me what to do when we get to Baton Rouge . . . me and my cow. . . . There she is, brindled like . . . see? She's going to have a calf. She'll get trampled to death sure . . . sure!"

Down on the barge before us, where the negroes are camped, an aged negro man has lumped down among drums of gasoline and bundles tied up with clothes-lines. A young negro girl kneels beside him, putting a cup to his lips. The searchlight moves on, blotting out the picture.

We settle down to sleep as best we can, waiting for safety, and sunrise, and dry land.

Show-boat

Kent and Margaret Lighty

Kent and Margaret Lighty came down the river in a
shantyboat—a sort of houseboat that generally has no
motor and flows with the current—but equipped also
with a motorboat (the *Salamander*). Among their adventures in Louisiana waters was this encounter above
Baton Rouge with a showboat, still a feature on the
Mississippi in the 1930s.

We were reading tranquilly under open windows,
early in the afternoon (hard to believe that this May midday had come in January), when suddenly a strange, sweet sound startled us. Faint, high, and clear
a melody drifted. . . . It seemed literally far off in the sky, above the world. We
looked at each other. There wasn't a town within thought or a dwelling in ear-
shot. There was, there could be, only one possibility: a show-boat was steaming up the river.

The next minute we were untying the *Salamander,* and then aboard, flying
up-stream in the direction of that shrill remote sound. Oh yes, it was the calliope a show-boat uses to announce that it is coming in to port somewhere;
the loud, clear, triumphant calliope that can be heard in all the cabins and
plantation houses for miles around.

It was. From the tip of the island we looked down the main channel and
there, just nosing into a laborious landing, was a great white steamboat pushing a bigger, bulkier, more glittering white boat before it. We took the glass
and on the roof of the Texas deck[9] of the tow saw the calliope itself, with its
own little puff of steam rising and an erect, earnest little figure in a broad-

---

9. The steamboat deck containing pilot house and officers' cabins.

brimmed black hat vehemently thumping out "The Land Where the Wurz-burger Flows." Coming closer, we picked out letters painted large on the boats: *Chaperon,* that was the steamer. And *Hollywood,* the floating theater. That seemed a silly name to give it.

As we scrambled aboard, a small freckled lad offered a handbill. This announced:

CLEAN—MORAL—REFINED

HOLLYWOOD

SHOWBOAT

Proudly Presents

"The Hoodlum"

In 3 acts

It's a Charming Story of Intrigue and Romance

and

HIGH CLASS VAUDEVILLE

We tucked it in a pocket, firmly determined to witness this prodigy in due time, and walked forward. Here was an entirely correct and conventional theater entrance, electric-light strings and all. Comedy grinned in a great crescent on one side of the lobby, Tragedy mourned on the other. Behind a little ticket window was B. F. Menke, the owner.

He was glad to see us. Indeed he was. Anybody that liked the river. We were to make ourselves at home, spend the afternoon with them, take dinner aboard, and have a look at their show to-night. Meet the cast.

"Boy!" For the freckled lad had softly followed us. "Call Mr. Cole."

Possibly every show-boat has its Mr. Cole, but it is extremely doubtful what this one would have done without him. For this young man, in addition to doing a stint at the calliope (in the profession, of course, it rhymes with "heliotrope") each day as they made a new landing, and for three fifteen-minute periods before every show, was the producer and also the juvenile lead. In addition he painted scenery and performed upon the slide trombone and the drums, by turns, during intermission. He is probably doing one or another of these things as you read this, for he told us he was content with show-boat life. Having come up from the "mud" shows, through a brief turn on the concert stage, to vaudeville, and during the war period having entertained soldiers in France, he knew what it was all about, and he was sticking with the river.

To be sure, it was an exacting life while the show was on. No performer, and not even a deck-hand or a fireman, was hired for duty unless he was especially versatile. All the actors played in the orchestra before the show, and in the intermissions some went down the aisles selling candy; and some did vaudeville stunts between the acts.

The steamboat hands served as ushers, he told us as we crossed to the *Chaperon*. And the spirit of the theater followed us right into the boiler-room. Prowling noiselessly there, we were not at first observed, and this is what we heard:

"What did you do with that money?" This came threateningly from the vicinity of the coal-pile.

"What money?" from a coil of rope.

"You know very well what money. . . . "

It was just one of the scenes from the show-boat repertory, floating in the boiler-room. A deck-hand, after long months of ushering, would probably make as capable an understudy as anybody else. There was no room for dead timber on so compact a unit as a show-boat. The result was a closely shared life, and, it seemed to us, an unusually friendly one.

We were beginning to understand why this gifted young Jack of all trades who led us around liked the life. They worked hard while they worked, but in between there were always the long idle journeys down the bayous, from one isolated village to the next, and then up the great river.

In the star's dressing-room, which was also her state-room, of course, we found the women of the cast making fudge and pecan pralines over a portable alcohol stove, to send to the mother of one of them, back in a Pennsylvania village. While the sweet mixture bubbled they were studying the spring fashion catalogue of a mail-order house, just brought over the levee from the tiny post-office and store behind, and some one triumphantly discovered a neat little ensemble—"just the thing to wear around the boat, my dear." The woman who played heavies was the wife of Mr. Cole. Indeed, we discovered that all the actors came, as you might say, in pairs. It was an economy of space, an important consideration in a migratory theater, as he gravely explained. They were happy, because apparently they were gipsies by temperament or by long force of habit. There were few things they hadn't tried. Some, like Cole, had served their time in the old wagon shows, others had played in carnivals and circuses, and a few were vaudeville performers who had tired of hotels.

The fun began after dinner, when from the plantation houses far and wide, from the village store, and from the negro cabins, a flickering trail of lanterns and electric torches wound over the levee and down the *Hollywood* stage-plank. They were all there, and they were all in their seats early. Two of the actresses were selling candy from the stage long before curtain-time. Some boxes entitled the purchasers to prizes and soon laps bulged with Indian blankets and plumed kewpie dolls. Then the candy girls disappeared, turning up again almost immediately in the orchestra with the rest of the cast. Programs rustled to the strains of the Blue Danube and the audience puzzled as they read:

Is a Rube always a Rube?
Is a Crook always Bad?
Is a Suspect always Guilty?
Is a Hoodlum always a Hoodlum?

The curtain rang up on the melodrama that was to tell us all this. And from there on it was just a stampede of entertainment; and a stampede of appreciation and participation on our side of the footlights. "The entire scene of the play," we had read, "takes place in the gathering room of Peter Argyle's estate on the outskirts of New York City." Here were all of us, away down on the Mississippi River, privileged to look in on that magnificent gathering room and the goings on—"gripping, full of heart interest, love and devotion, and chuck-full of good clean comedy"—of its metropolitan habitues. It was immense. We hooted, clapped, booed, wept in sudden oases of silence, stamped, almost fainted of laughter. All of us, the country lawyer and his wife and the troop of youngsters seated, seriatim, between them, the village idiot, the cotton-pickers, were having the time of our lives.

Afterward, the cast had coffee, made over the same alcohol stove, in one of the state-rooms, and together we swapped stories about the river, for many of their habitual stands had been our mooring-places. There was an air of leisure and easy friendliness, a ruminative pulling at pipes and sipping at cups. Another day was over, another evening of strenuous, highly cooperative, nervous work was done. The night could be as long as they chose, as long as their stories and ours would make it. For them it did not matter; the steamboat would be on its way by dawn, and when they awakened it might be puffing them along fifty miles up-stream from here. Meanwhile there were guests, who lived on the river like themselves. The coffee-pot was passed around again.

An imperative call came then for Cole, a call from forward where the "boss" had his room:

" 'Casey Jones' on the calliope! Give us 'Casey Jones'!"

Cole leaped to his feet, snatched up his big black hat, necessary to the correct execution of this role, and was bounding across to the steamboat, up through the moonlight to her Texas deck. The shrill, insistent notes of "Casey Jones" sprang out over the midnight river, so shrill, so gay, they almost drowned out an undertone of rhythmic splashing. Leaning over the rail, we saw, sharp against dark water, the sprinkled lights of the *Belle*. Her captain was a friend of the show-boat owner; this was a greeting. She passed us close, and the last notes of the ballad died, gave us her salute of three crisp blasts. Then three more as she splashed up the channel.

It was time for us to be going, too, to be saying good-by. Strange how hard it was sometimes to break a chance meeting. We'd never see each other again, of course, but we'd all talked together over coffee and tobacco, and in some kind of way we'd become friends. They leaned over the rails with their flashlights to watch us untie the *Salamander*. The rising moon, just slanting over the "floating palace," cut out their silhouettes, shouting and laughing good-by, as we looked back. We sped off then over the dark water, around the island, and down to our silent bayou.

Canoeing the Mississippi

EDDY L. HARRIS

Harris, an African American journalist, canoed down
the Mississippi, starting in Minnesota, in the 1980s.
Bobbing about the great river in a tiny canoe, dwarfed
by seagoing vessels, he provides a unique perspective
on the lower Mississippi as it is today: between New
Orleans and Baton Rouge stretches a major port.
Oceangoing ships ascend as far as Baton Rouge; cargo
from and to places farther upstream are transhipped
in barges.

The realm of the barges ends at Baton Rouge. From
Baton Rouge on south, the river is much deeper and the bridges across the
river are higher and from now on the Mississippi can support the weight of
tankers that reach out to cargo the world.

I met my first tanker in the morning. Slipping from camp early in the mist,
two sharp bends in the river, and there she was. A massive red ship riding high
in the water. The *Hoegh Forum* from Oslo.

If those others were beasts, these huge things were behemoths twenty
stories tall and longer from end to end than any two stacks of barges strapped
together—towboats included. Bright red steel changing to a darker color below the water line, and orange rust sneaking through the paint all over. I could
almost smell the salty sea mingling with the Mississippi's muddy odor.

I moved away and watched the sharp front end of the ship peel away the
layers of water rushing to meet the bow. So totally unlike the river slapping at
the squared off ends of barges. The river moved aside for these machines, their
bows slicing right through the water and shoving aside a mountain ridge of
water that rushed toward me like a tidal wave. I waited for the damage to be

done and held on tight. Strange thing, though. The wake from these mammoths was high and swift, but not rough at all. Very gentle, in fact, and as long as I kept the front end of the canoe facing into the moving wall of water, I only bobbed gently up and down on the successive waves. I couldn't understand it and tried to explain it away by the depth of the river or the counterrotation of the tanker engine's screws or the easy way the tanker sliced through the water, but whatever it was, it felt great and a lot more fun to ride than the wake from the barges. . . .

I sailed into the valley of these tall ships: oil tankers, grain tankers, freighters. *Exxon Baytown, Enand Hope, Alonossos,* and some eastern vessel whose letters I couldn't read. But then came the *Professor Kostiukov* from Odessa. When she passed I was dead tired and my shoulder was giving me fits. But all the hands on the bridge came out to look. I could see they were watching me through binoculars and maybe wondering who I was or what I was doing. Maybe they thought I was a spy. Maybe they envied the freedom. No way could they get away with this in Mother Russia. Someone would suspect them of trying to escape—which was exactly what I was doing, but of a different kind. One of them came out with a camera and took pictures. They wouldn't believe this back home in the Ukraine. I straightened out and carried on as if I were strong and fresh and just starting out. I wanted them to be jealous. And then they waved down at me. One sailor put his fingers in his mouth and pierced the air with his joyous whistle, and that gave me real strength. I raised my arms overhead and they did the same. We were brothers on the water, rivermen, seafarers, sailors all. . . .

Later on that evening I came upon the *Delta Queen* again. She was moored at the shore, having landed to let her passengers off for an excursion to the plantations nearby. The *Queen* . . . was here for a day and would head back tonight for New Orleans again. The captain told me to find him in the city when I arrived tomorrow and he would take me aboard and show me around and buy me lunch. I told him I'd see him there.

The *Queen* passed me just as it got dark outside. She was all lit up like a party about to happen and I was feeling my way through the barges, moving and parked, and past all the industrial docks along the way. Once more I was out on the river after dark. I passed many spots that would have made suitable campsites, and certainly better than the one I finally ended up with, in the trees, on a hill, behind a parking lot of empty barges that had been loaded with some kind of grain and still smelled like it, barges that rocked back and forth all night long, clanking against one another, their ropes creaking constantly under the strain. But I could not bring myself to leave the river. I didn't care about the danger of canoeing after dark among all this crowd of rust and steel, I didn't care that I might run into something or get hit by something or fall over and drown. I wanted to stay on the river as long as I could tonight. It was going to be my last night on the river.

I wanted to stretch it out.

Tomorrow would be my last day.

The Invisible Corridor

B. C. HALL AND C. T. WOOD

> Hall and Wood drove much of the length of the Mississippi—taking various excursions on the river as they went—because of their interest in its history and romance. Along the way they talked to many who worked on or simply lived along it. The chapter reprinted here from their *Big Muddy: Down the Mississippi Through America's Heartland* is telling commentary on the lingering past and on the ecological concerns of today.

Highway 61 widens into a freeway and takes you all the way to New Orleans. The rains didn't let up and we had to feel our way along until we got to a turnoff that would take us to State Highway 44, called here simply the River Road. It's a good blacktop road and it meanders precisely with the river along the edge of the earthen levee. It's a beautiful levee, neatly clipped and as green and soothing as fresh mint, with cattle grazing lazily on the slopes behind a chain-link fence.

Just south of Baton Rouge begins a procession of beautiful old antebellum houses and estates, most open for tours at about five or six dollars a walkthrough. We were told at a state tourist center that firms specializing in restoration have taken over most of the old houses and have made them profitable attractions. We stopped and chatted with a group coming out from a tour and one person said she thought it was "really nice for those families who've owned the mansions for ages to open them up for us."

The chemical corridor has actually already begun above Baton Rouge; it runs through the city in an almost uninterrupted line to New Orleans. Before striking out for the levee we had swung over on the west bank to pass by Ethyl Corporation, B. F. Goodrich, American Cynanamid, Dow, Cos-Mar, Copolymer, Fina, Arcadian, BASF, Borden. We were just getting started, for there were others to see down the river: Georgia Gulf, Kaiser, Marathon, Melamine, Monsanto, Nalco, Triad, Texaco, Exxon again, Union Carbide, Uniroyal, Vulcan, Shell. And we probably missed some.

The charm of the antebellum mansions back in their cupular groves of tall live oaks and Spanish moss suddenly changes as in a movie montage and you're thrown upon an industrial expanse. One minute you're driving along the frontage of Tara, and the next you see an Orwellian phantom—an undressed pile of steel and sheet metal with octopus arms and bulgy pipes and conveyor belts leaning against the river. Here all of America's Fortune 500s churn out the products of daily life, from prescription drugs and videotapes to the wax coating on milk cartons.

The sugarcane fields begin just south of Baton Rouge and grow south and west through the land called Acadia, home of the Cajuns. The cane was head-high as we passed through and was sucking up the rain and turning a rich, dark green as it moved off toward the bayous along the river. In the fall the cane will grow as tall as trees and turn amber at harvest. In Twain's time the heavens would have been choked with thick black smoke from the bagasse fires, but now the cane farmers don't burn the cropped cane; they use stalk and all for feed and fertilizer.[10] We passed sugarcane fields planted right up to the walls of the chemical plants; sloughs of stagnant black water seeped into the fields.

The River Road hugs so close to the levee that occasionally we could look out and see the Mississippi. Huge oceangoing ships were in the deep channel and we made out one old red tanker with Russian markings; later we would see Japanese and Norwegian ships. This portion of the Mississippi is international and the big foreign ships can get upriver as far as Baton Rouge; the ones we saw were oil tankers.

All the little towns on the levee seemed oblivious to the fact that they are plugged into the chemical corridor. We stopped in a town called Prairieville after passing other large estates, interspersed among humble little houses. At

---

10. Bagasse is the residue of the cane stalks after the juice has been squeezed out. Today it is often used to fuel the fires of a grinding mill. The fires visitors see in cane country are those used to burn the leaves off the stalks once cane has been cut in the fields.

an old-fashioned corner grocery we listened to some men talking about football, the Saints of New Orleans; the men weren't at all interested in our questions as to how they feel about the chemical companies. "Who cares about
'em?" one young man said. In Prairieville we passed a playground of basket-
ball courts someone had thought to name after baseball great Jackie Robinson. We wondered how Jackie got all the way down to Louisiana; in his era he
wouldn't have been allowed to play ball here.

Billows of white smoke rose off the BASF Corporation refinery next along
the levee, and around a bend we came to the outsized Borden plant. Now followed Uniroyal, jammed up against the river. As we passed these plants we saw
big rusting cast-iron pipes running over the levee to the river, carrying off the
wastewater. The plants take in enormous amounts of water and return it to
the river, and it is this process that so disturbs the environmentalists. Posted
on the levee were NO TRESPASSING signs. Security cars came along the River
Road every so often; it's not a private road but you have to believe it is the
province of the companies. We had learned in Baton Rouge that all the big
companies on the corridor are extra-sensitive, almost paranoid about sabo-
tage. We just stopped and asked a security guard about the matter and he said,
"It's understandable, with all the explosions they have."

Next came an oddity. The road sign said, GILLIS W. LONG HANSEN'S DIS-
EASE CENTER. A white gravel road led up over the levee; we took it and came
down to a ferry landing. Three pickup trucks were waiting to get on the ferry.
The sign by the ferry said, CARVILLE. We had come upon what was once
called a leper colony, the only one of its kind in America. Leprosy, or Hansen's
disease, is not totally a thing of the past. Cases crop up and when they do,
those afflicted are brought here for treatment, across the river at Carville. The
treatment center sits on a remote little island of its own among the chemical
plants.

We got out and talked to the people waiting in the pickups. One man, who
was on his way to work across the river, said he didn't think they allowed visitors at the Hansen center. He was right, and we didn't need to bother those
people. In another pickup two men sat reading the morning newspaper; they
worked at a plant near Carville. We asked them how they liked their jobs and
one said blandly, "The work's hard but okay." The other said, "Sheeit, they
pay dog-do."

Rain was coming down harder and through it we proceeded into a kind of
surreal fog. We didn't even need to conjure up visions from Kafka; it was vivid

enough like an American gothic turned dark, and there sat a leper colony in the middle of it all.

The levee road winds on past more antebellum estates with prominent signs announcing guided tours daily. Because it was raining so hard, we didn't see a great many tourists taking in the shows, and somehow we didn't think too many people would be coming to tour chemical plants and refineries. We saw no signs by the plants inviting guests. We did see more cattle grazing on the levee and more rusty pipes going to the river. At the big, rambling BASF plant an extra-tall chain-link fence stretched along the levee. BASF wants no sightseers and puts up NO TRESPASSING signs about every hundred yards. Evidently the companies own, or think they own, the levee. Maybe they hold lifetime leases.

State Road 44 winds on toward New Orleans, and still more pre–Civil War mansions appear. We passed through the town of Donaldsonville, where a high arching bridge connects to the western shore of the river; the sugarcane fields come on again to the levee, thickening like a jungle. The Burnside plant ahead looks as if it will block the highway, and actually it spreads across it, so we drove right through the plant. They were making asphalt and the world around the giant plant was totally blackened. Heavy viscid smoke concealed the sky and did not dissipate even in the stiff wind and steady rain. We passed a honky tonk at Donaldsonville called Duke's Place, with a sign that said, COME PARTY.

Marinas along this stretch of the corridor offer boats and pirogues for rent and a few pleasure boats were berthed in the little harbors. The estates in the vicinity seemed so affluent that we were reminded of the silk-stocking strip of the upper river. But the look here is a bit deceiving. Nowhere is the contrast more pronounced than in the picturesque little place called Good Hope.

In the early 1980s calamity struck the quiet town of Good Hope. A series of spills at the big Good Hope refinery left the town on the brink of annihilation. Fires broke out one after another until there were so many that the river itself, local people claimed, caught fire. In the end a hundred fires struck the Good Hope plant, and there was so much combustible material pumping out that there was simply no way to stop the inferno. We spoke to one local resident who said the fires kept breaking out for weeks, months. That was back in 1982. In an edition devoted primarily to the chemical corridor's problems, *Newsweek* reported in 1990 that the Good Hope Refinery was ordered shut down and that the company had bought and closed the adjacent public school. *Newsweek* also reported that Georgia Gulf bought out forty families who lived in Reveilletown and settled a class-action suit out of court.[11] Dow Chemical is trying to buy up as many communities as possible, we learned in Baton Rouge.

Something of a buy-out and buy-off mentality seems to be taking hold of the chemical companies along the corridor. "Maybe their thinking is that they will be absolved when they remove all the citizens," a veteran newspaper reporter in Baton Rouge told us. "Some of those boys higher up in the companies think they are now untouchable."

We stopped at the closed elementary school in Good Hope. It's gone a little shoddy because it's just sitting there. Spills, explosions and fires have been so commonplace that any new one hardly rates a headline in the state papers. The town of Good Hope is pretty enough still, and people live here and go about their business. They weren't very talkative or neighborly, and we could understand that after all the fires and the evacuations. With the refinery closed, the town is just about dead too, and in a very real way it reminded us of Times Beach.[12] A few people were hanging around, hanging on. The harbor wasn't doing much business with its pirogue rentals. One fellow told us they were thinking of renaming the town, and that would be a step toward reality.

The rain came harder again and to get in out of it we took a tour of one of the antebellum mansions. The place was called the San Francisco House; it was just down the way from Good Hope and wedged in among Cargill, Marathon and Dow.

The tour guides at the San Francisco House were gracious; there was a fair turnout of tourists despite the rain, and the old plantation proved to be a unique diversion. The house has nothing whatsoever to do with the city of the Golden Gate. Instead, it derived its name from the French slang expression *sans fruscins,* "without a cent." That's what the original owner of the plantation claimed his wife left him after she spent his money furnishing the place. Before the Civil War, the San Francisco plantation was part of several parcels of land dating back to the original French colonies, though the big house itself wasn't built until the mid 1850s—in time for Mark Twain perhaps to no-

11. "Troubled Waters," *Newsweek,* April 16, 1990, pp. 66–69, 71–73, 75, 77, 79–80 (esp. 77, 79).

12. A Missouri town that suffered an environmental disaster and that figured earlier in their book.

tice it during his piloting days. The house sits just a hundred yards off the riverbank. Most of the features in the mansion were designed for ostentation; the owner put down crushed brick in the dining hall to make it look like a rich carpet, and the crown molding of the ceiling was done in polished cypress that has an amazing resemblance to marble.

The plantation owner's name was Edmond Marmillion. His family had owned other estates in the area and his lineage dated to the settlers who came here with Bienville. Marmillion consolidated the smaller estates into one big sugarcane plantation. The slave quarters are still out back and the house itself is a galleried affair in the French Creole style; it has an enormous roof ventilated by a band of louvers at the attic floor. Much of the house is the original work. Marmillion had three daughters, the tour brochure says. Two of them never married, not a surprising fact considering that the Civil War wiped out most of the South's male population.

As we went past the Cargill plant down the road, the second shift was just going on. We saw white men and black men and dark sons of Acadia. They all looked hardy and they didn't hurry to get in out of the rain. Marmillion would have welcomed them in.

The corridor ends without announcement; the levee road curves and takes you back out to Highway 61. We couldn't be sure, of course, but we had the idea that the chemical and oil companies like the presence of all the elegant mansions along the corridor—they lend a needed look of credibility.

The tour of the chemical corridor is not really an unpleasant drive, and we almost found ourselves going emotionally numb. In 1989 when the Greenpeace people toured the river, they were anything but numb. They studied in detail all the companies here and made many shocking accusations and formidable disclosures, using the EPA and other official agencies as sources of data. Greenpeace indicted all the companies for gross water and air pollution. Dow Chemical at Plaquemine, for instance, has a daily wastewater flow, says Greenpeace, of 452 million gallons and the plant generated 98 million pounds of hazardous waste a year and released more than 6 million pounds of hydrocarbons into the air. Dupont at Laplace, Louisiana, had a daily wastewater flow of 57 million gallons and released 1.6 million pounds of toxic waste into the environment. Greenpeace's lists fill a good-sized book and the statistics are so stupefying that they become almost ludicrous. Greenpeace also drew some damning conclusions in its cancer studies along the corridor, and it was over this critical point that Greenpeace became a victim of its own overwhelming statistics. It pinpointed the corridor as having the highest rate of mortality from cancer and infant death in the Mississippi basin. And the Chemical Association jumped on Greenpeace, saying it had "committed scientific malpractice" because it couldn't prove its claims.

The Association went on record that the chemical companies return water to the river in better shape than when they draw it out. The Association was aided by local public health officials in Louisiana who said that "there might be a cancer problem on the Corridor but it is a small one." Greenpeace had intended its river survey to put the country on alert about the poisoning of the national waterway. The actual result was to alert the chemical industry that it needed to improve its public image. . . .

The sun came out the morning we headed down Old 61 again but it disappeared by midday and the rain set in hard again. Weather bulletins were coming thick and fast on the radio. Flash floods had hit the suburbs of New Orleans, now just a few miles away, and two lanes of the interstate into the city had been closed. We were thinking that maybe we'd have the threat of a hurricane. Maybe we'd get to the Crescent City in time to see what one of those parties was all about.[13]

13. Some Louisianians gather with friends during hurricanes and—unable to go anywhere else during the fierce storm—"party" while it rages outside.

Travel Update

Mary Ann Sternberg's *Along the River Road: Past and Present on Louisiana's Historic Byway* (Baton Rouge, 1996), provides the contemporary traveler with an exceptionally fine guide to the River Road (which, as Sternberg makes clear, is actually a series of roads). The Mississippi River can, of course, be seen from any number of places. Roads run along the river for many miles, at times virtually on the edge of the levees, at times swerving away and running at a distance from the banks. The river cannot, however, be driven along in the same sense that the Loire, say, or the Columbia can be driven along, because there are high levees that prevent the river's being seen from the road. There are roads along the top of the levee in some places, but they are mostly dirt or gravel and are used for restricted purposes. The flow of the river creates a natural levee; early settlers along the river were required to maintain levees because the Mississippi rises dramatically due to spring thaws farther north. The levee system has been strengthened over the years in response to major floods—such as the one Lyle Saxon wrote of—and the levees today are massive.

Thus, to see the river it is necessary to find vantage points: bridges, the Moon Walk and River Walk in New Orleans, the lawn of the Old State Capitol in Baton Rouge, the various levee-top paths and roads. The State Capitol in Baton Rouge offers an observatory deck from which visitors can get a nice perspective on not only the Mississippi but also the surrounding countryside. There are also boat trips on the river, mostly out of New Orleans, often on vessels carefully built to resemble old-time riverboats. And Louisiana state and local government entities continue to operate ferries at various points. Once free, they now commonly charge a modest fee (though usually only in one direction), and they offer rides across the great stream that are, if direct and thus short, pleasant and in tune with the everyday life of the region. One ferry (still free for pedestrians) leaves from the foot of Canal Street in New Orleans and crosses to Algiers. Foot passengers can ride round trip without ever leaving the boat. The upper decks offer superb views of the French Quarter and downtown New Orleans as well as of the river itself.

One particularly interesting vantage point for seeing the river that reminds us of the Mississippi's incredible power as a natural force is the Old River Control Structure in lower Concordia Parish. Owing to the physics of river flow, the Mississippi has continually changed its course over the centuries and is still doing so. In 1831 steamboatman Captain Henry Shreve cut through a neck of land created by a loop in the meandering river bed near where the Red River flowed into and the Atchafalaya River flowed out of the Mississippi. The Mississippi's main channel followed Shreve's cut, and the old loop came to be called Old River (where Lyle Saxon's account of the 1927 flood opens), part of it eventually silting up. Soon the Red no longer emptied into the Mississippi but into the Atchafalaya, though Old River was a connection that allowed for some Mississippi water to still go down the Atchafalaya. After 1839 the Atchafalaya was cleared of obstructions that had limited its flow, and more and more Mississippi water entered its banks. Because the Atchafalaya now offered a shorter route to the Gulf of Mexico than the Mississippi's present channel and because rivers often shift course to find shorter routes, it seemed possible that the Mississippi might change its route—inundating the Atchafalaya Basin, turning the Mississippi's current lower channel into a saltwater estuary, and wreaking economic and social havoc.

Alcée Fortier mused on this possibility in the 1890s (see Chapter 6). There was so much concern by the 1950s that the Mississippi River Commission recommended the building of a structure—in effect a dam controlling a specially dug "outflow channel"—to regulate the flow of the Mississippi into the Atchafalaya. Old River was dammed to prevent the Mississippi from changing course into the Atchafalaya, and a lock was built to allow for navigation between the rivers. However, through the 1970s flood conditions sorely tested the structures, and an auxiliary structure was built in 1981 to further strengthen the defenses. The possibility that the structures could fail and the Mississippi again change its course—with disastrous consequences—remains, giving a visit to the control structure a touch of the dramatic. Louisiana 15 crosses all the structures, though there is no tour of the facilities available. Just upriver from the low sill structure is a shell-paved parking lot that allows a view of the Mississippi and the outflow channel.

As B. C. Hall and C. T. Wood suggest, the stretch of river country from just above Baton Rouge to New Orleans is an odd mixture of the industrial and the ancient. Stately plantation houses and lesser homes—both of which can be found neat or run-down—alternate with petrochemical and other

manufacturing and shipping facilities. The surreal effect is heightened by escaping steam, strangely colored piles of minerals, warning lights, and by the
seeming absence of human habitation at the highly mechanized plants. The
mixture is not without its fascination. As Eddy Harris discovered, huge seagoing vessels put in at the plants; if the river is high, one can drive along the
River Road and look up at giant boats tethered to the bank. Of course the
presence of industry has created environmental problems, as Hall and Wood
also note. According to figures published in 1991, 136 petrochemical plants
in an 80 mile stretch of river dumped 900 million pounds of toxins into the
river the previous year.

San Francisco Plantation, mentioned by Hall and Wood, is a superb example of classic "steamboat Gothic" architecture with astoundingly elaborate
trim. Located on Louisiana 44 at Reserve, it has been very well restored and is
open for tours. Also open for tours (Monday–Friday, twice daily; inquire for
times) is the Gillis W. Long Hansen's Disease Center, so it is surprising that
Hall and Wood thought this facility did not encourage visitors. The center is,
however, likely to be closed, and the site dedicated to other use as the population of patients steadily shrinks owing to medical advances.

The Louisiana State Capitol, mocked by Twain, was designed by James Dakin and completed in 1852. It burned in 1862 while occupied by Federal
troops during the Civil War (hence Twain's remark that he hoped dynamite
would finish the place off) and was restored in 1880. It is a masterpiece of
Gothic-revival architecture. The restoration added cast-iron turrets that intensified the pseudomedieval aspect of the building and that Twain no doubt
saw in 1882. Dakin was a codesigner of the St. Charles Hotel in New Orleans, to which so many nineteenth-century travelers went. See Chapter 7 for
more information on the building today and also Arthur Scully, Jr., *James Dakin, Architect: His Career in New York and the South* (Baton Rouge, 1973).

Louisiana 39, running down the eastern bank of the river below New Orleans, is more a country road than Louisiana 23, which runs down the western
bank and is four-lane and speedy in most places. Louisiana 23 does stretch
farther south. Venice is the last town actually on the river that is reachable by
this road, which continues a short distance, unceremoniously terminating at
an oil company facility. A visitor can charter a boat at Venice to go on to Pilot
Town (which houses the river pilots who take oceangoing ships in and out of
port) or to see the jetties at the very ends of the Mississippi. The exact location
where LaSalle's expedition raised their cross is not known, but a Plaquemines

Chitimacha Indian baskets, from a history of New Orleans for visitors

From Grace King, *New Orleans: The Place and the People* (New York, 1895)

Parish tradition has it that this was done on the site of the present-day town of Venice.

Native Americans, not surprisingly, figure most prominently in the travel accounts of the French colonial period, when the aboriginal inhabitants of Louisiana were an important presence in the lives of the arriving Europeans. As time passed they became more and more peripheral, sometimes pushed to marginal places, sometimes absorbed into the general culture, sometimes discriminated against or ignored. There is still a definite Native American presence in Louisiana, however—over 18,000 Louisianians were listed as such in the 1990 census, with three federally recognized and five state-recognized tribal groups; currently Louisiana has one of the largest Native American populations in the South and among states east of the Mississippi. There are important, active Native American archaeological sites in the state as well.

Poverty Point (the derivation of the name is uncertain) in the northeast corner of the state is among the most significant sites in North America. Now a state commemorative area, the site was the largest early prehistoric settlement in North America and contains extensive earthworks, including a massive mound in the shape of a bird, several smaller mounds, and six concentric rings that spread out from the main mound (these rings were discovered in

1953 from aerial photographs). Located on Bayou Macon, an old bed of the Arkansas River, Poverty Point was at its height from 2,000 to 1,000 B.C.E. and was probably a hub and port that traded widely (materials brought from the Great Lakes, the Appalachians, and the Gulf Coast have all been associated with the site). Visitors can climb on the great mound, which is covered by trees, and walk to various parts of the site. Relatively little is known about the culture that lived there or the purpose of the mounds, so the place, though not an especially dramatic one, takes on some of the mystery that accrues to ruins from the dimly understood past. A museum and film at the visitor center on the site add to intellectual understanding of Poverty Point.

Also of considerable interest is the Marksville Site, also a state commemorative area. The mounds there were built by a southern extension of the Hopewell Culture, and the site is typical of their ceremonial centers. Visitors pass through an ordinary Marksville neighborhood, then through low earthworks to enter the site, where the mounds rise up like ancient riddles (though in fact there has been much excavation to study them). An old channel of the Mississippi (when the river flowed this way from 4,000 to 2,500 B.C.E.) can be seen from the grounds. A small museum provides further information. Also in Marksville is the present location of the Tunica-Biloxi reservation, which contains the tribal museum that houses the famous Tunica Treasure. The museum is in a moated mound that imitates the Marksville site structures—its entrance flanked by sculptures of alligator guardians—so that one goes into the earth to see the treasure that came out of the earth.

The treasure came from a site in West Feliciana Parish, where it was dug up in the 1960s by a treasure hunter who located a Tunica burial ground. Ownership of the grave goods was in dispute for a number of years as the tribe attempted to gain title, which they finally did. In colonial times the Tunica were closely allied to the French and had profitable trading relations with them, providing the Europeans with pelts, salt, and horses. They amassed much wealth in the form of European trade goods, which composed the treasure that gradually was buried with deceased tribe members. The museum is full of thousands of glass beads from Venice and Amsterdam, French- and English-made ceramics, European manufactured iron and copper vessels, and firearms and other weapons. The Tunica Treasure is an extremely important collection of colonial-era trade goods and gives even the casual visitor some idea of the cultural interchange of those times.

Few traces remain of the earliest French settlement, but a re-creation of

Fort St. Jean Baptist provides a most interesting focus for interpreting that period. Located in Natchitoches, this state commemorative area was based on detailed plans of the original fort and other archival materials. Situated a few hundred yards from what is believed to be the actual historical site of the fort, the present reconstruction is an almost startling vision of the past. The whole is completely surrounded by a stockade of pointed logs set in the earth (unlike the originals, these were treated to resist decay; early French settlers did not immediately learn that poles and beams could not be put into Louisiana's moist soil without quickly deteriorating), over which peep rooftops and the diminutive steeple of the settlement's church. Inside are various structures: the commandant's house, barracks, storehouses, outdoor oven, powder magazine. Eighteenth-century construction techniques were used in the building, and the interiors are rudely furnished befitting a military outpost that became a trading center. The complex on the banks of Cane River, a strange contrast to apartments and other modern houses on the opposite side, is the only complete French-colonial fort—albeit a reproduction—in the United States.

Mississippi steamboats became increasingly less significant as passenger vessels when railroads and then highways expanded to provide transport for people, though a number operated well into the twentieth century. Today, the only remaining river steamers are operated by the Delta Queen Steamship Company, which has three boats that offer pleasure cruises of two to fourteen nights' duration. One of these, the *Delta Queen* (encountered by Eddy L. Harris), has been in operation since 1927 (on the Mississippi since the 1940s) and thus takes us back to older days of steamboat travel. The other two, the *Mississippi Queen* and the *American Queen,* were launched in 1976 and 1995, respectively, built specifically for modern cruises. Ironically perhaps, the *American Queen* is the largest steamboat ever built. The company traces its history back to 1890, when it was founded as the "Greene Line," by husband and wife Gordon and Mary Greene, both licensed river pilots. The ships were then operated out of Cincinnati, hauling both freight and passengers. The company relocated to New Orleans in 1985 because so many of its passengers originated their cruising in Louisiana, which, even in this latter day, remains the key terminus for river steamboats. Delta Queen boats cruise on a number of rivers throughout the American heartland.

Showboats plied the Missisippi for over one hundred years. The first bona fide showboat was launched in 1831, and the last was operating into the early 1940s. In their day they presented dramatic performances including Shakespeare; comedy, music, and dance acts; and even equestrian performances on "circus" boats. By the 1930s, however, their staple was exaggerated melodrama like that seen by Kent and Margaret Lighty. Additional information can be found in Philip Graham, *Showboats: The History of an American Institution* (Austin, 1951). Occasional troupes of actors have made their way down the Mississippi more recently, and day tour boats out of New Orleans sometimes provide entertainment, including concerts on their steam calliopes.

Gambling has returned to the Mississippi—though certainly not in a form George Devol would recognize—with the launching of a number of gambling boats based in various locations along the river. In Louisiana there are boats on the Mississippi in New Orleans and Baton Rouge, all designed to resemble traditional riverboats. In Shreveport and Bossier City, they are docked on the Red River. They are required by law to cruise periodically but often do not actually do so. These boats offer slot machines and table games.

The 1927 flood, which inundated a vast area and displaced thousands, is the subject of a history by Pete Daniel, *Deep'n as It Come: The 1927 Mississippi River Flood* (New York, 1977). Glenn R. Conrad and Carl A. Brasseaux's *Crevasse: The 1927 Flood in Acadiana* (Lafayette, La., 1994) includes much photodocumentation of the great flood. Bayou des Glaises and Bayou Choupique, mentioned by Saxon, are in Avoyelles Parish. Bayou des Glaises was heavily leveed; breaks in the levees at several places precipitated the massive flooding that Saxon describes.

2

A Splendid Bedlam
of a City: New Orleans

New Orleans, the Crescent City—so called because of the bend in the Mississippi it's built upon—became a favored destination for travelers early on. Younger than the great cities of the Eastern seaboard, not even the oldest in Louisiana—it was founded in 1718, after Natchitoches and Baton Rouge—it developed as the metropolis of the Mississippi Valley and as one of the few true cities the South had before the end of the nineteenth century. Its size, its location—both a port of entry and the terminus for river steamers—and its reputation as a singular place made it a magnet for visitors. Before the Civil War, its mild winters and pleasant social life made it a popular temporary winter residence for thousands, especially the well-to-do from other parts of the South.

In the nineteenth century those who came—for whatever reason—were sometimes surprised that New Orleans could exist where it does. Sitting in a swampy morass, located below sea level, flooded when the rains came—it was a most unhealthy place. (One eighteenth-century visitor, the English captain Philip

Pittman—whose description of the city is the earliest reprinted here—thought the true metropolis of the lower Mississippi would arise farther upstream, where the river then flowed into Bayou Manchac.) And certainly there have been visitors who were sharp critics, usually on moral grounds—not only did the city teem with secular life on the Sabbath, but indeed it had become known as a place where the sins of the flesh were tolerated and the living was easy (a reputation that holds today). Thus the Englishman J. Benwell called the city "as vile a place as any under the sun . . . [where] the renegades of all nations" flocked to gambling houses, made "violence and bloodshed indigenous," and crowded the saloons.[1] But many visitors, even staid Anglo-Saxons, turned a more forgiving and interested eye toward the diversions and frequently were intrigued by the pace of life and diversity of the population.

Many who describe their arrival in the city or their progress through it cannot but convey their excitement at the bustling activity, the animated life. They write of bells ringing, military bands playing, balloons being sent aloft, fireworks set off, cafés, billiard parlors, the tumult of the levee, the socializing at the St. Charles Hotel, the ceaseless activity of the markets. Margaret Hunter Hall, who visited in 1828 with her husband, Captain Basil Hall, wrote of the city's "air of cheerfulness and gaiety" and "the lively, French tone heard in the streets." Kate Conyngham, a northern governess accompanying her southern charge to town in the 1850s, called it "this splendid bedlam of a city." The Russian Aleksandr Borisovich Lakier thought that "New Orleans more than any other city [in America] recalls the outdoor street life of southern Europe." The prominence of Carnival by the mid-nineteenth century and the love the residents had for balls from an early period (they "repair . . . to forget their cares in dancing" John Davis said in 1806) added to the impression of New Orleans as a lively, action-filled place, an impression that only intensifies as the years go on. New Orleans "has always meant gayety," Dorothy Childs Hogner commented in the 1930s, and the Crescent City is still where the nation—the South, in particular—comes to celebrate, leave off inhibitions, and enjoy a vital, if at times faintly decadent, urban environment.[2]

1. J. Benwell, *An Englishman's Travels in America: His Observations of Life and Manners in the Free and Slave States* (London, n.d.), 115.

2. Una Pope-Hennessy, ed., *The Aristocratic Journey: Being the Outspoken Letters of Mrs. Basil Hall Written During a Fourteen Months' Sojourn in America, 1827–1828* (New York, 1931), 252; J. H. Ingraham, ed., *The Sunny South; or, the Southerner at Home, Embracing Five*

Part of the city's vitality has stemmed from its ethnic diversity and related sense of foreignness—a feeling in part engendered by the long-dominant French Creole culture. The Englishman who identified himself in print merely as "A Rugbean" comments: "New Orleans strikes a traveller more than any city in the Union, from its possessing so many foreign features." William Kingsford found "even the American part of the city" to be "full of interest"; but "in the narrow French streets of the Creole population . . . and the varied appearance of the people . . . you are made to feel that you are a traveller." Frederick Law Olmsted took note of signs in various languages and observed: "Three taverns, bearing the sign of 'The Pig and Whistle,' indicated the recent English, a cabaret called the Universal Republic, with a red flag, the French, and the Gasthaus zum Rhein Platz, the Teutonic contribution . . . ."[3] The French Market area ("a traditional curiosity to visitors," Will H. Coleman says of it in his 1885 guidebook) seemed an especially polyglot sort of place. Coleman says that at the market one "might study the world. Every race that the world boasts is here, and a good many that are nowhere else."

In denoting people found "nowhere else," Coleman probably meant the Crescent City's African American population, "creolized" into a varying array of skin colors that seem to have fascinated visitors. Perhaps not so foreign as the recent arrivals who babbled in a dozen tongues, New Orleans blacks (many of whom did speak French or Creole) were another important element in the exoticism travelers perceived when they encountered such events as Congo Square gatherings of song and dance or quadroon balls. In earlier days frontiersmen were also a fixture on the scene, and as recently as 1880 Ernst von Hesse-Warteg found Texan and Mexican cowboys, as well as other backwoods types, at the cockfight he attended.

Pittman's description reminds us that in the eighteenth century the city was still rather a modest settlement. By 1817 William Darby is extolling New Orleans as a singular place: "There are few places where human life can be enjoyed with more pleasure." A little later Arthur Singleton and Donald Mac-

Years' Experience of a Northern Governess in the Land of the Sugar and the Cotton (Philadelphia, 1860), 322; Arnold Schrier and Joyce Story, trans. and eds., *A Russian Looks at America: The Journey of Aleksandr Borisovich Lakier in 1857,* (Chicago, 1979), 235; John Davis, *Travels in Louisiana and the Floridas in the Year 1802* (New York, 1806), 27; Hogner, *South to Padre,* 35.

3. "A Rugbean," *Transatlantic Rambles,* 69–70; William Kingsford, *Impressions of the West and South, During a Six Weeks Holiday* (Toronto, 1858), 64; Frederick Law Olmsted, *A Journey in the Seaboard Slave States* (New York, 1856), 584.

Donald write of a bustling, intriguing place with bagpipers on the levee and hawkers of parrots. Other writers focus on particular encounters or phases of life. A. Oakey Hall, a "Manhattaner in New Orleans," tackles the city's notoriously wet weather and attendant mosquito problems with whimsy. Benjamin Latrobe describes the exotic African American gatherings in Congo Square. Whereas he seems to have stumbled upon this musical scene, over 130 years later Simone de Beauvoir actively seeks out "real jazz" in its birthplace.

As the most exotic part of New Orleans, the French Quarter—the Vieux Carré, the abode of the Creoles—has been the subject of special attention. De Beauvoir favored it (finding her grand hotel on the other side of Canal Street too enormously American for her taste). George Augustus Sala, writing in the 1880s, calls our attention to the Frenchness of the Quarter, pointing out the details of a Gallic existence that still flourished despite decades of American rule. The bohemian place the Quarter had become in the 1920s is evoked by William Faulkner—who came to New Orleans for the literary life—and another notable American novelist, Walker Percy, catches a later Quarter of tourists, antique shops, and the occasional movie star in his fictional amble. Though Joy Harjo's poem seems to take on the entire city—and much else— the Quarter has centrality as she imagines a Spanish conquistador drinking on Bourbon Street long after his supposed death.

George F. Scheer III is the most recent traveler writer reprinted here. Though he writes of staying in New Orleans for only a couple of days in 1991, his account is a surprisingly full one. Not only do his travels take him all over the city, but his perception of what he encounters offers telling insight into the New Orleans of today—its "air of decay," its hints of tension amidst the charm.

Gay living, urban vitality, and ethnic exoticism, combined with an overlay of historical romance (exploited by such local writers as George Washington Cable and Grace King) and an abundance of architectural charm and subtropical ambience, have established New Orleans as a major travel destination. Hence a great deal has been written about visiting the Crescent City. In this section we only suggest some of the general impressions traveler writers have had at different times.

New Orleans in the 1760s

Philip Pittman

Captain Pittman came to Louisiana in 1763 to explore areas north of New Orleans that had just been ceded to Britain. From *The Present State of the European Settlements on the Mississippi* (1770).

New Orleans stands on the east side of the river, and in 30° north latitude; its situation is extremely well chosen, as it has a very easy communication with the northern parts of Louisiana . . . by means of the Bayouk of St. John, a little creek, which is navigable for small vessels drawing less than six feet water, six miles up from the lake Ponchartain, where there is a landing-place, at which the vessels load and unload; and this is about two miles from the city. . . . The town is secured from the inundations of the river by a raised bank, generally called the Levee; and this extends from the *Detour des Anglois*,[4] to the upper settlement of the Germans,[5] which is a distance of more than fifty miles, and a good coach-road all the way. The Levee before the town is repaired at the public expence, and each inhabitant keeps that part in repair which is opposite to his own plantation. Having described the situation of the city of New Orleans, I will proceed to its plan of construction.

The parade is a large square, in the middle of that part of the town which fronts the river; in the back part of the square is the church dedicated to St. Louis, a very poor building, framed with wood; it is in so ruinous a condition that divine service has not been performed in it since the year 1766, one of the king's store-houses being at present used for that purpose. The capuchins are the curates of New Orleans; on the left hand side of the church they had a

4. A section of the Mississippi River below New Orleans, today called English Turn, where English ships seeking to interfere with early French colonization efforts were turned back.

5. Germans were encouraged to settle along the Mississippi just upriver from New Orleans; that area was long referred to as the German Coast, though culturally these early Germans were largely assimilated by the French.

A corner of Jackson Square with the levee beyond

From George A. Sala, *America Revisited* (London, 1883)

very handsome and commodious brick house, which is totally deserted and gone to ruin; they now live on their plantation, and in a hired house in town. On the right hand side of the church is the prison and guard-house, which are very strong and good buildings. . . . The square is open to the river. . . . All the streets are perfectly straight, and cross each other at right angles, and these divide the town into fixty-six squares, eleven in length by the river's side, and six in depth. . . . The intendant's house and gardens take up the right side of the parade, the left side is occupied by the king's store-houses and an artillery-yard. There is at present no building . . . for the governor; his general residence is in a large house, which was formerly the property of the company who were the proprietors of Louisiana. . . . The convent of the Ursulines and general hospital, which is attended by the nuns, occupy the two left hand squares facing the river: these buildings are strong and plain, well answering the purposes for which they were designed. The general plan of building in the town, is with timber frames filled up with brick; and most of the houses are but of one floor, raised about eight feet from the ground, with large galleries round them, and the cellars under the floors level with the ground; it is impossible to have any subterraneous buildings, as they would be constantly full of water. I imagine that there are betwixt seven and eight hundred houses in the town, most of which have gardens. The squares at the back and sides of the town are mostly laid out in gardens; the orange-trees, with which they are planted, are not unpleasant objects, and in the Spring afford an agreeable smell.

There are, exclusive of the slaves, about seven thousand inhabitants in town, of all ages and sexes.

New Orleans billiards parlor, by Auguste Hervieu. Frances Trollope had passed through New Orleans in 1827, recollecting some of her impressions of Louisiana for the novel in which this illustration appears. Hervieu had accompanied her.

From Frances Trollope, *The Life and Adventures of Jonathan Jefferson Whitlaw; or, Scenes on the Mississippi* (London, 1836), reproduction courtesy Special Collections, LSU Libraries

Where Human Life Can Be Enjoyed

WILLIAM DARBY

Darby (1775–1854) was a noted frontier geographer who originally came to Louisiana to survey land for planters and speculators. He traveled extensively in the state and region, eventually producing *A Geographical Description of the State of Louisiana, the Southern Part of the State of Mississippi, and Territory of Alabama.* This excerpt is taken from the second edition (1817).

No city perhaps on the globe, in an equal number of human beings, presents a greater contrast of national manners, language, and complexion, than does New Orleans. The proportion between the whites and men of mixed cast or black, is nearly equal. As a nation, the French among the whites are yet most numerous and wealthy; next will be the Anglo-Americans; thirdly, the natives of the British Isles. There are but few Spaniards or Portuguese—some Italians; and a scattering of individuals of all the civilized nations of Europe.

Much distortion of opinion has existed, and is not yet eradicated in other parts of the United States respecting public morals and manners in New Orleans. Divested of pre-conceived ideas on the subject, an observing man will find little to condemn in New-Orleans, more than in other commercial cities; and will find that noble distinction of all active communities, acuteness of conception, urbanity of manners, and polished exterior.

There are few places where human life can be enjoyed with more pleasure, or employed with more pecuniary profit.

Congo Square

BENJAMIN LATROBE

Latrobe (1764–1820) was a noted architect who was in New Orleans at various times in connection with architectural projects. He left a number of journals written during his time in Louisiana between 1818 and 1820, along with sketches and watercolors. Here he describes his 1819 encounter with one of the gatherings held by the city's slave population, who were allowed to get together on Sundays at Congo Square to sing and dance.

This long dissertation has been suggested by my accidentally stumbling upon the assembly of negroes which I am told every Sunday afternoon meets on the Common in the rear of the city. My object was to take a walk with Mr. Coulter on the bank of the Canal Carondelet as far as the Bayou St. John. In going up St. Peters Street & approaching the common I heard a most extraordinary noise, which I supposed to proceed from some horse mill, the horses trampling on a wooden floor. I found, however, on emerging from the houses onto the Common, that it proceeded from a crowd of 5 or 600 persons assembled in an open space or public square. I went to the spot & crowded near enough to see the performance. All those who were engaged in the business seemed to be *blacks*. I did not observe a dozen yellow faces. They were formed into circular groupes [*sic*] in the midst of four of which, which I examined (but there were more of them), was a ring, the largest not 10 feet in diameter. In the first were two women dancing. They held each a coarse handkerchief extended by the corners in their hands, & *set* to each other in a miserably dull & slow figure, hardly moving their feet or

From *The Journals of Benjamin Latrobe, 1799–1820: From Philadelphia to New Orleans,* by Benjamin Latrobe, ed. Edward C. Carter II, John C. Van Horne, and Lee Formwalt. Copyright © 1980 by Yale University Press. Reprinted by permission of Yale University Press.

bodies. The music consisted of two drums and a stringed instrument. An old man sat astride of a cylindrical drum about a foot in diameter, & beat it with incredible quickness with the edge of his hand & fingers. The other drum was an open staved thing held between the knees & beaten in the same manner. They made an incredible noise. The most curious instrument, however, was a stringed instrument which no doubt was imported from Africa. On the top of the finger board was the rude figure of a man in a sitting posture, & two pegs behind him to which the strings were fastened. The body was a calabash. It was played upon by a very little old man, apparently 80 or 90 years old.

The women squalled out a burthen to the playing at intervals, consisting of two notes, as the negroes, working in our cities, respond to the song of their leader. Most of the circles contained the same sort of dancers. One was larger, in which a ring of a dozen women walked, by way of dancing, round the music in the center. But the instruments were of a different construction. One, which from the color of the wood seemed new, consisted of a block cut into something of the form of a cricket bat with a long and deep mortice down the Center. The thing made a considerable noise, being beaten lustily on the side by a short stick. In the same Orchestra was a square drum looking like a stool, which made an abominably loud noise: also a Calabash with a round hole in it, the hole studded with brass nails which were beaten by a woman with two short sticks.

A Man sang an uncouth song which I suppose was in some African language, for it was not french, and the Women screamed a detestable burthen on one single note. The allowed amusements of Sunday, have, it seems, perpetuated here, those of Africa among its inhabitants. I have never seen anything more brutally savage, and at the same time dull and stupid than this whole exhibition. Continuing my walk about a mile along the Canal, and returning after Sunset near the same spot, the noise was still heard. There was not the least disorder among the croud, nor do I learn, on enquiry, that these weekly meetings of the negroes have ever produced any mischief.

Parrots, Spider-Monkeys, and Sun Umbrellas

ARTHUR SINGLETON

From *Letters from the South and West* (1824), a collection of colorful and informative missives Singleton wrote to his brother as he traveled, which he later published.

Along the levee, hang cages of canary, and mocking birds, for sale. Here you may see the little Congolese parrots, not bigger than sparrows, of a fine shape, with their gaudy, but beautiful plumage. I saw here a China macaw, larger than a pheasant, with twelve inches of sweeping tail feathers, and a superb vivid plumage of red, yellow, green, blue, and their shades. It was said, that he could talk Chinese . . . but he spake not a word unto me. The owner asked thirty dollars for the bird. . . . I also saw here, a curious animal . . . called sapajou [spider monkey], which suspends itself by its tail. The gentlemen carry sun-umbrellas. The levee is a fine evening promenade for the ladies. The ladies wear no head-dresses in fair sky; but modest becoming white or black lace veils. There are some beautiful brunette girls here; and the French mademoiselles have a peculiar soft drawling, but rather insinuating tone of voice. The negresses wear checked turbans, of gay colours. . . . The other evening, on the levee, I met a Highlander playing on his Scotch bagpipe. . . . When near, the sounds are powerful; and the player would lift high his legs, and briskly step backward and forward in fine enthusiasm.

As to the morals of this city, the word is obsolete. On the Sunday we arrived, a balloon, with a live lamb in the car, and aerial fireworks, were to be exhibited, by permission of the mayor. . . . Sunday is the busy holiday, when the theatre, and the circus, have the most spectators, as then they least value the time. Duels are very fashionable, if they can contrive an affront; such as:—"How dared you to spit as I was passing?"—"How dared you to pass as I was spitting?" or, "You shall not sneeze where I am!" This would make a pleasant duel. There is a corner called Cadiz, a rendezvous for assassins, and no inquiry made.

The Levee

Donald MacDonald

The Scotsman Donald MacDonald (1791–1872) was involved in the creation of the utopian New Harmony settlement in Indiana. He traveled in North America, coming to Louisiana (to take ship for Charleston via Havana) in March of 1826.

The Levee which protects the town is covered with shells and small stones and made into a hard terrace, behind which runs a wide road, separated from the first street or row of houses by an open space of a mile in length but only two or three hundred ft. wide. On this ground stand the custom house, the large stone market houses & some warehouses. During the first half of the year trade is very brisk, the Levee being covered with bales of . . . cotton, casks of sugar & tobacco, coffee & rice, carts driving in every direction with goods, and shipping of all descriptions lying by the river bank. While I remained at New Orleans, there were never less than 12 or 15 steamboats lying there, and several times in the course of the day, the guns of those arriving and departing were heard in every part of the town. . . .

Above the steamboats lye a great number of keel & flat boats & other small craft, which have brought raw materials & provisions of all kinds down the river. . . .

The Levee is a place of lounge for strangers, and it is a common practice, to ramble from steam boat to steam boat. . . . The captains therefore have their cabins in fine order, & spirits & water at the service of those who come on board to admire their boats, I saw several very large boats superbly fitted up . . . and constructed on so large a scale as to afford accommodations which quite surprise a stranger.

From *The Diaries of Donald MacDonald, 1824–1826,* by Donald MacDonald. Originally published by the Indiana Historical Society in 1942. Reprinted by permission of the Indiana Historical Society.

Rain and Mosquitoes

A. Oakey Hall

Hall (1826–1898) was New York–born and, in fact, mayor of New York in the latter years of the nineteenth century, as well as a successful lawyer, writer, and editor. He had family connections in New Orleans and was in the Crescent City from 1845 to 1848 studying and practicing law. He published his recollections of life in the city as *The Manhattaner in New Orleans; or, Phases of "Crescent City" Life* (1851), a witty memoir of his sojourn that discourses on such subjects as charivaris and—as in this excerpt—the extremes of climate.

I have been upon the Catskills when the roof of the Mountain-House [hotel] reverberated with the peltings of the rain, and when my spasmodic dreams were crowded by floating visions of drowning men and images of diluvian arks. I have worn out several umbrellas in my day; and overshoe-shod I have paddled the causeways of various cities; and so seen something of rain. But I never realized the capacity of the clouds for water until "going through a course" of the wet season in New Orleans. When there was little squeamishness, or modesty, or gentlemanly consideration in the rain-drops. When the latter rarely gave due and generous notice of intention to commence action. When small glimpses of hope for an early cessation during progress were afforded. When the rain was now dogged, obstinate and persevering; and now the rapidly succeeding showers charged the earth like reserve after reserve of cavalry in a battle.

The soil of the Crescent City, in the driest time of the seasons, is filled with humidity (and this to its utmost capacity, at two feet from the surface;) and under favor of these aforementioned showers, soon overflows. Shunning the river, the choking gutters send their burdens swamp-ward, littering the angles of pavement with clumps of cotton and wool, heads of barrels, hogsheads sometimes; broken paper-boxes, bits of pasteboard, twine and bagging rope; all which the ever-thirsty swamp licked, in course of time, into its capacious maw.

If you are a stranger in the city, and the clouds have liberally dispensed their favors all the night; and all unconscious to yourself the monotony of the falling rain has beguiled you into a late nap, and you arise at ten o'clock to view the prospect without . . . you have queer sights to look at. . . .

Pedestrians are standing on divers corners in a dreadful state of uncertainty, looking gloomily from their boots to the surging floods before them; now and then consulting watches, making feints to jump, and balking; until urged on by the still more dreadful visions of protested bills, undunned accounts, and lost bargains. . . . Astonished eastern men gazing from office windows, and turning to their Bibles (if any they have) for statistics respecting Noah's ark. Piano strumming misses in the by streets are executing "Home, sweet Home" (how soothingly the melody vibrates the out-door air.) Valiant bank runners and collecting clerks wading (apparently unconcerned) through Canal-street, jostling nicely-poised umbrellas, or skilfully navigating them . . . about the tall heads and wide-brimmed, hats (the latter sometimes knocked off with provoking ease,) and low balconies, and projecting signs, and nuisances of awning posts. Here and there fat men who are victims of circumstance are seen with large umbrellas—canopies, morelike, of silk and whalebone—in narrow streets, caught and brought hard up by a pile of bricks or a stack of boxes. . . .

Anon, the earth would seem tired of "staying herself with flagons," and as if by telegraphic direction the heavens would suspend their rain-drops. Then the air would become chilly, and the ascending moisture hang in fog as low as the lamp posts; the chimney-tops, and the St. Charles' [hotel] Dome, and the tops of the flag-staffs skulk in a misty obscurity.

And again, when brisk allusions to that clearing-up shower had circulated through the city, the rain would once more descend in torrents, and set at defiance all deductions and calculations of meteorology.

I never take up a New Orleans newspaper, and read from the price current of the day the words, "in consequence of the weather yesterday out-door operations were suspended, and sales of produce were limited," but I know directly that the said "yesterday" was a day like the one above described. . . .

Of course, where such a swampy soil and so much rain is found, that eighth plague to modern Egyptians, the mosquito tribe (insect, and not Indians) are to be discovered without great scrutiny. Your mosquito is a sad drawback in the sunny days and pleasant nights of a New Orleans exile. The mosquito! whose bark is perhaps more disagreeable than his bite.

The month of March in the Crescent City, whether he comes in lamb-like or lion-like, brings mosquitoes, which by April have completely colonized bedrooms, drawing-rooms, and saloons; nay, "all out-doors" besides. And of two classes. One for night duty, one for the tasks of daylight; both equally systematic in all the details of their operations. When twilight deepens, the class that have slept all day in obscure retreats behind curtains, and in wardrobes, and in the shadows of furniture, sally forth and dance about with a noise like the humming of a boarding school of tops. Then is reading a suspended recreation. Old gloves are a treasure. The presence of a veteran cigar-maker is a prize. Fans are a luxury. Woe to that person who becomes immersed in thought, or interested in conversation, or overcome by drowsiness in exposed situations. In ten minutes' time mosquitoes have duly marked him as a rash man; and on the morrow his mirror will become suggestive of small-pox; and his cologne bottle and flesh brush will find active employment in the duties of the toilet.

One retires to rest, and, with as much of the rapidity of lightning as can be employed by nervous fingers, draws his bar of netting and duly tucks it in; forming a wall secure against the assaults and mining and sapping operations of the whole mosquito army. Behind this he lies until morning, and can sing to his heart's content . . . with an orchestral accompaniment whose only fault is its monotony.

There is much of science to be displayed in getting beneath this netting of the bed so that none of the hungry swarms accompany you. I found it no bad plan to institute a feigned attack upon one side, thus drawing thitherward every insect in the room; and then making a rapid march for the other side escape them thence into the snug quarters of your bed. Or taking a corner seat for a few moments as if about to read; and when the wily insects are beguiled towards you make the same rapid march for the further corner of the bed. Perhaps often there will be a few mosquitoes who have already obtained an entrance, (admitted to the bar under some new constitution and without an examination,) after ingeniously plotting and planing through the daylight like the burglars they are. They must be carefully assassinated, while some good friend without or your body-servant holds the light in assistance of the tedious search that must sometimes supervene before the prey be ensnared. In default of the friend or the body servant, a little experience, and an attentive ear, will make you a sharp-shooter even in the shade of night, as, guided by the humming of the enemy, you track him to execution.

Old jokers will tell you of mosquitoes who contemptuously spurn bars and netting; and who will crib your bed of straw or even mattress hair, and suck you (julep wise) from without. . . .

But joking and metaphor aside, the mosquitoes of New Orleans deserve a distinct niche in the temple of its history. They are parts and parcels of its population . . . and far before all men, women, and children in point of numbers.

The French Quarter

GEORGE AUGUSTUS SALA

From *America Revisited* (1882), the author's lively account of an extensive tour of the United States. Sala (1828–1895) was a well-known English travel writer.

Satisfied with being nothing but a wandering alien, I took the streets . . . as they came, and derived ineffable delight from their contemplation. . . . Occasionally in the French quarter, you are forcibly reminded of the all-dominating influence of the Anglo-Saxon language, institutions, and character. . . . Still, square after square, block after block, and street after street are French, and Old French. Of course, remembering how and by whom Louisiana was settled, it is as absurd to feel astonished at finding so many reproductions in an American city of French life and manners as it was for the Englishman, who landed at Boulogne, to express his surprise at finding the little children prattling French so fluently; yet I do not scruple to own that I grew to be lost in pleasant amazement when I surveyed a genuine French *pharmacie* in the Rue de Chartres. It seemed to have been transported bodily from the Rue du Bac—say, or from the Rue St. Louis au Marais. A delicious *pharmacie*. None of your new, fashionable impertinent chemists' shops, glaring with parti-colored bottles as big as locomotive lamps, garish with carving, gilding, and plate-glass, and distracting you with advertisements and specimens of the newest adjuncts to the toilet and the most favourite quack nostrums.

. . . Here in this old French *pharmacie,* all was subdued, composed, and serene. No doubt you could obtain *sinapismes* and *vésicatoires* and *tisanes* enow, if you asked for them; but nothing was advertised in an obtrusively alluring manner. In the dim recesses of the store, you could discern rows of shelves laden with tall old white gallipots; and about the whole place there was a gentle soporific odour of aromatic drugs—just such an odour as that which pervades the Egyptian drug market in the Bezesteen in Stamboul—a perfume of henna and haschish, of frankincense and myrrh, of benzoin and gum tagacanth, with just the slightest suspicion of rhubarb. . . . A grave and baldheaded gentleman sat in a rocking chair at the door of the *pharmacie,* reading the *Abeille de la Nouvelle Orléans.* His equally grave spouse was enthroned, spectacled, behind the counter perusing the *Propagateur Catholique.* I entered and made a trifling purchase of Spanish licorice as a pretext for converse in a tongue well beloved by me. It was consolatory to hear cents spoken of as "centimes" and to find a dollar called a "piastre." Surely I was very far from the land of "notions" and dry goods, of corn cakes and cock-tails.

Next in interest to the *pharmacien* was the *épicier.* I need scarcely say that the "corner grocery" is a very notable institution in every American town. . . . At the New Orleans' grocers, in the French quarter, I found . . . a plentiful supply of things alcoholic; but the products of France *la bien-aimée* pleasantly

French Market scene

From Edward King, "The Great South: Old and New Louisiana," *Scribner's Monthly,* November, 1873, reproduction courtesy Special Collections, LSU Libraries

predominated. Chartreuse, green, yellow, and white, absinthe and cassis, vermouth and parfait amour—all the alcoholic frivolities of the people who are continually sipping stimulants, and who never get tipsy.

. . . Here you are at once reminded that the tropics are over the way, or round the corner, so to speak. The coffee made in New Orleans is the most aromatic and the most grateful to the palate that I have ever tasted; and I am told that it comes from the *tierra caliente* about Cordova in Mexico. Still there is a large variety of other coffees—Java, Puerto Rico, Rio, Jamaica, and Hayti among the number—from which to choose. . . .

Modistes and *couturières*—French to the backbone—I mean to the staylace and the back hair, abound in the French quarter. "Celine" hangs out her hat in connection with "robes." "Alphonsine" proclaims the Parisian elegance of her "dentelles et fleurs artificielles." "Pauline" simply says, on a pretty *pancarte*, "chapeaux." . . .

. . . Deeper and deeper into the French quarter do I dive. The friendly *pédicure,* with the effigy of a human foot highly gilt, invites me to enter his establishment. I almost wish that I had corns in order to have them cut *à la Française.* In almost every "block" or "insula" of houses there is a French *café* or an *estaminet.* The clicking of billiard balls is continuous. The *cafés* lack Parisian splendour; but they are trim and neat, and very different in their appearance to the groggeries . . . and the customers quench their thirst with *orgeat, bavaroises, sirop de groseille,* and other non-intoxicants. . . . There are numbers of little French stationers' shops and *cabinets de lecture.* . . . The very pencils and pens are French; the ink is the "encre de la Petit Vertu." Little cheap French chap-books and *livres d'images* abound. . . . The shops for the sale of votive offerings—*immortelles, billets d'enterrement, lettres de faire part*—and "objets religieux" generally, are numerous. Gaily-painted plaster images of Madonnas, saints, and angels are intermingled with rosaries and scapularies, holy water fonts, electro-plated shrines, oratory lamps, and *paroissiens;* and these last became so plentiful that I fancied myself in the *parvis* or close of some old Continental cathedral.

The French Market

Will H. Coleman

Coleman, a New York bookseller who once lived in
New Orleans, published the *Historical Sketchbook and
Guide to New Orleans and Environs* (1885) for visitors
to the World's Industrial and Cotton Centennial Exposition. He pulled together material by several hands,
including Lafcadio Hearn's. S. Frederick Starr and
Delia LaBarre recently attributed to Hearn this romantic piece about the vibrant market so many visitors to
the city have written about, though Hearn's standard
bibliographers have not.

The French market has become a traditional curiosity
to visitors to New Orleans, as one of the most original features of the city, and
it is considered one of the first duties of a stranger to visit it.

As you near Jackson square a stream of busy-looking people appears, laden
with baskets and bundles. Following this current of life, you are whirled forward to the corner, opposite the market. Here a stout old lady of heavy build,
ornamented with a bonnet like a basket of vegetables, dashes across, followed
by her daughter, a rosy-faced, stout-shouldered, masculine young woman.
Business is everything to them, and as they pass over the cozy mud they lift
their dresses high, high enough to attract the attention of the neighboring
men. You follow in their footsteps into the market; at its entrance is a marble-
topped stand, over which hangs the title and sign of the Café Rapide, with a
painting, illustrative of the title, of many persons devouring their food with
dangerous and terrifying celerity. Here you take your seat for a cup of coffee
or chocolate, and glance around you.

A man might here study the world. Every race that the world boasts is here,
and a good many races that are nowhere else. The strangest and most complicated mixture of negro and Caucasian blood, with negroes washed white, and

white men that mulattoes would scorn to claim as of their own particular hybrid.

The dresses are as varied as the faces; the baskets even are of every race, some stout and portly, others delicate and adorned with ribbons and ornaments; some, again, old, wheezy and decayed, through whose worn ribs might be seen solemn and melancholy cabbages, turnips and potatoes, crammed and jostled together in ruthless imprisonment. The butchers scorn to use all those blandishments that the lower grades of market society make use of to attract purchasers. Like Mahomet, the mountain must come to them. From the ceiling hang endless ropes of spider's webs, numberless flies, and incalculable dirt. The stalls are deeply worn by the scraping process; in some yawn pits, apparently bottomless; and lastly, the floor of the market is not at all clean, but covered with mud and dirt from the feet of its patrons. Through the crowd lurk some skeleton-dogs, vainly hoping, by some happy accident, to secure a dainty morsel.

At the end of the market lie, sleep, eat and trade a half-dozen Indians.[6] In olden days these Natchez, Choctaws and Creeks were numbered by the thousands, but they have melted away into mulattoes. The lazy, unstudied attitude of these Red Roses, these daughters of the forest is not exactly in accordance with the poetic idea one used to drink in, in his earlier days. Indian females are formless, and the bag that they wear has no pretensions to fitting. When in addition they have hung around them bundles, beads, babies, and other curiosities, they fail to arouse our poetic sentiments.

Still following the drift of the crowd, you enter the Bazaar market, the newest of this batch of old buildings that are collectively honored with the title of market. It is in a tolerably good state of preservation. The architect had high and ambitious views, evidenced by two tin cupolas that rise like domes from the market-house. . . . A string of youthful merchants stretched across the street from the Bazaar to the vegetable market. Though but a dozen or so years of age, they have learned all the "tricks of the trade," and overwhelm you with good bargains, and almost extort your money from you.

At the angle of the vegetable market is the chicken repository. The dead chickens hang downward from the roof; the live ones are cooped up, and chant endless rounds of music. This market is the most cosmopolitan of all.

---

6. Native Americans, predominantly Choctaws from across Lake Pontchartrain, were a well-known presence at the French Market, where they sold baskets and herbs.

The air is broken by every language—English, French, Italian and German, varied by gombo languages of every shade; languages whose whole vocabulary embraces but a few dozen words, the major part of which are expressive, emphatic and terrific oaths.[7]

Nor are the materials for sale less varied. Piles of cabbages, turnips and strange vegetables adorn each side. Monstrous cheeses smile from every corner; the walls are festooned with bananas, etc.; while fish, bread, flour, and even alligators, have each appropriate tables. The bright sun leaks drowsily through the spider webs, producing a sad, sleepy light; the monotonous cries of the boys, *"cinq à dix sous,"* "two cents apiece, Madame," keeps on as endlessly as Tennyson's brook, and the crowd jostles you with baskets and bundles until you drop into some neighboring stall for a bite, or make your way altogether out of the market. . . .

. . . There is a large class of people who raise their own vegetables and bring them to this place for sale in carts. At about two or three o'clock in the morning the sounds of many loaded carts are heard jolting on the streets. They travel generally at that pace commonly practiced at fashionable funerals. They creak and rumble in a characteristic manner as they go up the street, for their drivers are ostentatiously plodding and methodical. These drivers look sleepy; the horses and mules look about half asleep; even the carts seem as though they objected to being pulled out of their sheds and dragged through the darkness at that unheard-of hour. Of these drivers, some are men and some are women.

On the arrival of the loads of vegetables at the market, the carts back up to the curbstones, the sleepy drivers descend, and the work of unloading and arranging the vegetables on the stall counters commences. The women with their limp petticoats and dresses, damp with the dews of the morning, gathered about their thick-set limbs, arrange the vegetables to their taste.

Flat white-headed cabbages, whose phrenology is striking, if cabbages may be considered phrenologically, are placed in long rows above one another on the stall counters where they rest, demure, stolid and uniform in appearance as the heads in the modern pictures of the old-time English charity schools. These men and women handle the cabbages in a manner more delicate and re-

7. Louisianians use the term *gumbo* to mean a mixture (like the soup most commonly designated by the word). However, the Creole spoken primarily by African Americans has been specifically referred to as gumbo or gumbo French; in this instance it seems to mean something like a pidgin.

spectful than that they use toward the other vegetables. The bags of potatoes, baskets of beans, bunches of carrots, beets and other stuffs are pitched unceremoniously on the stands, while numerous humble flat squashes are chucked unostentatiously beneath the stands as if there were no people in the world who had any regard for squash. . . .

In Billingsgate [the London market] it is said that the "heavenly gift divine—the power of speech"—is a faculty habitually abused. Here the abuse is more flagrant, for not "king's English" alone is subjected to pretty rough handling, but every language spoken on the globe is slanged, docked, or insulted by uncivilized innovations on its original purity. This commingling of languages is swelled to an absolute uproar by sunrise, when the market-goers begin to arrive. Aristocratic old gentlemen with their broadcloth, polished manners and boots puffed in and out; fat females with fat baskets hanging on their fat arms, waddle to and fro; footmen, waiters, maids and small boys come and go away. Nearly all trades, professions, colors and castes are represented with baskets on their arms. . . .

There are several marble-top tables about, in different parts of the market; four-legged stools are standing in rows alongside of these. Many little white cups and saucers are in a line near the edge of the tables. These are the coffee stands. A big steaming urn, with a faucet to it, is in the centre of each table, while various dishes, containing bread, beefsteaks, even bacon and greens, are scattered over the marble top. These are not very neat-looking tables, for some of their parts are not in keeping with the others. Thus the marble top looks white and nicely polished, the cups and saucers look bright as porcelain, but the legs and bodies of the tables are uncanny in the extreme.

They are streaked with grease, or the polish is worn off at regular intervals where the stools are placed along side of them. The legs might look better; stray cabbage leaves and other waste material, scattered around their feet, give these legs a half-unclean, negligent appearance that borders on depravity. But then this is the market, and the wilted cabbage leaves are a part of the place. The tall stools, too, have this semi-negligent aspect. They are brightly polished on the top of their seats unavoidably, but their rungs and legs are scratched and scraped by iron shoe-pegs, or just the least bit discolored by mud. With the odors of the aromatic coffee, steaming from the urns, is mingled a peculiar market smell. . . .

Strangers who come into town late at night, bringing into the city with them their rural tastes and appetites, like to get a bite of something early in the morning. So they, too, often patronize the coffee stands. Some of these have a rural lack of assurance which they failed to leave at their homes, and they look very modest when they climb the high stools. They hesitate in answering to the question whether they'll take *"café au lait"* or *"café noir;"* they believe, however, they'll take "the first." The respectable keeper of the coffee stand has a pitying look in his eye for the ignorance of country people. The stranger of this class gets through, fumbles awkwardly in his pocket for the necessary pay; then gives place to the man of display, who pulls in on his purse here to gratify a taste for the ornamental somewhere else. . . .

Sometimes old rich men come here to get cheap breakfasts; for certainly black coffee, "five cents a cup," and warm beefsteaks, are as nourishing and wholesome as broiled mutton chops, soft boiled eggs, and the thigh of a spring chicken, even if it is the least bit noisy down here, and smells more like a market than a restaurant.

Episode

WILLIAM FAULKNER

Nobel Prize–winner Faulkner (1897–1962) sojourned in New Orleans in the 1920s, participating in the lively literary scene that existed then. He wrote the following sketch, which captures something of the everyday life of the French Quarter of those days, for the New Orleans *Times-Picayune* in 1925. Later he collaborated with William Spratling, on *Sherwood Anderson and Other Famous Creoles*. Spratling, who is best known for the silver later produced by his Mexican workshops, taught architecture at Tulane University and was the illustrator for the book.

Every day at noon they pass. He in a brushed suit and a gray hat, never collarless nor tieless, she in a neat cotton print dress and a sunbonnet. I have seen her any number of times, sitting and rocking upon wooden porches before the crude, shabby cottages among my own hills in Mississippi.

They are at least sixty. He is blind and his gait is halting and brittle. Talking in a steady stream, gesturing with her knotty hand, she leads him daily to the cathedral to beg; at sunset she returns for him and takes him home. I had not seen her face until Spratling from the balcony called to her. She looked to both sides and then behind her without discovering us. At Spratling's second call she looked up.

Her face is brown, and timeless and merry as a gnome's and toothless: her nose and chin know each other.

"Are you in a hurry?" he asked.

"Why?" she replied brightly.

"Episode," by William Faulkner, originally published in the August 16, 1925, issue of the New Orleans *Times-Picayune*. Reprinted by permission of the *Times-Picayune*.

"I'd like to sketch you."

She watched his face keenly, not comprehending.

"I'd like to make a picture of you," he explained.

"Come down," she replied promptly, smiling. She spoke to the man with her and he obediently tried to sit down upon the narrow concrete base of the garden fence. He fell heavily and a passer-by helped her raise him to his feet. I left Spratling feverishly seeking a pencil and descended with a chair for him, and I saw that she was actually trembling—not with age, but with pleased vanity.

"Assiz [sit; from *s'asseoir*], Joe," she ordered, and he sat down, his sightless face filled with that remote godlike calm known only to the blind. Spratling with his sketch pad appeared. She took her place beside the seated man with her hand on his shoulder: one knew immediately that they had been photographed so on their wedding day.

She was a bride again; with that ability for fine fabling which death alone can rob us of, she was once more dressed in silk (or its equivalent) and jewels, a wreath and a veil, and probably a bouquet. She was a bride again, young and fair, with her trembling hand on young Joe's shoulder; Joe beside her was once more something to shake her heart with dread and adoration and vanity—something to be a little frightened of.

A casual passer-by felt it and stopped to look at them. Even blind Joe felt it through her hand on his shoulder. Her dream clothed him, too, in youth and pride; he too assumed that fixed and impossible attitude of the male and his bride being photographed in the year 1880.

"No, no," Spratling told her, "not like that." Her face fell. "Turn toward him, look at him," he added quickly.

She obeyed, still facing us.

"Turn your head too; look at him."

"But you can't see my face then," she objected.

"Yes, I can. Besides, I'll draw your face later."

Appeased, her smile broke her face into a million tiny wrinkles, like an etching, and she took the position he wanted.

At once she became maternal. She was no longer a bride; she had been married long enough to know that Joe was not anything to be either loved or feared very passionately, but on the contrary he was something to be a little disparaging of; that after all he was only a large, blundering child. (You knew she had borne children by now—perhaps lost one.) But he was hers and another would be as bad probably, so she would make the best of it, remembering other days.

And Joe, again taking her mood through her hand on his shoulder, was no longer the dominating male. And he too, remembering other days when he had come to her for comfort, took her new dream. His arrogance dissolved from him and he sat quiet under her touch, helpless yet needing no help, sightless and calm as a god who has seen both life and death and found nothing of particular importance in either of them.

Spratling finished.

"Now the face," she reminded him quickly. And now there was something in her face that was not her face. It partook of something in time, in the race, ambiguous, enigmatic. Was she posing? I wondered, watching her. She was facing Spratling, but I don't believe her eyes saw him, nor the wall behind him. Her eyes were contemplative, yet personal—it was as if someone had whispered a sublime and colossal joke in the ear of an idol.

Spratling finished, and her face became the face of a woman of sixty, toothless and merry as a gnome's. She came over to see the sketch, taking it in her hands.

"Got any money?" Spratling asked me.

I had fifteen cents. She returned the picture without comment and took the coins.

"Thank you," she said. She touched her husband and he rose. "Thank you for the chair," she nodded and smiled at me, and I watched them move slowly down the alley, wondering what I had seen in her face—or had I seen anything at all. I turned to Spratling. "Let's see it."

He was staring at the sketch. "Hell," he said. I looked at it. And then I knew what I had seen in her face. The full-face sketch had exactly the same expression as the Mona Lisa.

Real Jazz

SIMONE DE BEAUVOIR

This eminent French woman of letters spent four
months traveling about the United States in the 1950s.
She was often uncomfortable with the American culture of that period and does not hesitate to say so.
However, de Beauvoir (1908–1986) found much in
New Orleans to please her; she comments on the jazz
scene and on race relations, bringing her unique perspective to bear upon the city.

March 30th

Each time, I felt crushed by the terrible opulence of the large American hotels: one could spend an entire life in one of these hotels without ever leaving:
florists, candy stores, bookshops, beauty salons, manicurists, stenographers,
typists, all are at one's service; and in this particular hotel there were several
different restaurants, bars, cafés and dance floors. It was a neutral zone, like
the international concessions of the Far East.

But we had only to cross the street and there we were in the French Quarter,
the center of New Orleans. The old colonial city was built as if by architectural planning, like a modern city, but its streets are lined with one- and two-
storied houses which remind one of France and Spain; they have the serenity
of Anjou or Touraine, and the beautiful, green, wrought iron balconies remind one of the balconies of Cordova or the iron window grilles of Arab palaces; an Andalusian warmth pervades the silence. Here the exotic is no longer
Mexican or Indian: it is French.[8] The French names on the gravestones, on
street signs and over shops seem archaic; and in the curio shops, instead of

8. De Beauvoir had just come from the Southwest.

tomahawks and Indian masks, they sell oil lamps, Sevres vases and the art objects of a civilization as remote as that of the Hopi or the Navajo Indians: pearl necklaces and barbaric headdresses, porcelain and chandeliers, strange idols. Many houses have their legends: here is the house of the blacksmith, the house of Jean Lafitte, the pirate, the house reserved for Napoleon which falsely uses his name; not far is The Old Absinthe House. All have been converted into bars, now quiet and empty in the morning sun, and there are several streets where every second door is that of a bar or nightclub.

There are many bookshops in this part of town; the tiny shops overflow onto the sidewalks; entire bins of old, soiled volumes are for sale. There are also many curio shops and confectioners: in front of one door a large Negro woman, cut out of cardboard and wearing a bandana around her head, smiles and points greedily at some creole specialty. We went to see a small theater that has remained unchanged since the eighteenth century and where French plays are given from time to time. And we came out into a square as pure and simple as the Place des Vosges in Paris. All the splendor of the old houses is found in the delicate, green tracery that borders the terraces. . . .

We did not want to miss the spirit of New Orleans nor the secret of its nights. In the streets of the Vieux Carré through which we strolled in the evening, we saw advertisements of Mexican and Hawaiian bands and stripteasers; now we wanted to hear real jazz played by a Negro band; or wasn't there any left in America? . . .

With as much wisdom as we could muster we consulted our pocket guide, and our first choice was lucky. The Vieux Carré restaurant where we dined enchanted us. The room was decorated with marine paintings; hanging from the ceiling above the fireplace were miniature frigates with full sails and rigging. At the end of the room was a dark, decorated patio with tables hidden among trees and lit with lamps. We were given creole food prepared in the grand manner, and occasionally we saw the blue flame of burning brandy flickering in the dark and ice melting slowly in the glowing vapors of some cherry flavored liqueur.

The Vieux Carré began to wake up; doormen in splendid uniforms stood outside the nightclubs; the bars were open, and one could see the glint of whiskey standing on the counters; from the street we could hear the clinking of glasses and the jukeboxes. Where should we go? We were attracted by the decor of the Napoleon House and went inside, but there was no band. The owner was extremely pleasant to us because we were French, and we told him

The tap dancer Porkchop in a New Orleans club, by Ralston Crawford

By permission of the Historic New Orleans Collection, Museum/Research Center, acc. no. 1983.33.4

that we wanted to hear a good Negro band. He recommended The Old Absinthe House. The first room was a tiny bar whose walls and ceilings were covered with calling cards and international banknotes. In the second room were a few tables and a bandstand with a Negro trio: piano, guitar and double bass. We were enchanted at once; this music was different from the music at Café Society or even in Harlem; the Negro trio played with passion, for themselves. The few people there were not elegant; they did not really constitute an audience, since there were but a few couples and a few families who were probably traveling through New Orleans, and they seemed out of place here. The band did not try to excite or play up to them but just played in a way that seemed right for itself; when the double bass player—a Negro youth not more than eighteen, in spite of his corpulence—sometimes closed his eyes and seemed lost in another world, it was not an act: he obeyed only the music and his feelings. Listening intently to the band were two dark-haired white men. They joked with the musicians between the numbers. They were different from the other people there and reminded us of the book by Dorothy Baker, *Young Man With A Horn;*[9] they probably were a part of that young generation, stifled by American civilization, and for which jazz is a means of escape. They stared back at us, for undoubtedly there was something strange about our being there.

Meanwhile, we cheerfully drank zombies. This formidable cocktail originated in New Orleans; this drink is named after the living dead, heroes of numerous horror stories, whose legend was born in the South.[10] (I was told that more than one adult in Louisiana and Georgia still believes in the existence of these living dead: they can only find eternal repose by being stabbed in the chest with the tip of a sword.) . . .

Our friendship with the two dark young men was progressing; we applauded with the same enthusiasm, exchanged a few words, and now they were sitting at our table. R. was Italian, C. Spanish, and R., by some miracle, was just the Young Man With the Horn we had pictured. He came from a very poor family and, when still a boy, had joined the Navy and become a trum-

9. Dorothy Baker, *Young Man with a Horn* (Boston, 1938). This first novel told the story of a young jazz trumpeter tragically at odds with society. Loosely based on the life of Bix Beiderbecke, it was widely praised.

10. The zombie of folklore, though not unknown in Louisiana, originated in the Caribbean, not the American South. On the process of zombification, see Wade Davis, *The Serpent and the Rainbow* (New York, 1987).

peter in a Naval band; he still had a year to serve and wanted very much to become a professional musician. He had taken a few courses at the Philadelphia Conservatory and thought the city quite wonderful. He spoke with enthusiasm not only of jazz but also of Ravel, Stravinsky and Béla Bártok. His reading had been limited, yet the book he enjoyed most was James Joyce's *Ulysses*. He was twenty-two. Of all the young men of his age I had met in America, he was the first who was young in heart.

There was no possibility of inviting the musicians to have a drink with us at our table. We spoke to them from our seats. Two of them had French wives, that is, women descended from the Creoles. They spoke some archaic French. We talked with them and asked them to play old tunes. We stayed for some time, but we wanted to discover other places. The band implored us to leave R. and C. with them, because they liked to play for people who loved and understood jazz. We made them give us some addresses, and our new friends promised to act as guides the following evening.

We were overwhelmed by our good luck; the raucous night no longer frightened us, we had tamed it; this time we were part of it, and we were no longer in the sad group of the excluded. . . .

We went to another bar which, apparently, was the hangout of artists and bohemians; we were struck by the large number of homosexuals who were staggering around the bar. One of them was slyly approaching a young couple. He pretended to flirt with the woman but always managed to lean on the husband's shoulder. A young Negro, half-drunk, strummed the piano and played old jazz in a very moving style. The place was seething with people who seemed soaked in alcohol; but vice and drunkenness wore light colors here. The atmosphere was not heavy; on the contrary, it seemed fresh and gay—or was this gaiety ours? The night was warm in the streets under the gray sky. Gradually the nightclubs closed but we didn't feel like going to sleep, we felt so alive. We sat down at the counter of a wretched bar where a dwarf with a coffee-colored face frenziedly played an old piano. Two tramps danced on the sidewalk. When the piano was silent and they had left we went back to the hotel as we could think of nothing else to do.

March 31st

In the morning we returned to the places we had seen the day before. . . .

We dined in a patio, different from the one we saw yesterday but just as delightful. We were struck by the color of the sky: it was pearl gray, luminous as the dawn, as if lighted by some mysterious searchlight. Once we were back in the street we understood: a soft mist enveloped the city. Tall buildings on the other side of Canal Street had retreated; they were far away and ghostly. The mist smothered the neon signs, but it made a screen above the roofs where all the lights were reflected. The sky was almost white, the air quite moist. It was gentle but stifling and seemed to presage a storm.

We met our friends again at *The Old Absinthe House*. We were proud of their company, proud to feel ourselves in league, not with the people who listened dumbly, but with the musicians. There were more people tonight: some attentive students, bored couples and gay parties. At one of the tables an old gentleman began to sing. He had a fresh, pink complexion and fine white hair, gold-rimmed spectacles and an air of quiet assurance that comes from a well-stuffed pocketbook. He was of a common and particularly detestable type. The band obligingly accompanied him. He began another song, and I got mad. The little Italian smiled; he explained that anyone in the audience had the right to sing providing he paid for it: the money went to the musicians. And I saw indeed that the obtrusive singer had put his dollars on the piano; he loved music in a strange way.

R. and C. wanted to go to a nightclub reserved for colored people to which they had entree. But it was Holy Week, and New Orleans is a pious city. Tonight the place was closed. They took us to another bar in the *Vieux Carré* where there was a good Negro band with saxophone and trumpet; the trumpeter was young and played with youthful zest. He had a natural gift, so complete in itself that his whole being seemed to be concentrated on each note. It is here in these unostentatious nightclubs and among these unknown players that jazz attains a real dignity, far more so than in Carnegie Hall or the Savoy: there is no showmanship, no exhibitionism, and no commercial flavor. It is, on the contrary, a mode of life and a *raison d'etre;* it gives to art, poetry and printed music the pathetic privilege of making immediate contact, like the moments whose very substance it transfigures. If these men's lives are often so tormented it is because, instead of holding off death at arm's length like other artists, they are conscious at every moment of the marriage of life and death. It was against this background—the background of death—that the inspired music of the young trumpeter rose up. You could not listen to him merely with your brain, for he conjured up an experience in which you felt you had to let yourself go utterly. He conjured it up, but in what a desert! The people here have not even the respectful enthusiasm of concert-goers; they are amused by jazz and despise it on racial grounds, their prejudices being as firmly rooted in their morality as in their money. It was with a similar arrogance that the great lords of the past amused themselves—with buffoons and jesters. R. questioned the trumpeter, they exchanged a few words, and the dark face lit up; he smiled at us as he played. Like the musicians at *The Old Absinthe House,* he felt he must play for someone, and it was a chance he seldom got.

The band stopped playing. A beautiful young woman with raven hair walked onto the platform; she began to dance and take off her clothes slowly, following the prescribed rites of burlesque. From a corner a middle-aged woman watched her indifferently: it was the girl's mother. We heard that the dancer was of good family, had studied much, and was intelligent and cultured; but in New Orleans, strippers are readily surrounded by legendary auras. This girl, however, was beautiful and attractive. The more she took off, the more forbidding grew the looks around her; they expressed detached curiosity, polite but bored; when she abandoned her panties, keeping only the "patch"—a spangled triangle held by a silken thread—the atmosphere was so charged with morality that one might have been in church.

Our friends were anxious to take us to the colored district. A taxi brought us to the other end of town, and we entered a dance hall where the proprietor, who knew R., welcomed us; but there was no band, because of Holy Week, and the colored people sitting in the bar appeared unfriendly. We would not burden them with our presence, so we left, and as we were on our way out we heard them laughing rudely. We walked through the hostile streets on foot in this part of town, where we were enemies through no fault of our own and yet responsible, despite ourselves, because of the color of our skin and all that it implied. R. told us that, despite the charm of New Orleans, he could not bear to live here on account of racial prejudices and that he would go back north as soon as possible. We walked for a long time. The pink of the azaleas glowed dully through the mist; the sky shed a white light. One could not see as far as the end of the street. The damp air clung to one's skin, and the smell of dead leaves lay heavy on the ground. We stopped at a bar and, while drinking whiskey, talked till dawn.

In the Quarter

WALKER PERCY

Though noted novelist Walker Percy (1916–1990) was born in Mississippi, most of his novels have Louisiana settings—he spent the latter part of his life in Covington, across Lake Pontchartrain from New Orleans. The following piece is from *The Moviegoer;* in it the novel's protagonist and narrator Binx Bolling lands in the French Quarter, having taken a bus in from Gentilly, the neighborhood where he lives. Though his fictional journey is intracity and thus short, he finds a world of travelers from elsewhere—shoppers, honeymooners, movie star William Holden—and relates an incident that draws them together in the particular ambience of the Quarter.

I alight at Esplanade in a smell of roasting coffee and creosote and walk up Royal Street. The lower Quarter is the best part. The ironwork on the balconies sags like rotten lace. Little French cottages hide behind high walls. Through deep sweating carriageways one catches glimpses of courtyards gone to jungle.

Today I am in luck. Who should come out of Pirate's Alley half a block ahead of me but William Holden!

Holden crosses Royal and turns toward Canal. As yet he is unnoticed. The tourists are either browsing along antique shops or snapping pictures of balconies. No doubt he is on his way to Galatoire's for lunch. He is an attractive fellow with his ordinary good looks, very sun tanned, walking along hands in pockets, raincoat slung over one shoulder. Presently he passes a young couple, who are now between me and him. Now we go along, the four of us, not twenty feet apart. It takes two seconds to size up the couple. They are twenty, twenty-one, and on their honeymoon. Not Southern. Probably Northeast. He wears a jacket with leather elbow patches, pipestem pants, dirty white shoes, and affects the kind of rolling seafaring gait you see in Northern college boys. Both are plain. He has thick lips, cropped reddish hair and skin to match. She is mousy. They are not really happy. He is afraid their honeymoon is too conventional, that they are just another honeymoon couple. No doubt he figured it would be fun to drive down the Shenandoah Valley to New Orleans and escape the honeymooners at Niagara Falls and Saratoga. Now fifteen hundred miles from home they find themselves surrounded by couples from Memphis and Chicago. He is anxious; he is threatened from every side. Each stranger he passes is a reproach to him, every doorway a threat. What is wrong? he wonders. She is unhappy but for a different reason, because he is unhappy and she knows it but doesn't know why.

Now they spot Holden. The girl nudges her companion. The boy perks up for a second, but seeing Holden doesn't really help him. On the contrary. He can only contrast Holden's resplendent reality with his own shadowy and precarious existence. Obviously he is more miserable than ever. What a deal, he must be thinking, trailing along behind a movie star—we might just as well be rubbernecking in Hollywood.

Holden slaps his pockets for a match. He has stopped behind some ladies looking at iron furniture on the sidewalk. They look like housewives from Hattiesburg come down for a day of shopping. He asks for a match; they shake their heads and then recognize him. There follows much blushing and confusion. But nobody can find a match for Holden. By now the couple have caught up with him. The boy holds out a light, nods briefly to Holden's thanks, then passes on without a flicker of recognition. Holden walks along between them for a second; he and the boy talk briefly, look up at the sky, shake their heads. Holden gives them a pat on the shoulder and moves on ahead.

The boy has done it! He has won title to his own existence, as plenary an existence now as Holden's, by refusing to be stampeded like the ladies from Hattiesburg. He is a citizen like Holden; two men of the world they are. All at once the world is open to him. Nobody threatens from patio and alley. His girl is open to him too. He puts his arm around her neck, noodles her head. She feels the difference too. She had not known what was wrong nor how it was righted but she knows now that all is well.

Holden has turned down Toulouse shedding light as he goes. An aura of heightened reality moves with him and all who fall within it feel it. Now everyone is aware of him. He creates a regular eddy among the tourists and barkeeps and B-girls who come running to the doors of the joints.

I am attracted to movie stars but not for the usual reasons. I have no desire to speak to Holden or get his autograph. It is their peculiar reality which astounds me. The Yankee boy is well aware of it, even though he pretends to ignore Holden. Clearly he would like nothing better than to take Holden over to his fraternity house in the most casual way. "Bill, I want you to meet Phil. Phil, Bill Holden," he would say and go sauntering off in the best seafaring style.

New Orleans

JOY HARJO

A noted Native American poet, Harjo is of the Creek tribe. In the poem below she mentions Hernando de Soto, whose early Spanish expedition reached present-day Louisiana only after de Soto himself had died in 1542. His body was buried in the Mississippi—so that the local Indians, rendered hostile by the actions of the Spaniards, would not learn of his death—but Harjo imagines him alive, drinking in the French Quarter.

This is the South. I look for evidence
of other Creeks, for remnants of voices,
or for tobacco brown bones to come wandering
down Conti Street, Royale, or Decatur.
Near the French Market I see a blue horse
caught frozen in stone in the middle of
a square. Brought in by the Spanish on
an endless ocean voyage he became mad
and crazy. They caught him in blue
rock, said
        don't talk.

I know it wasn't just a horse
        that went crazy.

Nearby is a shop with ivory and knives.
There are red rocks. The man behind the
counter has no idea that he is inside

magic stones. He should find out before
they destroy him. These things
have memory,
                        you know.

I have a memory.
                        It swims deep in blood,
a delta in the skin. It swims out of Oklahoma,
deep the Mississippi River. It carries my
feet to these places: the French Quarter,
stale rooms, the sun behind the thick and moist
clouds, and I hear boats hauling themselves up
and down the river.

My spirit comes here to drink.
My spirit comes here to drink.
Blood is the undercurrent.
There are voices buried in the Mississippi
mud. There are ancestors and future children
buried beneath the currents stirred up by
pleasure boats going up and down.
There are stories here made of memory.

I remember DeSoto. He is buried somewhere in
this river, his bones sunk like the golden
treasure he traveled half the earth to find,
came looking for gold cities, for shining streets
of beaten gold to dance on with silk ladies.

He should have stayed home.

                        (Creeks knew of him for miles
                        before he came into town.
                        Dreamed of silver blades
                        and crosses.)

And knew he was one of the ones who yearned
for something his heart wasn't big enough
to handle.
>   (And DeSoto thought it was gold.)

The Creeks lived in earth towns,
>   not gold,
>   spun children, not gold.
That's not what DeSoto thought he wanted to see.
The Creeks knew it, and drowned him in
>   the Mississippi River
>   so he wouldn't have to drown himself.

Maybe his body is what I am looking for
as evidence. To know in another way
that my memory is alive.
But he must have got away, somehow,
because I have seen New Orleans,
the lace and silk buildings,
trolley cars on beaten silver paths,
graves that rise up out of soft earth in the rain,
shops that sell black mammy dolls
holding white babies.

And I know I have seen DeSoto,
>   having a drink on Bourbon Street,
>   mad and crazy
>   dancing with a woman as gold
>   as the river bottom.

Between Trains

GEORGE F. SCHEER III

Having grown up in the age of the automobile, Scheer took a notion to see his country via the older mode of rail travel. He wrote about his train journeys in *Booked on the Morning Train: A Journey Through America.* This book, from which the following is taken, practically begins with his entry into New Orleans on the train called the Crescent just as the city is waking up. Despite his short stay in the city, he provides a remarkably insightful and informative account of modern New Orleans.

Not only is New Orleans the end of the line for the Crescent from the East Coast, but for the City of New Orleans from Chicago and the Sunset Limited from Los Angeles as well. New Orleans is also the end of the line for conformity. Puritan values and the Protestant ethic get off somewhere north of Lake Pontchartrain. The dollar is legal tender in New Orleans and people there work, many of them no doubt work hard, but the city as a culture doesn't celebrate work as a virtue. Necessary maybe, sometimes even enjoyable, but not necessarily good for the soul or constructive of character. New Orleans is not about saving souls or building character.

From a pay phone in Union Station on Loyola Avenue, I phoned an old friend who had been living in New Orleans for a few years. Jim is a traveler and a wanderer. I've known him for nearly twenty years and he is well into his third page of my address book by now, with mailing addresses ranging from New Jersey to Minnesota, San Francisco, Hawaii, and Fiji. Unlike many wanderers who glance across the surface of the earth, Jim sets root everywhere he

Children playing in front of double-shotgun houses in New Orleans, 1943, by John Vachon

Photograph courtesy Library of Congress

stops, immersing himself in his surroundings with a ravenous curiosity. I have come to expect that Jim will know more about a city or a country, having lived there six months, than all but a few natives.

"George, you made it," he said from work, where I reached him. "I can't talk now. I've arranged for you to stay in a quintessential New Orleans house on Governor Nicholls Street in the Tremé, near the French Quarter. This house was built in the 1820s. Marcia, a friend of mine, grew up there and owns it now. You'll meet her later. Why don't you walk around in the Quarter this evening. You know your way around. I'll meet you when I get off at eleven." . . .

When Jim drove up in a borrowed Plymouth Horizon, my watch read one-thirty. I had forgotten the time change: New Orleans was on Central time and I was still on Eastern. Schlemiel goes to Warsaw. The rube leaves home. It was still early, only a bit after midnight—the train had not been late, after all.

So we took a drive. After retrieving my bags from Union Station, we skirted the Quarter, turned away from the river on Bayou Road and followed it past the fairgrounds. Through back streets we made our way over to Bayou St. John, a long and placid tendril of water that flows through the city into Lake Pontchartrain. Jim pointed out to me the Caribbean cottages that were the first plantation houses along the Bayou. With the car windows down, the sweet night air flowed through the car. After the heat of the bright afternoon and the still humidity of the Quarter, it felt good to lean back and let it wash over me.

Afterward, we drove back toward the Quarter and parked at the corner of Governor Nicholls Street. "This is it," Jim said, indicating with a glance the high brick wall on our side of the street. Tangled vines scaled the chipped and crumbling masonry. A wooden gate, midway along the wall, was the only breach. Inside I saw what might have been a movie set for Poe's "Fall of the House of Usher." A brick walk, narrow and uneven, led from the gate to the front steps of an antebellum mansion in decay. On either side of the walk were fallow garden plots edged with soldier rows of crumbling bricks. Against the inner wall vines grew uncultivated and unkempt. The entire scene was lit with a soft, pale glow that might have been moonlight.

More than the faded paint, more than the dark windows, something made that house a forbidding presence. There is about much of New Orleans an air of decay. Paint peels so quickly it hardly seems worth the bother. Vegetation threatens to reclaim the city, vines tugging at every wall and crumbling the sidewalks. Lizards and cockroaches are the living things best adapted to the climate. It's a climate that breeds mosquitoes. And it breeds indolence and madness.

I followed Jim along a narrow brick passageway squeezed between the house and the banana plants along the wall. At the rear, we crossed a brick patio under a broad magnolia tree to a two-story frame outbuilding with a balcony drooping off the upper story.

"I think she's going to put you in the slave quarters." Jim opened the door and we stepped into a rustic kitchen. He found a note, meant for us, on the spindly, painted wood table near the hearth. "She wants you to take her bedroom in the main house. I guess she's staying here in the slave quarters. Follow me."

Back out and through the yard we went, as quietly as possible. We climbed the back stairs and came into a long hall that ran straight through the first floor of the house, from the rear door to the front. To the left a sweeping staircase climbed up one wall, turned and continued up the side wall, and turned again and climbed out of sight to the second floor. The ceiling was too high to take its measure.

"I think this is her room." Jim tentatively pushed open one of a pair of French doors, looked in, then opened it wide, beckoning me to follow. Inside was a once-handsome room, now nearly bare. A mattress and springs, made with serviceable linen and a quilt, a massive, scarred wooden desk, an armoire, a sewing table, and an ironing board were the only furnishings. A battered box fan stood on the floor in the corner. Hanging over the mantle were two masks, grotesque exaggerations of the human visage, waiting there like a coat or scarf that the owner could grab on his way out the door.

"I met Marcia through a friend who works at the coffeehouse," Jim said. "She came to New Orleans as a girl when her father was named director of the New Orleans Museum of Art, and she grew up here in this house. The neighborhood was genteel then. Now she lives in California most of the year, but she keeps coming back to try to restore the house."

Jim and I made plans to meet the next afternoon at the restaurant where he worked. "The weather should be good. I'll borrow a bike for you and we'll take a ground-level tour of the city."

Jim left and I was alone. I turned out the lights and then turned one back on, a floor lamp next to the bed. I wasn't ready to sleep in that house in the dark. I looked for something to read and found a paperback copy of Janet Flanner's memoirs from Paris. A shiny black roach crawled over my leg and continued across the bedspread. I gently flicked it across the room. My dreams turn violent if I sleep in a warm room, so I switched on the fan and aimed it toward the bed. It began to turn, slowly at first, and then picked up speed, roaring in the empty house, the rattle of its bearings drumming the resonant wood floor and echoing off the ceiling. I regretted the noise. I had no wish to be noticed until morning. But I was gummy with sweat from the long train ride and my long evening's ramble through the Quarter, and the air in the tall room was still and thick.

I dreamed of ghostly figures drifting in ones and twos through the hall and peering in at me while I slept. I dreamed of a succubus in a hideous mask. The heat, perhaps. . . .

I awoke early, after only a few hours of uneasy sleep, eager to see my surroundings in daylight and to meet my hostess. Through the tall French doors of the bedroom, I walked into the vacant hall, where daylight flooded through from the panes on either side of the front door and washed down the passage to the open rear doors. In the night, a few hours before, I had imagined hideous spirits in that hall. The cleansing early light was as encouraging as morning coffee. Through the open doorway I could see the green of tropical plants in the backyard. It was sunny when I wandered out the back door into the yard and still cool enough so that the sun felt good. Across the yard the door to the slave quarters stood open. A slight woman with graying hair sat at a table beneath a window, writing in longhand in the light from the window.

"Good morning, you must be Jim's friend," she said. "I'm Marcia. Come in and have some coffee. Do you mind coffee and chicory?" She was wearing baggy, black cotton trousers, soft black shoes, and a mannish white shirt, rolled up at the sleeves.

"I would love coffee and chicory," I said, standing awkwardly near the door. "On my very first visit to New Orleans, my father took me to a little steak house where I discovered New Orleans coffee. I drank about eight cups, black, and it took him two days to get me detoxed."

"It's a small pot, but we can make another." She laughed, and a few wisps of her hair, which was pulled back severely behind her head, came loose and fell across her face and she brushed them back with a girlish gesture.

The process of making coffee gave us both something to do for a couple of minutes. When it was ready we each took a mug. I sat down on the hearth where the bricks were still cool from the night air; she returned to her desk. She asked about my trip and, since she seemed genuinely curious, I told her my plans and we talked about the possibilities. She had an enthusiasm that we unfairly think of as youthful. The conversation turned gradually to other things: New Orleans, of course, the house, and her childhood there. We made a second pot of coffee, and then another.

She was restoring the old house, fighting that hopeless war on several fronts, excavating the basement and plastering the kitchen and trying just to battle time to a standstill everywhere else. Her background in art constrained her to restore the crumbling house as one would a fine painting, destroying nothing that could be saved, no matter what pains were required, and adding nothing inauthentic. She was no dilettante: on my way back through the kitchen I saw the scaffolding she had erected and the arduous job she had begun of restoring the lathing and replastering the ceiling.

Soon the sun that had been slanting into the doorway was overhead and the heat of day drifted in through the doors and windows. We departed in our respective directions: she, on her moped, to fetch supplies from the hardware store; I, on foot, for the Quarter. I closed the front gate carefully behind me, turned right, and stepped out lively down Governor Nicholls Street toward the river. As I crossed Rampart Street, I passed a delicately dressed man strolling with his well-bred dog on a leash. Like most residents of the Quarter he had mastered the ability to ignore tourists as beneath notice, scarcely sufferable annoyances, like cockroaches, the price to be paid for living where others can only visit. . . .

For an hour I strolled through the Garden District, where every home is a showplace. These were the homes that the Creoles, considering their owners nouveaux riches, derisively called Prairie Palaces. Along Magazine Street, on the edge of the Irish Channel, the opulence of the Garden District began to fray at the edges. The iron fences were bare of decorative hedges, and finally they gave way entirely to chain link—practical, ugly, and unthinkable in the Garden District.

As I walked along Magazine Street, I saw a choice example of New Orleans' most significant contribution to residential architecture. The Garden District offers well-kept examples of a smorgasbord of architectural styles: Italianate, Queen Anne, Greek Revival, and others. The French Quarter is a heady, unpolluted concentration of ornate Old World architecture. But the salient creation of New Orleans is the shotgun, that frame-and-board archetype of the mobile home: rooms lined up one behind the other in a soldier course, from the front of the lot to the rear, with no hallway, only a series of doors from each room into the one behind. Along Magazine Street I saw a classic of the genre, a dilapidated double shotgun in a bald gritty yard separated from the street by a chain link fence on which climbed only a few hardy weeds. From every window along each side of the house a window air conditioner drooped, and two electric meters were tacked to the outside wall halfway to the rear. . . .

We ended our night at the Napoleon House on Chartres Street. We shared a muffuletta and I had a Guinness and we didn't talk much. Our energy was flagging and we were both thinking ahead to the following day. It was Friday night and drinkers crowded the bar, but the weekend had no meaning for either of us. Jim was due at work early and I was booked on the afternoon train, headed north. I wouldn't see him again.

I slept until midmorning. I found Marcia on scaffolding in the kitchen, wearing spattered pants and shirt and pulling chunks of plaster from the lathing in the ceiling. It came off in her hands in flakes and clumps, exposing the strips of wood beneath, like whitecooked flesh from the rib cage of a fish.

She looked down at me and wiped her hands on her trousers. "I left some coffee on for you this morning," she said. "It's probably soot and ash by now. Make some more if you like. I'm going to keep at this for a little while. When's your train?"

"Between four and five this afternoon. I'll have to check the time."

"Why don't you sit out in the garden? I'll join you when I'm through here. Or when I can't stand it any longer. I'll never be through."

I found the coffee, simmered to sludge, still on the stove, poured an immediate dose, then started a fresh pot. I dragged an old wooden chair with a cane seat, pieces of the cane snapped and curled like busted banjo strings, a few feet into a patch of sunlight. The cat of the house, an old tom named Percy, lay about with me, moving from one sun-warmed patch of brick to another. He dozed with one eye propped open to a slit, occasionally switching his tail in warning to a young male kitten recently brought to the house by one of the renters. The kitten was uncertain of himself, and Percy encouraged the little usurper to believe that his life hung by a thread.

Marcia came out of the house, disappeared into the kitchen of the slave quarters, and returned with a few sliced tomatoes, some leftovers, and a couple of bottles of beer. We ate lunch at the table under the magnolia tree in the back garden. I could feel my ambition for the afternoon slipping away.

She brushed a few flecks of plaster off her shirt. "Ah, yes, we preserve things down here, it's all we do." She was looking over my shoulder at the house and she was smiling, but there was resignation and a touch of despair in her voice. "I don't want to run a museum. That's what my parents did. I found an old letter from my mother, 'Well,' she said, 'you just have to keep the place up. It's like an old pet.' She was right. You can't restore its youth and vigor, you just have to make it comfortable in its infirmity."

"Jim calls it 'the virtue of decay.'"

"Is it virtue? It all returns to the earth. I know this to be true. I think the house will outdo me, though." She sounded wistful.

We had finished the beers and the small bottle of wine I had saved from my complimentary basket on the run down to New Orleans. The house that had seemed so gloomy, so indifferent, that first night now seemed warm and comfortable. The peeling paint and crumbling plaster, the overgrown wall, the neglected garden full of big banana trees and tiny green lizards all now seemed in order, in keeping with the city. Behind the garden wall, those "convent walls," as Marcia called them, I felt the same security that she felt. I was coming under the same spell. I was beginning to understand why, in the face of all reason, in the face of hostility surrounding her, in the face of upkeep beyond reason and taxing to exhaustion, she soldiered on, returning every year to patch the old place together.

Marcia smiled. "It's hard to leave, isn't it? New Orleans gives you a million excuses, excuses for not working, excuses for not leaving."

"I've got a four forty-five train. I'd better go call a cab."

"Yes, you'd better."

I went into the house and called the taxi company she had suggested and we carried my bags to the front garden. On the porch, next to the door frame, was a plaque. I had noticed it the day before.

The Meilleur-Goldthwaite House, erected 1828–1829. The residence of William F. Goldthwaite, antiquarian, 1859–1889. The site was once part of the plantation of Claude Tremé, where the first brickyard in New Orleans had been established in 1725 by the Company of the Indies.

We stood and waited just inside the gate. "The taxi drivers won't wait for you if you're not ready to go. They don't like to hang around in this neighborhood. Danger is a part of life in New Orleans. So much violence. Black and white people live side by side all over New Orleans, but whites still fear blacks and blacks are still angry over four hundred years of mistreatment. In little ways . . . they throw their trash in front of my gate, as if to say, 'Here, you pick up after me now.' And every day, I go and pick it up. It's my lesson in humility." On the way to Union Station the taxi driver said, "Summers are very hard on us here." It was a short ride, but it broke the spell.

Travel Update

New Orleans is one of the most visited cities in the United States. The prospective visitor can find a more than adequate array of detailed information on what to see and do. The major guidebook publishers, such as Fodor and Birnbaum, have standard Louisiana and New Orleans volumes that include hotel and restaurant information. The locally published *Pelican Guide to New Orleans,* by Thomas K. Griffin with an introduction by Mayor Sidney Barthelemy (Gretna, La., 1991), is a good source of information, and *New Orleans: Yesterday and Today,* by Walter G. Cowan, John C. Chase, Charles L. Dufour, O. K. LeBlanc, and John Wilds (Baton Rouge, 1983), is strong on historical background and culturally significant sites; this latter volume has short chapters on such topics as the cemeteries, literature, the Civil War, and Mardi Gras. The *New Orleans City Guide* (Boston, 1938), part of the American Guide Series produced under the auspices of the Depression-era Federal Writers' Project, is in many ways out of date but nonetheless a classic with a gold mine of still-useful information. It was republished (New York, 1983) as *The WPA Guide to New Orleans,* with an updating introduction by the staff of the Historic New Orleans Collection. Stanley Clisby Arthur's 1936 *Old New Orleans* has been reprinted, edited by Susan Cole Doré (using a 1955 printing of the 1944 revision), with the subtitle "Walking Tours of the French Quarter" (Gretna, La., 1990). The book is still very sound and informative as an architectural guide, Doré having noted various changes that have taken place; it is enhanced by illustrations by several noted artists, including Morris Henry Hobbs, Joseph Pennell, Knute Heldner, and Clarence Millet. *New Orleans,* by Bethany Ewald Bultman, with photographs by Richard Sexton (Oakland, 1994), is lavishly illustrated with mostly color photographs. Though it includes standard information on hotels, museums, restaurants, and shops, it is especially strong on local color and "inside" information. *Frommer's Irreverent Guide to New Orleans,* by Guy Leblanc (New York, 1996), is similar and attempts to give particularly frank information. Though *Passport's Guide to Ethnic New Orleans,* by Martin Hintz (Lincolnwood, Ill., 1995), also includes standard tourist data, it emphasizes local culture and ethnicity, as its subtitle, *A Complete Guide to the Many Faces and Cultures of New Orleans,* indicates.

Though obviously there is a world of things to see in New Orleans and no guidebook or travel account can deal with them all, the writers whose work has been included in this section managed to cover quite a bit of ground, having turned their attentions to many of the city's most important sights.

Most of what Philip Pittman saw in the 1760s no longer exists—a disastrous fire swept through the city in 1788 destroying, among other things, the church Pittman found so unprepossessing (itself the second on the site, replacing one destroyed by a hurricane in 1723). The present St. Louis Cathedral was completed in 1794 and considerably modified between 1845 and 1851, and it does dominate the square ("the parade") that Pittman knew as the center of town. Indeed, the church, which was designated a cathedral when Louisiana became a separate Catholic diocese, is a center of religious life as well as visitor interest. The grayish cream structure with its slate-roofed spires topped by delicate ironwork is the dominant focus of the square, the clock a utilitarian accent on this spiritual landmark. Inside, the cathedral is pleasant rather than spectacularly beautiful, comfortably parochial rather than grand (and, in many ways, it is still a parish church for this old neighborhood).

The square itself, today officially called Jackson Square (in the past called the Place d'Armes or Plaza de Armas, depending on French or Spanish rule), is a lovely, lively space teeming with tourists as well as French Quarter residents. It is ringed by interesting shops, sidewalk artists who offer portraits and other paintings, and—in recent times—psychics and tarot readers. Flanking the cathedral are two historically important buildings: to the right (if one is facing the church) is the Presbytere, which replaced the Capuchin monastery noted by Pittman. The Presbytere was begun in 1793 or 1794 as a *casa curial,* or ecclesiastical residence ("presbytère" in French), though it was not used for that purpose and was not finished until 1813, well into the American period. On the other side of the cathedral is the Cabildo, the *Casa Capitular* ("Capitol House," or headquarters) of the Spaniards, built in 1795 on the site of an earlier administrative building constructed a few years after Pittman's visit. Both buildings are operated by the Louisina State Museum and are open to the public; each contains exhibits relating to Louisiana history and culture, and each provides a good view of Jackson Square from its second floor.

The upriver and downriver sides of the square are occupied by the Pontalba

Buildings, built in 1849 and sometimes called the first apartment buildings in the United States. These large but graceful red-brick structures contain shops and apartment residences and provide the square's nineteenth-century faces. One of the apartments in the Lower (downriver) Pontalba Building has been restored by the state museum to show the public something of nineteenth-century life in this part of the Crescent City; this is the "1850 House," whose entrance is through the museum's gift shop. The Baroness de Pontalba, who commissioned the buildings, was also responsible for the further transformation of the square from military parade ground and assembly place to public gardens. Today the fenced square is a central focus of the Vieux Carré for tourists and residents alike, beautiful on sunny days and with a reserved elegance. An equestrian statue of Andrew Jackson is the square's centerpiece, surely the "blue horse" of Joy Harjo's poem (though she conveniently omits the presence of the general atop his steed).

Between and behind the cathedral, Presbytere, and Cabildo are several alleyways. One (formerly St. Anthony's Alley) is called Père Antoine Alley for a beloved local priest, the others Cabildo Alley and Pirate's Alley (formerly Orleans Alley and seeming to have no historical connection with piracy; Percy's Binx Bolling passes it before seeing movie star William Holden). This is an especially charming little section and was the setting for William Faulkner's 1925 episode with William Spratling and his artistic subjects. Faulkner lived at 624 Pirate's Alley, where a plaque marks the house; according to a drawing in Faulkner and Spratling's book, this part of the Vieux Carré was particularly popular with the writers and artists of that generation. The Faulkner House Books shop has operated in the building for some years now, specializing in Faulkneriana and Louisiana and southern literature. (Earlier editions of Arthur's *Old New Orleans* have a nice sketch of the alley by Spratling.) Across the alley and just behind the cathedral, the peaceful St. Anthony's Garden offers a tiny oasis. It was once, however, a popular spot for the duels that addicted New Orleans gentlemen in the eighteenth and nineteenth centuries, as Arthur Singleton mentions. Where his rough Cadiz corner was located remains unclear. In City Park, one of the two famous Dueling Oaks still stands, identified by a sign. Long before there was a park here and while this spot was far outside the city, this also was a noted place for settling affairs of honor.

Vast City Park is located at the lake end of Esplanade, the street that marks the downriver boundary of the French Quarter (as Canal Street does the

French Market scene, by Nils Hogner

From Dorothy C. Hogner, *South to Padre,* copyright © 1936 by Lothrop, Lee & Shepard Books. By permission of Lothrop, Lee & Shepard Books, a division of William Morrow & Company, Inc.

upriver). Esplanade is a stately boulevard (where Percy's character begins his Quarter excursion) lined by many splendid old houses. Though some sections have become run-down, it still offers an interesting drive. Before reaching City Park (which also houses the New Orleans Museum of Art and various amusement and recreation areas), Esplanade crosses Bayou St. John, which Pittman mentions. He was enthusiastic about the bayou as an avenue for reaching "the northern parts of Louisiana" because it and the lake offered access to areas that had just come under British control. Of course the Mississippi still offered the main route north. He calls it the Bayou*k* of St. John because the word *bayou* is derived from the Choctaw *bayuk,* meaning a stream. This bayou is connected to Lake Pontchartrain and provided early access to New Orleans: ships could sail from French settlements farther east along the Gulf Coast and into the lake, thus avoiding the arduous trip up the swift current of the Mississippi. In 1795 the Carondelet Canal, which Benjamin Latrobe was making for on his stroll when he encountered the Congo Square festivities, was opened to connect Bayou St. John to the city by water. It has long since been filled in, like most of the city's canals.

Because of the bayou's early importance, a number of structures lined its banks, a few of which still remain. Most notable of these is the Pitot House built in 1799, now open as a museum (though hours are limited). The French-colonial structure has white plastered walls, green shutters and jalousies, and uneven galleries, and sits behind a raggedy *pieux* fence (typical of French Louisiana). It was the residence of the first elected mayor of New Orleans, James Pitot. (George F. Scheer calls such houses "Caribbean cottages," but that is something of a misnomer. Louisiana Creole architecture has much in common with that of the West Indies, but it is not simply derivative of Caribbean forms.) Another eighteenth-century Creole house sits at the corner of Grand Route St. John, and the 1834 Greek-revival mansion that is now the rectory for Our Lady of the Rosary Roman Catholic Church tends to dominate the scene. The impressive, tarnish green dome of the church itself, located on Esplanade, towers over the neighborhood. Up and down the wide, placid bayou, the architecture mirrors many periods—colonial structures, 1930s bungalows, 1950s ranch houses, and ultrabland modernity are all represented. A trestle-style footbridge spans the bayou, and in the distance can be seen a few downtown skyscrapers, so at variance with the low-rise, ancient neighborhood.

The only building Pittman mentions that still exists (the disastrous fire of 1788 stopped just short of it) is the Ursuline Convent. Located at Chartres and Ursulines Streets in the French Quarter, it is considered by many the oldest building in the Mississippi Valley. The Ursulines came to Louisiana in 1727. Their convent, built in 1749, has since served various church purposes; for a time it was the residence of the Archbishop of New Orleans. Beautifully restored in recent years, it can be toured at set times, allowing the modern visitor to see more than Pittman could. The grayish cream building with gray shutters is striking: more massive than most buildings in the area, hidden behind high walls, fronted by neat, geometrically arranged hedges. At one end it seems to devour the small church, now called Our Lady of Victory, once the chapel of the archbishops.

The French Market, which by Will Coleman's time in the late nineteenth century had become of such interest to visitors that he included a whole chapter on it in his guide, is still a popular attraction. The site of the market—today between Decatur Street and the railroad tracks that run near the bank of the Mississippi—was probably a market of sorts even in Pittman's time, for tradition has it that this was once an Indian trading place. The first actual structure was the meat market, erected in 1813, followed by the vegetable market in 1823 and by other structures later. Both the meat and vegetable markets still stand, though in altered form. The bazaar market, which Coleman mentions, sold clothing and dry goods but was destoyed by a hurricane in 1915. What is today called the bazaar market was built in the 1930s by the Works Progress Administration. Major renovations were undertaken in the 1930s and 1970s. The landmark Red Stores were a privately built, commercial part of the market; they were destroyed, though a reconstruction was undertaken in 1976. A structure closely resembling the original now stands on the same site between the main market buildings and the railroad tracks. Increasingly the market has become tourist-centered, with souvenir shops replacing older businesses, but one segment continues to sell fruits and vegetables—the farmers' market, also a 1930s WPA project—and a flea market that operates at the downriver end has brought a bustle and tumult in the general spirit of the market's headier days. Alligator meat is no longer sold (nor are birds, some of which Audubon bought here to be his models), but one can find superb pralines and such Louisiana delicacies as sugarcane and mirlitons, a squashlike member of the cucumber family. The Café du Monde, at the end of the market across from Jackson Square (the meat market, where the coffee stalls traditionally were located), is the last vestige of the coffee stands Coleman presents as an integral part of the scene, and it is a most popular stop (at all hours of the day and night) for coffee and beignets, the New Orleans "doughnuts" eaten with powdered sugar, which are the sole food item offered. Another coffee stand, the venerable Morning Call, moved to a suburban area called Fat City, where it continues its life in a strip mall. Its proprietors moved it, fittings and all, recreating something of its old appearance. Given its almost exclusively local clientele, it is still a quintessential New Orleans experience. As George Scheer discovered, Orleanians like to mix their coffee with chicory. That is by no means the only way they prepare it, though they do take their coffee seriously and use dark, strong roasts. Hence at the coffee stands people almost invariably drink it *au lait* (about half hot milk).

The Mississippi River levee attracted the attentions of most visitors to New Orleans. Paintings, prints, and photographs depicting its heyday show a river front chockablock with river boats and oceangoing vessels and a quay alive with stevedores shifting cotton bales and other cargo. Oyster boats from the coastal country also once put in here at a special landing, and the levee swarmed with human life, as Donald MacDonald and Arthur Singleton make plain. Today the shipping is gone, having given way to modern wharves up- and downstream (and, indeed, the shape of the riverbank itself has changed here—the river was formerly much closer to the U.S. Customs House on Canal Street, a massive gray structure with Egyptian accents where novelist George Washington Cable worked as an official). However, the area remains lively, with walkways and plazas along the river stretching from the downriver end of the Quarter through the Riverwalk commercial development. A new street car line runs here also, on old railroad tracks. Visitors may not find any hawkers of parrots, as did Singleton, but the collection of humanity along the river remains colorful. And though there are no longer riverboat captains who pass out free drinks to prospective passengers, a few excursion boats built to resemble the old river palaces give a distant hint of what once lined the levee.

The general ambience of the French Quarter has charmed visitors for a long time; the area continues to fascinate those who come and, like Percy's characters, saunter past the numerous Royal Street antique shops or famous restaurants like Galatoire's (209 Bourbon Street), though of course it has changed over the years. George Augustus Sala noted its strongly French flavor, but even as he strolled there the section was rapidly losing its Gallic population (which was being increasingly Americanized while also moving to other parts of the city), Italians becoming the area's dominant ethnic group. The French-language newspapers he saw passed away with the French signage that charmed him (though the *Abeille* was published into the 1920s, the *Propagateur Catholique* ceased publication soon after Sala's visit). By the time Faulkner moved in, the Quarter was something of a slum, attractive to artists because the living was cheap. It never lost its interest for tourists, however, and preservationists understood its powerful underlying attraction—it has made a comeback as a fashionable residential area and magnet for tourism. It still has neighborhood groceries that serve a mixed bag of residents, and the Pharmacy Museum on Chartres Street, formerly the *pharmacie* established by Louis Dufilho, recreates the sort of establishment Sala so enjoyed. Bookstores—commented on by both Sala and Simone de Beauvoir—especially those specializing in used and antiquarian volumes, settle in comfortable Quarter locations where browsers are welcome. Despite the changes, the Quarter still strikes visitors as remarkably French, or at least old world or non-American, factors that instantly won the heart of de Beauvoir, among others.

She was especially interested in the Quarter's more raffish side: the jazz clubs, the bars, the night life. Indeed, though it once had the religious-articles stores Sala saw, this central part of New Orleans has long had a reputation for gaiety—and even downright wickedness (Storyville, the legal red light district that was closed down in 1917, lay just outside the Quarter, centering on Basin Street; it was later razed, as if only complete destruction could wipe away its stain). The Quarter still enjoys a vital celebratory atmosphere such as de Beauvoir observed, ranging from the seedy to the boisterous to the elegant. Along Bourbon Street, T-shirt shops elbow strip clubs that vie with fine restaurants. Strains of jazz and country-western slip through doorways and windows. An endless procession of tourists and locals marches through the night, making the rounds of bars or just basking in the neon light of the city where America comes to sin.

De Beauvoir found several notable old New Orleans bars. The Old Absinthe House has been serving refreshments since 1870, though it received that name twenty years later. Absinthe is a liqueur made from wormwood, and it had great vogue in New Orleans—where, in fact, much of the world's supply of the stuff was consumed until it was outlawed because it was thought to cause brain damage. (One can still order an absinthe frappe, but it will be made from a less dangerous substitute called Herbsaint.) Actually there are two bars called the Old Absinthe House. The one located at Bourbon and Bienville Streets is the older establishment. During Prohibition, the actual *bar* itself was moved and became the focus for the other establshment of the same name at Bourbon and Conti. From her description, it would seem that de Beauvoir went to the second of these two. Lafitte's Blacksmith Shop is located at 941 Bourbon, beyond the street's noisiest blocks, and derives its name from the tradition—lacking historical verification—that famed pirate Jean Lafitte and his brother Pierre operated a smithy here as a front for their illegal activities. It is an eighteenth-century structure built of *briquette-entre-poteaux* (brick-between-posts, which Pittman noted as the dominant mode of construction in the eighteenth century), a traditional Louisiana construction technique. Cool and dark, it is found by some to be a bit dank, by others unspeakably romantic.

The Napoleon House at 500 Chartres Street, where Scheer and his friend Jim shared a muffaletta (a splendid, giant sandwich made of meats, cheeses, and pickled vegetables, said by some to have been invented at the Central Grocery on Decatur Street), is also steeped in tradition. The story goes that a plot was hatched by certain New Orleanians to rescue the exiled Napoleon from St. Helena and bring him to Louisiana, where the Chartres Street building would become his residence—but the emperor died before the plan could be effected. Historical substantiation for the story may be slight, but the building is a fine one, with a distinctive belvedere topping a third floor, both added well after Napoleon's day. The bar, staffed by ancient waiters, is very popular. Customers fan out into several areas, and music is provided by an old phonograph. The absence of anything resembling maintenance or refurbishment of the premises seems to add to its charm, giving patrons a sense that they are experiencing an older New Orleans, a neighborhood watering hole untouched by tourist flash.

New Orleans has nurtured a vital tradition of music making, and music can be found in various milieux. A number of French Quarter locations provide "traditional" New Orleans jazz as well as other forms of music, local and not-so-local. The most famous venue for traditional jazz is Preservation Hall (726 St. Peter Street, a tavern in the early nineteenth century), which was founded by a transplanted northern businessman with a passionate love of classic Crescent City jazz and the will to preserve what he feared was a dying tradition. Old-time jazzmen have performed here for years now, and crowds line up outside for several performances a night. Uptown, the Maple Leaf Bar and Tipitina's have become known for presenting local music, and several clubs in the Faubourg Marigny have established followings as popular jazz spots. Unlike during de Beauvoir's day, there are magazines devoted to New Orleans music, including *Offbeat,* which provides good coverage of the scene, *Jazzbeat,* and *New Orleans Music,* which is produced, oddly, in England. In addition, the New Orleans Jazz Society publishes *Second Line.* A "Jazz Map of New Orleans," prepared by Karl Koenig (Abita Springs, La., n.d.), locates sites significant to the history of jazz. Congo Square, which Benjamin Latrobe stumbled on, was a place where slaves and free African Americans were permitted to gather and dance and make music, and it probably played a key role in the ultimate development of jazz and the continuation of African forms in American music. It was located outside what is today the Municipal Auditorium at Armstrong Park, just outside the French Quarter. The best historical treatment of Congo Square is Jerah Johnson's *Congo Square in New Orleans* (New Orleans, 1995).

George Scheer III is almost alone among traveler writers included in this section in getting outside the Vieux Carré (admittedly the heart of old New

Orleans). The house he stayed in on Governor Nicholls Street is in a district called Tremé, located on the opposite side of North Rampart Street from the French Quarter. One of the first areas to be built when the city expanded, it was developed particularly by free people of color and has a heritage of jazz-musician residents. Tremé has been a recent focus for gentrification because of its stately old houses as well as more modest ones—but it is regarded by some New Orleanians as a bit unsafe. Many old New Orleans houses have slave quarter wings or outbuildings that have been converted in recent times to apartments. Bayou Road, which Scheer followed to the Fairgrounds (important not only for racing but because the wildly popular Jazz and Heritage Festival is held here), angles off from Governor Nicholls.

Scheer also managed to get Uptown, the area upriver of Canal Street, particularly the gracious neighborhoods off St. Charles Avenue (served by a streetcar line that is the oldest operating light rail line in the world and that provides a popular method of seeing this part of town at a leisurely pace). The Garden District is the area developed by the wealthier Americans who began to flood into New Orleans after the United States acquired Louisiana. According to historical lore, they were unwelcomed by the downtown Creoles and thus had to build their own neighborhood. The area is full of substantial residences—amazingly large mansions with rambling wings, mysterious walls, and formal porticos—and the layout differs radically from that of the tightly packed Quarter. Many houses enjoy sprawling gardens, which, combined with lush but decidedly upscale trees, shrubs, and vines, make the section worthy of its name. The borders of the district are St. Charles Avenue, Jackson Avenue, Louisiana Avenue, and Magazine Street, but much of the rest of the Uptown area is impressively grand; the Historic New Orleans Collection has published a map that provides information on sights along the streetcar route. Magazine, also noted by Scheer, is a long but winding and narrow commercial thoroughfare. In recent years it has become a center for antique shops and art galleries. The Irish Channel, historically a "tough," white, working-class area, lies on the opposite side of Magazine, uptown of Louisiana Avenue. Despite its humble associations, it—like so many parts of New Orleans—has considerable charm.

The shotgun house, which Scheer calls "the salient creation of New Orleans," did not originate in the Crescent City, though it is certainly an important feature of the urban landscape. Shotguns are one room wide and several deep. The name is often said to derive from the fact that one could shoot a shotgun at the front of the house and the shot would pass through the row of rooms and out the back. It may in fact derive from an African word for house, *to-gun*. See John M. Vlach, "Shotgun Houses," *Natural History,* XXXVI (February, 1977), 50–57.

The rain A. Oakey Hall describes in such appalled detail still falls in all its subtropical splendor. Although drainage has been greatly improved since his day, the rain can yet be formidable, easily flooding parked cars left in low spots or near clogged drains. The city commonly gets about sixty inches of rain annually, with heavier precipitation in the summer and winter months. With the use of screens and air conditioning so common today, the mosquito threat is no longer extreme. There is an active mosquito control program with widespread outdoor spraying and constant monitoring of the mosquito population to guard against disease-bearing varieties (yellow fever was the deadly scourge of New Orleans in the eighteenth and nineteenth centuries). Roaches such as Scheer encountered, however, remain omnipresent and often are surprisingly large. Local folklore insists that Louisiana has a greater variety than any other state, though Floridians in particular have reason to disagree.

3

A HAUNTING THING: PLANTATION REALMS

Carolyn Ramsey, in the book that chronicles her journeys in search of Cajun culture, refers to a plantation on Bayou Lafourche as "a haunting thing." The plantation buildings—what was left when she saw them in the 1950s—were "desolate," were "brooding ruins." She found this place haunting in the sense that it seemed a shadow from the past, a thing of "magnificence," now only an abandoned hulk but evoking strong feelings of a past life, of a grandeur vanished. In a similar spirit photographer Clarence John Laughlin called his book about the River Road plantations *Ghosts Along the Mississippi.*[1]

Today the term *plantation* is often used loosely to mean the "big house" itself, the antebellum mansion, which may be in ruins or deserted, lived in or only visited by tourists; which may sit on a sizable piece of land, perhaps with a few outbuildings, but in compar-

1. Carolyn Ramsey, *Cajuns on the Bayous,* illus. Alex Imphang (New York, 1957), 90–91; Clarence John Laughlin, *Ghosts Along the Mississippi: An Essay in the Poetic Interpretation of Louisiana's Plantation Architecture* (New York, 1948).

ative isolation, divorced from the swath of fields stretching expansively away. We tend to forget that *plantation* implies planting, that these great houses were merely a part—though surely a central part—of agricultural enterprises whose vastness often made the houses themselves seem almost insignificant. Plantations, as we generally understand them, came into existence with European colonial expansion in the fifteenth century as colonizers sought ways to organize agricultural labor on a grand scale to produce wealth. Though there is great variety among plantations, the plantation as an institution is "an agricultural factory" with a "dependable labor supply" (not necessarily slaves, though that is the form it took in the pre–Civil War American South).[2] Though historians argue whether the plantation was capitalist or precapitalist, it did require capital expenditures—often considerable ones—to produce a market crop (usually one principal crop, with most plantations growing a variety of others). In Louisiana, sugarcane was the chief plantation crop for much of the nineteenth century, though cotton was also important. If it were large enough, a plantation was a virtual village, a "self-contained . . . world unto itself" as Ernst von Hesse-Wartegg puts it, going on to say that its "boundaries, its fences, become its Pillars of Hercules. Its tiny populace lives an independent and self-sustaining life unlike any other."

As an institution, the plantation continued into recent times, adjusting to changing historical and economic forces. Pieces reprinted in this section reflect visions of the plantation at various stages, from antebellum days to the present, and focus on both the narrow definition of plantation as great house and the broader concept of agricultural factory and on the accompanying lifestyle and culture of the plantation realms of Louisiana.

Antebellum travelers steaming down the Mississippi often commented on the parade of plantations they saw. The great houses were impressive, a sign of civilization and prosperity (in 1860 Louisiana had the highest concentration of wealth in the South—the second highest in the nation—based on the economy of its rich plantations, especially the sugar estates). Although many travelers contented themselves with looking from afar, there was great interest in actually visiting a plantation, in seeing its operations and way of life close

2. William Hampton Adams, "Historical Perspectives on the Southern Plantation: Labor Systems, Settlement Systems, and Foodways," in *One World, One Institution,* ed. Sue Eakin and John Tarver (Baton Rouge, 1989), 28.

up. To do so was comparatively easy, for the planters were notably hospitable and welcomed visitors into their somewhat cut-off little kingdoms.

The way of life that visitors found often enchanted them, for it seemed luxurious and different (if a bit monotonous). "The carriages, the games—tennis and cricket—everything, *everything* is here!" writes Hesse-Wartegg. J. Milton Mackie, a Yankee who went south to Louisiana before the war for the warm winter, was to enthuse over the "cheerful, affectionate faces," "the sight of French porcelain, powder puff, and pomatum," and the "air of good nature [that] pervades the house, the service of which is performed by Africans, whose mouths are ready to grin with cheerful ivory at the first kind word addressed to them" (though, he added, there would be "neither ball nor opera" in the vicinity, so life could become rather routine).[3]

The writers included in this section certainly comment on the social life and amenities of the plantation. Eliza Ripley remembers Valcour Aime's famous plantation as a place of attentive servants with foot baths, steaming tisanes, or herbal teas, and café au lait; fabulous gardens (with a miniature river and—wonder of wonders in dead-flat south Louisiana—an artificial mountain!); and gilt clocks sent from Paris. It is all a "fairyland" she regrets leaving. W. H. Russell, the English journalist edging his way through the uncertain atmosphere of 1861, is clearly amused by the liberality with which morning mint juleps are served, interested in the evening gathering of politics-talking planters on his host's verandah, and impressed by the guest quarters' four bedrooms, sitting room, and library.

Yet despite the attention they paid to social life, these writers are by no means ignorant of the plantation as a working establishment. Russell is more than respectful of the agricultural wealth he finds himself amid. He is also well aware of the slave labor force, whose quarters he tours (a not uncommon activity for antebellum plantation visits). The most careful attention to the aspect of work, however, is given by Edward King, who looks at a sugar house, talks to the overseer, and tells us a little of the sugar-making process. King, of course, was in Louisiana after the war, in the 1870s, so his report gives us the plantation after its heyday, suggesting some of the strains the institution was under and noting a move toward mechanization.

Today there are numerous working plantations in Louisiana, some proper-

3. J. Milton Mackie, *From Cape Cod to Dixie and the Tropics* (New York, 1864), 184.

ties intact since antebellum times, some owned by the same family for generations. But nowadays they are highly mechanized and in many ways not unlike
any other big farming operation. If we define a plantation in terms of a large
labor force, then the plantation is increasingly a thing of the past. Perhaps, the
last true plantation in Louisiana is Avery Island, whose traditional mode of
weighing the crop and paying the field laborers (who picked it by hand) is described by Richard Schweid. The Avery Island crop is atypical: peppers used
in making the famous Tabasco-brand hot sauce. And the island, though
sugarcane has been grown there, is an atypical plantation in other ways: it is
tied to a salt mine, hot sauce factory, and oil wells. Yet its use of a large force
of field workers to hand pick the crop keeps it closer to the old plantation
way—as does its existence as something vaguely like a feudal domain, con-
trolled by one family whose ancestors carved it out of the coastal wilderness,
discovered the salt, invented the hot sauce, developed a world-wide business,
and contributed much to Louisiana's culture and natural environment.

The plantation evolved as a key symbol of the Old South even as the New
South took shape and many plantations declined—land broken up, houses allowed to fall into ruins (such as Ramsey found) due to the economic devasta-
tion brought on by the war and later hard times. No doubt it was this symbolic mystique that brought so many visitors to Shadows-on-the-Teche in
New Iberia (not to mention the charisma of its last owner). Henry Miller
takes us in 1941 into this famous house to spend time with the last of the line
to own it, Weeks Hall. The Shadows is an unusual house, and Weeks Hall was
a very unusual man, a painter and intellectual whose frequent visitors included celebrated artists and literati. Hall was devoted to a legacy he inherited, a legacy that was embodied in the house, and Miller's odd portrait of
man and structure brings the plantation saga into modern times: The land is
mostly gone, the last of the family line is alone (Hall had no children),
strangers are attracted to the wonderful house as its last occupant struggles to
understand his place in time. Like the Shadows, the plantation house in general seems both an anachronism and a timeless treasure. Perhaps that is its ultimate position in the Louisiana landscape.

Plantation houses haunt Louisiana in many ways, though in recent years
historic restoration and hordes of lively visitors have combined to dispell the
architectural melancholy of emptiness and decay that Carolyn Ramsey saw.
They haunt as a looming presence in the cultural landscape: reminders of the
slave society that was at the heart of plantation existence and has left a legacy

of problems between the races; reminders of a very different way of life—conceived as gracious, romantic, chivalric for those who enjoyed its fruits; reminders of things lost and pains suffered and beauties enacted and pleasures enjoyed. As such, these great houses must be observed, visited, imagined, understood, come to terms with—for they are central symbols as well as real places.

A Visit to Valcour Aime Plantation

ELIZA RIPLEY

Eliza Ripley (1832–1912) was the daughter of a prominent New Orleans jurist. In her old age, she wrote recollections of her childhood—including this one of her trip in 1847 to the Aime plantation—in *Social Life in Old New Orleans* (1912). Valcour Aime was viewed as the very model of a Louisiana *grand seigneur,* and his plantation, Petit Versailles, was celebrated, especially for its superb gardens. We begin on the steamboat taking Ripley's party—herself, her aunt, and a family friend called "the doctor"—upriver.

M. Champomier is on board. Everybody knows *le vieux* Champomier.[4] He mingles with all, conspicuously carries his memorandum book and pencil, and we all know he is "on business bent," getting from any and every available source statistics of the year's crop of sugar. Whether he acted for a corporation, or it was his individual enterprise, I never knew, but he visited the planters, traveled up and down and all around the sugar region, and in the spring compiled and computed and published in a small, paper-covered book (price $5) the name and address of every planter and the amount of sugar made on each individual estate. "Champomier's report" was considered as authentic as need be for the planter to know what his neighbor's crop actually amounted to, and the city merchant to adjust his mortgages and loans on a safe basis.

It was after midnight when the plank was thrown out to touch the levee of the Valcour Aime plantation; midnight in late March, 1847. Deckhands steadied the wabbling plank till three persons and their little baggage were

4. This was P. A. Champomier, whose annual volumes published in New Orleans had such titles as *Statement of the Sugar Crop of Louisiana* and *Statement of the Sugar Crop Made in Louisiana.*

Louisiana plantation house, by Mircea Vasiliu

From Emily Kimbrough, *So Near and Yet So Far,* copyright © 1955 by Emily Kimbrough Wrench, renewed 1983 by Emily Kimbrough. Reproduced by permission of Harper-Collins Publishers, Inc.

safely landed ashore. A tram (as it is called to-day) was awaiting the doctor, Tante Lise and myself, then a girl of fifteen. Darkies with torches preceded and followed us to the house, not so far away, only a short walk, but Tante Lise must not be permitted to walk at that hour of the night. The tram was nothing more than a flat car, fitted for the occasion with seats, on a short railroad leading to the sugar refinery, which I believe was the first in the state. A dusky housekeeper received us at the house. Not knowing at what hour we might appear, the family had retired. *Belle Creole,* as may be supposed, had no fixed schedule of arrivals or departures. Fires were already alight in our rooms, affording a cheery welcome. Before we were ready for bed basins of hot water were brought for the inevitable foot bath of the Creole. Something warm to drink, a *tisane* probably—I remember I thought it might be ambrosia, fit for the gods, it was so deliciously refreshing. Then I was tenderly tucked into bed, and told to "*dormez bien,*" which I straightway proceeded to do.

The sun was already proclaiming a bright spring day when I inhaled the odor, and opened my eyes to a full-blown rose on my pillow; and gracious, how good! a steaming cup of *café au lait.* On our descent to the breakfast room we received an effusive and cordial greeting from M. and Mme. Valcour, and their daughter Félicie, a girl of my own age. The air was redolent of the delicious odor of roses, the windows open to the floor upon the garden, the floor of the room not one step higher than the garden walks. The Valcour Aime house was a two-story structure. The long, main building faced, of course, the roadway and the river; there was a long L at each end, running back, thus forming three sides of a square court. A broad and partly jalousied balcony extended entirely around the three sides of the building, fronting the court. This balcony afforded the entrances to a seemingly endless series of living and sleeping rooms, the whole house being, so to say, one room deep only. The first floor, flush with the ground, was entirely paved with square blocks of stone or brick. There were to be found the small and the grand dining rooms, the master's office and den and the various and sundry domestic departments. The salon opened on the second floor balcony. The paved court below was protected by the deep balconies and an awning. The assemblage of all the family and the favorite resort of their multitudinous guests, madame's basket, mademoiselle's embroidery frame, the box of cigars, the comfortable lounging chairs, were to be found in that entrancing court.

M. Valcour, tall and graceful, was at that time in the prime of life, and was my (romantic) ideal of a French marquis; Mme. Valcour, inclined to *embonpoint* [plumpness] and vivacious, kissed me and called me "*ma petite,*" though I was quite her height. But the charm of my visit to that incomparable mansion, the like of which is not to be found on the Mississippi River to-day, was the daughter, Félicie, who at once took me under her wing and entertained me as only a well-bred young girl can. She showed me all over the premises, opening door after door, that I could see how adequate the accommodations for the guests who frequently filled the house; into the salon that I might see and listen to the chimes of the gilt clock Gabie had sent from Paris. Gabriel Aime, the only son, was then in Europe. Sweet Félicie never tired of talking of Gabie and showing me the pretty trifles from abroad (so far away then) he had sent home from time to time. She sent for the key, and opened the door of Gabie's room, that I might see how he had left it, and, "Mamma won't have a thing changed; she wants him to find his gun and boots and cap just where he left them." Girl-like, she confided to me that she would be a young lady when Gabie came, and they would have a house in the city and a box at the opera, for Gabie loved music.[5]

By this time a number of the Roman family arrived. M. Valcour's oldest daughter had married Gov. Roman's son, and a flock of Roman grandchildren came with their parents to welcome the doctor and Tante Lise, and incidentally the young girl with them. The Valcours and Romans were closely related, independent of the marriage of their children. Both families being related to Tante Lise also, there was a great reunion and rejoicing when the tante made her annual visit. The governess, a New England woman, was accorded a holiday, in which Félicie participated. . . .

Félicie and I, with a whole escort of followers explored the spacious grounds, considered the finest in Louisiana. There was a miniature river, meandering in and out and around the beautifully kept parterres, the tiny banks of which were an unbroken mass of blooming violets. A long-legged man might have been able to step across this tiny stream, but it was spanned at intervals by bridges of various designs, some rustic, some stone, but all furnished with parapets, so one would not tumble in and drown, as a little Roman remarked. If it had not been before Perry's expedition to Japan, at any rate before his report was printed and circulated, one might have supposed M. Valcour received his inspiration in landscape gardening from the queer little Eastern people. There were summer houses draped with strange, foreign-looking vines; a pagoda on a mound, the entrance of which was reached by a flight of steps. It was an octagonal building, with stained-glass windows, and it struck my inexperienced eye as a very wonderful and surprising bit of architecture. Further on was—a mountain! covered from base to top with beds of blooming violets. A narrow, winding path led to the summit from which a comprehensive view was obtained of the extensive grounds, bounded by a series of conservatories. It was enchanting. There I saw for the first time the magnolia frascati, at that date a real rarity. . . .

Next morning the *Belle Creole* was due, and our visit to fairyland was draw-

5. Gabriel Aime was born in 1826. His early death from yellow fever is said to have been such a blow to his father that Valcour lost interest in his plantation and in life.

ing to a close. The call, "*la Vapeur*" [the steamboat], rushed us to the landing in the tram, the "whole pack in full cry" of the Roman children running by the side and calling adieu to dear Tante Lise. We gingerly walked the plank, in single file. The boat backed out to get her leeway, and once more for a moment we were in full view of the house. Two figures fluttered handkerchiefs from the balcony, Mme. Valcour and Félicie waving a last adieu—alas! a last. On entering the cabin, behold the ubiquitous M. Champomier, with his everlasting book and pencil. As he greeted the doctor I heard (in French, of course), "Can you tell me the exact amount of ———?" I fled, and at the rear end of the boat I had one more last glimpse of Valcour Aime's plantation. Alas! the last.

St. James Parish Plantations

W. H. RUSSELL

After a sojourn in New Orleans, Russell (1820–1907) went up the Mississippi in 1861 visiting sugar plantations. Here we include the account of his visit to the estate of Governor Alfred Roman (a relation of Valcour Aime, as Eliza Ripley points out in the preceding selection) and then to that of Irish-born John Burnside, across the river. On the eve of the Civil War, Russell was, of course, seeing the plantation world in slavery's last days. From *My Diary North and South* (1863).

At half-past three P.M. the steamer ran alongside the levee at the right bank, and discharged me at "Cahabanooze," in the Indian tongue, or "The ducks' sleeping-place," together with an English merchant of New Orleans, M. La Ville Beaufevre, son-in-law of Governor Roman, and his wife. The Governor was waiting to receive us in the levee, and led the way through a gate in the paling which separated his ground from the roadside, towards the house, a substantial, square, two-storied mansion, with a verandah all round it, embosomed amid venerable trees, and surrounded by magnolias. By way of explaining the proximity of his house to the river, M. Roman told me that a considerable portion of the garden in front had a short time ago been carried off by the Mississippi; nor is he at all sure the house itself will not share the same fate; I hope sincerely it may not. My quarters were in a detached house, complete in itself, containing four bedrooms, library, and sitting-room, close to the mansion, and surrounded, like it, by fine trees.

After we had sat for some time in the shade of the finest group, M. Roman, or, as he is called, the Governor—once a captain always a captain—asked me whether I would like to visit the slave quarters. I assented, and the Governor led the way to a high paling at the back of the house, inside which the scraping of the fiddles was audible. As we passed the back of the mansion some young women flitted past in snow-white dresses, crinolines, pink sashes, and gaudily coloured handkerchiefs on their heads; who were, the Governor told me, the domestic servants going off to a dance at the sugar-house; he lets his slaves dance every Sunday. The American planters who are not Catholics, although they do not make the slaves work on Sunday except there is something to do, rarely grant them the indulgence of a dance, but a few permit them some hours of relaxation on each Saturday afternoon.

We entered, by a wicket gate, a square enclosure, lined with Negro huts, built of wood. They are not furnished with windows—a wooden slide or grating admits all the air a Negro desires. There is a partition dividing the hut into two departments, one of which is used as the sleeping-room, and contains a truckle bedstead and a mattress stuffed with cotton wool, or the hair-like fibres of dried Spanish moss. The wardrobes of the inmates hang from nails or pegs driven into the wall. The other room is furnished with a dresser, on which are arranged a few articles of crockery and kitchen utensils. Sometimes there is a table in addition to the plain wooden chairs, more or less dilapidated, constituting the furniture—a hearth, in connection with a brick chimney outside the cottage, in which, hot as the clay may be, some embers are sure to be found burning. The ground round the huts was covered with litter and dust, heaps of old shoes, fragments of clothing and feathers, amidst which pigs and poultry were recreating. Curs of low degree scampered in and out of the shade, or around two huge dogs, *chiens de garde,* which are let loose at night to guard against the precincts; belly-deep, in a pool of stagnant water, thirty or forty mules were swinking in the sun and enjoying their day of rest.

The huts of the Negroes engaged in the house are separated from those of the slaves devoted to field-labour out of doors by a wooden paling. I looked into several of the houses, but somehow or other I felt a repugnance, I dare say unjustifiable, to examine the pentralia, although invited—indeed, urged to do so by the Governor. It was not that I expected to come upon anything dreadful, but I could not divest myself of some regard for the feelings of the poor creatures, slaves though they were, who stood by, shy, curtseying, and silent, as I broke in upon their family circle, felt their beds, and turned over their clothing. What right had I to do so?

Swarms of flies, tin cooking utensils attracting them by remnants of molasses, crockery, broken and old, on the dressers, more or less old clothes were found in all the huts; not a sign of ornament or decoration was visible; not the most tawdry print, image of Virgin or Saviour; not a prayerbook or printed

Gathering the Cane,
by J. W. Orr

From T. B. Thorpe, "Sugar
and the Sugar Region of
Louisiana," *Harper's
Monthly,* November, 1853

volume. The slaves are not encouraged, or indeed permitted to read, and some communities of slave-owners punish heavily those attempting to instruct them.

It struck me more and more, however, as I examined the expression of the faces of the slaves, that deep dejection is the prevailing, if not universal, characteristic of the race. Here there were abundant evidences that they were all well treated; they had good clothing of its kind, food, and a master who wittingly could do them no injustice, as he is, I am sure, incapable of it. Still, they all looked sad, and even the old woman who boasted that she had held her old owner in her arms when he was an infant did not smile cheerfully, as the nurse at home would have done at the sight of her ancient charge.

In the evening several officers of M. Alfred Roman's company and neighbouring planters dropped in, and we sat out in the verandah, illuminated by the flashing fireflies, and talking politics. I was struck by the profound silence which reigned all around us, except a low rushing sound, like that made by the wind blowing over cornfields, which came from the mighty river before us. Nothing else was audible but the sound of our own voices and the distant bark of a dog. After the steamer which bore us had passed on, I do not believe a single boat floated up or down the stream, and but one solitary planter, in his gig or buggy, traversed the road, which lay between the garden palings and the bank of the great river. . . .

At five o'clock this morning, having been awakened an hour earlier by a wonderful chorus of riotous mockingbirds, my old Negro attendant brought in my bath of Mississippi water which, Nile-like, casts down a strong deposit, and becomes as clear, if not so sweet, after standing. "Le seigneur vous attend"; and already I saw, outside my window, the Governor mounted on a stout cob, and a nice chestnut horse waiting, led by a slave. Early as it was, the sun felt excessively hot, and I envied the Governor his slouched hat as we rode through the fields, crisp with dew. In a few minutes our horses were traversing narrow alleys between the tall fields of maize, which rose far above our heads. This corn . . . is the principal food of the Negroes; and every planter lays down a sufficient quantity to afford him, on the average, a supply all the year round. Outside this spread vast fields, hedgeless, wall-less, and unfenced, where the green cane was just learning to wave its long shoots in the wind—a lake of bright green sugar-sprouts, along the margin of which, in the distance, rose an unbroken boundary of forest, two miles in depth, up to the swampy morass, all to be cleared and turned into arable land in process of time. From the river front to this forest, the fields of rich loam, unfathomable, and yielding from one to one and a half hogsheads of sugar per acre under cultivation, extend for a mile and a half in depth. In the midst of this expanse white dots were visible. Those are the gangs of hands at work—we will see what they are at presently. When the Indian corn is not good, peas are sowed, alternately, between the stalks, and are considered to be of much benefit; and when the cane is bad, corn is sowed with it, for the same object. Before we came up to the gangs we passed a cart on the road containing a large cask, a bucket full of molasses, a pail of hominy, or boiled Indian corn, and a quantity of tin pannikins. The cask contained water for the Negroes, and the other vessels held the materials for their breakfast; in addition to which, they generally have each a dried fish. The food was ample, and looked wholesome; such as any labouring man would be well content with.

We returned to the house in time for breakfast, for which our early cup of coffee and biscuit and the ride had been good preparation. Here was old France again. One might imagine a lord of the seventeenth century in his hall, but for the black faces of the servitors and the strange dishes of tropical origin. There was the old French abundance, the numerous dishes and efflorescence of napkins, and the long-necked bottles of Bordeaux, with a steady current of pleasant small talk. . . .

At the ferry-house I was attended by one stout young slave, who was to row me over. . . . I bade good-bye to my friend Roman, and sat down in my boat, which was forced by the Negro against the stream close to the bank, in order to get a good start across to the other side. The view from my lonely position was curious, but not at all picturesque. The world was bounded on both sides by a high bank, which constricted the broad river, just as if one were sailing down an open sewer of enormous length and breadth. Above the bank rose the tops of tall trees and the chimneys of sugar-houses, and that was all to be seen save the sky.

A quarter of an hour brought us to the levee on the other side. I ascended the bank, and across the road, directly in front, appeared a carriage gateway and wickets of wood, painted white, in a line of palings of the same material, which extends up and down the road far as the eye could see, and guarded wide-spread fields of maize and sugar-cane. An avenue lined with trees, with branches close set, drooping and overarching a walk paved with red brick, led to the house, the porch of which was visible at the extremity of the lawn, with clustering flowers, rose jessamine, and creepers clinging to the pillars supporting the verandah. The view from the belvedere on the roof was one of the most striking of its kind in the world.

If an English agriculturist could see six thousand acres of the finest land in one field, unbroken by hedge or boundary, and covered with the most magnificent crops of tasseling Indian corn and sprouting sugar-cane, as level as a billiard-table, he would surely doubt his senses. But here is literally such a sight—six thousand acres, better tilled than the finest patch in all the Lothians, green as Meath pastures, which can be turned up for a hundred years to come without requiring manure, of depth practically unlimited, and yielding an average profit on what is sold off it of at least £20 an acre, at the old prices and usual yield of sugar. Rising up in the midst of the verdure are the white lines of the Negro cottages and the plantation offices and sugarhouses, which look like large public edifices in the distance. My host was not ostentatiously proud in telling me that in the year 1857, he had purchased this estate for £300,000 and an adjacent property, of eight thousand acres, for £150,000, and that he had left Belfast in early youth, poor and unfriended, to seek his fortune, and indeed scarcely knowing what fortune meant, in the New World. In fact, he had invested in these purchases the greater part, but not all, of the profits arising from the business in New Orleans, which he inherited from his master; of which there still remained a solid nucleus in the shape of a great woolen magazine and country house. He is not yet fifty years of age, and his confidence in the great future of sugar induced him to embark this enormous fortune in an estate which the blockade has stricken with paralysis. I cannot doubt, however, that he regrets he did not invest his money in a certain great estate in the North of Ireland, which he had nearly decided on buying. Six thousand acres on this one estate all covered with sugar-cane, and sixteen thousand acres more of Indian corn, to feed the slaves; these were great possessions, but not less than eighteen thousand acres still remained, covered with brake and forest, and swampy, to be reclaimed and turned into gold. As easy to persuade the owner of such wealth that slavery is indefensible as to have convinced the Norman baron that the Saxon churl who tilled his lands ought to be his equal.

The smart Negro who waited on me this morning spoke English. I asked him if he knew how to read and write. "We must not do that, sir." "Where were you born?" "I were raised on the plantation, Massa, but I have been to New Orleans"; and then he added, with an air of pride, "I s'pose, sir, Massa Burnside not take less than fifteen hundred for me." Downstairs to breakfast, the luxuries of which are fish, prawns, and red meat which has been sent for to Donaldsonville by boat rowed down by an old Negro. Breakfast over, I walked down to the yard, where the horses were waiting, and proceeded to visit the saccharine principality. Mr. Seal, the overseer of this portion of the estate, was my guide, if not philosopher and friend.

Mr. Seal conducted me to a kind of forcing-house where the young Negroes are kept in charge of certain old crones too old for work, whilst their parents are away in the cane and Indian corn. A host of children of both sexes were seated in the verandah of a large wooden shed, or playing around it, very happily and noisily. I was glad to see the boys and girls of nine, ten, and eleven years of age were at this season, at all events, exempted from the cruel fate which befalls poor children of their age in the mining and manufacturing districts of England. At the sight of the overseer the little ones came forward in tumultuous glee, babbling out, "Massa Seal," and evidently pleased to see him.

As a jolly agriculturist looks at his yearlings or young beeves, the kindly overseer, lolling in his saddle, pointed with his whip to the glistening fat ribs and corpulent paunches of his woolly-headed flock. "There's not a plantation in the State," quoth he, "can show such a lot of young niggers. The way to get them right is not to work the mothers too hard when they are near their time; to give them plenty to eat, and not to send them to the fields too soon." He told me the increase was about five per cent per annum. The children were quite sufficiently clad, ran about round us, patted the horses, felt our legs, tried to climb up on the stirrup, and twinkled their black and ochry eyes at Massa Seal. Some were exceedingly fair. He talked about their colour and complexion quite openly; nor did it seem to strike him that there was any particular turpitude in the white man who had left his offspring as slaves on the plantation.

. . . My chattel Joe . . . awoke me to a bath of Mississippi water with huge lumps of ice in it, to which he recommended a mint-julep as an adjunct. It was not here that I was first exposed to an ordeal of mint julep, for in the early morning a stranger in a Southern planter's house may expect the offer of a glassful of brandy, sugar, and peppermint beneath an island of ice—an obligatory panacea for all the evils of climate. After it has been disposed of, Pompey may come up again with glass number two: "Massa say fever very bad this morning—much dew." It is possible that the degenerate Anglo-Saxon stomach has not the fine tone and temper of that of an Hibernian friend of mine, who considered the finest thing to counteract the effects of a little excess was a tumbler of hot whisky and water the moment the sufferer opened his eyes in the morning. Therefore, the kindly offering may be rejected. But on one occasion before breakfast the Negro brought up mint julep number three, the acceptance of which he enforced by the emphatic declaration, "Massa says, sir, you had better take this, because it'll be the last he make before breakfast."

Breakfast is served: there is on the table a profusion of dishes—grilled fowl, prawns, eggs and ham, fish from New Orleans, potted salmon from England, preserved meats from France, claret, iced water, coffee and tea, varieties of hominy, mush, and African vegetable preparations. Then come the newspapers, which are perused eagerly with ejaculations, "Do you hear what they are doing now—infernal villains! that Lincoln must be mad!" and the like.

Magnolia Plantation

EDWARD KING

King (1848–1896) was a journalist who traveled in the South in 1873 and 1874 to report on the region for *Scribner's* magazine. His writings were recast as *The Great South* (1875), from which this excerpt is taken. His book has been called "the most useful" and the "most carefully conceived and executed" of Reconstruction-era travel accounts.[6] This account of his 1873 visit to a sugar plantation shows slaves replaced by wage labor—black and imported Chinese[7]—and attempts to mechanize, the plantation "lamenting past grandeur" but still a vast agricultural enterprise.

The "Magnolia" plantation of Mr. Lawrence is a fair type of the larger and better class; it lies low down to the river's level, and seems to court inundation. Stepping from the wharf, across a green lawn, the sugar-house first greets the eye, an immense solid building, crammed with costly machinery. Not far from it are the neat, white cottages occupied by the laborers; there is the kitchen where the field-hands come to their meals; there are the sheds where the carts are housed, and the cane is brought to be crushed; and, ranging in front of a cane-field containing many hundreds of acres, is a great orange orchard, the branches of whose odorous trees bear literally golden fruit; for, with but little care, they yield their owner an annual income of $25,000.

The massive oaks and graceful magnolias surrounding the planter's man-

6. W. Magruder Drake and Robert F. Jones, Editors' Introduction to *The Great South*, by Edward King (Baton Rouge, 1972), xxi.

7. A shortage of labor brought Chinese workers to Louisiana sugar plantations beginning in 1871, when seventy were brought from Alabama, where they had been working on railroad construction. See Lucy M. Cohen, *Chinese in the Post–Civil War South* (Baton Rouge, 1984).

sion give grateful shade; roses and all the rarer blossoms perfume the air; the river current hums a gentle monotone, which, mingled with the music of the myriad insect life, and vaguely heard on the lawn and in the cool corridors of the house, seems lamenting past grandeur and prophesying of future greatness. For it was a grand and lordly life, that of the owner of a sugar plantation; filled with culture, pleasure, and the refinements of living—but now!

Afield, in Mr. Lawrence's plantation, and in some others, one may see the steam-plough at work, ripping up the rich soil. Great stationary engines pull it rapidly from end to end of the tracts; and the darkies, mounted on the swiftly-rolling machine, skillfully guide its sharp blades and force them into the furrows. Ere long, doubtless, steam-ploughs will be generally introduced on Louisiana Sugar estates. Four of these stationary engines, built at Leeds, England, and supplied with water brought from the river in mule carts, suffice to do the work upon the ample plantation of Mr. Lawrence.

As to the details of plantation work, the negroes, evidently, do not attend to them with quite the thoroughness exacted under the rigid discipline of slavery. Evidences of neglect, in considerable variety, offer themselves to the critical eye. Entering the sugar-house, the amiable planter will present you to a venerable, mahogany-looking individual in garments stained with saccharine juices, and with a little tone of pride in his voice will tell you that "this is Nelson, overseer of this place, who has been here, man and boy, forty years, and who knows more about the process of sugar-making than any one else on the plantation."

Nelson will, therefore, conduct you into the outer shed, and, while showing you the huge rollers under which the canes, when carted in from the fields in November or December, are crushed, will impress upon you the danger of early winter frosts which may baffle every hope of profit, will explain to you how difficult and how full of risks is the culture of the juicy reed, which must be nursed through twelve or thirteen weary months, and may leave but a meagre result. He will take you across the delightfully-shaded way into one of the fields, passing on the walk a cheery Chinaman wearing a smile which is seven times childlike and bland, and point you to the stalks of the cane left at the last harvest to lie all winter in the furrows and furnish young sprouts for the spring. These shapely and rich-colored stalks have joints every few inches along their whole length, from which spring out the new buds of promise. When the spring ploughing begins, these stalks are laid along the beds of the drills, and each shoot, as it makes its appearance, is carefully watched and cultured that it may produce a new cane, a great portion of the crop being thus reserved, each year, for seed.

The complaisant overseer will give you a profusion of details as to how the cane, if safe from the accidents of the seasons, is cut down at its perfection and brought to the sugar-house; how all hands, black and white, join, for many days, in "hauling" it from the fields, and then keep the mill going for a week night and day; how there is high wassail and good cheer in the intervals of the work, and every nerve is strained to the utmost for the completion of the task. He will show you the great crushers which bring the sweetness out of the fresh canes as they are carried forward upon an endless series of rollers, and will then point out the furnace into which the refuse is thrown to be burned, thus furnishing the motive power for crushing the stalks and for all the minor and subordinate mechanical details in the processes of the manufacture. The *bag-gasse,* as this refuse is called, usually furnishes steam enough for this purpose, and leaves nothing but a kind of coke in the ash-pit of the furnace; no coal being used except in the refining mill's furnace.

Out from the crushed arteries of the cane wells a thick, impure liquid, which demands immediate attention to preserve it from spoiling; and then the clarifying process is begun and continued, by the aid of hundreds of inge-nious mechanisms whose names even you will not remember when Nelson takes you into the refinery.

You enter a set of huge chambers, the floors of which are sticky with sugar, and watch the juice passing through various processes. There are the great open trays, traversed by copper and iron steam-pipes; there are the filter-pans filled with bone dust, from which the liquid trickles down. Now it wanders through separators and then through bone dust again, onward toward granu-lation in the vacuum pans, and then into coolers, where the sugar is kept in a half liquid state by means of revolving paddles, until, finally, it comes to the vessels, in which, by rapid whirlings, all the molasses is thrown out; and the molasses, leaving the dry sugar ready for commerce, goes meandering among the pipes under the floors, and round and round again through the whirling machines, until there is no suspicion of sweetness in it, and it is ignomini-ously discharged.

It seems a pity that such fine machinery should be in use only during one sixth of the year, as it would be injured far less by being kept constantly run-ning than by remaining idle. The new steam-mills are, in every point of view, so vastly superior to the old horse-mills, that they have been adopted on the greater portion of the sugar plantations and are desired by every planter; but they are so enormously expensive, that cooperative or joint ownership is, in many cases, essential.

The division of the large plantations into small farms seems, sooner or later, inevitable; as no one owner can, under the new condition of things, make the necessary and continuous outlay. In a few years the cane now crushed at one of these immense sugar-houses in the winter months will belong, in small lots, to a hundred different men, instead of to the one aristocratic and wealthy planter, as under the old regime.

Plantation Life in Southern Louisiana

ERNST VON HESSE-WARTEGG

Hesse-Wartegg (1854–1918) was a German diplomat, journalist, and world traveler who married an American actress and whose writing was admired by Mark Twain. He published an important travel account in German soon after a trip to the lower Mississippi region. He was an observant and engaging writer; his is one of the best Louisiana travel accounts of the second half of the nineteenth century. Like King, Hesse-Wartegg shows the plantation in postslavery transition, with white as well as black laborers, though many features he describes would have been familiar to antebellum travelers.

To experience the plantation in its own right, we must have recourse to Creole hospitality on one of these many plantations. For, self-contained, this way of life revolves about itself in a world unto itself. Its boundaries, its fences, become its Pillars of Hercules. Its tiny populace lives an independent and self-sustaining life unlike any other, cut off from everything in the world outside. Political events, new ideas of consequence, wars, revolutions: little of them gets this far. These people devote every effort and all aspiration to the few hundred acres of sugarcane between their homes and the Mississippi's "swamps." Doors are by and large open to the tourist. Planters welcome visitors, especially Europeans. After all, these plantations doze in a quiet, remote corner of the world, so peaceful, so removed from life elsewhere, so seldom visited by travelers, that the resident family considers a visit an occasion almost to celebrate. The longer the visit, the more their happiness.

They look upon the guest as a member of the family; only with heavy hearts do they let him go.

Blissful peace reigns, winter and summer. The planter's lovely, spacious home rises not far behind the levee that shields the land from the mighty Mississippi's floods. A road follows the levee, but through the garden's trees, dense with subtropical foliage, the house can scarcely be seen from it. We walk toward the house across a soft lawn replete with flowers. The house beckons from its distance, like an idyll incarnate. Old, thick walls, tall windows with green jalousies closed, and broad verandahs running all the way around: it seems rather like a chateau out of the French Middle Ages. Skyscraper magnolias throw it into deep shade. Stately palms thrust slim trunks out of a thicket of mandarin oranges. Aloes enclose with ponderous leaves the wide, sanded terrace in front of the house. Rosebushes cover the fences with a riot of blooms. The garden continues to the right in a forest of orange trees a mile long. At the peak of blossom now, in February, they exude an intoxicating fragrance. Peacocks and turkeys strut back and forth on the greensward in bright sunlight. Now and then the cries of these birds shatter the peace and quiet of a perfect pastoral scene.

The women of the house do us the most cordial of honors in the absence of the planter at work with his overseers and Negroes in the fields. Elegance and refinement remain with the aristocratic and once proud Creole race. Stripped of power, bereft of wealth, they remain well bred nonetheless.

Something more than a stone's throw from the house, a few dozen tiny houses duplicate one another. Frequent floods and wet soil forbid cellars and walled foundations. Therefore, these houses, like many buildings on the delta, seem built on stilts. Though they form a group, they obey no pattern; nor do they touch—to deter the spread of fire. A larger one serves as infirmary, another as church. This is the so-called "*quarter*," home to the Negroes, former slaves. Here they live in families, and the children romp outside the houses and in the fields. Negroes take a certain pride in their houses, "*home*" to them. They appoint them with all sorts of little pictures, colored paper, old furniture, and rags of curtain and carpet. . . .

An hour later [after morning call on the bell], work in the fields proceeds apace. Blacks work with blacks, whites with whites, as segregated as in housing. People and their many mules, under a sun that blazes down in a broil, suffer in the oppressive fire of February. Horses cannot stand [hard work in] such heat. None are used except those the overseers ride about the fields while supervising. The overseer plies no longer the fearsome lash. Former slaves look up at him freely without fear when he remarks on their work and urges them to more. Backs no longer bend in fright at the sound of discipline and punishment galloping toward them. The curse and the crack of the whip have stilled—song, joke, mirth, serenity instead.

What a difference between then and now, slavery and freedom! The black man's work has been lightened, too. Pairs of steam engines, pulling plows of twenty and more bottoms, turn the soil and relieve the former slave of the hardest labor. Steam and the machine do all [of the worst work]. Dredges clear the mucky, alligator-infested ditches on the edge of the forest. Steam and the machine have made the Negro a human being.

The huge bell sounds noon. It can be heard for miles. Men toss work aside, a hundred mules bray for joy, and every able fellow leaps onto the best at hand. They gallop—bounce, bounce—to the quarter. We must wonder—*ouch!*— how these guys can sit such gross beasts, without saddle, without bridle, astride those bony backs. The beasts know the way for sure. Into the yard they thunder like troops of cavalry. In a trice the yard resembles a military camp in a rage of hustle and hustle.

Horses and mules line up and get fed. Long tables groan under steaming soups and platters of meat and vegetables. White field-hands and white sugar-mill workers eat apart from blacks. For a while not a sound [from people] except the rattle of knives and forks. Dozens of big, black porkers grunt around the tables. Dogs, chickens, little pigs, pigeons, and the rest of the animals have rendezvoused, too. Only the proud peacocks and aristocratic turkeys keep their dignified distance, removed in the garden like Spanish grandees. People take meals al fresco, year in, year out [whatever the month or seasons] under this warm and cloudless Italian sky, never risking that the soup get cold.

Back to the field, everybody, an hour later, back to pulling weeds.

Much calmer at the house. Boring, if you will. The day consists of reading and a few strolls. What of the hammocks swaying in the breeze between limbs of splendid magnolias? On the river do not a few small, slim boats dance on currents beside the dock? Are there several hunting rifles leaning near the door in the house? Is that not a target among the fat, bushy, thorny aloes? Are there various riding horses pawing the ground in the stable? The carriages, the games—tennis and cricket—everything, *everything* is here! But the proud, placid, pale women vegetate in easy chairs among grandly elegant furniture in the great hall. They stare into space. They press their foreheads against the glass of windows and . . . ? This is no joyous, delighted *dolce far niente* [sweetness of doing nothing], not at all. *Far niente*—idleness, yes. As for *dolce,* of the sweetness the women know nothing. There used to be a plantation way of life. It is dead.

Things change when foreign guests arrive! The planter's wife, a Creole daughter, knows what she must do then. With what grace she greets them, such kindness! New life seems to have come to her. Callers, society, companionship are what she needs. She has them now. She enjoys them. Each day holds a new delight when guests are here, every day its own surprise, because the program changes daily.

Today several horses wait saddled at the verandah outside the glass of the tall, wide door. To morning coffee the women come dressed for riding. A tour on horseback awaits us: out to the cypress forests along the bayou on the other side of the plantation. There (on the edge of the narrow land between here and the Mississippi) lie the famous swamps, the subtropical, half-submerged, primeval forests and their bewitching vegetation and rare animal life.

"The Shadows"

HENRY MILLER

Henry Miller (1891–1980) looms as an important figure in mid-twentieth-century American literature, best known for such novels as *The Tropic of Cancer* and *Nexus,* noted for their frank treatment of sexuality. His piece about visiting the Louisiana great house known as Shadows-on-the-Teche—and its master, Weeks Hall—is from *The Air-Conditioned Nightmare,* Miller's account of a tour of the United States. By the time of Miller's visit in 1941, the Shadows was surrounded by the city of New Iberia, but originally it had been the center of a small plantation where vegetables and firewood were grown. It was home to the Weeks family, whose vast sugar estate—originally a Spanish land grant—was located elsewhere, at Weeks Island. Artist Weeks Hall, scion of plantation aristocracy and a bachelor, was the house's last resident. He spent his time there receiving numerous celebrated guests and restoring his ancestral home.

It was in Paris that I first began to dream of visiting New Iberia—in the Café de Versailles, Montparnasse, to be exact. It was Abe Rattner, the painter, who put the bug in my head. All evening he had been relating his experiences as a camouflage artist in the world war. Suddenly, by some strange transition, he began talking about his friend Weeks Hall who he said lived in a strange part of the world, in this place called New Iberia, near Avery Island. His description of his friend, of the house he lived in and the country roundabout, was so vivid, so out of the world, as we say, that then and there I resolved to go to Louisiana one day and see with my own eyes the wonders he was describing.

I left Paris three months before the war broke out, to spend a Sabbatical year in Greece. Little did I dream then that I would encounter Abe Rattner in New York or plan with him this tour of America which I am now embarked upon. A singular coincidence, too, that he should have been able to accompany me on this trip only as far as New Iberia! Looking back upon it all, it almost seems as though everything had been planned and arranged by some unseen power.

We arrived at "The Shadows" towards dusk on a day in January. Our host was waiting for us at a gas station on the highway, in front of the house. He had been waiting to intercept us in order, as he explained, to have us enter the grounds from the rear. I saw at once that he was a character, a rich, amiable personality, such as my friend Rattner had so faithfully portrayed. Everything had to be done in a prescribed way, not because he was domineering or tyrannical, but because he wanted his guests to derive the utmost from every situation or event.

"The Shadows," as the house is called, is not at all in the traditional Louisiana style of architecture. Technically it would be defined as of the Roman Doric order, but to speak in architectural language of a house which is as organically alive, sensuous, and mellow as a great tree is to kill its charm. For me, perhaps because of the rich pinkish brick which gives to the whole atmosphere of the place a warm, radiant glow, "The Shadows" at once summoned to my mind the image of Corinth which I also had the good fortune to come upon towards the close of day. The wonderful masonry columns, so sturdy and yet so graceful, so full of dignity and simplicity, were also reminiscent of Corinth. Corinth has always been synonymous for me with opulence, a roseate, insidious opulence, fragrant with the heavy bloom of Summer.

All through the South I had been made aware again and again of the magnificence of a recent past. The days of the great plantations bequeathed to the brief and bleak pattern of our American life a color and warmth suggestive, in certain ways, of that lurid, violent epoch in Europe known as the Renaissance. In America, as Weeks Hall puts it, the great houses followed the great crops: in Virginia tobacco, in South Carolina rice, in Mississippi cotton, in Louisiana sugar. Supporting it all, a living foundation, like a great column of blood, was the labor of the slaves. The very bricks of which the walls of the

Woodlawn Plantation, Louisiana, 1941

Photograph by Edward Weston, © 1981 Center for Creative Photography, Arizona Board of Regents

famous houses are made were shaped by the hands of the Negroes. Following the bayous the landscape is dotted with the cabined shacks of those who gave their sweat and blood to help create a world of extravagant splendor. The pretensions which were born of this munificence, and which still endure amidst the soulless ruins of the great pillared houses, are rotting away, but the cabins remain. The Negro is anchored to the soil; his way of life has changed hardly at all since the great debacle. He is the real owner of the land, despite all titular changes of possession. No matter what the whites say, the South could not exist without the easy, casual servitude of the blacks. The blacks are the weak and flexible backbone of this decapitated region of America.

It had been a wonderful ride up from New Orleans, past towns and villages with strange French names, such as Paradis and Des Allemands, at first following the dangerous winding road that runs beside the levee, then later the meandering Bayou Black and finally the Bayou Teche. It was early in January and hot as blazes though a few days previously, coming into New Orleans, the cold was so mean and penetrating that our teeth were chattering. New Iberia is in the very heart of the Acadian country, just a few miles from St. Martinsville where the memories of Evangeline color the atmosphere.

January in Louisiana! Already the first signs of Spring were manifesting themselves in the cabin door-yards: the paper-white narcissus and the German iris whose pale gray-green spikes are topped by a sort of disdainful white plume. In the transparent black waters of the bayous the indestructible cypress, symbol of silence and death, stands knee-deep. The sky is everywhere, dominating everything. How different the sky as one travels from region to region! What tremendous changes between Charleston, Asheville, Biloxi, Pensacola, Aiken, Vicksburg, St. Martinsville! Always the live oak, the cypress, the chinaball tree; always the swamp, the clearing, the jungle; cotton, rice, sugar cane; thickets of bamboo, banana trees, gum trees, magnolias, cucumber trees, swamp myrtle, sassafras. A wild profusion of flowers: camellias, azaleas, roses of all kinds, salvias, the giant spider lily, the aspidistra, jasmine, Michaelmas daisies; snakes, screech-owls, raccoons; moons of frightening dimensions, lurid, pregnant, heavy as mercury. And like a leitmotif to the immensity of sky are the tangled masses of Spanish moss, that peculiar spawn of the South which is allied to the pineapple family. An epiphyte, rather than a parasite, it lives an independent existence, sustaining itself on air and moisture; it flourishes just as triumphantly on a dead tree or a telegraph wire as on the live oak. "None but the Chinese," says Weeks Hall, "can ever hope to paint this moss. It has a baffling secret of line and mass which has never been remotely approached. It is as difficult to do as a veronica. The live oaks tolerate it—they do not seem to be at one with it. But to the Louisiana cypress it seems to want to act as a bodyguard. A strange phenomenon." It is also a profitable one, as the mattress and upholstery industry of Louisiana would indicate.

There are people from the North and the Mid-West who actually shudder when they first come upon the giant bewhiskered live oaks; they sense something dismal and forbidding in them. But when one sees them in majestic, stately rows, as on the great estates around Beaufort, S.C., or at Biloxi—at Biloxi they come to apotheosis!—one must bow down before them in humble adoration for they are, if not the monarchs of the tree world, certainly the sages or the magi.

It was in the shade of one of these great trees that the three of us stood admiring the back of the house. I say the three of us because our host—and that is one of the things I like about Weeks Hall—can stop and examine the place he lives in any hour of the day or night. He can talk for hours about any detail of the house or gardens; he speaks almost as if it were his own creation, though the house and the trees which surround it came into existence over a century ago. It is all that remains of estates which once comprised several thousand acres, including Weeks Island, a Spanish royal grant made to David Weeks by Baron Carondelet in 1792. The entrance to the property, now reduced to three acres, is on Main Street, which is a continuation of Highway 90. Driving past it in a car one would never in the world suspect what lies hidden behind the dense hedge of bamboo which encircles the grounds.

As we stood there talking, Theophile came up to inform our friend that some women were at the front gate demanding permission to visit the grounds. "Tell them I'm out," said our host. "The tourists!" he said wryly, turning to Rattner. "They pour through here like ants; they overrun the place. Thousands and thousands of them—it's like the plague." And then he began to relate one anecdote after another about the women who insist on inspecting the rooms, which is forbidden. "They would follow me into the bathroom," he said, "if I permitted them. It's almost impossible to have any privacy when you live in a place like this." Most of them were from the Middle West, I gathered. They were the type one sees in Paris, Rome, Florence, Egypt, Shanghai—harmless souls who have a mania for seeing the world and gathering information about anything and everything. A curious thing about these show places, and I have visited a number of them, is that the owners, despite the martyrdom inflicted upon them by the steady hordes of visitors, almost never feel at liberty to exclude the public. They all seem to possess a sense of guilt about living alone in such ancient splendor. Some of course can not afford to spurn the modest revenue which this traffic brings, but for the most part there exists a feeling of obligation towards the public, whether conscious or unconscious.

Later, in looking over the register, I came across many interesting names, that of Paul Claudel surprising me not a little. "Claudel, ah yes! He said a wonderful thing about the camellia—how in Japan, when the blossom falls, they speak of it as a beheading." He went on to talk about the camellia, of which he has some marvelous varieties, including the largest Lady Hume's Blush in America. Its rarity, I was informed, is almost legendary; a plant of this size, in fact, is comparable to a black pearl. He dwelt at length on the tones and colors, the Lady Hume's Blush, he insisted, being of the palest pink ivory, whereas the Madame Strekaloff was of a peach-blossom pink streaked with rose, a rose with reddish stripes. He spoke of the tight little blossoms which might have been born under the glass domes of wax flowers. "The new varieties are lush but never sensuous; they have a beauty which forbids. They are coldly unaffected by praise and admiration. Pink cabbages, that's what they are!" And so on and so forth. It seemed to me that the man had given his life to the study of camellias, to say nothing of his wealth. But the more I listened to him the more I realized that he had an almost encyclopaedic knowledge about a great diversity of things. A superabundant vitality also, which permits him, when he feels inclined to talk, to continue like a fount from morning till night. He had always been a great talker, I learned, even before the injury to his arm limited his painting. That first evening, after the dishes had been cleared away, I watched him in fascination as he paced up and down the room, lighting one cigarette after another—he smokes almost a hundred a day—and telling us of his travels, his dreams, his weaknesses and vices, his passions, his prejudices, his ambitions, his observations, his studies, his frustrations. At three in the morning, when we finally begged leave to retire, he was wide awake, making himself a fresh cup of black coffee which he shares with his dog, and preparing to take a stroll about the garden and meditate on things past and future. One of the weaknesses, shall I call it, which sometimes comes upon him in the wee hours of the morning is the desire to telephone some one in California or Oregon or Boston. The anecdotes about these early morning enthusiasms of his are related from one end of the country to the other. Telephoning is not the only one of his imperative impulses; the others are even more spectacular, more weird, such as impersonating a non-existent idiot twin brother . . .

When the guests retire he communes with the dog. There is an unholy sort of bond between them, something quite out of the ordinary. I have forgotten the dog's name—Spot or Queenie, some common name like that. She is an English setter, a bitch, and rather seedy now and smelly, though it would break her master's heart if he should hear me say a thing like that. Weeks Hall's contention about this Alice or Elsie is this—that she does not know that she is a dog. According to him, she does not like other dogs, doesn't even recognize them, so to speak. He contends that she has the most beautiful manners—the manners of a lady. Perhaps. I am no judge of dogs. But of one thing I am in agreement with him—she has absolutely human eyes. That her coat is like falling water, that her ears remind you of Mrs. Browning's portrait, that she makes things handsome with her casual languor—such subtleties are beyond me. But when you look into her eyes, no matter how much or how little you know about dogs, you must confess that this puzzling creature is no ordinary bitch. She looks at you with the soulful eyes of some departed human who has been condemned to crawl about on all fours in the body of this most companionable setter. Weeks Hall would have it that she is sad because of her inability to speak, but the feeling she gave me was that she was sad because nobody except her master had the intelligence to recognize her as a human being and not just a dog. I could never look her in the eyes for more than a few moments at a time. The expression, which I have caught now and then on the face of a writer or painter suddenly interrupted in the midst of an inspiration, was that of a wanderer between two worlds. It was the sort of look which makes one desire to withdraw discreetly, lest the separation between body and soul become irreparable.

The next morning, after breakfast, as I was about to open a door which had blown shut, I saw to my astonishment the signatures in pencil on the back of the door of hundreds of celebrities, written in every scrawl imaginable. Of course we had to add our own to the collection. I signed mine under that of a Hungarian named Bloor Schleppey, a fascinating name which unleashed a story about the door that is worth recounting. The present names, it seems, are all of recent origin. Originally there was an even more scintillating array of names, but about the time of Bloor Schleppey, perhaps because the name had such an uncommon effect upon our host, the latter, after a debauch lasting several days, was so disgusted with the condition of the house that he ordered the servants to clean it from top to bottom. "I want it to be immaculate when I wake up," were his orders. They tried to tell him that it was impossible to put a house of such proportions in order in such a short space of time. There were only two of them. "Well, then, hire a gang," said our host. And they did. And when he awoke from his slumber the house was indeed spic and span, as he had commanded it to be. Certain things, to be sure, had disappeared, what with the zeal and frenzy of the house-cleaners. The real coup came when he observed, in the course of his inspection, that the door with the names had been washed down and the names obliterated. That was a blow. At first he stormed and cussed, but when he had quieted down suddenly an inspiration came to him. He would unhinge the door, crate it, and send it on a round robin to be re-signed by his distinguished visitors. What a journey! The idea was so fascinating that presently he began to think it was too good a treat to offer a mere door—he would go himself from place to place, carrying the door along, and begging like a monk for a fresh signature. Some of the visitors had come from China, some from Africa, some from India. Better to supervise it personally than entrust it to the post or express agencies. Nobody, as far as he knew, had ever travelled around the world with a door. It would be quite a feat, a sensation in fact. To find Bloor Schleppey, that would be something. God only knew where he had disappeared. The others he thought of as relatively fixed, like certain stars. But Bloor Schleppey—he hadn't the faintest idea where Bloor Schleppey had departed to. And then as he was planning his itinerary—a delight which lasted for weeks—who should arrive, unheralded, in the dead of night, accompanied by three great Danes on a leash, but Bloor Schleppey himself! Well, to make the story short, the door was put back on its hinges, Bloor Schleppey inscribed his signature again, and the idea of a world tour with a door on his back gradually faded away, like all whimsical ideas. A strange thing about the people identified with this door, which I feel compelled to add in conclusion, is this—that many of them, as if in answer to a silent summons, have returned to sign their names again. It may also be, of course, that some of them were summoned back by an early morning telephone call—who can say?

In the course of a century or more curious events must naturally have occurred in a remote and idyllic domain of this sort. At night, lying in the center of a huge four-poster bed staring at the brass ornament in the center of the tester, the stillness of the house seemed the stillness not of an empty house but of one in which a great family was sleeping the profound and peaceful sleep of the dead. Awakened from a light sleep by the buzz of a mosquito I would get to thinking about the statues in the garden, about that fluid, silent communion which went on like music between these guardians of the Four Seasons. Sometimes I would get up and go out on the broad balcony overlooking the garden, stand there half-naked puffing a cigarette, hypnotized by the warmth, the silence, the fragrance which enveloped me. So many strange, startling phrases were dropped in the course of a day—they would come back to me at night and plague me. Little remarks, such as the one he dropped about the pool, for instance. "A dozen square feet of pool mean more to them than all the soil: it is a transparent mystery." The pool! It brought back memories of the dead fountain which graces the entrance to the now abandoned Mississippi Lunatic Asylum. I know that water is soothing to the insane, just as music is. A little pool in an enclosed and enchanted garden, such as this one, is an inexhaustible source of wonder and magic. One evening standing thus in a dream, I remembered that there was a type-written description of the place framed and posted near the pool. I descended the outer staircase and with the aid of a match I read the thing through. I re-read the paragraph about the garden, as though it contained some magic incantation. Here it is:

> "A rectangular formal garden to the east of the house is enclosed by a clipped bamboo hedge and is bordered by walks of hand-shaped brick, at the four corners of which are marble statues of the Four Seasons which were once in the gardens of the old Hester plantation. The center of the grass rectangle has a clump of old Camellia trees planted when the house was built. The signed marble sundial is inscribed with the French adage—'Abundance is the Daughter of Economy and Work', and is dated 1827."

A heady mist had descended. I walked cautiously in my bare feet for the old bricks were slippery with moss. As I got to the far corner of the rectangle the light of the moon broke full and clear on the serene face of the goddess there enshrined. I leaned over impulsively and kissed the marble lips. It was a strange sensation. I went to each of them in turn and kissed their cold, chaste lips. Then I strolled back to the trellised garden house which lies on the banks of the Bayou Teche. The scene before my eyes was that of a Chinese painting. Sky and water had become one: the whole world was floating in a nebular mist. It was indescribably beautiful and bewitching. I could scarcely believe that I was in America. In a moment or so a river boat loomed up, her colored lights scattering the dense mist into a frayed kaleidoscope of ribboned light. The deep fog horn sounded and was echoed by the hooting of invisible owls. To the left the draw-bridge slowly raised its broken span, the soft edges illumined by fulgurant lights of red and green. Slowly, like a white bird, the river boat glided past my vision, and in her wake the mist closed in, bearing down the sky, a fistful of frightened stars, the heavy wet limbs of the moss-covered trees, the density of night, and watery, smothered sounds. I went back to bed and lay there not just wide awake but super-conscious, alive in every tip and pore of my being. The portrait of an ancestor stared at me from the wall—a Manchu portrait, with the dress folded and pressed in the frame. I could hear Weeks Hall's booming voice saying to me: "I should like to do a garden which would not be a seed-catalogue by daylight, but strange, sculptural blossoms by night, things hanging in trees and moving like metronomes, transparent plastics in geometrical shapes, silhouettes lit by lights and changing with the changing hours. A garden is a show—why not make one enormous garden, one big, changing show?" I lay there wondering about those several thousand letters and documents which he had exhumed from the garret and stored in the Archives at Baton Rouge. What a story they would make! And the garret itself—that enormous room on the third floor with the forty trunks! Forty trunks, with the hair still intact on the bear-skin hides. Containing enormous hat boxes for the tall hats of the fifties, a stereoscope of mahogany and pictures for it taken in the sixties, fencing foils, shotgun cases, an old telescope, early side-saddles, dog baskets, linen dancing cloths with rings to fit over the carpets in the drawing room, banjos, guitars, zithers. Doll trunks too, and a doll house replica of the great house itself. All smelling dry and lightly fragrant. The smell of age, not of dust.

A strange place, the attic, with twelve huge closets and the ceiling slanting throughout the length of the house. Strange house. To get to any room you had to walk through every other room of the house. Nine doors leading outside—more than one finds in most public buildings. The both staircases originally built on the outside—a somewhat mad idea. No central hall. A row of three identical double wooden doors placed in the dead center of the grave facade on the ground floor.

And the strange Mr. Persac, the itinerant painter who left a brace of microscopically done wash drawings in black enamel gilt frames on the walls of the reception room where we held our nightly pow-wows. Up and down the country, especially the Teche region, he wandered, just a few years before the War between the States. Making pictures of the great houses and living on the fat of the land. An honest painter who, when the task got beyond his powers would cut out a figure from a magazine and paste it on the picture. Thus in one of his masterpieces the child standing by the garden gate has disappeared—but the balloon which she held in her hand is still visible. I adore the work of these travelling artists. How infinitely more agreeable and enriching than the life of the present day artist! How much more genuine and congenial their work than the pretentious efforts of our contemporaries! Think of the simple lunch that was served them in the old plantation days. I cull a menu at random from one of Lyle Saxon's books on old Louisiana: "a slice of bread and butter spread with marmalade or guava jelly, accompanied by a slab of jujube paste and washed down with lemonade or orange-flower syrup or tamarind juice." . . .

Well, Monsieur Persac or Persat, whichever it was, I felicitate you for having had the good fortune to be born in such times! I hope you are chewing the cud of these rich and pleasant memories in the Bardo beyond. When morning comes I shall go down to the reception room and look again at the balloon which is suspended above the gate. If I am in good fettle I will look around for a little child capable of holding such a beautiful balloon and I will paste her back in the picture as I know you would wish me to do. May you rest in peace! . . .

As I was about to go to my room Weeks called me from the studio, the only room he had not yet shown me. "Are you very tired?" he asked. "No, not too tired," I answered. . . .

He lit a fresh cigarette. Paced nervously back and forth. He wanted to say something . . . he wanted to say a lot of things . . . *everything*, if I would only be patient and not run away. He began again, haltingly, clumsily, feeling his way like a man groping through a dark and winding passage.

"Look, this arm!" and he held it out for me to look at intently. "Smashed. Smashed for good. A terrible thing. One moment you have an arm there, the next moment it's a pulpy mess. I suppose the truth is that it was only good for the derrick-use which other arms are good for. This arm was perhaps too slick, too clever; it made me paint like a gambler deals and shuffles the cards. Perhaps my mind is too slick and too brittle. Not disciplined enough. And I know I won't improve it by my mania for research. That's just a pretext to forestall the day when I must really begin to paint. I know all that—but what are you going to do? Here I am living alone in a big house, a place which overwhelms me. The house is too much for me. I want to live in one room somewhere, without all these cares and responsibilities which I seem to have assumed from my forbears. How am I going to do it? Shutting myself up in this room is no solution. Even if I can't see them or hear them I know there are people outside clamoring to get in. And perhaps I ought to see them, talk to them, listen to them, worry about what they're worrying about. How should I know? After all they're not all fools. Maybe if I were the man I'd like to be I wouldn't have to set foot outside this door—the world would come to me. Maybe I'd paint under the worst conditions—perhaps right out there in the garden with all the sightseers crowding around me and asking me a thousand and one irrelevant questions. Who knows but that, if I were deadly in earnest, they would let me alone, leave me in peace, without saying a word to them? Somehow people always recognize value. Take Swedenborg, for example. He never locked his door. People came and when they saw him they went away quietly, reverently, unwilling to disturb him though they had travelled, some of them, thousands of miles to ask him for help and guidance." With his good hand he took hold of the smashed arm and gazed at it, as though it belonged to some other person. "Can one change one's own nature—that's the question? Well, eventually this arm may act as the pole does for the tight-rope walker. *The balance*—if we don't have it within we've got to find it without. I'm glad you came here . . . you've done me a world of good. God, when I was listening to you all talk about Paris I realized all I had missed these years. You won't find anything much in New Orleans, except the past. We've got *one* painter—that's Dr. Souchon.[8] I want you to meet him. . . . I guess it's pretty late. You want to go to bed, don't you? I could talk all night, of course. I don't need much sleep. And since you all came here I can't sleep at all. I have a thousand questions to ask. I want to make up for all the time I've lost."

I had difficulty myself in going to sleep. It seemed cruel to leave a man stranded like that on a peak of exaltation. Rattner had prepared me for his exuberance and vitality; but not for his inexhaustible hunger. This hunger of his touched me deeply. He was a man who knew no stint. He gave just as recklessly and abundantly as he demanded. He was an artist to the finger-tips, no doubt about that. And his problems were no ordinary ones. He had probed too deeply. Fame and success would mean nothing to a man like that. He was in search of something which eluded all definition. Already, in certain do-

---

8. Miller writes about visiting Souchon in another part of *The Air-Conditioned Nightmare.*

mains, he had amassed the knowledge of a savant. And what was more, he saw the relatedness of all things. Naturally he could not be content in executing a masterful painting. He wanted to revolutionize things. He wanted to bring painting back to its original estate—painting for painting's sake. In a sense it might be said of him that he had already completed his great work. He had transformed the house and grounds, through his passion for creation, into one of the most distinctive pieces of art which America can boast of. He was living and breathing in his own masterpiece, not knowing it, not realizing the extent and sufficiency of it. By his enthusiasm and generosity he had inspired other painters to do their work—had given birth to them, one might say. And still he was restless, longing to express himself surely and completely. I admired him and pitied him, both. I felt his presence all through the house, flooding it like some powerful magic fluid. He had created that which in turn would recreate him. That hermetically sealed studio—what was it in fact if not a symbolic expression of his own locked-in self? The studio could never contain him, any more than the house itself; he had outgrown the place, overflowed the bounds. He was a self-convicted prisoner inhabiting the aura of his own creation. Some day he would awaken, free himself of the snares and delusions which had gathered in the wake of creation. Some day he would look around and realize that he was free; then he would be able to decide calmly and quietly whether to remain or to go. I hoped that he would remain, that as the last link in the ancestral chain he would close the circle and by realizing the significance of his act expand the circle and circumference of his life to infinite dimensions.

When I took leave of him a day or two later I had the impression, from the look he gave me, that he had come to this conclusion himself. I left knowing that I would always find him at a moment's notice anywhere any time.

"No need to telephone me in the middle of the night, Weeks. As long as you remain centered I am at your side eternally. No need to say good-bye or good luck! Just continue being what you are. May peace be with you!"

Weighing and Paying

Richard Schweid

Schweid (b. 1946)—who grew up in Tennessee, where the food was not highly spiced—was living in Oregon and looking for some ingredient to add zing to his table. He found Tabasco Sauce and was drawn to Louisiana to explore the hot sauce industry. He was in the state in 1977 and 1978, and again in 1986, and recounts his discoveries in *Hot Peppers: Cajuns and Capsicum in New Iberia, Louisiana,* from which the following is taken. In this excerpt he writes of one traditional field activity on Avery Island, where the McIlhenny Company makes Tabasco and grows the peppers that go into it. Though the crop is an unusual one, we do get a sense of the fundamentals of plantation existence—work in the fields—in the modern age. The "he" of the first sentence is Walter McIlhenny, president of the family-owned McIlhenny Company.

He suggested I see some Avery Island tradition at work, and used the phone to summon Edmund McIlhenny into the office. He asked Edmund to take me along for the weighing of the day's harvest. Walter, himself, had ritually performed this task every afternoon for twenty-five harvest seasons, but with his health not at its best he delegated it to his younger relatives. He solemnly assured me that I was about to witness the manner in which pepper pickers on Avery Island had been paid for their day's labor, "since beyond any living memory." . . .

The men of the McIlhenny family do not take off their jackets and ties when they go into the fields. On the afternoon that Edmund drove me out to watch the pickers get paid, he was wearing a green, herringbone tweed jacket and a dark tie. It had been air-conditioned and cool in the office building, but outside it was over eighty degrees.

Edmund had the ruddy face and light brown hair of his family. He looked, in fact, remarkably like his namesake, the company's founder, in a surviving portrait from the 1850s. Edmund was thirty-four years old. He was born and raised in New Orleans, and graduated from Tulane Law School. He interned in Washington, D.C., with Senator Joe Clark of Pennsylvania, then returned to New Orleans where he practiced law. He had been living on Avery Island with his wife and two children since 1975. He did not seem to miss city life and described himself, with a chuckle, as a retired member of the Louisiana State Bar.

We were riding in one of the McIlhenny's fleet of blue, late-model, American sedans. The road was gravel and we left a cloud of dust in the air behind us. In 1910, the pepper fields came right up to the walls of the old factory, but they have receded and it took a ten-minute ride along the narrow island road to reach them. During the harvest season, old school buses came into New Iberia from Avery Island at 5:30 every morning but Sunday, to give the pickers a ride out to the pepper fields. There was an hour for a meal in the middle of the day, and the work stopped at 3:45.

Edmund and I arrived at the fields shortly after four o'clock. Thirteen acres of tabasco peppers were coming ripe under the bright, afternoon sun. Pepper bushes, three-feet high, were loaded with red and green, erect pods as far as the eye could see. A dirt road, called the headland, ran down one side of each field, alongside the ends of the rows. The pickers were beside the headland, sitting on overturned buckets, or on the ground with boxes of scarlet peppers around them. The boxes looked as old as any of the traditions in force on Avery Island. They were wooden, two feet long and a foot deep, sturdy and worn. Each weighed eight pounds when empty.

The pickers were all black, almost all women over forty-five. There were a handful of young women, and a few old men. There was not a young man in sight. The women wore bonnets or kerchiefs. The sun-bleached reds and blues of their headgear bobbed and flashed in the hot, dusty air, as they patiently waited for the weighing of the day's work to begin.

I had a moment's impression of peace and well-being, compounded by the smell of the warm soil and the sight of people resting beside their harvests. It disappeared as I focused on the pickers, the sweat cooling on their faces, the exhaustion in their eyes, the bone-tired postures into which their bodies had settled. During the summer months, and on Saturdays during the fall, black high school students, boys and girls, often came out to pick. Their supply of energy was unlimited and they shouted, chattered, and horsed around during the midday meal or while waiting for the McIlhennys to begin weighing. But it was a weekday; most of the pickers had gray hair. A sense of their fatigue was palpable.

All eyes were on Edmund and I as we got out of the car and walked down the headland. At the far end were two trucks and a number of men dressed in the tan uniforms of permanent McIlhenny Company employees. Edmund exchanged greetings with the pickers as we walked by them, speaking to many by name.

When we reached the trucks at the bottom of the headland, I notice a two-wheeled cart was attached by a trailer hitch to the first truck. A large platform scale was mounted on the cart. Paul McIlhenny was waiting for us beside it. He and Edmund were first cousins, of nearly the same age, and they bore a strong resemblance to one another. Paul was dressed in a blazer, gray flannels, and a dark tie. There was a bit of banter between them about who would weigh and who would pay, until Paul conceded that it was his turn to weigh. He climbed into the cart and sat down behind the scales on a little, three-legged milking stool.

The truck pulled the cart slowly up the headland, stopping at each picker and box of peppers. One of the company men walked in front of the truck and poked a stick down through the peppers in the boxes to make sure the picker had not loaded them with rocks in the bottom. When the truck stopped, a company man would lift a box onto the scale. Paul adjusted the weight on the scale's beam and solemnly called out the number of pounds. The box was removed and stacked on the bed of the second truck, which was following behind. Paul seemed slightly ill-at-ease and out-of-place, perched in the cart on a low stool, thumbing the scale.

The truck lurched forward and stopped every few feet so a box could be hoisted up to the scale. I watched as Paul weighed a box. The woman who had picked that box of peppers stood on the ground, gazing up toward his flushed, sweaty face, her eyes stopping somewhere around the knot in his tie, as he fiddled with the weights.

"Sixty-five," he called out. An employee inside the truck recorded the weight, subtracting eight pounds for the box, and punched it on a card.

The woman was at least fifty, and she had spent her day picking those fifty-seven pounds of peppers. She smiled, her face streaked with sweat under her red bonnet, "How y'all doin' Mistah Paul?"

"Fine thanks, Miss Rose. Made yourself a little money today, I guess. Gonna see you tomorrow, aren't we?"

She laughed. "Course you will, Mistah Paul. If I ain't out here, you know my health done give out. You jist know ah be done for if ah ain't here."

She took her punched card from a hand waving it out the window of the truck's cab, and walked up the headlands to Edmund McIlhenny, who stood by another gray, late-model sedan. This one had an open cash box on the hood. Edmund took her punched card, wrote down her name and how much she had picked in a large ledger, and counted $16.10 into her palm. Miss Rose received it in silence, signed her X in the ledger beside her name, and climbed wearily aboard the school bus to wait for her ride back to New Iberia.

The school buses were painted olive green, and had "The McIlhenny Company" printed on their sides. By the time everyone had been paid in the traditional manner, and the bus had rattled its slow way back to New Iberia, it would already be five o'clock, with barely enough time left for these women to start getting supper on the stove once they got home.

While the truck pulled Paul slowly up the headland, I spoke with Willie Dore, the field foreman at Avery Island. He was in his middle forties. French was his first language and he spoke English with a thick, Cajun accent. To my ears, the English spoken in southern Louisiana is second only to that spoken in the Caribbean in the loveliness of its tones. Words seem to roll off the tongue, making softer and less harsh sounds than those of English spoken elsewhere. No matter whether the conversation is only about the weather or last night's television show, the song of the spoken words makes them sound like poetry.

Willie Dore was wearing a white shirt, open at the collar, and a broad-brimmed hat. He had light, freckled skin and the hat kept him shaded. People here, as in many white, rural societies around the world, regard the lightest, whitest skin as the most desirable. Despite the subtropical heat, they do not like to go under the hot sun with bare arms, or uncovered heads. They are baffled by city folks who lie exposed beneath blazing rays in order to turn darker.

Willie was grateful for the security offered him by the McIlhenny Company. He was a loyal and devoted employee. "I was born on Avery Island. When my daddy and family left I was five years old, and when we came back I was nineteen. I been here ever since. My daddy had worked here about ten years, and then went to share farming. But there wasn't no money in it, and we wanted to come to work where they paid every week and at least you could see money. Farming, you wouldn't see it until the end of the year, and then just maybe you'd see some. So when we got back here I just stayed on."

He shook his head, sadly. "There were about fifty or sixty out here pickin' today. I got work for a hundred and twenny. See that ole lady who's weighin' out now? She's been pickin' over fifty years. Strong and healthy like an ole mule, *cher*. Still be the same people picking. I believe after these people die, nobody be comin' out a-tall. They need to fine a good machine, but Lord, this one they got now be jist a bit better than nothing. It's slow and the machine gotta use so much pressure it always be knockin' the greens off the bush."

Willie Dore had been growing tabasco peppers for a long time. Like any farmer, he could remember some good years and some bad ones, but he could not remember a season when everything went right. "The ideal weather for peppers to grow in would be a half inch of rain every week and then sunshine. Clouds now and then, a little clouds, but I'm talking the ideal. If you have sunshine, it's all right, but if it be cloudy it's better, 'cause your moisture stays. If your wind go south your moisture comes up, if it goes north then it comes down. The last couple of days we had that wind from the north, and right now the rows be dry, dry, dry. That stops the crop from growing right there. Oh yes, *cher*, that completely stop it.

"This year we was late gettin' started 'cause we had cold nights for the longest time. Lord, we not usually seein' that many cold nights. Your pepper plant likes to grow at night, in the warm night air. We put 'em out this year in April, but at night it was real cold, right in the fifties for a long time. Usually these nights be much warmer and we start pickin' in the last week of July, but this year we didn't get goin' until the middle of August.

"So that be three weeks we was late gettin' started with our pickin'. You losin' that, plus you losin' the time when you able to get the kids to come out and pick. This is why we always strain so much to have a good start, so we can have the kids for a month before they go back to school. That's when we make our good pickin'. After they be back in school, we not gettin' much in the way of hand-pickers, but when the kids are pickin' you can get a hundred and twenny people out here."

By 1986, things had changed. The McIlhennys purposely waited until school resumed to begin picking Avery Island peppers, so that they would not have to fool with adolescents and their horseplay. There was plenty of available adult labor—deadly serious about the work—and it did not pay to have kids out there just picking half a box a day.

When the oil patch slowed down in 1981, and the first wave of laid-off workers came to the end of their unemployment benefits a year later, people began to trickle to the pepper fields when the picking season rolled around. Another factor in the increased supply of labor was the growing presence of southeast Asian refugees in southern Louisiana. While the Vietnamese have generally chosen to make their livelihoods on the water by fishing and shrimping, many of the first-generation refugees from land-locked Laos gravitated into filling what little demand existed for agricultural labor.

Even though Willie Dore could count on drawing from 160–200 pickers out to the field on any given day during the 1986 harvest season—three times as many as 1978, and many of them strong men in their 30s and 40s—it was clear that the days when the McIlhenny Company supplied its needs with home-grown peppers were gone for good. Latin Americans performed the same day's labor for about one-tenth the wage, and even with the cost of transportation the company came out way ahead by growing in Latin America. About ninety-eight percent of the peppers that the McIlhenny Company turned into mash in 1985 were grown and harvested in Latin America.

Harvesting is only one step in the yearly cycle of the peppers. Traditionally, on Avery Island, all phases of this cycle were done by hand, from the greenhouse in January, to the turning over into the ground of the frozen, bare, pepper bushes in December.

"When we plant, we got a machine that makes a little hole to put the plant in, but that's it," said Willie Dore. "Everything else by hand, don'tcha know? One person puts it in the hole and another comes along behind and covers it up.

"Then you got your weeding and that has to be done. It's a good thing they be comin' out with chemicals we can use. If it wouldn't be for herbicides the farmers would be in a hell of a shape, *cher.* It takes a long time to clear one of 'em with the government, you know? We got one clear, and one practically clear. Should be clear next year.

"This time of year we start to get that north wind and the weeds won't grow anymore, but a lot of the time I'm stuck with too many acres where you can hardly see the peppers for the weeds that grew up before that north wind came. The pickers don't want to pick where you have a lot of grass 'cause that's where the snakes be. You be busy pickin' and never notice the darn thing. No, *cher,* I wouldn't like to pick in grass, myself. People will pick about half way down the bush and that's it. They not goin' no lower. That snake gonna have to jump to get their hand. Might get their leg but not their hand."

He laughed. "You know in all my time here I never heard of nobody actually gettin' bitten by a snake. We've got all kinds here, including rattlesnakes, but nobody ever been bit. So really the snakes are not that bad, but I guess none of the pickers wants to be the first."

Travel Update

Plantations—or, at any rate, plantation houses—are a near obsession for many Louisianians today. They visit these houses as assiduously as out-of-state tourists do and have their favorite ones for touring, for driving by, for bringing their out-of-town friends and relatives to see. Though at one time many of these mansions were allowed to deteriorate (and though some still remain endangered), today both individuals and organizations maintain considerable interest in restoring plantation houses and keeping them up. As B. C. Hall and C. T. Wood note, plantations as tourist attractions are big business (and yield more than the "modest revenue" Henry Miller noted). The literature on Louisiana plantations includes such landmark books as *Old Plantation Houses in Louisiana* (New York, 1927), with a text by Natalie Scott, particularly appealing because of delightful illustrations by William Spratling; and David King Gleason's *Plantation Homes of Louisiana and the Natchez Area* (Baton Rouge, 1982), with lavish color photographs. (Architect and artist Spratling makes an appearance in William Faulkner's "Episode.")

There are literally dozens of Louisiana plantation houses open to the public, a great many along the Mississippi, Bayous Teche and Lafourche, the Red River, and other streams (as the earliest routes of communication and transit, the waterways continued to provide the most efficient means for shipping huge quantities of cotton and sugar to market until the advent of railroads). Whereas earlier travelers often remarked on the plantation houses they could see from the water, today tall levees obstruct views from boats and often restrict river views from the houses. Sternberg's *The Pelican Guide to Louisiana* provides reasonably up-to-date information on many houses. Lyle Saxon's "tour" of a number of them in his *Old Louisiana* (New York, 1929), though well out of date, is pleasant reading, with information on particular houses interspersed with chapters on plantation lore.

Of the plantation houses visited by the writers in this volume, Valcour Aime's Petit Versailles burned. Its site, however, can be found less than two miles downriver from the famous Oak Alley Plantation on Louisiana 18.

Running alongside the campus of St. James Junior High School is Valcour-Aime Street. The site of Aime's celebrated gardens is now a wooded rectangle enclosed by an iron fence, located down this street and behind the sugarcane field that fronts the highway. The property is owned by a landscape architect who may restore the gardens. (The gardens at Avery Island also include a pagoda, though what Aime's looked like is anyone's guess.) Governor Roman's house is also gone. Just as he feared (as confided to Russell), it was claimed by the river. There is a historical marker on the site of the plantation (at "Cabahanoce Plantation" on Louisiana 18, near the junction of Louisiana 912 and the present-day post office for St. James). One plantation house with Roman and Aime connections does survive and flourish, however, and it is one of the grand jewels of the River Road and of southern architecture: Oak Alley, which was built by Governor Roman's brother, J. T. Roman, between 1837 and 1839. The view of it from the highway is one of the most glorious in Louisiana, twenty-eight astonishingly large live oaks running in two rows up to the delicate pink house, framing its front. Entering the plantation grounds, one has the prospect of (in the right season) a wall of waving sugarcane on one side and the house on the other, a multicolumned Greek-revival structure that would be at home on the dust jacket of a historical novel. The Roman family sold the house after the war, and it was restored in the 1920s by Josephine and Andrew Stewart, who made numerous changes (moving an entire stairway, for example) and who provided its present furnishings (though an exquisite Roman-family cradle can be found in one bedroom). Rows of oaks in back of the house were planted by J. T. Roman, though those in the front predate the house or any other structure (and their presence is thus something of a mystery). Several movies have been filmed there, most recently *Interview with the Vampire*.

The St. Joseph Plantation Store, located between Oak Alley and the Valcour Aime site, sits on a plantation made up of those Aime gave two of his daughters. It is one of few continuously functioning plantation stores in Louisiana and is said to be the only such on the Mississippi. (Plantation stores were, of course, a postslavery institution set up to provide newly free plantation laborers with supplies.) The Olivier Plantation Store on Weeks Island Road outside New Iberia has not functioned continuously and is today a gift shop (operated by descendants of the original owners), but it is well preserved and full of many old items the store once stocked, as well as volumes of old ledgers.

Alive and well—alone among the houses Russell stayed in—is John Burn-side's residence, Houmas House, on the east bank of the river. The mansion was built in 1840 as a grandiose addition to a smaller house built in the 1790s. Burnside had purchased the property (including 556 slaves) in 1858, only a few years before Russell's visit. Burnside died in 1881, and the house was part of a working plantation until around 1920. In 1940 the house was purchased by Dr. George B. Crozat, a New Orleans dentist and inventor, who wanted it for a weekend and retirement place. Although a handful of the original fur-nishings remain (a highchair and a Burnside bookmark, for example), the present interior is largely Crozat's creation. Crozat did have exquisite taste, and because he and his family made themselves at home there (one floor is still occupied by the family), Houmas House has more of a lived-in feel than many restored plantation homes. The grounds are pretty and can be wan-dered through or seen from the front verandah, which is more or less on a level with the top of the Mississippi levee. There is also a good example of a *garçon-nière* (the segregated living quarters of the young, unmarried men of the family).

Donaldsonville, mentioned by Russell, is located on the west bank of the Mississippi and is the seat of Ascension Parish, which borders St. James. It was for a short time capital of Louisiana.

Oak Alley and Houmas House are Greek-revival structures, representing a style of architecture found throughout the South and introduced into Louisi-ana by American planters who came into the state in increasing numbers in the nineteenth century. Magnolia Mound in Baton Rouge (on Nicholson Drive between downtown and the Louisana State University campus) is quite different in style, an excellent representative of the older, Creole-style planta-tion house (sometimes called the West Indian style). Creole-style houses could be quite large, but Magnolia Mound, though beautiful, is fairly modest and thus indicative that many plantation residences were not fabulously grand. Built around 1791, the house has been documented and restored with particular care. As its name implies, it sits on raised ground, which would have protected it from Mississippi flooding, behind several superb live oaks. The walls are of *bousillage,* a mixture of mud and Spanish moss, and the re-storers have left off a portion of the plaster in one room so that visitors can see this material. The house sits on 17 acres, but the original plantation had 930 and ran from the present-day Mississippi River Bridge to the LSU campus. The overseer's house has been moved back on to the property, and a slave cabin from another plantation is being restored on the grounds. The separate kitchen (plantation house kitchens were usually separate structures because of the heat they generated and the threat of fire) is a reproduction, where cooking demonstations are given. There are several other living history programs, and in the site's visitor center are models of various plantation buildings and an exhibit on the history of Creole architecture. Magnolia Mound should not be confused with Magnolia Plantation (visited by both King and Hesse-Wartegg), which was located downriver from New Orleans.

The orange trees noted by Russell were a feature remarked on by many travelers. Small groves, the last vestiges of the plantation orchards, are found almost exclusively below New Orleans in Plaquemines Parish. Today the Louisiana orange crop is comparatively small and consumed mostly locally; the climate is a little too cold for oranges, and the crop has periodically been wiped out. There are numerous stands that sell oranges and other crops, however.

Weeks Hall, last master of Shadows-on-the-Teche, died in 1958. The house, fortunately, remains, and is open to the public on a regular basis. In his final days Hall sought to ensure the future of the Shadows by raising an endowment and finding an organization to take the house over; the National Trust for Historic Preservation now operates the property. The house now has the feel of a town residence and sits on the main street of New Iberia, close to downtown on the edge of a historic district. The gardens are not overgrown as Miller implies they were in 1941, but retain a fine lushness; one can imagine an earlier generation of tourists trying to peer in through thick foliage. A delightful rectangular gazebo overlooks Bayou Teche, and a second floor loggia (enclosed when Miller visited) overlooks the rear garden. Miller is mistaken in saying that the Shadows "is not at all in the traditional Louisiana style of architecture." Though the architectural details are indeed neoclassical revival, the floor plan is French colonial (*cabinet* rooms in the rear and no central hallways, for example), so that the house is something of a combination of the Creole and the American. (Many doors opening onto a gallery are a common feature of Creole houses, not an eccentricity as Miller suggests.) Likewise, it is surprising that Miller thought the name of painter Marie Adrien Persac might be Persat. Persac (who painted many Louisiana scenes) had a style remarkable for its precision (including his signature). The paintings Miller refers to still hang in the house. Persac (*ca.* 1822/24–1873) was a lithographer and photographer as well as painter and did his popular gouache paintings of plantation houses, like those of the Shadows, in the early 1860s. The vast collection of documents relating to the Weeks family that were preserved at the Shadows (comprising over 10,000 items) are now housed in the Special Collections archives at the Louisiana State University Library as the Weeks (David, and Family) Papers. For a biography of Weeks Hall, see Morris Raphael, *Weeks Hall: The Master of the Shadows* (New Iberia, 1981).

Weeks Hall is buried in the little family cemetery in the front garden. His studio in the ground floor has been preserved, and the door Miller makes much of is still there, with the signatures of the likes of Walt Disney and Tex Ritter. Several whose work is reprinted in this volume also visited and signed: Sherwood Anderson, Caroline Durieux, Harnett Kane, and Lyle Saxon (who writes about visiting Hall in *The Friends of Joe Gilmore and The Friends of Lyle Saxon*, written with Robert Tallant [New York, 1948]). Miller himself signed, adding the message: "Keep the aspidistras flying" (evidently a reference to George Orwell's novel of that title).

A major problem in understanding Louisiana plantations is that the romance and architectural splendor of the big house have been emphasized to contemporary visitors at the expense of the idea of the plantation as a complex and a community—the big house divorced from its historical surroundings, from fields, outbuildings, laborers, and their quarters. Henry Miller observed that the great houses were rotting away while the slave and sharecropper cabins remained, but by the 1990s that situation had reversed, and the cabins are increasingly disappearing from the landscape. It is possible, however, to get something of the larger picture of plantation life by visiting places where attempts are being made to preserve aspects of plantation settings beyond the venue of the big house, such as the Louisiana State University Museum of Rural Life in Baton Rouge and Laurel Valley Plantation Village at Thibodaux. Laurel Valley, currently owned by a nonprofit organization, includes over seventy structures from its days as a plantation community, including quarters houses, a school, and a store (which displays plantation-related tools and serves as a gift shop for the facility), and is thought to be the largest surviving plantation-manufacturing complex in the South. The plantation was devastated during the Civil War, when its original big house was destroyed, and much of what survives dates from the late nineteenth century, when the sugar plantation underwent a revival (and when many of its workers were not blacks but Cajuns). The store and some other structures front Louisiana 308 on Bayou Lafourche, but the heart of the complex lies down a straight road through cane fields. The ruins of the old sugar mill, now little more than an arched brick wall, stand overlooking the quarters houses, small cabins in several styles with rusting metal roofs. They are fenced off pending possible restoration, so presently there is little to see up close. And though they presently are, in a sense, abandoned leftovers, they offer a genuine sense that a plantation was a clustered community, with workers and their families living in the lee of the work areas and the center of the crops. Plantation field equipment, including two engines for the "dummy" trains that carried cane in from the fields, are on display near the store.

Another way to understand plantations in historical perspective is to have a contemporary look at the crops that were important in their evolution. The key plantation crop noted by the travelers in this section—sugarcane—continues to be important in Louisiana and to provide familiar color to the landscape. In recent years, cotton—the other major antebellum crop—has generated nearly $600 million per year in revenues and sugarcane over $400 million. Because it requires a warmer climate, cane is grown in parishes in the extreme southern part of the state, while cotton grows farther north. Both are harvested in the fall, an interesting and lovely time to visit Louisiana—to see the lush, green walls of cane and the acres and acres of white puffs of cotton as well as the processes of harvesting (now largely mechanized). Cane that has fallen from trucks on the way to the mills litters the roadside.

Cotton ginning—which separates seeds from lint—is also much changed since plantation times, but a visit to a Louisiana gin is still interesting. Such gins as the Frogmore Cotton Gin in Frogmore (near Natchez, Mississippi) and the Producer's Mutual Cotton Gin in Cheneyville offer tours. Today cotton comes to a gin in a module, or huge rectangular pile (formed by machine) that can be seen sitting in fields. Visitors can watch as the cotton is sucked up by vacuums, flows like spumes of water down chutes, is layered and compacted into bales (which today are plastic-wrapped), and finally is rolled out into warehouse areas, while workers use computer terminals to track the operation.

The original cotton gin was a fairly simple machine. A small, early-nineteenth-century gin is on display at the Louisiana State Museum in New Orleans. A much larger gin, made in 1885 by the Gullett Gin Works of Amite, Louisiana—at the time the largest gin manufacturer in the country—is located at the Old Hickory Village museum complex in Jackson. Future plans call for its reactivation for historical demonstrations.

Sugarcane is perhaps a more romantic crop, given that it is less common in the United States than cotton and that it has such a graceful, tropical form. Historically its cultivation was very labor intensive, so that its production required the institution of the large plantation, which could muster many workers—originally slaves, later wage laborers who commonly lived in quarters on the plantation. Today cultivation is largely mechanized (though some still plant the cane—which grows from stalks, not seeds—by hand). The large labor force is no longer required, and cane cultivation has become more like other forms of farming. Some old sugar plantations continue to be operated solely by their owners. In some cases the owners lease the land to farmers in whole or in part; in other cases the larger holdings have been broken up into smaller ones (as Edward King anticipated).

In antebellum days many plantations operated their own sugar mills. Today there are only about twenty grinding mills in the whole state (some cooperative, also as King anticipated) each serving various properties. The cane is cut mechanically, then set fire to in the fields (to burn off the leaves), a practice that creates a characteristic smokey smell in sugar country during the harvest. It is loaded into big carts and taken to the mill (which in grinding season operates day and night for up to eighty-five days) to join the phalanxes of others waiting in regimented rows to be unloaded. Cane samples in each cart are extracted by suction for testing sugar content, and the cane is then unloaded, washed, shredded, and crushed by rollers to extract the sweet juice. It is put into tins where lime is added and solids are removed, then boiled in vacuum pans till the water evaporates and a dark syrup remains. This is cooked until it crystallizes, a centrifuge separating molasses from the granular raw sugar. This concludes the process at the grinding mill. At the separate sugar refinery (there are two in Louisiana), the raw sugar is refined into the white, powdered, and brown sugars familiar to consumers. (King describes a grinding mill, not a refinery.)

Several grinding mills, such as the Dugas and LeBlanc Sugar Mill in Paincourtville, will give visitors tours, but usually only with special, advance arrangements. A grinding mill in season is an awe-inspiring sight. Even from a distance the nearly frantic activity is apparent, an endless stream of cane carts pulling up to the rambling mill structure, which pumps smoke skyward as if straining to finish the job. (Today the smoke is mostly steam, mandated scrubbers working to eliminate the soot that poured from the stacks until a few years ago.) Up close the visitor can see mountains of cane being unloaded, run through a muddy waterfall for cleaning, then shuttled by conveyor belt into the building. Inside are the machines that chomp the cane to bits; brown rivers of cane juice flowing down sluices; bagasse being sidetracked to great, sparking ovens where it's burned to provide the mill's fuel; vats with little round windows like old washing machines, where the sloshing juice is heated. Finally what looks like sludgy coal slides into centrifuges that separate molasses from crystallized sugar, and the raw sugar pours out into a gigantic warehouse where Caterpillar tractors move it into piles that look like huge sand dunes.

In addition to visiting operating mills, it is possible to see the remains of an old mill at Fontainebleau State Park near Mandeville; the West Baton Rouge Museum in Port Allen has a scale model of a mill, which was produced by several companies that made equipment for sugar refining for the 1904 Louisiana Purchase Exhibition in New Orleans. The museum has various sugar plantation artifacts, including a "dummy" train and the horse-drawn pumper that was the fire department for a local plantation. The visitor center at Longfellow-Evangeline State Commemorative Area in St. Martinville includes an exhibit on historical sugar making; the Creole-style plantation house for the Olivier sugar plantation is also on the grounds.

Avery Island is a major Louisiana attraction. It is reached by Louisiana 329 from nearby New Iberia. This road goes through agricultural country, and the terrain seems increasingly remote and marshy until the island (which is actually a salt dome, one of the so-called Five Islands of the Louisiana coastal marsh country) rises up in the near distance, a striking contrast to the flatness of the surrounding countryside. Bayou Petit Anse flows around part of the place, making it seem like an actual island, and the visitor crosses the bayou on a toll bridge. Because the island is entirely McIlhenny private property, access is restricted, but one may visit the wonderful Jungle Gardens, a parklike domain cut out of the island wilderness by E. A. McIlhenny, a noted naturalist and conservationist largely responsible for saving snowy egrets from extinction. Gravel roads take visitors past a wealth of Oriental holly, sixty-four varieties of bamboo, azaleas, irises, and camellias, alligators basking in pools, and other wildlife (including the egrets of "Bird City," an area of nesting platforms to which a vast bird population returns every year after wintering in Central and South America). The Tabasco Sauce factory, a graceful brick building that seems almost domestic despite its great size, can also be toured (its gift shop offers a great array of Tabasco-related wares). Increasingly, the

McIlhenny Company has come to use peppers imported from Honduras and Colombia, but peppers are still hand-picked on the island and weighed in the manner Schweid describes. The local peppers are considered "the heart and soul" of the McIlhenny operation, used "to test agricultural practices . . . and to maintain the stock that originally came out of Mexico."[9] A salt mine also operates on the island, and oil was discovered there in the 1940s.

The Autry House in Dubach in north Louisiana's Grant Parish is an interesting remnant of plantation living of another sort, the very small operation having been run with only a few slaves under frontier conditions. Made of hand-hewn logs in dogtrot form (with an open breezeway between two "pen" rooms, or square rooms), it was built in 1848. Its owners grew cotton and raised and hunted their own food. Restored, it has a simple dignity but reminds us that many Louisiana planters lived not in grand mansions but in humbler dwellings.

9. Diane M. Moore, *The Treasures of Avery Island* (Lafayette, 1990).

4

TELLING THE STORY OF OUR LIVES: THE AFRICAN AMERICAN PRESENCE

In his memoir of a visit to a great Louisiana sugar estate, Sherwood Anderson tells the strange tale of how he passed himself off to some of the blacks on the plantation as a man of partial African American ancestry passing for white. One of them approves of his supposed deception and tells him that it is important for him, as a writer, to engage in "telling the story of our lives," that is, the story of African Americans. Anderson, of course, was deceiving not the whites but the blacks, and he does not tell us much of the black story (though in this memoir he does conceive the idea that the blacks really own the southern land in some fundamental, spiritual sense that goes beyond the fact of white legal possession). How well other visitors to Louisiana have told the stories of the African Americans they encountered is an interesting question.

The vast majority of those who came to Louisiana and wrote about it were white, and it might be argued that they have not told the black story fully: that only the rare black visitor-writer like Zora Neale Hurston or Solomon Northup—who, as a free black man kidnapped into slavery, sojourned in Louisiana under conditions both remarkable and appallingly common—could have the insight to tell the story as it should be told; or that only native or long-resident writers and artists, both black and white—Ernest Gaines, Anne Rice, Michael P. Smith, Bruce Brice, Malaika Favorite, Walker Percy—could express the story of African American Louisiana or the tangled interrelation of black and white (and sometimes Native American) that produced jazz and zydeco and gumbo, Mardi Gras and voodoo, cruel misperceptions and curious alignments, casual ignorance and intimate interdependence. (It is, in any event, illuminating to compare Northup's account of Louisiana slave celebrations with that of white commentator Fred Mather,[1] or Hurston's experience with voodoo and that of Charles Dudley Warner, both included later in this volume.)

Be that as it may, the African American presence in Louisiana struck many travelers—struck them as a powerful part of the local essence. If visitors did not understand black culture or black lives, they at least realized that African Americans were a prominent feature of Louisiana's social landscape. If black people were an exotic other, they were hardly an invisible one: they were noted as curiosities, like the alligators, palmettos, and the use of the French language. The German journalist Frederich Ratzel echoed the impressions of many other visitors when he wrote of New Orleans: "The colored people provide the dominant features of street life here. . . . As dealers of fruit, flowers, and confectionery goods, as bootblacks, porters, coachmen . . . they are found everywhere. In fact, they constitute the main body of people in the street. . . ."[2]

Before the Civil War, visitors were fascinated by slavery in particular, for many of them were northern or European (and often of an antislavery turn of mind). Thus Fredrika Bremer felt impelled to see slave markets and auctions, and writers like J. Benwell (who saw slaves being whipped by a black driver even before he stepped off the steamboat in Louisiana) commented upon the treatment of slaves.[3] The great naturalist John James Audubon, who observed more than birds, writes of a runaway slave family he encountered in his be-

1. Fred Mather, *In the Louisiana Lowlands: A Sketch of Plantation Life, Fishing and Camping Just After the Civil War, and Other Tales* (New York, 1900), 86–96.

2. Friedrich Ratzel, *Sketches of Urban and Cultural Life in North America,* trans. and ed. Stewart A. Stehlin (New Brunswick, 1988), 214.

3. Benwell, *An Englishman's Travels in America.*

loved Louisiana woods (an encounter that contrasts slaves' kindness and hospitality with a system that cruelly separated their families).

In New Orleans, visitors found one of the great emporiums of the slave trade, but slavery, of course, was not limited to Louisiana. What was unique in pre–Civil War Louisiana was the existence of a large and well-defined community of "free people of color," whose odd, liminal status intrigued visitors. Many of these "free mulattos"—the descendants of slaves and French or Spanish masters (whose ideas about slavery and race differed from those of Anglo-Saxon Americans)—were rich and well-educated, some slave-holding planters themselves (as Frederick Law Olmsted learns when he travels along Cane River). Yet laws restricted their rights and freedoms, and mores limited their social lives. Perhaps most interesting of all, however, was their ongoing relation with the community of white Creoles, especially through the institution of *plaçage,* the formalized taking of a free woman of color as a mistress by a white man. Visitors were always writing of the *ménages* created by such unions and of the "quadroon balls" to which the men could bring their mistresses or at which liaisons could be effected (and to which distinguished visitors like the Duke of Saxe-Weimar-Eisenach might go, at least for a quick look).

In the years after emancipation, African Americans were still carefully noted by travelers in Louisiana. Captain Willard Glazier, who canoed down the Mississippi in 1881, could not "say enough in praise of the genuine hospitality of the negroes we came in contact with" at such places as Fairview, where he spent the night with an African American family who were engaged in a local religious revival.[4] In more recent years, thoughtful white traveler writers have looked at the larger picture of black-white relations as they have changed. John Steinbeck, whose novels closely examined American society in the 1930s, writes here of his experience in Louisiana in the throes of desegregation in the 1960s, when some local whites resisted with obscene fury the opening of "their" schools to African Americans. Steinbeck ends with the story of an odd meeting with another local white, whom he calls "Monsieur Ci Gît," a meeting that evokes the sadness of the past and comments on the difficulties of the then-present, the difficulties of changing worldview and at-

---

4. Willard Glazier, *Down the Great River; Embracing an Account of the True Source of the Mississippi* (Philadelphia, 1889), 411–12.

titude. If Steinbeck leaves us with a sense of uncertainty about the future, Frederick Turner takes us into the 1990s with his visit to the old quadroon ballroom—now part of a modern hotel—a half-hidden symbol of race in Louisiana. Though his encounter with a modern-day "Creole of color" is a short and casual one, he finds the seeds of a spirit of reconciliation that, if not the final word in telling the story of African Americans in Louisiana, at least gives us a glimpse of a present in which blacks and whites may yet coexist.

The Runaway

John James Audubon

Audubon (1785–1851), the great naturalist and artist, traveled widely to produce his celebrated illustrations. Louisiana was an especially beloved place for him, and he spent a good deal of time in the area around St. Francisville, where the incident described here took place. From *Ornithological Biography* (1834).

Late in the afternoon of one of those sultry days which render the atmosphere of the Louisiana swamps pregnant with baneful effluvia, I directed my course towards my distant home, laden with a pack, consisting of five or six Wood Ibises, and a heavy gun, the weight of which, even in those days, when my natural powers were unimpaired, prevented me from moving with much speed. Reaching the banks of a miry bayou, only a few yards in breadth, but of which I could not ascertain the depth, on account of the muddiness of its waters, I thought it might be dangerous to wade through it with my burden, for which reason, throwing to the opposite side each of my heavy birds in succession, together with my gun, powder-flask, and shot-bag, and drawing my hunting-knife from its scabbard, to defend myself, if need should be, against Alligators, I entered the water, followed by my faithful dog. As I advanced carefully, and slowly, "Plato" swam around me, enjoying the refreshing influence of the liquid element that cooled his fatigued and heated frame. The water deepened, as did the mire of its bed; but with a stroke or two I gained the shore.

Scarcely had I stood erect on the opposite bank, when my dog ran to me, exhibiting marks of terror; his eyes seeming ready to burst from their sockets, and his mouth grinning with the expression of hatred, while his feelings found vent in a stifled growl. Thinking that all this was produced by the scent of a Wolf or Bear, I stooped to take up my gun, when a stentorian voice commanded me to "stand still, or die!" Such a *qui vive* in these woods was as unexpected as it was rare. I instantly raised and cocked my gun; and although I did not yet perceive the individual who had thus issued so peremptory a mandate, I felt determined to combat with him for the free passage of the grounds. Presently a tall, firmly built negro emerged from the bushy underwood, where until that moment he must have been crouched, and in a louder voice repeated his injunction. Had I pressed a trigger, his life would have instantly terminated; but observing that the gun which he aimed at my breast, was a wretched, rusty piece, from which fire could not readily be produced, I felt little fear, and therefore did not judge it necessary to proceed at once to extremities. I laid my gun at my side, tapped my dog quietly, and asked the man what he wanted.

My forbearance, and the stranger's long habit of submission, produced the most powerful effect on his mind. "Master," said he, "I am a runaway; I might perhaps shoot you down; but God forbids it, for I feel just now as if I saw him ready to pass his judgment against me for such a foul deed, and I ask mercy at your hands. For God's sake, do not kill me, master!" "And why," answered I, "have you left your quarters, where certainly you must have fared better than in these unwholesome swamps?" "Master, my story is a short, but a sorrowful one. My camp is close by, and, as I know you cannot reach home this night, if you will follow me there, depend upon *my honor* you shall be safe until the morning, when I will carry your birds, if you choose, to the great road."

The large, intelligent eyes of the negro, the complacency of his manners, and the tones of his voice, I thought invited me to venture; and as I felt that I was at least his equal, while moreover, I had my dog to second me, I answered that I would *follow him*. He observed the emphasis laid on the words, the meaning of which he seemed to understand so thoroughly that, turning to me, he said, "There, master, take my butcher's knife, while I throw away the flint and priming from my gun!" Reader, I felt confounded: this was too much for me: I refused the knife, and told him to keep his piece ready, in case we might accidentally meet a Cougar or a Bear.

Generosity exists everywhere. The greatest monarch acknowledges its impulse, and all around him, from the lowliest menial to the proud nobles that encircle his throne, at times experience that overpowering sentiment. I offered to shake hands with the runaway. "Master," said he, "I beg you thanks," and with this he gave me a squeeze that alike impressed me with the goodness of his heart and his great physical strength. From that moment we proceeded through the woods together. My dog smelt at him several times, but as he heard me speak in my usual tone of voice, he soon left us and rambled around as long as my whistle was unused. As we proceeded, I observed that he was guiding me towards the setting of the sun, and quite contrary to my homeward course. I remarked this to him, when he with the greatest simplicity replied, "Merely for our security."

After trudging along for some distance, and crossing several bayous, at all of which he threw his gun and knife to the opposite bank, and stood still until I had got over, we came to the borders of an immense cane-brake, from which I had, on former occasions, driven and killed several Deer. We entered, as I had frequently done before, now erect, then on "all fours." He regularly led the way, divided here and there the tangled stalks, and, whenever we reached a fallen tree, assisted me in getting over it, with all possible care. I saw that he was a perfect Indian in his knowledge of the woods, for he kept a direct course as precisely as any "Red-skin" I ever travelled with. All of a sudden he emitted a loud shriek, not unlike that of an Owl, which so surprised me, that I once more instantly levelled my gun. "No harm, master, I only give notice to my wife and children I am coming." A tremulous answer of the same nature gently echoed through the tree tops. The runaway's lips separated with an expression of gentleness and delight, when his beautiful set of ivory teeth seemed to smile through the dusk of evening that was thickening around us. "Master," said he, "my wife, though black, is as beautiful to me as the President's wife is to him; she is my queen, and I look on our young ones as so many princes; but you shall see them all, for here they are, thank God."

There, in the heart of the cane-brake, I found a regular camp. A small fire was lighted, and on its embers lay gridling some large slices of venison. A lad nine or ten years old was blowing the ashes from some fine sweet potatoes. Various articles of household furniture were carefully disposed around, and a large pallet of Bear and Deer skins, seemed to be the resting-place of the whole family. The wife raised not her eyes towards mine, and the little ones, three in number, retired into a corner, like so many discomfited Raccoons; but the Runaway, bold, and apparently happy, spoke to them in such cheering words, that at once one and all seemed to regard me as one sent by Providence to relieve them from all their troubles. My clothes were hung up by them to dry, and the negro asked if he might clean and grease my gun, which I permitted him to do, while the wife threw a large piece of Deer's flesh to my dog, which the children were already caressing.

Only think of my situation, reader! Here I was, ten miles at least from home, and four or five from the nearest plantation, in the camp of runaway slaves, and quite at their mercy. My eyes involuntarily followed their motions, but as I thought I perceived in them a strong desire to make me their confidant and friend, I gradually relinquished all suspicions. The venison and potatoes looked quite tempting, and by this time I was in a condition to relish much less savory fare; so, on being humbly asked to divide the viands before us, I partook of as hearty a meal as I had ever done in my life.

Supper over, the fire was completely extinguished, and a small lighted pine-knot placed in a hollowed calabash. Seeing that both the husband and the wife were desirous of communicating something to me, I at once and fearlessly desired them to unburden their minds, when the Runaway told me a tale of which the following is the substance.

About eighteen months before, a planter, residing not very far off, having met with some losses, was obliged to expose his slaves at a public sale. The value of his negroes was well known, and on the appointed day the auctioneer laid them out in small lots, or offered them singly, in the manner which he judged most advantageous to their owner. The Runaway, who was well known as being the most valuable next to his wife, was put up by himself for sale, and brought an immoderate price. For his wife, who came next and alone, eight hundred dollars were bidden and paid down. Then the children were exposed, and, on account of their breed, brought high prices. The rest of the slaves went off at rates corresponding to their qualifications.

The Runaway chanced to be bought by the overseer of the plantation; the wife was bought by an individual residing about a hundred miles off, and the children went to different places along the river. The heart of the husband and father failed him under this dire calamity. For a while he pined in sorrow under his new master; but having marked down in his memory the names of the different persons who had purchased each dear portion of his family he feigned illness, if indeed, he whose affections had been so grievously blasted could be said to feign it, refrained from food for several days, and was little regarded by the overseer, who felt himself disappointed in what he had considered a bargain.

On a stormy night, when the elements raged with all the fury of a hurricane, the poor negro made his escape, and being well acquainted with all the neighboring swamps, at once made directly for the cane-brake in the centre of which I found his camp. A few nights afterwards he gained the abode of his wife, and the very next after their meeting, he led her away. The children, one after another, he succeeded in stealing, until at last the whole of the objects of his love were under his care.

To provide for five individuals was no easy task in those wilds, which after the first notice was given of the wonderful disappearance of this extraordinary family, were daily ransacked by armed planters. Necessity, it is said, will bring the Wolf from the forest. The Runaway seems to have well understood the maxim, for under the cover of night he approached his first master's plantation, where he had ever been treated with the greatest kindness. The house-servants knew him too well not to aid him to the best of their power, and at the approach of each morning he returned to his camp with an ample supply of provisions. One day, while in search of wild fruits, he found a Bear dead before the muzzle of a gun that had been set for the purpose. Both articles he carried to his home. His friends at the plantation managed to supply him with some ammunition, and on damp and cloudy days he first ventured to hunt around his camp. Possessed of courage and activity, he gradually became more careless, and rambled further in search of game. It was on one of his excursions that I met him, and he assured me the noise which I made in passing the bayou had caused him to lose the chance of killing a fine Deer, "although," said he, "my old musket misses fire sadly too often."

The Runaways, after disclosing their secret to me, both rose from their seat, with eyes full of tears. "Good master, for God's sake, do something for us and our children," they sobbed forth with one accord. Their little ones lay sound asleep in the fearlessness of their innocence. Who could have heard such a tale without emotion? I promised them my most cordial assistance. They both sat up that night to watch my repose, and I slept close to their urchins, as if on a bed of the softest down.

Day broke so fair, so pure, and so gladdening that I told them such heavenly appearances were ominous of good, and that I scarcely doubted of obtaining their full pardon. I desired them to take their children with them, and promised to accompany them to the plantation of their first master. They gladly obeyed. My Ibises were hung round their camp, and, as a memento of my having been there, I notched several trees; after which I bade adieu, perhaps for the last time, to that cane-brake. We soon reached the plantation, the owner of which, with whom I was well acquainted, received me with all the generous kindness of a Louisiana planter. Ere an hour had elapsed, the Runaway and his family were looked upon as his own. He afterwards repurchased them from their owners, and treated them with his former kindness; so that they were rendered as happy as slaves generally are in that country, and continued to cherish that attachment to each other which had led to their adventures. Since this event happened, it has, I have been informed, become illegal to separate slave families without their consent.

Slave Markets

FREDRIKA BREMER

Bremer (1801–1865), a talented observer, was a well-connected Swedish traveler who spent about a month in Louisiana on a tour of the United States and the Caribbean. She aimed at giving a view of domestic life and was antislavery in her outlook. From *The Homes of the New World: Impressions of America,* trans. Mary Howitt (1854).

And now, while the weather is bad, and the great world is paying visits and compliments, and polite gentlemen are sunning themselves in the beautiful smiles of elegant ladies, in gas-lighted drawing-rooms, I will, at my ease, converse with you about the occurrences of the last few days, about the slave-market and a slave-auction at which I have been present.

I saw nothing especially repulsive in these places excepting the whole thing; and I can not help feeling a sort of astonishment that such a thing and such scenes are possible in a community calling itself Christian. It seems to me sometimes as if it could not be reality—as if it were a dream.

The great slave-market is held in several houses situated in a particular part of the city. One is soon aware of their neighborhood from the groups of colored men and women, of all shades between black and light yellow, which stand or sit unemployed at the doors. Accompanied by my kind doctor, I visited some of these houses. We saw at one of them the slave-keeper or owner—a kind, good-tempered man, who boasted of the good appearance of his people. The slaves were summoned into a large hall, and arranged in two rows. They were well fed and clothed, but I have heard it said by the people here that they have a very different appearance when they are brought hither, chained together two and two, in long rows, after many days' fatiguing marches.

African American
lady in New Orleans

From George A. Sala,
America Revisited
(London, 1883)

I observed among the men some really athletic figures, with good countenances and remarkably good foreheads, broad and high. The slightest kind
word or joke called forth a sunny smile, full of good humor, on their countenances, and revealed a shining row of beautiful pearl-like teeth. There was
one negro in particular—his price was two thousand dollars—to whom I
took a great fancy, and I said aloud that "I liked that boy, and I was sure we
should be good friends."

"Oh yes, Missis!" with a good, cordial laugh.

Among the women, who were few in number in comparison with the men
(there might be from seventy to eighty of them), there were some very pretty
light mulattoes. A gentleman took one of the prettiest of them by the chin,
and opened her mouth to see the state of her gums and teeth, with no more
ceremony than if she had been a horse. Had I been in her place, I believe that

I should have bitten his thumb, so much did I feel myself irritated by his behavior, in which he evidently, no more than she, found any thing offensive.
Such is the custom of the place.

My inquiries from these poor human chattels confined themselves to the
question of whence they came. Most of them came from Missouri and Kentucky. As I was constantly attended by the slave-keeper, I could not ask for any
biographical information, nor could I, in any case, have been certain that
what I here received was to be relied upon. . . .

On the 31st of December I went with my kind and estimable physician to
witness a slave-auction, which took place not far from my abode. It was held
at one of the small auction-rooms which are found in various parts of New
Orleans. The principal scene of slave-auctions is a splendid rotunda, the magnificent dome of which is worthy to resound with songs of freedom. I once
went there with Mr. Lerner H., to be present at a great slave-auction; but we
arrived too late.

Dr. D. and I entered a large and somewhat cold and dirty hall, on the basement story of a house, and where a great number of people were assembled.
About twenty gentlemenlike men stood in a half circle around a dirty wooden
platform, which for the moment was unoccupied. On each side, by the wall,
stood a number of black men and women, silent and serious. The whole assembly was silent, and it seemed to me as if a heavy gray cloud rested upon it.
One heard through the open door the rain falling heavily in the street. The
gentlemen looked askance at me with a gloomy expression, and probably
wished that they could send me to the North Pole.

Two gentlemen hastily entered; one of them, a tall, stout man, with a gay
and good-tempered aspect, evidently a *bon vivant,* ascended the auction platform. I was told that he was an Englishman, and I can believe it from his
blooming complexion, which was not American. He came apparently from a
good breakfast, and he seemed to be actively employed in swallowing his last
mouthful. He took the auctioneer's hammer in his hand, and addressed the
assembly much as follows:

"The slaves which I have now to sell, for what price I can get, are a few
home-slaves, all the property of one master. This gentleman having given his
bond for a friend who afterward became bankrupt, has been obliged to meet
his responsibilities by parting with his faithful servants. These slaves are thus
sold, not in consequence of any faults which they possess, or for any deficien-
cies. They are all faithful and excellent servants, and nothing but hard neces-

sity would have compelled their master to part with them. They are worth the highest price, and he who purchases them may be sure that he increases the prosperity of his family."

After this he beckoned to a woman among the blacks to come forward, and he gave her his hand to mount upon the platform, where she remained standing beside him. She was a tall, well-grown mulatto, with a handsome but sorrowful countenance, and a remarkably modest, noble demeanor. She bore on her arm a young sleeping child, upon which, during the whole auction ceremonial, she kept her eyes immovably riveted, with her head cast down. She wore a gray dress made to the throat, and a pale yellow handkerchief, checked with brown, was tied round her head.

The auctioneer now began to laud this woman's good qualities, her skill, and her abilities, to the assembly. He praised her character, her good disposition, order, fidelity; her uncommon qualifications for taking care of a house; her piety, her talents, and remarked that the child which she bore at her breast, and which was to be sold with her, also increased her value. After this he shouted with a loud voice, "Now, gentlemen, how much for this very superior woman, this remarkable, &c., &c., and her child?"

He pointed with his outstretched arm and fore-finger from one to another of the gentlemen who stood around, and first one and then another replied to his appeal with a short silent nod, and all the while he continued in this style:

"Do you offer me five hundred dollars? Gentlemen, I am offered five hundred dollars for this superior woman and her child. It is a sum not to be thought of! She, with her child, is worth double that money. Five hundred and fifty, six hundred, six hundred and fifty, six hundred and sixty, six hundred and seventy. My good gentlemen, why do you not at once say seven hundred dollars for this uncommonly superior woman and her child? Seven hundred dollars—it is downright robbery! She would never have been sold at that price if her master had not been so unfortunate," &c., &c.

The hammer fell heavily; the woman and her child were sold for seven hundred dollars to one of those dark silent figures before her. Who he was; whether he was good or bad; whether he would lead her into tolerable or intolerable slavery—of all this, the bought and sold woman and mother knew as little as I did, neither to what part of the world he would take her. And the father of her child—where was he?

With eyes still riveted upon that sleeping child, with dejected but yet submissive mien, the handsome mulatto stepped down from the auction-platform to take her stand beside the wall, but on the opposite side of the room.

Next, a very dark young negro girl stepped upon the platform. She wore a bright yellow handkerchief tied very daintily round her head, so that the two ends stood out like little wings, one on each side. Her figure was remarkably trim and neat, and her eyes glanced round the assembly both boldly and inquiringly.

The auctioneer exalted her merits likewise, and then exclaimed, "How much for this very lively young girl?"

She was soon sold, and, if I recollect rightly, for three hundred and fifty dollars.

After her a young man took his place on the platform. "He was a mulatto, and had a remarkably good countenance, expressive of gentleness and refinement. He had been servant in his former master's family, had been brought up by him, was greatly beloved by him, and deserved to be so—a most excellent young man!"

He sold for six hundred dollars.

After this came an elderly woman, who had also one of those good-natured, excellent countenances so common among the black population, and whose demeanor and general appearance showed that she too had been in the service of a good master, and, having been accustomed to gentle treatment, had become gentle and happy. All these slaves, as well as the young girl, who looked pert rather than good, bore the impression of having been accustomed to an affectionate family life.

And now, what was to be their future fate? How bitterly, if they fell into the hands of the wicked, would they feel the difference between then and now—how horrible would be their lot! The mother in particular, whose whole soul was centered in her child, and who, perhaps, would have soon to see that child sold away, far away from her—what would be her state of mind! . . .

The master had been good, the servants good also, attached, and faithful, and yet they were sold to whoever should buy them—sold like brute beasts!

Fear of a Slave Uprising

CHARLES CÉSAR ROBIN

> Little is known about Robin or why he was in Louisiana in 1804 and 1805, but he left a very full account of the travels he made just as the transition to American rule was taking place.

Some of the plantations at Point Coupee have more than one hundred Negroes, among which there may be only one or two white people with their wives and children. One cannot but experience uneasiness at this great disproportion. Here the white inhabitants are not, as in the city, in a position to aid each other. Dispersed on the plantations, they could not put down an uprising in a single place. They would be slaughtered one after the other. Without effective communication, the uprising would spread without difficulty from plantation to plantation. After such an uprising, the Negroes would have an immense country into which to retire. They could place vast regions of forests, lakes and river between them and these settlements. Going to the northwest they would reach regions inhabited by Indians who have little to do with Europeans whom they fear and dislike. There the Negroes would be safe, mingling with the Indians and enflaming their hatred for the white man and discouraging them from permitting either settlement or trade.

Something like these reflections are felt by the inhabitants of Point Coupee. They live among continual alarms. At night they patrol the countryside and everywhere they spy and listen in on the Negroes. The least suspicious matter, a few more fervent meetings, say, among the Negroes, redoubles their fears and multiplies the nocturnal patrollings and espionage. . . . One can see how gnawing is the anxiety, which far from diminishing with time, is growing, because the colored population is growing faster than that of the whites.

How the Slaves Celebrate Christmas

SOLOMON NORTHUP

Solomon Northup's presence in Louisiana was a singular one; the book he published about his experience is an extraordinary document. Northup (1808–?) was a free black man who was kidnapped into slavery; he spent years laboring on Louisiana plantations before being rescued. His perspective on African Americans is thus a unique one indeed. From *Ten Years a Slave* (1853).

The only respite from constant labor the slave has through the whole year, is during the Christmas holidays. Epps [Northup's master] allowed us three—others allow four, five and six days, according to the measure of their generosity. It is the only time to which they look forward with any interest or pleasure. They are glad when night comes, not only because it brings them a few hours repose, but because it brings them one day nearer Christmas. It is hailed with equal delight by the old and the young; even Uncle Abram ceases to glorify Andrew Jackson, and Patsey forgets her many sorrows, amid the general hilarity of the holidays. It is the time of feasting, and frolicking, and fiddling—the carnival season with the children of bondage. They are the only days when they are allowed a little restricted liberty, and heartily indeed do they enjoy it.

It is the custom for one planter to give a "Christmas supper," inviting the slaves from neighboring plantations to join his own on the occasion; for instance, one year it is given by Epps, the next by Marshall, the next by Hawkins, and so on. Usually from three to five hundred are assembled, coming together on foot, in carts, on horseback, on mules, riding double and triple, sometimes a boy and girls, at others a girl and two boys, and at others again a boy, a girl and an old woman. Uncle Abram astride a mule, with Aunt Phebe and Patsey behind him, trotting towards a Christmas supper, would be no uncommon sight on Bayou Boeuf.

New Orleans street vendor

From Charles Dudley Warner, "New Orleans," *Harper's Monthly*, January, 1887

Then, too, "of all days i' the year," they array themselves in their best attire. The cotton coat has been washed clean, the stump of a tallow candle has been applied to the shoes, and if so fortunate as to possess a rimless or a crownless hat, it is placed jauntily on the head. They are welcomed with equal cordiality, however, if they come bare-headed and barefooted to the feast. As a general thing, the women wear handkerchiefs tied about their heads, but if chance has thrown in their way a fiery red ribbon, or a cast-off bonnet of their mistress' grandmother, it is sure to be worn on such occasions. Red—the deep blood red—is decidedly the favorite color among the enslaved damsels of my acquaintance. If a red ribbon does not encircle the neck, you will be certain to find all the hair of their woolly heads tied up with red strings of one sort or another.

The table is spread in the open air, and loaded with varieties of meat and piles of vegetables. Bacon and corn meal at such times are dispensed with. Sometimes the cooking is performed in the kitchen on the plantation, at others in the shade of wide branching trees. In the latter case, a ditch is dug in the ground, and wood laid in and burned until it is filled with glowing coals, over which chickens, ducks, turkeys, pigs, and not unfrequently the entire body of a wild ox are roasted. They are furnished also with flour, of which biscuits are made, and often with peach and other preserves, with tarts, and every manner and description of pies, except the mince, that being an article of pastry as yet unknown among them. Only the slave who has lived all the years on his scanty allowance of meal and bacon, can appreciate such suppers. White people in great numbers assemble to witness the gastronomical enjoyments.

They seat themselves at the rustic table—the males on one side, the females on the other. The two between whom there may have been an exchange of tenderness, invariably manage to sit opposite; for the omnipresent Cupid disdains not to hurl his arrows into the simple hearts of slaves. Unalloyed and exulting happiness lights up the dark faces of them all. The ivory teeth, contrasting with their black complexions, exhibit two long, white streaks the whole extent of the table. All round the bountiful board a multitude of eyes roll in ecstacy. Giggling and laughter and the clattering of cutlery and crockery succeed. Cuffee's elbow hunches his neighbor's side, impelled by an involuntary impulse of delight; Nelly shakes her finger at Sambo and laughs, she knows not why, and so the fun and merriment flow on.

When the viands have disappeared, and the hungry maws of the children of toil are satisfied, then, next in the order of amusement, is the Christmas dance. . . .

On that particular Christmas I have now in my mind, a description whereof will serve as a description of the day generally, Miss Lively and Mr. Sam, the first belonging to Stewart, the latter to Roberts, started the ball. It was well known that Sam cherished an ardent passion for Lively, as also did one of Marshall's and another of Carey's boys; for Lively was lively indeed, and a heart-breaking coquette withal. It was a victory for Sam Roberts, when, rising from the repast, she gave him her hand for the first "figure" in preference to either of his rivals. They were somewhat crestfallen, and shaking their heads angrily, rather intimated they would like to pitch into Mr. Sam and hurt him badly. But not an emotion of wrath ruffled the placid bosom of Samuel as his legs flew like drum-sticks down the outside and up the middle, by the side of his bewitching partner. The whole company cheered them vociferously, and, excited with the applause, they continued "tearing down" after all the others had become exhausted and halted a moment to recover breath. But Sam's superhuman exertions overcame him finally, leaving Lively alone, yet whirling like a top. Thereupon one of Sam's rivals, Pete Marshall, dashed in, and, with might and main, leaped and shuffled and threw himself into every conceivable shape, as if determined to show Miss Lively and all the world that Sam Roberts was of no account.

Pete's affection, however, was greater than his discretion. Such violent exercise took the breath out of him directly, and he dropped like an empty bag. Then was the time for Harry Carey to try his hand; but Lively also soon outwinded him, amidst hurrahs and shouts, fully sustaining her well-earned reputation of being the "fastest gal" on the bayou.

One "set" off another takes its place, he or she remaining on the floor longest receiving the most uproarious commendation, and so the dancing continues until broad daylight. It does not cease with the sound of the fiddle, but in that case they set up a music peculiar to themselves. This is called "patting," accompanied with one of those unmeaning songs, composed rather for its adaptation to a certain tune or a measure, than for the purpose of expressing any distinct idea. The patting is performed by striking the hands on the knees, then striking the hands together, then striking the right shoulder with one hand, the left with the other—all the while keeping time with the feet, and singing, perhaps, this song:

> "Harper's creek and roarin' ribber,
> Thar, my dear, we'll live forebber;
> Den we'll go to de Ingin Nation,
> All I want in dis creation,
> Is pretty little wife and big plantation.

Chorus. Up dat oak and down dat ribber,
　　　　Two overseers and one little nigger"

Or, if these words are not adapted to the tune called for, it may be that "Old Hog Eye" *is*—a rather solemn and startling specimen of versification, not, however, to be appreciated unless heard at the South. It runneth as follows:

> "Who's been here since I've been gone?
> Pretty little gal wid a josey on.
> 　　Hog eye!
> 　　Old Hog Eye.
> 　　And Hosey too!
> Never see de like since I was born,
> Here comes a little gal wid a josey on
> 　　Hog Eye!
> 　　Old Hog Eye!
> 　　And Hosey too!"

Or, maybe the following, perhaps, equally nonsensical, but full of melody, nevertheless, as it flows from the negro's mouth:

> "Ebo Dick and Jurdan's Jo,
> Them two niggers stole my yo'.
> *Chorus.*　Hop Jim along,
> 　　　Walk Jim along,
> 　　　Talk Jim along," &c.
> Old black Dan, as black as tar,
> He dam glad he was not dar.
> 　　Hop Jim along," &c.

During the remaining holidays succeeding Christmas, they are provided with passes, and permitted to go where they please within a limited distance, or they may remain and labor on the plantation, in which case they are paid for it. It is very rarely, however, that the latter alternative is accepted. They may be seen at these times hurrying in all directions, as happy looking mortals as can be found on the face of the earth. They are different beings from what they are in the field; the temporary relaxation, the brief deliverance from fear, and from the lash, producing an entire metamorphosis in their appearance and demeanor. In visiting, riding, renewing old friendships, or, perchance, reviving some old attachment or pursuing whatever pleasure may suggest itself, the time is occupied. Such is "southern life as it is," three days in the year, as I found it—the other three hundred and sixty-two being days of weariness, and fear, and suffering, and unremitting labor.

The Cheerleaders

JOHN STEINBECK

Nobel Prize–winner Steinbeck (1902–1968) felt that, though he had written much about America, he had perhaps lost touch with its realities. So, late in his career, he set out on a cross-country journey of rediscovery, driving a pick-up fitted out like a camper (dubbed Rocinante after Don Quixote's horse) and accompanied only by his poodle, Charley. This selection is drawn from the popular travel book that came out of that trip, *Travels with Charley in Search of America,* and recounts his observation of the 1960 school desegregation crisis he made a special point to witness.

While I was still in Texas, late in 1960, the incident most reported and pictured in the newspapers was the matriculation of a couple of tiny Negro children in a New Orleans school. Behind these small dark mites were the law's majesty and the law's power to enforce—both the scales and the sword were allied with the infants—while against them were three hundred years of fear and terror of change in a changing world. I had seen photographs in the papers every day and motion pictures on the television screen. What made the newsmen love the story was a group of stout middle-aged women who, by some curious definition of the word "mother," gathered every day to scream invectives at children. Further, a small group of them had become so expert that they were known as the Cheerleaders, and a crowd gathered every day to enjoy and to applaud their performance.

This strange drama seemed so improbable that I felt I had to see it. It had the same draw as a five-legged calf or a two-headed foetus at a sideshow, a distortion of normal life we have always found so interesting that we will pay to see it, perhaps to prove to ourselves that we have the proper number of legs or heads. In the New Orleans show, I felt all the amusement of the improbable abnormal, but also a kind of horror that it could be so.

At this time the winter which had been following my track ever since I left home suddenly struck with a black norther. It brought ice and freezing sleet and sheeted the highways with dark ice. . . .

Now we stopped dawdling and laid our wheels to the road and went. We could not go fast because of the ice, but we drove relentlessly, hardly glancing at the passing of Texas beside us. . . .

And then I was in Louisiana, with Lake Charles away to the side in the dark, but my lights glittered on ice and glinted on diamond frost, and those people who forever trudge the roads at night were mounded over with cloth against the cold. I dogged it on through Lafayette and Morgan City and came in the early dawn to Houma, which is pronounced Homer and is in my memory one of the pleasantest places in the world. There lives my old friend Doctor St. Martin, a gentle, learned man, a Cajun who has lifted babies and cured colic among the shell-heap Cajuns for miles around.[5] I guess he knows more about Cajuns than anyone living, but I remembered with longing other gifts of Doctor St. Martin. He makes the best and most subtle martini in the world by a process approximating magic. The only part of his formula I know is that he uses distilled water for his ice and distills it himself to be sure. I have eaten black duck at his table—two St. Martin martinis and a brace of black duck with a burgundy delivered from the bottle as a baby might be delivered, and this in a darkened house where the shades have been closed at dawn and the cool night air preserved. At that table with its silver soft and dull, shining as pewter, I remember the raised glass of the grape's holy blood, the stem caressed by the doctor's strong artist fingers, and even now I can hear the sweet little health and welcome in the singing language of Acadia which once was French and now is itself. This picture filled my frosty windshield, and if there had been traffic would have made me a dangerous driver. But it was pale yellow frozen dawn in Houma and I knew that if I stopped to pay my respects, my will and my determination would drift away on the particular lotus St. Mar-

5. Steinbeck is probably referring to Thad St. Martin, author of *Madame Toussaint's Wedding Day* (New Orleans, 1936).

tin purveys and we would be speaking of timeless matters when the evening came, and another evening. And so I only bowed in the direction of my friend and scudded on toward New Orleans, for I wanted to catch a show of the Cheerleaders.

Even I know better than to drive a car near trouble, particularly Rocinante, with New York license plates. Only yesterday a reporter had been beaten and his camera smashed, for even convinced voters are reluctant to have their moment of history recorded and preserved.

So, well on the edge of town I drove into a parking lot. The attendant came to my window. "Man, oh man, I thought you had a nigger in there. Man, oh man, it's a dog. I see that big old black face and I think it's a big old nigger."

"His face is blue-gray when he's clean," I said coldly.

"Well I see some blue-gray niggers and they wasn't clean. New York, eh?"

It seemed to me a chill like the morning air came into his voice. "Just driving through," I said. "I want to park for a couple of hours. Think you can get me a taxi?"

"Tell you what I bet. I bet you're going to see the Cheerleaders."

"That's right."

"Well, I hope you're not one of those trouble-makers or reporters."

"I just want to see it."

"Man, oh man, you going to see something. Ain't those Cheerleaders something? Man, oh, man, you never heard nothing like it when they get going."

I locked Charley in Rocinante's house after giving the attendant a tour of the premises, a drink of whisky, and a dollar. "Be kind of careful about opening the door when I'm away," I said. "Charley takes his job pretty seriously. You might lose a hand." This was an outrageous lie, of course, but the man said, "Yes, sir. You don't catch me fooling around with no strange dog."

The taxi driver, a sallow, yellowish man, shriveled like a chickpea with the cold, said, "I wouldn't take you more than a couple of blocks near. I don't go to have my cab wrecked."

"Is it that bad?"

"It ain't is it. It's can it get. And it can get that bad."

"When do they get going?"

He looked at his watch. "Except it's cold, they been coming in since dawn. It's quarter to. You won't miss nothing except it's cold."

I had camouflaged myself in an old blue jacket and my British navy cap on the supposition that in a seaport no one ever looks at a sailor any more than a waiter is inspected in a restaurant. In his natural haunts a sailor has no face and certainly no plans beyond getting drunk and maybe in jail for fighting. . . .

"Where you from?" the driver asked with a complete lack of interest.

"Liverpool."

"Limey, huh? Well, you'll be all right. It's the goddamn New York Jews cause all the trouble."

I found myself with a British inflection and by no means one of Liverpool. "Jews—what? How do they cause trouble?"

"Why, hell, mister. We know how to take care of this. Everybody's happy and getting along fine. Why I *like* niggers. And them goddamn New York Jews come in and stir the niggers up. They just stay in New York there wouldn't be no trouble. Ought to take them out."

"You mean lynch them?"

"I don't mean nothing else, mister."

He let me out and I started to walk away. "Don't try to get too close, mister," he called after me. "Just you enjoy it but don't mix in."

"Thanks," I said, and killed the "awfully" that came to my tongue.

As I walked toward the school I was in a stream of people all white and all going in my direction. They walked intently like people going to a fire after it has been burning for some time. They beat their hands against their hips or hugged them under coats, and many men had scarves under their hats and covering their ears.

Across the street from the school the police had set up wooden barriers to keep the crowd back, and they paraded back and forth, ignoring the jokes called to them. The front of the school was deserted but along the curb United States marshals were spaced, not in uniform but wearing armbands to identify them. Their guns bulged decently under their coats but their eyes darted about nervously, inspecting faces. It seemed to me that they inspected me to see if I was a regular, and then abandoned me as unimportant.

It was apparent where the Cheerleaders were, because people shoved forward to try to get near them. They had a favored place at the barricade directly across from the school entrance, and in that area a concentration of police stamped their feet and slapped their hands together in unaccustomed gloves.

Suddenly I was pushed violently and a cry went up: "Here she comes. Let her through. . . . Come on, move back. Let her through. Where you been? You're late for school. Where you been, Nellie?"

The name was not Nellie. I forget what it was. But she shoved through the dense crowd quite near enough to me so that I could see her coat of imitation fleece and her gold earrings. She was not tall, but her body was ample and full-busted. I judge she was about fifty. She was heavily powdered, which made the line of her double chin look very dark.

She wore a ferocious smile and pushed her way through the milling people, holding a fistful of clippings high in her hand to keep them from being crushed. Since it was her left hand I looked particularly for a wedding ring, and saw that there was none. I slipped in behind her to get carried along by her wave, but the crush was dense and I was given a warning too. "Watch it, sailor, everybody wants to hear."

Nellie was received with shouts of greeting. I don't know how many Cheerleaders there were. There was no fixed line between the Cheerleaders and the crowd behind them. What I could see was that a group was passing newspaper clippings back and forth and reading them aloud with little squeals of delight.

Now the crowd grew restless, as an audience does when the clock goes past curtain time. Men all around me looked at their watches. I looked at mine. It was three minutes to nine.

The show opened on time. Sound of sirens. Motorcycle cops. Then two big black cars filled with big men in blond felt hats pulled up in front of the school. The crowd seemed to hold its breath. Four big marshals got out of each car and from somewhere in the automobiles they extracted the littlest Negro girl you ever saw, dressed in shining starchy white, with new white shoes on feet so little they were almost round. Her face and little legs were very black against the white.

The big marshals stood her on the curb and a jangle of jeering shrieks went up from behind the barricades. The little girl did not look at the howling crowd but from the side the whites of her eyes showed like those of a frightened fawn. The men turned her around like a doll, and then the strange procession moved up the broad walk toward the school, and the child was even more a mite because the men were so big. Then the girl made a curious hop, and I think I know what it was. I think in her whole life she had not gone ten steps without skipping, but now in the middle of her first skip the weight bore her down and her little round feet took measured, reluctant steps between the tall guards. Slowly they climbed the steps and entered the school.

The papers had printed that the jibes and jeers were cruel and sometimes obscene, and so they were, but this was not the big show. The crowd was waiting for the white man who dared to bring his white child to school. And here he came along the guarded walk, a tall man dressed in light gray, leading his frightened child by the hand. His body was tensed as a strong leaf spring drawn to the breaking strain; his face was grave and gray, and his eyes were on the ground immediately ahead of him. The muscles of his cheeks stood out from clenched jaws, a man afraid who by his will held his fears in check as a great rider directs a panicked horse.

A shrill, grating voice rang out. The yelling was not in chorus. Each took a turn and at the end of each the crowd broke into howls and roars and whistles of applause. This is what they had come to see and hear.

No newspaper had printed the words these women shouted. It was indicated that they were indelicate, some even said obscene. On television the sound track was made to blur or had crowd noises cut in to cover. But now I heard the words, bestial and filthy and degenerate. In a long and unprotected life I have seen and heard the vomitings of demoniac humans before. Why then did these screams fill me with a shocked and sickened horror?

The words written down are dirty, carefully and selectedly filthy. But there was something far worse here than dirt, a kind of frightening witches' Sabbath. Here was no spontaneous cry of anger, of insane rage.

Perhaps that is what made me sick with weary nausea. Here was no principle good or bad, no direction. These blowzy women with their little hats and their clippings hungered for attention. They wanted to be admired. They simpered in happy, almost innocent triumph when they were applauded. Theirs was the demented cruelty of egocentric children, and somehow this made their insensate beastliness much more heartbreaking. These were not mothers, not even women. They were crazy actors playing to a crazy audience.

The crowd behind the barrier roared and cheered and pounded one another with joy. The nervous strolling police watched for any break over the barrier. Their lips were tight but a few of them smiled and quickly unsmiled. Across the street the U.S. marshals stood unmoving. The gray-clothed man's legs had speeded for a second, but he reined them down with his will and walked them up the school pavement.

The crowd quieted and the next cheer lady had her turn. Her voice was the bellow of a bull, a deep and powerful shout with flat edges like a circus barker's voice. There is no need to set down her words. The pattern was the same; only the rhythm and tonal quality were different. Anyone who has been near the theater would know that these speeches were not spontaneous. They were tried and memorized and carefully rehearsed. This was theater. I watched the intent faces of the listening crowd and they were the faces of an audience. When there was applause, it was for a performer.

My body churned with weary nausea, but I could not let an illness blind me after I had come so far to look and to hear. And suddenly I knew something was wrong and distorted and out of drawing. I knew New Orleans, I have over the years had many friends there, thoughtful, gentle people, with a tradition of kindness and courtesy. I remembered Lyle Saxon, a huge man of soft laughter.[6] How many days I have spent with Roark Bradford, who took Louisiana sounds and sights and created God and the Green Pastures to which He leadeth us.[7] I looked in the crowd for such faces of such people and they were not there. I've seen this kind bellow for blood at a prize fight, have orgasms when a man is gored in the bull ring, stare with vicarious lust at a highway accident, stand patiently in line for the privilege of watching any pain or any agony. But where were the others—the ones who would be proud they were of a species with the gray man—the ones whose arms would ache to gather up the small, scared black mite?

I don't know where they were. Perhaps they felt as helpless as I did, but they left New Orleans misrepresented to the world. The crowd, no doubt, rushed home to see themselves on television, and what they saw went out all over the world, unchallenged by the other things I know are there. . . .

The show was over and the river of us began to move away. Second show would be when school closing bell rang and the little black face had to look out at her accusers again. I was in New Orleans of the great restaurants. I know them all and most of them know me. And I could no more have gone to

6. See Chapters 1 and 10 for writing by Saxon and information concerning him.

7. Roark Bradford (1896–1948) wrote *Ol' Man Adam an' His Children*, a popular book that was adapted by Marc Connelly for his Pulitzer Prize–winning play *The Green Pastures*. Though Steinbeck is not a writer particularly associated with Louisiana, he did spend some time in the state; he was married to his second wife, Gwyn, at Lyle Saxon's house on Madison Street in 1943.

Gallatoir's for an omelet and champagne than I could have danced on a grave. Even setting this down on paper has raised the weary, hopeless nausea in me again. It is not written to amuse. It does not amuse me.

I bought a poor-boy sandwich and got out of town. Not too far along I found a pleasant resting place where I could sit and munch and contemplate and stare out over the stately brown, slow-moving Father of Waters as my spirit required. Charley did not wander about but sat and pressed his shoulder against my knee, and he does that only when I am ill, so I suppose I was ill with a kind of sorrow.

I lost track of time, but a while after the sun had passed top a man came walking and we exchanged good afternoons. He was a neatly dressed man well along in years, with a Greco face and fine wind-lifted white hair and a clipped white mustache. I asked him to join me, and when he accepted I went into my house and set coffee to cooking and, remembering how Roark Bradford liked it, I doubled the dosage, two heaping tablespoons of coffee to each cup and two heaping for the pot. I cracked an egg and cupped out the yolk and dropped white and shells into the pot, for I know nothing that polishes coffee and makes it shine like that. The air was still very cold and a cold night was coming, so that the brew, rising from cold water to a rolling boil, gave the good smell that competes successfully with other good smells.

My guest was satisfied, and he warmed his hands against the plastic cup. "By your license, you're a stranger here," he said. "How do you come to know about coffee?"

"I learned on Bourbon Street from giants in the earth," I said. "But they would have asked the bean of a darker roast and they would have liked a little chicory for bite."

"You do know," he said. "You're not a stranger after all. And can you make diablo?"

"For parties, yes. You come from here?"

"More generations than I can prove beyond doubt, except classified under *ci gît* in St. Louis."[8]

"I see. You're of that breed. I'm glad you stopped by. I used to know St. Louis, even collected epitaphs." . . .

" . . . Are you traveling for pleasure?"

---

8. *Ci-gît* ("here lies") is a standard phrase on Louisiana French tombstones; St. Louis is a cemetery in New Orleans.

"I was until today. I saw the Cheerleaders."

"Oh, yes, I see," he said, and a weight and a darkness fell on him.

"What's going to happen?"

"I don't know. I just don't know. I don't dare think about it. Why do I have to think about it? Let the others take care of it."

"Can you see an end?"

"Oh, certainly an end. It's the means—it's the means. But you're from the North. This isn't your problem."

"I guess it's everybody's problem. It isn't local. Would you have another cup of coffee and talk to me about it? I don't have a position. I mean I want to hear."

"There's nothing to learn," he said. "It seems to change its face with who you are and where you've been and how you feel—not think, but feel. You didn't like what you saw?"

"Would you?"

"Maybe less than you because I know all of its aching past and some of its stinking future. That's an ugly word, sir, but there's no other."

"The Negroes want to be people. Are you against that?"

"Bless you, no, sir. But to get to be people they must fight those who are satisfied to be people."

"You mean the Negroes won't be satisfied with any gain?"

"Are you? Is anyone you know?"

"Would you be content to let them be people?"

"Content enough, but I wouldn't understand it. I've got too many *ci gîts* here. How can I tell you? Well, suppose your dog here, he looks a very intelligent dog—"

"He is."

"Well, suppose he could talk and stand on his hind legs. Maybe he could do very well in every way. Perhaps you could invite him to dinner, but could you think of him as people?"

"Do you mean, how would I like my sister to marry him?"

He laughed. "I'm only telling you how hard it is to change a feeling about things. And will you believe that it will be just as hard for Negroes to change their feeling about us as it is for us to change about them? This isn't new. It's been going on a long time."

"Anyway, the subject skims the joy off a pan of conversation."

"That it does, sir. I think I'm what you might call an enlightened Southerner mistaking an insult for a compliment. As such a new-born hybrid, I know what will happen over the ages. It's starting now in Africa and in Asia."

"You mean absorption—the Negroes will disappear?"

"If they outnumber us, we will disappear, or more likely both will disappear into something new."

"And meanwhile?"

"It's the meanwhile frightens me, sir. The ancients placed love and war in the hands of closely related gods. That was no accident. That, sir, was a profound knowledge of man."

"You reason well."

"The ones you saw today do not reason at all. They're the ones who may alert the god."

"Then you do think it can't happen in peace?"

"I don't know," he cried. "I guess that's the worst. I just don't know. Sometimes I long to assume my rightful title Ci Gît."

"I wish you would ride along with me. Are you on the move?"

"No. I have a little place just off there below that grove. I spend a lot of time there, mostly reading—old things—mostly looking at—old things. It's my intentional method of avoiding the issue because I'm afraid of it."

"I guess we all do some of that."

He smiled. "I have an old Negro couple as old as I am to take care of me. And sometimes in the evening we forget. They forget to envy me and I forget they might, and we are just three pleasant ... things living together and smelling the flowers."

"Things," I repeated. "That's interesting—not man and beast, not black and white, but pleasant things. My wife told me of an old old man who said, 'I remember a time when Negroes had no souls. It was much better and easier then. Now it's confusing.'"

"I don't remember, but it must be so. It is my guess that we can cut and divide our inherited guilt like a birthday cake," he said, and save for the mustache he looked like the Greco San Pablo who holds the closed book in his hands. "Surely my ancestors had slaves, but it is possible that yours caught them and sold them to us."

"I have a puritan strain that might well have done so."

"If by force you make a creature live and work like a beast, you must think of him as a beast, else empathy would drive you mad. Once you have classified him in your mind, your feelings are safe." He stared at the river, and the breeze stirred his hair like white smoke. "And if your heart has human vestiges of courage and anger, which in a man are virtues, then you have fear of a dangerous beast, and since your heart has intelligence and inventiveness and the ability to conceal them, you live with terror. Then you must crush his manlike tendencies and make of him the docile beast you want. And if you can teach your child from the beginning about the beast, he will not share your bewilderment."

"I've been told the good old-time Negro sang and danced and was content."

"He also ran away. The fugitive laws suggest how often."

"You're not what the North thinks of as a Southerner."

"Perhaps not. But I'm not alone." He stood up and dusted his trousers with his fingers. "No—not alone. I'll go along to my pleasant things now."

"I have not asked your name, sir, nor offered mine."

"Ci Gît," he said. "Monsieur Ci Gît—a big family, a common name."

When he went away I felt a sweetness like music, if music could pleasure the skin with a little chill.

A Certain Meeting South

SHERWOOD ANDERSON

Celebrated author Sherwood Anderson (1876–1941)
is most associated with the Middle West, but he began
spending winters in New Orleans in 1922.

I was in a rich man's house. I was a guest there and they were being very nice to me.

It was a great country house in the South and there were many Negro servants.

Everything was beautifully arranged, very formal. The people of the house did not meet at breakfast. There were several other guests and everyone breakfasted in his room.

They met later in the day. They walked, they rode horses, played games, drank together.

In the evening, often, there was music. The master of the house arranged to have some of the Negroes come in the evening to sing.

They did not come into the house. There was a wide veranda on which the whites sat while the Negro men and women stood at some distance, half hidden among trees. . . .

The Negro people were under trees, in the darkness. They sang Negro spirituals. They sang Negro work songs.

The singing was very beautiful. The voices seemed to run away into the dark distance, under the trees, across distant fields. The voices ran away and came back. Their voices were along the ground, in the grass. They were in the treetops.

Voices called to each other. There was one high clear Negro woman's voice that seemed to go up to the stars in the blue black Southern sky.

It did something to me. It seemed to me that, for the first time, I saw something clearly. I sat among the other guests in the rich man's house thinking what were to me new thoughts. My thoughts concerned the land on which stood the great house in which I was a guest.

The house was in the so-called Sugar Bowl in the lower delta country of the Mississippi.

There were many acres of sugar cane fields stretched away from the river and the door. In the distance there were forests—in a low swampy land—forests of cypress and gum trees.

It was a dark land, a strange rich land. The Negroes had been there a long time. The Negroes singing that night, standing in the darkness in a grove of live oaks hung with ghostly moss, had been born on the land.

From childhood they had worked in the fields. Their ancestors had been slaves on the land. It was under their finger nails, in the creases of their flesh, in their crinkly hair, in their eyebrows.

As I sat that night listening to the singing Negroes something came clear to me. It concerned ownership.

How could a man really own land, own trees, own grass, own flowing water of rivers? The land had been there so long.

There was a rich man who had money and what a strange thing money. The man had been shrewd. He had, no doubt, a certain talent, the talent of acquisitiveness. There had been in him an instinct that had enabled him to see certain opportunities. At a certain critical moment he had bought certain stocks.

Then, at just the right moment, he had sold them and bought other stocks.

Stocks were like money itself. They were pieces of paper with words printed upon them.

In the case of money, the picture of some man, a president.

Oh, the power of words.

"I promise to pay," etc., etc.

You could burn the pieces of paper and they were gone.

The land remained. The trees, the grass, the flowing brown water of the river remained.

Burn the trees and they would grow again.

The land was there before man came. It would be there when there were no men left.

But there were certain people, the poor whites of the South, the Negroes,

Musicians near
New Iberia, 1938,
by Russell Lee

Photograph courtesy
Library of Congress

slaves and free, farmers of my own native Middle West who worked their own fields, who were related to the land.

There had been a marriage, man and the land.

The land was in them as a lover is in his sweetheart in the embrace of love.

So, as far as there is ownership, it is their land as a man's wife is his wife.

The thought set down here, coming to me as it did in a certain house in the South on a certain night, was no doubt not a new thought in the world but such thoughts mean nothing to a man when set down in books, when expounded by some speaker, some political revolutionist. The thought was in the throat of the Negro singers, it was in the trees under which they stood in the Southern night. It explained so much of the South—the landed aristocrats, the predatory Whites, the secret hatreds, the insistence upon white supremacy, the secret jealousy of something the Negroes had, something that had come into them from the land as it sifted through their black fingers. I was suddenly quite sure that the man sitting beside me that night, my host, the rich man, deep down within himself would have given all his wealth to have been, not as he was, the overlord, but one of the brown men, a man closer to the land, living simply as an animal lives.

He had gone about seeking something he did not have. What did all of his buying of pictures, his collecting of objects of art, of first editions mean?

It meant obviously an attempt to buy his way out of one world into another, to, at any rate, get a little closer.

He had even said something of the sort to me. . . .

However the rich man had been patient with me. He had invited me to be his guest. This was in the winter and I was hungry for the South and the sun. I had been given a separate house, at the foot of a path lined with bushes. It was by a little quiet bayou.

I slept there and, as it was winter, there were no mosquitoes.

In the early morning an old Negro woman, very black, a huge old woman with big hips, came to me. The door and the windows of my little one-room house were open and there was a sharp tinge of frost in the air.

The old woman had brought me a pot of hot black coffee. She built a wood fire in the fireplace.

I was in bed, drinking my coffee. I began a conversation with the old woman. She had lived as a child in the West Indies. A kind of friendship sprang up between her and me. I lied to her, told her I had Negro blood in my veins. It was a trick I had got from my father.

If you are with a Catholic, become, for the time a Catholic, if with a Swede, a Swede, if with an Irishman, Irish. There was, I told the old black woman, a grandfather who having much white blood had gone North and had gone white. The old woman was not to tell my secret.

"You see I am here, a guest. You come here and wait on me. I can go up to the big house, can dine there. By law, by all the social customs of the South, I am really like you, a Negro."

There was something established between me and the Negro servants about the rich white man's house. The servants were always coming secretly to my little house. I was presumed to be at work there, creating masterpieces. The rich man and his other guests were impressed. I must not be disturbed.

I was getting many stories out of the lives of the Negroes on the place. It pleased them that I was, as they thought, cheating the whites. I was gathering up all the servants' tales.

There was one young Negro woman, very straight and strong of body, who came often secretly to my cabin. She had stolen a bottle of champagne which she brought to me. Sometimes she came late at night when I was in bed. She had brought some delicacy from the kitchen.

She came in and sat on the edge of my bed. She had heard the white guests speaking of me and my work.

She was impressed.

"So you are really one of us. They look up to you. You should be telling the story of our lives."

There was one of the guests, a young white man who had married a rich woman much older than himself. He was after the young Negro woman.

He was giving her money.

He had given her a ten dollar bill. Once when she went into his bedroom he came in there.

She had gone in the late morning to make up the bed, to arrange the room, and he had been watching for her coming.

He was somewhere about the house or he was sitting with the other guests on a terrace before the house and when she went upstairs, to arrange the rooms, she made a point of letting him see her.

She said he always sat in the late morning where he could see her going up the stairway. He was a great horseman. He had on riding breeches. There was always something he had left in his room, so he followed her up.

She said, "I let him kiss me. I let him hold me in his arms. I keep promising him I will meet him outdoors at night.

"I am not married but I tell him I am. I tell him my husband is watching me.

"I pretend I am crazy about him. When he is holding me in his arms I cry a little and when I do he always gives me money.

"He has given me several presents. He thinks he is going to get me but I am only fooling with him."

The young Negro woman was sitting on the edge of my bed. She laughed, the laugh of a Negro woman. I was smoking cigarettes and she asked for one. She sat smoking with me. She told me little human stories of the rich man, his wife, the other white guests. One night she came at two in the morning. It was her woman's time. She had become the daughter of the moon. She explained that it was always a terrible time for her.

She was in great pain. She said that the great pain lasted but a few hours, but that, at such times, she could not bear to be alone.

"I want someone to be with me and hold my hand and I do not want a woman. I want a man."

I put her into my bed and, having put on my bathrobe, sat beside her holding her hand.

She kept groaning. Tears ran down her cheeks. It was a cold clear moonlit night and the moonlight came in through the open door. I could feel with her the spasms of pain. When they came her hand gripped my hand so that the fingers ached. It was like a childbirth. When it had passed she got up and I returned to my bed. She had gone out of my little house but presently returned. She had been with me nearly three hours and soon day would come. I felt curiously close to her.

She came running into the cabin and kissed me on the cheek. I was smoking a cigarette.

"I guess it is better for you to stay white. If you took one of us in, for example, it would spoil it all.

"It is better for you to stay white. You get all the best of it by being white."

For a moment she stood thus beside my bed, in the moonlight. She was of a light brown color and the moonlight, coming through the door, made highlights on her brown skin. She stood thus, in silence, for a time, looking down at me. To her it was inconceivable that a white man, a real white, could tell a lie, claiming Negro blood. She believed my lie. She wanted me to go on fooling the whites. She went slowly out of my cabin and while I remained a guest in that place she did not return to me.

Children of Mulattoe Family Returning Home After an Afternoon of Fishing in Cane River, 1940, by Marion Post Wolcott

Free People of Color

FREDERICK LAW OLMSTED

From *A Journey in the Seaboard Slave States* (1856). Here Olmsted has been traveling by the steamboat *Dalmau*.

There are also, in the vicinity, a large number of free-colored planters. In going down Cane River, the Dalmau called at several of their plantations, to take on cotton, and the captain told me that in fifteen miles of a well-settled and cultivated country, on the bank of the river, beginning ten miles below Nachitoches, he did not know but one pure-blooded white man. The plantations appeared no way different from the generality of those of the white Creoles; and on some of them were large, handsome, and comfortable houses. These free-colored people are all descended from the progeny of old French or Spanish planters, and their negro slaves. Such a progeny, born before Louisiana was annexed to the United States, and the descendants of it, are entitled to freedom. . . .

The driver of the stage from Nachitoches towards Alexandria, described them as being rather distant and reserved towards white people with whom they were not well acquainted; but said, that he had often staid over night at their houses, and knew them intimately, and he was nowhere else so well treated, and he never saw more gentleman-like people. He appeared to have been especially impressed by the domestic and social happiness he had witnessed in their houses. . . .

The barber of the Dalmau was a handsome light coloured young man. While he was once dressing my hair he said to me:

"You are an Eastern man, I think, sir."

"Yes: how did you know?"

"There's something in the appearance of an Eastern man that I generally know him by."

"Couldn't you tell me what it is?"

"Well, sir, there's more refinement in an Eastern man, both in his look and his manner, than in a Southerner, in general—Are you from Massachusetts or New York, sir?"

"New York."

"I lived in New York myself, one year: at West Troy."

"Ah—what were you doing there?"

"I was at school, sir."

Perceiving from this that he was a free-man, I asked if he preferred living at the South to the North. He said he didn't like the Northern winter, and he was born and bred in Louisiana, and felt more at home there. Finally he said his best reason was, that a colored man could make more money in Louisiana than at the North. There were no white barbers there, and a barber was paid nearly four times as much for his work as he was at the North.

"I presume you have no family?"

"No, sir."

"If you should marry, would you not find it more agreeable to live at the North?"

"I'd never marry in Louisiana, sir."

"Why not?"

"Because I'd never be married to any but a virtuous woman, and there are no virtuous women among the colored people here!"

"What do you mean?"

"There are very few, sir."

"What, among the free?"

"Very few, sir. There are some very rich colored people, planters, some of them are worth four or five hundred thousand dollars. Among them I suppose there are virtuous women; but they are very few. You see, sir, it's no disgrace to a colored girl to *plaçer*.[9] It's considered hardly anything different from marrying."

I asked if he knew any of the colored planters on Cane River. He did and had relatives among them. He thought there were virtuous girls there. They were rich, too, some of them. He said they rather avoided white people, because they could not associate pleasantly with them. They were uncertain of their position with them, and were afraid, if they were not reserved, they would be thought to be taking liberties, and would be subject to insults,

9. That is, enter into a formalized sexual arrangement with a white man.

which they could not very well resent. Yet there were some white people that they knew well, with whom they associated a good deal, and pleasantly. White men, sometimes, married a rich colored girl; but he never knew a colored man to marry a white girl. (I subsequently heard of one such case.) He said that colored people could associate with whites much more easily and comfortably at the South than the North; this was one reason he preferred to live at the South. He was kept at a greater distance from white people, and more insulted, on account of his color, at the North than in Louisiana. He thought the colored people at Cane River were thriving and happy. . . .

He asked if I knew what the colored people at the North had concluded about emigration. He did not incline to go to Africa himself; but he would like to live in a community where he was on an equality with the rest, and he preferred it should be in a warm climate. He didn't want to go out of the United States. He was an American, and he didn't want to be anything else.

He did not think the slaves were fit to be freed all at once. They ought to be somewhat educated, and gradually emancipated, and sent to Africa. They would never come to anything here, because the white people would never give them a chance.

The Quadroon Ball

THE DUKE OF SAXE-WEIMAR-EISENACH

The German Duke of Saxe-Weimar-Eisenach (1792–1862), who traveled in America in 1825 and 1826, comments here on briefly leaving a white ball to attend a quadroon ball. These balls were a social institution tied in with the Louisiana custom of *plaçage.* Men could bring their mistresses to the balls, or liaisons with women could be effected.

The . . . men . . . stayed only a short time, preferring to escape to a so-called "Quaterons Ball" which they find more amusing and where they do not have to stand on ceremony. There were, as a result, soon many more women than men.

A "quateron" (octoroon) is the offspring of a mestizo mother and a white father, just as the mestizo is the child of a mulatto and a white man.[10] The "quaterons" are almost completely white. There would be no way of recognizing them by their complexion, for they are often fairer than the Creoles. Black hair and eyes are generally the signs of their status, although some are quite blond. The ball is attended by the free "quaterons." Yet the deepest prejudice

From *This Was America: True Accounts of People and Places, Manners and Customs, as Recorded by European Travelers to the Western Shore in the Eighteenth, Nineteenth, and Twentieth Centuries,* ed. Oscar Handlin. Originally published by Harvard University Press. Copyright © 1949 by the President and Fellows of Harvard College. Reprinted by permission of Oscar Handlin.

10. The Louisiana French had precise terms for designating particular racial admixtures. The Duke, however, seems to have been confused as to usage. The Spanish term *mestizo* was not used. A mulatto was the child of a white parent and a black, a quateron (quadroon) that of a white and a mulatto (that is, someone considered "one-fourth black"). An octoroon (confused here with a quateron) was someone considered "one-eighth black."

reigns against them on account of their colored origin; the white women particularly feel or affect a strong repugnance to them.

Marriage between colored and white people is forbidden by the laws of the state. Yet the "quaterons," for their part, look upon the Negroes and mulattoes as inferiors and are unwilling to mix with them. The girls therefore have no other recourse than to become the mistresses of white men. The "quaterons" regard such attachment as the equivalent of marriage. They would not think of entering upon it other than with a formal contract in which the man engages to pay a stipulated sum to the mother or father of the girl. The latter even assumes the name of her lover and regards the affair with more faithfulness than many a woman whose marriage was sealed in a church.

Some of these women have inherited from their fathers and lovers, and possess considerable fortunes. Their status is nevertheless always very depressed. They must not ride in the street in coaches, and their lovers can bring them to the balls in their own conveyances only after nightfall. They must never sit opposite a white lady, nor may they enter a room without express permission. The whites have the right to have these unfortunates whipped like slaves for infractions for which there are two witnesses. But many of these girls are much more carefully educated than the whites, behave with more polish and more politeness, and make their lovers happier than white wives their husbands. And yet these white ladies speak of these unfortunate depressed creatures with great disdain, even bitterness. Because of the depth of these prejudices, many fathers send their daughters, conceived after this manner, to France where good education and wealth are no impediments to the attainment of a respectable place.

Only the colored women are admitted to the "Quateron Ball"; the men of that caste are excluded by the whites. To endow these dances with the qualities of good society, a high admission fee, two dollars, is fixed, so that only the upper class of men can attend. I found this ball much more decent than the white masquerade. The colored ladies were under the oversight of their mothers; they were elegantly dressed; and they behaved themselves with decorum and modesty. Both counter-dances and waltzes were performed, and most of the girls danced very well. I could not remain very long for fear of spoiling my reputation in New Orleans, and returned to the masquerade. I had also to be careful lest I mention to any white woman where I had been. Were it known that a foreigner who has entree to good society resorted to such a ball, he would receive a very cold treatment from the white ladies.

The Quadroon Ballroom

FREDERICK TURNER

> From *Spirit of Place: The Making of an American Literary Landscape*. Turner (b. 1943) is a poet and literary critic.

Down at the white end of Orleans Street was the Orleans Ballroom, one of the sites of the quadroon balls. These days it's called the Bourbon Orleans Hotel, but the building is the same one, and the ballroom still exists on the second floor. . . . The Orleans Ballroom symbolized the whole system of racism and caste that once made New Orleans so unique and that still, in muffled but real ways, is a part of this city. You heard it said, for instance that in the 1984 mayoralty, it was really the blacks against the colored Creoles, and that Sidney Barthelemy's election was due to the whites' preference for the colored Creoles, their fears of what might happen if State Senator William Jefferson (who is black) were to win. It might not be true. . . . But the fact that such things can still be soberly—or even snidely—said tells you . . . the past lives here, intensely so. I wanted to see it living on in the grand ballroom and to make this my last stop in the city.

The day was bright and sunny, the subtropical sun on this late spring morning still withholding its full powers, the air soft under a blanket of blue. The Bourbon Orleans sits at the corner of Royal and Orleans, and along the iron railings of the garden behind the cathedral you could see the sidewalk artists setting up their pitiful paintings. A shop a door off the corner had its doors flung wide, its tape player up, and Bessie Smith shouted into the heedless sun of the banquette. Inside the hotel I was told by the manager I'd have to wait until a meeting of AT&T broke up in the ballroom above. I occupied myself by copying the text of the historical plaque outside the main entrance.

"Former site," it read, "of Holy Family Sisters' Convent, the old Orleans Ball-room, built in 1817, served a number of purposes over the decades." There wasn't enough space, apparently, to list them all, no mention being made of the quadroon balls held here. It did mention that the property was purchased for the convent for colored nuns through the philanthropy of Thomy Lafon. It didn't say Lafon was a Creole of color, child of a French father and Haitian mother. . . .

When the manager summoned me with the news that I could go up, he told a bellhop, Richard Thomas, to show me the way. A muscular young man in his stiff-collared uniform jacket with a bushy Afro, Thomas bounded up the curving stairs two at a time ahead of me, then waited patiently at the door of the ballroom, a high-ceilinged affair about half as long as a football field. We walked in and stood in a moment's silence amidst the neat clutter of the just-departed telephone executives who were now happily at some nearby res-taurant, perhaps savoring the heady reward of that first luncheon drink. Thomas told me he was New Orleans born, and so I asked him what he knew of the ballroom's history. He told me it had been built by the nineteenth-century financier John Davis at a then astronomical price of $60,000 and that it was "the place where men bought their mistresses." After that, he said, it had been a convent.

"You must yourself be of mixed blood," I said then, "to judge from your looks."

"I am," he said with a smile. "I'm what we call here a Creole." I asked him then what it felt like to work in this place, knowing what he did of its history, what it felt like to show this room to a stranger and have him ask about it.

"Well," he said without much pause, "if you want to know whether I feel bad about it, the answer is no. I feel like I fit in here, you know? I feel like I understand this. It gives me a good feeling to be working here, some way.

"Say," he said suddenly, "how'd you like to go out on the balcony there to get a feel of the place?" I hesitated. "Come on," he laughed, "you're not that old. You can climb this sill. Come on." And he preceded me, clambering nim-bly up onto the broad, waist-high sill, then dropping down through the open window to the balcony. I followed.

Now we were once again into the bright soft air with the cathedral garden on our left, the green of Congo Square down the street on our right, and be-neath us the busyness of a spring day's noontime. "They used to go over there to settle up when they had arguments about their mistresses," Richard

Thomas was saying, nodding in the direction of the small garden. The sounds of Bessie's blues filled in the silence as we regarded the scene.

"Well," I said shortly, "up at the other end is Congo Square." And we looked squarely at each other then, two strangers united in being Americans and so sharing, however obliquely, a history. "And here we are," I resumed, "on a balcony of a place where they used to sell quadroons. And the last two mayors have been of mixed race like you."

He laughed a full, throaty laugh. "Yeah. It just goes to show." What, I wondered aloud, did it show? "It shows," Thomas said forcefully but without heat, "that what you look like doesn't count anymore. It's what's inside that counts. It's an individual thing." I said I thought that was the right point and we went in then, crossed the empty ballroom, and, descending the graceful stairs, reentered the rush of the present in which the past so often seems but fiction.

Travel Update

African Americans, who in slavery times constituted about half the population of Louisiana, have had a singular importance in southern society and culture. Clearly they fascinated many northern white and European travelers who came to the American South. Unfortunately, African American culture seldom has been offered as a focus for tourism, and sites and events important to black life seldom have been publicized—in Louisiana or elsewhere. Places and artifacts important to African American culture often have not even been preserved. This situation is changing, and the Louisiana Office of Tourism has published a small but very useful guide, *Our Culture Abounds: A Pictorial Directory of Louisiana's African-American Attractions,* later reissued in an expanded and somewhat different form as *The Fabric of Our Culture.* There is also a private organization working to document information on sites significant to black culture and history (the African American Site Identification Project), and the emerging Jazz Heritage National Park promises to call increasing attention to black Louisiana, as the Jean Lafitte National Park has done for Cajun Louisiana. *Our Culture Abounds/The Fabric of Our Culture* divides the state into regions and provides information on famous people (such as Ernest Gaines, Jelly Roll Morton, and Clementine Hunter), historical sites, and restaurants specializing in African American cuisine. *American Visions* magazine included a special 1995 advertising supplement for Louisiana attractions that was tailored to African American interests.

There are now several small museums in the state devoted to black culture and history. The River Road African American Museum and Gallery occupies space on the grounds of Tezcuco Plantation near Darrow. Materials on display relate particularly to the area and include such things as lodge publications, information on the roles played by African American benevolent societies, and lists of the slaves of John Burnside (whose plantation W. H. Russell visited in 1861). There is a display on Leonard Julien, the black man who invented the mechanical sugar planter in 1964. A mammy doll and a COLORED SERVED IN REAR sign remind visitors of a history of problematic race relations, while information on a local bricklayer marks the importance African Americans have had in Louisiana as craftspersons and artisans.

The Arna Bontemps House is located at Third and St. James Streets in Alexandria. Bontemps, author of such books as *Black Thunder* and *Chariot in the Sky* and a participant in the Harlem Renaissance, was born in the house (though it was moved to this site). There is a small exhibit about Bontemps and space for circulating art and historical exhibits. In Monroe, the Ouachita African American Museum (503 Plum Street) offers revolving exhibits of black artwork and related materials. The Louisiana State Museum in New Orleans includes information about African Americans in several exhibits and displays items ranging from slave collars and a tignon (the kerchief worn by African American women) to portraits of well-to-do people of color.

In some ways the most extraordinary site associated with African Americans in Louisiana is Melrose Plantation on Cane River. Originally it was called Yucca Plantation and was founded and run by a dynasty of people of African (though also of French) heritage, who came to form the nucleus from which grew the community of "Creoles of color" on the Cane River about whom Olmsted writes. The matriarch of the Yucca dynasty was the slave Marie Thérèze Coincoin, who managed to attain her freedom and then buy freedom for her children, most of them fathered by the Frenchman Pierre Metoyer. Metoyer secured land from a Spanish grant for her, and she and her offspring became slaveholders themselves, planting indigo and tobacco and also exporting fat from the black bears then numerous in the area. The Yucca plantation house was constructed around 1790 and is still extant, a small, typically Creole structure with front and rear galleries (and dirt floors until the 1920s). Other early plantation structures at Melrose include the distinctive African House, which served the Metoyers as a tobacco barn, supply room, and slave jail (and which is controversial architecturally, some claiming the building is directly based on African models, others that it is typically Creole despite its seemingly unusual form); another, unrestored barn; and a spring house.

Yucca is situated behind the big house at Melrose. The big house was built by Marie Thérèze's son Louis Metoyer and was finished in 1833, by which time the Metoyers had become prosperous planters. The property was lost by the family in the 1840s (the name change came later) but may have been one of the "large, handsome, and comfortable houses" where Olmstead's steamboat put in. The Metoyer family continued to expand, however, partly by intermarrying with free people of color from New Orleans; by the time of Olmstead's tour in 1853 there was indeed "a large number of free-colored planters." The "mulatto" community of the area, called Isle Brevelle, has continued to exist, its members having remained socially apart from both whites and blacks in the area. The community's life centers around St. Augustine Church (near Melrose but on the opposite side of the Cane), which houses a wonderful portrait of Augustin Metoyer (brother of Louis), whose plantation was also on the opposite shore from Melrose. It shows an African American man of dignity and means, dressed like the white plantation patriarchs of his day. According to local lore, the painting was saved for the community in the 1940s (when it was due to be auctioned and was eagerly sought for its historical importance by collectors and museums) by the parish priest, whose eloquent speech on the picture's meaning to the community dissuaded others from bidding on it. Lyle Saxon wrote a novel about the Cane River Creole community of his own day, *Children of Strangers* (Boston, 1937), and the connection between Cane River and New Orleans Creoles of color figures in Anne Rice's *Feast of All Saints* (New York, 1981). *The Forgotten People: Cane River's Creoles of Color,* by Gary B. Mills (Baton Rouge, 1977), is a history of the community.

Melrose had a second period of significance, which came in the twentieth century under the ownership of the extraordinary Cammie Garrett Henry, who formed a kind of colony there by inviting artists and writers to stay and work in cabins on the property. Writers included in this volume who stayed there are William Faulkner, Sherwood Anderson, and John Steinbeck, while Harnett Kane and Lyle Saxon had long associations with the place (Saxon lived for a time in Yucca). Other artists who went include writers Grace King, Frances Parkinson Keyes, and Gwen Bristow; photographer Doris Ulmann; actress Margaret Sullivan; and painter Alberta Kinsey. The Metoyer big house was a standard Creole-style structure, but the Henrys modified its appearance considerably by adding six-sided, tower like *garçonnières* on each end and a large rear addition.

Although Melrose was largely a white domain in the Henry period, the place did assume an importance in African American cultural history again through Clementine Hunter. A field hand who became Mrs. Henry's cook about 1938, Clementine Hunter took up painting, initially using supplies thrown away by Alberta Kinsey. She developed into an important artist, whose primitivist paintings depict folklife and other aspects of everyday existence in the world she knew (wash days, harvests, baptisms) as well as religious motifs. Melrose has a number of her paintings on display, including a series of murals in the second story of the African House, and there are plans for a Clementine Hunter museum in Natchitoches.

The Cane River area also has legendary associations with Harriet Beecher Stowe. According to local tradition, she visited the area and patterned the plantation in *Uncle Tom's Cabin* after what she observed. This story is not historically substantiated and may have been started by Dr. Samuel Scruggs, a local physician. Nonetheless, there was once a cabin in the vicinity that was claimed as Uncle Tom's, and one local plantation is still called Little Eva after the character in the novel.

Another remarkable locus for African American connections in central Louisiana is the Solomon Northup Trail; signage and a guidebook allow visitors to follow Northup's sojourn in Louisiana. His story is itself such a remarkable one, and his book such an important document, that following his presence can be a uniquely significant experience. Prepared by Sue Eakin, the guidebook (*Northup Trail through Central Louisiana*) identifies various extant sites, including the place where the slave festivities Northup describes are said to have taken place (now just a field near Ashland Plantation house). The Epps House was moved in the 1960s from the plantation where Northup spent most of his time into the town of Bunkie; it can be found on U.S. 1 where it sits amid commercial properties, though unfortunately it is closed and has deteriorated. A simple structure, it mirrors the fact that the plantation cluster along Bayou Boeuf where Northup lived (not to be confused with the Bayou Boeuf seen by James K. Hosmer during his Civil War travels) included many rather modest holdings. Open to the public in the area are two plantation houses dating from Northup's time, both considerably more grand than the Epps House: Walnut Grove had associations with people Northup mentions; Loyd Hall was simply part of the larger Bayou Boeuf community. Both are in nearby Cheneyville.

Though African Americans have played many roles in Louisiana society, and though there was from early times a significant population of urban free people of color in New Orleans, the plantation is a central fact in the African American history of the state. It is the institution that brought Africans there in the first place and the venue where most African Americans in Louisiana carried out their lives until well after the Civil War. Unfortunately, plantations that are open to visitors today more often than not feature only the big house of the planter and provide little insight into the lives of the African Americans who were once the majority of the population on virtually every such estate. There are, however, a few places where one can obtain a fuller idea of the quarters and other precincts that were the focus for African American lives on the plantation.

One such place is the Louisiana State University Museum of Rural Life in Baton Rouge (entrance from Essen Lane near Interstate 10). This museum in part aims to portray the plantation "backstage" through a group of buildings on the former Windrush Plantation, which was donated to LSU by the Burden family to be used for agricultural research. Steele Burden, a member of the family and at one time the university's landscape architect, assembled the plantation structures from several other Louisiana sites. They include an overseer's house, quarters cabins, a church, and a syrup mill.

The West Baton Rouge Museum in Port Allen has a slave cabin from nearby Allendale Plantation on display, tucked away behind the main museum building. It contains tools, household utensils, and other items used by plantation blacks, and such furnishings as a rope bed. The house, constructed *ca.* 1850, is spacious, has wide-planked floors, and would have been provided to favored slaves. Today it is a focus for cooking and other educational demonstrations. In addition, some owners of plantations that are open for tours are beginning to understand the need to present a picture of the plantation as something more than a house and to include aspects of African American plantation life. For example, a slave cabin brought in from another site is being restored at Magnolia Mound in Baton Rouge.

Another key factor in antebellum African American life was, of course, the slave market, and—as Fredrika Bremer makes clear—New Orleans was an important center for the slave trade. Perhaps because of the inhumanity this trade represented, there is little to mark the sites of the markets. Two of the most significant, however, operated right in important hotels, the St. Louis and the St. Charles. The St. Louis (which became the place where the Reconstruction-era, black-dominated legislature met for a time) was torn down in 1916; the present Royal Orleans Hotel occupies the same site. The St. Charles Hotel was situated on the "American," or uptown, side of Canal Street on St. Charles between Common and Gravier. Solomon Northup writes of being held before market in a slave "pen" in New Orleans that was probably located across the street from the St. Charles Hotel, the third incarnation of which was demolished in 1973 and replaced by an office building.

The school where John Steinbeck observed the "Cheerleaders" was the William Frantz Elementary School, which was integrated in November of 1960. The events Steinbeck writes about also inspired Norman Rockwell's well-known painting of a tiny black child surrounded by U.S. marshals. Today the school (located at 3811 North Galvez) has an all-black enrollment.

The former quadroon ballroom is, as Frederick Turner says, part of a modern hotel, the Bourbon Orleans (just behind St. Louis Cathedral, entrance on Orleans Street). Inquiries can be made at the hotel about seeing it.

The Amistad Research Center, housed at Tulane University in New Orleans, contains the largest collection in the United States of historical materials pertaining to African Americans and race relations.

Our Culture Abounds/The Fabric of Our Culture lists festivals, such as the Baton Rouge Blues Festival, where African American culture is featured.

5

Never So Many Travel
Accounts: The War

The Civil War was limited to a period of but four
years, yet as E. Merton Coulter has said, "Not again
until the twentieth century, if then, were there as
many travelers in the South . . . as during the Civil
War. . . . And never have so many travel accounts been
written dealing with so short a period of American life
as appeared on the Confederacy." Coulter's own bibli-
ography lists nearly five hundred such war-years accounts, well over fifty of them including travels in
Louisiana.[1]

These are, of course, strangely unique travel accounts. They speak of unprecedented conditions and
unusual circumstances. They are less apt than the accounts of peacetime travelers to casually observe the
passing scene, more likely to recount personal involvement in the difficulties and dramatic events of the
times. Though they tell us something of what Louisiana was like in those years, they tell us more about

1. E. Merton Coulter, *Travels in the Confederacy: A Bibliog-*
raphy (Baton Rouge, 1994), x.

what it was like to be *a person* in Louisiana then, how conditions and actions and great historical developments affected those who traveled as refugees and combatants. Selections from Civil War travel accounts are included in this book precisely because their authors saw things happening in Louisiana that none had seen before nor have since. And we must remember that these events, in their larger context, changed the place forever, ending the slave-based plantation society of earlier times, thrusting African Americans into a new universe, devastating the Louisiana economy, transforming ways of living—all consequences that would have profound effects on the observations of later visitors.

Renowned British journalist W. H. Russell observed Louisiana at the outset of the war, in the days just before battles and Yankee occupation actually descended upon New Orleans and much of the rest of the state. His commentary is full of the initial enthusiasm for fight that prevailed in the Crescent City at that time—companies of volunteers being raised, seamstresses busy making uniforms, members of the body politic dreaming of ridding themselves of Yankee abolitionists—though also hints of hardship and confusion. But a year later, Eliza McHatton-Ripley (who had a charming stay on Valcour Aime's legendary Petit Versailles in the 1840s) finds herself forced off her own plantation near Baton Rouge. She tells of the travels of a refugee—of a slave who steals her child's pony, loyal slaves who warn of Federal pickets, the uncertainty of being taken in by strangers—before finally meeting with a stream of other southerners fleeing the invaders, carrying bits and pieces of their worldly goods.

Soldiers on both sides give their accounts. James K. Hosmer, in the Forty-second Massachusetts Volunteers, presents in part an idyllic Louisiana, telling how he marched along a lovely bayou in country he imagined to be like Holland, a place with fine mansions, prosperous-looking settlements, cool water, and bright skies. Except for the obvious military context, his account almost could be an enthusiastic peacetime journey along Bayou Lafourche in the mid–nineteenth century. Yet he also writes of the extreme discomforts of wartime traveling—camped in a swamp in the midst of a subtropical downpour in the Florida Parishes—of his uneasiness over foraging (and, in writings not reprinted here, of the deaths of his friends and comrades). James Blessington joined the southern cause and the Confederate Army in Texas and spent most of the war in Louisiana. Christmas of 1863 found him near Marksville; he writes of the camp life he observed there, the placing of pickets to foil enemy advances offset by the gaiety and reverence occasioned by the holiday season. Yet not offset very far, for these camp festivities seem those of men who have traveled far from home, men taken into Louisiana by hard circumstances trying to ward off the loneliness of being away.

Blessington notes that he and his fellows were paid in Confederate money the day after Christmas, and its worthlessness seems a counterweight to the enthusiasm for the war that Russell had seen two years before. So does Sarah Morgan Dawson's final journey of 1863. A truly ardent Confederate, she, like Eliza Ripley, had fled Baton Rouge, though she and her family sojourned at Clinton and other places in the Florida Parishes. Finally they felt the need to cross Lake Pontchartrain to New Orleans and—ironically—the protection of a Unionist brother. The voyage by schooner ends with their taking the hated oath of allegiance to the United States, administered by a Yankee officer. It seems a personal surrender little envisioned by Louisianians in the headier days of Russell's visit. It also seems emblematic of much of the traveling that took place in Louisiana (and in the South) during the war: full of turmoil and touched by uncertainty and sorrow.

New Orleans, Just After Secession

W. H. RUSSELL

> British war correspondent W. H. Russell (1820–1907) was sent to the United States to cover the secession crisis for the London *Times*. While he was in the country, the Civil War broke out. In New Orleans in May of 1861, he recorded the initial enthusiasms and turmoils we read about here, including the raising of troops. From *My Diary North and South* (1863).

The streets [of New Orleans] are full of Turcos, Zouaves, Chasseurs;[2] walls are covered with placards of volunteer companies: there are Pickwick rifles, La Fayette, Beauregard, MacMahon guards, Irish, German, Italian, and Spanish, and native volunteers. . . . Tailors are busy night and day making uniforms. I went into a shop with the [British] consul for some shirts—the mistress and all her seamstresses were busy preparing flags as hard as the sewing machine could stitch them, and could attend to no business for the present. . . .

The respectable people of the city are menaced with two internal evils in consequence of the destitution caused by the stoppage of trade with the North and with Europe. The municipal authorities, for want of funds, threaten to close the city schools, and to disband the police; at the same time, employers refuse to pay their workmen on the ground of inability. The British Consulate was thronged today by Irish, English, and Scotch, entreating to be sent North or to Europe. The stories told by some of these poor fellows were most pitiable, and were vouched for by facts and papers; but Mr. Moore has no funds at his disposal to enable him to comply with their prayers. Nothing

---

2. Turcos were soldiers whose uniforms were modeled on those of Turkish or Greek regiments; Zouaves were infantry whose "Oriental" uniforms were modeled on those of elite French regiments noted for their precision in drill; Chasseurs are cavalry or light infantry skilled in rapid deployment.

remains for them but to enlist. For the third or fourth time I heard cases of British subjects being forcibly carried off to fill the ranks of so-called volunteer companies and regiments. In some instances they have been knocked down, bound, and confined in barracks, till in despair they consented to serve. Those who have friends aware of their condition were relieved by the interference of the Consul; but there are many, no doubt, thus coerced and placed in involuntary servitude without his knowledge.

The great commercial community of New Orleans, which now feels the pressure of the blockade, depends on the interference of the European Powers next October. They have among them men who refuse to pay their debts to Northern houses, but they deny that they intend to repudiate, and promise to pay all who are not black Republicans when the war is over. Repudiation is a word out of favour, as they feel the character of the Southern State and of Mr. Jefferson Davis himself has been much injured in Europe by the breach of honesty and honour of which they have been guilty; but I am assured on all sides that every State will eventually redeem all its obligations. Meantime, money here is fast vanishing. Bills on New York are worth nothing, and bills on England are at eighteen per cent discount from the par value of gold; but the people of this city will endure all this and much more to escape from the hated rule of the Yankees.

Through the present gloom come the rays of a glorious future, which shall see a grand slave confederacy enclosing the Gulf in its arms, and swelling to the shores of the Potomac and Chesapeake, with the entire control of the Mississippi and a monopoly of the great staples on which so much of the manufacture and commerce of England and France depend. They believe themselves, in fact, to be masters of the destiny of the world. Cotton is king—not alone king, but czar; and coupled with the gratification and profit to be derived from this mighty agency, they look forward with intense satisfaction to the complete humiliation of their hated enemies in the New England States, to the destruction of their usurious rival New York, and to the impoverishment and ruin of the states which have excited their enmity by personal liberty bills, and have outraged and insulted them by harboring abolitionists and an anti-slavery press.

Having made some purchases, and paid all my visits, I returned to prepare for my voyage up the Mississippi.

Fleeing the Yankees

ELIZA MCHATTON-RIPLEY

Eliza McHatton-Ripley (1832–1912)—who published a later book as Eliza Ripley—was living on Arlington Plantation near Baton Rouge when Union troops, having already taken New Orleans, invaded the area. Her husband, in direct violation of Federal regulations, sent some of their slaves to her brother's plantation. As this rendered him liable to arrest, he fled beyond Federal reach, and soon thereafter, in 1862, McHatton-Ripley found herself fleeing the area with her two small children in the company of a young boy, Willy, and slaves Dave, who drove, and Sabe, the nurse-maid. Later the family reached Texas and waited out the war there and in Mexico and Cuba. But McHatton-Ripley's account of her initial flight—in her *From Flag to Flag*, published in 1889—provides a picture of the obvious confusion and difficulties of travel under Federal occupation.

I rode away from Arlington, leaving the sugar-house crowded to its utmost capacity with the entire crop of sugar and molasses of the previous year for which we had been unable to find a market within "our lines," leaving cattle grazing in the fields, sheep wandering over the levee, doors and windows flung wide open, furniture in the rooms, clothes too fine for me to wear now hanging in the armoires, china in the closets, pictures on the walls, beds unmade, table spread. It was late in the afternoon of that bright, clear, bracing day, December 18, 1862, that I bade Arlington adieu forever! . . .

By evening we reached the end of Gartness Lane, and a black head popped out of the bushes. "Don't go dat road, pickets down dar!" so we turned up the

General Banks' Army in the Advance on Shreveport, La.: Crossing Cane River, March 31, 1864

From *Leslie's Illustrated Civil War* (Jackson, Miss., 1992)

road we wanted to go down. When it was quite dark, we reached a house, where we asked to remain all night, and there to my intense astonishment I met our overseer, who, instead of remaining on the plantation attending to his duties, had taken flight on the first appearance of the Federals. He had departed without the slightest notification, leaving me to do the best I could, without the help of a living soul but little Willy; seeking a place of safety for his worthless self, and in that place of safety I found him at night—waiting for me!

I was too dejected, helpless, and cowed, to say anything more than that I was pleased to see him, and would he be good enough to help Willy feed the mules; and be sure to put Dave in a safe place, as he was my only dependence for a driver until I could join my husband?

The next morning, the first thing I heard was, that Dave had stolen Henry's pony and absconded! Words fail to express my indignation. . . .

The rest comes to my mind in vague confusion. Recollections of woolly heads popping out of bushes at every cross-road, and sending us the roundabout way, with the whisper, "Pickets down dat road!" temporary bridges over impassable places, felled trees shoved aside, fences taken down for us to pass through woods and fields to come to an open road, and the oftrepeated warning, "Pickets down dar!"—it is all now like a dim, troubled dream. On the third day we emerged on a broad highway, where were wagons loaded with furniture, beds, bundles, cooking-utensils, articles of clothing, old trunks and barrels overflowing with hastily collected household effects, being laboriously drawn by broken-down, emaciated horses, whose days of active service had long since departed. A few decrepit, bedraggled, dejected women, with whole families of shivering children, walked the dusty roadside.

A Very Swarthy and Travel-Stained Warrior

JAMES K. HOSMER

James Hosmer (1834–1927) later became a historian of some note, but during the war served with the Forty-second Massachusetts Volunteers. Hosmer had a real feel for describing the Louisiana he saw in 1863, and his account of his experiences, *The Color-Guard* (1864), is an attractively written one. He interacted rather intensely with the Louisiana environment, encountering both the tempestuous wet weather in the Florida Parishes in mid-March and the extreme beauty along Bayou Lafourche in April. As this excerpt opens he is on the edges of the fighting around Port Hudson; later the scene shifts to the march down Bayou Lafourche and then to the vicinity of Opelousas. Hosmer expresses obvious ambivalence toward the foraging activities of the Union forces that caused much destruction to Louisiana. After his visit to an abandoned plantation near Opelousas to forage, he was himself briefly arrested and jailed.

[March]

Yesterday we were sure of a battle; but the enemy fell back before us. Now, why were we falling back before them? We halt every half-hour or so; when every one is on his back in a moment. As I noticed the day before, the road becomes strewn with knapsacks and blankets; but fewer men fall out, for they fear capture by the enemy. In the middle of the afternoon, it begins to rain. I never knew it rain so hard: there was a general uncorking among the clouds. The road becomes a deep pudding and the gutters are rivers. We are wet to the skin. I throw my left arm against my breast-pocket to shield (as much as I can) my portfolio, which has my precious paper and pencils. By great care I partly succeed; but every thing else is soaked. Boots become filled with water that runs from the clothes into them. The army splashes on through the rain, dreary and disheartened. Some of the officers give up their horses to tired soldiers, and shoulder muskets.

At five o'clock we reach a field, where we are to encamp. Gen. Banks assigned it when he passed in the morning. Since then, creation has put on a new face; but we must obey orders. In we turn, therefore, into a swamp, to pass the most tedious night of our lives. A dreary Louisiana swamp! The space had been cleared, and was full of charred stumps and logs, half floating, half lying in the mud. . . . We waded and stumbled forward to the middle of this dreary quagmire. Could we stop here for the night? We had marched very rapidly ten or twelve miles, most of the way in heavy order; and were exhausted. The roads were almost impassable: moreover, the general had left orders for us to stay here. We had no choice.

Wet to the skin, I threw off my knapsack and equipments into the mud, too tired to hold them. We managed, as night fell, to get a fire started in a charred stump. . . . Frequently the rain would pour in sheets; when the fire, in spite of all we could do, would dwindle down to a mere spark.

About ten o'clock, I managed to make a little coffee. Then putting my knapsack into the mud, in the highest and dryest spot I could find, drawing my two blankets about my shoulders, and my rubber havelock over my ears, I sat down for the night. As I sat on my knapsack, it settled down into the mud until it just kept me out of the pool. My boots sank half-way to the tops. I rested my elbows on my knees, and chewed the cud of misery. Once in a while, some one waded forth after wood. On every stump and log were figures wrapped up in rubber blankets, trying to sleep. . . .

Nothing was ever more wretched; and, when morning came at last,—swimming up through the pouring heavens to us,—such a half-drowned, haggard, bedraggled set as the regiment was, horse and men! We had the consolation of thinking we had touched bottom of misery at any rate. Any lower deep there surely cannot be. Snakes and crabs, no proper food or drink, wet to the skin, the deadly vine weeping its "venomous dew" upon us,—there could be nothing further down. Mildewed, frowzy, horrible! . . .

This matter of foraging is a hard one. I have seen now what a scourge to a country an invading army is. We were turned loose. As I shall presently record, the Government, under our guns, collected a large amount of cotton; and we were suffered to kill cattle, pigs, and poultry. All this marauding went on ruthlessly and wastefully. We left the road behind us foul with the odor of decaying carcasses. Cattle were killed, a quarter or so taken out of them, and the remainder left to the buzzards. So with sheep and poultry. Pigs were bayoneted, sugar-houses plundered of sugar and molasses, private dwellings entered; and, if any resistance was offered by the owner, his arms were wrested from him, and he overmastered. To be sure, there can be no doubt of the sympathy of all these people with the rebel cause. We saw nothing of any young white men,—only old men, negroes, and women left behind by the young men when they entered the Confederate army. I have not heard that any were actually slain in these marauding expeditions, or that insult was offered to any white woman; but property was handled, destroyed, or taken, without scruple.

I took no part in any active foraging, though I own I was more than once a partaker in the booty. It was, in fact, our only way to live. Government-bread and poor bacon were really insufficient to support strength under our work and exposure. . . . If I did no active foraging, it was, perhaps, due more to want of enterprise, and because there were enough others to do it, than because my conscience stood in the way. Am I demoralized? But it was the only way to live. Our rations were insufficient, and the commissary-department seemed to expect we should find a good part of our food for ourselves. It is, indeed, sad; and there was enough that was pathetic. War is horrible, and this feature of plunder is one of its horrors. . . .

[April]

—This forenoon, we are encamped at Donaldsonville,—a point fifty or sixty miles below Baton Rouge, on the western bank of the great river. The neighborhood of this town, and the country along the Bayou La Fourche, which here opens out of the Mississippi, is said to be the garden of Louisiana.

The landscape just about the camp here must be very like Holland. The tents are pitched in a perfectly level field,—stretching, without a fence, far and wide, with only here and there a tree. Along one side of the field runs the bayou, behind its Levee. The water now brims up nearly to the edge of this Levee, though on the land side there must be a slope of six or eight feet from the top of the bank to the surface of the land. If an opening were made in the Levee, our camp would be instantly drowned by the rush of waters. Sloops and schooners of considerable tonnage sail up and down the bayou, and one full-sized clipper ship lies at anchor just opposite us. To see these craft, we are obliged to look up. The water-line on the bayou is about on a level with our eyes; so that the hulls and rigging of the vessels are in the air, over our heads. At the mouth of the bayou is a fort, with pointed angles, smoothly cut, and turfed with green. It is very regularly built, with ditch, counterscarp, bastion, and berme. This again, I imagine, is a feature which this landscape has in common with that of the Low Countries. . . .

Of course, we have very little idea where we are going, or what we are going to encounter; for we are the soldiers of a general who keeps his own counsel. In a day or two we expect to march from here to Thibodeaux, and thence onward to Berwick Bay. . . . We marched in the moonlight aboard the transport that was to bring us here, two or three nights ago. I lay on the upper deck, propped up by my knapsack, and took my farewell of the buildings on the Levee [at Baton Rouge]. . . .

—At Assumpcion [later] (I guess at the spelling). Charming,—perfectly charming,—day, place, sensations. We have marched twelve or thirteen miles since nine o'clock this morning, through the sweetest of regions, with the sweetest of air. Now we pause for the night,—the landscape still the mild, verdant, level expanse which made me think of Holland . . . the grand bayou, deep and swift, riding along above the heads of the people. Here and there, the current, eating into the bank, leaves only a mere spadeful between the rush of the stream and the plain below it. . . . Among our indispensibles . . . a few of us carry certain new arrangements . . . we have bought a coffee pot, a frying-pan, and a kettle for boiling. Wivers carries the coffee-pot slung at his side: sergeant Bivins carries the frying-pan strapped on his back. . . . I have, strapped to my belt, the boiler; its crocky bottom painting thunder-clouds on the blue of my right thigh, as it swings to and fro. It will hold two or three quarts, and is up to flour, meal, eggs, oysters, or any thing which shall come to the omniverous haversack of the campaigner. . . .

The conditions for marching to-day are excellent . . . the currents of northern air broke through . . . in a perfect *crevasse* of coolness, inundating all these Louisiana lowlands with its refreshing tide; so that, although we marched fast, the drops of sweat were beaten back, and the locks of the soldier, not plastered to his forehead, danced in a jolly manner in the breeze of home.

I have seen this day what I have not seen before,—estates which come up to what I have imagined about the homes of princely planters, two or three of them. The first we came upon was on the opposite side of the bayou. I was marching, not in the road, but along the ridge of the Levee, whence I could overlook the long column, the sugar-fields, and the distant wood. . . . While thus marching,—the bayou a foot or two from my path on one side, the road six or eight feet down on the other,—I caught sight of thick shrubbery, a chenille embroidery of green tufting the bare level plain. Then came into view a towering roof, and the stately palings of an enclosure befitting a princely domain. As we came opposite, down a long avenue, the perspective led the eye within the open portal of a splendid mansion; from whose hall, ladies and children looked across at the marching army. Meantime the air was full of sweet scents: for tropic plants, like Eastern princes, stretched forth their arms from the enclosure, and with odorous gifts flattered the passers-by; and a tree full of bell-shaped blossoms—the airy "campanile" of the garden showing rows on rows of little purple chimes—"tolled incense" to us. One or two domains like this I saw, and many more less splendid, yet which were neat and pretty. . . .

We shall carry home a much more favorable impression as to the resources and civilization of this State than we should have had if we had not passed through this country of the La Fourche. . . . It is thickly peopled; the plantations succeeeding one another as do the farms in any populous agricultural region of the North.

Seldom does the army march under circumstances so delightful. The miles were not weary ones. . . . On one side rose the slope of the Levee. . . . When the column halted, we could run up the slope, then stoop to the cool bayou to drink, or to wash face, hands, and feet. On our right . . . we passed, now houses of moderate size, bare of elegance—sometimes even squalid in appearance; now, again, mansions of comfortable look; and, not infrequently, beautiful seats, set high up to preserve them from danger in case of a crevasse, with colonnades ornamented tastefully with orange-groves and the glorious live-oak, with *trees* full of roses instead of bushes.

Plantation after plantation! Along the road were white palings, or often the pleasanter enclosure of a rose-hedge, with white roses all out, and the green of a richer depth than we know it. Sometimes the planter and his family looked out at us from behind a "protection" posted before them on the gate, seated upon the broad portico under the wide roof, beneath wide-spreading awnings, with open doors and windows behind. Then, between house and hedge, these marvellous gardens! Tall trees overhung them; with vines, sometimes nearly as thick as the trunks, twining, supple as serpents, from root

A Floating Hospital—Conveying Wounded Soldiers on a Raft After the Battle of Bayou Teche, La., January 15, 1863

From *Leslie's Illustrated Civil War* (Jackson, Miss., 1992)

to topmost bough,—twining, hanging in loops, knotted into coils. Then, underneath, flowers white and delicate, adorned with dewy jewels, scented with odors incomparable; flowers uncouth and spiny; the cactus, not here exotic, but "to the manor born," its gnarled and prickly stem thickly set with purple buds. The air would be pungent with sweetness as the column marched past.

Such tropic luxury of air and vegetation! These scents and zephyrs; the bird-songs we heard; the summer-blue of the heavens; the broad palm-leaves at the planter's portico; these blossoms of crimson and saffron and white; this slow-moving air, so burdened, and laboring under its freight of perfume . . . and I suppose, too, the foil of all these,—the miasma of the swamp close at hand, and the poisonous serpent lurking there.

When the garden was passed, generally we came to a huge gate, upon and about which would be clustered the negro force of the whole estate, old and young. From this a road ran, down which, at the distance of a quarter mile perhaps, we could see the white chimneys of the sugar mill; the village of negro cabins; then acres and acres of cane-field, stretching clear to the heavy forest on the verge of the horizon.

At noon yesterday, we came to Thibodeaux. As we entered the village, the drums struck up. The footsore men forgot to hobble; the melting men forgot their heat. We were all straight and soldierly; for the march was nearly finished. The streets of the village were full of people, upon whom it became us to make an impression; and the sound of the drum and fife is a spur to the soul. We were dusty and sweaty; but I think we made a good appearance. . . . We unfurled the two flags, and set them upright. The road, as we approached Thibodeaux, had been growing even more lovely; and now, in the village, the climax of beauty was reached.

To go from Baton Rouge to Thibodeaux is like changing from the outer petals to the heart of a full-blown rose. Baton Rouge, once fresh and pretty, is now curled up and withered by the heats of war; but the blossom grows fresher, and here in the centre is the reservoir of honey,—the place where the bee sucks. Each little cottage had its garden; every gable was embowered; every window and pilaster buried in vines; every garden gilt-edged with ripe oranges along the borders. Puffs of wind, like scented exquisites, sprang out over the blossoms,—the gayest sprites that ever were,—and, seizing for partners our two colors,—rather faded and dishevelled belles,—danced them up and down in a brisk measure. The streets of the village were full of its hybrid population. Very few jet-black ones there were, and not many thoroughly white, but throngs of mixed-blood,—from deep mulattoes, up through quadroon and octoroon, to fair boys and girls with complexion just made rich and vivid with a dash of the tiger-lily. . . .

—At the "Bayou Boeuf." The bayou is one of those characteristic Louisiana watercourses which do so differently from water in other parts of the world,—riding over a district, instead of boring its way through it. The land slopes back from the river-bank; so that the drainage of our camp is toward the swamp, a short distance in the rear, instead of toward the bayou. It is a dreamy afternoon. A heavy haze buries the distance, and veils even the trees and plantations a little way off on the other side of the stream. I sit on the huge root of a live-oak, whose heavy top hangs far out over the water, giving me a dense shade,—me and the brilliant little minnows that I see swimming up in the shoals in the quiet water, as I raise my eyes.

We did not leave Terre Bonne until yesterday forenoon; making the whole time of our stay there a day and a half. We were piled, thick as we could sit, upon platform-cars, and then brought eighteen miles to this point. The road was a level, broad-gauge track, over which the engine drew us rapidly. We had the best opportunity we have yet had of seeing a wild Louisiana morass. For a long distance, we went through a dense cypress-swamp,—such as we have not seen before,—a dense growth of cypresses, with a very heavy undergrowth between the tall trunks, and, beneath that, a thick mat of water-plants lying upon the surface of the fen. It was like a wall of vegetation, almost, on each side; through which, occasionally, we could see deep, dark bayous flowing, and black pools. Alligators several feet long lay on logs, or in the water, with their backs just rising above; and, on floating timbers and little islands of earth, snakes, single or in coils, lay basking in the sun. Later in the season, I suppose, we should have seen even larger numbers of this agreeable population. Huge vines, coiled into knots, bound the cypress-trunks and other growths into one mass of vegetation. We saw, too, numbers of palms; which here grow short, by stumps and pools, spreading abroad their wide-divided leaves, as if they were showing hands at cards. . . .

It was the fourth or fifth day of our stay there [at Opelousas]. I was tired of lying with the lizards under the shelter-tent: so, as Bivins and two of the corporals were going off on a sugar expedition, I joined them. We went to the "Swayze Place," where my companions had been before. They had given such accounts of its elegance as to arouse our interest. We made our way through a forest (killing a rattlesnake in our course), entered the plantation gate, passed through a rather squalid purlieu of negro huts, then came to the mansion itself,—a one-story dwelling, with neat veranda and some marks of taste, though house and surroundings lacked finish. The garden was a wreck; and through this we passed without hindrance, by the open door, into what had been elegantly furnished apartments. One had been a library; and the floor was strewn with a litter of valuable books. One had been a dining room, at one side of which stood a handsomely carved sideboard. In the parlor was a rich piano, and other furniture in keeping,—all overturned, scattered, and marred. We went into bedrooms, where were handsome canopied beds, and heavy furniture of rosewood. In one was a very large mirror, in which I caught a sight of a very swarthy and travel-stained warrior, whom I should never have recognized.

I hurried out with an uncomfortable feeling. The pillage and destruction were due in part to our soldiers, in part to the negroes. It was discreditable and painful. At the sugar-house was sugar going to waste. My companions took what they could carry in their blankets, and I took from the deserted garden a handfull of onions,—articles really necessary, short of rations as we were, and which we had been instructed we might take. Then we washed and filled our canteens from the broken bucket of the old well.

Christmas at Marksville

JOSEPH P. BLESSINGTON

Blessington joined the Confederate service in Texas and came into Louisiana with Walker's Texas division. He spent much of the war in Louisiana, fighting mostly in the vicinity of Alexandria and Monroe. In 1875 he published *The Campaigns of Walker's Texas Division,* from which this excerpt is taken. Here he writes about the Christmas of 1863, spent near Simmesport and Marksville. He conveys something of the loneliness of being away from home at that time of year and the attempt to transcend that loneliness in camp with music and religion.

Marched seventeen miles. Passed through Simmesport, and camped on Bayou De Glaize, about two miles and a half north of Simmesport. . . . A company from each regiment in the brigade was sent on picket at Simmesport, to protect the pontoon bridge in the Atchafalaya Bayou, and to be on lookout for the enemy. . . .

We will accompany a regiment going out on picket, in order to give our readers an idea of how the men got on. Their blankets are thrown over their shoulders; their guns are clean and bright; they take up the line of march in the direction of the enemy. Arriving within a few miles of the enemy, they halt and establish their reserve posts, while, further on, they place their pickets, with strict orders to keep a sharp lookout. It was night; the men had to scramble through the brush and trees, through ravines, to gain the different stations.

Thus, our pickets in front quietly . . . kept their posts. They are relieved every two hours, and go back to join their commands, who are grouped around a blazing fire in some ravine, sheltered from the enemy's observation. Here they refresh themselves out of their haversacks, and, perhaps, join in a game of cards, or listen to those wonderful tales that, like those of the "Arabian Nights," are got up for the entertainment of the company. . . .

We will proceed on our journey to Marksville, where Haws' and Randalls' Brigades are encamped, and see how they are enjoying Christmas. For the most part, the men were actively engaged during the day, by the duties and routines of camp-life. It is only at night that this busy hum of martial life and bustle sinks into repose. Then five thousand camp-fires glow and sparkle from hill and dale, looking, through the darkness of night, like the gas-lights of a city. The imagination can easily picture the scene. The sentinel's challenge, the sound of music from the bands, ring clearly and musically on the night air; and the camp-fires glow and flare, around which the men are grouped, singing, joking, and laughing, with a light-hearted ease, as if they knew "dull care." Most of them are full of practical jokes, light and sparkling as champagne, and had a gay faculty of taking the sunny side of everything. Near one of the huge fires a kind of arbor was nicely constructed of the branches of trees, which were so interwoven as to form a kind of wall. Inside this were seated a couple of fiddlers, making elegant music on their fiddles. Around the fire, groups were dancing jigs, reels, and doubles. Even the officers' colored servants had collected in a group by themselves, and, while some timed the music by slapping their hands on their knees, others were capering and whirling around in the most grotesque manner, showing their white teeth, as they grinned their delight, or "yah, yah"ed, at the boisterous fun.

It was no wonder that a great portion of the troops were gathered around there, for it was Christmas night, and home thoughts and home longings were crowding on them; and old scenes and fancies would arise, with sad and loving memories, until the heart grew weary, and even the truest and tenderest longed for home associations that blessed Christmas night. On the right of the camp-ground was another arbor, lately erected for prayer-meetings at night. It was beautifully lighted up with burning pine-knots. Gathered under the arbor were a number of soldiers, quietly and attentively listening to the words which fell from the lips of the preacher standing in their midst—the preacher with his gray locks and wrinkled brow showing the foot-prints of time. Amongst the groups of eager listeners were men just entering the threshold of life, yet whose vocations placed their feet upon the verge of the grave. The rows of tents, the black groupings of adjacent shelters, all made an impressive scene. Occasionally, mingling with the preacher's words, came laughter from some group assembled round a camp-fire near by, or a shout from some unthinking, free-hearted stroller about camp. Words rich with eloquent meaning rolled from that aged preacher's lips, like rippling waves of ocean, succesively, rapidly, breaking upon a sandy shore; the light of hidden power burned in his eyes, as he pleaded—warned his hearers of the life to come. . . . The exhortation finished, a closing hymn was sung, rolling its waves of fine melody out upon the night's still air, over the adjacent prairies . . . .

To-day [the day after Christmas], the troops received four months' pay, in Confederate money, a species of money not very useful to the soldier.

Taking the Oath

SARAH MORGAN DAWSON

Sarah Morgan Dawson (1842–1909) was living in Baton Rouge when the Federals occupied the area. An ardent supporter of the Confederate cause, she fled with members of her family (Eliza Ripley reports on entering the abandoned Morgan house to find it ransacked), spending time in various places in the Florida Parishes, including Clinton. The diary she kept at the time was published years later, in 1913, as *A Confederate Girl's Diary.* In 1863 she crossed Lake Pontchartrain from Bayou Bonfouca with others (including a woman who was transporting the encoffined body of her son) on a schooner to find refuge with a Unionist brother in New Orleans. New Orleans had been in Union hands since early in the war, so she was entering the lair of the enemy. Her journey across the lake ends with the trauma of taking the oath of allegiance to the United States, which she faces upon landing.

Yesterday we arrived [in New Orleans]; I thought we should never get here. Monday we had almost given up in despair, believing the schooner would never return. But in the evening, when all were gathered in our room discussing our hopes and fears, a sail was perceived at the mouth of the bayou, whereupon every one rushed out to see the boat land. I believe that I have not mentioned that this Bonfouca is on a bayou of the same name that runs within a few yards of this house. It is an Indian name signifying Winding River, which struck us as very appropriate when we watched the schooner sailing now to the left, now to the right, apparently through the green fields; for the high grass hid the course of the stream so that the faintest line was not perceptible, except just in front of the house. All was now bustle and confusion, packing, dressing, and writing last words to our friends at home, until half-past eleven, when we embarked.

This is my first experience of schooners, and I don't care if I never behold another. The cabin where Mr. Kennedy immediately carried me, was just the size of my bed at home (in the days I had a home) and just high enough to stand in. On each side of the short ladder, there was a mattress two feet wide. One of them Mrs. R—— had possession of already; the other was reserved for me. I gave the lower part of mine to Minna and Jennie, who spent the rest of the night fighting each other and kicking me.

Just before twelve we "weighed anchor" and I went on deck to take a last look at Dixie with the rest of the party. Every heart was full. Each left brothers, sisters, husband, children, or dear friends behind. We sang, "Farewell dear land," with a slight quaver in our voices, looked at the beautiful starlight shining on the last boundary of our glorious land, and, fervently and silently praying, passed out of sight.

God bless you, all you dear ones we have left in our beloved country! God bless and prosper you, and grant you the victory in the name of Jesus Christ.

I returned to my mattress, and this is the way we spent the night.

Mrs. R——, rocking and moaning as she sat up in bed, whined out her various ills with a minute description of each, ceasing the recital only to talk of her son's body which lay on deck. (Yesterday morning she was sitting crying on his coffin while a strange woman sat on its head eating her bread and cheese.) Mrs. Bull, one of the most intelligent and refined ladies I have yet met, who is perfectly devoted to me, sat by me, laughing and talking, trying her best to make every one comfortable and happy in her unobtrusive way. Mother talked to Mrs. R—— and cried at the thought of leaving her children fighting and suffering. The space between the two beds was occupied by three Irishwomen and Mrs. Ivy's two babies. The babies had commenced screaming as they were brought into the pen, at which I was not surprised. Having pitched their voices on the proper key, they never ceased shrieking, kicking, crying, throwing up, and going through the whole list of baby performances. The nurses scolded with shrill voices above the bedlam that had hushed even Mrs. R——'s complaints; Jennie and Minna quarreled, kicked, and cried; and as an aggravation to the previous discomforts, a broad-shouldered, perspiring Irishwoman sat just by my head, bracing herself against my pillow in the most unpleasant style. I endured it without flinching until about half-past three, when the condensed odor of a dozen different people and children became unendurable, and I staggered up on deck where Miriam and Mrs. Ivy had been wise enough to remain without venturing below. They laid me on a bench in the stern, rolled me up in shawls to keep off the heavy dew, and there I remained until daylight with them, as wide awake as ever.

At daylight there was a universal smoothing of heads, and straightening of dresses, besides arrangements made for the inspection of baggage. Being unwilling for any Christian to see such a book as this, I passed a piece of tape through the centre leaves, and made Miriam tie it under her hoops. At sunrise we were in sight of the houses at the lake end. It seemed as though we would never reach land.

I forgot to speak of our alarm as we got in the lake. No sooner had we fairly left the bayou than the sky suddenly became threatening. The captain shook his head and spoke of a very ugly night for the lake, which sent everybody's heart to their throats and alarmed us immeasurably. We got talking of the sailor's superstition of crossing the water with a corpse, until we persuaded ourselves that it was more than probable we would founder in the coming storm. But the severest storm we met was the one in the cabin; and all night the only wind was a head breeze, and the spicy gale from below.

When we at last entered the canal, I beheld the animal now so long unseen, the Yankee. In their dark blue uniforms, they stood around, but I thought of the dear gray coats, and even the pickets of Madisonville seemed nobler and greater men than these. Immediately a guard was placed on board, we whispering before he came, "Our dear Confederates, God bless them."

We had agreed among ourselves that come what would, we would preserve our dignity and self-respect, and do anything rather than create a scene among such people. It is well that we agreed. So we whispered quietly among ourselves, exhorting each other to pay no attention to the remarks the Yankees made about us as we passed, and acting the martyr to perfection, until we came to Hickock's Landing. Here there was a group of twenty Yankees. Two officers came up and asked us for papers; we said we had none. In five minutes one came back, and asked if we had taken the oath. No; we had never taken *any*. He then took down our names. Mother was alone in the coop. He asked if there was not another. The schooner had fifteen passengers, and we had given only fourteen names. Mother then came up and gave her name, going back soon after.

While one went after our passes, others came to examine our baggage. I could not but smile as an unfortunate young man got on his knees before our trunk and respectfully handled our dirty petticoats and stockings. "You have gone through it before," he said. "Of course, the Confederates searched it."— "Indeed, they did not touch it!" I exclaimed. They never think of doing such work."—"Miss, it is more mortifying to me than it can be to you," he answered. And I saw he was actually blushing. He did his work as delicately as possible, and when he returned the keys, asked if we had letters. I opened my box and put them into his hand. One came near getting me into serious trouble. It was sent by some one I never saw, with the assurance that it contained nothing objectionable. I gave it sealed to the man, who opened it, when it proved to be rather disagreeable, I judged from his language. He told me his captain must see it before he could let me have it, and carried it off. Presently he came back and told me it could not be returned. I told him to burn it then, as I neither knew the writer, the contents, nor those it was written to. "I may save you some difficulty if I destroy it," he remarked, whereupon he tore it up and flung it into the canal. I have since found I had cause to be grateful; for just after came an officer to see the young lady who brought that letter. I showed the pieces in the water, saying the young man had torn it up, which seemed to annoy him; it was to be sent to headquarters, he said.

Then came a bundle of papers on board carried by another, who standing in front of us, cried in a startling way, "Sarah Morgan!" "Here" (very quietly).—"Stand up!"—"I cannot" (firmly).—"Why not?"—"Unable" (decisively). After this brief dialogue, he went on with the others until all were standing except myself, when he delivered to each a strip of paper that informed the people that Miss, or Mrs. So-and-So had taken and subscribed the oath as Citizen of the United States. I thought that was all, and rejoiced at our escape. But after another pause he uncovered his head and told us to hold up our right hands. Half-crying, I covered my face with mine and prayed breathlessly for the boys and the Confederacy, so that I heard not a word he was saying until the question, "So help you God?" struck my ear. I shuddered and prayed harder. There came an awful pause in which not a lip was moved. Each felt as though in a nightmare, until, throwing down his blank book, the officer pronounced it "All right!" Strange to say, I experienced no change. I prayed as hard as ever for the boys and our country, and felt no nasty or disagreeable feeling which would have announced the process of turning Yankee.

Then it was that mother commenced. He turned to the mouth of the diminutive cave, and asked if she was ready to take the oath. "I suppose I have to, since I belong to you," she replied. "No, madam, you are not obliged; we force no one. Can you state your objections?" "Yes, I have three sons fighting against you, and you have robbed me, beggared me!" she exclaimed, launching into a speech in which Heaven knows what she did not say; there was little she left out, from her despoiled house to her sore hand, both of which she attributed to the at first amiable man, who was rapidly losing all patience. Faint with hunger, dizzy with sleeplessness, she had wrought on her own feelings until her nerves were beyond control. She was determined to carry it out, and crying and sobbing went through with it.

I neither spoke nor moved. . . . The officer walked off angrily and sent for a guard to have mother taken before General Bowens. Once through her speech, mother yielded to the entreaties of the ladies and professed herself ready to take the oath, since she was obliged to. "Madam, I did not invite you to come," said the polite officer, who refused to administer the oath; and putting several soldiers on board, ordered them to keep all on board until one could report to General Bowens. Mother retired to the cabin, while we still kept our seats above.

Oh, that monotonous, never-ending canal. We thought it would go on forever. At last we came to the basin in the centre of the city. Here was a position for ladies! Sitting like Irish emigrants on their earthly possessions, and coming in a schooner to New Orleans, which a year ago would have filled us with horror. Again the landing was reached, and again we were boarded by officers. I don't know how they knew of the difficulty mother had made, but they certainly did, and ordered that none should leave until the General's will was made known.

Mrs. Bull and Mrs. Ivy, after a long delay and many representations, at last prepared to leave. I was sitting in the spot I had occupied ever since before daylight, with nothing to support me above my hips. All of us had fasted since an early and light supper the night before; none had slept. I was growing so weak from these three causes, and the burning sun (for it was now twelve), that I could hardly speak when they came to tell me good-bye. Alarmed at my appearance, Mrs. Bull entreated the officer to allow me to leave the boat. No, he said; it was impossible; we should remain on board until General Bowens could come. We may get an answer in half an hour, or we may not get it for some time; and there we must stay until it came. "But this young lady has been ill for months; she is perfectly exhausted, and will faint if she is not removed immediately," pleaded Mrs. Bull. She did not know my powers of control. Faint! I would have expired silently first! The officer said those were his orders; I could not leave. "Do you think you are performing your duty as a gentleman and a Christian? This young lady has obtained her pass already, without the slightest difficulty," she persisted. Still he said he was acting according to orders. Not to be baffled, she begged that she might be allowed to take me to Brother, telling him who he was, while our trunk, Miriam, Tiche, and mother would remain as hostages. Then he gave a reluctant consent on condition I left my number, so he could go after me when I was wanted.

I don't know what good came of the consent, for there I was to remain until something, I don't know what, happened. I only know I was growing deathly sick and faint, and could hardly hold myself up, when some time after Mrs. Bull and Mrs. Ivy left (under the impression that I was to go immediately), a gentleman in citizen's clothes came to me and said he had obtained permission for me to wait General Bowens's orders in his office, a few steps from the schooner. Thankful for so much, I accepted his arm and slowly dragged myself along to the first shelter I had seen that day. By some wonderful condescension Miriam and mother were allowed to follow; and with the guard at the door, we waited there for half an hour more until our sentence could be received.

Miriam had written a line to Brother as soon as possible, telling him of the situation, and while we were waiting in this office, I half dead with fatigue, a carriage dashed up to the door, and out of it stepped Brother. I felt that all our troubles were over then. He looked so glad to see us that it seemed a pity to tell the disagreeable story that yet remained to be told. But once heard, he made all go right in a few moments. He got into the carriage with mother, to take her to General Bowens, while we got into another to come to the house. I saw no more of the guard or officer.

Travel Update

The vote for Louisiana secession was held in the Old State Capitol in Baton Rouge. The state cast its lot with the Confederacy, though local opposition to the Confederate government continued as the war proceeded (many small farmers saw little reason to protect the interests of the slaveholders, and many Acadians felt little connection to this "américain" conflict).

Louisiana was of strategic importance because of the significance of New Orleans as a port and because both sides sought to control the Mississippi River. New Orleans was captured by Admiral Farragut in April of 1862 in the most important Louisiana action of the war, which involved naval assaults on Forts Jackson and St. Philip, both of which had to be passed to reach the city itself. There were literally hundreds of skirmishes and battles in Louisiana, with armies operating not only up and down the Mississippi but also with Union forays down Bayou Teche and Bayou Lafourche and a campaign up the Red River. Grant's attack on Vicksburg also had a significant impact on the Louisiana side of the river.

A map, "The Civil War in Louisiana," has been published cooperatively by several government agencies, including the Louisiana Office of Tourism. In addition to the map itself, which shows campaigns, battle sites, and other places related to the war, the map folder includes much additional information regarding the conflict in Louisiana. There is a guide to Louisiana Civil War sites, Betty L. Morrison's *Louisiana Civil War Tour Guide* (Gretna, La., 1982). The two most important battlefields, however—Port Hudson and Mansfield—are given attention in *The Civil War Battlefield Guide,* ed. Frances H. Kennedy (Boston, 1990), which also contains a section on the Red River campaign. Parts of both battlefield sites are now state commemorative areas that provide visitor centers and educational activities and that maintain and explain battle landmarks. The remains of Fort Jackson also can be visited.

The Battle of Port Hudson was waged not because the town of Port Hudson itself had great strategic value but because of vast Confederate earthworks that were hastily constructed there—north of Baton Rouge on bluffs—to control the Mississippi. Union forces sought to capture it to ensure their own control, initiating the longest siege of the war. What survives at the present state commemorative area site (access from U.S. 61) are significant portions of the northern Confederate earthworks and corresponding Union positions (the map in *The Civil War Battlefield Guide* shows the state-owned area in relation to the larger battle site). The site has several components, including Fort Defiance, the remains of a lunette-type earthwork where the Fifteenth Arkansas Regiment and First Mississippi Light Artillery fought off two assaults in forty-eight days and endured the conditions of the siege. A visit to Fort Defiance gives one at least some sense of the kind of siege warfare that took place at Port Hudson. A concrete path leads to an elevated wooden walkway that goes over earthworks and through pleasant woods past mounted pictures of known combatants; there are also notations about saps and sniper towers. The walkway horseshoes visitors over the site, and, peering down like a latter-day voyeur, one gets an appreciation of what must have been the conditions of battle: Yankees creeping up numerous wild ravines (though trees were felled in them to discourage advances) and taking advantage of the wooded terrain while Confederates slipped out through a tunnel into their protective ditch to fire down at them. The visitor center offers a clear account of the battle, and reenactments and other living history events are regularly staged at the battlefield site. Outside the commemorative area, Port Hudson National Cemetery, which holds the bodies of Union dead from this and other battles, can be visited via Louisiana 3113 from U.S. 61.

The Battle of Mansfield and the associated Battle of Pleasant Hill were fought in 1864. One of the last major Confederate victories, the Mansfield battle blunted the Federal advance up the Red River, which had been launched to destroy factories in Shreveport and in Tyler and other Texas localities that produced most of the goods used by the Confederate armies west of the Mississippi, and to capture cotton-producing lands in Texas so that the cotton trade could be reopened under Union control. Union general Banks had left the protection of the fleet that had come up the Red with him and marched his troops away from the river and through the piney hills toward Shreveport. With his army spread out, Banks was attacked and forced to retreat, having expected no major resistance before Shreveport itself.

Actually, the battle was a series of engagements that took place over several days and in several places. The state commemorative area (easily reached from Interstate 49 by following well-posted signage) includes one major site, where the troops of Louisiana general Alfred Mouton charged across fields to attack Union forces massed along a split rail fence. Mouton was killed; General Camille de Polignac, a French prince in Confederate service and the "Lafayette of the South," assumed command and won the victory. Today the General Mouton Trail takes visitors over the ground of this engagement, now in pleasant pine woods, past a reconstructed rail fence. The visitor center displays information on the battle and the Red River campaign as well as other Civil War materials (weapons, photographs, medical instruments), and on the site there are monuments to Mouton, Polignac, and others. In the general vicinity, markers indicate the sites for other phases of the fighting.

Far to the south, on the Mississippi River below New Orleans, Fort Jackson is maintained by Plaquemines Parish and is located four miles south of the town of Buras on Louisiana 23. The fort was completed in 1832 to protect New Orleans and the Mississippi and complemented the older, Spanish-built Fort St. Philip on the opposite bank of the river. Lightly garrisoned, both were seized in 1861 by Confederate Louisiana, and Admiral David Farragut had to fight his way past them to capture New Orleans. Once New Orleans fell, the forts themselves surrendered, weakened by disease and a shortage of ammunition. Today the fort is an impressive structure (though it was in the recent past a flooded, snake-filled ruin). Though the citadel in the center of the fort was destroyed in the bombardment, the fort's inner walls are virtually intact, and a significant portion of the outer defenses also survive (and have peaceful picnic tables atop them these days; Fort Jackson serves the local community as a gathering place and as the venue for their Orange Festival). A moat with sluggish water and tropical vegetation separates inner and outer fortifications. A nearby Spanish-American War–era emplacement that overlooks the Mississippi is a good vantage point for overlooking the fort, too, as it is on a level with the top of the inner walls. A small bridge crosses the moat (originally spanned by a drawbridge), and a tunnel that seems to burrow into the earth leads the visitor into the fort's interior, where another Spanish-American War battery dominates the central space. Visitors can climb to the top of the cracked, pockmarked, red-brick inner walls and make a complete circuit of them, noting casemates for various guns, stairways leading up to the ramparts, and brick arches that support the ramparts. The fort was buried in rubble for years, and hills of dirt where large trees grow still nuzzle the walls, giving the whole place a gentle appearance. A levee constructed in the 1960s is as tall as the fort's walls; today the Mississippi can only be seen from the vantage point of the ramparts. There is a small museum in a former powder magazine that houses Civil War artifacts and where a brochure with suggested tour routes can be obtained. Fort St. Philip, across the Misissippi, is on private land that can be reached only by boat; what little is left of it above ground cannot be visited.

The Louisiana State Museum in New Orleans has extensive Civil War–related materials, and New Orleans also has a long-established (in fact, the nation's oldest) Civil War museum, the Confederate Memorial Hall at 929 Camp Street. As its name implies, it is also something of a shrine to the Confederacy, an impression reinforced by its stained glass windows and gothic-revival, churchlike interior with flags hanging high in the rafters. Indeed, Jefferson Davis lay in state here after his death in 1893. It is an excellent small museum with exhibit materials well-displayed in exquisite old cases. These materials range from the remains of the jowl of a hog killed in self-defense by Port Hudson defenders, to photographs, paintings, swords, rifles, pieces of Lee's camp silver, and Jefferson Davis memorabilia (his saddle and portmanteau, a crown of thorns woven and sent to him by Pope Pius IX, a portrait of his daughter who was a Mardi Gras queen). The museum is, appropriately, near Lee Circle, a landmark location since the end of the nineteenth century, where a statue of Robert E. Lee stands atop a lofty column. The statue faces a YMCA, and local lore has it that those initials are actually reminding the general, "Yankees may come again."

The Civil War Naval Museum is located, improbably enough, in landlocked Arcadia in north Louisiana's Bienville Parish. Located in a tiny building in the woods north of the town, the private museum contains carefully crafted models of over sixty Civil War ships, said to be the largest extant collection. All were built by the museum's founder, who makes model kits commercially and who provides knowledgable personal tours of the collection.

The town of Clinton, where Sarah Morgan Dawson stopped and which figures peripherally in James K. Hosmer's Louisiana war reminiscences, has a number of interesting antebellum buildings, including the famous Lawyers' Row and the columned courthouse so quintessentially southern that it was used in the film version of Faulkner's *The Sound and the Fury.* Dawson's route across Lake Pontchartrain from Bayou Bonfouca must have been very close to that followed today by U.S. 11 and the railroad tracks used by Amtrak trains entering New Orleans from the east. Hosmer's route from Donaldsonville can be roughly followed today by going down Louisiana 1 or Louisiana 308 (which run on opposite sides of Bayou Lafourche) to Thibodaux and then via Louisiana 20 and U.S. 90 to Morgan City and Berwick. The Parish of Terre Bonne is today written "Terrebonne." Bayou Boeuf, also mentioned by Hosmer but not to be confused with the other Bayou Boeuf along whose banks in central Louisiana Solomon Northup was enslaved, flows into the Atchafalaya River near Morgan City.

6

LAND PICTURESQUE AND FERTILE: CAJUN COUNTRY

The proliferation of Cajun restaurants in such far-flung places as New York and Australia, of advertisements for Cajun country tours, and of Cajun dishes on the menus even of mass-production, fast-food, chain eateries like Burger King indicates very clearly that Louisiana's Cajuns have been discovered by the rest of America and the world. Beginning in the 1970s (coinciding with a rising wave of ethnic pride), people outside Louisiana were made increasingly aware that in the rural bayou country of Louisiana lived a distinctive ethnic group called Cajuns, who spoke French and had their own discrete culture, their own distinctive—and highly appealing—music, cuisine, and worldview.

Of course, Cajuns had been living in Louisiana since the end of the eighteenth century. They came from France by way of Nova Scotia, then called Acadie (hence the evolution of the term: *Acadien, 'cadien, Cajun*). That once-French colony passed to British rule in the mid-eighteenth century, and the Acadians came into conflict with British imperial policies and interests. In 1755 they were expelled from this homeland by the English and thus began the tragic *grand dérangement* of their history: first they were uprooted, next dispersed to France, other English colonies, and the West Indies. Gradually some of them made their way to Louisiana, drawn by its already French culture and traditions (though by then it was a Spanish colony). The Spaniards saw these people as a group who could be a useful buffer against possible British incursion and encouraged them to settle.

Initially they settled as small farmers (*petits habitants*) along the Mississippi in what today are St. James and Ascension parishes and along Bayou Teche in what was known as the Attakapas district. As time went on, they moved into new areas—expanding within the Attakapas and into the prairies of the Opelousas district, for example—while they were also displaced from some of their earlier settlements by the growth of the sugarcane plantation economy of the Louisiana Creoles and incoming Anglo-Americans, which forced some Cajuns to move into more marginal lands such as the coastal marshes and the great Atchafalaya Basin swamp. Because of their common history, their linguistic distinctiveness, their perception of themselves as different from other Louisianians, their relative geographical isolation, and their maintenance of a traditional culture, the Cajuns remained a well-defined group—but their society was hardly static. They assimilated newcomers and were subjected to such acculturative forces as the coming of the railroads and settlers from the American Midwest in the last part of the nineteenth century, the development of a powerful oil industry after major local discoveries in 1901, and attempts by the educational bureaucracy after 1921 to suppress the French language. Yet Cajuns moved into the late twentieth century with a sense of themselves and were recognized by others as being a unique part of American society.

If the Cajuns were indeed "discovered" in the 1970s and 1980s—in the sense of becoming widely known—before then they hardly went unnoticed. Travelers from rather early days reported on them and their region. Charles César Robin, who was in Louisiana just at the time of the transfer from French to American rule, writes about Cajun settlements along the Mississippi and more extensively about his sojourn further west in the Attakapas country, where he may have intended to settle. Frederick Law Olmsted came across Acadians while traveling in the 1850s. His central interest was the slave economy, so he noticed the Acadians on the peripheries of the plantation world, where he thought they were deemed undesirables—whites who might not command the respect of the slaves or who might be poor role models for the work ethic. In 1847, though he himself never came to Louisiana, Henry Wadsworth Longfellow had published his celebrated epic poem about Acadian *dérangement* and reunion, *Evangeline.* Its considerable popularity gave nineteenth-century America an expanded sense of who the Acadians were, and ultimately it gave travelers a symbolic focus for trips to "the Teche country," as well as—indirectly—a specific "sacred" site to visit, the Evangeline Oak, and later, the Evangeline Monument in St. Martinville.

Still, before the twentieth century relatively few people made trips to Acadiana specifically to explore the life of the region. Charles Dudley Warner (whose description of New Orleans voodoo appears in Chapter 11) was one such traveler. After his stay in the Crescent City for the exposition of 1885, he spent Easter in St. Martinville, where he witnessed the holiday custom of egg paquing.[1] He also observed Acadian weaving and architecture and formed an opinion on Acadian cultural dominance and assimilation. Another was Alcée Fortier, whose account of his travels into Acadiana is particularly interesting because he was Louisiana French, though not Acadian, and because his focus as a student of French language and folklore is specifically cultural. Born into the Creole planter aristocracy of St. James Parish (his grandfather was Valcour Aime), Fortier was a well-educated Tulane academic. He writes how he "thought . . . the Acadians and their dialect . . . an interesting subject to study," and he noted various aspects of Acadian language, folklore, and custom during his short and rather casual visit. His affinity for this other French culture comes through, but so does the obvious fact that as an upper-caste urbanite and a traveler, he is still an outsider to this milieu.

By about the time of the First World War, attempts were being made to encourage motorists and other tourists to visit the "Evangeline Country." Later, the monumental travel guide *Louisiana: A Guide to the State,* published in 1941 but based on the research of the New Deal Federal Writers' Project, calls attention to the Cajuns as "the most homogeneous group" of Louisiana French and details aspects of their folkways.[2] The book's tours—which sug-

---

1. "Paquing," or "paquering," is an Easter tradition whose name derives from the French for Easter, *Pâques;* it involves a competition in which two opponents try to break each other's eggs by tapping them together. For more information, see Barry Ancelet, Jay Edwards, and Glen Pitre, *Cajun Country* (Jackson, Miss., 1991), 83.

2. Louisiana Writers' Project, *Louisiana: A Guide to the State* (New York, 1941), 86–87.

gest routes and sights for visitors—recommend various incursions into Cajun country.

In the 1940s and 1950s several writers devoted considerable attention to their contact with the Cajuns. They figured in several books written by journalist, novelist, and popular historian Harnett T. Kane. From his base in New Orleans, Kane made numerous trips to the Louisiana countryside, including Acadiana. In 1950 Frances Parkinson Keyes, best-selling author of innumerable historical novels, published *All This Is Louisiana*.[3] Keyes had come to the state to research several books, working from accommodations she leased on the grounds of a River Road plantation called the Cottage. Collaborating with photographer Elemore Morgan, Sr.—a Baton Rouge native who did a lot of the actual traveling—she wrote a kind of travelogue that takes readers around the state. Such aspects of Cajun life as pirogue races, Saturday-night dances, and Cajun houses figure prominently in her volume.

Then in the mid-1950s another journalist became intrigued by the ever-popular Evangeline story and wondered, "Where *are* Evangeline's people and what have they become?" This question led to extensive travels for Carolyn Ramsey and eventually her 1957 book, *Cajuns on the Bayous*. Around the same time a witty memoirist named Emily Kimbrough was recording her impressions of Louisiana travel in a book called *So Near and Yet So Far*. Well known for *Our Hearts Were Young and Gay*, which she coauthored with actress Cornelia Otis Skinner, Kimbrough came to Louisiana with a small group of friends, all middle-aged women. Her book is built around a dry humor of cultural difference—affluent outsiders encountering a state that seems so different from the rest of America ("so near and yet so far"). The portion reprinted here takes us to a *fais-do-do* (also described by Fortier over sixty years earlier), an important social institution. A *fais-do-do* is a dance that commonly lasts all night. Children are brought to an area designated the *parc aux petits,* and the term *fais-do-do* derives from Acadian French baby talk meaning "go to sleep." Though Kimbrough and her friends seem merely to have dropped in for a peek, she stresses the wish not to intrude or disturb local feelings—a valuable perspective for travelers who call on cultures not their own.

Until recent years visitors have tended to romanticize the Cajuns or to emphasize the most traditional elements of Cajun culture while ignoring Cajun

---

3. Frances Parkinson Keyes, *All This Is Louisiana: An Illustrated Story Book,* photographs by Elemore Morgan (New York, 1950).

society's complex, present-day shape. Indeed, some Cajuns themselves may seek to project such a romantic image to tourists. One recent traveler writer who avoids that road is William Least Heat Moon, who set out in the 1980s to visit little American towns off the main routes of travel. Heat Moon does indeed seem to be someone just passing through. Yet by stumbling into a bar scene in his search to find Cajun music, he gives us a glimpse of the modern underbelly of this part of the world and of the seedy but probably dynamic mixture of outsiders and locals that the oil industry has thrown together. Frederick Turner, on an odyssey along the Gulf Coast from the tip of Florida to the Yucatan, is also just passing through, but by managing to find articulate and thoughtful Barry Ancelet—"perhaps the essential Cajun of his time" (as well as a sharp critic of Heat Moon)—Turner turns his short stay in Acadiana into a look at some of the conflicts and pressures of contemporary Cajun society.

The Acadian Coast

CHARLES CÉSAR ROBIN

> When the Acadians first arrived in Louisiana, a num-
> ber of them settled along the banks of the Mississippi
> upriver from New Orleans. This area, which Robin
> describes, became known as the *côte française,* or Aca-
> dian Coast (as opposed to the German Coast, which
> had been settled upriver from the city earlier by immi-
> grants from Germany).

Twenty leagues above the city the Acadian coast be-
gins and runs another twenty up from there. Like the Germans they work
their own farms. Only a few of them have Negroes. Already the population
has risen so that the farms are sub-divided into strips of two or three arpents
of frontage. You must remember that each plot ran back forty arpents from
the river. Only about half that depth, however, is under cultivation, the rest
being inundated and covered with cypress and similar swamp vegetation.

Rice, corn, several kinds of beans, melons (in season), pumpkin, salted
pork and beef make up their principal diet. Their customs can be compared
to those of our farmers of Beauce and Brie. Good fellows! They do not show
the zeal in their work that their European confreres would, for on the one
hand, they are not pressed by necessity, and on the other hand, the lack of outlets for their product discourages them from greater efforts. However, they are
still Frenchmen, passionately loving their country, proud to work for it, and
showing a great predilection for its products.

Ordinarily their manner is reserved but they are no strangers to gaiety.
They love to dance most of all; more than any other people in the colony. At
one time during the year, they give balls for travelers and will go ten or fifteen

leagues to attend one. Everyone dances, even *Grandmère* and *Grandpère* no matter what the difficulties they must bear. There may be only a couple of fiddles[4] to play for the crowd, there may be only four candles for light, placed on wooden arms attached to the wall; nothing but long wooden benches to sit on, and only exceptionally a few bottles of *Taffia* [rum] diluted with water for refreshment. No matter, everyone dances. But always everyone has a helping of *Gumbo,* the Creole dish *par excellence*;[5] then "Good Night," "Good Evening," "So Long," "See you next week" (if it isn't sooner). One shoves off in his pirogue, his paddle in his hand; another gallops off on horseback, others who live nearer walk home singing and laughing. The Carmagnolle is the usual garment.[6] Clean clothes are a great luxury for them. The women wear a simple cotton dress and often in the summer they wear only a skirt. They go to dances barefoot, as they go to the fields, and even the men only wear shoes when they are dressed formally. As for learning they don't know what it is. Most of them cannot read.

Once past the Acadian coast the houses become more and more spaced out.

4. The Acadians developed a style of twin fiddling to amplify the sound of their music at noisy dances. Fortier found three fiddles at the dance he attended.

5. Gumbo is a hearty soup that begins with a flour-based roux and may contain any of a variety of ingredients: seafood, sausage, chicken, wild game, okra. It is commonly eaten with rice and sprinkled with sassafras powder (*filé*).

6. The carmagnole was a short coat as well as an outfit including such a coat popular with the French revolutionaries. This description does not seem to accord with the most commonly accepted conceptions of Acadian costume.

Acadians

FREDERICK LAW OLMSTED

In 1853 Olmsted (1822–1903) encountered Acadians
on the peripheries of the plantation world. The expansion of sugarcane plantations had pushed many of
them away from earlier areas of settlement; his account suggests the at-best ambivalent attitudes of the
displacing planters. He presents the Acadians at least
partially as carefree "vagabonds" who spend their lives
in more pleasant pursuits than constant work (an enduring stereotype). From *A Journey in the Seaboard
Slave States* (1856).

At one corner of Mr. R.'s plantation, there was a ham-
let of Acadians (descendants of the refugees of Acadia), about a dozen small
houses or huts, built of wood or clay in the old French peasant style. The residents owned small farms, on which they raised a little corn and rice; but
Mr. R. described them as lazy vagabonds, doing but little work, and spending
much time in shooting, fishing, and play. He wanted very much to buy all
their land, and get them to move away. He had already bought out some of
them, and had made arrangements to get hold of the land of some of the rest.
He was willing to pay them two or three times as much as their property was
actually worth, to get them to move off. As fast as he got possession, he destroyed their houses and gardens, removed their fences and trees, and brought
all their land into his cane-plantation.

Some of them were mechanics. One was a very good mason, and he employed him in building his sugar-works and refinery; but he would be glad to
get rid of them all, and should then depend entirely on slave mechanics—of
these he had several already and he could buy more when he needed them.

Why did he so dislike to have these poor people living near him? Because,
he said, they demoralized his negroes. The slaves seeing them living in appar-

ent comfort, without much property and without steady labor, could not help thinking that it was not necessary for men to work so hard as they themselves were obliged to; that if they were free they would not need to work. Besides, the intercourse of these people with the negroes was not favorable to good discipline. They would get the negroes to do them little services, and would pay them with luxuries which he did not wish them to have. It was better that negroes never saw anybody off their own plantation; that they had no intercourse with other white men than their owner or overseer; especially, it was best that they should not see white men who did not command their respect, and whom they did not always feel to be superior to themselves, and able to command them.

A Tour of the Acadian Country

Alcée Fortier

Born in St. James Parish, Fortier (1856–1914) had a distinguished academic career at Tulane University as a nationally known scholar of language, literature, and folklore. Though of Louisiana French background himself, he was not Acadian, so he approached the Cajuns sympathetically but as an urban outsider. He published this account of his travels in the Bayou Teche area (the Attakapas) of south Louisiana in *Louisiana Studies: Literature, Customs and Dialects, History and Education* (1894).

Having thought of the Acadians and their dialect as an interesting subject to study, I determined to pay a visit to the Attakapas country made classic by the genius of Longfellow. In the beginning of September, 1890, I left New Orleans at 7:30 A.M. by the Southern Pacific Railroad and arrived at St. Mary Parish after a journey of five hours. Along the route the train passed through fields of tall sugar cane, yellow corn and golden rice. Every now and then we crossed a bayou, or a marsh or a forest. Shortly after leaving the city we reached "Bayou des Allemands" named for the German settlers who had been sent to America by the famous John Law.[7] In the middle of the bayou is an island covered with trees and briers, on which is a hut which serves as a hunting lodge for the sportsmen, whose canoes for duck-shooting are to be seen everywhere. Trees grow to the edge of the water of all our bayous and render the smallest stream picturesque.

After passing another beautiful stream, Bayou Boeuf, we see a few of the Indian mounds which are so interesting to the archeologist and the ethnolo-

7. John Law (1671–1729) was a Scottish-born financier who formed the Mississippi Company to finance the colonization of Louisiana. The company became the focus of intense financial speculation, after which it collapsed (a debacle known as the "Mississippi Bubble").

Washday in Cajun
country, by A. R.
Waud

From *Harper's Weekly*,
October 20, 1866,
reproduction courtesy
Special Collections,
LSU Libraries

gist, and at Morgan City we cross the wide and turbid Atchafalaya, the rival of
the Mississippi, and which threatens, if not curbed by artificial means, to divert the waters of the great river from its present channel.[8]

A few miles after passing Morgan City I leave the train and am soon on a
plantation situated on both sides of the Teche. After dinner I take my little
nephews with me and we go to the bayou. There is in front of the house a
drawbridge which is opened every time a boat or raft passes. We sit on the
bridge and I look on the waters flowing beneath and I can hardly see the direction of the current. A few months before the bayou had been a torrent overflowing its left bank. St. Mary Parish is one of the most prosperous in Louisiana, and everywhere there are central sugar factories with the most modern
appliances, the powerful mills, or the diffusion process, and through this busy
scene of progress flow the tranquil waters of the Teche, its banks covered with
moss-grown live-oaks. Here is the same spectacle which the poet [Long-
fellow] has so admirably described. It is civilization now, but side by side with

8. See Chapter 2 for information on how this situation developed.

the primeval forest. Under the stately oaks the children run and play while I lie upon the grass and meditate. My thoughts return to the past and I imagine what must have been the feelings of the Acadians when they saw for the first time in 1765 the beautiful Attakapas country.

Not far from the plantation where I visited is a village called Charenton. It is but a hamlet, but it possesses a church and a convent of nuns. The good sisters of St. Joseph have established a school for girls which does great good to the neighborhood. The mother superior, a very agreeable and intelligent lady, is a descendant of the Acadians. Very near the village is a settlement of Indians. I observed them with curiosity, as they are the sole remnant of the Attakapas tribe, the fierce maneaters. Some of the squaws are handsome, and the men have the real Indian type, although I am told that the tribe is rapidly disappearing and mingling with the negroes. The women make very pretty reed cane baskets, quite different in design from those which the Choctaws sell at the French market in New Orleans; the men cultivate little patches of ground and sell fish and game. One hundred years ago the Indians were numerous on the Teche; they seem to have melted away without being molested. The mere contact of civilization was sufficient to cause them to vanish.[9] . . .

Two miles from Charenton is the Grand Lac, which I desired very much to see, so one morning at daybreak I started in a light buggy with the oldest of my nephews, a Sophomore of Tulane University. There is in reality no route leading to the lake; we had to pass for several miles through a forest on the bank of the Teche and it gave me great pleasure to see the bayou where it appeared most wild. After a ride of two hours we left the shore of the Teche and turning toward the interior we soon arrived at the lake. I felt delighted at the sight: before us stretched the blue waters, which a light breeze caused to undulate gently, and in the distance could be seen the sails of two schooners which seemed to be the wings of marine birds skimming the surface of the waves. All around the lake is a forest, and on the trees we could see the cardinal bird with

9. The Chitimachas, who unlike a number of other present-day Louisiana tribes lived in Louisiana when Europeans arrived, still have a reservation at Charenton, where they now also own a casino. They are renowned basket makers, and a few members of the tribe continue this tradition. Fortier is confused, however, about their identity; he speaks of them as the Attakapas, who lived farther west and acquired a reputation as cannibals. His confusion may have stemmed from the fact that the early French post at the site of St. Martinville was the *poste des Attakapas* and that this area is sometimes called "the Attakapas country."

his scarlet robe, the jay bird with his silver and blue jacket, the black bird with his golden epaulets, and what pleased me most, numberless mocking birds, those admirable songsters, which the impudent English sparrow is rapidly driving away from our Southern land.

Being so near the Atchafalaya, the Grand Lac is liable to overflows and, last spring, its water inundated a large extent of country. A levee made in great part with shells has been erected by the owner of the plantation immediately adjoining the lake, and as there are large oak trees on the bank, the place is a favorite resort in summer for pleasure seekers. While we were crossing a little bayou by means of a tree which the wind had thrown down and which served as a suspended bridge, we saw an old Indian on the other side. He appeared to us as the spirit of the lake summoned to protect it from the pale face, and already our imagination was taking its flight toward fairy land when we were suddenly brought back to reality by the voice of the red man, who was speaking to us in English. Never did our national idiom appear to me more prosaic than in the mouth of this descendant of the Attakapas. We hastened to leave him and turned our eyes again toward the Lake. Here my mind reverted to another scene and events long past presented themselves to me. In the year 1862, after the fall of New Orleans, our plantation being on the Mississippi, fifty-seven miles from the city, my father thought that it would be more prudent to put his family out of the reach of the invading army and he sent us to St. Mary parish, where there was a Confederate army to protect the Attakapas country. After a few months, however, the Federals spread over the country, and it was thought advisable that we should return home. My brother, aged seventeen, enlisted as a Confederate soldier in the Trans-Mississippi department, and my father started with the younger children on the return journey. We embarked in two large skiffs, with two Indians in each one as oarsmen, and we went down the Teche. The trip was most pleasant to me, as we passed through numberless bayous, stopping at night at the houses of friends, and taking our meals during the day under the shade of some large tree. I have no recollection of the route, which ended only at the mouth of Bayou Plaquemines, in Iberville parish, where there were carriages to take us home; but although only six years old at the time, I shall never forget the anxiety of my father, when, on entering the Grand Lac, the booming of a cannon was heard. It was thought to be a Federal gun-boat and our Indians were ordered to row most diligently. Twenty-eight years had passed since I had crossed the

Grand Lac as a fugitive, but yet on that September morning of 1890 I thought I heard still the voice of our devoted father encouraging his little children with his tender words of love.

While in St. Mary I had occasion to visit a number of planters, who received me very kindly; and who did all in their power to help me in my work. They introduced me to some Acadians and communicated to me a few characteristic expressions of the Acadian language. I was, however, anxious to see St. Martinsville, and, after promising to return to St. Mary, I took the train and went to the oldest town on the Teche. It was with real pleasure that I started on my journey; I had never gone to that part of Louisiana before and everything was new to me. I passed on my way Jeanerette and New Iberia in Iberia parish. They are both thriving towns, the latter especially, on account of its proximity to the celebrated salt mines on Avery Island. It has a handsome Catholic church, an elegant public high school and some beautiful private residences. . . .

I may add here that the Teche becomes a noble river shortly before mingling its waters with those of the rapid Atchafalaya. From Jeanerette to New Iberia the fields presented the same beautiful crops of cane, rice and corn which I had seen along the route from New Orleans; but after passing New Iberia, cotton begins to be seen, and I noticed in one patch of ground the curious fact of our four great staples growing side by side—cane, cotton, rice and corn. Such is the wonderful fertility of our soil.

St. Martinsville does not lie on the Southern Pacific Railroad, and it is only lately that it has been connected with the main line by a branch leading to the Teche. This may account for the stagnation of business in the town, which, before the war, was very prosperous. I had letters of introduction to several distinguished gentlemen, but I saw on arriving in that Creole town that a Creole needed no credentials to be well received. I found myself among friends, I may say, among relations, as all the persons I met knew my family and I knew theirs. French is essentially the language of the inhabitants and it is well spoken by the educated class. The latter speak English also, but the lower class speak the Acadian French mixed with the Creole patois[10] and a little English. In the interior settlements (*au large*) little or no English at all is spoken, and at Breaux Bridge, in St. Martin parish, and in the adjoining parish of Lafayette, French is taught together with English in the public schools. Although we de-

10. Fortier refers to the Creole spoken primarily by Afro-French Louisianians.

sire to see every child in Louisiana speak English we wish every one to speak French also, and I was very glad to see how the people of St. Martin are attached to their French. . . .

There is but one hotel in St. Martinsville; it is a large house with a wide gallery and massive brick columns. Everything is as in ante-bellum days; no register awaits the names of the guests, and the owner seems to have implicit confidence in the honesty of his boarders. As the criminal court was in session, the members of the jury were taking their dinners at the hotel when I arrived. There being no place at the table for me, I was given a comfortable rocking chair and I sat in the dining-room during the dinner of the jurors. As several of them were Acadians, I listened very attentively to their conversation and took notes while they were speaking. All of them spoke French, but the influence of English on their French was sometimes apparent. One of them, speaking of an important criminal case, said to the others: "Vous serez tous lockés (locked up) ce soir." Another, to express his contempt of the argument of a lawyer, said: "Ça, ça n'a pas grand fion avé moué" (that does not produce much effect on me); and his friend replied: "Il aura un bon bout (pronounced *boute*) encore avec cette affaire." Although I was very hungry, I was sorry to see the jurors leave the table to go to the court house to be *lockés*.[11]

After dinner I took a walk over the town, and never have I seen a more quiet and orderly place and one where there are so few bar-rooms. The life in that old Creole town reminded me of *autrefois* [former times], as depicted to me many times by my aged friends. There was not much animation in business, but order and decency remained everywhere and the people were uniformly affable and polite. I spent the evening very pleasantly with my host, his wife and his grandmother, conversing with the old lady about the past.

I awoke very early the next morning, and on opening the window of my room I saw a pretty sight: the bayou was just beneath, its waters green with water plants and rushes, and in the distance a prairie, above which was rising resplendent a September sun. A knock was heard at the door, and answering it I found a little negro girl bringing me a cup of real Creole coffee.

At a short distance from the hotel is the church, on the green before which stands the statue of the last curate, Father Jan, who died an octogenarian, beloved by his parishioners. The present priest, Father Langlois, is a botanist of

11. *Lockés* is, of course, being borrowed directly from the English. Fortier finds these phrases differing from standard French usage.

great merit who has made important discoveries in the flora of Louisiana . . . and I determined to pay him a visit. He received me very kindly and showed me his admirable botanical collections. I asked his permission to look over the church register, and on turning to the year 1765 I saw the record of the first child born of Acadian parents in St. Martin, probably the first born in Louisiana. . . .

There being such vast prairies in the Attakapas the Acadian settlers compared them with the wide expanse of the ocean and applied to them many nautical terms. They say *aller au large* [to go to sea], or *mettre à la voile* [to set sail] when they start to cross the prairie, and an island is, in their language, a piece of wooded ground in the prairie. I was shown *l'île des Cypres* while in St. Martin. It is in a prairie which is not far from the Grand Bois, an immense forest which begins in the Attakapas country and extends as far as the Arkansas line. In the Grand Bois, near St. Martinsville, are a number of lakes, of which one, Lake Catahoulou, is two and a half miles long and three-fourths of a mile wide. It is one hundred and ten feet deep and is said to be beautiful. It is a great place for hunting and fishing, but is full of alligators and gar-fish. I was shown an Acadian who, being in a canoe on a fishing excursion, was followed by a gar-fish twelve feet long. He seized an opportunity and jumped on the back of the fish, which dived with him to the bottom of the lake. On arising from the water our hero said to his terrified companions: "Now, he will not return." This individual was a real type and his conversation was very instructive in its quaintness. . . .

The eminent men that have arisen among the Acadians in Louisiana show what good elements there are in that race, but unfortunately, they are, as a rule, lacking in ambition. They are laborious, but they appear to be satisfied if, by cultivating their patch of ground with their sons, they manage to live with a little comfort. The mother and daughters attend to the household duties and weave that excellent fabric called the *cotonnade*. The greatest defect of the Acadians is the little interest they take in education; a great many are completely illiterate. As the public school system progresses, education will spread gradually among them, and being an intelligent race they will produce many men like Alexandre Mouton.[12] Education will, of course, destroy their dialect, so that the work of studying their peculiar customs and language must not be long delayed.

12. Mouton was governor of Louisiana from 1843 to 1846.

On Sunday, September 21, I went to church, where I saw the whole population of the town, and after bidding adieu to my newly made friends I left St. Martinsville, where I had met kind gentlemen and fair ladies, taking with me a good stock of Acadian expressions. A few hours later I was again in St. Mary parish. I wished this time to live in the prairie, where I thought there would be a better chance of observing the Acadians. The prairie is now entirely cultivated around Jeanerette and is dotted everywhere with the cottages of the small farmers and with the comfortable houses of the large planters. For a week I roamed all over the country with some friends who were kind enough to take me to the places of interest and to the persons who might help me in my work.

Having heard that every Saturday evening there was a ball in the prairie, I requested one of my friends to take me to see one. We arrived at 8 o'clock, but already the ball had begun. In the yard were vehicles of all sorts, but three-mule carts were most numerous. The ball room was a large hall with galleries all around it. When we entered it was crowded with persons dancing to the music of three fiddles. I was astonished to see that nothing was asked for entrance, but I was told that any white person decently dressed could come in. The man giving the entertainment derived his profits from the sale of refreshments. My friend, a wealthy young planter, born in the neighborhood, introduced me to many persons and I had a good chance to hear the Acadian dialect, as everybody there belonged to the Acadian race. I asked a pleasant looking man: "Votre fille est-elle ici!" He corrected me by replying: "Oui, ma *demoiselle* est là." However, he did not say *mes messieurs* for his sons, but spoke of them as *mes garçons,* although he showed me his *dame.*[13] We went together to the refreshment room, where were beer and lemonade, but I observed that the favorite drink was black coffee, which indeed was excellent. At midnight supper was served; it was chicken gombo with rice, the national Creole dish.

Most of the men appeared uncouth and awkward, but the young girls were really charming. They were elegant, well-dressed and exceedingly handsome. They had large and soft black eyes and beautiful black hair. Seeing how well they looked I was astonished and grieved to hear that probably very few of them could read or write. On listening to the conversation I could easily see

13. The gentleman is using very elegant language, calling his daughter "my young lady" rather than the standard *ma fille* and his wife "my lady" rather than the standard *ma femme.* He uses the standard phrase for his sons, however.

that they had no education. French was spoken by all, but occasionally English was heard.

After supper my friend asked me if I wanted to see *le parc aux petits.* I followed him without knowing what he meant and he took me to a room adjoining the dancing hall, where I saw a number of little children thrown on a bed and sleeping. The mothers who accompanied their daughters had left the little ones in the *parc aux petits* before passing to the dancing room, where I saw them the whole evening assembled together in one corner of the hall and watching over their daughters. *Le parc aux petits* interested me very much but I found the gambling room stranger still. There were about a dozen men at a table playing cards. One lamp suspended from the ceiling threw a dim light upon the players, who appeared at first very wild, with their broad-brimmed felt hats on their heads and their long untrimmed sun-burnt faces. There was, however, a kindly expression on every face, and everything was so quiet that I saw that the men were not professional gamblers. I saw the latter a little later, in a barn near by where they had taken refuge. About half a dozen men, playing on a rough board by the light of two candles. I understood that these were the black sheep of the crowd and we merely cast a glance at them.

I was desirous to see the end of the ball, but having been told that the break-up would only take place at 4 or 5 o'clock in the morning, we went away at 1 o'clock. I was well pleased with my evening and I admired the perfect order that reigned, considering that it was a public affair and open to all who wished to come without any entrance fee. My friend told me that when the dance was over the musicians would rise, and going out in the yard would fire several pistol shots in the air, crying out at the same time: *le bal est fini.*

The names of the children in Acadian families are quite as strange as the old Biblical names among the early Puritans, but much more harmonious. For instance, in one family the boy was called Duradon, and his five sisters answered to the names of Elfige, Enyone, Meridie, Ozeina and Fronie. A father who had a musical ear called his sons Valmir, Valmore, Valsin, Valcour and Valerien, while another, with a tincture of the classics, called his boy Deus, and his daughter Deussa.

All the Acadians are great riders and they and their little ponies never seem to be tired. They often have exciting races. Living is very cheap in the prairie and the small farmers produce on their farms almost everything they use. At the stores they exchange eggs and hens for city goods.

Several farmers in the prairie still have sugar houses with the old-fashioned mill, three perpendicular rollers turned by mules or horses. They have some means, but are so much attached to the old ways that they will not change. It will not be long, however, before the younger generation replaces the antiquated mill with the wonderful modern inventions.[14] The Acadians are an intelligent, peaceful and honest population; they are beginning to improve, indeed many of them, as already stated, have been distinguished, but as yet too many are without education. Let all Louisianians take to heart the cause of education and make a crusade against ignorance in our country parishes!

Before leaving the prairie I took advantage of my proximity to the gulf to pay a visit to Côte Blanche. The coast of Louisiana is flat, but in the Attakapas country five islands or elevations break the monotony.[15] These are rugged and abrupt and present some beautiful scenes. A few miles from the prairie is a forest called Cypremort; it is being cleared, and the land is admirably adapted to sugar cane. The road leading to Côte Blanche passes for three miles through the forest and along Cypremort Bayou, which is so shallow that large trees grow in it and the water merely trickles around them. On leaving the wood we enter on a trembling prairie[16] over which a road has been built, and we soon reach Côte Blanche. It is called an island, because on one side is the gulf and on the others is the trembling prairie. We ascended a bluff about one hundred feet high and beheld an enchanting scene. In the rear was the wood which we had just left, stretching like a curtain around the prairie; to the right and to the left were a number of hills, one of which was one hundred and fifty-seven feet high, covered with tall cane waving its green lances in the air, while in front of us stood the sugar house with large brick chimneys, the white house of the owner of the place, the small cottages of the negroes on both sides of a wide road, and a little farther, the blue waters of the gulf. I approached the edge of the bluff, and as I looked at the waves dashing against the shore and at

14. For discussion of an old-fashioned Louisiana sugar mill, see Calvin Claudel, "The Sugar Mill," *Georgia Review,* XVI (1962), 87–93. Edward King provides a description of the sort of mill Fortier would have thought modern in Chapter 3.

15. The Five Islands are Avery, Jefferson, Weeks, Côte Blanche, and Belle Isle, all of which are coastal saltdomes that provide islandlike elevations in the marsh.

16. *Trembling prairie* was commonly used as a term for *marsh* in nineteenth-century Louisiana.

the sun slowly setting in a cloudless sky, I exclaimed: "Lawrence,[17] destroyer of the Acadian homes, your cruelty has failed. This beautiful country was awaiting your victims. We have here no Bay of Fundy with its immense tides, no rocks, no snow, but we have a land picturesque and wonderfully fertile, a land where men are free—*our* Louisiana is better than *your* Acadia!"

17. Major Charles Lawrence was the British officer responsible for the Acadian expulsion from Nova Scotia.

The *Fais Do Do* at Mamou

EMILY KIMBROUGH

Kimbrough (b. 1899) authored several witty memoirs, including *Our Hearts Were Young and Gay* with Cornelia Otis Skinner. In the 1950s she toured Louisiana by car with a group of middle-aged women friends and with a guide (Fred); she wrote about the experience in *So Near and Yet So Far,* from which the following is reprinted. Mamou is on the prairies northwest of Lafayette, and thus the dance she writes about was in a different part of Acadiana from that Fortier visited.

The main street of Mamou at night looked like a scene from an old silent movie of a Western town. It was wide. I daresay it is wide in the daytime, too, but that night along its curbs was an assortment of vehicles I would have thought only Hollywood could have assembled as props. There were several kinds of horse-drawn carriages, each horse nodding into a feed bag. One drew a covered buggy, another an open cart, a third a two-seated carriage, and there were duplicates of these models. I saw a Model T Ford and the newest Cadillac. What I did not see was an open parking space. The Cajuns had come to town for their *fais do do.*

Clara drove slowly looking for a place but stopped at the sound of Sophy's horn behind us, and we all looked back. Sophy was beckoning us to follow. She pulled around ahead of us and turned into a side street.

Three people stood on the sidewalk, evidently waiting for us. They waved at our approach and pointed to two parking places. When we joined them we were introduced by Fred to one of the group called O. C. I learned later his

The main street of Mamou on the night of the *fais do do,* by Mircea Vasiliu

From Emily Kimbrough, *So Near and Yet So Far,* copyright © 1955 by Emily Kimbrough Wrench, renewed 1983 by Emily Kimbrough. Reproduced by permission of HarperCollins Publishers, Inc.

name is José, but that to the Cajuns he was O. C.[18] He and Fred had worked together on a tanker, but O. C. was a native Mamoun. O. C. introduced us to his companions, Mr. Reed and a Mrs. Reed, who was not his wife. Mr. Reed in fact had not met her before this evening. She was a reporter on a newspaper in a nearby town and O. C. had invited her to join us. I further discovered it was from Rosa to Fred to O. C. that the evening had been accomplished. All this was in our conversation as we walked back to the main street. When we reached it O. C. stopped in front of a lighted store, looked a little anxiously from one to the other of us, and respectfully asked if we would gather close

18.   More probably his name was Hosea, a fairly common Cajun name.

around him, so that he might tell us a few things. We huddled in a football playing clump, and O. C. in his Cajun English—and I cannot reproduce it— explained that at Mamou there are two halls for a *fais do do:* one for the old folks, the other a few doors down the street for the young people. We would visit each. The Cajuns were happy to have guests but did not like them to stare like sightseers that came in just to look. "Like at freaks. You see?" O. C. asked apologetically.

We assured him we did indeed, and wanted to do only what would be the least conspicuous.

O. C. grinned with relief. "Then we all go now," he suggested happily.

We crossed the street. There was no traffic moving on it. Obviously everybody was already there. We entered a building a few doors to our left. It was a one-story structure, the inside of rough wood. It, too, looked like a bar and dancehall from an early Western movie. The bar was the first room we entered off the street and it was crowded with standees several rows deep. We edged our way round them, and through a doorway into the room beyond that was the dancehall. There were tables and chairs around the edge of this and it was crowded, too, but O. C. led us all the way to the far end and found an empty table there just under the musicians' stand. We made a parade of some length, moving single file, but we attracted, I could see, no particular attention.

We had arrived during an intermission. We were no sooner seated than the music began again. Old-fashioned fiddle music, it was, the bows scraping the strings, harshly but vigorously, the melody unfamiliar. O. C. was standing behind me. He had chosen not to sit down; he wanted to keep an eye on everything going on, he explained.

He leaned down and spoke close to my ear. Above the music it was hard to hear him. "They play old French tunes," he said, "all Cajun music, especially 'Big Mamou.'"

After a few bars of the music the room began to fill. I saw O. C. had not exaggerated when he said the *fais do dos* in this hall were for the older folk. Though there were young couples, there were elderly people, too. Hands are not twisted and joints swollen from working only a few years. These faces were lined, the skin thickened by many seasons of labor in the sun. But the dancers carried themselves well and their feet were light on the floor. They did not combine in square dancing; they danced in couples. Here and there one showed off a few fancy steps, but for the most part they went round and round in a sort of two-step in quick time with much arm pumping. There was no cutting in, but the music stopped frequently for a general change of partners.

I beckoned O. C. and he leaned down again. "Am I right," I asked him, "that these people have worked all day and they'll dance here all night, and go back to work again? And they do this twice a week?"

O. C. shrugged his shoulders. "But of course, madame," he said, "they do not stop the work, but they must have fun to live, isn't it?"

"Yes," I said, "it is. It's wonderful."

Two of my friends caused a little trouble. Sophy became suddenly somewhat carried away by the music, and rising to her feet executed a little jig. This brought attention to our corner and I was forced to hiss at her to sit down. She complied instantly but regretfully, and I leaned forward to whisper to her, "I'm sorry, but they think you're imitating them. O. C. says so."

Sophy was chagrined. Nothing had been farther from her mind, she told O. C. across my shoulder, but she'd understood him to say anybody could dance, and the music had made her feel like dancing.

O. C. shrugged his shoulders again apologetically. "Generally it is two people."

A heavy-set, red-faced gentleman stood in front of Sophy and bowing offered her a glass of red wine, and with it simultaneously an invitation in French to dance.

Kat's voice cut through, sharp and clear, "Now, Sophy, you see, we can't have this."

Ellen's voice broke in. "Oh, isn't that lovely," she said, "I do hope you will, dear."

But Sophy was abashed, and though we prodded her, refused the offer politely, but firmly.

A few minutes later I saw we were again attracting attention; passing couples nudged one another and turned toward us. I followed the direction in which they were looking and saw at once the focal point of their interest. It was a bright focus: Darn's white gloves. She was pulling over her hands a fresh pair.

O. C. simultaneously saw what was happening and spoke in my ear again. "They don't wear gloves at *fais do dos.*"

I turned the suggestion into an order. "Take off those gloves. They're blinding everybody."

Darn peeled them off immediately and was so dismayed at having made a gaff, she half rose and tucked the gloves underneath her, evidently to make sure they were completely out of sight. A few minutes later she sat on her hands, too, probably because having embarrassed others by her gloves, she embarrassed herself without them.

O. C. suggested we might like to visit the other dancehall, and at the next intermission, Kat, Darn, Ellen, Sophy and I filed out behind O. C., the others deciding to stay where they were and hold our places.

The young people's *fais do do* was only a few doors away from the one we had just left. O. C. said this was to allow parents to keep an eye on their young and yet slip to the other hall for a few rounds themselves. A row of sheets made a curtain on the right of the entry. A couple parted these, and came out. Behind them and the curtains I saw a bar. Fred explained the State was going through a "clean-up" movement that had threatened to be troublesome for the *fais do dos,* because by law no children may enter a bar. But the Cajuns had resolved the difficulty by cutting off the bar by means of the line of sheets we saw. Presumably, this created for minors an impenetrable barrier. Fred also said the Cajuns had been surprised to learn of the repeal of Prohibition. They hadn't heard about Prohibition.

In the dancehall proper, benches against the wall circled the room. We could see through a door at the far end a little ice-cream parlor with boys and girls at tables having innocuous refreshments of sodas, Coke and the like.

The music began, the youngsters left their tables and in a minute the dance floor was crowded. Though I saw many on the floor who looked eighteen and a little over, I saw a good number I would have guessed to be not more than nine or ten.

O. C. confirmed my estimate. "They start at the very young," he told me, "and is very good reason for this. Mamas and papas bringing their boys and girls and looking at boys and girls from the other mamas and papas for making marriages. That is why you see mamas and papas all here, so nothing can go bad. But also so something can come good for future."

I asked what the mamas and papas did with their littler ones.

"Wait till music stop," O. C. said, "then take quick look down under benches."

I repeated this suggestion to my friends. When the music stopped we ducked our heads quickly, taking a surreptitious look. We saw the littlest ones, each rolled in a blanket. Babies were sleeping on the floor beneath the benches. The next older ones, O. C. said, were in rows on the floor in a room upstairs. "All family here," he added. "Nobody left behind."

The music began again. The dancers rushed to the floor. Their style was considerably more gymnastic than that of their elders up the street. There was nowhere for us to sit. We were in some peril from the arms and legs gyrating around us.

We returned to the more conservative gathering, what Sophy termed, "The Philadelphia Assembly" of the *fais do do*. We entered during an intermission and found a newcomer at our table. Emma introduced us all as friends without bothering about names. The new arrival was Cajun, speaking only French. She was handsome, only moderately tall but with a straight slim figure, clear smooth skin, bright blue eyes and a pompadour of hair almost as white as Darn's gloves. She wore a straight black dress and over it a bright red sweater.

Within a few minutes she had told us a good deal about herself, that she was in her seventies, she did not care to say just where in them, that she had been a widow for a considerable length of time but had begun to be tired of that single state, and had decided to come into town to look about for a husband. There were not many to be had, but there was some selection.

I asked if she would like to tell us how she would set about making her choice.

She bowed to me graciously and answered in French, "You would perhaps like to see?"

We assured her we would like it very much.

"Then watch," she told us, and rose from the table. She walked to an adjoining one and with a regal nod of the head and charming smile said to the group seated there, "You will permit? I shall return it untouched." As she said this she picked up a wine glass filled nearly to the brim with red wine, and with another nod turned and walked out on the dance floor.

"Play, if you please," she ordered in a firm commanding voice to the musicians on the platform. "A waltz."

Obediently, the musicians picked up their instruments, the leader stamped on the floor a few beats to mark the tempo, and the orchestra swung into a waltz.

Our friend bowed to each corner of the room much like Queen Elizabeth in the ceremony of her coronation, and then slowly raising the glass of wine, set it carefully on the top of her head. When it was placed there to her satisfaction, she withdrew her hand and began to waltz, slowly, and in perfect rhythm, turning this way and that, sometimes completely around. She circled the room. When she had returned to her starting point, she stopped, lifted her hand, removed the glass of wine, bowed again to the musicians. The music stopped. She walked to the table from which she had taken it, set the glass down in its original place, faced the room again and with a ravishing smile called out "*Voilà.*"

Pandemonium was the accolade she received—cheers, shouts, handclappings, stamping on the floor. We rose from our table simultaneously. No one of us needed to say to another, "This is the peak. Let's go remembering this."

We were able to reach her before the rest of the room closed in. "*Magnifique,*" we told her, and thanked her "*mille fois*" for a superb performance.

She acknowledged our tributes graciously and then added with a gamin's wink, "And now you see how it will be."

At the door we turned back and saw how it was: a queen making her selection from among her subjects begging from her any small favor she might bestow.

Cajun Music

William Least Heat Moon

> Heat Moon set out on a long journey across America to visit "those little towns that get on the map—if they get on at all—only because some cartographer has a blank space to fill."

If you've read Longfellow, you can't miss Cajunland once you get to the heart of it: Evangeline Downs (horses), Evangeline Speedway (autos), Evangeline Thruway (trucks), Evangeline Drive-in, and, someone had just said, the Sweet Evangeline Whorehouse.

I found my way among the Evangelines into an industrial area of Lafayette, a supply depot for bayou and offshore drilling operations. Along the streets were oil-rig outfitters where everything was sections of steel: pipes, frames, ladders, derricks, piles, cables, buoys, tanks. Crude oil opened Acadian Louisiana as nothing in the past three centuries had, and it seemed as if little could be left unfound in Cajun hamlets once quite literally backwaters.

Eric's, on the edge of the outfitters' district, was a windowless concrete-block box with a steel door and broken neon and a parking lot full of pickups, Cadillacs, and El Caminos ("cowboy Cadillacs"). But no French music.

I drank a Dixie and ate bar peanuts and asked the bartender where I could hear "chanky-chank," as Cajuns call their music. She, too, drew a map, but her knowledge gave out before she got to the destination. "It's called Tee's. It's down one of these roads, but they all look alike to me out there."

"Out there?"

"It's in the country. Follow my map and you'll be within a couple miles."

When I left she said good luck. The traveler should stand warned when he gets wished luck. I followed her map until the lights of Lafayette were just a glowing sky and the land was black. I wound about, crossing three identical bridges or crossing one bridge three times. I gave up and tried to find my way back to town and couldn't do that either.

Then a red glow like a campfire. A beer sign. Hearty music rolled out the open door of a small tavern, and a scent of simmering hot peppers steamed from the stovepipe chimney. I'd found Tee's. Inside, under a dim halo of yellow bug lights, an accordion (the heart of a Cajun band),[19] a fiddle, guitar, and a ting-a-ling (triangle) cranked out chanky-chank. The accordionist introduced the numbers as songs of *amour* or *joie* and the patrons cheered; but when he announced "*un chanson de marriage*," they booed him. Many times he cried out the Cajun motto, "*Laissez les bons temps rouler!*"[20]

While the good times rolled, I sat at the bar next to a man dying to talk. My Yankee ass and his were the only ones in the place. His name was Joe Seipel and his speech Great Lakes. I asked, "You from Wisconsin?"

"Minnesota. But I been here seven years working for P.H.I."

"What's P.H.I.?"

He put down his bottle and gave me an exaggerated, wide-eyed, open-mouthed look to indicate my shocking ignorance. "You gotta be kidding!"

"About what?"

"Petroleum Helicopters Incorporated!" He shook his head. "Jees!"

"Oh, that's right. What kind of helicoptering do you do?" I tried to talk between numbers, but he talked through it all.

"I don't fly. I'm a mechanic. But Stoney here flies out to the offshore rigs. Delivers materials, crews. You know."

The pilot, in his fifties, wore cowboy boots and a jaunty avocado jumpsuit. He was applying a practiced *Bridges-at-Toko-Ri* machismo to a hugely mammaried woman who had painted on a pair of arched, red lips the likes of which the true face of womankind has never known.

19. The accordion did not become a prominent feature in Cajun music until the latter part of the nineteenth century, when it was introduced into south Louisiana. Before that, the only instrument generally available was the fiddle. The guitar also came to rural America in general in the late nineteenth century, when it became an important element in the string bands popular then. The Cajun music most commonly heard today is a dance music, and the accordion—which actually went out of fashion in the 1930s until after World War II—is a dominant feature of the characteristic sound.

20. That is, "Let the good times roll"; for some this widely used phrase seems to characterize the supposed Cajun propensity for celebrating and enjoying life.

Seipel said, "I was just like you when I came here—dumb as hell. But I've read about Louisiana. Learned about Coonasses from that yellow book."

"What yellow book is that?"

"That one comes out every month."

"National Geographic?"

"That's it. They had a story on Coonasses."

"Did they explain the name 'Coonass'?"[21]

"I think they missed that."

A small, slue-footed Gallic man wearing a silky shirt with a pelican on it dragged an up-turned metal washtub next to the band and climbed on. I think he'd taken out his dentures. A mop handle with baling twine tied to it projected from the tub, and he thrust the stick about in rhythm with the music, plucking at the sound of a double bass.

"That's DeePaul[22] on the gut bucket," Seipel said. "He's not with the band."

After a couple of numbers on the tub, the small man hopped down and waltzed around the floor, quite alone, snapping his wrists, making sharp rapid clacks with four things that looked like big ivory dominoes.

"Those are the bones," Seipel said. "Sort of Cajun castanets."

When the band folded for the night, the little fellow sashayed to the lighted jukebox, drawn to it like a moth, and clacked the bones in fine syncopation, his red tongue flicking out the better to help him syncopate, his cropped orb of a head glowing darkly. Seipel hollered him over.

He showed how to hold the bones one on each side of the middle fingers, then flung out his wrist as if throwing off water and let loose a report like the crack of a bullwhip. "Try dem in you hands."

The bones were smooth like old jade. I laboriously inserted the four-inch counters between my fingers and snapped my wrist. *Cluk-cluk.* "Lousy," Seipel said. I tried again. *Cluk-cluk.* Wet sponges had more resonance. Seipel shook his head, so I handed them to him. He got them mounted, lashed out an arm, and a bone sailed across the room.

"You boys don't got it," DeePaul said, his words looping in the old Cajun way. DeePaul's name was in fact Paul Duhon. He had cut the clappers from a

21. The derivation of this term is obscure, but it has been a derogatory nickname for Cajuns. In recent years, however, some Cajuns have coopted it.

22. Probably his name was *TeePaul* or *Ti-Paul. Ti,* from *petit* (small), is commonly used by Cajuns to form diminutives of personal names.

certain leg bone in a steer and carved them down to proper shape and a precise thickness. "You got to have da right bone, or da sound she muffle. And da steer got to be big for da good ringin' bones."

I tried again. *Cluk-cluk.* "I work at dis forty years," Duhon said, "and just now do I start gettin' it right. Look at me, gettin' ole and just now gettin' good. Dat's why only ole, ole men play da good bones."

"Where'd you learn to make them?"

"Ole color man, he work on da rayroad. He got nuttin' but he love music so he play da bones. He play dem in da ole minstrel shows. He da one day call 'Mister Bones,' and it Mister Bones hisself he show me carvin'. Now people say, 'Come play us da bones in Shrevepoat.' But da bones just for fun."

"DeePaul flies kites," Seipel said. "Wants in the *Guinness Book.*"

"My kites day fly for time in da air, not how high. Someday I want people to be rememberin' Duhon. I want 'Duhon' wrote down."

"I can play the musical saw," Seipel said and called to the barmaid, "Got a saw here?" She pushed him a saltshaker. "What's this?"

"That's the salt you're yellin' for." Seipel and I laughed, holding on to the bar. Duhon went home. Everybody went home. The barmaid watched us wearily. "Okay," she said, "come on back for some hot stuff."

"Is this where we find out why they call themselves 'Coonasses'?" I said, and we laughed again, holding on to each other.

"All right, boys. Settle down." She led us not to a bedroom but to a large concrete-floor kitchen with an old picnic table under a yellow fluorescent tube. We sat and a young Cajun named Michael passed a long loaf of French bread. The woman put two bowls on the oil cloth and ladled up gumbo. Now, I've eaten my share of gumbo, but never had I tasted anything like that gumbo: the oysters were fresh and fat, the shrimp succulent, the spiced sausage meaty, okra sweet, rice soft, and the roux—the essence—the roux was right. We could almost stand our spoons on end in it.[23]

The roots of Cajun cookery come from Brittany and bear no resemblance to Parisian cuisine and not even much to the Creole cooking of New Orleans. Those are *haute cuisines* of the city, and Cajun food belongs to the country where things got mixed up over the generations. No one even knows the

---

23. Heat Moon seems to be referring to the liquid of the gumbo as the roux. The term actually refers to the starter for gumbo (and other dishes) made by browning white flour. C. Paige Gutierrez, in *Cajun Foodways* (Jackson, Miss., 1992), 52, comments, "A roux is not a finished dish by itself; rather a roux is a temporary product that becomes part of a finished dish."

source of the word *gumbo*. Some say it derives from an African word for okra, *chinggombo,* while others believe it a corruption of a Choctaw word for sassa-fras, *kombo,* the key seasoning.

The woman disappeared, so we ate gumbo and dipped bread and no one talked. A gray cat hopped on the bench between Seipel and me to watch each bite of both bowls we ate. Across the room, a fat, buffy mouse moved over the stove top and browsed for drippings from the big pot. The cat eyed it every so often but made no move away from our bowls. Seipel said, "I've enjoyed the hell out of tonight," and he laid out a small shrimp for the cat. Nothing more got spoken. We all went at the gumbo, each of us, Minnesotan, Cajun, cat, mouse, Missourian.

South of the South

Frederick Turner

In *A Border of Blue: Along the Gulf of Mexico from the Keys to the Yucatan,* from which this is taken, Turner recounts his travels along the entire Gulf Coast. In addition to this brief incursion into Cajun culture, the book also includes an interesting section on New Orleans jazz musicians.

December 30, a lead sky, and the whole region from mid-Texas south to the Gulf and east to the Florida panhandle sealed beneath it; fields a matching gray or else a dead yellow, standing water in most of them, barren trees like still smoke. On the marquee of the Piggly Wiggly in Lafayette, Louisiana, the transparent brilliance of Christmas had departed, leaving behind only the homely and familiar specials: SALT MEAT, BLACK EYES, 3-LITER COKE.

I had some time to kill before my appointment with Barry Ancelet[24] in Scott and filled it with mall shopping for inessential items and then with manic calisthenics in my motel room, pushing myself time and again up from the thin green carpeting, momentarily defying the clock and the gravity of sand that was running down on the year, the decade of the Eighties, and my own little allotment of mortality.

---

24. People who know Ancelet and this area have pointed out that a few of Turner's facts may be incorrect: Ancelet does not live on a dirt road, nor does his house have dormer windows. They suggest that for reasons of health Ancelet drinks little alcohol and that he has denied drinking the three beers in a row Turner credits him with. It may be that Turner was mis-remembering or that his writing was subtly shaped by his larger vision of this place and its inhabitants.

In the hamlet of Scott I had time, too, time to think about the impending appointment with Ancelet since I missed the turn for his dirt road both going and coming; time, that is, to reflect on the certainty that I was not wanted where I was going, that Ancelet's flat, inflectionless voice on the telephone had done everything this side of rudeness to warn one off. But in the subtly brutal way of a writer on the scent of material, I had ignored his signals, secretly trusting in my knowledge of the innate dignity of these Cajuns: if you didn't insult theirs they couldn't ultimately bring themselves to refuse you their common courtesy. That maybe was the trump the Texans had held, then played, when they'd come into this country back in the Twenties with their oil rigs, their sweet technology, their talk, and convinced cooperation from the Cajuns, sucking out oil and money and wetlands soil, then leaving. I knew Ancelet was perhaps the essential Cajun of his time, a young man who had so fully mastered the culture and history of his place that an hour spent in his company would be worth months of random travel here, years in a library. What I didn't know was what—if anything—he was prepared to share with me.

When we'd talked by phone and I'd stumbled through a description of my mission, concluding with a request to spend a few hours with him, he'd said that he was very busy: when he wasn't teaching at the University of South-western Louisiana, or writing, or putting on festivals of Cajun culture, he was at home with his wife and kids. "And whatever time's left over these days, I spend in a duck blind. My wife's understandably jealous of what free time I do have, and so am I." He let these last four words hang out there on the line, then seemed to leave something of an opening when he volunteered that Sat-urday nights he hosted a live-audience radio show in Eunice. I barreled through that space like a runaway truck, all but inviting myself to accompany him to Eunice the following Saturday.

So here Saturday was, and here I was now at his house, a traditional wooden one with narrow dormer windows, raised high above the flat fields. On its wide, west-facing gallery my only greeter was a bowlegged hound with a chalky blind eye. Presently a little boy burst from the door carrying a toy musket, and behind him, sauntering, lean, handsome, with great brooding eyes and a mustache that looked out of the century before, Barry Ancelet. He stood above me on the gallery, unsmiling and guarded as I made my way across the muddy yard, then opened the door by way of invitation, and we went into the kitchen. His wife said hello with what I thought was a careful smile, then announced she had to run down to the store for a pie tin but wouldn't be gone long. I had to wonder if I wouldn't miss her company.

Ancelet seated himself in a rocker and asked me what kind of book I thought I was writing, and after I'd tried again to explain it, he interrupted with "Oh, kind of a *Blue Highways* type thing."

Trying to curry some sort of favor, I said, "Well, kind of, I guess."

"You know," he said, "that's a book I truly hated. All that sorry self-searching: it left me cold. And, you know, if you're going to work the underside of places, like that guy did, you're not going to get the average people in there. I'm not going to speak about the people in the rest of the book, but I can tell you he didn't come near getting the average people from here in there." All this without looking at his visitor, rocking in cadence with his words, his fingers, too, tapping out some code in accompaniment on the rocker's lowest rung, *tap, pop, tap. . . .*

"How long are you going to be in this part of the country?" he asked, glancing at me now. I told him just a couple more days, that I'd already spent almost two weeks in Louisiana and felt I had to move on into Texas. He shook his head, looking more and more like a Gallicized Christopher Walken. "Do you think you can get to know a country in a couple of days?" He shook his head again, mourning the evident folly of the enterprise, this man living on ground prepared and fertilized by the lives and deaths of generations of ancestors and now called to wedge himself ever deeper into its rich, fecund soil. And what, after all, could I say to the thrust of his questions? What *were* a traveler's impressions worth, anyway, compared with the blood knowledge of one who had made his life the study of his native place? In the pleasant clutter of the kitchen, the little boy poking his musket under our chairs and into corners on a hunt, the quality of my own hunt seemed suddenly—though surely not for the first time—brought into an uncomfortably sharp relief.

I was saved from further such melancholy questions and musings by Mrs. Ancelet's reappearance, apologetically brandishing a small pie pan, the only size, she now explained, the store had in stock. "Well," she said at the sideboard and to no one in particular, "it'll just have to be a small pie."

Then we were out in Ancelet's spattered pickup, its front seat cluttered with hunting gear, and backing swiftly down the drive. "It's the second split of the duck and goose season," he said by way of explanation for the jackets, caps, boots, and cartridge box on the seat. He yanked the truck into first and spun out into the road's soft ruts. Rolling through the puddles toward the paved road, he told me that before we made the show in Eunice we'd be stopping at a friend's house where Ancelet was to pick up some tickets for tomorrow night's New Year's Eve dance. "I might have a bit of trouble finding him," he said. "He's my duck-hunting friend and I've never seen his place in the daylight." But he found it well enough, a beige house trailer marooned in an inlet of muddy water. Concrete block steps led up from the water to the trailer's door, but you still would have to find a way to get to them.

Ancelet had swung down from the cab and was about to slosh across when he jerked his head around. "Look there!" he exclaimed, dropping for an instant his reserve. "They're right over there!"

So they were: in the rice field across the road a great gathering of snow geese sat in the shallow water, and as we looked another long harrow came out of the north, braked over the field, then dropped quickly into it amid the cries and flutterings of those already settled. Ancelet stood there in the swimming light of the late afternoon, a man clearly torn between his present obligations and the sight of these beautiful creatures just a few hundred yards away. It wasn't, he explained when he'd come away with his tickets and turned the pickup north for Eunice, just the killing of them, the thrill of the hunt. Sometimes, he said, after he'd bagged his limit, he'd stay on in the blind, simply watching the great birds or taking photos of them.

It was forty-five minutes along the back roads to Eunice, and the plan I'd had in mind in inviting myself for this trip was to use the time to ask Ancelet about Cajun culture and his own intense involvement with it. Though our beginnings had not been promising, once I broached the subject, I found him a ready talker, personal in his approach to the culture and its preservation, impersonal in his delivery to this audience of one beside him: this, his manner said, is how it is, and I don't care especially who you are or what use you might eventually make of what I'm telling you.

At bottom, he saw himself and the Cajuns as an endangered species, endangered by the homogenizing forces of modernism, the economic erosion of traditional values and ways of living, endangered most particularly by the invasive presence of the English language. "To speak French today in Louisiana," he wanted me to understand, was a "daily decision. You go into a grocery store [motioning with a thumb at one that sat at a nameless crossroads], and you can say 'Give me some bread' or you can say 'Donnez-moi du pain,' and the storekeeper will give it to you, because it doesn't make any difference to him, he can do it either way. That's the choice you're faced with every day here." He slapped the steering wheel lightly with the flat of his hand. The Cajuns, he said, had been facing this choice for more than a century and a half, but especially so in the past fifty years.

Soon after the Louisiana Purchase, he claimed, the Louisiana Creoles had gotten what he called "the message." "The message was that the key to the future was in becoming Americanized. But out here the Cajuns didn't get that message. They were much more isolated by geography and occupation. Most of them were subsistence farmers, or else they were hunters or trappers or fishermen. Their economy was basically barter and they were just much farther removed from the stream of history. So, where the Creoles saw what was going to happen, the Cajuns didn't. When the Civil War came along, what do you think the desertion rate was among them? Eighty-five percent or higher. It wasn't that they sympathized with the Union forces. It just wasn't their war. When they were conscripted and put into uniform, they just walked home. It didn't have anything to do with them.

"Well, after the war matters began to change. For one thing, after the turn of the century they discovered oil at Jennings. Then they passed the Education Act in—I think—1916, and this meant free public education. The Cajuns, like a lot of other traditional peoples, had been resistant to education simply because if kids went, they might learn things their parents didn't know. But now the kids had to go to school, and when they did the first thing they learned was that they were forbidden to speak French. They couldn't speak it anywhere, not even on the playground. If they did, they were punished. Some of those kids suffered real trauma in those first days because they couldn't say they had to go to the bathroom and so they had to wet their pants." If Ancelet wasn't actually glaring at me now, he was certainly giving me a very direct stare. "This," he resumed, glancing back quickly at the road, then turning his glowing eyes on me again, "this is what America was up to then and what it's still up to: what I call homogenization and channeling. You try to take various ethnic groups and strip away their distinguishing differences, channel them into a narrower way of behavior and thinking so they'll fit in more easily with the national system." He quoted me some lines from that great bully boy of early twentieth-century nationalism, Theodore Roosevelt, to the effect that America had room for but one language—English—because the goal of the culture was to turn out what T. R. was pleased to style "Americans" and not some nation that might be mistaken for a rooming house of various ethnic groups.

"Then, while this process was going on and the oil industry was siphoning off the Cajuns into that line of work, away from their traditional ways, there was the new system of roads built by Huey Long, and suddenly you had coming into the country a whole new set of outside influences. And not only that, but people found they could take these same roads out. And there came in, too, radio, which has the inevitable tendency to standardize. Instead of making your own music, your own entertainment, it's all done for you, it's all done by others who don't share anything of your background. Well, after three generations of all this, traditional Cajun culture was pretty well eroded around here.

"Me, I was a little bit different, maybe. Both my father and mother worked out, which meant that my grandmother, my father's mother, one of the dearest people I've ever known—or ever will know—took care of me a lot, and all she spoke was French. So I grew up speaking it. My parents would come to pick me up at the end of a day, and they'd ask me something—in English—and I'd automatically answer back in French because I'd been talking with my grandmother all day. So they said, by the time I was getting ready to go to first grade (1957), 'Hey, we better teach this kid English.' They were a little worried, maybe. But I could speak both equally well, so they sort of gave up and spoke French with me. You have to understand that, because of the developments I've just mentioned, the French language here had become something parents spoke to each other at home and whenever they didn't want the kids to understand what was being said.

"When I went off to graduate school it was with the idea of coming back here and doing something, I didn't know what, but something that would in some way involve me with my roots. So, I ended up studying French, linguistic anthropology and folklore at Indiana. Then I came back here and was lucky enough to land a job at USL. I teach in the French department but we now have a much different emphasis than when I came here and was looked upon as something of a freak because I went around whistling or singing 'Jolie Blonde' [the Cajun cultural anthem]. We're now very involved with Francophone studies and French area studies, which means we study a number of cultures—Caribbean, African—where French is spoken."

He bristled when I asked him whether the French he'd grown up with was in fact a dialect. Did he, I wanted to know, teach his students in entry-level courses to speak French as he had learned it? "Many people," he said with asperity, had gone from here to France and to other French-speaking countries and had had "no trouble at all making themselves understood. They found they were perfectly able to order meals, sleep indoors, use public facilities. I teach French the same way I learned it, and there are now hundreds of students of mine going around pronouncing French the way they learned it in my classes."

Was it then all insult, I asked, to speak of Cajun French as a dialect? "No," he said shortly, "it's just wrong."

By now the muffled sun had sunk into the long prairies that stretched west into Texas, and the lights of the gas stations and convenience stores we passed were beginning to stand out. As we neared Eunice and the Liberty Theatre where Ancelet hosted the show, I asked him to tell me something about how the show had gotten started. It had been, he said, the joint idea of the town of Eunice and the National Park Service.[25] "But the Park Service wanted to do it in English. I told them, 'That's fine. But you've got the wrong guy here.' I wasn't interested in doing that. I wanted to do it in French, or I didn't want to do it at all. And this'll give you an idea of what I've been talking about: right up until the very last minute they were still trying to convince me to do it in English—and throw in a little French here and there, for the flavor. We had twenty minutes till air time, and they're *still* doing this! I said, 'Okay! Will you guys *just shut up*, and let me do what I'm going to do anyway, and then next Saturday night you can get someone else to do the show.'

"Well, I went on and started out in French, and the audience just went nuts! They hadn't heard anything like that in forty years or more. So, the show's in French—with a little English thrown in, for the flavor. We generally have a band or two, Cajun music or zydeco. We might have a storyteller. And generally we have a living recipe. That's someone who'll give out a recipe and explain it.

"The effect of this kind of a thing is to encourage the truly local, and not only that, but also to create conversation and cultural dialogue. You see people in the audience who're from the outside, and they'll be leaning over to ask, 'What'd he say? What'd he say?' And suddenly you've got a totally new situation. Suddenly the French-speaking people are in a new situation. They are the ones who have the knowledge. They are the ones who know what's going

25. This is because of the National Park Service's involvement in Jean Lafitte National Park, which has several facilities rather than a single area and which focuses upon the cultures of south Louisiana; see the Travel Update for more information.

on, and the effect of this is to encourage pride and interest and enthusiasm and a desire to perpetuate traditions."

Whatever congeries of motives it was that brought them here, the folks at Eunice had filled the Liberty Theatre's seats by six-fifteen for the show at seven o'clock. In the alley in back two bands leaned against vans or the building's walls, talking and practicing a few licks. The fire exit lights on either side of the stage door were reflected in the puddles at the bottom of the steps Ancelet and I now went up. There was a sizable crowd back there as well, including the mayor who stood beaming at the general shape of matters, resplendent in shirtsleeves and broad red suspenders. I asked him if there was any place nearby where I might get a cup of coffee.

"There isn't any coffee right around here," he said with his big smile, "but across the street you could get lots of other things." I went where he directed, settled for a can of Bud, and brought it backstage.

Out in the glow of the stage lights Barry Ancelet was casually seated atop a high stool. In an almost conversational tone he warmed up the house with a few jokes, the punches of which were lost on me with my cast-iron, graduate school French. But I was too embarrassed by this deficiency to ask any of those standing about me, laughing in the shadows, "What'd he say? What's the joke?" Perhaps quite as he had intended, Ancelet's jokes were at least partly on those like myself who couldn't get them, those who were emissaries from that wider world that in its almost thoughtless way had crowded this little one toward effective extinction.

Primed by Ancelet's short course in Cajun cultural survival, I felt through the next two hours at the Liberty a certain sort of ardor, amounting almost to a kind of fierceness, in this joyful celebration of communal Cajunness. It was easy enough to see that these people—the performers and their friends and relatives, their audience—were having a good time. What might have been missed by the outsiders, who also missed Ancelet's preliminary jokes, was the emotional intensity they had brought to this old brick building on a Saturday night in Louisiana's westerly parishes. Yet, once you looked and listened for it, it was there: there in the defiant metallic brashness of the old-style diatonic ac- cordions that had all but disappeared from Cajun instrumentation by the early 1940s but now were absolutely *de rigueur* for any self-respecting Cajun band; there in the high, inspired madness of the fiddlers, descendants of those nameless folk artists who more than a century ago had made for the Ishmae- lite Acadians the first esthetic accommodation to this new home, their heavy attack on their instruments wailing of exile, loss, the flat challenge of these unsung prairies and marshlands; there in the weathered faces of the audience, faces filled with surprise and joy and the remembered pain of having only yesterday been forbidden their native tongue and then disparaged as ignorant "coonasses."

After four bands performed, a pleasant-faced woman explained how to make a fruitcake, and Barry Ancelet took a solo turn on the accordion; then part of the crowd flowed backstage to congratulate the performers. An old man in a straw cowboy hat and bib overalls, holding a small boy's hand in his own rough paw, came up to the fiddler of the group Jambalaya and with a slight cock of the head patted the artist's arm. "We just so proud of you!" he said, and then simply stood there beaming.

I mentioned this episode to Ancelet as we whipped at what felt to me like dangerous speed back along the patched and bumpy roads from Eunice to Scott. To the south an oil field flare turned the night a cloudy carmine and all about us lightning was hitting into the sodden fields. "That kind of thing," he rejoined, "is the kind of thing you see all the time." His postperformance adrenal rush, sustained perhaps in some measure by the six-pack of beer we'd stopped for, induced in him what might have been a friendliness. "What this show does is tell these folks over and over again that this music, this whole culture, is beautiful and valuable simply because it is theirs." In the darkness of the lurching cab I heard the flat of his hand strike the steering wheel once again, and I could feel the glow of those eyes.

When I remarked on the uniform excellence of the four bands heard at the Liberty tonight, he told me that when they'd put on the first Cajun music festival in 1974, there had been no musicians in it who were under thirty, which, he said, "will give you another idea of what I meant about homogenizing and channeling. Cajun music—traditional Cajun music—was regarded then by young musicians as old-timey chankety-chank. Five years later at the same festival we had eight bands with musicians under thirty, and three of those bands had musicians in their early twenties." I said this reminded me of Allan Jaffe's experience with traditional jazz musicians at Preservation Hall: the more the old music was aired again, the more those who had known how to play it began to come out of the shadows, and eventually traditional New Orleans jazz made converts of younger musicians who had been playing in contemporary styles.

"Exactly. There were actually a lot more musicians out here than at first appeared. They had stopped playing, given it up, but when they heard it again, when there was a recognized outlet for it, when they saw it was honored, they began to come forward. And at the same time the kids were watching this development, and they began to say, 'Hey, I want to be up on the stage with that man! I want to play that music!' "

Now into his third beer, he suddenly turned back to a subject he'd dismissed earlier, my Gulf coast book, asking if I had a title for it yet. I said I'd thought about calling it *The Redneck Riviera,* but that the more I had gotten into the project, the more that seemed a smart-ass and inappropriate title.

"There was an anthropologist who used to be here," Ancelet said, "who claimed the Gulf coast was a world apart. He said it was 'south of the South.'[26] One of the things that sets it apart from the rest of the South is that it really wants to be a part of the Caribbean instead of the North American continent. The Gulf coast yearns toward the Caribbean. Look at our crops: rice, yams, citrus, sugarcane. They're really Caribbean, not North American. And with virtually every one of them we've had to fiddle around to try to make them grow here. Rice wasn't a commercial product here until the Americans made it one. Sugarcane, they had to fiddle around with it to make it commercially profitable. We really don't have the proper climate for these things—as we found out again just the other day when that hard freeze ruined the citrus crops. When that hard freeze hits, you can hear the trees just *popping.*

"But in spite of freezes and hurricanes and everything else, the Gulf coast seems to want to hang on somehow. Of course it gets harder every year, it seems. Every year there's less and less of the Gulf coast here. I don't know if you're aware of this, but we have a very serious shoreline erosion problem that is a direct result of the kind of channeling I've been talking about. They've channeled the Mississippi so much and built such a tremendous system of dikes and so on that the very thing that over the centuries made this such fertile farmland—the river—has been prevented from replenishing our lands. We're starving our shoreline to death."

He said other things, too, had been starved to death by the channeling of the Mississippi and the region's bayous and streams: traditions, communal

26. Ancelet may be referring to Nicholas R. Spitzer, who was Louisiana's state folklorist at one time; more recently, however, he has attributed the phrase to another folklorist, Gulf Coast native Paige Gutierrez.

ways. When I asked him for an example, he shot back that the tradition of hand fishing was a thing of the past because many of the region's watercourses had been so dredged and channeled that their flows were too swift either for the fish to make nests in their banks or for men to hope to catch them with their bare hands. And with the end of hand fishing, there had been an end to the community outings that had been an integral part of the practice.[27]

We rolled presently into the lights from Ancelet's house. He looked into the sack that had recently contained our beer and said flatly, "Well, we did that proud." Then he alighted and stood there in the gloom with the gallery lights etching his tall, spare form. We shook hands quickly.

"The name of your book," he said, turning to go, "is *South of the South*."

27. Handfishing involves going into the water and inserting one's hands into holes in the bank and hollow logs to catch fish. It was not limited to the Cajuns or Louisiana, who probably learned the art from local Native Americans, but was an important activity, especially as it was a part of social outings. A video by Cajun filmmaker Pat Mire (director) and Charles Bush, *"Anything I Catch": The Handfishing Story*, 1990, provides an introduction to the practice.

Travel Update

Cultural geographers and anthropologists have drawn maps to indicate the area of greatest French influence in Louisiana (see one in Nicholas R. Spitzer, ed., *Louisiana Folklife* [Baton Rouge, 1985], 351, for example), and a twenty-two-parish area officially has been designated Acadiana. Yet Cajun country really has no fixed boundaries, and the visitor may have difficulty in getting a good fix on it. Not only does it sprawl across a wide area, but its cultural landscape may not always seem particularly distinctive. Parts of it are hardly picturesque and may even strike the traveler as monotonous or ugly. Many non-Cajuns live here, some of whom—particularly African Americans—may even resent that the region's identity has become so closely linked with one ethnic group. Though its towns, villages, and people are increasingly oriented toward tourism and provide an especially friendly welcome to outsiders, there are not, as Barry Ancelet notes, "many orientation points for visitors."[28] Thus a journey to Acadiana must be planned carefully if one wants to come to terms with it as a culture area with a distinct way of life—and that seems to be the best reason for wanting to go there. However, there are some key sites and events in Cajun Country that can serve to anchor the visitor to an appreciation of the cultural landscape.

Cajun Country Guide, by Macon Fry and Julie Posner (New Orleans, 1993), is a comprehensive guide to everything from genteel bed and breakfasts to the savagery of cockfighting, and it can be very useful, especially for its relatively up-to-date information on eateries and entertainment. The visitor centers of the Jean Lafitte National Park complex in Lafayette, Eunice, and Thibodaux offer first-rate, up-to-date exhibits that introduce Cajun culture to those seriously interested in trying to understand where that culture came from and how it has developed. The Jean Lafitte Park, headquartered in New Orleans, is the first "cultural park" in the National Parks System, primarily emphasizing not the natural environment and scenic splendors but the

---

28. Barry Jean Ancelet, "Cultural Tourism in Cajun Country: Shotgun Wedding or Marriage Made in Heaven?" *Southern Folklore,* XLIX (1992), 258.

An Acadian Homestead in Louisiana, by A. R. Waud

From *Harper's Weekly,* July 20, 1867, reproduction courtesy Special Collections, LSU Libraries

society and cultures of an American region. Though its mandate takes in many cultural groups, outside of New Orleans it has strongly focused on the Acadian. The center in Lafayette (located in the shadow of Vermillionville, near the Lafayette airport) provides a general overview. The Eunice center (easy to find in the small downtown area next to the Liberty Theatre) emphasizes the life of the prairie Cajuns who fanned out to ranch and farm on those flat expanses between the marshes to the south and hilly pine forests to the north. The Thibodaux facility (on St. Mary Avenue in a large brick building overlooking Bayou Lafourche that also houses the public library and a performance center) features the bayou Cajuns, who settled the watery lands and the coast. It presents information on boats and the seafood industry, but each center duplicates basic information. The Lafayette center features a Canadian-made film, "The Cajun Way—Echoes of Acadia," which focuses mainly upon the Acadian expulsion from Canada and its aftermath by using impressionistic dramatizations of events.

The exhibits at all three centers are strong on both documentary photographs and artifacts (though in some cases these were created specifically for the displays) and take the visitor through a range of historical and cultural information. There is basic information on the Acadian migrations (with timelines) and on settlement patterns and influences (for example, the early prairie settlements hugged the bayous, while the railroads that came through in the late nineteenth century opened new possibilities for living and brought new, non-French groups to the area). Visitors can work their ways through a variety of informative and well-designed sections on a variety of topics. Cajun music, a distinctive tradition that has not only had a significant role locally but has been eagerly sought out by such travelers as Heat Moon, is the subject of a section exhibiting fiddles made out of cigar boxes, vintage recordings, and the information that two dozen radio stations broadcast chank-a-chank. Hunting is a Cajun passion, and there was a great tradition of decoy carving long unknown to decoy collectors; there are decoys on display in several stages of completion. Other display areas treat ancient traditions like home altars and the use of loquat leaves on Palm Sunday, the celebration of Groundhog Day as *la fête des crêpes* (when pancakes were made and eaten, with at least one tossed on top of the armoire for good luck), and the *traiteurs* who traditionally healed by touch, prayer, and herbal medications. Modern forces (like the oil industry) that have transformed south Louisiana life receive attention too, and other exhibit topics range from architecture to toys to foodways to agriculture to the intense love for dances observed by both Robin and Fortier. (The dances were the focus for gossip, courtship, cockfighting, and card playing, as well as for music and dance.) Signage in the exhibits is in English but with considerable French thrown in to stress the importance of that language and the ongoing bilingualism of the region. Recorded segments allow one to hear Cajun French spoken.

The Jean Lafitte exhibits provide an experience of Cajun country for the visitor, and if that experience suffers from the somewhat artificial form of museum displays, it also benefits from the richness of concentrating a mélange of objects, images, and information otherwise scattered—even lost. Two ambitious outdoor museums, both in the Lafayette area, provide a different sort of concentration of Cajun culture by pulling together buildings, furnishings, and other artifacts into environments where visitors can wander and use their imaginations to reconstruct earlier Cajun ways of life. Vermillionville is one of these museums, on the east side of town near the Jean Lafitte facility (the two make an effective combination). Opened in 1990, it contains an assortment of authentic and reproduction buildings laid out to represent a Cajun community in the 1790–1890 time period. Interpretation of past Cajun life is further aided by furnishings and by the presence of craftspeople who perform such tasks as weaving (there are both antique and reproduction looms) and quilting. An artificial bayou features pirogues and skiffs with the characteristically tall oarlocks that enabled a rower to stand while crossing a bayou. Cajun music is played periodically, and there is a restaurant on the premises. Acadian Village is the other museum, on the west side of Lafayette, and it is in many ways similar to Vermillionville. It, too, has both reproduction and authentic structures, and an artificial bayou flowing through the middle of things. There are, however, no regular living history dimensions, and the structures are used for exhibits (on such subjects as Dudley LeBlanc, legendary patent medicine promoter and advocate of Cajun history and culture) as well as for furnishings. Vermillionville offers guided tours; Acadian Village provides a printed sheet for self-guiding. Vermillionville is spacious and new; Acadian Village is cozy. Both put the visitor into environments that suggest the atmosphere of Cajun country in earlier times.

The premier event that regularly allows visitors to Acadiana to mingle with the locals and to sample their culture is the one Frederick Turner writes about, the "Rendez-Vous des Cajuns" radio show at Eunice. The show is still put on weekly (every Saturday from 6 P.M. to 8 P.M.), and Barry Ancelet still serves as its host, introducing the performers and maintaining a constant, humorous patter in Cajun French. There is a modest admission fee; tickets go on sale two hours before the show and cannot be bought further in advance. The Liberty Theatre (opened in 1924, listed on the Register of Historical Places) is itself worth a visit, a splendid small town version of the American film palace with such fripperies as faux marble columns, trompe-l'oeil Oriental vases, and wall paintings of faintly racy, frolicking ladies rather in the style of Roman frescoes. The audience comes early, may get to listen to the musicians warming up, and watches the show being set up. There is an air of amateurism throughout. An announcer may show up in a Park Ranger's uniform (the show is an aspect of Jean Lafitte Park programming). The stagehands may look grandmotherly. The musicians sit in the audience when they're not performing. People dance in front of the stage (Ancelet may have to come down from it to pour sawdust on the dance floor if that task has been forgotten). The audience may be boisterous and restless, with kids squirming or crying. It all seems rather in the spirit of the old-time dances. The performers usually include two bands—often one Cajun, one zydeco—plus someone who gives a recipe and maybe a storyteller. The musicians play in front of a painted backdrop that evokes the Cajun prairies and resembles an old, sepia-toned photograph, as though we're being taken back into the twenties or thirties, when Cajun country was less visited by outsiders.

Eunice is central to the Cajun prairies area and a good base for touring such places as Church Point, Mamou, Ville Platte, and Iota, with their little groceries that sell boudin and dance halls that thrive on chank-a-chank—set amidst the flat, wet fields that in part define life for the Cajuns and their Afro-French Creole neighbors in these still agricultural communities.

On Saturday mornings (8 to 11 A.M.) there is a radio broadcast with Cajun music from Fred's Lounge in Mamou, and there are numerous dance halls where the music can be heard. (It's surprising that Heat Moon had such difficulty in finding some, but he did make a rather lightning tour through the area.) D. I.'s on Louisiana 97 near Basile, Randol's in Lafayette, and Mulate's in Breaux Bridge are all well-established venues for music. Mulate's has a branch in Baton Rouge and one in New Orleans, though neither city has much historical connection with Cajun music. There are also a number of festivals, such as the Festival de Musique Acadien in Lafayette (held as part of Festivals Acadiens, third week of September), that feature music and other aspects of Cajun culture.

St. Martinville, in bayou country on the fabled Teche, is symbolically central to the Cajun experience. There is some irony in this, in that the town viewed itself as a sophisticated Creole "Petit Paris," as a place where "French from France"—including Napoleonic soldiers—settled, and in some degree held itself apart from Cajun country. It was, however, the site of the French trading post (the Poste des Atakapas), where the early Acadian refugees landed, and it could claim an important place from the Longfellow-created mythology. It contains the Evangeline Oak, said to be the meeting place of the historic counterparts of Longfellow's ill-fated lovers, Evangeline and Gabriel. Though no oak was so designated until some time between 1895 and 1902 (thus Fortier says nothing about it), and the present tree is the third one so designated (some time after 1910), it has become something of a shrine and sits in a tiny park on the banks of the Teche, a peaceful, shady spot where today Cajun musicians and raconteurs may gather. Adjacent to the park is a tourist information office that contains, among other things, signs taken from the store run by André Olivier, who was a major force in locally promoting the Evangeline story and knowledge of the Cajuns. Several traveler writers speak of him, including Carolyn Ramsey. On the other side of the park is the Old Castillo Hotel, where Fortier probably stayed and eavesdropped on the local French speakers. After some years as a girl's school, it is operating as a hotel again and has enormous rooms with exceptionally high ceilings, a restaurant, and a second-story verandah with nice views of the Evangeline Oak and brown-green bayou. Charles Dudley Warner also stayed there after leaving New Orleans to tour the Cajun country and writes of Mme. Castillo, who ran it then. St. Martinville has a pleasant central square in front of St. Martin de Tours church, whose little nook of a graveyard contains the Evangeline statue, placed near the spot thought to be the grave of Emmeline Labiche—said to be the real-life Evangeline—and modeled after movie star Dolores del Rio, who played Evangeline in the 1929 silent film. Fortier gives the town's name as St. Martinsville; though that is not the generally accepted spelling today, that spelling has been used periodically. Lake Catahoulou is not to be confused with Lake Catahoula in central Louisiana, which will be discussed in Chapter 7.

Highways run up and down both Bayou Teche and Bayou Lafourche, so the traveler can easily drive along either of these historically important streams to get a sense of bayou living. Bayou Lafourche is often referred to as "the longest street in the world." Alcée Fortier's route actually covered a lot of the most important places to visit in this area. He, of course, came from New Orleans by train; today Amtrak service uses the Southern Pacific route his train utilized, though today's traveler is probably more likely to use U.S. 90. Bayou des Allemands, which he mentions, runs from Lac des Allemands to Lake Salvador, forming in part the boundary line between St. Charles and Lafourche parishes. Bayou Boeuf is near Morgan City (and should not be confused with the Bayou Boeuf farther north, along whose banks Solomon Northup was enslaved). There is a cultural center for the Chitimacha Indians at Charenton, run in conjunction with the Jean Lafitte Park. Today there is a state park at Cypremort Point, which Fortier also visited. Grand Lac is located in the Atchafalaya Basin.

French is less widely used in Cajun country than in Fortier's day but still has considerable vitality, in part due to attempts made in recent years to preserve and revive its use. The visitor can still easily find French speakers.

The tradition of Cajun weaving that Fortier notes was a distinctive one that employed huge looms to weave cotton used in making clothing, coverlets, and blankets. Some of the work was characterized by the use of a naturally brown cotton that did not need to be dyed and produced cloth of a lovely café-au-lait color. There is some continuation of Acadian weaving by revivalist weaving groups. Examples can be found in museums, and that produced today can be purchased. For more information see Vaughn L. Glasgow, *L'Amour de Maman: La Tradition acadienne du tissage en Louisiane* (LaRochelle, France, 1983). Examples of the weaving and additional information on the tradition can also be found in the Jean Lafitte National Park exhibits.

Many would insist that despite important differences Cajun and Creole cooking have more in common than Heat Moon suggests. See Peter S. Feibleman *et al., American Cooking: Creole and Acadian* (New York, 1971). Visitors to Acadiana will surely want to sample the local food—probably again and again—and there are numerous restaurants in this American region in which good food is taken very seriously.

Books that are especially informative about Cajun culture and history include Barry Jean Ancelet, Jay Edwards, and Glen Pitre, *Cajun Country* (Jackson, Miss., 1991); C. Paige Gutierrez, *Cajun Foodways,* foreword Barry Jean Ancelet (Jackson, Miss., 1992); Glen Pitre, *The Crawfish Book* (Jackson, Miss., 1993); Barry Jean Ancelet and Elemore Morgan, Jr., *The Makers of Cajun Music/Musiciens cadiens et créoles* (Austin, Tex., 1983). Lauren C. Post's *Cajun Sketches from the Prairies of Southwest Louisiana* (Baton Rouge, 1962) is a minor classic. Turner Browne's *Louisiana Cajuns/Cajuns de la Louisiane* (Baton Rouge, 1977) and Philip Gould's *Today's Cajuns/Les Cadiens d'Asteur* (Lafayette, La., 1980) have been popular for their photographic depictions of Acadiana; Gould has also published *Cajun Music and Zydeco* (Baton Rouge, 1992).

7

RED CLAY HILLS AND PINEY-WOODS: CENTRAL AND NORTH LOUISIANA

Though countless travelers have written about New Orleans and south Louisiana, only a handful have commented on the northern reaches of the state. Remarks by two nineteenth-century travelers, Stephen Powers and Timothy Flint, are suggestive of why this might be so. The obscure Powers, whose chief claim to fame was that he walked across the United States from North Carolina to California, says of the country between the Ouachita and Red rivers that it was "much like Georgia—red clay hills and piney-woods." The better-known Flint, who spent considerable time in the Alexandria area, says "that two thirds of the state was covered with pine woods, of the same character as those in Florida."[1]

Because people often travel to see places that are in some manner particularly distinctive, those parts of Louisiana that have seemed simply like other parts

---

1. Stephen Powers, *Afoot and Alone: A Walk from Sea to Sea by the Southern Route* (Hartford, 1872), 102; Timothy Flint, *Recollections of the Last Ten Years in the Valley of the Mississippi*, ed. George R. Brooks (Carbondale, 1968), 236.

of the South have not caught the imagination like the Louisiana of endless marshes and trackless swamps. Even in Flint's day the stereotype of Louisiana as mostly marsh and swamp had currency, for he disputes it: "Very mistaken ideas have been entertained respecting this state," he wrote, "as though it were in great measure composed of alluvion and swamp." As he had discovered, huge chunks of the state—in the northern part—are predominantly piney hills (virtually the whole northwest quadrant, though the hills are hardly dramatic ones—the state's highest point, Mount Driskill, reaches but 535 feet above sea level), and elsewhere in the north there are flatwoods and blufflands, plantation lands along the Mississippi and the 15-mile-wide Red River Valley. But the stereotype has been an enduring one.

North Louisiana is geographically different from the southern part of the state, but the dissimilarities are not merely geographical. When Louisianians point out how the two parts of the state are unlike each other—and they often do, as A. J. Liebling discovered—they are more likely thinking of cultural differences. It is not that either part is culturally homogeneous. But the south is predominantly Latin- (primarily French-) influenced, Catholic, and perceived to be more relaxed about certain morality-tinged behaviors like drinking alcohol, while the north is historically Anglo-Saxon and Scotch-Irish, staunchly Protestant (with particular allegiance to the more evangelical churches), and perceived to be possessed of a strongly puritanical strain. The northern part does have its French influence (notably in the vicinity of Natchitoches), its Spanish influence (the Spanish colonial outpost Los Adais, near Robeline, was for a while the capital of Spanish Texas), and its smattering of ethnic groups. Yet north Louisiana culturally is predominantly Anglo, with a traditional culture that has much in common with that of the upland South generally (including, of course, a significant African American minority, with cultural interchange between them and the dominant whites). Historically, north Louisiana shared in the "log culture" of the southern mountains, with many earlier dwellings made out of abundantly available logs; in the musical traditions that eventually developed into country-western; in the camp meetings and religious revivals of the southern frontier. Though it has its plantation culture, with similarities and historical ties to the plantations of south Louisiana, it has been a place of mostly small holdings and yeoman farmers. (Each area's growing a different major plantation crop—sugar or cotton—also meant significant differences in their respective plantations.)

Because the people of north Louisiana seem to have so "much in common with other upland Southerners from east Texas to the Carolinas,"[2] they have not been able to compete for attention with the more exotic Creoles and Cajuns who live in the southern part of the state. If the northwestern part of the state is the piney hill country, there is nonetheless plenty of "alluvion and swamp" in northern Louisiana, especially in the eastern Delta parishes. Here the Mississippi itself and powerful tributaries such as the Black make the region a wet one, and here lie the legendary Mississippi River swamplands, such a barrier to earlier voyagers. Yet the popular imagination fixed upon south Louisiana as the land of swamps and water, and the hilly landscapes of the north attracted much less attention. There is much of considerable interest in north Louisiana, but fairly few traveler writers have devoted attention to it, and it has been far less visited than New Orleans or Acadiana.

Except in the Cane River area, French culture never took hold in north Louisiana, though the French colonists did attempt to settle the northern part of what became the state. They founded Natchitoches (in fact, the oldest city in the state) and had a post at what is today Monroe. It is this place, the Poste des Ouachitas, that Charles César Robin writes of visiting in 1804. He traveled to it from New Orleans by water—up the Mississippi, into the Red, then into other watercourses—and found a settlement that seemed to be flourishing in the wilderness. He went, of course, on the eve of the cession of Louisiana to the United States. What is today north Louisiana was otherwise very sparsely settled (even in 1810 there were well under ten thousand people in the area). However, the American takeover opened the region to an influx of settlers, who came mostly from Georgia, Alabama, South Carolina, Mississippi, and Tennessee. What Amos A. Parker found crossing from Natchez to Texas in 1834 was still in many ways a wilderness, but he writes of finding farmsteads in the woods and of pioneers moving west. What he describes is the expansion of the American frontier South. Thirty-five years later Samuel H. Lockett moved through yet another environment. Confederate veteran Lockett, a professor of engineering at the Louisiana State Seminary in Pineville (which was to move to Baton Rouge and become Louisiana State University), was employed to perform a topographical and geological survey. He set out for several months each year between 1869 and 1872 to map and to obtain geographical information. The north Louisiana he describes in his witty

2. Susan Roach-Lankford, "The Regional Folklife of North Louisiana," in *Louisiana Folklife: A Guide to the State*, ed. Nicholas R. Spitzer (Baton Rouge, 1985), 88.

and good-humored memoir is still primitive and wild in some ways—but no wilderness. It has many roads, however poor; it has railroads, towns, settled regions, numerous farms. It has passed from frontier South to deeply rural South. Thus three of the travelers whose accounts are included here show us the transformation of a region—from French outpost to settled southern America.

In the 1920s and 1930s north Louisiana was to bring forth a brand of politics that had a profound effect upon Louisiana, the South, and the nation. Initially basing his populism in the small farms and the disadvantaged lives of his region, Huey P. Long—born in Winn Parish—descended on Baton Rouge in a short but meteoric rise to power, the governorship, and the United States Senate. Though neither Long nor the northern part of the state has had a monopoly on the amazingly bizarre ways of Louisiana politics, with his showmanship, drive, and accomplishments he caught the public imagination as few others have. Stories are still told and arguments still rage about him (though he died in 1935, assassinated in the art deco State Capitol he commissioned), and he and his political heirs embody for many a byzantine tradition of outrageous political behavior. A. J. Liebling catches something of this tradition in his account of Earl Long, Huey's brother, himself a governor of the state and a man of grandly eccentric ways. Liebling came to Louisiana specifically to write about Earl for the *New Yorker;* here he recounts going to Alexandria in central Louisiana to hear one of Earl's stump speeches. In addition to commenting on north-south Louisiana differences, Liebling provides a stunning portrait of the strange political climate of Louisiana in 1959.

The Post of the Ouachita

CHARLES CÉSAR ROBIN

Robin traveled by water to this outpost, which is today the city of Monroe.

We arrived finally at the post of the Ouachita, 44 or 45 days after leaving the city [New Orleans]. The settlement of the district had been begun by the Canadians,[3] who followed the Arkansas River down and followed the prairie south to the Ouachita River. . . . The abundance of game that they found there, the large number of Indians who used the spot as a meeting place, the beautiful fields on the shores of a river, navigable in any season, determined some of them to settle there, and as a matter of fact these original Canadian settlers were still living there when I arrived.

For twenty-five years the Spanish Government had had a Commandant at the post.[4] The first was a Frenchman named Filiol who today has settled here. His successor, whom I found in command, is a Spanish officer named Cotard, a man of spirit and honor and of agreeable company. I received from him a most cordial welcome. At his insistence I stayed with him for the entire six weeks of my stay. His young and beautiful wife, a New Orleanian, presided over his household in a gracious manner. . . .

The Ouachita Post today has a population of only four hundred and fifty whites with fifty or sixty slaves. The settlements are mostly on the left bank of the river, where the natural prairies are to be found and clearing of the forests

From *Voyage to Louisiana,* by Charles César Robin, trans. Stuart O. Landry, Jr. Copyright © 1966 by Stuart O. Landry. Used by permission of the publisher, Pelican Publishing Company, Inc.

---

3. Some of the earlier French colonists, including Bienville and Iberville, were French Canadian by birth.

4. France ceded Louisiana to Spain in 1762, and the territory was Spanish-ruled until returned to France in 1800.

is not necessary. The right bank is, for the most part, either hilly or sandy, covered mostly with pines. The soil there is less suitable for agriculture, because being raised it is promptly leached by the rains after being cleared. The soil on the left bank, however, being flat and covered with a thick layer of humus overlying the reddish subsoil is fertile, and will be inexhaustible for a long time. The lands of the Ex-commandant Filiol, for example, have been cultivated for twenty-five years, without missing a year. They have been sown to corn with which are mixed pumpkins, melons, beans, and still give harvests as abundant as in the first year.

These settlements are spread out for twenty miles above the post. On the same side of the Ouachita are found the Bayou's communication with the river, circling across the prairie. One called *Bayou de Siard* and the other *Bayou Bartholomew*. The banks of both are thickly settled. . . .

With the Canadians settled in that distant region, are found several Spaniards from Mexico, some Irishmen, some Americans coming in via Natchez, and a small number of colonists born in France, some from San Domingo, some from Scioto,[5] and the United States.

The Canadians do little farming, they take the trouble only to grow a little corn to maintain themselves and a little cotton, which their women weave into clothes with which they clothe themselves. Their dominant activity, even today, is hunting. Toward December they disappear into the woods, where they remain until about Easter time. Then they reap the real harvest, and it might be a good one if almost all of them were not gamblers, drunkards and dissipators. This vagabond life in the woods hardly makes them amenable to work and a regular life. . . .

In the cabin which they have constructed, they store their amunition and a little corn. Some stay there as guards, the rest disperse through the woods to hunt deer and bear. They wander alone for days at a time or even weeks, sleeping under trees, stretching out beside the trunk or sleeping in hollow trees if it rains. If they become wet from crossing swamps or streams, they pay no attention. They live on game, which they skin out and hang up on trees to await them while they continue to hunt. Finally they carry their game back to the cabin, where sometimes they have horses to help carry their heavy loads.

What seems so remarkable is, that they do not lose their way in these immense forests, even when they are hunting for the first time. They always find

5. Scioto was a region in what is today the state of Ohio.

the skins they have pelted and the meat they have cached. I have questioned some of them to see if I could find out how they are able to do this, but they are unable to tell how.

Those who remain at the cabin dry the meat in strips, pelt the skins, drying them and making them pliable, extract the deer tallow from which they make beautiful candles, and melt down the bear oil which is used as a cooking fat throughout the colony, replacing olive oil. One bear yields up to eighty pots of oil. . . .

The hunters often form companies and go shares. Sometimes, one of them, a little more thrifty and well off than the others will advance all of the money for ammunition and supplies and hire the others. Their monthly wage varies, according to their hunting skills. . . . Many of the hunters are in debt for their guns, their powder and their clothes, and in fact have sold the bear skin before having killed the bear. For this reason their returns from hunting are always meagre, for they are forced to buy dearly what is advanced to them, and sell cheap, what they bring back.

And their most unfortunate vice is gambling. Several of these men have lost five or six hundred piastres in one night, and when this happens, they take to the woods again.

The Irish and the Americans are mostly occupied with raising cattle, swine and horses. Two or three of them have already introduced a better strain of horse, an activity much neglected in Louisiana.

The French families, helped by a few Negroes, are especially concerned with agriculture. Along with corn (which is the staple of the men and animals) they raise cotton, which however, did not seem to me to be as pure a white as I have seen elsewhere in Louisiana. Several have tried to grow wheat. They have tried different kinds, some from Mexico, some from the United States and some from the Arkansas River in the neighboring district. This culture is not very successful. The heavy dews during the flowering season seem to abort or blacken the grain. Some have tried dragging a tow rope every morning across the tips of the plants, but this precaution is time consuming and does not seem to completely avert the damage. . . .

M. Danemours, the former French Consul at Baltimore, had retired to the district several years before my visit and had set up a pretty little house. This man, noted for the nicety of his manners and cultivated mind, used several of his Negroes, whom his excessive indulgence had rendered unused to real work, to lay out an English formal garden in his fields. One must admit that the time and the site were ill chosen. There, where the essentials of life are everyone's preoccupation, where an opulent nature provides a varied and imposing scenery, who would think of disfiguring a spacious field with a tiny garden of coldly spaced groups of plants?

What more beautiful Formal Garden, in this immense forest, than this same field itself, regularly divided into squares of corn, cotton, melons and pumpkins? Near cities, when the eye is fatigued by symetrical figures, one should there reproduce deliberate irregularities. For, while, not far from Paris, I took pleasure in walking in rustic groves, here in Louisiana I delighted in strolling along an avenue of sycamores neatly aligned by the same M. Danemours. In these cool shades I had the illusion of being in my native land.

Crossing Central Louisiana

AMOS A. PARKER

> Traveling by stagecoach and boat, Parker (1791–1893)
> left New Hampshire desirous of seeing "some portion
> of the unknown and unsettled regions of the West and
> the South." He left a steamboat at Natchez (together
> with a gentleman he met on the boat) to go overland
> on horseback to Texas through Louisiana, an adven-
> turous trek through what was then (in 1834) still
> sparsely settled, little-known country. From *Trip to the
> West and Texas* (1835).

Having provided ourselves with horses, portman-
teaus, fireworks, &c. and obtained the necessary directions, we took an early
start; crossed the Mississippi in a ferry boat, for which we were taxed half a
dollar each; and took the road to Alexandria. We had some ill-forbodings
about the great Mississippi swamp; for just as we were about to cross the river,
a gentleman, of whom we made some enquiries respecting the route, told us
he thought it now impossible to travel through it in consequence of the rains
which had recently fallen. But we were all equipped to go by land, and this,
our only route; and therefore, we determined, at all events, to push forward.

There is a road from the mouth of Red River, along its bank to Alexandria,
and this, we were afterwards informed, is the best route; but it was seventy
miles below us; and whoever takes it, must go down in a boat.

Our route lay, for the first six miles, up the river near its bank; and then we
turned more to the west. We passed half a dozen cotton plantations, some
quite large, and saw an army of negroes picking it. . . .

Our route now lay through a dense forest—and the ground generally so
miry that we could only ride on a walk. Sometimes we came to the thick canebrakes, about twenty feet high, and overhanging our narrow path. Sometimes
we found the palmetto, which exactly resembles a large green, open fan,

standing on a stem a foot high, and so thick that we could hardly ride through them, or see any path at all. Sometimes, we came to a sheet of water one hundred yards wide, in which a horse would plunge to the saddle skirts, and for awhile become stuck fast; and again we would find a cypress swamp, full of cypress knees and mud. Indeed it is the worst swamp I ever travelled over, before or since; and sometimes, I thought our horses were stuck too fast ever to move again.

These cypress knees are quite a curiosity. They start from the roots of the tree, grow from two to four feet high, about the size of a man's arm, but rather larger at the bottom, and are smooth, without a leaf or branch. They look like a parcel of small posts, with the bark growing over the top end; and are so thick, that it is troublesome to ride among them. The cause or use of this anomaly in nature I cannot divine.

Eighteen miles from Natchez, we came to two log houses and a small stream, called the Tensaw. We crossed the ferry, about twice the length of the boat in width, and paid, half a dollar each for ferriage. We had now twelve miles to go to find a stopping place for the night, and all the way through dense forest of lofty trees; and it was three o'clock in the afternoon. The first half of the distance was decent travelling, although we could not ride much of the way, faster than a walk. Then we came to a wet and miry road.

It began to grow dark in the woods. The trees were quite thick, and hung full of Spanish moss; and there was no moon in the sky. The wolf, the wildcat, and the owl, had pitched their tune for the night; and soon, thick darkness shrouded around our path. The heavens were clear; yet so dense were the foliage and moss, that it was seldom I could find a loop hole, through which a star might cast its rays upon us. I never had been in such a gloomy situation before. We were in a path, to us untravelled; and by its appearance, seldom travelled by man. We had shoals of muddy water to cross, and sloughs of mud to wallow through. And then the night was so dark, and the track so faint, we frequently lost it, and found it again with difficulty. It was ten o'clock at night when we arrived on the shore of a lake, and saw a light on the other side.—We raised the ferryman after awhile, and he came out and took us over.

This lake is about a mile wide, and twelve long, and must have once been the channel of the Mississippi. The ferriage here was half a dollar each. On the other side, we found a good house, and a genteel family within. They soon provided for us an excellent supper, which was very acceptable after a ride of thirty miles over such an execrable road. Not being much used to travelling on horse-back, I felt excessively fatigued and retired immediately to bed. My companion and myself had each of us a good bed, and we slept soundly until after sunrise.

The morning was fine, so we walked awhile along the shore of the lake, before breakfast. It was about the twentieth of November, yet the air felt as mild as a morning in June. . . .

This gentleman has a fine cotton plantation of rich alluvial land. His house is built facing the lake, on an Indian mound, levelled down to the height of about six feet. We took breakfast with the family in a large portico on the back side of the house. It was a good breakfast, on a neat bread table, and the lady at the head performed the honors of it with an ease and grace seldom equalled. We performed our parts to a charm, both in eating the breakfast, and complimenting the hostess. . . .

Immediately after leaving this gentleman's plantation, we passed into a dense forest and found a muddy path. In about six miles we found some sandy land and pine timber and here we left what is called the Mississippi swamp. We soon came to the outlet of the lake, which we had to ford. The water was deep, and the shores deep mud. It was a difficult job to make a horse wallow through. We were told that a horse got swamped and died in the mud, a few feet from where we crossed.

We came to the banks of the Washita River, following it down three miles, and crossed over to Harrisonburg. The town is built on a level plain on the west bank of the river; but it contains not more than twenty houses. This river empties into Red River, and is navigable for steamboats a long distance above the village. It is forty-two miles west of Natchez. . . .

We rode twenty-five miles over a rolling sandy country, generally covered with pine woods; and stopped at night with a gentleman who had . . . been there nineteen years; had cleared a large plantation; raised cotton, corn and cattle; had eight or ten negroes, and possessed the necessaries of life in abundance. But he still lived in a log house, without a glass window in it. . . . It was not just such a house as I should be contented in, for nineteen years, and possessing the wealth he had.—It, however, was to his taste; and for aught I could see, he was as happy as those who live in much better houses.

To-day we travelled thirty-three miles to Alexandria, just one hundred miles from Natchez. The first forty was Mississippi swamp, excellent land, but a good deal of it too low for cultivation; the last sixty miles was, with few exceptions, hilly, sandy, pitch pine woods. We passed only a few good plantations. Occasionally, we found a small prairie of poor soil, and a deserted log house. It was indeed the most dreary road I ever travelled. In the last day's travel, we passed two small rivers; one we crossed in a ferry boat; and to our special wonder, we found quite a decent bridge over the other.

Red River is rightly named; it is almost as red as blood, caused by the red soil through which it passes. It is quite a large stream; but the water is too brackish to drink, or for culinary purposes. The only resource of the inhabitants of Alexandria is to catch rain water, for which they have enormous cisterns. We crossed the river opposite the town in a ferry boat, and found the current about as strong as that of the Mississippi. . . .

Alexandria is pleasantly situated on a level plain the south side of Red River, one hundred and four miles from its mouth, and three hundred and twenty-nine from New Orleans. It is regularly laid out in squares; has a court house, three hotels, eight or ten stores, two or three groceries, and a number of good dwelling houses. Its chief export is cotton, and that of the first quality. Red River cotton commands the highest price in market. I saw a large number of bales piled on the river bank, and wagon loads coming in.

Gentlemen and ladies, in pleasure carriages and on horseback, were riding through the streets; and the hotels were full of guests. It appears to be a place of business and of pleasure; of much wealth, and in a rich neighborhood. This place and Natchitoches, seventy-five miles above it, are the only towns of any size in this section of the country. . . .

About a mile above the place, we left Red River, and travelled the road on the bank of Bayou Rapide for twenty-five miles, to the mansion house of a Mr. Henderson, where we stayed over night. . . .

From Mr. Henderson's, an intelligent gentleman, well acquainted with the country, travelled with us three or four days on our route; and from whom we obtained much information. This day, we travelled forty miles through an unbroken forest of pitch pine. The land is sandy, gently undulating, but seldom rocky. The trees were of good size, but not so thick together as to prevent the grass from growing beneath them; or the traveller from seeing a great distance as he passes along. . . .

At night, we came to the house of a planter, near a small river. He had a hundred acres cleared of river bottom land, which had been planted with cotton and corn; a large stock of cattle and hogs, which ranged in the woods. He had lived here twelve years, was worth twenty thousand dollars; yet still, lived in a log house with only two rooms, and without a window in it. Our supper was fried beef, fried greens, sweet potatoes, corn bread and a cup of coffee, without milk or sugar; which we ate by the light of the fire, as he had neither candle or a lamp. Our fellow traveller told us that we had now got out of the region of what we should call comfortable fare; and we might expect to find it worse, rather than better, all the way through Texas. Our lodging was on a comfortable bed made of Spanish moss; and our breakfast exactly like our supper, which we ate with the doors open to give us light. Our bill was a dollar each, for supper, breakfast, lodging and horsekeeping. . . .

After passing the river and about a mile of bottom land, we came to the pine woods again. . . .

This day's travel was through the pine woods, except at some few places where we found a small clearing and a log house, near some small stream. . . . About the middle of the afternoon, we came out on the Mexican road, three miles south of the garrison. It appeared to be a road a good deal travelled by wagons, as well as on horseback; some places running through swamps and muddy; occasionally, a bridge over the most miry streams; but generally in a state of Nature. The land became some better, and we passed more settlements.

At night, we stopped at a log house kept by a widow. She had, living with her, two sons and one daughter. The house had no windows, and but one room in it. Near it, was a small kitchen where a negro woman did the cooking. Our fare was very similar to that of the night before, except the old lady had a candle on the table at supper. There were four beds in the room, where we all slept—the lady and her daughter in one bed—her two sons in another—and we three travellers in the other two. I hope the delicate nerves of my fair readers may not greatly be disturbed at this; if they are, they must close the book, and read no further; for if I must tell "the whole truth," I shall be obliged to state, that during the thirty following nights, I often slept in the same room with one or more ladies!

The old lady had about twenty acres cleared and cultivated with corn; but the land is not the first rate. The fact is, all along Missouri, Arkansas and Louisiana, after you get sixty or seventy miles west of the Mississippi river, you come to light, sandy, hilly land. . . .

We took an early start, and travelled on. . . .

We passed a number of covered wagons, generally with four horses, loaded with goods and families bound to Texas. They invariably lodge out doors over night. They carry their own provisions with them and select some spot where there is plenty of wood and water, build up a fire, cook their meals, turn their horses or oxen loose to feed on the prairie, or in the woods, and camp down on the grass by the side of the fire. I saw some who had been thirty and forty and sixty days on the road; from Missouri, Illinois, Indiana, &c. and said they had not put up at a house for a single night. . . .

About noon to-day, we came to the Sabine river, the dividing line between the United States and Texas. We had now travelled from Natchez two hundred and twenty-five miles on horseback; and this, the seventh day since we started. I had now become used to the saddle; and saving the muddy roads and miry streams which we sometimes found, I enjoyed the trip very well. I was surprised to find the Sabine so small a river. I should think it was not more than one third as large as Red River. It is a deep muddy stream, and gentle current. We were paddled across the river by a woman who was a "right smart" one, and landed at last on the shore of Texas.

Manner in Which the Survey Was Made

SAMUEL H. LOCKETT

Colonel Lockett (1837–1891) was a Confederate engineering officer who after the war assumed duties on the faculty of Louisiana State Seminary in Pineville and later in Baton Rouge. In addition to his teaching, he was asked to undertake a topographical survey of Louisiana in concert with Professor Frederick V. Hopkins (referred to as "the Doctor" in Lockett's account), who would do a geological survey. They set out in 1869. Over several years Lockett was to travel over much of the state and to write both a geographical description and an account of his travels. That account is witty, amusing, and full of interesting details about the places and people he encountered and about the vicissitudes of journeying. The excerpts here are from his travels in 1869 from his Pineville base north to Harrisonburg and then Monroe and, in 1872, from Delhi to Carroll Parish and then Winnfield en route to Pineville. On the earlier journey his means of conveyance was an old ambulance, the only vehicle that could be found for his survey work.

[1869]

It is not my intention to give a detailed account of every day's travel during the summer's explorations nor of those which followed it, but I shall endeavor, without being tedious, to convey to the reader a clear idea of the manner in which the survey was conducted by transcribing so much of my itineraries as may be necessary for that purpose.

From the state Seminary we took the Harrisonburg road, the objective point of our first day's journey being the Buffalo or White Sulphur Springs on Trout Creek in Catahoula Parish.[6] Professor S—— of the Seminary accompanied us to spend one night with us in camp and enjoy one day's angling in Trout Creek.[7] This first day's journey gave us a very fair foretaste of the trials and labors awaiting us. The first down-hill we came to, our driver let the ambulance and mules obey the force of gravity unimpeded by check-rein or brake, and when asked why he did not "hold his team back," did not know what was meant by "holding back"; and when he had the meaning of the term explained to him, did not see how it was possible for it to do any good as "the trouble was the ambulance had run down the hill too fast, and if he had pulled on the reins it was perfectly plain that it would have gone down all the faster." "Pretty fair physics," thought I, "but very poor driving."

"Did you ever drive before?"

"No!" From that time onward, the Doctor or I took the reins save when the road was smooth and level.

Three miles from our starting point we came to Flacon Bayou. Recent high water had carried away the bridge, but there was, in the language of the people of the country, a "good ford." That is, the water was not very deep, the bottom not very boggy nor very full of logs, and the banks on either side did not slope at a greater angle than forty-five degrees. After a reconnaissance it was decided that, considering our load, the banks were nevertheless too steep to be tried as they then stood. So out came the geological pick and spade, and in about an hour and a half we did more work on that road than the Police Jury of Rapides Parish had done since the war.[8] Professor S—— lent us a helping hand, but I think this little episode came very near preventing him from seeing the topographical and geological survey of the state of Louisiana one day on its journey. During the ascent on the other side of Flacon Bayou, the first of a long series of breakages occurred. The leathern strap that prevents too great play in the singletree snapped as our gallant mules swayed from side

6. The parish lines were not the same in Lockett's Day as they are today; then Catahoula Parish covered much more ground.

7. William A. Seay, who taught subjects ranging from constitutional law to Greek at the seminary; Lockett later identifies him by name.

8. A police jury is the governing council of a Louisiana parish.

to side in their mighty efforts. But this was a small matter; a good stout twist of tarred rope soon replaced the broken strap, and we rolled on our way, rejoicing that we had safely overcome one difficulty and feeling more confidence in our ability to struggle with others that we might yet encounter.

Nothing more occurred, however, today to disturb the quietness of a long drive through a barren longleaf pine country. We crossed Little Clear Creek, Big Creek, and Little River in safety. Little River was crossed at La Croix's Ferry, and as it is a beautiful navigable stream it was deemed of sufficient importance to make it an item in the survey. . . . Here, at La Croix's Ferry, we saw two sights of some interest, namely: a tremendous raft of pine and cypress trees floating slowly along on its way to New Orleans, and a country trading boat consisting of a small cabin built on a common ferry-flat which was rowed from point to point along the river with its cargo of cheap whiskey, groceries, dry-goods, hardware, and notions. The motive power was a man and a boy at the oars, and the ruling, governing, guiding spirit of the whole affair was a very tall woman standing like a statue in the stern of the boat, rudder in hand. . . .

We reached the Sulphur Springs about dusk, having made a journey of twenty-two miles. This, considering our early start, was not a very brave day's work, but we consoled ourselves with the thought that the time lost at Flacon and the halt at Little River would readily account for our apparently slow progress. We confidently expected to make between twenty-five and thirty miles a day when uninterrupted.

We selected for our first campground a grassy knoll about a hundred yards from the Sulphur Springs and pitched tent, built fire, fed our team, and then began to think of something to eat for ourselves.

We found that our driver, who was also to be our cook, was as innocent of knowing anything of the culinary art as he was of that in which Jehu was so proficient; so of that part of the survey, also, the Doctor and I found it necessary to take immediate charge. Poor Clamp, the driver, was an honest, earnest, intelligent young man, exceedingly anxious to accompany us on our journeyings through the state for the scientific interest he took in the survey, and thought that driving, cooking, taking care of a team, and performing all sorts of camp service would be a matter of but slight importance as regards the trouble it would give him, and were duties that any sensible man could attend to if he wished. His discovery that such was not the case was a considerable disappointment and source of mortification to him.

Fish Fry Along Cane River, 1940, by Marion Post Wolcott

Photograph courtesy Library of Congress

On realizing that I had to assume the duties of chief cook, I determined to prepare for our good appetites an equally good supper. I accordingly called upon Mrs. Ward, the proprietress of the springs, to see if I could obtain from her something better than we had in our larder. I found the lady sitting on the portico of the only habitable cabin among a dozen or more that surrounded the spring. She was knitting, and to my very politest "Good evening, Madam" replied by knitting with redoubled vigor and a half audible salutation of "Good evening, Sir," in a tone of voice that very much diminished the ardor of my expectations. However, I was hungry and, taking courage, began, "We wish to purchase some provisions, Madam. Have you any eggs?" "No," was the reply, "can't keep any chickens here for the owls and *varmints*."

"Have you any fresh milk?"

"No! cows don't come up exceptin' when they want saltin'."

"Have you any vegetables, green corn, sweet, or Irish potatoes?"

"No! the drouth has done dried up the garden long ago."

"You can let us have a little corn-meal, can't you?"

"No, I can't, there ain't more'n a peck in the house and I don't know when I'll get any more."

"Well, Madam, haven't you got something that you could let us have to eat?"

"I suppose I could let you have some fish, they've just brought in a parcel from the creek."

"Nothing would suit us better, how many can you spare?"

"Oh, as many as you want, fish ain't scarce in these parts."

"We will take a dozen of them, what are they worth?"

"Anything you've a mind to give, I reckon they might be worth a quarter or a half dollar."

"Very well, say a half, and let us have the fish."

In a few minutes the fish were produced, and such a string old Izaak Walton himself never dreamt of catching. Soon the first twelve were "shucked" off for us; some of them still "alive and kicking," and a more magnificent lot of lusty trout I never before had seen. They varied from ten to eighteen inches in length and weighed between one and four pounds apiece. I thought they could make rather a large supper for four men, but recollecting that Professor S—— was of the number and thinking we might need something of the kind to add to our breakfast, I gathered up my spoils and returned to camp. The Doctor and Professor S—— with immense enthusiasm and energy, went to work scaling and cleaning the fish while I, as the most experienced *cuisinier* of the party, set to work making the coffee and getting the frying pan in readiness. We had some few loaves of baker's bread, a box of hard crackers, a small jar of western butter, salt and pepper *ad libitum*, and in about an hour from the beginning of our labors, six of the trout were nicely fried and pronounced by all parties "done to a T." We sat down on the grass and ate, but there were not many fragments to be gathered up after that feast. And thus ended the first day's field operations of the Topographical and Geological Survey of the State of Louisiana. . . .

After supper [on the subsequent day after the day of fishing], we held a long consultation with Mr. Dan Shaw, the keeper of the saloon of the Buffalo Springs, in regard to the route we had better take in our examination of Catahoula Parish. Mr. Shaw was thoroughly acquainted with the country through which we would have to travel; it mattered not what direction we might take. In fact, there was little of Louisiana that he did not know. Though he was now keeping a saloon on a very small scale at the Buffalo or Catahoula White Sulphur Springs, in the midst of the interminable pine hills, with probably an average of one customer a day, yet he had spent an exceedingly active life. He had been a saloon keeper in New Orleans during its palmiest days, had been a large wholesale, retail, and importing liquor dealer, had during the late war been a government agent for the obtaining and distillation of spirituous liquors for the Confederate government, managing and possessing in his own right Confederate money by the bushel or barrel full; and even now he said, he owned several thousand acres of land in Louisiana, yet we find him in a wilderness, apparently perfectly contented, sitting in a rickety, crazy, ready-to-tumble-down cabin, playing solitaire with a pack of greasy cards, with one barrel of whiskey and a dozen bottles of ale for his stock in trade, and but little prospect of needing an early replenishment of his stores. He told us of many localities that we would be interested in visiting, and among others, of a coal bed on Castor Bayou near its junction with Dugdemona River. From his account of this region we determined to make it our next objective, and, after having made arrangements for an early start the next morning, we retired to our pallets in our tent feeling sufficiently fatigued to insure sound slumbers in spite of the fact that there would be but one blanket between our persons and the ground. . . .

Tuesday . . . we took the road to Harrisonburg. During the entire day we journeyed through a level country called by the people "Hog Wallow Land" from its intense muddiness in wet weather; but as it was now midsummer and perfectly dry, we found the roads in good order and had for once a pleasant and safe drive. . . . We passed just beyond the confines of this tract, and camped near a beautiful, bold spring hard by the house of a Widow Francis. This camp-ground was the most pleasant one we found during our summer's campaign. Our tent was pitched in an abandoned field thickly covered by a forest of old-field pines whose slender leaves falling upon the smooth sward made a natural carpet as soft and clean as one of Brussels manufacture. In front of us was the gushing spring, its waters gurgling down a channel cut in grey sandstone, with a dense growth of magnolia bays and gum trees surrounding it. The next morning at the first peep of dawn there came from that clump of trees the sweetest music I ever listened to. It was alive with mockingbirds and sweet-singing thrushes, and the whole atmosphere seemed literally permeated by the melody that came from their tuneful throats.

Wednesday we got back into the rugged, hilly country, and five miles before we reached Harrisonburg, another breakdown in the ambulance brought us to a sudden halt. Leaving Clamp in camp, the Doctor and I saddled up our mules and went on to Harrisonburg with the broken irons. There was but one blacksmith in Harrisonburg, and he was of the newly enfranchised class, by no means of an energetic or industrious disposition. I tried to get him to work at once and hoped to keep him at it throughout the night as we were getting impatient at losing so much time. But it was five P.M. when we reached his shop. His fire was out, his day's work was done, and no amount of persuasion, no promises of extra pay could induce him to strike a blow on our work before the next morning. . . .

On the morrow we succeeded in getting our . . . vulcan under headway in the fabrication of the irons by 8 o'clock, and then took a survey of the country around the village. The Pine Hills terminate at this point in a fine, bold bluff about 120 feet in height. This afforded the Doctor a good opportunity to study the strata of the hill formation. While he was thus engaged I made a sketch from the summit of the bluff of Harrisonburg and the Ouachita Valley. . . .

At noon the progress made by the smith was so insignificant we determined to lose no more time in waiting upon him, so after dinner we crossed the Ouachita River to make an equestrian tour of Sicily Island. We found this a beautiful country and enjoyed very much our ride over its level roads, among its flourishing plantations, and through its magnificent groves. We stayed one night on the island and were hospitably entertained free of charge by Dr. Lovelace. We completed the circuit of the island and returned to Harrisonburg by 3 P.M. the next day. Our work was still unfinished, but his sable lordship said he would be ready for us in a few minutes. These few minutes lengthened themselves out till nearly dark, and in returning to camp we got badly lost. But for the sagacity of our mules we would have had to spend the night in the woods supperless and uncovered, save by the leafy trees and the unclouded sky. After we had exhausted all our own powers of guessing which of several roads that we sucessively tried and became doubtful about was the right one—we finally gave reins aloose to our animals, and they carried us without hesitation to camp which we reached just before midnight. . . .

As we had in some manner excited the direful wrath of the Fates, our ill luck still pursued. When we tried to put our new irons into their places, we found it impossible to make them fit. No amount of straining and twisting and turning produced any effect. If I had had an anvil and forge I was sure I could make the necessary changes. But how could these things be improvised?

We tried it in the following manner. We made a huge fire of dried oak twigs and the bark of an old oak tree that lay near camp—bark makes probably a hotter fire than any other kind of woody material—and into this we plunged our refractory irons. Now for an anvil. A large green stump—that is, the stump of a freshly fallen tree—fortunately, stood but a few feet from the fire. Into this our axe was sunk as far as a blow with all of my strength could drive it, and my anvil was made. In less than an hour the irons were at a pretty fair white heat, and with hammer in one hand and a monkey wrench in the other to act as a pair of tongs, I made my first effort at playing the part of a blacksmith. Well, reader, I got those irons into their places, and when the old ambulance was sold a year afterwards those irons were still just where and how I had placed them. Other parts of it gave way, but the "hounds" never occasioned us another moment's trouble. . . .

Saturday evening . . . found us on Lost Creek near Mr. J. W. Meridith's. Here we remained through Sunday, and on Monday rode with Mr. Meredith to the Lone Grave Bluff on the Ouachita. This bluff which stands immediately opposite the estate of ex-Governor Hyams, is the highest on the Ouachita River. It is named for the solitary grave that stands on its summit at least 135 feet above the surface of the waters. The grave is covered by a simple, stuccoed tomb which records the fact that Mrs. Graves lies buried there. From Colonel Meridith, who assisted at the funeral of this lady, we learned the story of her remains being laid in so conspicuous but solitary a resting place. She was the wife of an Alabamian who came to Louisiana in 1845, and obtained employment as manager of one of Governor Hyams' plantations. This was the first year of their wedded life, and often they would cross the river and clamber to the top of the bluff and spend a quiet Sabbath afternoon gazing upon the broad fields of cotton and corn that the young husband took as much pride in tending as if they were his own, and in watching for the steamers that were passing up and down the winding channel of the Ouachita which could be seen for miles in its meanderings to the north and south.

Ere the year had passed the new-made wife sickened, and having a presentiment that she would not recover, begged to be buried on the highest point of the bluff opposite to their home so that she might still look down upon the scene of their happiness. She died and her wishes were carried out, and now her lone grave gleams white among the dark pines that surround it and attracts the attention of every one who voyages upon the Ouachita. . . .

We reached Monroe . . . and I shipped Clamp and the ambulance, tent, and camp equipage by the first boat back to Alexandria. The Doctor and I kept the mules and riding saddles, and bought us a pair of saddlebags apiece in Monroe, and put ourselves in the lightest possible traveling order.

From Monroe we took a run out on the North Louisiana and Texas Railroad to Delhi to study the intervening country and the Bayou Maçon Hills. . . .

[1872]

From Delhi I went up into Carroll Parish, stopping on the way at Mrs. Jackson's on Bayou Maçon where I remained Saturday afternoon and Sunday. In the vicinity of Mrs. Jackson's I examined a number of Indian mounds, took a sketch of Bayou Maçon, and tried my fishing tackle in its waters with very poor success. Monday I went on to Floyd, the old courthouse site, and called on Colonel Hiram Lott living one mile west of the town. From Colonel Lott I obtained a great deal of information about several parishes in the northeastern part of Louisiana. From this point I turned southward and traveled through the parishes of Richland and Franklin.

In returning through Delhi I witnessed a wedding that was characterized by some rather peculiar, not to say ludicrous, features. An Irishman was to be married to one of the rosy country girls of the parish of Richland and came to Delhi to get a magistrate to perform the ceremony. He was informed that he would have to go to Rayville, the courthouse town, for a license. Off he put on a mule at a break-neck gallop, leaving his soon-to-be bride at the magistrate's house. Rayville was seven miles distant. In about two hours our gallant son of Erin returned to Delhi, both he and his mule reeking with perspiration. Every one supposed he had his license and was preparing to congratulate Pat on his quick trip and the speedy approach of his nuptials, when lo! he exclaimed, "Bedad, I forgot the girl's name. I told thim she was named Sophrony, and they asked me Sophrony what? 'Sophrony what?' sez I, 'and faith ain't that name enough!' But they said to me no, it wan't enough to git a license on and to save me sowl I couldn't think of any ither name she iver had, and I have come to see if she has got any ither." They gave Pat his sweetheart's surname on a piece of paper and off he started again for Rayville. Meantime the news of the affair and Pat's queer blunder got abroad in the village, and when he returned the second time about 2 P.M., half of the population of Delhi was at the magistrate's office to witness the making of the twain one flesh. I was at the hotel and was invited to be present. The ceremony was very simple, but sufficiently solemn for all practicable purposes, and had the great merit of not keeping Pat and his blushing bride long before the eyes of the numerous curious spectators. . . .

My next objective point was Winnfield in the parish of Winn. To get to Winnfield I had to travel some fearful roads. In the first place there was our old friend of our first summer's survey, Bayou Castor, to be forded at one of those fearful fords already sufficiently noticed. Then came a hilly, thinly settled country with roads, apparently selecting the steepest parts of the ridges for ascent and descent, all washed and gullied or else full of roots and stumps. I made the trip, however, to Winnfield by the end of another week without any serious damage to myself, my horse, or buggy. The day I reached my destination I stopped for dinner at quite a neat-looking log house in the pine woods. I found it occupied by an old man and two young women. After dinner when I got my pipe out for a smoke and offered the old gentleman some Perique tobacco, his heart opened unto me, and he told me something of his history. He had lived on the low lands on Bayou Maçon before the war, owning a good farm and some few slaves. The approach of the federal army had caused him to fly from his home, and he "refugeed" into Texas. There he remained till the war closed and then started back home. His former slaves did not return with him, and when he got to Winnfield he heard that all of the bottom lands were under water, and learning that the place where he now lived was for sale cheap, he bought, stopped his teams, unloaded, and settled.

I asked him if he purposed remaining in such a poor country. "Oh yes," he said, "it is poor, but very healthy, and I reckon I can make enough for me and my wife and child to live on. The youngest of those two women you saw at the table is my wife, the other is my daughter by another wife. I've got lots of children, but they are all grown up and married and gone off to themselves but this one; she stays with me to help my wife. I have been very unfortunate, sir, in my wives; I have lost four of them, but thank the Lord I have always been fortunate in soon getting another good one after one of them was taken away. I've never been longer than six months without a wife since I was first married, and I never intend to be longer than that, no matter how old I get to be."

By this time my pipe was exhausted, and I told the old gentleman I thought I had better hitch up my horse and drive ahead. I wanted to get out into the woods again where I could have a good, broad smile all to myself without any fear of hurting the good old man's feelings. In a few hours after I had left my much-married host, I reached Winnfield, the courthouse town of Winn Parish. It was Saturday, the third day of August. I had intended to pass through Winnfield and go on to the house of Mr. Luke Radeschiche, the father of one of our university graduates, to spend the approaching Sunday. But on inquiring the road, I was informed that a bridge across Kiesche Creek between me and my desired destination was washed away, and, in consequence, a detour would be necessary which would add many miles to my journey. While hesitating about taking this increased journey, Mr. R. B. Williams, recorder of the parish, introduced himself to me and invited me to spend the night and next day with him. This kind invitation I gladly accepted and went with Mr. Williams a mile out of town to his house.

The following day we rode on horseback to old Mr. Radeschiche's crossing at the site of the broken bridge by a deep ford. Old Mr. Radeschiche is an Italian who settled in Winn Parish while the Redman still claimed it for a hunting ground. When he built his cabin on Kiesche Creek his nearest white neighbor was ten miles distant. He had seen all the changes take place by which the country around him had been transformed from a perfectly unbroken wilderness, with wild beasts and equally wild Indians its only denizens, into a civilized and thickly settled community. He had a great many anecdotes to tell of his early life, which were all the more interesting for being narrated in a broken language, part English, part Spanish, part French, and part Italian. The old gentleman entertained us with great hospitality and made my Sunday with him one of the pleasantest and most interesting of all my travels.

The next morning, after an excellent breakfast, I started on a long drive through the longleaf Pine Hills for Alexandria on Red River. The country I was to traverse was thinly settled, and I was told in the outset to try to make it convenient to get to old Mr. Nugent's about nightfall, as his was the only house on the road where I would be likely to get accommodations. I reached Mr. Nugent's about an hour before sundown, and found his own family literally crowded out of house and home by a huge concourse of people. You would have imagined that a wedding or a funeral was about to take place, or that a prodigal son had returned and all the relatives and friends of the family had gathered together to welcome him home, but you would have been wrong, reader, in any of these suppositions. There was a camp meeting within a mile of Mr. Nugent's and the crowd of persons I saw in his yard, on the gallery of his house, and with their heads poking out of the windows of all the rooms, as I drove up, were only some of his neighbors from ten or twelve miles around that had come over after meeting to spend the night. I did not have the hardihood to ask for lodgings after seeing how many there were ahead of me. I stopped and asked the distance to the next house. "Only seven miles," was the reply. I knew that was more than I could make by dark, and more too than I ought to expect of my horse, over a sandy, hilly road in the hot month of August, so I next asked how far was it to the first water. I was told that the road ran along a ridge, but water could be found almost anywhere by turning off the road and descending to some of the side hollows. I at once made up my mind to go on a short distance and camp by myself in the woods. Fortunately I had supplied myself with a day's forage for my horse, and Mr. Nugent gave me, free of charge, a half dozen big biscuits and a goodly supply of barbecued beef.

I drove on a half or three-quarters of a mile from Nugent's house, turned off from the road, and in a few hundred yards found a clear spring with its trickling branch between two spurs of the main ridge. Here I unhitched and went into a solitary camp. I had no bed clothes with me, not even an overcoat, so that the cushions of my buggy seats were the only materials wherewith to make my simple couch. My carpetsack served me for a pillow. After feeding and watering my horse and partaking of half of my biscuits and beef, I arranged my bed under a small, brushy blackjack oak, lit my pipe and prepared to make myself comfortable for the night. I avoided lighting a fire, knowing it would attract a swarm of bugs, beetles, and flies of all kinds. With this precaution I thought I would make a pretty fair night of it, but I was doomed to disappointment. I had scarcely laid down before whole armies of wood-ticks and all manner of creeping things began to crawl over me, and I was compelled to abandon the soft leaf-covered ground and take refuge in the buggy. Here I doubled up on the seat and made a desperate effort to get to sleep. But the mosquitoes from the water near by soon found my retreat and sang their sharp songs in my ears. I tied my handkerchief over my head and tried again to compose myself to slumber, for I was tired and very sleepy. I believe I did get a little nap, but my position was such a cramped one that I soon waked up with my limbs benumbed and stiff. Then I filled my pipe and took a good, long smoke, changed my attitude on my narrow, and by no means procrustean, bed and took another short nap, to awaken soon, feeling still more cramped and benumbed. And thus I dragged out the night. The owls kept me company in my wakefulness and were hooting all around me throughout the night. You may be sure, reader, that I got a pretty early start from that camp the next morning. Day had hardly dawned before I was on the road again. I have read in books of romance of travelers and hunters, camping all alone in the deep woods, and it did not seem to be a very unpleasant way of passing a night, but I am free to confess that I am sufficiently satisfied with my experience in that direction not to wish to try it again.

The next day, about five o'clock, I reached the site of the old State Seminary, passed directly in front of the quarters I had once occupied as my home, drove by the ruins of our once magnificent school building, and hurried on with sad feelings to the house of Mr. Seay, one of our old-time colleagues, before the demon of fire had driven us from the pine woods. I stopped with Mr. Seay and his kind lady several days and had a most refreshing rest.

Nothing But a Little Pissant

A. J. LIEBLING

In his day a celebrated journalist, Liebling (1904–1963) came to Louisiana in 1959 to write about Earl Long for the *New Yorker* magazine. Governor Long—brother of the state's assassinated former governor and senator, the highly controversial populist Huey P. Long—was himself an eccentric and controversial figure. By the time of Liebling's visit, Long had been attracting national attention for his erratic behavior. He was, in fact, committed to an asylum in Galveston, Texas, and then to the Louisiana state mental hospital at Mandeville, but he was able to engineer his release and—because he was still governor—dismiss the state official who might challenge that release. Here Liebling writes of going to Alexandria—"Alick" in local parlance—to follow a Long election campaign, in the company of Tom Sancton, a local journalist. He makes some cogent comments on the state's north-south cultural divisions as well. From *The Earl of Louisiana,* Liebling's account of his observations of Long during his Louisiana visit.

. . . The distance from New Orleans to Alexandria is about 190 miles. The first 90 miles, from New Orleans to Baton Rouge, are on a throughway, a straight, fast road on the east side of the Mississippi, far enough back from the bank to avoid meanders, and high enough over the marshes to obviate bridges. There is nothing worth a long look. The bayous parallel the road on either side like stagnant, weed-strangled ditches, but their life is discreetly subsurface—snapping turtles, garfish, water moccasins and alligators. The mammals are water rats and muskrats and nutria, a third kind of rat. The nutria, particularly ferocious, is expropriating the other rats. Bird life, on the day we drove through, was a patrol of turkey buzzards looking down for rat cadavers. There pressed down on the landscape a smell like water that householders have inadvertently left flowers in while they went off for a summer holiday. It was an ideal setting for talk about politics.

The old station wagon slammed along like an old selling plater that knows a course by heart.

"It's the most complex state in the South," my companion said. "In just about every one of the others you have the same battle between the poor-to-middling farmers on the poor lands—generally in the hills—that didn't justify an investment in slaves before the war, and the descendants of the rich planters on the rich lands, who held slaves by the dozen to the gross. Slaves were a mighty expensive form of agricultural machinery, with a high rate of depreciation. You could only use them to advantage on land that produced a cash crop. We had that same basic conflict, and it lasted longer than anywhere else, for reasons I'm going to give, but in addition, we have a lot that are all our own. In the other states it was just between poor Anglo-Saxon Protestant whites and rich Anglo-Saxon Protestant whites. But here we got poor French Catholic whites and poor Anglo-Saxon whites and rich French Catholic whites and rich Anglo-Saxon Protestant whites. Sometimes the Catholic French get together against the Anglo-Saxon Protestants and sometimes the rich of both faiths get together against the poor, or the poor against the rich.

"And there's always been another problem in Louisiana that no other Southern state has. There are other large collections of people living close together in the South, but they are not big cities, just overgrown country towns like Atlanta. They may have corruption, but not sophistication. They lack the urban psychology, like ancient Athens, that is different, hostile, and superior, and that the countryman resents and distrusts. So you get a split along another line—you got not only poor rural French Catholic, rich rural white Protestant, rich rural French Catholic, and poor rural white Protestant, but poor urban Catholic, not exclusively French, rich urban Catholic, poor urban Protestant (mainly Negro) and rich urban Protestant. Making out a ticket is tricky.

"Alick, in Rapides Parish, is the political navel of the state, right in the middle." (Alick is Alexandria.) "Southern, bilingual, French Catholic Louisiana, the land of the bougalees, shades into Northern monolingual, Anglo-Saxon Protestant Louisiana, the land of the rednecks. But in Rapides itself and the parishes across the center of the state you get both kinds. So there's always a lot of politicking and name-calling in Alick, and when Earl picked it to stump in he showed he was ready to fight."

He sounded as complacent as a man I remembered on the road to Baalbek, telling me of the Ten Varieties soup of politico-religious divisions within the Lebanon.

The old car banged along. Its speedometer was not working, but it had a clock in its head, like an old horse that an old trainer, set in his ways, has worked a mile in 1.47 every Wednesday morning since it was three years old.

"Orleans Parish—that's the city of New Orleans—and Jefferson, across the river, which is its dormitory country—have about a quarter of a million voters between them," my instructor said. "That's between twenty-five and thirty per cent of the state vote. All the parishes north of a line through Rapides have maybe twenty per cent and all the parishes south of it and west of the Mississippi maybe twenty to twenty-five. The central chunk, on an axis from Alick to Baton Rouge and on east, has the balance of strength. To get a majority of votes on the first primary, a candidate got to win big in one of the four regions and make it close in the others, or win big in three and lose big in one. They're so different and so opposed historically that it's hard to imagine a candidate running evenly in all four. Old Earl was so strong in 1956 that he ran almost even in the metropolis. For an upstate candidate that's great. He won easy everyplace else.

"If Earl is too sick to run, a Catholic from New Orleans like Morrison might win big in New Orleans and south Louisiana, but he would be snowed under in the north, and he would have to run like hell in Alick and Baton Rouge to make it. So probably there would be no winner the first time around, and then, in the runoff between the two high men, anything could happen. Generally all the losers gang up against the top guy. Hard to name a favorite in the betting until the day before the second runoff, and then often you're wrong anyway."

"Then how did Huey Long put all the bits and pieces together?" I asked.

"Huey got all the poor people over on one side," my friend said. "And there were a lot more of them. He made the poor redneck and the poor Frenchman and the poor Negro see that what they had in common was more important for voting purposes than the differences. The differences couldn't be changed by ballots. The Depression helped, of course.

"When people are living good again they can afford to fight over unessentials. The regime that ran Louisiana right on from the Purchase discouraged the idea that a man had the right to live decently. It was new stuff down here when Huey put it out: 'Share Our Wealth'; 'Every Man a King'; and remember, he got to be Governor four years before Franklin D. Roosevelt was elected President. Huey got after the out-state oil companies and the in-state oil companies, and the old-family bench and bar that held with the out-state money, and anybody that gave him an argument for any reason he blackened with being a hireling of Standard Oil. I don't know how much money he made out of it, but certainly less than a lot of politicians make taking the easy money side.

"And whether he did it all because he loved the sense of power is moot—you could say the same thing against any leader you didn't like. I think up North you got the idea that the man who killed him became a popular hero, like William Tell or Charlotte Corday. Incidentally, Charlotte Corday wouldn't have won any Gallup polls in Paris in her day. There were editorials that said, 'Louisiana heaved a sigh of relief and raised her tear-stained head from the dust.'

"But, in fact, Dick Leche and Earl Long, who ran for Governor and Lieutenant Governor on the Long ticket in 1936, got sixty-seven and a tenth per cent of the popular vote, even though there was a fight among the Long people themselves and Leche was next to unknown then. That was a better percentage than even Roosevelt got against Landon that year. The vote came straight from the tear-stained head."

We got hungry and stopped at a glass-and-Monel-metal hangar that advertised "Shrimp, BarBQue, PoBoy" (this last the Louisiana term for what we call Italian hero sandwiches). The BarBQue was out, the shrimps stiff with inedible batter, the coffee desperate. Southern cooking, outside New Orleans, is just about where Frederick Law Olmsted left it when he wrote *The Cotton Kingdom.* A PoBoy at Mumfrey's in New Orleans is a portable banquet. In the South proper, it is a crippling blow to the intestine.

"We're hitting a new culture belt," I said. "This is the kind of cooking that goes right on up the center of the United States with the Mississippi until it hits the Great Lakes. It's nearer akin to what we'd get in a roadside diner in La

Grange, Illinois, than to the poorest oyster bar in New Orleans, sixty miles behind us."

Tom, New Orleans born, of parents born there, said, "You're right on that. We're Mediterranean. I've never been to Greece or Italy, but I'm sure I'd be at home there as soon as I landed."

He would, too, I thought. New Orleans resembles Genoa or Marseilles, or Beirut or the Egyptian Alexandria more than it does New York, although all seaports resemble one another more than they can resemble any place in the interior. Like Havana and Port-au-Prince, New Orleans is within the orbit of a Hellenistic world that never touched the North Atlantic. The Mediterranean, Caribbean and Gulf of Mexico form a homogeneous, though interrupted, sea. New York and Cherbourg and Bergen are in a separate thalassic system. . . .

The middle of Louisiana is where the culture of one great thalassic littoral impinges on the other, and a fellow running for Governor has got to straddle the line between them.

When Tom and I were sufficiently disgusted with the coffee of the inland-dwellers, we resumed our ride, bypassing the center of Baton Rouge to cross the Mississippi by the Baton Rouge bridge, and after that leaving the monotony of the throughway for the state roads with their complete lack of variety. By now I had begun to sneak compulsive glances at my watch. We had left New Orleans at four, and Earl was slated to speak at eight. The owner of the old station wagon had said he could make it to Alick in four hours easy. It began to look not all that easy.

I tried to estimate the station wagon's speed by clocking it between signposts. From "Bunkie, 27 Mi." To "Bunkie, 20 Mi.," I caught it in a consoling seven minutes, but the next post, a good bit farther on, said "Bunkie, 23." Bunkie is the leading bourgade between Baton Rouge and Alick—it has a population of 4,666—but there were other one-street-of-storefronts towns that the road ran through. By now it was dusk and the stores were lighted, so that, coming out of the dark, we galloped episodically between plywood maple-finished bedroom suites in the windows on one side of the street and mannequins with $7.98 dresses on the other, scaring from our course gaunt hounds that looked like Kabyle dogs.

The entrance to Alick was little more impressive than these others, except for two electric signs. One was a straw-hatted spook flapping great wings over the Hocus-Pocus Liquor Store and the other a symbolic giraffe and dachshund over a used-car lot. They disappeared at every other flash in favor of a legend: "High Quality, Low Prices."

Hurrying through otherwise undistinguished streets, we passed between cars parked thick along the approaches to the courthouse square and heard the loud-speaker blaring long before we got there. Somebody was on the platform in front of the courthouse steps, standing too close to the microphone and blasting. The crowd, massed immediately around the speaker's stand, thinned out toward the sidewalks.

My companion let me out and drove on to find a parking space, and I ran onto the lawn for my first look at the Imam in the flesh. As I crossed over to the forum, a boy handed me a pink throwaway, which I examined when I got within range of the light diffused from the floodlamps over the platform:

GOVERNOR LONG SPEAKS
Governor Long Opens Campaign for Re-Election

Come Out and Bring All your friends to hear the truth.
Come out and see Governor Long in person. Nothing will
be said to offend or hurt anyone.

The Governor, on the platform, was saying to somebody I could not see over in the other wing of the audience:

"If you don't shut up your claptrap, I'm going to have you forcibly removed. You just nothing but a common hoodlum and a heckler."

"Amen," an old man in front of me yelled. "Give it to him, Earl."

Whoever it was that Earl was talking to in the crowd had no microphone, so we couldn't hear him, but he must have answered in tones audible to the Governor, because the latter shouted into the mike:

"I knew your daddy, Camille Gravel, and he was a fine man.[9] But you trying to make yourself a big man, and you nothing but a little pissant."

"Amen, Earl," the old man yelled. "Give it to him."

The fellow in the crowd, now identified for me as a lawyer from Alick who was the Democratic National Committeeman from Louisiana, must have spoken again, for the Governor thundered:

"Mr. Gravel, I got nothing against you personally. Now you keep quiet and

9. Camille Gravel (b. 1915) had a long political career in Louisiana, including service as executive counsel and executive assistant to Governor Edwin Edwards.

I won't mention your name. If you don't I'll have you removed as a common damn nuisance." He paused for the answer we couldn't hear and then bellowed:

"If *you* so popular, why don't *you* run for Governor?"

It sounded like a dialogue between a man with the horrors and his hallucinations. But the National Committeeman, Earl's interlocutor, was there in the flesh. He had brought his ten children, and they were all mad at the Governor.

The night was like a heavy blanket pressed down on the lawn. Men stood in their sleeveless, collarless shirts, and sweat caked the talcum powder on the backs of the women's necks. Anti-Long newspapers the next day conceded the crowd was between three and four thousand, so there may well have been more. Plenty of Negroes, always in little groups, were scattered among the whites, an example, I suppose, of Harry Golden's "vertical integration," because in public gatherings where there are seats, the two colors are always separated into blocs.[10]

"That's the way I like to see it," the Governor said, from the stand. "Not all our colored friends in one spot and white friends in another. I'm the best friend the poor white man, and the middle-class white man, and the rich white man—so long as he behave himself—and the poor colored man, ever had in the State of Loosiana. And if the NAACP and that little pea-headed nut Willie Rainach will just leave us alone, then *sen*sible people, not cranks, can get along in a *reas*onable way. That Rainach wants to fight the Civil War all over again."[11]

There were two colored couples, middle-aged, in front of me, next to the old white man who didn't like Gravel, and now one of the colored men shouted "Amen!" The old white man gave him a reproving look, but he couldn't bawl him out for agreeing with a Long. Nobody can object to *reas*onable and *sen*sible, but Long hadn't said what he thought *reas*onable and *sen*sible were, and it occurred to me that he probably never would.

10. Harry Golden (1902–81) was a journalist and humorist who for years edited the anomalous *Carolina Israelite*. The term "vertical integration" refers to his whimsically offered idea that since whites (in segregation days) did not seem to object to blacks being with them in public places so long as the blacks were standing (for example, when serving them), all chairs should be abolished from public places.

11. Willie Rainach was a state senator whom Earl Long considered a racial extremist.

I had been looking at him with an amateur clinical eye since I got there, and his physical condition seemed to me to have improved several hundred per cent since his stump appearance with Joe Sims on the Fourth of July.[12] Late hours and a diet of salted watermelon, buttermilk, and Vienna sausages cut up in chicken broth had put a dozen pounds back on his bones. Walking between grandstands and paddocks had legged him up, and he pranced under the floodlights that must have raised the temperature to a hundred and ten or so. I remembered when I had seen first the referee, Ruby Goldstein, and then the great Sugar Ray Robinson himself collapse under the heat of similar lights in a ring on a less oppressive night in New York.

Uncle Earl wore a jacket, shirt and tie, a pattern of statesmanlike conventionality on a night when everybody off the platform was coatless and tieless. The tie itself was a quiet pattern of inkblots against an olive-and-pearl background, perhaps a souvenir Rorschach test from Galveston.[13] The suit, a black job that dated from the days when he was fat and sassy, hung loosely about him as once it had upon a peg in the supermarket where the Governor liked to buy his clothes.

He left the dude role to Morrison.[14] And in fact, before the evening was over, he said:

"I see Dellasoups has been elected one of the ten best-dressed men in America. He has fifty-dollar neckties and four-hundred-dollar suits. A four-hundred-dollar suit on old Uncle Earl would look like socks on a rooster."

It is difficult to report a speech by Uncle Earl chronologically, listing the thoughts in order of appearance. They chased one another on and off the stage like characters in a Shakespearean battle scene, full of alarums and sorties. But Morrison, good roads and old-age pensions popped in quite often.

Of Dodd, the State Auditor, a quondam ally and now a declared rival for the Governorship, he said, "I hear Big Bad Bill Dodd has been talking about inefficiency and waste in this administration. Ohyeah. Ohyeah. Well let me

12. Joe Sims was the attorney who got Long released from the state mental hospital with a writ of habeas corpus.

13. Location of the Texas insane asylum where Long was committed until released by a judge with the understanding that the governor would enter a Louisiana institution.

14. deLesseps S. Morrison—whose first name Earl Long liked to parody as "Dellasoups"—was four times mayor of New Orleans and ran several unsuccessful campaigns for governor; he was killed in a plane crash in 1964.

tell you, Big Bad Bill has at least six streamlined deadheads on his payroll that couldn't even find Bill's office if they had to. But they can find that *Post Office* every month to get their salary check—Ohyeah."

It was after the "*reas*onable and *sen*sible" bit that he went into his general declaration of tolerance. "I'm not against anybody for reasons of race, creed, or any ism he might believe in except nuttism, skingameism or communism," he said.

"I'm glad to see so many of my fine Catholic friends here—they been so kind to me I sometimes say I consider myself forty per cent Catholic and sixty per cent Baptist" (this is a fairly accurate reflection of the composition of the electorate). "But I'm in favor of *every* religion with the possible exception of snake-chunking. Anybody that so presumes on how he stands with Providence that he will let a snake bite him, I say he deserves what he's got coming to him." The snake-chunkers, a small, fanatic cult, do not believe in voting.

"Amen, Earl," the old man said.

The expressions on the Governor's face changed with the poetry of his thought, now benign, now mischievous, now indignant. Only the moist hazel eyes remained the same, fixed on a spot above and to the rear of the audience as if expecting momentarily the arrival of a posse.

"I don't *need* this job," he said. "I don't *need* money." He stopped and winked. "I don't miss it except when I run out."

There were shouts of laughter, the effect he courted.

"Amen, Earl. You tell 'em, Earl."

His face turned serious, as if he had not expected to be so cruelly misunderstood.

"I'm serious about that," he said. "You know I'm no goody-goody. But if I have ever misappropriated one cent, by abuse of my office, and anyone can prove it, I'll resign.

"I know lots of ways to make a living. I know how to be a lawyer, and a danged good one. I know how to be a traveling salesman. I know how to pick cotton, and have many times, although I've seen the days when to get my hundred pounds I had to put a watermelon in the bag."

There were gales of tolerant laughter now, even from farmers who would shoot any of their own help they found cheating on weight.

"All I ask," he said, with the honesty throbbing in his voice like a musical saw, "is a chance once again to help the fine people of the Great State of Loosiana, and to continue to serve them as their Governor."

Even a group of great louts in T shirts, perhaps high-school football players, were silent and by now impressed; earlier in the address they had made a few feeble attempts at heckling, like yelling, "Hey, Earl, what's in the glass?" when the Governor paused for a drink of water. These boys might be from well-to-do anti-Long families, but they had the endemic Southern (and Arabic) taste for oratory, and they knew a master when they heard him.

Mr. Gravel, down near the platform, must have again attracted the Governor's attention, but now Uncle Earl, the creature of his own voice, was in a benign mood from offering his own body to the Great State of Loosiana.

"Mr. Gravel," he said, "you got ten beautiful children there, I wish you would lend five of them to me to bring up." It was one of Earl's well-publicized sorrows that he, like the Shah of Iran then, had no legitimate heir, and he handed peppermint candies or small change to all children he saw, even in years when there was no election. "He bought those candies by grosses of dozens," an ex-associate told me.

Mr. Gravel, still inaudible except to Earl, must have declined this overture, because the Governor shouted to the crowd: "He used to be a nice fellow, but now he just a goddamn hoodlum!"

"Leave him alone, Earl, we come to hear *you* talk!" the old man near me shouted back.

"I was in Minneannapolis once, talking to the Governor of Minnesota, a great expert on insanity," Uncle Earl said, "and he told me an astonishing fact—there are ten times as many crazy people in Minnesota as Louisiana. I suppose that is on account of the cold climate. They cannot go around in their shirt sleeves all year around, go huntin' and fishin' in all seasons, as we do. We got a wonderful climate," he said, and paused to wipe the sweat from his face with a handkerchief soaked in Coca-Cola, which he poured from a bottle out of a bucket of ice handed him by one of the lesser candidates on his ticket. The bugs soaring up at the edge of the lighted area and converging on the floodlights formed a haze as thick as a beaded curtain.

"On account we got so few crazy people, we can afford to let Camille Gravel run around."

"Leave him up, Earl," the old man yelled. "You got him licked."

"Some sapsuckers talk about cutting down taxes," the Governor said, apropos of nothing he had been talking about. "Where are they going to start cutting expenses? On the *spastic* school?" (When any opponent suggests a cut in welfare expenditures, Earl accuses him of wanting to take it out on the spastics. This is the equivalent of charging the fellow would sell his mother for glue.) "They want to cut down on the *spastics?* On the little children, enjoying the school lunches? Or on those fine old people, white-haired against the sunset of life—" and he bowed his own white head for a split second—"who enjoy the most generous state pensions in the United States?"

"We got the finest roads, finest schools, finest hospitals in the country—yet there are rich men who complain. They are so tight you can hear 'em squeak when they walk. They wouldn't give a nickel to see a earthquake. They sit there swallowin' hundred-dollar bills like a bullfrog swallows minners—if you chunked them as many as they want they'd bust."

"Amen, Earl," the old man said. "God have mercy on the poor people."

"Of course, I know many *fine* rich people," the Governor said, perhaps thinking of his campaign contributors. "But the most of them are like a rich old feller I knew down in Plaquemines Parish, who died one night and never done nobody no good in his life, and yet, when the Devil come to get him, he took an appeal to St. Peter.

" 'I done some good things on earth,' he said. 'Once, on a cold day in about 1913, I gave a blind man a nickel.' St. Peter looked all through the records, and at last, on page four hundred and seventy-one, he found the entry. 'That ain't enough to make up for a misspent life,' he said. 'But wait,' the rich man says. 'Now I remember, in 1922 I give five cents to a poor widow woman that had no carfare.' St. Peter's clerk checked the book again, and on page thirteen hundred and seventy-one, after pages and pages of how this old stumpwormer loan-sharked the poor, he found the record of that nickel.

" 'That ain't neither enough,' St. Peter said. But the mean old thing yelled, *'Don't* sentence me yet. In about 1931 I give a nickel to the Red Cross.' The clerk found that entry, too. So he said to St. Peter, 'Your Honor, what are we going to do with him?' "

The crowd hung on Uncle Earl's lips the way the bugs hovered in the light.

"You know what St. Peter said?" the Governor, the only one in the courthouse square who knew the answer, asked. There was, naturally, no reply.

"He said: 'Give him back his fifteen cents and tell him to go to Hell.' "

He had the crowd with him now, and he dropped it.

"Folks," he said, "I know you didn't come here just to hear me talk. If this big mouth of mine ever shut up I'd be in a devil of a fix. I want to introduce to you some of the fine *sincere* candidates that are running with me on my ticket. My ticket and the independent candidates I have endorsed are trained, skilled, and have the wisdom and experience to make you honest, loyal and sincere public servants."

He turned to the triple row of men and women who sat behind him on undertaker's chairs, the men swabbing, the women dabbing, at their faces with handkerchiefs, while the Governor talked like an intrepid trainer who turns his back on his troupe of performing animals.

A reporter who had his watch on the Governor said that his talk had lasted fifty-seven minutes, and he was not even blowing.

"And first," he said, "I want to introduce to you the man I have selected to serve under me as Lieutenant Governor during my next term of office—a fine Frenchmun, a fine Catholic, the father of twenty-three children, Mr. Oscar Guidry."

The number of children was politically significant, since it indicated that Mr. Guidry was a practicing, not a *soi-disant*, Catholic. The candidate for Lieutenant Governor had to be a Frenchman and a Catholic, because Uncle Earl was neither.

Mr. Guidry, a short, stocky man who reminded me of a muscular owl, arose from his chair like a Mr. Bones called to front center by Mr. Interlocutor. He appeared embarrassed, and he whispered rapidly to Uncle Earl.

"Oscar says he has only fourteen children," the Governor announced. "But that's a good beginning."

Mr. Guidry whispered again, agitated, and Earl said, "But he is a member of a family of twenty-three brothers and sisters." He turned away, as if washing his hands of the whole affair, and sat down.

Mr. Guidry, throwing back his head and clasping his hands in front of him, as if about to intone the "Marseillaise," began with a rush, sounding all his aitches:

"I am *honored* to be associated with the Gret Governeur of the Gret Stet on his tiquette. Those who have conspired against him, fearing to shoot him with a pistol-ball . . ." and he was off, but Earl, seated directly behind him, was mugging and catching flies, monopolizing attention like an old vaudeville star cast in a play with a gang of Method actors.

Pulling his chair slightly out of line, he crossed his legs and turned his profile to the audience, first plucking at his sleeves, which came down about as far as his thumbnails, then, when he had disengaged his hands, picking his nose while he looked over at Alick's leading hotel, the Bentley, across the street, described by the Louisiana State Guide as "a six-story building of brick and stone, with a columned facade and a richly decorated interior." He stared at it as if it contained some absorbing riddle.

When he had finished with his nose, he began to bathe his face, his temples and the back of his neck with Coca-Cola from the cold bottle, sloshing it on like iced cologne.

"Cool yourself off, Earl," a voice piped up from the crowd, and the Governor shouted back, "I'm a red-hot poppa."

When he had wet himself down sufficiently, he drank the heel-tap and set the bottle down. Then he lit a cigarette and smoked, dramatically, with the butt held between his thumb and middle finger and the other fingers raised, in the manner of a ventriloquist. While he smoked right-handed he pulled out his handkerchief and blotted his wet face with his left.

He sat unheeding of the rumpus raised by his adherents, like a player in a jazz band who has finished his solo, or a flashy halfback who poses on the bench while the defensive team is in. The candidates ranted and bellowed, putting across a few telling although familiar points.

"In the great state of Texas, biggest and richest in the United States, there is an old-age pension of thirty-one dollars a month. Here in Loosiana we got seventy-two."

But the bored crowd stood fast, knowing that a whistle would blow and the star would throw off his blanket and come onto the field again to run rings around the forces of Mammon. Sure enough, after what seemed to me an endless session of subordinate rant, the Governor threw away the last of a chain of cigarettes and shook his head like a man waking up on a park bench and remembering where he is. He got up and walked to the microphone so fast that the man using it had barely time to say "I thank you" before the Governor took it away from him.

"You shall know the truth, and the truth shall set you free," the Governor said, "but you will never get to know the truth by reading the Alexandria *Town Talk*. You all read in that paper that I am crazy. Ohyeah. Do I look any crazier than I ever did? I been accused of saying the fella that owns that paper is a kept man. Maybe he ain't, but I'd like to be kep' as good as he is. He married a rich woman. That's about the best way I know to save yourself about ninety-eight years' hard work."

"Amen, Earl, it's the truth," the old man in front of me cried, and the Negroes laughed at what was apparently a well-established local joke.

"Maybe some of you are here because you've never seen a man out of a nuthouse before," the Governor said tolerantly. "Maybe you want to see a man who has been stuck thirty-eight times with needles. Oh, the first man stuck me, stuck me right through the britches. He didn't get me in the fat part, either, and oh, how it hurt! Maybe I lost a little weight, but you would have, too. Occasionally I say hell or damn, but if it had happened to you all, you'd say worse than that. Christ on the Cross Himself never suffered worse than poor old Earl!

"Oh, not that I'm fit to walk in Christ's shoes!" he bellowed to preclude any confusion. "I'm not good enough, when a fellow slugs me on one cheek, to turn the other side of my scheming head. I'm going to slug him back."

"Amen, Earl. You tell him, Earl. Who you goin' to hit first, Earl?"

House on a cotton plantation in the Delta parishes, 1937, by Dorothea Lange

Photograph courtesy Library of Congress

"Down there in that court in Texas in Galveston before that Texas judge, I felt like Christ between the two thieves. He reared back his head and he said, 'Father forgive them, for they know not what they do!'"

At this point he was interrupted by wild handclapping from a group of elderly ladies wearing print dresses, white gloves, straw hats and Spaceman eyeglasses, who had been seated quietly on the platform through the earlier proceedings. They were under the impression that it was an original line.

I next remember the Governor in his seat again, head down, exhausted, having given his all to the electorate, in a pose like Bannister after running the first four-minute mile. It occurred to me that he was like old blind Pete Herman fighting on heart alone, by a trained reflex. Pete is a friend of the Governor's.

As Earl sat there, one of the assisting speakers, a fellow with a strong voice, grabbed the microphone and declaimed the family battle ode, "Invictus."

When the man came to the part where it says:

"Under the bludgeonings of fate
Ma haid is bloody, but *unbowed*"

Earl flung up his head like a wild horse and got up like a fighter about to go into a dance to prove he hasn't been hurt. He called for a show of hands by everybody who was going to vote for him, and I waved both of mine.

I left him surrounded by children to whom he was passing out coins, "a quarter to the white kids and a nickel to the niggers."

My companion had rejoined me after parking the car, and we walked together through the breaking crowd.

"How could his wife have done him like she done?"[15] a woman was asking another, and a man was saying, "Got to give da ol' dawg what's coming to him."

My friend saw Gravel, a handsome, tanned man in a white sports shirt and black slacks, standing where the lawn ended at the pavement, and walked over to him. Two or three reporters were already there, asking Gravel what he had said when Earl said what.

The National Committeeman said he had come to hear the speech because

15. Mrs. Long had played a role in the attempts to commit the governor.

two or three men close to Earl had called him up and warned him that Earl was going to blacken his name.

"I wanted to be there to nail the lie," he said. He said Earl started the argument.

Six or eight of the ten Gravel children played hide-and-seek around their father's legs, and as he talked, another boy, about eleven years old, ran up and said to a slightly younger girl, his sister, "The Governor wanted to give me a quarter, but I wouldn't take it."

"Why not?" the girl asked, and I decided she had a bigger political future than her brother.

Gravel said he had to go home because there was a wedding reception there, and the rest of us walked back toward the Bentley, where all the rocking chairs on the porch were already occupied. The row of glowing cigar ends swaying in unison reminded me of the Tiller Girls in a glow-worm number.

Travel Update

Samuel Lockett's topographical excursion as excerpted here covers interesting sections of central and north Louisiana. Lockett started out from Pineville, where he was based at the Louisiana State Seminary, and covered much ground. Today's traveler might *roughly* replicate his travels here by proceeding from Pineville (across the Red River from the larger city of Alexandria) on Louisiana 28 (passing the Alexandria airport) and then on U.S. 84 to Jonesville. This route goes past Catahoula Lake (not mentioned by Lockett—who actually traveled on the other side of the lake—and not visible from the present-day road). The traveler will notice the swampy terrain and the presence of various levees and that 128 is built up above the surrounding countryside. This is overflow country, into which rising waters from the lake and from nearby rivers can move. (The Little River and Bayou Flacon are both connected to Catahoula Lake.) It is very wet country, the sort of land that might be termed "hog wallow land." Near Jonesville several rivers meet, and we are reminded again of the overpowering importance of waterways in Louisiana, even though this is far from the "bayou country" of the Cajuns.

Louisiana 124 and then a short jog on Louisiana 8 brings one to Harrisonburg, an old town Amos Parker visited some years before Lockett. Though Lockett does not say so, the approach to Harrisonburg from the south is startling because the traveler, after crossing miles of some of the flattest and lowest country imaginable, comes upon what seems like a giant hill, upon which the town's cemetery is located. This brings us to the very edge of the hill country that fills the northwestern part of the state. (Lockett mentions mounting this hill for the view.) Harrisonburg has preserved the old Sargeant Hotel, a modest but interesting structure that was a hostelry for steamboat passengers traveling on the Ouachita River. Its dates are uncertain (Lockett does not mention it), though it was known to be operating prior to 1910, and it retains a pinch of the flavor of travel in these parts in earlier times.

Lockett made a side trip to Sicily Island while his ambulance was being fixed in Harrisonburg. Today Louisiana 8 leads there, for a short time along the banks of the Ouachita, upon whose waters towboats and barges have replaced the steamboats. In Louisiana the name *island* has been conferred on various geographic features that are not actually islands; Sicily Island is "a high area between the Ouachita and Mississippi Rivers" at one end of the Maçon Ridge (which is made up of gravel long ago deposited by the Mississippi and extending up into Arkansas).[16]

After returning to Harrisonburg, Lockett proceeded further up the Ouachita. The modern traveler could go along Louisiana 124, which comes close to that river in places (the tiny ferry at Duty is a relic from the past) and also goes through hill country, which in places seems strikingly remote (the road is unpaved in stretches). Louisiana 126 carries one over to U.S. 165, which proceeds through Columbia (noted by Lockett and near where he locates Lone Grave Bluff) to Monroe.

From Monroe, Lockett went to Delhi by rail. Interstate 20 more or less parallels the railroad track (there is no longer passenger service in the area) and takes one out of the hill country into the flat plantation lands of the Delta parishes. He also went up into West and East Carroll parishes (where the town of Lake Providence is a charming old settlement and where Poverty Point, one of the most important Indian sites in North America, is situated; see Chapter 1).

Following Lockett's travels today takes one through interesting and varied parts of central and north Louisiana—swampy overflow country, rugged (if low) hills, pine woods, and Delta agricultural land. Lockett produced "The Louisiana State University Topographical Map of Louisiana" (published in 1873 by Colton and Co. of New York), which locates many of the places he visited.

Amos Parker, going west, covered some of the same country as Lockett did later. He too put in at Harrisonburg and proceeded to Alexandria. From Alexandria a modern-day traveler might roughly approximate his route (which, of course, is difficult to follow because there were so few well-established towns or other landmarks in his day) by driving west on Louisiana 28 then cutting northwest on highway 118. This route will take one through parts of the Kisatchie National Forest, providing some sense of this part of the state as Parker saw it. One should proceed north on U.S. 171 to Louisiana 6 at Many. This highway follows—though by no means precisely—the way of the old Spanish *Camino Real* from Natchitoches to Texas, and the route suggested

16. Darwin Spearing, *Roadside Geology of Louisiana* (Missoula, Mont., 1995), 201.

brings one to it just below Fort Jessup (like Parker came to it). There is a state commemorative area that contains ruins and reconstructions of the fort, which was built in 1822 by Zachary Taylor and served as an American outpost on the edge of the United States and as a staging area during the Mexican War. This general area was the neutral zone, or no man's land, between the Spanish and French (later American) territories whose borders were ill-defined. It was a haven for those who sought to live beyond the reach of government and had a reputation as a wild place. Though not on Parker's route and built in 1848, later than his journey, the Autry House (see Chapter 3) near Dubach in Grant Parish is an example of the sort of humble north Louisiana frontier dwellings he encountered.

The Earl K. Long State Commemorative Area in Winnfield—birthplace of Huey and Earl Long—is made up of a small plazalike space with a statue of Earl and a pavilion. It can be a focal point for looking at the origins of these two brothers, but for greater insight into Louisiana politics in general, a visit to the Old State Capitol in Baton Rouge—recently renovated into a still-developing museum called the Center for Political and Governmental History—is called for. Obviously a fitting site for such a museum, the capitol is—despite Mark Twain's poking fun at it—a marvelous structure, an important example of Gothic-revival architecture and the work of noted architect James Dakin. Inside, multicolored light flows in from a colored-glass skylight, and a cast-metal, winding staircase dominates the central area of the building in a striking manner.

The Old State Capitol was abandoned after the new art deco skyscraper capitol was completed in 1932—part of Huey Long's ambitious plans to re-create the state (it was also the place of his assassination). Used for various purposes since then, the old capitol's latest restoration utilizes as display areas certain of the actual rooms originally used for governmental functions. Thus, for example, the governor's office has been furnished as such. In addition, there is a display about Louisiana governors. Visitors can call up film clips and recordings, such as excerpts from speeches by Huey and Earl (including Earl's famous "Socks on a Rooster" remark that Liebling quotes), as well as a clip of another colorful governor, country-western singing star Jimmie Davis, singing his trademark song, "You Are My Sunshine" (in earlier and later performances). Other displays include footage of the turmoil of the civil rights struggle in Louisiana and a room devoted to Huey Long's still-controversial murder. This exhibit is set in a small chamber in one of the building's turrets, where the presence of the murder weapon and the dark, tomblike setting add a touch of eerieness to the informative display.

The New State Capitol is open to the public and can be fun to observe when the legislature is in session. Hordes of lobbyists congregate while state officials come and go. Long is buried in the gardens, and pockmarks from the bullets fired during Long's assasination can still be seen in the wall near where he was shot.

The Old Governor's Mansion—also built by Huey and resembling the White House, supposedly a reflection of his presidential ambitions—is a few blocks from the Old State Capitol (on North Boulevard) and contains rooms related to various Louisiana governors.

The well-known photographer Philip Gould has produced a lavish volume that documents in color photographs the history and political life of the Louisiana capitols, *Louisiana's Capitols: The Power and the Beauty* (Lafayette, La., 1995). Huey Long's life and career have been definitively chronicled and analyzed in *Huey Long,* Pulitzer Prize-winning masterwork of Louisiana State University historian T. Harry Williams (New York, 1970). There are also excellent video documentaries on both Longs: Ken Burns (director) and Richard Kilberg, *Huey Long,* 1985, and Rick Smith (director), *Uncle Earl,* 1986. Earl, as played by Paul Newman, was the subject of the feature film *Blaze* (1989), a rather fictionalized version of his escapades and particularly his relationship with the stripper Blaze Starr. Huey has long been thought to have been the inspiration for Robert Penn Warren's epic political novel, *All the King's Men* (1946). Huey Long penned his own autobiography, *Every Man a King: The Autobiography of Huey P. Long* (New Orleans, 1933), which, though self-promoting, is nonetheless a fascinating document. Earl lost the election of 1959 observed by Liebling.

The Bentley Hotel—where Liebling concludes the account of his journey to Alexandria—was indeed a central gathering place for many years. Built in 1908 and expanded in the 1930s, it fell prey to the general decline of downtown areas in the 1960s and closed its doors in the early 1970s. It was, however, refurbished and reopened in the 1980s and continues as a grand hotel. It has exquisite public areas. There are no longer any rockers on the porch, but the porch itself remains an impressive outdoor space. The hotel also played a significant role in accommodating the military during the massive field maneuvers that took place in central Louisiana just before and during World War II.

8

Where All Things Seem to Dream: Bayou, Marsh, Coast

Traveling by train into New Orleans in 1871 on a tour of the post-war South, Robert Somers took particular note of Louisiana as a place of water. He noted the "trembling prairies"—the marshes—as "watery mazes spreading on all sides." The train, he said, "comes to places where lagoons expand over miles of territory, and rivers seem to lose themselves in unseen channels amidst the weltering waters." At stations he encountered "floating houses [that] have penetrated by patient navigation from some dry shore with goods and groceries, powder and shot" and "men and boys . . . always jumping into canoes . . . and paddling their way in all directions." The train seemed "to be running directly into the sea," and came to "still more lakes and serpentines." "Nature," he observed, "here consists of amphibious beings."

Even when he got to firmer land closer to the city he found "hoary cypresses standing in pools of water" and "shallow swamps." Ensconced finally in his Crescent City hotel, he heard heavy rain at night. In the morning: "Throwing open the casement, the street is seen to be several feet deep in flood . . . a smooth canal-like surface of water overspreads the avenue." In the city he became aware of the pumps that helped to keep the city sufficiently drained and found crawfish chimneys in people's gardens. Awestruck by all this wetness, Somers whimsically says: "I have put the question whether . . . New Orleans may not be a floating island." But locals at most admitted that the city "does mayhap swing a little."[1]

He is hardly the only traveler who wrote to stress how wet New Orleans was. "Divine" Sarah Bernhardt, in the city for theatrical performances, found the place inundated. She claimed that she saw an alligator, water snakes, and boys crawfishing in the streets. Struck by the profusion of drainage and other canals, the Soviet journalists Il'ya Il'f and Eugene Petrov compared the city to Venice, as had Lady Emmeline Stuart Wortley many years before.[2]

But if Louisiana's great metropolis has evoked such observations, the state as a whole has been viewed even more so as a watery place, as a region practically defined by water, and Louisiana's watery environs have caught the attention of many travelers. To the visitor, much of the southern part of the state may seem like a "floating island" (indeed, there are only a handful of places where the coast can actually be seen from a road, so pervasive is the marsh country).

In reality, of course, many parts of Louisiana are no more moist than other places in the Deep South. But the Louisiana of the imagination is often the Louisiana of the bayou country, the alligator-infested swamps, the coastal marshes, and that is the vision of the state that has so often attracted visitors. (*Bayou* is simply a local term for stream—borrowed by the French from the Choctaw language. However, because of the prominence of such streams topographically and in local life, the very term *the bayous* has come to suggest something more: the wet environment as a whole.)

The stereotype of Louisiana as a place of wetness should not be terribly surprising in view of the reality of its geography and climate. Louisiana is the end point of the Mississippi River drainage basin, the fourth largest such basin in the world (after the Amazon, Congo, and Nile). The river drains 41 percent of the continental United States—an area ranging from Montana to New York—31 states in all, plus 2 Canadian provinces. The state's coast is vir-

---

1. Robert Somers, *Southern States Since the War, 1870–1* (London, 1871), 189–94.

2. Sarah Bernhardt, *Ma Double Vie* (Paris, 1907), 545ff; Il'f and Petrov, *Little Golden America*, 271; Lady Emmeline Stuart Wortley, *Travels in the United States etc. During 1849 and 1850* (New York, 1851), 126.

tually covered by marshes (estimates of their extent range from over 2.5 million to about 4 million acres), 41 percent of the nation's total marshland. In addition, there are approximately 1 million acres of swamp (forested wetland, as opposed to the grassy wetland of the marsh), and in the Atchafalaya the state has the largest river-basin swamp in the United States (though now contained within protective levees, historically it was even larger). Louisiana has what geographers call humid subtropical weather (in fact, among southern states, "Louisiana alone meets the qualifications" for this type of climate "perfectly"), which means there is "abundant precipitation."[3] New Orleans and south Louisiana generally get nearly 60 inches a year, and the southeastern portion of the state—the area of maximum precipitation—has gotten nearly 100 (in 1991, when the state as a whole got over 80).

A tremendous amount of water, then, does make its way through Louisiana, and a particular natural environment has resulted (though not a single terrain; the great river-basin swamp of the Atchafalaya, for example, is in many respects different from the coastal marshes, though to the casual observer they may seem similar). In addition, humans in Louisiana have created ways of life adapted to their watery surroundings, and the state thus has had a unique cultural environment as well. The swampers, the shrimpers and oystermen, the marshland trappers engage in lives that have fascinated outsiders and attracted travelers for years. The denizens of bayou country have a singular place in the Louisiana of the mind, and the selections in this chapter, while they speak of the natural environment, concentrate on the human side of coast and swamp.

For some early travelers the swamps and marshes were obstacles rather than goals, but there have been many visitors who have tried to know them for their own beauty and presence. In the nineteenth century such visitors had to be hardier and more enterprising than the general run of tourists. Back then casual travelers seldom got outside New Orleans, though the antebellum English author Matilda Charlotte Houstoun, for example, arranged for a tour of the marshes and the coast, going with a planter friend to see some of the more remote coastal plantations. Her account weaves through coastal marshlands and bays, giving us a picture of the often indefinable coastline where marshland meets the Gulf of Mexico. A couple of decades later, that confirmed ro-

3. Fred B. Kniffen and Sam Hilliard, *Louisiana, Its Land and People* (Baton Rouge, 1988), 19.

mantic Lafcadio Hearn heard news of a settlement of "Malays" in the swamp-lands and organized an expedition to find it, finally coming to the strange "lacustrine village" of St. Malo on Lake Borgne, with its isolated Oriental residents wresting livings from the water and from gambling at cards and a game similar to bingo. Elsewhere, in his short novel *Chita: A Memory of Last Island*, Hearn is eloquent about the "strange land [of] winding waterways" and the coast. He speaks of it as a place "where all things seem to dream," evoking the glorious colors of the coastal waters under sunny, azure skies, all of which may seem unreal.)[4]

In this chapter Ben Lucian Burman provides an overview of Louisiana water culture, moving from the rivers, swamps, and bayous of the central part of the state into the Atchafalaya Basin and down into the coastal marshes, the land becoming increasingly watery as he moves south; Kate Chopin's fictional journey from Grand Isle to Chênière Caminada presents the coastal waters and simple way of life she observed there in the 1870s. In Chopin's day Grand Isle was in part a resort for the New Orleans French-speaking bourgeoisie. That way of life was destroyed by the hurricane of 1893; the Grand Isle Charles Tenney Jackson writes about in 1914 is a very different sort of place. He presents the local culture as idyllic, as a land of cucumber farmers, fishermen, and turtle raisers who coexist happily despite racial differences and who while the night away with dances and parties.

Carolyn Ramsey and Christopher Hallowell look more closely at the working lives of swampers and coastal dwellers. Both writers—Ramsey in the 1950s, Hallowell in the 1970s—set out to find contemporary Cajuns to limn a portrait of them. Though the Cajuns are by no means the only group to inhabit Louisiana's water country (various traveler writers have stressed the multiculturalism of the swamp and marsh dwellers), they have been a dominant cultural influence, and Ramsey and Hallowell both noted the centrality of water occupations to their lives. Ramsey takes us into the swamps with moss pickers (Spanish moss was used commercially for furniture stuffing), while Hallowell gets us aboard a coastal oyster lugger working out of Bayou du Large.

4. Lafcadio Hearn, "St. Malo," in *An American Miscellany*, ed. Albert Mordell (2 vols.; New York, 1924), II, 89–102; Lafcadio Hearn, *Chita: A Memory of Last Island* (New York, 1917), 3, 153.

A World Apart

BEN LUCIAN BURMAN

Burman (1895–1984) wrote *Children of Noah: Glimpses of Unknown America,* from which this piece is taken, as a portrait of some of the common folk who "form the backbone of the South." He describes himself as an inveterate roamer and the book as "the result of my journeying." Here he provides a portrait of Louisiana fishermen and "swampers," moving from the rivers of central Louisiana to the Atchafalaya further south and on to the coastal marshes—drawing not upon a particular journey but upon composite memories from several. As a result we get a sort of travelogue through several layers of Louisiana water life. The reader may be surprised to learn that many Louisiana fishermen have made their livings from freshwater sources in addition to the more stereotypical Gulf.

There are four rivers at Jonesville. Here the Tensas, Little River, and Ouachita come together to form the Black. All are full of the succulent catfish and the huge buffalo. The inhabitants say there are as many fishermen as fish, and of more unusual varieties. . . .

Most of the shantyboats[5] which house the fishermen have gone from Jones-

5. A shantyboat is a folk houseboat, generally not powered by an engine. Kentucky artist Harlan Hubbard wrote two books about shantyboat life: *Shantyboat: A River Way of Life* (New York, 1953) and *Shantyboat on the Bayous* (Lexington, 1990), which deals with a Louisiana voyage.

ville to Cocodra Swamp on Red River, or found a place on the other smaller streams that wind through the neighboring wilderness. Numerous fishboats connect Jonesville with these tiny settlements, going out at frequent intervals to collect the catch.

A voyage on one of these odd vessels is like a trip through the African jungle. All day the traveler glides beside the vast, brooding forest, the trees bearing long festoons of Spanish moss with buzzards perched grimly on the branches. Now and then a cabin shows in a clearing or a shantyboat is moored to a tree, with half a dozen hoop nets piled on the near-by shore. A fisherman rows out and drops a load of catfish or buffalo onto the scales at the bow of the fishboat. The young pilot notes the weight, and dumps the catch into the ice-filled hold.

Occasionally there is a woman who has taken the place of her ailing husband at the nets, now and then a Negro with limbs like Hercules. Always as the boat comes to a halt, the young pilot passes out the flour and canned goods or a gaudy lamp or pillow cover he had been asked to procure on a previous excursion. For here in the swamps, where there are no roads, the fishboat is still the only link with the far-off world of the towns. . . .

Cocodra is typical of a Mississippi [river] fishing settlement. A long row of shantyboats and cabins is set along the riverbank, some almost completely hidden by the cypresses. Beyond stretches Cocodra Swamp, a tangled, gloomy jungle, one of the last outposts of the almost vanished . . . wilderness.

Here and there are scanty fields for growing a little corn and potatoes and cotton; every fisherman in the region is a farmer as well. Occasionally there is a narrow earthen mound, higher than the roofs of the buildings; this is a refuge, where the few pigs and cows may find safety in floodtime. For Cocodra is overflow country, and all life has to be conducted with the knowledge that each spring the rains will swell the streams up the Valley, and the earth will vanish under a muddy sea. Even the houses are not like other dwellings. They are built on Choctaws, great hollow logs that rise slowly with the flooding water; when the tide recedes the building comes down gradually once more to the land. Occasionally, if the house in its floating moments is not tied properly to a neighboring tree, there will be difficulty. I stayed once in a home on Choctaws where the kitchen, a separate structure from the main building, had been roped insecurely. When the waters fell and the dwelling came to rest, the kitchen was a full city block away. There it remained for an entire season, while the harassed women folk of the family carried the meals across the gap, until there came a new flood and the house was made whole again.

It is not an easy life, that of the swamp dweller. There is no electricity, and no running water. The only fuel is fire wood, cut with an ax from the forest. Yet here the fisherman lives quietly, happily, much as his ancestors lived a hundred years ago. Each day he runs his lines and puts his catch in the latticed fish boxes showing before his cabin door; intent he waits until his keen ears hear the fishboat chugging down the river. Constantly he must patch the great rents in his nets, torn by a marauding garfish or a hungry alligator; regularly he must dip the tackle in his tar vats to keep the hemp from rotting. He is proud of his blackened hands.

"Ain't a good fisherman unless he's covered with tar," is a Cocodra proverb.

When he tends his little crops, it is often by the signs of the moon in the ancient way of his forefathers. Again and again I have heard a fisherman farmer tell how, if he observes the signs in his planting, he can make his corn grow six or eight or twelve feet high, as accurately as though it were measured with a ruler; he can likewise at will make the ears appear high or low on the budding stalk. Almanacs which explain these lunar signs are still a treasure in almost every household.

Inseparable from the fisherman is his hound, here the famous Catahoula hog dog, an animal that legend crowns the undisptuted king of the Mississipi swamps.[6] They are sad, moth-eaten creatures, these Catahoulas, even more melancholy in appearance than the doleful bloodhound, bony as skeletons from their ceaseless chasing in the gloomy woods. The most prized of the breed bears a fabulous name, the "glass-eye, leopard type"; this is because of his faded spots, which suggest that some unhappy sire in the dim past might have been a bird dog.

Yet despite the animal's sorry appearance, his master regards him with affection and veneration. For the Catahoula is a vital part of the swamp dweller's life. The dog helps him hunt his coon and possum, and gives him comfort on his lonely vigils; he guards the swampman's wife and children, and warns them of the rattlesnake and the occasional panther. But most important of all he presides over the hogs.

6. Catahoulas are a "folk breed" bred in Louisiana to herd hogs and cattle. According to some accounts, they are descendants of dogs brought by the Spaniards. Today the Catahoula is the official Louisiana state dog.

Each spring, to save feed, the fishermen put out their hogs to forage in the wilderness. When fall approaches, there is a great roundup that covers all the swamp. It is the Catahoula hog dogs who take complete charge of the occasion. For several days they range through the tangled trees, where a man could never make his way. Working sometimes as a team, sometimes alone, with almost human intelligence they drive any hog they come upon to the pen of the nearest farmer, though the dog may be twenty miles from the point where he started. When all the pigs in the woods have been thus collected, the swamp dwellers make the rounds of their neighbors, and inspecting the crude brands, sort out their grunting property. Soon after, they put the animals in a little barge, and attaching a gasboat, start for their homes on the river; while the Catahoula sits serenely in the stern beside his master, content with a labor well done.

The women of the swamps, like their husbands, remind the observer of the pioneer folk who set out in their covered wagons for California. Patiently they go about their household duties, roasting their coffee, and baking their corn bread, often working in the fields when the male members of the family are busy at their tasks on the water. In their spare moments some sew fancy coverlets to lay over their handmade beds; others knit the hoop nets stretched out like giant spider webs before every doorway. They are self-reliant as the men, prepared to take over their husbands' duties in any emergency.

Some are unusually versatile, like my old friend Aunt Mollie, whom I visited on her shantyboat, neat as any parlor. Now nearing ninety, in her busy career Aunt Mollie had been fisherman and trapper, as well as Holiness preacher, midwife, and teacher for all her swamp-dwelling neighbors.

Her blue eyes still peered brightly out of her withered face, as she brought some coffee and crackling corn bread, and set them on a table.

"Yessir, people used to pay me a dollar a head to learn their children reading and writing," she declared. "Now they comes around some places in boats to git the children and take 'em to a regular school. Everybody says I could git a job quick in one of them new schools. They says them teachers gits paid plenty more a head than I was gitting for learning 'em. But I don't like living around a town."

There is a touching quality about many of these swamp-dwellers, a simplicity that seems almost unbelievable in the stern world of today, where the great cities so often breed only aloofness and self-interest. On one occasion I traveled for several hours with a poor fisherman who at my request was taking me to a distant point in his rickety gasboat. When at the end of the long trip I asked how much I owed, he looked at me in surprise. "I couldn't charge you no money for that, brother. You and me was just having a good time talking."

And nothing I could do would make him change his mind.

They are deeply religious, and even though they cannot read, always possess a large, much-thumbed Bible. When a literate stranger passes they are apt to ask him to quote and interpret some of the more familiar passages. . . .

South of Jonesville and Cocodra lies another fishing area, the basin of the Atchafalaya, a wilderness that stretches from Red River to the Gulf. This is a bleak and melancholy region, where many an outlaw is said to be still roaming, with a high price on his uneasy head. So trackless are the swamps, so twisting the waterways, that years ago a steamboat was stolen from New Orleans and hidden in its recesses; to this day the vessel has never been discovered. Occasionally along a remote inlet, I have come upon some sinister figure tramping with gun on his shoulder, who avoids all the usual courtesies of honest men, and quickly disappears into the brush. . . .

As the traveler moves into the southern reaches of the Atchafalaya, the scene begins to change, and so do the fishermen. The sun grows hotter. The Spanish moss thickens. It is the land of Evangeline, the bayou country of the Cajuns. Everywhere pirogues, the fisherman's swift craft that is a direct descendant of the Indian dugout, dart in silvery flashes back and forth across the glassy streams. Often from a shantyboat door there drifts the sound of a voice speaking French.

These bayou fishermen are spread over much of lower Louisiana. A unique colony is found near the placid town of Plaquemine, where towering locks lift towboats from the Mississippi into the smaller waterways on their course to Texas. A narrow road twists and winds until it reaches a tiny ferry anchored in a stream known as Bayou Sorel. On the ferry is painted a cryptic sign: TRAVEL AT YOUR OWN RISK. NO DRUNKS AFTER 7.00 P.M.

The traveler, crossing on the awkward craft, comes upon a startling sight. A wide levee is built paralleling the bayou. In either direction, as far as the eye can reach, it is lined with the habitations of fishermen—houses, cabins, and shantyboats of every description, some floating in the water, and others pulled up on the land. A pile of nets and a tarpot stand on the bank near each picturesque dwelling; craft of all kinds, flatboats, gasboats, skiffs, pirogues, travel like a school of feeding minnows through the quiet water. Here and there a larger craft lumbers on its way, the vessel of a dealer, collecting the usual catfish and buffalo. Trucks, heavy laden with fishy cargoes, rumble down the levee, the drivers calling out jovially to the grizzled figures dragging their tackle across the sticky clay. It is a fisherman's paradise.

Most of the inhabitants are frontier types, like the dwellers at Jonesville and Black River and Cocodra; now and then there is a family whose deep-accented speech had its origin in a fishing village of distant Normandy.[7] But a short distance down the vanishing road the inhabitants change abruptly. Here at Bayou Pigeon, the "End of the World," where the swamps begin to turn into the great Louisiana marshes, is a new fisherman's heaven. Here all are French, a gayer people than their Anglo-Saxon neighbors; a visitor speaking English to the older generation would not be understood. In these few miles are two thousand fishermen living as their fellows to the north in a world apart.

As the Gulf comes nearer, the marshes stretch in all directions to the horizon. More fishing communities appear at the mouth of each lazy inlet. There are Frenchmen like those who were so busy one Christmas they could not stop their labors, and pious folk, unwilling to forget the day of the good infant Jesus, later celebrated their Christmas during Lent.[8] There are Indians, and strange men dark with Spanish blood and brawny Yugoslavs in their oyster camps, who drink tall glasses of orange wine, and talk of harvesting oyster crops as farmers talk of harvesting corn. There are the shrimp fleets, with crews from the ends of the earth, who sail their boats through heat and hurricane, and never ask the reason. Together they form a collection of colorful individuals whose like can rarely be seen in America.

7. Longfellow's *Evangeline* created the incorrect idea that the Acadians had originally come from Normandy. In fact, most came from the provinces of the French Centre-Oeust region.

8. Burman seems to be referring to residents of Bayou du Large near Houma who, unable to celebrate Christmas in December in the 1920s and 1930s because the men of the community were away for trapping season, began holding Christmas festivities in February or March. However, this particular community is not French but Anglo-Celtic; their ancestors may have migrated from Mississippi or Tennessee.

Moss Pickers of the Lafourche Interior

CAROLYN RAMSEY

> Journalist Carolyn Ramsey was interested in the history of the Cajuns and wondered what had become of them in twentieth-century Louisiana. Her book *Cajuns on the Bayou* tells about her travels to find the essence of Cajun life in the mid-1950s. This piece reveals much about the economics and seasonal work round of the Atchafalaya Basin. Though her travels took place in fairly modern times, the isolation of the areas she describes makes the time frame seem earlier; such parts of Louisiana were—and still are in some instances—remote. Spanish moss, the gathering of which she describes, has been used in making various folk artifacts—such as dolls and even shoes—though in the fifties it was gathered mostly to sell, after curing, as a furniture stuffing.

I got there by moss truck, one belonging to the merchant, Honoré St. Germaine, who is known as "the moss king of Pierre Part." A kindly friend in Napoleonville arranged for me to ride in the seat of an empty truck that was returning to its village after delivering a load of moss "on the front."

As we bounced along the rutted, oyster-shell road, the driver told me something of the moss industry. I was to learn that this was not only the chief support of his village, but the favorite conversational topic of his fellow-villagers of Pierre Part.

Near the end of the road the landscape took on an unreal, story-book picturesqueness. It was like something off a picture postcard, or an illustration out of a children's book. Everything seemed to be in miniature. We crossed on a curving bridge over the tiniest bayou I had ever seen. . . . The houses which lined these banks were quaintly-shaped, small as model houses, and had little yellow curtains flying out the windows and doors. The pirogues seemed infinitesimal. The campboats were strange one-room affairs with open, sunken, barge-like decks. These were the boats of the moss pickers who towed them behind sputtering johnboats into the deeper cypress swamps to pull the grey shrouds from the trees.

Only the oaks seemed of normal size, and they were enormous, stretching their tortured feet along the bayou bank, dipping into the musky earth for support, and swinging their huge limbs out boldly to join with limbs of other oak trees across the narrow bayou.

With a tremendous shudder the moss truck came to a stop beside the long, white wooden bridge which stretched across Pierre Part Bay. It seemed to me I had never seen such a beautiful village as Pierre Part, which lay on either side of the wide stream.

"*Eh bien, Mam'selle,*" said the weary, dark-skinned lad who drove the truck. "Me, I mus' leave da truck 'ere by the sto' galerie for tonight. You find Father Toups over dere, by the church, him."

Across the river, dominating the village landscape, stood the Catholic Church, its stark white beauty reflected in the bayou waters. Here, I was told, the natives rowed in to Mass from miles around, from settlements that never had seen a gravel road or an automobile.

I walked across the bridge toward the church, watching youngsters and oldsters alike standing up to propel the big skiffs which the truck driver had called *péniches*. They rowed with peculiarly graceful strokes, bending forward on the long oars, straightening up to pull strongly and send the *péniche* foward with a steady rhythm.

Tied to a landing in front of the church was one of the strangest chapels I have ever seen. It was built on a houseboat with a roomy porch deck running all way round, a wooden cross nailed to its roof peak. It was painted shining white with green-trimmed windows. *Mary Star of the Sea* was her name, painted in neat red letters on her roomy sides.

At tiny communities all along the deep interior bayous, at every place *Mary*

The mail boat pulling into bayou landings, by Mircea Vasiliu

From Emily Kimbrough, *So Near and Yet So Far,* copyright © 1955 by Emily Kimbrough Wrench, renewed 1983 by Emily Kimbrough. Reproduced by permission of HarperCollins Publishers, Inc.

Star of the Sea could safely make a landing, the Cajuns flocked out of the swamps and came joyfully to Mass in this trim chapel. Inside she had a small but fully appointed altar and benches for fifty worshippers. Others stood along the bayou banks and listened as the priest said the solemn words. Here too, Father Toups performed weddings, held funerals, christenings and confirmations, and here he give them counsel on all matters spiritual and temporal.

Beside the floating chapel I found Father Toups, buried elbow-deep in the motor of a long bateau tied near by. This bateau bore the name *St. Francis Xa-*

vier and was the boat that Father Toups used to tow his chapel to faraway, down-the-bayou missions accessible only by water.

The broad-shouldered priest laid down his monkey wrench, ran a big hand over his sweaty, grease-stained brow, straightened his crumpled cassock, and smiled at me. Though he was a strong, brusque man with deep-set, intense eyes, his smile glowed like a child's. In an instant I thought I knew why he was the best-loved man in the bayou country.

"This is my penance, *Mam'selle,*" he said. "*St. Frances Xavier* leads me a bad life, him."

Father Toups found a hospitable family who agreed to let me stay in their home, for of course there was no regular place for an outsider from "the front" to stay in Pierre Part.

For three days I slept in the master bedroom, with a mosquito net shrouding the sides of the four-poster. The family served me coffee in bed at dawn, and chocolate at breakfast out of a big steaming bowl in the center of the table from which each member of the family dipped his own. They told me their oldest yarns, their latest gossips. Let me sit on their sto' *galerie* which was the center of life in Pierre Part. Took me with them crab fishing and alligator hunting.

I met Elijah Miller, historian of the swamps, the only man who was "set on book-larnin'." I soon was haunted by a charming little sprite, Anita Foret, an intelligent and ambitious child of twelve. She volunteered her services as guide for the chance to practice on me "da Engleesh" which she had learned in six months' schooling in Napoleonville. Anita lived with her mother, the village dressmaker, and her little brother of whom she was intensely proud. Their home was a one-room house set up a foot off the ground on six round logs.

Through these friends I made many others—oldsters full of superstitions and youngsters eager over the new school bus which was taking them "to the front" to school. All of them spoke constantly of the moss—picking, drying, ginning—which was their chief source of income. Like the French I met all over the bayou country, these moss pickers seemed to derive as much pleasure from their work as from their play.

"Mam'selle, I have many *noncs* (uncles)," Anita told me one day. "All da bes' moss pickers in Pierre Part is my *noncs, oui.* My *nonc* Étienne, he aks me yesterday if you like to go wid the moss fleet nex' Monday. He say he take you and me and *maman* and we leave lil Antoine with *Tante* Suzette. You like that, *Mam'selle?*"

While it was still dark on Monday morning we gathered on Étienne's barge. They had given him the place of honor, the lead barge, because he had guests aboard. *Nonc* Étienne turned out to be a mere youth of nineteen, young like most of the moss pickers, for this was arduous work. He had a slim grace, powerful shoulders, and a way of tossing his dark head back in laughter that was beautiful.

We sat on the deck of the broad, flat craft, slapped at monstrous mosquitoes and waited for the sun to rise.

. . . In all the bayous of South Louisiana there was hardly a village so busy as Pierre Part on a Monday morning. . . .

The moss fleet, leaving for its week's work in the swamps, was a sight worth seeing. We were off at last, moving slowly down the wiggling, hyacinth-lined Bayou Pierre Part. From off the wider stretches of Pierre Part Bay came more gasboats, moss barges, derricks and skiffs, all to join our parade. We made a strange procession. In the muggy dawn the barges loomed up like monsters, with squat ugly cabins and lean empty flanks. Following these were swaying skiffs which held the spindly legs of derrick platforms from which the moss pickers would work. Ahead of all, the stub-nosed gasboats spluttered greasily and pulled at the towlines. Fifteen to twenty barges fell into the weird parade, towed by as many gasboats and followed by as many derrick boats and *péniches*.

I stood up in the barge to watch the fantastic procession wind sinuously along the bayou. The sun rose at last and put a glistening touch to the wakes of our strange craft.

We were heading into the smaller waters of the Atchafalaya Basin, to a region of tortuous bayous, dark, hidden sloughs and wild, shallow lakes. . . .

As we moved slowly toward the inner swamps, the landscape grew more grotesque, its cypress and oaks more heavily laden with long, thick moss. No one knew why the Spanish moss of the Pierre Part swamps was different, richer and stronger, than that from any other region. Some special combination of atmosphere and general terrain perhaps. Yet no one denied that these deep swamps, far from salty Gulf breezes, produced the finest there was. Long of staple, it averaged five feet when cured, whereas in other regions the average was as low as five inches. There were a few spots where the strands grew as long, but of a weaker fibre.

I had lots of time to hear about the moss, for we had to travel the whole of Monday before we reached the spot where we were to work. Like great waddling turtles the barges lurched down the narrow waterways, followed by their brood of smaller boats. A whole day of such travel and we covered only thirty miles!

My friends talked incessantly while the sputtering gasboat pulled us deeper into the swamps through a green and grey world of trees, moss and water.

We traveled mostly on narrow "float roads" cut many years ago by lumber companies who had robbed this swamp of its richest timber. Cypress stumps were not pulled up to make this watery path. They were simply sawed off at the surface during low water periods. Covered now by rising spring tides, the jagged stumps lay treacherous and evil beneath us, ready to gore the hulls of barges and gasboats if the men should misjudge the water's depth. Swamps of the Great Basin are interlaced with such float roads. I wondered what this weird place must look like to the big white cranes that flew lazily above and around us—perhaps like a green city, crisscrossed with murky brown avenues and smaller watery alleys.

Étienne and Jacques were arguing hotly over which trees produced the best moss.

"*Mais oui,* the cypress she grow da longest, strongest strand of any," insisted Étienne. "Me, I seen da strands fifteen, sometimes twenty feet long after they was cured."

"*Mon dieu,* man," said Jacques, "but t'ink of da bulk in them oak tree. She lose weight in curing, yes, but what you care when you got the bulk."

Probably, I concluded, it was to the picker's advantage to gather oak moss for bulk, but to the buyer's and ginner's advantage to get the more durable cypress moss. Also, I learned, the loss in poundage varied with the section in which it was picked. Moss grown in Lake Verette and in Des Allemands, both only a few miles from Pierre Part, lost seven-to-one in weight during the curing, while at Pierre Part the loss was only three-to-one.

Although these boys, and their companions on the barges that followed behind us, were following the traditions of their fathers, trained in the trade they loved best, they could tell me little of the beginnings of this industry nor how it developed. The men of today remembered that their fathers were moss pickers before them. They remembered well when the moss was floated out to market on giant barges that would dwarf the little one upon whose deck we sat. Not until 1932 was there any road leading out from Pierre Part to the market towns "along the front" of Bayou Lafourche. In those days, before the gravel road put the village in touch with the outside world, the moss industry was run on the plantation system—one man furnishing supplies and taking a percentage in exactly the same fashion as on a cotton plantation. But the new road brought in more buyers who saw golden opportunities in the moss business. They broke the one-man monopoly. Now there is no gin at all in Pierre Part. The cured moss is carried out by truck to two gins in towns on the front.

There were only about half a dozen moss gins in all South Louisiana. Ginning was a fairly simple process, consisting chiefly of cleaning twigs and extraneous materials from the moss, then baling it for shipment to Eastern markets where it was used for upholstery material in automobiles and furniture.

Étienne said that a good moss picker averaged about seventy-five dollars per month for his work.

Anita's *maman*, a shriveled little woman of forty-five who looked sixty, explained that moss picking was always a family affair. Papa found that he could get the most from his children's work in this way, since young boys were agile in the big swamp trees and to them moss picking was a game. A boy could cure the moss as well as a man.

Étienne interrupted, flashing his smile and flexing his muscles proudly.

"Since fo' year now Jacques and me been partners—since my brother Ophille got drowned in the alligator hole—and since we fi'teen year old we can pick more moss in a day than any grown man, for sure. All da boys like dat, can pick more dan mens."

I learned that a barge like the one we rode cost the family about two hundred dollars and that they paid another hundred and fifty for the gasboat and motor, and twenty-five a piece for several derrick boats.

"Dat's our whole rig, *mais oui*, and when da price she drop to da bottom, it seem one helluva lotta rig, *Mam'selle*."

Dusk crept swiftly upon us now as we drew near to the rich woods which were our destination. Gigantic cypresses stood like ghouls along the float roads, silently dragging their shrouds of heavy moss in the water.

Étienne climbed to the cabin roof and signalled that the fleet should tie up here. The bulky barges stopped, made their towlines fast to trees on the edge of the float road. Night closed down suddenly on our caravan, and each barge became its little world within a sea of blackness. We moved swiftly to tighten our door and window against the dronings of merciless mosquitoes. I looked through the cracked pane of our single window. Lamps glowed dimly in the small opening of our sister barges.

"*C'est bon,*" said Étienne as he looked around to see that all was shipshape. We felt very cozy inside the little cabin with its narrow bunks double-decked against the walls and bedrolls on the floor for the boys.

Jacques ducked outside and brought in the catfish he had caught that afternoon on a troll line and which we had towed for three hours along the barge's shank.

"*C'est magnifique!*" shouted Étienne, catching the catfish away from Jacques and dancing a little jig with it as he presented it to *Maman* Foret.

The stoop-shouldered little lady bent coaxingly over the one-burner oil stove. Anita worked on the tiny table nearby, cutting onions, green peppers, opening cans of tomato paste and tomato purée. Her mother put the rice in the big black iron pot. The catfish went into a stew with the delicacies cut up by Anita.

Étienne and Jacques did everything they could to hurry the cooks, and soon the feast was ready—two big pots placed in the center of the table and each fellow serving his own plate.

The food was wonderful.

"*Maman's coobyawn,*[9] it's da best in all Pierre Part," bragged Anita.

Étienne slapped his stomach and groaned with delight.

"Da bes' in da word is what you mean, *chère,* and I'm here to guarantee ya."

I hastened to agree. By now I felt myself something of a connoisseur of French bayou cookery. Catfish court bouillon was without doubt the ultimate delicacy in a land where every woman, and most of "the mens," excelled in cookery magic. And of all the catfish court bouillons I had eaten none seemed to compare with *Maman* Foret's, cooked on that one-burner oil stove in the moss picker's cabin.

After the meal we sat quietly for awhile, then turned to the bunks and crawled in with our clothes on. Étienne and Jacques sighed wearily and soon their heavy breathing told they slept. From the other barges came the faint echoes of keen, high laughter ringing across the waters. Then faintly came the

9. *Court bouillion* is a stewlike fish soup.

sounds of music from an accordion and a young voice singing a plaintive French love song. . . .

Finally the songs grew fainter . . . and after a little while they stopped.

From out in the swamps came the growls of the big bull 'gators and the piercing wails of screech owls. Gradually the swamp came alive with night sounds, as lights blinked out in the cabins and sleep settled on the moss fleet.

The moss pickers were up in the early dawn. Some of them detached gasboats from the barges and, with derrick boats and skiffs in tow, set out along the many small alleys which cut off from the main float road. Some moved barges and whole rigs further into the woods and went their separate ways to seek the rich moss harvest.

Étienne and Jacques moved our barge a little way down the float road and, with two other rigs nearby, prepared to detach the derrick boats and climb onto their spindly ladders. Anita, Maman and I watched from the barge deck.

Soon the great, silent trees were alive with little men. They stood aloft in the tall derrick boats and gathered moss in armloads. They stood in swaying skiffs and fished the moss from the trees with long, hooked poles. They dug their spiked boots into trunks and clambered up to the highest limbs, tearing off the clinging moss and throwing it to the tiny boats below.

The trees were tall and sometimes the little men climbed a hundred feet into the air. I shuddered as I watched. *Maman* smiled sadly at me, seeing that, and spoke very quietly. "My husban', *Mam'selle,* he fall out a tree taller than dat one dere. Ninety feet down, he fell. He broke 'is back, him, and die before they can get him into the barge. Anita was only *une petite* girl, maybe four-five, when it happen."

Anita patted her *maman's* shoulder.

"Many mens fall from da trees, *Mam'selle,* and sometimes they get drowned. But mens they love da trees. Father Toups he say it's not jus' to make da money they climb 'em. He say the mens sometimes t'ink the bigges' trees is . . . how you say, dat, *Mam'selle* . . . a challeenge?"

Then Anita told about the time Father Toups himself was gathering moss with his parishioners. He fell from the top of a fifty foot tree. He sprang out of the water, shook his fist at the giant cypress, dug his spiked boots into the trunk and cried:

"*Tonnerre!* So you t'row me out, *hein?* Well, *un* moment, my fine, sweet cypress. I show you who clim' who!"

By now the derrick boats and skiffs were stacked high with the silvery para-site.[10] Moss pickers towed smaller boats back to the barges, piled their load into big empty decks and cooked their lunches on cabin stoves. In the after-noon they set out again, and returned at dusk with their second boatload for the day.

A man could pick one thousand pounds of green moss in a day, but in the evening his back ached fearfully and he lay down wearily on his hard cabin floor, thankful for the protective folds of his mosquito nets.

For two days our pickers combed the cypress brakes. Sometimes the group stayed out three or four days, but because Anita, *Maman* Foret and I were along they made this a shorter trip.

Now, with barges of the whole fleet stacked high—for the boys had worked hard and this had been a good trip—they made tow lines fast to the gasboats and turned our caravan back toward the village.

Thursday nights and Friday mornings the fleet usually returned, in pairs, trios and larger groups, creeping carefully along the bayous. The most excit-ing part of the work was over. Now came the drudgery of unloading and the long slow process of curing.

I had noticed that each time Étienne or Jacques brought in a skiff-load of moss, they stacked their own moss in a separate place on the barge deck. So with every man in the fleet. Although to me the barge loads looked like one big unit when they were complete, each of the boys knew exactly where his "rank" began and ended.

We made the long trip in from the moss-picking grounds even more slowly than we had gone out. With the barges loaded ten to fifteen feet in the air with solid blocks of grey moss, and pulled by gasboats followed by the swaying der-rick boats, we must have been a weird and beautiful sight to behold. Sitting on the roof of our cabin I had a fair view. But I kept wishing I had the wings of the big white cranes which flew down the quiet bayou waters ahead of us. What a view they must have had!

By Thursday noon we were back in the village. Along Bayou Pierre Part the clumsy barges dropped one by one out of the procession, as each was tied to the landing in front of its own home.

10. Spanish moss is not a parasite but an epiphyte of the pineapple family. It is not gener-ally harmful to the host trees, except that its weight sometimes causes branches to break off.

Each man unloaded his own part of the crop, dumping it first into the bayou waters. Here it must soak for a week. After Étienne and Jacques had each unloaded his week's harvest into the bayou, they took the afternoon off to spend it over a few beers in Honoré St. Germaine's cafe by the bank of Pierre Part Bay.

Next morning they were back at work. Many of the boys in the moss fleet did not have the laborious job of curing their own moss, for this was usually handled by fathers, grandfathers and little brothers. But Étienne and Jacques had both been orphaned, by the same fierce hurricane that had swept over the village five years before, and although Étienne had a bright-faced little wife and a laughing baby son of five months in his tiny houseboat home on the bay, he had no older man to share his labors.

Now the two young fellows must drag their last week's load from out of the bayou. This moss, streaked a sickly yellow from its week-long soaking, must be stacked in beds for curing along the bayou bank. In front of all the houses along the bayou were many of these beds. They looked like giant toadstools or like big black igloos, adding to the strangeness of the village landscape. Each bed represented a week's picking in the swamps. A man's prosperity was measured by the number of moss beds lying before his cabin, and Étienne was proud of those which lay on the bank beside his campboat home. He figured he must have two to four hundred dollars there—and this, *Mam'selle*, was no little fortune for a family man of nineteen!

To moss pickers the curing process was still filled with mystery and wonder. Though for generations they have seen the velvety bark shed from the strong, wiry, black inner strands, a moss bed was still something of a miracle to them.

There was an art in this curing, as in turning any rough material into a finished product. Old men must know and must teach the boys just when the bed should be "turned." Sun and rain and wind must be judged. A man must know the seasons and must be able to judge the effects of slow heat engendered by nature. In winter the process took longer. Sometimes the bed was left for two months before it was turned. After this turning it might stay another month in beds before it was completely cured. In summer the same process might be completed with two turnings in a mere six weeks. When sun and inner heat have dried the moss completely, it must be wet with bucket-loads of water from the bayou, so that the sun can steam again into the bed.

The heat inside one of these moss beds is blistering. Étienne showed me how he could hardly hold his hand in the heart of a moss bed without being scorched.

When curing was completed, the moss was hung out to dry. Now the village took on its fantastic look, like a fairy town in a child's picture book. Lacy black draperies festooned every fence. Finally the product was ready for sale.

Étienne and Jacques had a favorite among the four moss buyers who operated out of Pierre Part. This man always bragged on their moss, how clean it was, how free of sticks and twigs that would add to the poundage once it reached the gin in Napoleonville. This buyer made half a cent per pound for carrying their product to the moss gins, and he had to be careful of his buying if he was to keep a profit. Each time the moss was handled, loading into the trucks, unloading at the gins, it lost weight.

It was time to say goodbye to Étienne and Jacques, to little Anita and *Maman* Foret. All of us felt sad. Anita turned her face away so I wouldn't see her tears.

I walked by the church for the last time, and found Father Toups again fussing with the motor of *St. Francis Xavier.*

Covered with grease to his elbows, the husky priest pulled his hands from the engine, lifted them palm-up to the heavens and sighed.

"It is my penance, *Mam'selle. St. Francis,* he do me bad again!" Then his face lighted up in that wonderful child's smile of his, and he said:

"And how you find it wit da moss pickers, *Mam'selle?* You find yo' true Cajun out there in the moss grounds, *hein?*"

Dance of the Oyster Luggers

CHRISTOPHER HALLOWELL

From *People of the Bayou: Cajun Life in Lost America,*
which Hallowell (b. 1945) wrote as an investigation
into contemporary Cajun life and its historical background. Though his is not a travel book as such, Hallowell does write of his extensive travels with local
people to have a look at how they made their livings as
trappers and fishermen in traditional coastal marsh
and swamp environments. The excerpt here provides a
sense of the working lives of the oystermen of the region. Bayou du Large is located not far from Houma.

. . . At daybreak, Jim's oyster luggers—the *Jerrie Allen,*
the *Clayton,* and a nameless smaller boat of hybrid design—crept in single file
down Bayou du Large. Only ghosts of the community's ordinary life were visible through the whiteness. Corners of buildings, telephone poles, moored
shrimp boats, and occasional parked vehicles slid into view and disappeared
like things half remembered. Branches of dead cypress trees, naked but for
hanging snarls of Spanish moss, reached down out of the white opacity to
grapple for the boats. The silence was chilling. Not until the luggers reached
Lake Mechant did the sun break through, tearing at the fog to reveal a flat expanse of muddy and sullen water whose far shores hid below the horizon. In
this calm solitude, the three small boats were no more than toys steaming
across a vast bathtub. They could almost have been miniature replicas of the
Mississippi River steamboats of a century ago, minus the twin smokestacks
and the paddle wheels. The *Clayton* was a classic craft. She fairly danced on
the water, her round-bottomed fifty-foot hull supporting an overhanging

deck upturned fore and aft to give her a deceptively light appearance considering her ample beam. Her foredeck was roofed with canvas stretched tight and flat over a pipe framework. Rounded about the bow, it gave the boat an airy outline. A little semicircular cabin with portholes and windows rose from the stern, and a cockeyed stack above the roof bespoke a welcoming warmth. Amidships, the gunwales had been built up with a latticework of freshly painted white boards to prevent the oyster sacks from falling overboard. The latticework and the awning are the identifying marks of any Gulf oyster lugger.

Luggers dredging for oysters present an even lovelier sight. When we reached Buckskin Bayou, opposite Jim's cabin, they began a kind of dance, circling lazily over the reef in an intricate series of movements of which family tradition, competition, the boats' design, and the abundance or scarcity of oysters are all a part. Each lugger carries a captain and a crew of two. The Daisy men were the captains, and their cousins and nephews from along the bayou made up the crew. They were far hungrier for a job in the marsh than for one that would take them out to the oil platforms, even though the pay on the marsh was poor—a dollar a sack—and they had to work fifteen or sixteen hours a day. During that time, if they were lucky, they might make forty or fifty dollars.

As the futures of sons revolve about the lives of fathers, so Willie and Dwight circled their luggers around the *Jerrie Allen* with Jim at the helm. The *Jerrie Allen* was the focal point; the two other luggers responded to her movements as though connected to her by a gossamer cord. Dredges scraped the oysters from the bottom as she circled up and down the bayou. At times the other two boats passed within twenty feet of her, and at others, they were a hundred or more yards distant; but there was no doubt that the movements of all three boats were connected. If their courses had been etched into the bayou's surface, the design would have been a mesh of interwoven circles.

When any two of the luggers approached one another, just barely avoiding a collision, the crews would exchange a fierce banter grounded in competition, hard work, and the hope for just one more sack of oysters. Back and forth it went, at first a tumble of shouted gibberish above the creak of the dredges, dying away as the boats drew apart, and then shutting off as abruptly as a spigot. . . .

On the deck of each lugger, the dance set into motion by the dredging was precise, repetitive, and exhausting. It was choreographed to the groan of the winches and the thud of oysters tumbling onto the decks. Oyster luggers have two wheels to steer by, one in the cabin and the other just aft of the bow. At the forward wheel, the captain reigns over a tiny domain—two rusting dredges and a work space no larger than a Ping-Pong table. His winch controls are within easy reach, but his movements as one dredge is dropped and the other is raised are a continuous bending, lifting, stretching, kneeling, and rising from one side of the lugger to the other. The dredges look like oversized garden rakes, each with a chain-and-nylon net attached, and are suspended by an iron frame. When one of these contraptions breaks the surface, looking vaguely like some prehistoric monster, the captain washes its haul of oysters in the boat's bow wave. The ancient chain and pulley scream as though being tortured while the heavy thing comes aboard over metal rollers. Oysters fall upon the deck with a hollow thud until the net has been shaken empty and the monster heaved overboard to continue its scavenging. The captain takes a moment just then to steer his vessel and maintain its circular path—but no more than a moment—before he is down on his hands and knees with a culling hammer, helping the crew break apart the clusters. Oysters come out of the dredges cemented to each other or to the remains of their ancestors. Under the mud that still clings, they look more like flat stones than the covering of what may be the most sensual food known to man.

The crew stay on hands and knees as the tap-tap of their hammers cleaves apart the mass of shells. Occasionally, the rhythm is broken as a beautifully patterned crab—a victim of the dredge—is tossed into a bucket for the night's meal or when the men stop to shovel the growing pile of oysters into a wire basket. When the basket is full, they stretch a burlap bag over its top and heave the whole thing upward and over until the limp strands are near to bursting. Except for interruptions, the tap-tapping is so persistent that the momentary pause is felt as a stillness, regardless of the groaning winches, the rumbling engines, and the shouted banter.

For two days, from before dawn until nightfall, the luggers circled up and down Buckskin Bayou. When the Daisys turned the expedition back toward Bayou du Large, they had a cargo of several hundred sacks of oysters, worth a couple of thousand dollars. The small, precise rhythms of culling and the grander ones of circling will be repeated virtually every day of the year except on Sundays and during the trapping season. . . .

The trip from Buckskin Bayou is a long one—hour after hour of chugging back across Lake Mechant and up the meanders of Bayou du Large to the line

Oyster boat, by Russell Lindsay Speakman

From Harold Speakman, *Mostly Mississippi* (New York, 1928)

of houses that makes up Jim's community. Lake Mechant lives up to its name, which means "cruel lake," as the head wind sends scudding rollers crashing against the luggers' flared bows and onto their decks. The boats tumble into the troughs and hit against the lake's muddy bottom. There is no sign of human beings save for the floats of crab traps sprinkled over the frothing surface. Given the slowness of the boats and the absence of human intervention, the trip is much the same as it would have been a century ago. Several hours after leaving Buckskin Bayou, the first signs of civilization come into view—lonely buildings on skinny legs above a spit of land on the edge of Lake Mechant, looking as fragile as sandpipers. On summer and fall weekends, fishermen and hunters crowd into the camps and roar around the lake and the bayous in their outboards. Jim shakes his head when he speaks of them. All the camps follow the same design—a cabin, usually painted green, with a slightly pitched roof and a cypress wood cistern off to one side; a dock jutting into the bayou; and a boardwalk joining the dock to the cabin. Many of the buildings have incongruously silly names painted above their doors—Kitty Kat Two, Home on the Bayou, Poochie's Retreat, Heart's Throb. Now they are all deserted, their docks empty of boats and life-preserver-garbed children, windows shuttered, doors padlocked. Their silence blends with the desolation of the marsh. It occurs to me that the little colony might be a colonial outpost, a failed experiment about to yield to the way of the marsh in disposing of unwanted objects.

As the luggers move from the lake into the calmly flowing waters of Bayou du Large, the colony vanishes around the bend far more quickly than it appeared. Only a sagging electricity line is visible as evidence of human penetration into this hostile region. Willow and hackberry trees grow along the levees, interspersed with palmettoes just above the cattle-shorn grass. The stubby palms with their richly green, fan-shaped leaves have a prehistoric look that is reinforced by the acres of coarse marsh grass stretching beyond the levees. We are passing through a forgotten world, nibbled at by floods and cattle, abandoned by humanity except for a thin electrical line that for the time being serves no purpose.

But civilization is sure to come. Along the bayou, the first house is apparently of pioneer vintage—a tiny structure covered with light brown asphalt shingles, roofed with tin strips, its cockeyed door painted aquamarine. The ground in front, which slopes toward a wharf, has been rooted up by pigs and clucked over by nesting hens. Now, only a lone mongrel is to be seen. The wharf's pilings are twisted and gnarled and its planks treacherously pitted with holes. Barnacle-encrusted whitewall tires buffer it at the edge. Back of the house, cattle with some zebu in their lineage and horses with exposed ribs rub against a fence patchworked together out of tires, planks, logs, milk crates, and netting, as though everything floating down the bayou had been snagged for that makeshift purpose.

At the end of the Bayou du Large road half a mile farther up the bayou, a tumbledown tin boat shed leans above the water on rotted pilings. Fifty yards beyond, the half-submerged and much rotted hull of the *McMarie,* probably a fine oyster lugger in her day, lies careened on the mud, no more graceful now than the two rusting refrigerators and the one ancient stove that are her neighbors.

Trucks hauling oysters lurch along the pavement of what now looks like any other two-lane road. The docks are piled with people waving the luggers homeward.

"How did you do there, Jim? You look like you got a few sacks on them boats all right."

"Them oysters taste good an' salty? They got a truck up there near yer house."

"Yer first time out an' you done cleaned out yer reefs. You can take the rest of the year off."

Oyster luggers by the dozen line the bayou below the road, and piles of oyster shells are a midden for future archeologists. Finally, the towering shrimp boats, *Miss Lila, Mr. Reese,* and *Little Kelly,* come into view, so grand in appearance that they seem to overpower the bayou itself. Little houses like Jim's line the road, tucked close together. A school bus stops every few hundred yards to let off children who, though they look like any other American children, will grow up to be trappers, shrimp- and oystermen, and boat builders like their fathers and older brothers.

Cruising the Marshes and Coast

MATILDA CHARLOTTE HOUSTOUN

Houstoun (1815–1872) was a prolific author of novels and travel accounts. Like many other nineteenth-century English visitors, she was interested in observing slavery and came to New Orleans; unlike most of the others, she arranged for a trip into the coastal marshes to more remote places, arranging to sail on a small local steamer called the *Dime*. This vessel took her through canals and natural waterways into Barataria Bay, and she proceeded by schooner as far as the barrier island of Grand Terre before heading back. From *Hesperos; or, Travels in the West* (1850).

The scene became more novel and curious, the farther we progressed; imagine an infinite number of confused cross *water* roads, a species of natural canals, which grew more and more intricate in their turnings and windings as we slowly wended our way through them. Sometimes these aquatic paths were wide and sometimes narrow, and on either side were flat, reedy, and most unwholesome-looking banks, raised but a few inches above the level of the water, while occasionally, but at rare intervals, the tall trees quite overshadowed our way. How the engineer and the steersman, who formed our crew, contrived to find their way through the puzzling sameness of this intricate navigation, was a mystery to the rest of the party on board: *they*, however, never seemed at a loss, but without any apparent land or water mark to direct them, they steadily pursued their course, the water sometimes widening into broad lakes, and at others becoming contracted into so narrow a channel, that our boat brushed the long flag-like rushes on either side in her passage through. . . .

. . . Towards the middle of the day the channels became gradually wider, till at length we came to the open sea, "without a mark, without a bound!" And how fresh and clear and healthy it seemed, when contrasted with the muddy canals, and rushy weedy streams we had been passing through. A long low island, by name Barataria, was the place to which we were bound; it was inhabited by an old Spaniard, Don Ribiera, by name, who would be happy, we were told, to give us shelter for the night. No sooner was our craft in sight, than the Don, on hospitable thoughts intent, sent off a boat to bring us to his house, which was about a mile from the place where we were.

The greater part of the island of Barataria is planted with sugar cane, which is said to produce a very fine crop, and there is no doubt that the property might be made still more valuable than it is, by expending a comparatively small sum of money in redeeming a portion of the land from the occasional encroachments of the sea, owing to which it is at present rendered useless for any purposes of cultivation. The whole of the island is extremely low, so much

Shantyboat moored in bayou country, by Harlan Hubbard. Hubbard and his wife went down the Mississippi in a shantyboat in the 1950s and later took their vessel along the intracoastal waterway and other Louisiana waterways, ending their journey in Delcambre.

From Harlan Hubbard, *Shantyboat on the Bayous* (Lexington, Ky., 1990), copyright © 1990 by the University Press of Kentucky, by permission of Don Wallis

so as to be scarcely visible till you arrive very near it, but when once landed there is a good deal to admire, particularly in the thick groves of orange trees which grow in every direction. . . .

We were conducted through a grove of orange-trees to a small house, about three hundred yards from that occupied by Don Ribiera and his dark family; and from which, through the trees, we could catch glimpses of the blue waters of the then tranquil gulf. The Don endeavoured to make us as comfortable as circumstances would permit, and gave us a profusion of eggs and oysters— the only food, excepting occasionally some tolerable fish, in which he constantly indulged. At night, when I adjourned to our lonely little dwelling, which (after the departure of half a dozen chattering and most persevering black attendants) we had all to ourselves, I greatly enjoyed the breath of the cool sea-breeze as it blew over the delicious blossoms of the orange-trees; the latter were loaded with fruit and blossom, and the night air was quite heavy with perfume. . . .

We remained three days on the famed island of Barataria, riding on horseback daily, and making our observations on the state and condition of the negroes. . . .

We took our departure in a very pretty and fast sailing schooner of about twenty tons. . . .

We had nothing in our schooner, by way of cargo, but Indian corn; this was thrown loosely into the vessel, which was not decked, and as the husks were still on the corn, the *produce* formed an agreeable seat. On it we reclined in luxurious indolence . . . and a favourable breeze wafting us gently over the smooth and sunlit sea; we all agreed that it was real and positive enjoyment, and were very far from wishing our sail to be terminated, when we came in sight of some more low land, on which was the sugar plantation belonging to our friend, Mr. B——. . . .

Mr. B——'s overseer, on the island, resided in a small house not far from the beach, and was blessed with a black wife, and a large family of dingy children.

Soon after our arrival, I, with considerable difficulty, mounted the most enormous horse it was ever my fate to see, (the creature measured eighteen hands,) and rode to inspect a fort of great strength, which the American Government are constructing at an immense cost, and no inconsiderable difficulty, on this desolate spot, but except this erection, which (though not as yet in a very advanced state) spoke highly for "Uncle Sam's" energy and liberality, where public works are concerned, there was little on the island to see, or to remark upon.[11]

We returned to the house, and enjoyed a plentiful, if not a refined supper, during which the black lady stood behind the chair of her lord and master the overseer, without being allowed to partake of the repast, though the children, to the number of seven, sat round the table perfectly happy, and quite at their ease.

As in the island of Barataria, we slept in a detached house, for which arrangement I confess I was not at all sorry. . . .

We rose at five o'clock the following morning, and . . . embarked in a small boat which was to convey us through a most intricate navigation. . . . Our boat was a small, four oared one and as it was quite doubtful how long our voyage might be prolonged, we took with us a good stock of provisions. There was a sail in the boat, which was occasionally of use, but when hoisted it required such constant shifting, owing to the frequent turns in the channels, through which we were obliged to thread our way, that it rather delayed than hastened our progress.

The sun was darting fierce rays over our heads, and we had no awning; but there was a pleasant breeze to keep us alive, and our boatmen rowed cheerily on towards the narrow waters. About twelve o'clock, and when the sun was at its height, I was aroused from a reverie, in which I was pondering on "things" not only "long enough ago," but also far enough off, by the sudden stopping of our craft, and by the announcement made by one of our boatmen, in a loud whisper, that there was an alligator close to us. And there, true enough, he was—a monstrous animal—within a dozen yards of the boat, and basking on the bank, in happy unconsciousness of our approach. One of our rifles was out in a moment, but the hideous reptile was too quick for us, for being doubtless awoke by the noise of the boat going through the water, he raised his ugly head, and even before the rifle could be levelled at him, was splashing away in the stream with astonishing rapidity. . . .

Towards four in the afternoon, exhausted, hungry, and parched by the almost tropical heat of the sun, we reached such a pleasant grove of thick evergreen oaks, that we determined to run our boat into a creek, which apparently traversed the wood from one side to the other, and there remain to rest ourselves. With considerable difficulty we forced our way through the thick and

11. Fort Livingston on Grand Terre.

Swamp Scene Near New Orleans, by C. Spiegle

From Will H. Coleman, ed., *Historical Sketch Book and Guide to New Orleans* (New York, 1885)

overhanging branches of trees; but when we were fairly in, and sheltered in our little harbour, the delicious change in the atmosphere, and the enchanting beauty of the spot, repaid even those who had toiled the most for all their exertions. The branches of the live oaks literally interlaced each other over our heads, making (with the variety of beautiful creeping plants budding with their early green) a screen, through which the rays of the sun strove in vain to penetrate. The palmetto spread out its graceful fan-like leaves above the short turf, and the air resounded with the song of many birds, already beginning to build their nests among the mossy branches of the oaks. The bright scarlet plumage *cardinal,* or Virginian nightingale, as it hopped about in search of food, and the more subdued, but still brilliant coloured *blue-bird,* gave life and animation to the scene; nor must the graceful active little squirrels be forgotten, as they sprang from bough to bough with fearless agility.

The ilexes were of gigantic size, and the short velvet-like turf was so prettily diversified by patches of ornamental shrubs, that one found it difficult to believe that the hand of man had not done something towards *bringing out,* and making the most of the great natural beauties of this singularly picturesque spot. Here, then, and near to the abode of what we immediately saw must be that of an Indian family, we agreed to dine, and if possible enjoy a *siesta* after our fatigues. We chose the opposite side of the stream from that on which the pretty little log hut had been erected, for we did not choose to deprive ourselves of the charm which its *presence* added to the picture before us. We arranged our repast under the boughs of a farspreading live oak, there where the "rill ran o'er, and round, fern, flowers and ivy creep." . . .

I hardly know when we should have found it in our hearts to leave our rural banquet hall, had not the encroachments of myriads of mosquitoes warned us that it was time to depart. The sting of those spiteful little creatures, and the fact of two of our party having encountered snakes within a few yards of the spot where we had been dining, decided us to continue our voyage without further delay. We had no one with us skilled in the capture of the rattlesnake. . . .

As we descended to our boat, we saw two Indians standing before the door of their hut, who were contemplating us with great composure, and without any apparent surprise. Their costume was a very scanty one, consisting merely of a short blanket thrown over one shoulder, and drawn round their persons; their limbs were bare, with the exception of the moccasins worn on the legs, and little red and blue paint traced on the dark skin of their muscular arms. Their faces were free from any such disfigurement, and the head of each was encircled by a species of *fillet,* of what metal composed I know not, but it *glittered like gold,* and gave the wearers a decidedly dignified appearance. One was quite a young man, and the other was probably his father, as he was middle-aged, and the two were strikingly alike; we left them standing on the bank, their brilliant head-dresses shining in the light of the setting sun, and neither of them deigning to turn their heads to watch us, as we rowed on through the creek.

Grand Isle

CHARLES TENNEY JACKSON

Jackson (1874–?) and an acquaintance called Hen impulsively decided to "get a canoe and paddle around the Gulf of Mexico" to get away from humdrum lives in the North. In *The Fountain of Youth* (1914) he recounts their adventures during three months in Louisiana waters (paddling a johnboat and a pirogue; their canoe perished en route to the South). Toward the end of their time they reached Grand Isle—not far from Grand Terre, which Houstoun reached. This selection from Jackson's book describes their idyllic stay in a primitive paradise. Grand Isle is the only settled barrier island in Louisiana, with Barataria Bay on one side, the Gulf of Mexico on the other. In the selection by Kate Chopin following this one, the travelers start out from Grand Isle.

Grand Isle is a unique municipality . . . it is one hundred and fifty years old, but in all that time it has never occurred to the natives to build a street. So there is no street—not one. Between the shaded gardens and neat, miniature fields are narrow lanes, but so narrow that two of the high-wheeled carts, which are the only means of carriage, can hardly pass. And these only run from "beach to bay" across the isle! Lengthwise there are no streets whatever. . . . When you shop on Grand Isle, you pass into your neighbor's lot, meander among the oaks and oleanders to another stile, through it and another until you come to the "sto'."

Well, we meandered down the bay path, turned into a lane, into a lot and were proudly introduced to Dr. Seay. We were hospitably received, and the vivacious young daughter of the house fitted us out with oysters and macaroni. Then we idled and discussed Grand Isle and our adventures until the heat of the day was broken, when the Doctor hitched up his cart and transported all our luggage to the outer beach. There, within a hundred yards of the tumbling surf, we put up the little silk tent among the gorgeous oleander bloom. Then we rested and watched the great round moon draw up from the sea—soft and benignantly shining as were the airs blown over the water. Somewhere back in the quiet gardens we heard the music of the Sunday evening ball. It was fine. We sat before the tent, listening to the surf on the yellow sands before us, watched the moon-path on the water, felt that soft breeze up from Yucatan six hundred miles due south, and voted old, tumble-down, carefree Grand Isle the place we had been looking for.

"I don't care if I never go home," murmured Hen—and went to sleep there on the spot all night, without taking the trouble to go to bed.

What sleeps! And eats! Even if a chap had injured his social standing by paddling around the wilderness with no coat. . . .

Next day we wandered about and had breakfast and much further information at the Doctor's. He was a New Orleans physician who had come down to the south coast islands years ago for his health, though the islanders were too healthy to make a good living. However, the Doctor gardened, as did all the neighbors, and the amount of stuff that can be taken off these tiny two-acre farms of Grand Isle is amazing. In the early spring, cucumbers; in the fall, cauliflower; and both the earliest raised in the United States and shipped principally to Chicago markets for distribution. Between croppings, the islanders fish and trap, and nearly every truck-gardener has his "seine share"[12] in one of the luggers.

In the evening I drove with Doctor Seay in his pony cart up and down the nine-mile curve of beach with the surf racing under the wheels. At either end the oak *chênière*[13] dwindled away to mere sandy reaches with a few dead trees slanting northward as the storms had left them. At the east end of the island is Grande Terre Pass, and at the other Caminada, and from these outlets the tides rush fiercely, draining all the vast inland of swamps and lakes reaching from the river to the Gulf. This and Grand Terre Island are still romantically entwined with the feats of Jean La Fitte, whose pirate ships took refuge here from raids on the Caribbean; and where, later, the slave ships fled when the

12. That is, a share in the profits of the catch.

13. A chênier, or chênière (from which Chênière Caminada took its name), is a sandy ridge along the coast or in the marshes upon which oak trees often grow. As solid, slightly raised ground in marsh country, chêniers were the locations for settlements.

British and Yankee sloops-of-war tried to break up the traffic. Here, as in all treasure-haunted Barataria, the tales still linger of La Fitte's hidden gold[14] and of the days when cargoes of African savages were thrown to the sharks in the back bayous rather than have them captured by the authorities.

The ancient landing place, the foundations of the house, and the old round tower or cistern of bricks at Rigaud's landing on the bay shore are given a date of 1780 in local legend, which is years before Pierre and Jean La Fitte, the gentleman adventurers, fled from France to lend their dubious fortunes to the thrifty Creole smuggler-traders of New Orleans. . . .

Hen and I grew highly interested. It is true that to-day but few of the old pirate remains are here. The fort on Grand Terre, where Jean long defied the puny Republic of Madison's day to take him, and from which he, at length, led a thousand buccaneers to the defense of New Orleans on Andrew Jackson's promise of amnesty, has long since been engulfed by the waves.[15] But there are a few old families about whom legends cluster—the Rigauds and Chigazolas—as being descended from the adventurers of La Fitte, though now these are the usual kindly, courteous islanders we met everywhere. Hen and I went to the west end of the island in quest of this ancient stock and came upon our buccaneers peacefully sorting cucumbers under the oak shade instead of slitting windpipes or relating hairbreadth 'scapes.

We sat down to listen to the soft Creole patois.[16] And in no time shy boys were bringing gifts—garden stuff and berries, and were saying that they had heard of us! The schoolteacher had told them about two Yankees she had seen almost four months ago starting from Barataria with a pirogue and a silk tent, headed for Grand Island—and where had we been all this time?

That was flattering. To have these strangers interested in our wanderings. We were quite celebrated at once, and began relating Homeric tales—and inquiring about the fishing.

Not that I cared a rap about fishing. Hen went off the next morning . . . but

14. Jackson had been picking up stories of buried treasure from the outset of his trip, and indeed the prominence of Jean Lafitte and piracy and smuggling as local activities have associated the area with treasure lore, as Chopin also notes.

15. Lafitte did have a headquarters on Grand Terre, not to be confused with the fort built later by the United States government, Fort Livingston, whose remains do still exist.

16. When applied to language in Louisiana, the term *Creole* generally refers to the French Creole spoken by African Americans, though also by some Cajuns and known to many of the white Creoles who spoke standard French. Jackson may have been hearing Cajun French.

I idled about the oak grove gardens and the sto's and the galleries. We had had a splendid dip in the surf before breakfast, much to the astonishment of the islanders, who never went in the sea until July unless they fell in. But the bathing was great. Some unfortunate day Grand Isle will be discovered and muddled over with hotels and tourists, and its warm, gentle surf all cluttered up with summer girls. May Hen not be there to see. Or I either! The charm of that *dolce far niente* [sweetness of doing nothing] is still with me. . . .

They had no jail. They had no church. I asked the official what was done when there was trouble. He related an exciting story.

"Wan time der was a Manilaman named José. Wan time dis José he coom here and feesh, and he drink wine. *Eheu!* Dat red wine he drink! I put dat José on a feesh boat wan time when he drink too much red wine, and he went away—I dun-no."

The higher life had an even more agitating legend. Once there was a church. It seemed that a priest came to the island and got everyone to help build the church. Everyone did, and when the church was up the happy islanders discovered how the uplift had brought the serpent into Eden. Who was to worship in the church? White, "light mixed," "dark mixed," or "just nigger"?

It was the happy isle's one legend of general contention. They wrangled and raged and no one could make head or tail of the controversy, until finally some unknown Solomon settled the matter by burning the church down one night. Again peace reigned, and never since has Grand Isle bothered its head about religion.

Wealth, too, seemed to lose its distinction here. Everyone on the island worked—easily, independently, buoyantly, and made a living. The richest man on the island, except John Ludwig, the terrapin king, was one who owned ten beach shore lots. But everyone worked, either at the "cucs" or the fishing or in the "sto's." Grand Isle will make a fine study for some economist, bad luck to him.

Ludwig's terrapin farm was a collection of sheds out on the bay shore marshes, and in it were six thousand small diamond backed turtles. The terrapin king bought every terrapin that the hunters brought to him, held them in his shed and shipped them North by boat and rail whenever an order came. The business made him wealthy, even as the outside world rates wealth. Terrapin occasionally bring him forty dollars a dozen and he pays about a dollar apiece. Ludwig—Creole, for all his German name—was an intelligent and courteous man. He had outside correspondents in business, and had been to New York and Philadelphia. To his store, the principal one on the island, came most of the inhabitants for advice, and when the fishing was bad or the crop poor, the general patrone carried them through the season on his books. And he lost little. People were honest, he told me.

At Ludwig's store was the only bar. But it had none of the character of a saloon. No loafers were about it; no barkeeper either. If one wanted a drink the proprietor or one of the boys in the store passed into the annex, served you, and came out. Or, if busy, they told you to help yourself and pay out in the store. More than likely half-a-dozen handsome children were playing "keep house" or something of the kind in the barroom, and no man would be in it all day long.

There were four more stores on the island, each set back in its own shady grove and hedged about with magnolia, oleander, and roses. If one went from Ludwig's to Adams's or Nacari's stores one went over stiles and through gates on a veritable lover's path, winding in and out with no pretense of street or sidewalk. The Arcadian simplicity of Grand Isle was refreshing, as fine as the hospitality of its people.

Hen and I bathed of mornings in that surf, idled, smoked, wandered, sat on the galleries, talked boats and fishing, storms and cucumbers, all of a week ere we knew it had gone. Once we mentioned that we really ought to be going and there was a kindly murmur of dissent. Go? Why we had only just come! Besides, Saturday the *Hazel* boat came back and there would be a ball Saturday night, Sunday, and Sunday night. Sunday all the bayou boat men would be in, and the seine crews and the island would give itself to gayety. So we agreed to stay, not having any particular place to go.

We had enjoyed the beach camp. For ten days the southwest breeze blew off the Gulf night and day, and our little silk tent bellied out like a paper bag. We slept without [mosquito] bars, which was remarkable at this season of the year for the sea wind kept every mosquito away. It is the occasional west winds that bring the scourge off La Fourche marshes—I have visited Grand Isle since when they were intolerable for a time.

We heard a good deal about the two balls on Saturday night. Our fair young friends who radiated about the Doctor's were, of course, going to their own ball; but some of the young chaps privately informed us that there would be cake and sherbet and the prettiest girls at the other.

Hen and I determined we would see both. And when we went we were totally unable to see any difference in the quiet, fun-loving folk at the two pavilions. There were not a dozen young people at the white ball; but we did the honors and then slipped away through the moonlight to the other, stopping at the sto' for a measure of wine and a word with the elders grouped about on the gallerie benches. There was always laughter, gentle badinage in the soft *patois*, and room for a friend. . . .

The ballroom was a long pavilion open on every side and with oleanders and roses hanging in over the gallerie railing, rough, unpainted, lit by side lamps hung here and there. At one was the "music," an accordeon and a fiddle, and around the floor waltzed dreamily the youth and beauty of Grand Isle.

We were heartily welcomed. We could sit in the "grape arbeh," or we could dance. And there would be sherbet and cake and also gumbo. Did we think it was too warm a night for gumbo?

Never. It was a fine night for anything. Even Hen warmed up as he saw the little girls in white with the orange blossoms in their hair waltzing about the old floor. All of the family giving the ball were busied. M'sieu was deftly shaving one guest in an ante-room, Madame was stirring the gumbo, the children were in ecstasies over the sherbet—it was sho' a grand ball. . . .

We stayed at the ball until midnight. It was very fine out on the gallerie, the flower-decked girls, the moonlight, the odors of the south and the boom of the surf on the island sands, and the droning music. In the shadows some fellow played a guitar, and the entire assemblage was low-voiced and gentle, with no boisterousness nor drinking nor a jarring note. We liked the ball immensely, and went away to camp satisfied.

Sunday morning we idled at the sto' watching the cocks fight in the yards and the mule carts creak in from the bay shore where a gas boat was being unloaded. The anchorage was so shallow that the boats could not come close in, so at low tide the mule carts were driven out to the lighters and the freight loaded in them. Another line of half a dozen carts was ambling out of the narrow, shady lanes loaded with cucumbers to go, the next day, to New Orleans and the North.

The Sunday idlers on the gallerie watched the work with languid comments. I asked them why a wharf had never been built to do away with this laborious lightering, and they seemed astonished. We found that Grand Islanders had a pleasing faith that some day a railroad would find its way down the leagues of swamp forest and salt marsh to the coast, a great hotel would be built, and their fortunes would be made. Not a man would sell an arpent of land. They could sit on the gallerie and dream of their long, beautiful beach cleaned and gay with winter visitors, the oak groves and oleander lined lanes set with modern cottages, and the thrifty folk amassing money from their ancient holdings. This pleasant mood of the lotus eaters we found among them all. They were absolutely the happiest people it has ever been my fortune to see.

Sailing to Chênière Caminada

KATE CHOPIN

Kate O'Flaherty Chopin (1850–1940) was born in St. Louis but married a Louisiana Creole and lived in New Orleans and Cloutierville before returning to her native city. Her famous novel, *The Awakening,* was published in 1899 and soon created controversy because of how Chopin dealt with marriage and female sexuality. The novel opens on Grand Isle at the end of the nineteenth century, during its days as a great summer resort for New Orleans Creoles. The excerpt here tells of the visit the main character, Edna Pontellier, takes with a young man named Robert to nearby Chênière Caminada, a coastal settlement (which was virtually wiped out in the legendary, murderous hurricane of 1893). Though this journey is a fictional one, Chopin's narrative catches nicely the spirit of that part of the Louisiana coast and the laziness of a sojourn there—in the nineteenth century or later.

Sailing across the bay to the *Chênière Caminada,* Edna felt as if she were being borne away from some anchorage which had held her fast, whose chains had been loosening—had snapped the night before when the mystic spirit was abroad, leaving her free to drift whithersoever she chose to set her sails. . . .

"Let us go to Grande Terre to-morrow?" said Robert in a low voice.

"What shall we do there?"

"Climb up the hill to the old fort and look at the little wriggling gold snakes, and watch the lizards sun themselves."

She gazed away toward Grande Terre and thought she would like to be alone there with Robert, in the sun, listening to the ocean's roar and watching the slimy lizards writhe in and out among the ruins of the old fort.

"And the next day or the next we can sail to the Bayou Brulow," he went on.

"What shall we do there?"

"Anything—cast bait for fish."

"No; we'll go back to Grande Terre. Let the fish alone."

"We'll go wherever you like," he said. "I'll have Tonie come over and help me patch and trim my boat. We shall not need Beaudelet nor any one. Are you afraid of the pirogue?"

"Oh, no."

"Then I'll take you some night in the pirogue when the moon shines. Maybe your Gulf spirit will whisper to you in which of these islands the treasures are hidden—direct you to the very spot, perhaps."

"And in a day we should be rich!" she laughed. "I'd give it all to you, the pirate gold and every bit of treasure we could dig up. I think you would know how to spend it. Pirate gold isn't a thing to be hoarded or utilized. It is something to squander and throw to the four winds, for the fun of seeing the golden specks fly."

"We'd share it, and scatter it together," he said. His face flushed.

They all went together up to the quaint little Gothic church of Our Lady of Lourdes, gleaming all brown and yellow with paint in the sun's glare. . . .

A feeling of oppression and drowsiness overcame Edna during the service. Her head began to ache, and the lights on the altar swayed before her eyes. Another time she might have made an effort to regain her composure; but her one thought was to quit the stifling atmosphere of the church and reach the open air. She arose, climbing over Robert's feet with a muttered apology. Old Monsieur Farival, flurried, curious, stood up, but upon seeing that Robert had followed Mrs. Pontellier, he sank back into his seat. . . .

"I felt giddy and almost overcome," Edna said, lifting her hands instinctively to her head and pushing her straw hat up from her forehead. "I couldn't have stayed through the service." They were outside in the shadow of the church. Robert was full of solicitude.

"It was folly to have thought of going in the first place, let alone staying. Come over to Madame Antoine's; you can rest there." He took her arm and led her away, looking anxiously and continuously down into her face.

How still it was, with only the voice of the sea whispering through the reeds that grew in the salt-water pools! The long line of little gray, weather-beaten houses nestled peacefully among the orange trees. It must always have been God's day on that low, drowsy island, Edna thought. They stopped, leaning over a jagged fence made of sea-drift, to ask for water. A youth, a mild-faced Acadian, was drawing water from the cistern, which was nothing more than a rusty buoy, with an opening on one side, sunk in the ground. The water which the youth handed to them in a tin pail was not cold to taste, but it was cool to her heated face, and it greatly revived and refreshed her.

Madame Antoine's cot[tage] was at the far end of the village. She welcomed them with all the native hospitality, as she would have opened her door to let the sunlight in. She was fat, and walked heavily and clumsily across the floor. She could speak no English, but when Robert made her understand that the lady who accompanied him was ill and desired to rest, she was all eagerness to make Edna feel at home and to dispose of her comfortably.

The whole place was immaculately clean, and the big, four-posted bed, snow-white, invited one to repose. It stood in a small side room which looked out across a narrow grass plot toward the shed, where there was a disabled boat lying keel upward.

Madame Antoine had not gone to mass. Her son Tonie had, but she supposed he would soon be back, and she invited Robert to be seated and wait for him. But he went and sat outside the door and smoked. Madame Antoine busied herself in the large front room preparing dinner. She was boiling mullets over a few red coals in the huge fireplace.

Edna, left alone in the little side room, loosened her clothes, removing the greater part of them. She bathed her face, her neck and arms in the basin that stood between the windows. She took off her shoes and stockings and stretched herself in the very center of the high, white bed. How luxurious it felt to rest thus in a strange, quaint bed, with its sweet country odor of laurel lingering about the sheets and mattress. She stretched her strong limbs that ached a little. She ran her fingers through her loosened hair for a while. She looked at her round arms as she held them straight up and rubbed them one after the other, observing closely, as if it were something she saw for the first time, the fine, firm quality and texture of her flesh. She clasped her hands easily above her head, and it was thus she fell asleep.

She slept lightly at first, half awake and drowsily attentive to the things about her. She could hear Madame Antoine's heavy, scraping tread as she walked back and forth on the sanded floor. Some chickens were clucking outside the windows, scratching for bits of gravel in the grass. Later she half heard the voices of Robert and Tonie talking under the shed. She did not stir. Even her eyelids rested numb and heavily over her sleepy eyes. The voices went on—Tonie's slow, Acadian drawl, Robert's quick, soft, smooth French. She understood French imperfectly unless directly addressed, and the voices were only part of the other drowsy, muffled sounds lulling her senses.

When Edna awoke it was with the conviction that she had slept long and soundly. The voices were hushed under the shed. Madame Antoine's step was no longer to be heard in the adjoining room. Even the chickens had gone elsewhere to scratch and cluck. The mosquito bar was drawn over her; the old woman had come in while she slept and let down the bar. Edna arose quietly from the bed, and looking between the curtains of the window, she saw by the slanting rays of the sun that the afternoon was far advanced. Robert was out there under the shed, reclining in the shade against the sloping keel of the overturned boat. He was reading from a book. Tonie was no longer with him. She wondered what had become of the rest of the party. She peeped out at him two or three times as she stood washing herself in the little basin between the windows.

Madame Antoine had laid some coarse, clean towels upon a chair, and had placed a box of *poudre de riz* within easy reach. Edna dabbed the powder upon her nose and cheeks as she looked at herself closely in the little distorted mirror which hung on the wall above the basin. Her eyes were bright and wide awake and her face glowed.

When she had completed her toilet she walked into the adjoining room. She was very hungry. No one was there. But there was a cloth spread upon the table that stood against the wall, and a cover was laid for one, with a crusty brown loaf and a bottle of wine beside the plate. Edna bit a piece from the brown loaf, tearing it with her strong, white teeth. She poured some of the wine into the glass and drank it down. Then she went softly out of doors, and plucking an orange from the low-hanging bough of a tree, threw it at Robert, who did not know she was awake and up.

An illumination broke over his whole face when he saw her and joined her under the orange tree.

"How many years have I slept?" she inquired. "The whole island seems changed. A new race of beings must have sprung up, leaving only you and me as past relics. How many ages ago did Madame Antoine and Tonie die and when did our people from Grand Isle disappear from the earth?"

He familiarly adjusted a ruffle upon her shoulder.

"You have slept precisely one hundred years. I was left here to guard your slumbers; and for one hundred years I have been out under the shed reading a book. The only evil I couldn't prevent was to keep a broiled fowl from drying up."

"If it had turned to stone, still will I eat it," said Edna, moving with him into the house. "But really, what has become of Monsieur Farival and the others?"

"Gone hours ago. When they found that you were sleeping they thought it best not to awake you. Any way, I wouldn't have let them. What was I here for?" . . . .

"Where are Madame Antoine and her son?" asked Edna.

"Gone to Vespers, and to visit some friends, I believe. I am to take you back in Tonie's boat whenever you are ready to go."

He stirred the smoldering ashes till the broiled fowl began to sizzle afresh. He served her with no mean repast, dripping the coffee anew and sharing it with her. Madame Antoine had cooked little else than the mullets, but while Edna slept Robert had foraged the island. He was childishly gratified to discover her appetite, and to see the relish with which she ate the food which he had procured for her.

"Shall we go right away?" she asked, after draining her glass and brushing together the crumbs of the crusty loaf.

"The sun isn't as low as it will be in two hours," he answered.

"The sun will be gone in two hours."

"Well, let it go; who cares?"

They waited a good while under the orange trees, till Madame Antoine came back, panting, waddling, with a thousand apologies to explain her absence. Tonie did not dare to return. He was shy, and would not willingly face any woman except his mother.

It was very pleasant to stay there under the orange trees, while the sun dipped lower and lower, turning the western sky to flaming copper and gold. The shadows lengthened and crept out like stealthy, grotesque monsters across the grass.

Edna and Robert both sat upon the ground—that is, he lay upon the ground beside her, occasionally picking at the hem of her muslin gown.

Madame Antoine seated her fat body, broad and squat, upon a bench beside the door. She had been talking all the afternoon, and had wound herself up to the story-telling pitch.

And what stories she told them! But twice in her life she had left the *Chênière Caminada*, and then for the briefest span. All her years she had squatted and waddled there upon the island, gathering legends of the Baratarians and the sea. The night came on, with the moon to lighten it. Edna could hear the whispering voices of dead men and the click of muffled gold.

When she and Robert stepped into Tonie's boat, with the red lateen sail, misty spirit forms were prowling in the shadows and among the reeds, and upon the water were phantom ships, speeding to cover.

Travel Update

See the Travel Update for "Sportsman's Paradise: Wildlife and the Natural Environment," which incorporates information relevant to the selections in this chapter.

9

Sportsman's Paradise: Wildlife and the Natural Environment

"Sportsman's Paradise" is a slogan that for many years has emblazoned Louisiana's auto license plates. Like many such slogans, it's a boast. Yet it's also a justifiable description that calls attention not merely to the local devotion to hunting and fishing but to the richness of Louisiana's natural environment, which has been observed by numerous travelers and visitors.

Not all such visitors have been powerfully or pleasantly attracted by that environment. Especially in early days, it could seem an impediment to travel or settlement, a fearsome wilderness full of dangerous creatures and unstable bogs. "Crossing the Mississippi Swamps," for example, a short account published in a periodical in 1853 by an anonymous Methodist minister, is a vivid description of the terrors of the wilderness that make it seem not far removed from hell itself. Edouard de Montulé's account of his hunting expedition just outside New Orleans in 1817, on which he suddenly found himself engulfed in a universe of slithering, poisonous snakes, also reverberates with the dangers of the environment.[1] The anonymous author of "Ibis-Shooting in Louisiana" relates a harrowing tale of being trapped on an island (he was unable to swim) and besieged by biting insects and threatening alligators; he was able to escape, he tells us, by inflating alligator entrails to make a raft and then floating back to his lost boat—an ending to his plight that evokes frontier tall tales.

But to others, natural Louisiana has been a paradise, or at least a splendid experience. Even the hapless island-trapped writer was initially enthusiastic about the bird life he encountered and a landscape that allowed him to fancy "that I was the first human being who had ever found a motive for propelling a boat through . . . this solitary stream." For the great naturalist John James Audubon, Louisiana was a magical place, and when he had left it he often thought back on it fondly. In the 1920s journalist Irvin S. Cobb, writing in *Some United States*—a sort of travelogue of his favorite American places— was to call Louisiana "the truest tropics to be found in the Union." He went on to compare it to lower Florida, which had "a sandiness and a sparsity of verdure which seem barren and skimpy when compared with the luxuriousness of growth and the variety of faunal life on the Gulf Shore west and southwest of New Orleans." In Louisiana, he says,

> are to be encountered in sizable flocks rare wading birds which practically are extinct elsewhere in America—the scarlet ibis and the glossy, and the snowy heron and the roseate spoonbill, and once in a while—although I never saw one myself—a few specimens of that most gorgeous of all the long-legged fowl, the flamingo. And on Avery Island are black bears larger than any other black bears in the world—bears regarded by naturalists as forming a separate and distinct species.[2]

Cobb's assessment accords well with the statistic George H. Lowery gives in his *Louisiana Birds:* 377 bird species have been found in Louisiana, "more than half of all the birds known in North America, north of Mexico." It should be no great surprise, then, that of Audubon's 435 plates in *Birds of*

---

1. "Crossing the Mississippi Swamp," in *Travels in the Old South, Selected from the Periodicals of the Times,* ed. L. Eugene Schwaab and Jacqueline Bull (2 vols.; Lexington, Ky., 1973), I, 163–65; Edouard de Montulé, *Travels in America, 1816–1817,* trans. Edward D. Seeber (Bloomington, Ind., 1951), 79–81.

2. Irvin S. Cobb, *Some United States: A Series of Stops in Various Parts of This Nation with One Excursion Across the Line* (New York, 1926), 384–85.

America, at least 167 are "definitively known to have been done in Louisiana." In his *Mammals of Louisiana,* Lowery also lists an interesting variety, ranging from armadillos to bears, cougars, bobcats, deer, red wolves, coyotes, and— offshore—dolphins as well as a number of commercially trapped fur-bearing animals. The significance of Louisiana as a fur-producing state is indeed indicative of the abundance of animal life as well as of the richness of the environment that supports it. (Louisiana is "today the leading fur-producing area on the North American continent," Lowery wrote in 1974, adding that its production "has amounted to as much as 65 percent of the total for all the rest of the United States," despite our stereotype that furs come from the "frozen north," not the coastal marshes of the Gulf of Mexico.)[3]

Travelers, however, have been more likely to notice another Louisiana creature that has become almost emblematic of the state—the alligator. The earliest French explorers were fascinated by *Alligator mississippiensis* (to use the scientific name of the only member of the family Crocodylidae found in Louisiana). Paul du Ru was surprised to hear in 1700 that Indians swam with alligators, while Pierre de Charlevoix saw them all along the Mississippi he came down in the 1720s. Perhaps because he had his provisions snatched by a gator near Red River, Jean Bernard Bossu was especially intrigued by them, noting various bits of lore about them that he had picked up. Nineteenth-century visitors were equally attentive to the alligator. Christian Schultz, for example, wrote about them as food, while Charlotte Matilda Houstoun, journeying through the marshes to visit coastal plantations, was obviously thrilled by the alligator she saw. For the 1980s, Peter Jenkins, staying in Louisiana during his protracted coast-to-coast walk, went out with a commercial alligator hunter; his account of that experience in *The Walk West* is an exciting one.[4]

De Montulé was, of course, hunting alligators when he stumbled upon the

3. George H. Lowery, Jr., *Louisiana Birds,* illus. Robert E. Tucker (Baton Rouge, 1955), 26, 4; George H. Lowery, Jr., *The Mammals of Louisiana and Its Adjacent Waters,* illus. H. Douglas Pratt (Baton Rouge, 1974), 21.

4. Paul du Ru, "Extract from a *Journal de Voyage,*" trans. Olivia Blanchard (Typescript in Special Collections, Louisiana State University Library), x; Pierre de Charlevoix, *Journal of a Voyage to North-America* (2 vols.; Ann Arbor, 1966), II, 251; Jean Bernard Bossu, "New Voyages in North America," trans. Olivia Blanchard (Typescript in Special Collections, Louisiana State University Library), 52–57; Christian Schultz, *Travels on an Inland Voyage* (2 vols.; New York, 1810), II, 177–79; Peter Jenkins and Barbara Jenkins, *The Walk West: A Walk Across America 2* (New York, 1981), 110–15.

snakes, a reminder of what has taken many into the Louisiana wilds in the first place: sport. Indeed, many of the most interesting accounts of the Louisiana wilds, at least before the twentieth century, were produced by hunters. Theodore Roosevelt came after the Louisiana black bear; his report in this section of his adventures in the north-Louisiana canebrakes not far from the Mississippi is a minor classic among hunting accounts. Clifton Johnson went after alligator. His account here of that foray reminds us of how close Louisianians often are to the wild; he got to the hunting grounds, right out of the metropolis of New Orleans, just by taking a little suburban railroad line out to the country. That was about 1907, but even today "everywhere in Louisiana people are in intimate contact with the world of reptiles and amphibians; even within the city limits of the largest city, New Orleans, one can find a good variety of amphibians and reptiles, even alligators and poisonous snakes" (though visitors are highly unlikely to encounter any unless they are trying to find them).[5]

Though hunting and fishing continue to be pursued avidly by locals and visitors alike, there has been increasing interest in the appreciation of the natural environment quite apart from its value as a venue for sport. Audubon, of course, shot many of the specimens he painted (though others he purchased at the French Market in New Orleans, which in his day was supplied by market hunters with an incredible array of edible wild game), and even he "killed tirelessly for sport."[6] Yet his name has come to be associated with the larger appreciation of wildlife and with its conservation. It is this—his gentler side, we might say—that figures in Mary Durant and Michael Harwood's quest for Audubon's lingering presence in West Feliciana Parish, while they also make clear the continuing abundance of bird life in this area that he knew and loved so intensely. Audubon's influence is still felt in Louisiana in many ways, including—if indirectly—in a project undertaken by another regional visitor to the state, Margaret Stones, a botanical artist based in London who over an extensive period of time spent part of each year in Louisiana producing the splendid watercolors for *The Flora of Louisiana*.[7] Initiated by Louisiana State University with specially designated funds, this was meant to be an Audubon-

5. Harold A. Dundee and Douglas A. Rossman, *The Amphibians and Reptiles of Louisiana*, illus. Eugene C. Beckham (Baton Rouge, 1989), ix.

6. Roulhac Toledano, "Audubon in Louisiana," in *Audubon in Louisiana* (New Orleans, 1966), n.p.

7. Margaret Stones, *Flora of Louisiana* (Baton Rouge, 1991).

like presentation of the state's flora, like *Birds of America* in aesthetic as well as taxonomic significance. It certainly is indicative of Louisiana's floral glories (for example, the state boasts well over 3,000 varieties of wildflowers[8]), even if such fauna as alligators, crawfish, and pelicans (Louisiana is nicknamed "The Pelican State") figure more prominently in the public imagination.

Louisiana today provides possibilities for experiencing nature in many ways—hiking designated nature trails, canoeing, bird watching. The contemporary person perhaps most associated with discovering this natural environment shares the tradition of Audubon as naturalist-artist, though he is photographer rather than painter. This is C. C. Lockwood, who in his book *Discovering Louisiana* divides the state into five habitats: hills and piney woods; scenic rivers and lakes; swamps and bottomlands; prairies, cheniers, bogs, and salt domes; and coastal Louisiana. Hardly a scientific division, but one that rings true for many and reminds us that Louisiana is not merely a few prominent species or a sportsman's paradise or the land of swamp and marsh—as popular stereotype has it—but a compound of highly complex environments. This section concludes with Lockwood's composite account of travels on Louisiana's scenic rivers and lakes.

8. See Clair A. Brown, *Wildflowers of Louisiana and Adjacent States* (Baton Rouge, 1972).

Ibis-Shooting in Louisiana

Anonymous

From *Harper's Monthly*, November, 1853.

The ibis *(tantalus)* is one of the most curious and interesting of American birds: it is a creature of the warm climates, and is not found in either the northern or middle States—the tropics, and the countries contiguous to them are its range. Louisiana, from its low elevation, possesses almost a tropical climate, and the ibis, of several varieties, is to be there met with in considerable numbers.

There are few sorts of game I have not followed with horse, hound, or gun; and, among other sports, I have gone ibis-shooting: it was not so much for the sport, however, as that I wished to obtain some specimens for mounting. An adventure befell me in one of these excursions that may interest the reader. The southern part of the State of Louisiana is one vast labyrinth of swamps, bayous, and lagoons. These bayous are sluggish streams that glide sleepily along, sometimes running one way, and sometimes the very opposite, according to the season. Many of them are outlets of the great Mississippi, which begins to shed off its waters more than three hundred miles from its mouth. These bayous are deep, sometimes narrow, sometimes wide, with islets in their midst. They and their contiguous swamps are the great habitat of the alligator and the fresh-water shark—the gar. Numerous species of water and wading fowl fly over them, and plunge through their dark tide. Here you may see the red flamingo, the egret, the trumpeter-swan, the blue-heron, the wild-goose, the crane, the snake-bird, the pelican, and the ibis; you may likewise see the osprey, and the white-headed eagle robbing him of his prey. These swamps and bayous produce abundantly fish, reptile, and insect, and are, consequently, the favorite resort of hundreds of birds which prey upon these creatures. In some places, the bayous form a complete net-work over the country, which you may traverse with a small boat in almost any direction; indeed, this is the means by which many settlements communicate with each other. As

An ibis

From "Ibis-Shooting in
Louisiana," *Harper's
Monthly,* November, 1853

you approach southward toward the Gulf, you get clear of the timber; and
within some fifty miles of the sea, there is not a tree to be seen.

It was near the edge of this open country I went ibis-shooting. I had set out
from a small French or Creole settlement, with no other company than my
gun; even without a dog, as my favorite spaniel had the day before been bitten
by an alligator while swimming across a bayou. I went of course in a boat, a
light skiff, such as is commonly used by the inhabitants of the country.

Occasionally using the paddles, I allowed myself to float some four or five
miles down the main bayou; but as the birds I was in search of did not appear,
I struck into a "branch," and sculled myself up stream. This carried me
through a solitary region, with marshes stretching as far as the eye could see,
covered with tall reeds. There was no habitation, nor aught that betokened the

presence of man. It was just possible that I was the first human being who had ever found a motive for propelling a boat through the dark waters of this solitary stream. As I advanced, I fell in with my game; and I succeeded in bagging several, both of the great wood-ibis and the white species. I also shot a fine white-headed eagle *(Falco leucocephalus)*, which came soaring over my boat, unconscious of danger. But the bird which I most wanted seemed that which could not be obtained. I wanted the scarlet ibis.

I think I had rowed some three miles upstream, and was about to take in my oars and leave my boat to float back again, when I perceived that, a little further up, the bayou widened. Curiosity prompted me to continue; and after pulling a few hundred strokes further, I found myself at the end of an oblong lake, a mile or so in length. It was deep, dark, marshy around the shores, and full of alligators. I saw their ugly forms and long serrated backs, as they floated about in all parts of it, hungrily hunting for fish, and eating one another; but all this was nothing new, for I had witnessed similar scenes during the whole of my excursion. What drew my attention most, was a small islet near the middle of the lake, upon one end of which stood a row of upright forms of a bright scarlet color: these red creatures were the very objects I was in search of. They might be flamingoes: I could not tell at that distance. So much the better, if I could only succeed in getting a shot at them; but these creatures are even more wary than the ibis; and as the islet was low, and altogether without cover, it was not likely they would allow me to come within range; nevertheless, I was determined to make the attempt. I rowed up the lake, occasionally turning my head to see if the game had taken the alarm. The sun was hot and dazzling; and as the bright scarlet was magnified by refraction, I fancied for a long time they were flamingoes. This fancy was dissipated as I drew near. The outlines of the bills, like the blade of a sabre, convinced me they were the ibis; besides, I now saw that they were only about three feet in height, while the flamingoes stand five. There were a dozen of them in all. These were balancing themselves, as is their usual habit, on one leg, apparently asleep, or honed in deep thought. They were on the upper extremity of the islet, while I was approaching it from below. It was not above sixty yards across; and could I only reach the point nearest me, I knew my gun would throw shot to kill at that distance. I feared the stroke of the sculls would start them, and I pulled slowly and cautiously. Perhaps the great heat—for it was as hot a day as I can remember—had rendered them torpid or lazy. Whether or not, they sat still until the cut-water of my skiff touched the bank of the islet. I drew my gun up cautiously, took aim, and fired both barrels almost simultaneously. When the smoke cleared out of my eyes, I saw that all the birds had flown off except one, that lay stretched out by the edge of the water. Gun in hand, I leaped out of the boat, and ran across the islet to bag my game. This occupied but a few minutes; and I was turning to go back to the skiff, when, to my consternation, I saw it out upon the lake, and rapidly floating downward! In my haste I had left it unfastened, and the bayou current had carried it off. It was still but a hundred yards off, but it might as well have been a hundred miles, for at that time I could not swim a stroke.

My first impulse was to rush down to the lake, and after the boat; this impulse was checked on arriving at the water's edge, which I saw at a glance was fathoms in depth. Quick reflection told me that the boat was gone—irrecoverably gone!

I did not at first comprehend the full peril of my situation; nor will you. I was on an islet, in a lake, only half a mile from its shores—alone, it is true, and without a boat, but what of that? Many a man had been so before, with not an idea of danger. These were first thoughts, natural enough; but they rapidly gave place to others of a far different character. When I gazed after my boat now beyond recovery—when I looked around, and saw that the lake lay in the middle of an interminable swamp the shores of which, even could I have reached them, did not seem to promise me footing—when I reflected that, being unable to swim, I could not reach them—that upon the islet there was neither tree, nor log, nor bush; not a stick out of which I might make a raft—I say, when I reflected upon all these things, there arose in my mind a feeling of well-defined and absolute horror.

It is true, I was only in a lake, a mile or so in width; but so far as the peril and helplessness of my situation were concerned, I might as well have been upon a rock in the middle the Atlantic. I knew that there was no settlement within miles—miles of pathless swamp. I knew that no one could either see or hear me—no one was at all likely to come near the lake; indeed I felt satisfied that my faithless boat was the first keel that had ever cut its waters. The very tameness of the birds wheeling round my head was evidence of this. I felt satisfied too, that without some one to help me, I should never go out from that lake: I must die on the islet, or drown in attempting to leave it.

These reflections rolled rapidly over my startled soul. The facts were clear, the hypothesis definite, the sequence certain; there was no ambiguity, no suppositious hinge upon which I could hang a hope; no, not one. I could not even expect that I should be missed and sought for: there was no one to search for me. The simple *habitans* of the village I had left knew me not—I was a stranger among them; they only knew me as a stranger, and fancied me a strange individual; one who made lonely excursions, and brought home bunches of weeds, with birds, insects, and reptiles, which they had never before seen, although gathered at their own doors. My absence, besides, would be nothing new to them, even though it lasted for days: I had often been absent before, a week at a time. There was no hope of my being missed.

I have said that these reflections came and passed quickly. In less than a minute my affrighted soul was in full possession of them, and almost yielded itself to despair. I shouted, but rather involuntarily than with any hope that I should be heard; I shouted loudly and fiercely: my answer—the echoes of my own voice, the shriek of the osprey, and the maniac laugh of the white-headed eagle.

I ceased to shout, threw my gun to the earth, and tottered down beside it. . . .

I lay in a state of stupor—almost unconscious; how long I know not, but many hours I am certain: I knew this by the sun—it was going down when I awoke, if I may so term the recovery of my stricken senses. I was aroused by a strange circumstance: I was surrounded by dark objects of hideous shape and hue—reptiles they were. They had been before my eyes for some time, but I had not seen them. I had only a dreamy sort of consciousness of their presence; but I heard them at length: my ear was in better tune, and the strange noises they uttered reached my intellect. It sounded like the blowing of great bellows, with now and then a note harsher and louder, like the roaring of a bull. This startled me, and I looked up and bent my eyes upon the objects: they were forms of the *corocdilidae,* the giant lizards; they were alligators.

Huge ones they were, many of them; and many were they in number—a hundred at least were crawling over the islet, before, behind, and on all sides around me. Their long gaunt jaws and channeled snouts extended forward so as almost to touch my body; and their eyes, usually leaden, seemed now to glare.

Impelled by this new danger, I sprang to my feet, when, recognizing the upright form of man, the reptiles scuttled off, and plunging hurriedly into the lake, hid their hideous bodies under the water.

The incident in some measure revived me. I saw that I was not alone: there was company even in the crocodiles. I gradually became more myself; and began to reflect with some degree of coolness of the circumstances that surrounded me. My eyes wandered over the islet; every inch of it came under my glance; every object upon it was scrutinized—the moulted feathers of wildfowl, the pieces of mud, the fresh-water mussels *(unios)* strewed upon its beach—all were examined. Still the barren answer—no means of escape.

The islet was but the head of a sand-bar, formed by the eddy—perhaps gathered together within the year. It was bare of herbage, with the exception of a few tufts of grass. There was neither tree nor bush upon it—not a stick. A raft indeed! There was not wood enough to make a raft that would have floated a frog. The idea of a raft was but briefly entertained; such a thought had certainly crossed my mind, but a single glance round the islet dispelled it before it had taken shape.

I paced my prison from end to end; from side to side I walked it over. I tried the water's depth; on all sides I sounded it, wading recklessly in; every where it deepened rapidly as I advanced. Three lengths of myself from the islet's edge, and I was up to the neck. The huge reptiles swam around, snorting and blowing; they were bolder in this element. I could not have waded safely ashore, even had the water been shallow. To swim it—no—even though I swam like a duck, they would have closed upon and quartered me before I could have made a dozen strokes. Horrified by their demonstrations, I hurried back upon dry ground; and paced the islet with dripping garments.

I continued walking until night, which gathered around me dark and dismal. With night came new voices—the hideous voices of the nocturnal swamp; the qua-qua of the night-heron, the screech of the swamp-owl, the cry of the bittern, the el-l-uk of the great water-toad, the tinkling of the bell-frog, and the chirp of the savanna-cricket—all fell upon my ear. Sounds still harsher and more hideous were heard around me—the plashing of the alligator, and the roaring of his voice; these reminded me that I must not go to sleep. To sleep! I durst not have slept for a single instant. Even when I lay for a few minutes motionless, the dark reptiles came crawling round me—so close that I could have put forth my hand and touched them.

At intervals, I sprang to my feet, shouted, swept my gun around, and chased them back to the water, into which they betook themselves with a sullen plunge, but with little semblance of fear. At each fresh demonstration on my part they showed less alarm, until I could no longer drive them either with shouts or threatening gestures. They only retreated a few feet forming an irregular circle round me. Thus hemmed in, I became frightened in turn. I loaded my gun and fired: I killed none. They are impervious to a bullet, except in the eye, or under the forearm. It was too dark to aim at these parts; and my shots glanced harmlessly from the pyramidal scales of their bodies. The loud report, however, and the blaze frightened them, and they fled, to return again after a long interval. I was asleep when they returned, I had gone to sleep in spite of my efforts to keep awake. I was startled by the touch of something cold; and half-stifled by a strong musky odor that filled the air. I threw out my arms; my fingers rested upon an object slippery and clammy: it was one of these monsters—one of gigantic size. He had crawled close alongside me, and was preparing to make his attack; as I saw that he was bent in the form of a bow, and I knew that these creatures assume that attitude when about to strike their victim. I was just in time to spring aside, and avoid the stroke of his powerful tail, that the next moment swept the ground where I had lain. Again I fired, and he with the rest once more retreated to the lake.

All thoughts of going to sleep were at an end. Not that I felt wakeful; on the contrary, wearied with my day's exertion—for I had had a long pull under a hot tropical sun—I could have lain down upon the earth, in the mud, any where, and slept in an instant. Nothing but the dread certainty of my peril kept me awake. Once again before morning, I was compelled to battle with the hideous reptiles, and chase them away with a shot from my gun.

Morning came at length, but with it no change in my perilous position. The light only showed me my island prison, but revealed no way of escape from it. Indeed, the change could not be called for the better, for the fervid rays of an almost vertical sun burned down upon me until my skin blistered. I was already speckled by the bites of a thousand swamp-flies and musquitoes, that all night long had preyed upon me. There was not a cloud in the heavens to shade me; and the sunbeams smote the surface of the dead bayou with a double intensity. Toward evening, I began to hunger; no wonder at that: I had not eaten since leaving the village settlement. To assuage thirst, I drank the water of the lake, turbid and slimy as it was. I drank it in large quantities, for it was hot, and only moistened my palate without quenching the craving of my appetite. Of water there was enough; I had more to fear from want of food.

What could I eat? The ibis. But how to cook it? There was nothing wherewith to make a fire—not a stick. No matter for that. Cooking is a modern invention, a luxury for pampered palates. I divested the ibis of its brilliant plumage, and ate it raw. I spoiled my specimen, but at the time there was little thought of that: there was not much of the naturalist left in me. I anathematized the hour I had ever imbibed such a taste; I wished Audubon, and Buffon, and Cuvier,[9] up to their necks in a swamp. The ibis did not weigh above three pounds, bones and all. It served me for a second meal, a breakfast; but at this *déjeuner sans fourchette*[10] I picked the bones.

What next! starve? No—not yet. In the battles I had had with the alligators on the second night, one of them had received a shot that proved mortal. The hideous carcass of the reptile lay dead upon the beach. I need not starve; I could eat that. Such were my reflections. I must hunger, though, before I could bring myself to touch the musky morsel. Two more days' fasting conquered my squeamishness. I drew out my knife, cut a steak from the alligator's tail, and ate it—not the one I had first killed, but a second; the other was now putrid, rapidly decomposing under the hot sun: its odor filled the islet.

The stench had grown intolerable. There was not a breath of air stirring, otherwise I might have shunned it by keeping to windward. The whole atmosphere of the islet, as well as a large circle around it, was impregnated with the fearful effluvium. I could bear it no longer. With the aid of my gun, I pushed the half-decomposed carcass into the lake; perhaps the current might carry it away. It did: I had the gratification to see it float off. This circumstance led me into a train of reflections. Why did the body of the alligator float? It was swollen—inflated with gases.

An idea shot suddenly through my mind, one of those brilliant ideas—the children of necessity. I thought of the floating alligator, of its intestines—what if I inflated them? Yes, yes! buoys and bladders, floats and life-preservers! that was the thought. I would open the alligators, make a buoy of their intestines, and that would bear me from the islet!

I did not lose a moment's time; I was full of energy: hope had given me new life. My gun was loaded—a huge crocodile that swam near the shore received the shot in his eye. I dragged him on beach; with my knife I laid open his entrails. Few they were, but enough for my purpose. A plume-quill from the wing of the ibis served me for a blow-pipe. I saw the bladder-like skin expand, until I was surrounded by objects like great sausages. These were tied together and fastened to my body, and then, with a plunge, I entered the waters of the

9. Georges-Louis Leclerc, comte de Buffon (1707–88), and Georges, Baron Cuvier (1769–1832), were noted French naturalists.

10. "Dinner without a fork"; however, the author is punning: *fourchette* can also mean the breastbone of a bird and *déjeuner à la fourchette* means a meat (or substantial) breakfast.

lake, and floated downward. I had tied on my life-preservers in such a way that I sat in the water in an upright position, holding my gun with both hands. This I intended to have used as a club in case I should be attacked by the alligators; these creatures lie in a half-torpid state, and to my joy I was not molested. Half an hour's drifting with the current carried me to the end of the lake, and I found myself at the debouchure of the bayou. Here, to my great delight, I saw my boat in the swamp, where it had been caught and held fast by the sedges. A few minutes more, and I had swung myself over the gunwale, and was sculling with eager strokes down the smooth waters of the bayou.

Alligator Hunting

CLIFTON JOHNSON

Johnson (1865–1940) was a prolific author of popular travel books that emphasized country life. He was able to find his alligator hunting simply by taking a train a little distance out of New Orleans. From *Highways and Byways of the Mississippi Valley* (1906). On an earlier excursion to the countryside, he had found his guide, Jake.

I made arrangements with Jake to go on an alligator hunt, and early one morning . . . I again was at the little station amid the swamplands.

. . . He [Jake] said the trip would be too boggy for my clothing, and he took me to his hut and furnished me with some of his garments, including a great heavy pair of shoes. For his own footwear he decided to put on rubber boots. He found a pair and discarded them because they lacked holes and the heat would make them unendurable. Another pair, however, was exhumed which were satisfactorily leaky, and he pulled them on. Then he adjusted a bag over one shoulder, stuck a hatchet into his belt, and took in his hand a slender iron rod, six feet long and hooked at one end.

Off we went along "the dirt road," intending to go to a hunting-camp Jake had seven miles off in the wilds. The road was a narrow trail of single cart width, with streaks of grass and weeds growing between the wheel tracks, and it was hedged in on either side by the rankest kind of a jungle, in which canes were predominant. This was the main highway of the region, but it ran off into nowhere, and grew more and more grassy as we advanced. Sometimes we walked in the shade of lofty, moss-hung trees,—live-oaks, gums, magnolias, and cypress,—sometimes through blasted tracts devastated by recent fires. Ordinarily these fires only burn till nightfall, and then are extinguished by the heavy dew. The woods were vocal with bird songs, and buzzards were soaring high in the ether.

"Hit's tolerable hot," remarked Jake; and so it was, for the sun shone clear and burning, and the breeze that fluttered the treetop leafage did not penetrate into the forest depths of cane and briers and palmetto scrub. The heat was not our only discomfort. Hordes of ravenous mosquitoes assailed us and could not be kept from our hands and faces except by persistent fighting. The creatures lit on our clothing and clung to it and prodded with their poisoned lances in savage eagerness.

After a few miles we turned off from the dirt road into an indistinct path, and waded through mucky lowlands to a dark silent bayou, which we crossed on some half-sunken logs embedded in the mud of its shallows. On we went, following the irregular windings of the path, long-legged Jake striding on ahead and I coming after, taking care to step along briskly enough not to be left behind in that lonely wilderness.

Presently Jake stopped and cut a cane a dozen or fifteen feet long that he intended to use as a prod when we came to the marshes where the alligators lurked. A little farther on the trees and woody undergrowth disappeared, and we had before us the marshlands, spreading away like a green endless sea to the horizon, an unbroken level of saw-grass, flags, and prairie canes. Last year's growths had all been burned off during the winter except for a few scattering stalks, tall and withered and rustling in the wind. The rank new shoots were waist high and grew in tufts from the charred stubs. These stubs were a foot tall and the size of one's fist, and they were set in mud that varied from a watery thinness to a stiff consistency. What sweaty, weary work it was pushing through that monotony of mud and coarse grasses! It made the breath come hard and fast and the muscles ache.

We went perhaps a mile, and then Jake said I might wait where I was until he had done a little investigating. I was glad enough to stop, and I stood still and looked around. Far behind me was the forest whence we had come, and all about was the vast waste of marsh which could have seemed utterly deserted if I had not now and then heard the lonely cries of waterfowl. Jake had disappeared from sight, but I occasionally saw the long pole he carried reaching up above the marsh growths. When that too was gone from view, I was a trifle uneasy in the forsaken and unfamiliar void, and I questioned whether, left to my own resources, I could find my way back by the devious and scarcely distinguishable path through the barbaric swamps.

Alligator hunting
from a steamboat

From Willard Glazier,
Down the Great River
(Philadelphia, 1889)

By and by I saw smoke curling up from the marsh grass. Jake had set it on
fire to clear a path and make walking and seeing easier. I hoped the fire would
not burn in my direction; for if it forged ahead with any rapidity I could not
have gotten away from it. Anything more than a snail's pace was impossible in
such a sticky mud and resisting stubble. But I need not have feared. So little
of the marsh growths was dry enough for the flames to lick up that the fire
made slight headway.

Finally I heard a distant shout. Jake had got on the trail of an alligator, and I plodded in his direction. The soil became more watery and I sank half leg deep. Several times I had to call to Jake before I came in sight of him, to make sure of his whereabouts. He was on the borders of a narrow channel of brown water that he spoke of as an "alligator slue," and which the alligator used as a highway when in search of food. The creature had a hole just aside from the slue, and Jake ran his pole half its length into the muddy cavity to let the inmate know that something was going on. Then he bent over, and holding his nose between his thumb and finger grunted with a peculiar guttural in imitation of the voice of an old alligator. He cautioned me to keep perfectly still. Near by was a muskrat's home—a heap of dry reeds. A water moccasin came from somewhere and stopped, startled at the sight of us, and then slid hastily away. We roused a marsh hen which uttered a harsh cry and fluttered up into view and with frightened wings sped to safety.

Jake watched the water intently, repeating the grunting at intervals. There was a slight movement at the surface, and he made a sudden grab and out came a little alligator a foot long. He grunted again and secured another little fellow, and pretty soon a third. Then the ground quivered faintly and the long pole trembled.

"That's the big one—the mother," whispered Jake, and resumed his vocal gymnastics.

In a few moments there was just the least ruffling of the water, and before I could discern the cause Jake had plunged in both hands and was pulling forth a seven-foot monster firmly gripped by the jaws. But it was bedaubed with clay so that it was very slippery, and when it gave a sudden twist and turn Jake lost his hold. The beast rolled over into the slue, and with a vigorous splash of its muscular tail sent the water flying over us and in a twinkling was back in its hole.

Jake was mad, and he made some remarks more vigorous than elegant and began thrusting his iron rod into the soil. He could prod the creature out, he said, but as that was likely to injure it he soon decided to try the persuasion of his voice once more.

This time he imitated the cries of the little alligators. The monster responded to this appeal to its maternal instinct, and Jake caught it in the same way as before, drew it out on the mud, and jumped on its back. Then he took a cord from his pocket, tied its mouth fast shut and fastened its legs over its back and had the beast at his mercy. It was the personification of ugliness, yet

I could not help feeling sorry for it and sorrier still for the little alligators, with their soft bodies and pathetic eyes. In the unmitigated loneliness of the bog, the pleasures of life were not very apparent. Nevertheless, I suppose these creatures are in their nature suited to the environment. Jake said the marshes were pretty thickly populated with them, and that there were at least forty big ones in a lagoon not far from where we were.

My comrade had put the little alligators into the sack he had brought, and he now fastened it around himself and hoisted the big beast on his shoulder. Then he staggered away through the mire and shallow pools and slues toward the comparatively firm ground of the swamp—and what a relief it was when we escaped from the dismal barren of the marshlands!

In the Louisiana Canebrakes

THEODORE ROOSEVELT

Twenty-fifth president of the United States, Theodore
Roosevelt (1858–1919) was a legendary sportsman
who wrote about sporting expeditions he made in
many parts of the world; he hunted in Louisiana in
1907. From *Scribner's Magazine,* January, 1908.

In October, 1907, I spent a fortnight in the cane-
brakes of northern Louisiana, my hosts being Messrs. John M. Parker and
John A. McIlhenny. Surgeon General Rixey, of the United States Navy, and
Dr. Alexander Lambert were with me. I was especially anxious to kill a bear in
these canebrakes after the fashion of the old southern planters, who for a century past have followed the bear with horse and hound and horn in Louisiana,
Mississippi and Arkansas.

Our first camp was on Tensas Bayou. This is in the heart of the great alluvial bottom-land created during the countless ages through which the mighty
Mississippi has poured out of the heart of the continent. . . .

Beyond the end of cultivation towers the great forest. Wherever the water
stands in pools, and by the edges of the lakes and bayous, the giant cypress
loom aloft, rivalled in size by some of the red gums and white oaks. In stature,
in towering majesty, they are unsurpassed by any trees of our eastern forests;
lordlier kings of the green-leaved world are not to be found until we reach the
sequoias and redwoods of the Sierras. Among them grow many other trees—
hackberry, thorn, honey locust, tupelo, pecan, and ash. In the cypress sloughs
the singular knees of the trees stand two or three feet above the black ooze.
Palmettos grow thickly in places. The canebrakes stretch along the slight rises
of ground, often extending for miles, forming one of the most striking and
interesting features of the country. They choke out other growths, the feath-
ery, graceful canes standing in ranks, tall, slender, serried, each but a few

inches from his brother, and springing to a height of fifteen or twenty feet. They look like bamboos;[11] they are well-nigh impenetrable to a man on horseback; even on foot they make difficult walking unless free use is made of the heavy bush-knife. It is impossible to see through them for more than fifteen or twenty paces, and often for not half that distance. Bears make their lairs in them, and they are the refuge for hunted things. Outside of them, in the swamp, bushes of many kinds grow thick among the tall trees, and vines and creepers climb the trunks and hang in trailing festoons from the branches. Here, likewise, the bush-knife is in constant play, as the skilled horsemen thread their way, often at a gallop, in and out among the great tree trunks, and through the dense, tangled, thorny undergrowth.

In the lakes and larger bayous we saw alligators and garfish; and monstrous snapping turtles, fearsome brutes of the slime, as heavy as a man, and with huge, horny beaks that with a single snap could take off a man's hand or foot. One of the planters with us had lost part of his hand by the bite of an alligator, and had seen a companion seized by the foot by a huge garfish from which he was rescued with the utmost difficulty by his fellow swimmers. There were black bass in the waters, too, and they gave us many a good meal. Thick-bodied water moccasins, foul and dangerous, kept near the water; and farther back in the swamp we found and killed rattlesnakes and copperheads.

Coon and 'possum were very plentiful, and in the streams there were minks and a few otters. Black squirrels barked in the tops of the tall trees or descended to the ground to gather nuts or gnaw the shed deer antlers—the latter a habit they shared with the wood rats. To me the most interesting of the smaller mammals, however, were the swamp rabbits, which are thoroughly amphibious in their habits, not only swimming but diving, and taking to the water almost as freely as if they were muskrats. They lived in the depths of the woods and beside the lonely bayous.

Birds were plentiful. Mocking-birds abounded in the clearings, where, among many sparrows of more common kind, I saw the painted finch, the gaudily colored brother of our little indigo bunting, though at this season his plumage was faded and dim. In the thick woods where we hunted there were many cardinal birds and winter wrens, both in full song. Thrashers were even more common; but so cautious that it was rather difficult to see them, in spite

11. What Roosevelt was seeing was in fact American bamboo.

of their incessant clucking and calling and their occasional bursts of song. There were crowds of warblers and vireos of many different kinds, evidently migrants from the North, and generally silent. The most characteristic birds, however, were the woodpeckers, of which there were seven or eight species, the commonest around our camp being the handsome redbellied, the brother of the red-head which we saw in the clearings. The most notable birds and those which most interested me were the great ivory-billed woodpeckers. Of these I saw three, all of them in groves of giant cypress; their brilliant white bills contrasted finely with the black of their general plumage. They were noisy but wary, and they seemed to me to set off the wildness of the swamp as much as any of the beasts of the chase. Among the birds of prey the commonest were the barred owls, which I have never elsewhere found so plentiful. Their hooting and yelling were heard all around us throughout the night, and once one of them hooted at intervals for several minutes at mid-day. One of these owls had caught and was devouring a snake in the late afternoon, while it was still daylight. In the dark nights and still mornings and evenings their cries seemed strange and unearthly, the long hoots varied by screeches and by all kinds of uncanny noises.

At our first camp our tents were pitched by the bayou. For four days the weather was hot, with steaming rains; after that it grew cool and clear. Huge biting flies, bigger than bees, attacked our horses; but the insect plagues, so veritable a scourge in this country during the months of warm weather, had well-nigh vanished in the first few weeks of the fall.

The morning after we reached camp we were joined by Ben Lilley, the hunter, a spare, full-bearded man, with wild, gentle blue eyes and a frame of steel and whipcord. I never met any other man so indifferent to fatigue and hardship. He equalled Cooper's Deerslayer in woodcraft, in hardihood, in simplicity—and also in loquacity. The morning he joined us in camp, he had come on foot through the thick woods, followed by his two dogs, and had neither eaten nor drunk for twenty-four hours, for he did not like to drink the swamp water. It had rained hard throughout the night and he had no shelter, no rubber coat, nothing but the clothes he was wearing, and the ground was too wet for him to lie on; so he perched in a crooked tree in the beating rain, much as if he had been a wild turkey. But he was not in the least tired when he struck camp; and though he slept an hour after breakfast, it was chiefly because he had nothing else to do, inasmuch as it was Sunday, on which day he never hunted nor labored. He could run through the woods like a buck, was far more enduring, and quite as indifferent to weather, though he was over fifty years old. He had trapped and hunted throughout almost all the half-century of his life, and on trail of game he was as sure as his own hounds. His observations on wild creatures were singularly close and accurate. He was particularly fond of the chase of the bear, which he followed by himself, with one or two dogs; often he would be on the trail of his quarry for days at a time, lying down to sleep wherever night overtook him; and he had killed over a hundred and twenty bears.

Late in the evening of the same day we were joined by two gentlemen, to whom we owed the success of our hunt. They were Messrs. Clive and Harley Metcalf, planters from Mississippi, men in the prime of life, thorough woodsmen and hunters, skilled marksmen, and utterly fearless horsemen. For a quarter of a century they had hunted bear and deer with horse and hound, and were masters of the art. They brought with them their pack of bear hounds, only one, however, being a thoroughly staunch and seasoned veteran. The pack was under the immediate control of a negro hunter, Holt Collier, in his own way as remarkable a character as Ben Lilley. He was a man of sixty and could neither read nor write, but he had all the dignity of an African chief, and for half a century he had been a bear hunter, having killed or assisted in killing over three thousand bears. He had been born a slave on the Hinds plantation, his father, an old man when he was born, having been the body-servant and cook of "old General Hinds," as he called him, when the latter fought under Jackson at New Orleans. When ten years old Holt had been taken on the horse behind his young master, the Hinds of that day, on a bear hunt, when he killed his first bear. In the Civil War he had not only followed his master to battle as his body-servant, but had acted under him as sharpshooter against the Union soldiers. After the war he continued to stay with his master until the latter died, and had then been adopted by the Metcalfs; and he felt that he had brought them up, and treated them with that mixture of affection and grumbling respect which an old nurse shows toward the lad who has ceased being a child. The two Metcalfs and Holt understood one another thoroughly, and understood their hounds and the game their hounds followed almost as thoroughly.

They had killed many deer and wildcat, and now and then a panther; but their favorite game was the black bear, which, until within a very few years, was extraordinarily plentiful in the swamps and canebrakes on both sides of the lower Mississippi, and which is still found here and there, although in greatly diminished numbers. In Louisiana and Mississippi, the bears go into their dens toward the end of January, usually in hollow trees, often very high up in living trees, but often also in great logs that lie rotting on the ground. They come forth toward the end of April, the cubs having been born in the interval. At this time the bears are nearly as fat, so my informants said, as when they enter their dens in January; but they lose their fat very rapidly. On first coming out in the spring they usually eat ash buds and the tender young cane called mutton cane, and at that season they generally refuse to eat the acorns even when they are plentiful. According to my informants it is at this season that they are most apt to take to killing stock, almost always the hogs which run wild or semi-wild in the woods. They are very individual in their habits, however; many of them never touch stock, while others, usually old he-bears, may kill numbers of hogs; in one case an old he-bear began this hog killing just as soon as he left his den. In the summer months they find but little to eat, and it is at this season that they are most industrious in hunting for grubs, insects, frogs and small mammals. In some neighborhoods they do not eat fish, while in other places, perhaps not far away, they not only greedily eat dead fish, but will themselves kill fish if they can find them in shallow pools left by the receding waters. As soon as the mast is on the ground they begin to feed upon it, and when the acorns and pecans are plentiful they eat nothing else, though at first berries of all kinds and grapes are eaten also. When in November they have begun only to eat the acorns they put on fat as no other wild animal does, and by the end of December a full-grown bear may weigh at least twice as much as it does in August, the difference being as great as between a very fat and a lean hog. Old he-bears which in August weigh three hundred pounds and upwards will, toward the end of December, weigh six hundred pounds and even more in exceptional cases.

Bears vary greatly in their habits in different localities, in addition to the individual variation among those of the same neighborhood. Around Avery Island, John McIlhenny's plantation, the bears only appear from June to November; there they never kill hogs, but feed at first on corn and then on sugarcane, doing immense damage in the fields, quite as much as hogs would do. But when we were on the Tensas we visited a family of settlers who lived right in the midst of the forest ten miles from any neighbors; and although bears were plentiful around them they never molested their corn-fields—in which the coons, however, did great damage.

A big bear is cunning, and is a dangerous fighter to the dogs. It is only in exceptional cases, however, that these black bears, even when wounded and at bay, are dangerous to men, in spite of their formidable strength. Each of the hunters with whom I was camped had been charged by one or two among the scores of hundreds of bears he had slain, but no one of them had ever been injured, although they knew other men who had been injured. Their immunity was due to their own skill and coolness; for when the dogs were around the bear hunter invariably ran close in so as to kill the bear at once and save the pack. Each of the Metcalfs had on one occasion killed a large bear with a knife, when the hounds had seized it and the man dared not fire for fear of shooting one of them. They had in their younger days hunted with a General Hamberlin, a Mississippi planter whom they well knew, who was then already an old man. He was passionately addicted to the chase of the bear, not only because of the sport it afforded, but also in a certain way as a matter of vengeance; for his father, also a keen bear hunter, had been killed by a bear. It was an old he, which he had wounded and which had been bayed by the dogs; it attacked him, throwing him down and biting him so severely that he died a couple of days later. This was in 1847. . . .

For several days we hunted perserveringly around this camp on the Tensas Bayou, but without success. Deer abounded, but we could find no bear; and of the deer we killed only what we actually needed for use in camp. . . .

But no bear were to be found. We waited long hours on likely stands. We rode around the canebrakes through the swampy jungle, or threaded our way across them on trails cut by the heavy wood-knives of my companions: but we found nothing. Until the trails were cut the canebrakes were impenetrable to a horse and were difficult enough to a man on foot. On going through them it seemed as if we must be in the tropics; the silence, the stillness, the heat, and the obscurity, all combining to give a certain eeriness to the task, as we chopped our winding way slowly through the dense mass of close-growing, feather-fronded stalks. Each of the hunters prided himself on his skill with the horn, which was an essential adjunct of the hunt, used both to summon and control the hounds, and for signalling among the hunters themselves. The tones of many of the horns were full and musical; and it was pleasant to hear them as they wailed to one another, backwards and forwards, across the great streches of lonely swamp and forest.

A few days convinced us that it was a waste of time to stay longer where we were. Accordingly, early one morning we hunters started for a new camp fifteen or twenty miles to the southward, on Bear Lake. We took the hounds with us, and each man carried what he chose or could in his saddle-pockets, while his slicker was on his horse's back behind him. Otherwise we took absolutely nothing in the way of supplies, and the negroes with the tents and camp equipage were three days before they overtook us. On our way down we were joined by Major Amacker and Dr. Miller, with a small pack of cat hounds. These were good deer dogs, and they ran down and killed on the ground a good-sized bobcat, a wild-cat, as it is called in the South. It was a male and weighed twenty-three and a half pounds. It had just killed and eaten a large rabbit. The stomachs of the deer we killed, by the way, contained acorns and leaves.

Our new camp was beautifully situated on the bold, steep bank of Bear Lake—a tranquil stretch of water, part of an old river-bed, a couple of hundred yards broad, with a winding length of several miles. Giant cypress grew at the edge of the water; the singular cypress knees rising in every direction round about, while at the bottoms of the trunks themselves were often cavernous hollows opening beneath the surface of water, some of them serving as dens for alligators. There was a waxing moon, so that the nights were as beautiful as the days.

From our new camp we hunted as steadily as from the old. We saw bear sign, but not much of it, and only one or two fresh tracks. One day the hounds jumped a bear, probably a yearling from the way it ran; for at this season a yearling or a two-year-old will run almost like a deer, keeping to the thick cane as long as it can and then bolting across through the bushes of the ordinary swamp land until it can reach another canebrake. After a three hours' run this particular animal managed to get clear away without one of the hunters ever seeing it, and it ran until all the dogs were tired out. A day or two afterwards one of the other members of the party shot a small yearling—that is, a bear which would have been two years old the following February. It was very lean, weighing but fifty-five pounds. The finely-chewed acorns in its stomach showed that it was already beginning to find mast.

We had seen the tracks of an old she in the neighborhood, and the next morning we started to hunt her out. I went with Clive Metcalf. We had been joined overnight by Mr. Ichabod Osborn and his son Tom, two Louisiana planters, with six or eight hounds—or rather bear dogs, for in these packs most of the animals are of mixed blood, and, as with all packs that are used in the genuine hunting of the wilderness, pedigree counts for nothing as compared with steadiness, courage and intelligence. There were only two of the new dogs that were really staunch bear dogs. The father of Ichabod Osborn had taken up the plantation upon which they were living in 1811, only a few years after Louisiana became a part of the United States, and young Osborn was now the third in line from father to son who had steadily hunted bears in this immediate neighborhood.

On reaching the cypress slough near which the tracks of the old she had been seen the day before, Clive Metcalf and I separated from the others and rode off at a lively pace between two of the canebrakes. After an hour or two's wait we heard, very far off, the notes of one of the loudest-mouthed hounds, and instantly rode toward it, until we could make out the babel of the pack. Some hard galloping brought us opposite the point toward which they were heading—for experienced hunters can often tell the probable line of a bear's flight, and the spots at which it will break cover. But on this occasion the bear shied off from leaving the thick cane and doubled back; and soon the hounds were once more out of hearing, while we galloped desperately around the edge of the cane. The tough woods-horses kept their feet like cats as they leaped logs, plunged through bushes, and dodged in and out among the tree trunks; and we had all we could do to prevent the vines from lifting us out of the saddle, while the thorns tore our hands and faces. Hither and thither we went, now at a trot, now at a run, now stopping to listen for the pack. Occasionally we could hear the hounds, and then off we would go racing through the forest toward the point for which we thought they were heading. Finally, after a couple of hours of this, we came up on one side of a canebrake on the other side of which we could hear, not only the pack, but the yelling and cheering of Harley Metcalf and Tom Osborn and one or two of the negro hunters, all of whom were trying to keep the dogs up to their work in the thick cane. Again we rode ahead, and now in a few minutes were rewarded by hearing the leading dogs come to bay in the thickest of the cover. Having galloped as near to the spot as we could we threw ourselves off the horses and plunged into the cane, trying to cause as little disturbance as possible, but of course utterly unable to avoid making some noise. Before we were within gunshot, however, we could tell by the sounds that the bear had once again started, making what is called a "walking bay." Clive Metcalf, a finished bear-hunter, was speedily able to determine what the bear's probable course would be, and we stole through the cane until we came to a spot near which he thought the quarry would pass. Then we crouched down, I with my rifle at the ready. Nor did we have long to wait. Peering through the thick-growing stalks I suddenly made out the dim outline of the bear coming straight toward us; and noiselessly I cocked and half-raised my rifle, waiting for a clearer chance. In a few seconds it came; the bear turned almost broadside to me, and walked forward very stiff-legged, almost as if on tiptoe, now and then looking back at the nearest dogs. These were two in number—Rowdy, a very deep-voiced hound, in the lead, and Queen, a shrill-tongued brindled female, a little behind. Once or twice the bear paused as she looked back at them, evidently hoping that they would come so near that by a sudden race she could catch one of them. But they were too wary.

All this took but a few moments, and as I saw the bear quite distinctly some twenty yards off, I fired for behind the shoulder. Although I could see her outline, yet the cane was so thick that my sight was on it and not on the bear itself. But I knew my bullet would go true; and, sure enough, at the crack of the rifle the bear stumbled and fell forward, the bullet having passed through both lungs and out at the opposite side. Immediately the dogs came running forward at full speed, and we raced forward likewise lest the pack should receive damage. The bear had but a minute or two to live, yet even in that time more than one valuable hound might lose its life; so when within half a dozen steps of the black, angered beast, I fired again, breaking the spine at the root of the neck; and down went the bear, stark dead, slain in the canebrake in true hunter fashion. One by one the hounds struggled up and fell on their dead quarry, the noise of the worry filling the air. Then we dragged the bear out to the edge of the cane, and my companion wound his horn to summon the other hunters.

This was a big she-bear, very lean, and weighing two hundred and two pounds. In her stomach were palmetto berries, beetles, and a little mutton cane, but chiefly acorns chewed up in a fine brown mass. . . .

After the death of my bear I had only a couple of days left. We spent them a long distance from camp, having to cross two bayous before we got to the hunting grounds. I missed a shot at a deer, seeing little more than the flicker of its white tail through the dense bushes; and the pack caught and killed a very lean two-year-old bear weighing eighty pounds. Near a beautiful pond called Panther Lake we found a deer-lick, the ground not merely bare, but furrowed into hollows by the tongues of the countless generations of deer that had frequented the place. We also passed a huge mound, the only hillock in the entire district; it was the work of man, for it had been built in the unknown past by those unknown people whom we call mound-builders. On the trip, all told, we killed and brought into camp three bear, six deer, a wild-cat, a turkey, a possum and a dozen squirrels; and we ate everything except the wildcat.

On the Road with John James Audubon

MARY DURANT AND MICHAEL HARWOOD

Durant and Harwood traveled 35,000 miles over thirteen months, mostly by car, generally camping, to visit places known to John James Audubon. The great naturalist and artist did much of his work in Louisiana and is particularly associated with the area around St. Francisville in West Feliciana Parish. Here Durant and Harwood write about their stay in that area, their initials indicating their respective contributions. As the selection opens, they are attending the annual Audubon Pilgrimage in St. Francisville, an event that celebrates the naturalist and offers tours of the historic homes of the area.

MH: After lunch in the parish house of Grace Episcopal Church, we take the house tour and pause to look at some plant or other at a front yard, and a young woman in hoopskirts invites us to see the garden. With her little daughter—also in costume—tagging along and Mary and our guide talking about flowers, we go around back. The shady garden and its gazebo overlook a deep glade, thick with vines and live oaks and willows and garlands of lavender-gray wisteria in bloom.

Prothonotary warblers nest in the gazebo, says our guide. *Where?* cries yours truly, who has never seen a prothonotary warbler. Oh, they'll nest in *anything,* she says. She points to the containers hung in the gazebo—old enamel coffee pots and a large glass jar on its side; and hollow gourds have been put out for them on the other side of the house. All empty, of course, now; the season's a bit early yet.

This is not what you'd call the classic nesting territory of the prothonotary warbler. Tree-holes near water are said to be preferred. And it's disconcerting to learn that a bird I've waited many years to find in the northeast (it seldom wanders closer to New England than southern Jersey and western New York) is so ridiculously easy to come by here and is as vulgar and tame in its domestic habits as a house sparrow.

Back at the West Feliciana Historical Society, our new friend Mary Ellen Young rubs a little salt in the wound. She's seen prothonotary warblers try to build a nest in the pocket of a pair of her husband's khaki pants hanging on the clothesline. Another year, she had to chase one out of the house, where it appeared to be prospecting for a home.

Well, for all the good its plenitude and tameness has done me, it might as well be rare and shy. Our traveling companion JJA [Audubon] counsels patience: "I have observed their arrival in Louisiana to take place, according to the state of the weather, from the middle of March to the first of April." George H. Lowery, Jr., in his *Louisiana Birds* says the warbler arrives in small numbers the first week of March. Today is March 13. Any day now . . .

March 19. What a brilliant orange-yellow head! Saw my first prothonotary at the edge of Audubon Lake, early this morning, after hearing it sing. And what an elegant texture too. The bird looks as if it might have arrived *poured,* like cream. Golden head, the gold gracefully shading into the pewter wings and tail; not a wingbar or any sharp, contrasting mark anywhere, except the bright black eyes in the bright yellow face. No painter I know of has ever done the bird justice, and that includes JJA.

MD: Sweet olive blooms in gardens throughout West Feliciana, as it did in Natchez, drenchingly fragrant. "Our sweet olive," says Mary Ellen Young. "When you walk out in the morning, there it is to greet you." She takes an unabashedly personal view of birds and flowers, as I tend to do. I recognize the relationship. "Our trillies," she says, speaking of the toadshade trillium. "Our golden warblers," when she speaks of the prothonotaries. But when it comes to robins, ah, that is another matter. "They are *your* robins," she explains to me, because their homeland is in the north where they nest and raise their broods. Here, they are merely winter visitors, feasting on the red berries of pyracanthus and holly, and here it's not the first robin that counts, but the last.

"That means good weather is on the way," says Mary Ellen. "We're delighted to see them go."

To think of all the songs, the prose, and the poetry—from Longfellow, Thoreau, Lowell, Emily Dickinson, Holmes, Burroughs, et al.—that eulogize the robin as the herald of spring ("When the red-red-robin comes bob-bob-bobbin' along") and not a word of it means anything at this end of the continent.

Today we went in search of a waterfall, an Audubon landmark we had known nothing about until now. Our lead came from an article in the historical society's files—"Audubon in West Feliciana," written in 1912 by a local resident, Miss Sarah Turnbull Stirling, who . . . had gathered stories about the Audubons. Miss Stirling included the memoir of a sentimental journey John Woodhouse Audubon made to West Feliciana some twenty years after the family left. Victor, it must be remembered, was here only briefly before going north to Shippingport to his mercantile apprenticeship, so this was John's terrain, his home from the age of eleven to sixteen.[12]

"How he rushed around to places of 'Auld lang syne,' remembering everything." He visited the plantations where he and his mother had lived and he met with childhood friends. "He quite disdained a horse and walked to all the old haunts. . . . He did not think there were as many birds as when he was a boy, and would exclaim again and again at the 'beauty' of the Magnolia Grandiflora and said it was the most beautiful tree in the world. . . . His face would beam with delight as he related the sports of his boyhood, and he would exclaim 'West Feliciana is one of the brightest spots on earth to me.'" He found his way to the place where his father had watched "the habits of the beaver" and took particular note of the red clay from which his father had made a "fine paint." He went to "Bayou Sara Creek," where he and his father used to bathe and fish, then on to the Roberts' property where there was a waterfall known as the "silver bath"—"a favorite resort for the men and boys of that day."

The Roberts' property, upcountry in the hills, is still in the same family, and old Frank Roberts now lives there alone. He has no phone. We'd have to drive out and hope that he'd be around. Mary Ellen Young got directions from her son, who's in real estate and knows every corner of the parish. North of

12. Victor was Audubon's older son, John his younger.

town, a dirt road that winds to the top of the ridge. To the right, a negro cabin (a herd of burly hogs rooting among the trees), and just beyond, to the left, an old dogtrot[13] farmhouse set back on a low rise, a few gray weatherworn outbuildings to the side.

There were no signs of life about the place, so we walked up past the orderly vegetable garden to the house where a tiger tomcat slept on the porch, and I, as the lady of a party arriving unannounced at the home of an old man who wasn't expecting visitors, waited on the steps where I was joined by the cat, who smoothed his whiskers and arched his flanks against the timbers that supported the porch roof. Mike knocked and called Hello and finally Frank Roberts came to the door in immaculate khaki pants and khaki shirt and rubber boots, and he said he'd been taking a nap, that's what took him so long. He was as welcoming to strangers as his cat, who turned out to have been a stray and Frank Roberts had taken him in because there was no reason not to.

The Roberts have lived here close to two hundred years, he told us. His great-great-grandfather came down from Georgia with a wagon and mules. No, he hadn't heard of John James Audubon, but whatever our reasons for wanting to see the waterfall, he'd be pleased to show us the way. . . .

There were several big fire-ant hills near the vegetable garden, and Mr. Roberts said he scalded them out with boiling water and he'd known them to eat baby chicks and pick a new-born calf clean to the bone.[14] His corn, okra, and cabbages had just sprouted and the deer would be coming in soon to eat the shoots. He'd have to put up a scare-pants pretty quick.

Across the road, a path ran along the spine of a steep ridge, and Frank Roberts led the way, bounding ahead through his woods, lightfooted as a boy. He pointed out yaupon, cypress, and huckleberry as we passed. "Huckleberries make the best pie there is." Then he pointed below through the trees, and we caught sight of a brook and heard the sound of splashing water. It was a fine place in summer, he said, to take a bath and cool off. "Once you're in it, you can't leave."

Michael and I scrabbled down into the gorge and followed the narrow stony stream bed to the falls. The water, cold and clear, sluiced through a cut

13. A dogtrot is a type of folk house that consists of enclosed "pen" rooms with a breezeway between them.

14. Fire ants are relatively recent immigrants to Louisiana, having apparently arrived in some kind of cargo from South America in the 1950s. They build large mounds and sting humans who blunder near them.

in the rocks and fell to a shallow, sandy-bottomed pool twenty feet below. Magnolia trees grow on the opposite bank, one bough spreading outward over the pool, and when they come into bloom in late spring, what a sight that must be. Waterfalls are mesmerizing. We lingered, looking up at the frothing column of water that sprang away from the ridge and leaped into the catch basin at our feet, both of us smitten by the possibility of a ghostly image of John James Audubon and his young son naked in the "silver bath."

We took a wide loop back to town through the Sleepy Hollow Woods. Another ridge-top dirt road, deep wild gullies to the side. Live oaks and sycamores hung with Spanish moss. Silverbells, dog-wood, red buckeye. Jessamine, cross-vine, and wild wisteria topping the trees. Vines to the tenth power.

MH: JJA often had a terrible time identifying and describing bird songs. Here in West Feliciana Parish, where he spent so much time observing and listening and watching, I can hear the ruby-crowned kinglets all over the place; it's a sweet, perky, insistent song, quite loud for a character only about as long as my thumb. Audubon says he didn't hear one sing until he got to Labrador in the summer of 1833. That can't be right. He must have heard the song many times here, from wintering and migrating kinglets; however, it mixes in nicely with other common songs—of the tufted titmouse and Carolina wren and yellowthroat—and he often failed to link singer to music. Good binoculars are useful for making such connections, and of course he lacked binoculars. But he could frequently get close to singing birds. If *I* can, he could. On the other hand, chance plays a huge role in the study of birds. So he must simply have missed, for many years, an ordinary experience—an eye-level encounter with a singing ruby-crowned kinglet; the same sort of missed connection has happened to me with various bird species, for no good reason and for years at a stretch.

Time marches on, all right. Just downstream of Bayou Sara and St. Francisville, Gulf States Utilities is building a nuclear power plant with fearful urgency. There has been some opposition to the project in the parish, we understand, but it's not enough so far to bring things to a halt. Tonight, having seen bright lights in that neighborhood from the ferry landing,[15] and later hearing the roar of distant engines as we finished supper, we put two and two together

15. One of the Mississippi River ferries crosses from St. Francisville to New Roads.

and went to investigate. It turns out the contractor is working nights to get the nuke built. From a bridge at what must be the fringe of the site, we watched monstrous earthmoving equipment grinding across freshly flattened and graded earth, in the glare of floodlights.

MD: You know, Audubon was startlingly prescient on the subject of *Progress.* As we watched the armies of the night levelling and rearranging the West Feliciana landscape, I thought of an impassioned outcry he wrote against mankind's "increasing ravages on Nature." He predicted that neither the stream, the swamp, the river, nor the mountain "will be seen in a century hence as I see them now." Rivers would be turned from their courses, the hills reduced to swamp level, and the swamp itself "become covered with a fortress of a thousand guns." There would be no more fish, he wrote; no more deer; the magnolia would almost vanish from Louisiana forests; millions of birds be driven away or destroyed by man, and "the eagle scarce ever alight."

MH: March 21. A calm and sunny day, which we spent housekeeping. I have not yet seen a second prothonotary. My first of two days ago must have been much in the van; either that, or I am *still* missing the bird. Robins, yellow-rumped warblers, dark-eyed juncoes remain in Louisiana today; along the east coast and in the Appalachians all have begun to move by now, and surely each morning here I must be seeing twenty-four-hour segments of a stream flowing north, not just winter residents. Well, at least, having come all this way myself, I have a much better feel for the great distances these little migrants have to cover in a short time each spring.

My uncertainty about birds is a metaphor for our experience in West Feliciana Parish. Two weeks may be long enough to absorb the flavor of a strange community and its history, but as to the specifics, that is a different matter. Here is a basic problem for historian, biographer, reporter. Something embarrassingly obvious and essential may be missed.

That was a basic problem for Audubon, too, most of his life; covering so much ground and so much unfamiliar scientific territory, he was usually short on time. He sometimes discovered rarities and didn't come across ordinary things and so drew conclusions about birds based on evidence that later turned out to have been insufficient.

Altogether, the historian who reaches for the essence of people risks clutching chimeras. Each generation has its peculiar attitudes, and those who write about a person or an era from the perspective of a different generation have to look through a double prism, at least—a dizzying effort. Biography written even so short a time ago as 1900 bears little relation to "modern" biography at its best: critical, psychological, scholarly, documented, indexed. So, when looking for specific information, one hates to have to depend on formal biographies written in the middle of the last century, for instance; much of it is pure puffery, childlike hero-worship. Then, when history is reduced to local common denominators—as when an illustrious personage becomes a key part of a community's self-image—it takes on a hearsay, gossipy quality that may eventually lead it miles away from the truth. On top of everything, the biographer brings personal blind spots to the task, or hasn't read enough, or has taken inaccurate notes, or too frequently goes by intuition instead of research and crosschecking. It's as easy as spilling the salt. Example: just this week we found a locally written biography of Audubon in which the lady author speaks of JJA's use of *thee* and *thou* when he wrote to Lucy, and she ascribes it to his French background—a leap of faith, unprovable. Audubon's most important English teacher was his Quaker wife, who probably thee and thou'd him plenty. I have this cautionary tale very much on my mind as we leave St. Francisville. I've spent the last few days blundering around looking for JJA in the litter of facts and suppositions we've collected. Mary seems much more sure than I am of how they add up—what sort of a man he was. For me he fades in and out all along our route.

Traveling on the Natural and Scenic Streams System

C. C. Lockwood

C. C. Lockwood (b. 1949) has attained considerable acclaim as a nature photographer, photo-journalist, and conservationist. This account of travels on Louisiana's scenic waterways is from his *Discovering Louisiana* but was originally occasioned by an assignment for *Louisiana Life* magazine to report on nine of the forty-nine streams that compose the Louisiana Natural and Scenic Streams System. This system was created in 1970 by Act 398 of the Louisiana Legislature to protect certain waterways from channelization, clearing, and the construction of reservoirs. Lockwood's observations go beyond reporting on those streams, however, to evoke the obvious richness of Louisiana's natural environment today.

Adventure is rampant on the varied rivers that compose the system. In Allen Parish, my bare feet have squeaked in the quartz sand on the Whiskey Chitto. In contrast, I have slapped mosquitoes and photographed alligators while standing in knee-deep mud at the edge of Bayou Penchant. Between Shreveport and Minden, I have paddled through the morning fog on Bayou Dorcheat and gazed at the rusty fall colors of cypress and sweet gum. Dodging lightning bolts from a summer thunderstorm on the Tangipahoa River was a lot less fun than finding spiderflowers to photograph or swimming in the rocky rapids below the falls on Bayou Kisatchie.

One of my favorite spring flowers is known naturally only in streamside communities of Washington Parish. I hiked and searched the banks of the Pushepatapa Creek one April day to find this shrub. The clean stream bends around so much you would think that it crosses back over itself like a carpenter's folding ruler. It seems as if you walk miles to progress a few yards in one direction.

The lovely white and pink flowers of the mountain laurel were easy to find. Between intermittent sparkling white sandbars, this locally common shrub was in full bloom. Close inspection revealed this flower's secret of reproductive success. Its stamens (male parts) are locked into the petals. As the flower opens, the petals release the stamens in catapultlike action to fire the pollen into the pistil (female part), thus fertilizing the flower. An insect landing on the petal can do the same thing.

Some branches, chock-full of flowers, dangled over the stream that is one of Louisiana's best creeks for small-mouth bass. The streamside vegetation here is rich and dense, a shaded, cool, hardwood community that's important to the species of plants here as well as the fish. . . .

Downstream, the community along the Pushepatapa changes to higher banks and a more open, drier habitat. Here the turkey oak grows. There are only fifty, maybe a hundred small oaks of this species in the entire state. This small area mimics like-habitats in Florida where the turkey oak is more common. Why did they name it turkey oak? Simple—the leaves look like a turkey footprint. . . .

With its towering hardwoods, cypress, and pines, its steep, sandy banks, its clear, cold water, and its constant switchbacks, the Saline is the Miss America of our scenic rivers. Its beauty is spellbinding, but a canoe trip here is not one I would recommend to the faint of heart.

Robert Murry and I put my battered but nicely camouflaged seventeen-year-old Gruman canoe in at Cloud Crossing, a campsite in the Kisatchie National Forest.[16] One of the canoeing guidebooks describes this as a leisurely ten-mile, six-hour trip. After twelve hours, thirty-nine minor obstacles, twenty-three pull-unders, seventeen pull-overs, and four portages, we arrived at the abandoned saltworks just east of Goldonna, dead tired but with a deep feeling of accomplishment. . . .

Perhaps most significant when considering the beauty of Saline Bayou is the abundance of mature trees. This is rare, because generally trees are harvested in a national forest when they reach maturity. George Tannehill, a

16. The Kisatchie is the only national forest in Louisiana and is divided into several areas.

ranger with the U.S. Forest Service in the Winn District of Kisatchie National Forest from 1935 to 1973, was partial to the Saline Bayou bottoms and would not let trees be marked for cutting in this area.

Tales like this from Robert Murry, a wildlife ecologist at Fort Polk, made me forget the rough going. Robert knew this area and all the scenic rivers well, because he studied them when he was with the Department of Wildlife and Fisheries at the time Act 398 was being drafted and passed.

Robert Murry once paddled down the Tangipahoa River with [secretary of the Interior] James Watt in the front of his canoe. Watt, who was then director of the Bureau of Outdoor Recreation under President Nixon, was trying to tell Robert, an avid spotted-bass fisherman, to cast in the middle of the river as they do in Wyoming. After a few fly-fishing attempts with a casting rod, Watt gave up, telling Robert, "If you're going to catch fish, you're going to catch fish, no matter how good you are, and I'm not going to catch any today."

Palmetto palm

From Grace King, *New Orleans: The Place and the People* (New York, 1895)

Among the most interesting things we ran into on our paddle down the Saline were a couple of seven-foot ten-inch cypress knees. Throughout our ten-mile trip, the bayou was about twenty feet wide. It was the narrowest of the nineteen rivers I have traveled.

This narrowness, along with the tall, mature trees, gave Saline Bayou a magical atmosphere. A thunderstorm had rolled in while we were loading up at Cloud Crossing, and the wind and rain filled the air with sweet smells and sounds. I drank it all in and knew I soon would come back to stretch and strain my muscles again to navigate my canoe down this lovely waterway.

On another of many camping trips to Cloud Crossing, I doused my cooking fire and lay on my back, wrapped in a wool blanket. Orion was passing overhead, and I imagined that the tall pointed pines were rocket ships ready to blast me to the great hunter's belt. After that wild ride, the pines turned back to trees, and I focused on their needles and wondered if a millionaire changed all his bills into needles, would they fill a pine tree? I contemplated that important question until I dozed off under the stars.

Whenever I think I'm getting too old to battle logjams on small bayous, I remember my canoeing partner on Bayou L'Outre. Dr. J. Robert ("Chic") Fowler, slim, handsome, straight as a two-by-four from a virgin longleaf log and sharp as the tack he was when he retired twenty-seven years ago as head of the Department of Zoology at Louisiana Tech. Chic has caught about as many fish on the L'Outre as charter-boat captain Charley Hardison has caught in the Gulf. How? Well, he's been at it for almost all of his ninety-one years. Bert Jones, a L'Outre fan, came along for the adventure.

It was Bert's Old Town canoe, but Dr. Fowler told Bert to get in the front and fish. Then he told me to get in the middle and take pictures, and he would do all the paddling. We paid attention to our elder, and as we took off, I thought the L'Outre looked to be just as lovely as Saline Bayou.

The high banks were lined with oaks, pine, and baldcypress. One was so twisted, it looked like a peppermint stick. The water was as clear as tap water, and we could see small-mouth bass, carp, bluegill, snapping turtles, and a couple of "no-necks," as Bert called small cottonmouths. The water level was low, and the going got tougher as we proceeded downstream. The L'Outre braided into two, three, even five channels at intervals, and with our combined woodsmanship the three of us usually picked the best channel. I'd never admit we had to backtrack once.

Red-bellied, pileated, and downy woodpeckers drummed trees above while we pulled over fallen trunks below. The sweet gums were well chewed by beavers. We passed over two dams and one lodge. Soon the ringed sweet gums would fall over the bayous, creating more wildlife habitat and making for harder paddling.

Then just as we were noticing the heat of the day, a paddle jammed between a cypress stump and the canoe. Over we went. I jerked to the surface, trying to keep my camera dry, then swung around to look for Bert and Dr. Fowler. Bert was looking straight at Chic's hat floating on the surface. Before either of us could move, up popped the nonagenarian, right under his hat. All was well.

While drying out on the bank, we saw another no-neck. This one was on dry ground, eating a toad. I noticed the toad was being eaten legs first. When a snake eats a fish, it always swallows the fish head first to avoid the sharp dorsal fins. After we were under way again, I saw the cardinal flower in bloom. It's one of my favorites, for it's the reddest of reds. Some say it signals summer's end.

Our estimated six-hour trip was already approximately eight hours as we portaged around a major logjam. Back in the water, we paddled around a midstream cypress giant—hollow, though—and Bert said, "Be quiet. I usually see deer up ahead."

Two bends later, we saw that he was right. A spike and two does were under a magnificent longleaf pine. As our canoe quietly edged up to the bank, one doe snorted and pounded the ground with a front foot. We sat still and watched as she continued her warning signal. The three soon became bored with us and ambled off. I climbed ashore to measure the big pine. It took two hugs and an extra foot to get around it. I like those big ones. Imagine standing there for over a hundred years, watching those deer . . . why, he's probably even seen a red wolf.

Dr. Fowler pushed onward, and finally Bert and I started to help. It wasn't long before I had a blowout in my ancient running-hiking-wading shoes. Bert taped the sole to my foot with the expertise of an NFL trainer. But the sand and the water of the L'Outre proved mightier than the adhesive tape.

It was eleven hours later and dark when we pulled out of the river. After seven portages, four pull-unders, and forty-seven minor obstacles, Mr. Jones wasn't even breathing hard. Chic and I, though not admitting it, knew we would feel the effects of our adventure in the morning. But we all agreed there that the L'Outre is one special river.

I had spent the day before with Dr. Fowler on Pope Lake, another part of the L'Outre. Doc caught a few fish and told me in his clear, carefree voice stories of teaching, family, friends, fishing, travels, and wildlife. The professor explained the bubble trail of the buffalo fish as it fed along the bottom. He told me of teaching Dr. George Lowery, LSU's famous ornithologist, in an ecology class and later being in the Singer tract in 1943 when one of the last official sightings of the ivory-billed woodpecker was made. Doc saw three. I admit I was jealous.

Pope Lake is lined with some big second-growth tupelo, and I got some nice images of those trees as the leaves first began to fall. Leaves from the streamside vegetation are just as important as the shade factor for water temperature and photoperiod. The detritus, decomposed leaf litter, is the basis of the food chain. Lakes can make their own food; moving streams can't.

Pope Lake is just a wide place in the L'Outre, and is one type of lake in Louisiana. Lakes such as this are caused by logjams and terrain. Here a wide low area above a narrower part of the stream with not much drop in elevation becomes a lake.

Other types of lakes in Louisiana include cutoffs or oxbows, formed by abandoned channels in a river. Bluff lakes are caused by a depression between a bluff and the natural levee of a nearby river. Then there are round and lagoonal lakes in the marsh and near the Gulf. And finally there are reservoirs or artificial lakes such as Toledo Bend.

Toledo Bend Reservoir, covering 284 square miles, is the fifth-largest man-made lake in the United States. We share it with Texas, as it was made by damming the Sabine River, which separated Texas and Louisiana. This river is actually still the Texas-Louisiana border, but you can barely distinguish the old channels meandering through dead cypress trees in the center of the lake. . . .

I went fishing with Roy [Webb] one foggy October morning, and he told me stories of the early Toledo Bend days as he maneuvered his small bass boat through the stumps. Even cypress die in water that is too deep for too long. The scene was like the set of a Steven Spielberg movie: fog shrouding dead cypress that resembled disfigured monsters. Up in the branches, double-crested cormorants roosted, their necks crooked, silhouetted against the gray mist. I wouldn't have been surprised to see Vincent Price come paddling out of the fog in a floating coffin.

Roy caught a few fish in between showing me around and said I ought to come back in the winter if I wanted to see more birds.

Later near the dam, I visited with Herbert Peavy, who loves to talk and can keep up with you on any subject. He is an arrowhead collector, gold miner, rodeoer, hunter, junk collector, storeowner, and eagle lover. His dream: to get a twelve-foot rattlesnake, stuff it, and tour the USA, charging a dollar a head to see it.

Herbert and I paddled a small bateau down the Sabine River from the dam, looking for eagles. We saw two eagles and two osprey that day and put up my blind on a set of rapids called Second Rocks. I returned the next three days to sit and wait for the eagles to come feed on the fish I staked out as bait. Eagles flew by, but only vultures stopped to snack on my smorgasbord.

Leaving the blind late one afternoon, I sneaked up on some wild pigs. I crept carefully to within eight feet of six piglets and watched them root around for acorns before the big sow snorted danger and they bounded away. Wild pigs are quite common in a lot of Louisiana's forests. I have seen them in the Pearl River Swamp as well as the Atchafalaya.

They are born yard pigs but escape or are let go to forage on their own. After a few generations, though, they are just as wild as a Russian black boar, some growing tusks. They eat about anything. In some areas, they can cause real problems. They destroy plants, roots and all. Wild pigs, traveling in groups with big appetites, can destroy whole areas.

Eagles that winter at Toledo Bend are especially fond of the area below the power station, for the fish injured in the turbines are easy prey. Northern bald eagles also winter on Cross Lake and Caddo Lake as well as other north Louisiana lakes.

The winner of the Spanish Moss Award, if there was one, would be Lake Bistineau. A natural lake that has been helped by an earthen dam, it was formed by a rift in the Red River. Before man's help, the water level in Bistineau varied as much as the Atchafalaya Basin, depending on the season.

Before the Red River logjam was removed,[17] steamboats from New Orleans used to travel Loggy Bayou to Lake Bistineau, then up Bayou Dorcheat to Overton, then the Webster Parish seat and a center of commerce. . . .

Miller Lake and 15,000,000 blackbirds. What a show! Now I didn't personally count them, but the U.S. Fish and Wildlife Service estimates

17. This logjam, then called the Red River Raft, had been created by tremendous quantities of trees and other materials that had floated downriver over the years and become stuck. It stretched for 180 miles above Natchitoches and blocked all navigation until removed by Captain Henry Shreve between 1831 and 1840.

15,000,000 blackbirds at Miller Lake and statewide at least twenty-seven other roosts with over 1,000,000 birds. After visiting Miller Lake twice during the winter roosting season, I won't refute their figures.

First time. It was the Sunday before Christmas, and I was just returning from the Audubon Christmas bird count at Sabine National Wildlife Refuge. A raging cold front had passed, and the winds were chipper, chilly, downright freezing from the northwest, especially over Miller Lake as I stood on the south levee. The sky was the bluest of blues as I watched a few blackbirds in the surrounding soybean fields. About 4:30 P.M., a small group of grackles appeared, followed by a flock of redwings. Then a gang of mixed blackbirds arrived and finally, by 5:00 P.M., the fields south of Miller Lake were covered with a fantastic, undulating blanket of blackbirds. As the northwester blew in at twenty-five miles an hour, the birds, weighing fifty-seven grams, could make headway only close to the ground. Coming to a fence, they would flare up to clear it, get caught in the wind, and tumble backwards like gymnasts running to the pommel horse and doing a backflip. After two or three false starts, the birds would finally get the angle to make the fence.

Fascinated with the show for some time, I finally turned to see where these determined fliers were going. It was then that I saw the leafless cypress and tupelo trees completely covered with millions of blackbirds.

Louisiana and Arkansas have the distinction of wintering more blackbirds than any other state. Today there are many more blackbirds than there were before man cleared the forest. Just like the coyote, the blackbird moved in and multiplied when the demand for cropland created more open space.

With more birds and bigger concentrations, the birds have caused problems when roosting near towns, but here at Miller Lake, they cause nobody any trouble.

To get a closer look at the treetops full of noisy birds, I had to come back in a boat. On my second trip, the day was almost as cold, just as clear, and promised a spectacular sunset. Drifting for two hours, I photographed the lovely nakedness of the water-tupelo trees and watched the coots skiddle across the lake. The coot must run across the water flapping its stumpy wings to get enough speed to take off.

In the spring, Miller Lake hosts a rookery of anhingas, little blue herons, and twenty thousand cattle egrets among the blooms of fragrant water lilies, water hyacinth, and buttonbush. But on a cold day in December, the lake is empty save for a few coots and skittish ducks.

From my position in the middle of the lake, the scene seemed to be transformed more quickly; once again, at 4:30 P.M. that emptiness was replaced by throngs of whirling blackbirds. One minute no birds, then birds were appearing from everywhere. They had no fear whatsoever. I suppose they feel safe in numbers. Buttonbushes ten feet away harbored thousands of blackbirds. I was soon surrounded. Alfred Hitchcock missed the best place when he filmed *The Birds*.

The previous day I had only seen the birds coming from the south. Now I saw them coming in from all directions. Looking west, I steadied my boat and framed a baldcypress loaded to the hilt. It resembled an overly ornate Christmas tree with a buzz of activity in the background. I couldn't shoot fast enough. I needed more cameras, film, tripods, hands, eyes, and imagination to capture the spectacle.

A group of five thousand birds would flush and then turn in perfect formation, then turn again as if they were one and settle in another tree a few feet away. . . .

It was wonderful to watch the blackbirds perform in front of the setting sun.

As the glow faded to dark, I wished for an encore, but was rewarded instead with my first glimpse of Halley's Comet above the evening star, Jupiter.

Travel Update

Given Louisiana's abundance of marsh and swamp, Louisianians who regularly boat, fish, and hunt today are in frequent contact with those natural environments. Visitors who want to engage in those pursuits can certainly do so. There are plenty of launching sites for those who have their own boats. There are fishing guides and charterboats in various places, including Lafitte, Westwego, and other towns near New Orleans.

State wildlife management areas are open for hunting and fishing as well as other forms of recreation (licenses and permits required). The *Louisiana Almanac* contains much information on hunting and fishing regulations, license fees (which differ for residents and nonresidents of the state), locations of public boat-launching facilities, and types of facilities available at various locations. However, the Louisiana Department of Wildlife and Fisheries should be consulted for the most up-to-date information. This agency can particularly provide information on wildlife management areas, including maps. Fishing is done virtually anywhere there is water. Among the most popular places are the Atchafalaya Basin, the huge Toledo Bend Reservoir on the Texas border (which C. C. Lockwood describes), False River near Baton Rouge (an oxbow lake, once a bed of the Mississippi), and swampy Lake Bistineau and Black Lake. In addition to using rod and reel, Louisianians enjoy using fishnets and crab and crawfish traps.

Teddy Roosevelt noted the relative decline of the bear population even in his own day; not surprisingly, it has precipitously declined since. The black bear does still exist in the wild, however, and recent years have seen concerted conservation efforts on the bears' behalf.

In northeast Louisiana, La. 580 cuts right across the country in East Carroll Parish where Teddy Roosevelt did his hunting in the canebrakes. In the interim, however, this land has been drained and cleared for agriculture (much as recently as the 1970s), so the modern visitor will see virtually nothing of the wilds he described except by looking up and down the several bayous the road crosses; they are still heavily wooded and give a faded sense of the ruggedness of this region in earlier days. (With the decline of soybean prices in recent years, there have been attempts to restore some of the cleared land to a wild state, but the overall impression of the area today is still overwhelmingly agricultural.) Though it is sometimes claimed that Roosevelt's refusing to shoot a small bear on his Louisiana excursion and the resulting publicity and editorial cartoons led to the creation of the now classic teddy bear toy by an East Coast manufacturer, that incident actually took place on an earlier hunt in Mississippi. On U.S. 65 near Sondheimer, a plaque marks the community of Roosevelt, which was named in honor of the president's visit.

Hunting of Louisiana black bears (considered a distinct subspecies of black bear) was stopped in the 1980s. These bears are now protected under the Endangered Species Act; there is also the Black Bear Conservation Committee. How many remain is not known, though the population is thought to be on the rise, and there are known to be breeding populations in the Tunica Hills and Pearl River Basin in the Florida Parishes, in the Atchafalaya Basin, and in the Tensas River Basin (Teddy Roosevelt's hunting grounds). Though bears have evidently been spotted not too far outside Baton Rouge, they are elusive and seldom seen; the Audubon Zoo in New Orleans is the best venue for finding one.

Though fortunately the black bear is now protected, Louisiana offers considerable opportunity for hunters of other game and, of course, for fishing. That hunters take about 150,000 whitetail dear annually is some indication of the state's abundance of game. The state has an 8-month hunting season running from late September to April (with particular seasons set for particular game within that time frame). Duck and waterfowl hunting is a particular local passion, especially in coastal regions. Alligators can no longer be hunted simply by taking a train to the outskirts of New Orleans, as Clifton Johnson did; the alligator has been considered at times an endangered species, and there have been periodic closures of alligator hunting season. Today they are hunted commercially for their hides; in 1990, for example, nearly 26,000 were taken. Although fur trapping does continue in the marsh country, this activity has seen a marked decline in recent years.

There are numerous possibilities for those who want to effortlessly encounter marsh- and swampland. There are now innumerable commercial swamp tour operators who work out of various localities, including Henderson and Patterson (for the Atchafalaya Basin), Houma, Kraemer/Thibodaux, Slidell (for Honey Island Swamp, which has its own legendary monster, a Bigfoot-type creature), Baton Rouge, and New Orleans.

Even those who do not wish to set foot in a boat can experience Louisiana's watery environments in other ways. For those who prefer not to leave the comfort of air-conditioning, the Aquarium of the Americas in New Orleans has exhibits that simulate natural contexts (and, indeed, show visitors underwater aspects that could not normally be seen in the wild). The most dramatic is a large tank re-creating the structure of an offshore drilling rig and the marine life that clusters around rigs (the drilling platforms create underwater habitats; in fact, much of Louisiana's salt-water sports fishing takes place around the platforms). In the aquarium tank, sharks laze on the sandy bottom while a large circle of fish move slowly around and around as if in a great choreographed promenade, shimmering silver in the dim light and shadow of encrusted girders that mimic the curves of a real rig. Various exhibits deal with other Louisiana habitats and creatures, from white alligators to ancient gar to catfish.

The Louisiana State University Museum of Natural History in Baton Rouge (in Foster Hall on the main LSU campus) offers another climate-controlled venue for approaching the Louisiana outdoors. The small facility (which actually has large and important collections of Louisiana specimens, many not on display) offers cases full of local mammals, amphibians, and reptiles perpetually suspended in taxidermic glory. Well-designed dioramas provide visitors entree into various re-created environments. "Waterfowl in a Louisiana Marsh in Early Spring," for example, provides a swatch of life based on the Sabine National Wildlife Refuge. Another diorama presents the Louisiana prairies long ago (intensive agriculture has so transformed them that virtually none remain in their original state). "In a Virgin Bottomland Forest" re-creates an environment in Madison Parish (not far from where Theodore Roosevelt hunted); such virgin forests existed in the state until the 1940s. "The Border of a Canebrake," with stuffed red timber wolf and Louisiana black bear, offers a view of the American bamboo Roosevelt had to hack his way through and of the fauna that most intrigued him. A hall of Louisiana bird specimens includes "most of the birds of Louisiana that are of regular occurrence."

For those willing to venture into the open air but who prefer not to leave a city, New Orleans' Audubon Zoo offers a pleasant re-creation of Louisiana wetland environments. Walks and walkways take visitors past various animals in simulated habitats. To make the point that the Louisiana swamps and marshes also contain a unique human habitat, the exhibit includes props indicative of the cultural landscape Louisianians have built in the wetlands: a Lafitte skiff, a fiberglass pirogue, a trapper's cabin, a moss-drying shed, a swamp campboat, signs warning against anchoring and dredging (ubiquitous in wetlands areas and usually indicating sunken pipe lines), an oil-field "Christmas tree" (used for capping off an oil well), a boat yard, even a stop sign full of bullet holes (as they seem frequently to be in the Louisiana countryside). Ordinary alligators fill a lagoon, while white alligators (these mutations were first discovered in 1987 and have become the celebrities of the crocodilian world) glow luminous in a special darkened area. Here is also the visitor's best chance to see a Louisiana black bear, such as Teddy Roosevelt stalked in northeast Louisiana.

The Barataria unit of Jean Lafitte National Park, located south of New Orleans in Marrero (on Louisiana 45) and easily reachable from the city, offers another specially prepared setting for observing the Louisiana wetlands environment. This part of the park (see also Chapter 6) was designed specifically to show visitors aspects of that environment. The visitor center includes a film that provides snippets of the culture of the coast, marsh, and bayous through song and interviews as well as visual images. In addition, there are displays relating to logging, trapping, moss picking, fishing, and swamp and marsh camps at the center. The facility has several trails that actually lead the visitor into local environments via paved paths and raised wooden walkways. For example, the Bayou Coquille Trail takes the visitor from the hardwood settings found on high-ground natural levees (in this case the levee of Bayou des Familles, once a bed of the Mississippi) through the cypress and tupelo-gum swamps that appear as the land slopes down, and finally to the treeless marshes (in this case those that stretch away to Lake Salvador). One passes the sluggish waters of Bayou Coquille (which connects to the larger Bayou des Familles), moves into gorgeous palmetto thickets (such thick understories are characteristic of levee backslopes), then to the shores of a canal beyond which is the marshland. Thus one passes through stages of the local environment (and can stop on various platforms where attention is called to special features of the landscape). A trail continues along the canal, whose genesis as a plantation drainage system and development as a logging canal remind us that the Louisiana wetlands have long been a focus of human interest. So does the placement at one point of cypress sinkers, logs that sank to the bottom after having been cut during logging operations in the area (the cypress was cut during the dry season, then floated out when the water rose). So does the fact that the trail at one point follows an abandoned oil-field road, as does the conjecture that these nearby bayous were the route by which pirate Jean Lafitte moved his smuggled wares to market. The Jean Lafitte preserve in Barataria thus provides easy access to an understanding of the wetlands in a pleasant setting. Park rangers provide guided walks daily and nighttime canoe trips each month at the time of the full moon. In Baton Rouge the Parks and Recreation Commission operates a modest but highly accessible swamp habitat in the midst of modern subdivisions. This is the Bluebonnet Swamp area (access from Bluebonnet Drive), which is still under development but includes a trail winding through the small swamp and a visitor center with displays.

Charlotte Matilda Houstoun had little sense of the geography of the region she traveled through. By Barataria Island she probably meant the island surrounded by the waters of Lake Salvador and several bayous on which the town of Barataria is located today. Barataria is used to refer to a larger, contiguous area, however.

In Cameron Parish in far southwest Louisiana, Sabine National Wildlife Refuge (on Louisiana 27) provides a concrete and wooden pathway into a tiny section of its vast 142,000 acres. From the pathway visitors can not only see the watery marshes stretching into the far distance but also observe numerous birds and the substantial population of alligators at close range. Louisiana 82, the road that passes closest to the coast in the western half of the state, provides interesting views of the coastal marshes as well as such features as the chenier called Pecan Island and passes by the Rockefeller Wildlife Refuge, an important site for migratory birds. The refuge headquarters contains an exhibit relating to a Spanish galleon lost off the Louisiana coast.

Elsewhere in Louisiana a number of accessible public areas provide entree to other natural environments. The Louisiana State Arboretum is located in Chicot State Park in Evangeline Parish (on Louisiana 3042 but with an entrance separate from the park's). It was founded in 1963 and is dedicated to presenting plants native to Louisiana. Several paths traverse the property, and one dips down into a lovely, wooded ravine. Numerous plants and trees ranging from yaupon and blackjack oak to witch hazel, American holly, and American bamboo are labeled and invite enjoyment. Near Saline in Bienville Parish is Briarwood, the former property of Caroline Dorman, the noted pioneer in Louisiana horticulture, forestry, and conservation. Now run by a private foundation and a resident curator, it consists of a number of trails through beautiful woods. Entrance is by a one-lane, unpaved road off Louisiana 9, and the property is seen via walking tours conducted by the knowledgable curator (vehicle available for those unable to walk). The area is planted with native American shrubs, trees, and plants, and one may also visit Dorman's rustic home and other buildings nestled in the lovely forest setting. Dorman was particularly devoted to promoting the Louisiana iris, so the iris gardens are especially fine.

Louisiana has a number of excellent state parks and preservation areas. Because they are varied, the visitor should consult a directory (the *Louisiana Tour Guide* contains a list with facilities indicated, and *The Pelican Guide* includes short descriptions). Most parks have campsites, some have rental cabins (Chicot and Lake Fausse Point, for example), and some have designated nature trails and guided tours.

As they note in their writings in this section, Kate Chopin and Charles Tenney Jackson found Grand Isle a special place. Neither would be likely to recognize it today. Indeed, even as Chopin wrote *The Awakening*, the island's role as a summer resort for the New Orleans bourgeoisie had ended, the great hurricane of 1893 having devastated the hotels with their comfortable cottages and main buildings—in some cases structures recycled from earlier plantation complexes—and their trams that took bathers down to the beach. Nor has the truck-farming life described by Jackson survived into the present day. The railroad that was anticipated by the islanders—probably because a never-realized plan to build one was floated a few years before Jackson's visit—never arrived, but a highway did, and the island is now connected to the mainland by a bridge and La. 1, so the place is far less remote. There is a Coast Guard station, an oil refinery, a state park, and a flourishing seafood industry, but the character of the island has been most shaped by the construction of cheek-by-jowl vacation houses ("camps" in Louisiana parlance), which their owners have christened with names like "Recovery Room," "Island Queen," "Six Pack," and "Raising Cane." Which is to say that, if the precise lifestyles and environments described by Chopin and Jackson are gone, something of the spirit they recorded remains, for the island is still a place where Louisianians go for some serious relaxing—fishing and boating, swimming and partying—in a hang-loose atmosphere.

The physical worlds known by Chopin and Jackson have not been entirely lost either. Tragically, Chênière Caminada, to which Robert takes Edna in the Chopin excerpt, has been. It was leveled by the storm of 1893 with horrendous loss of life (the location of the settlement was, roughly, the area the visitor passes through before crossing the bridge to the island, and there is a cemetery on the highway where storm victims were buried). But on Grand Isle itself, toward its center and down such streets as Ludwig Lane, Post Lane, and Cemetery Lane, remnants of the past can be found. These streets lead one from La. 1 into the groves of oaks and other trees that cluster on the spine of the island (they originally may have grown from acorns dropped by Native American hunters). The lanes seem to cut through the trees like tunnels, and here are old Creole-style houses, tiny orange groves, the winding lanes that Jackson thought bound the place together. (According to local lore, the residents of Chênière Caminada had cut their oak trees, whereas those of Grand Isle had not; when the storm of 1893 hit, Grand Isle was sheltered by its trees.) Ludwig Lane is named for the terrapin farmer Jackson mentions, and the building that contained his store is still on the lane (at the corner of Medical Avenue). His terrapin farm was just beyond in the direction of the bay. Grand Isle State Park preserves a segment of the island as open land, here also one can have a sense of what the island was like in earlier days: an expanse of beach and thickets of the scrubby vegetation that grows in sandy soil. In general, the island's beach is accessible, and there is much sport fishing—from the beach, from fishing piers, and from private and charter boats. Jackson's story about the local controversy over a church and the church's destruction seems not to be remembered on the island today. Today there is a church, dating from the 1920s, but at one time residents went to Chênière Caminada for services (as do Chopin's characters). If the story is true, the events may have taken place in the mid-nineteenth century.

Fort Livingston, to whose ruins Robert means to take Edna and which Houstoun mentions, still stands on nearby Grand Terre. This island—where Jean Lafitte had his piratical headquarters and which at one time had extensive sugar plantations—continues to be reachable only by private boat. However, the fort—a moated brick structure that has lost a portion of its wall to storms—can be seen from the observation tower at Grand Isle State Park (as can the state marine research facility, which is virtually the only other regular human presence on Grand Terre). The fort was begun in the 1830s and was still unfinished (and already obsolete) by the time of the Civil War (when it was briefly occupied by Confederate forces).

Farther inland in Catahoula Parish is Jonesville, where Ben Lucian Burman begins his tour of Louisiana waters. Though this is far from the area generally thought of as bayou country, it is, as he points out, in the heart of a water culture based on nearby rivers—four of which converge near the town. Today the town may seem sleepy, the stores on its old main street abandoned or taken over by church groups, but the presence of net-making companies testifies to the continued existence of river and swamp fisheries. A visitor can have a good view of the Black River by driving over the bridge on U.S. 84, and one can get a closer view of Little River flowing into the Black from Four Rivers Park, located downtown and entered through a gate in a flood wall; on the river side of the wall a neatly painted mural depicts the town and its close connection to the rivers.

Jonesville was one of three towns—the others being Simmesport and Melville, both on the Atchafalaya River—that were market centers for the commercial freshwater fisheries in this region. These fisheries developed around the turn of the twentieth century, when demand for fish in eastern cities combined with the extension of rail transportation into this part of Louisiana and the availability of ice so that shipping fish became feasible. This was an area of abundant supplies of fish—huge quantities of buffalo fish, catfish, drum, and freshwater sturgeon were caught and shipped over a long period. Largely because of the construction of levees and improved drainage, this fishing industry had declined by the time Burman was writing; in the 1960s, it looked to be in its last days. However, the visitor to Jonesville will still see the commercial net-making establishments that are indicative of the fact that some still pursue commercial fishing here. The shantyboats have, indeed, largely disappeared, but fishermen continue to make a living. Cocodrie Swamp (which Burman renders as Cocodra) is in Concordia Parish, but today the strongest surviving fishing community is based on Larto Lake. See H. F. Gregory, "The Black River Commercial Fisheries: A Study in Cultural Geography," *Louisiana Studies*, V (1966), 3–36, for more information.

The Atchafalaya Basin, also noted by Burman, is the largest river basin swamp in America. It has been the focus of fights over its conservation (drilling activity and attempts at agriculture within its boundaries having taken a toll on its natural beauty), and the Atchafalaya River is silting up as a result of channeling and the Old River Control Structure that sends a regulated flow into the river—without which, however, the Mississippi might have changed course into the Atchafalaya. Grand Lac, for example—which Alcée Fortier remembered as a site of his childhood Civil War excursion—is a considerably smaller body of water than when he saw it. Yet the basin is still an amazing area. The traveler can get an interesting quick look at it simply by driving across Interstate 10 from Grosse Tete to Henderson. It is also possible to drive down the Basin's levee from Henderson (access from other points as well; Lake Fausse Point State Park is reached via this road). On the east side of the basin, La. 75 will take one to such towns as Bayou Sorrel (where Burman encountered the ferry sign forbidding drunken passengers) and Bayou Pigeon. (Burman's sense of geography is askew when he suggests that it is near Bayou Pigeon that the swamps begin to merge into the coastal marshes.) This road runs past numerous camps, launching places, and moorings for those who go out into the basin by boat, whether for recreational or other purposes. Near the town of Plaquemine in Iberville Parish (and not far from Baton Rouge), this may be the area Burman has in mind when he writes of the "unique colony . . . found near" this "placid town." At one time the basin had its own communities and a population that made a living from a seasonal round of such activities as crawfishing, trapping, and frogging. Most of those people have moved to the rim of the basin, though many still use the basin's natural resources, engaging in such occupations as crawfishing and alligator hunting. The offshore oil industry, which uses workers for extended periods on Gulf of Mexico rigs and then gives them an equal number of days off, has enabled people to work in high-paying jobs while still letting them pursue traditional water occupations part-time. Campboats often are still anchored out in the basin, though many today are used only for weekend recreation.

Burman speaks of the Atchafalaya as "the land of Evangeline, the bayou country of the Cajuns." In fact, Evangeline is associated primarily with Bayou Teche, well to the west of the basin's present levees, and the country of the Cajuns is a much larger area—but the Basin does have the swampy character associated in the popular imagination with Cajuns and bayous (though Cajuns have hardly been the only group prominent in the basin). The pirogues Burman notes are dugouts particularly associated with Cajuns, a boat type borrowed from Louisiana Native Americans. They are still made and used, though are seldom dugouts; their form has been replicated in a type of pirogue made out of planks. No doubt people escaping the law have hidden out in the region, but Burman exaggerates and romanticizes the case. See Malcolm Comeaux, *Atchafalaya Swamp Life* (Baton Rouge, 1972), for more information and also C. C. Lockwood, *Atchafalaya, America's Largest River Basin Swamp* (Baton Rouge, 1981).

Napoleonville, where Carolyn Ramsey started her journey, is on Bayou Lafourche (and the location of Madewood Plantation, a grand and gracious house where Emily Kimbrough stayed). Pierre Part, the center of the Spanish moss industry in the 1950s, can be reached via La. 70 from Interstate 10 or Morgan City. Until a detour was constructed in the 1990s, the highway went through parts of Pierre Part that were quintessentially south Louisiana—little houses and docks lining the bayou—and this area can still be reached by leaving the main road. A nice view of Bayou Grosbec—suggestive of the great swampy expanses of the basin Ramsey writes about—can be had from the parking lot of the parish church. Moss gathering today is only sporadic, and the industry is a moribund one, the moss being used mostly in making local crafts items, such as dolls. The moss is cured by wetting and drying it and stripping the outer casing from the inner core; it has had various local folk uses and was particularly sought after as a commercial furniture stuffing. See Fred B. Kniffen and Malcolm Comeaux, *The Spanish Moss Folk Industry of Louisiana* (Baton Rouge, 1979), for more information. How remote this area once was is reflected not only in the term "Lafourche *interior*," but also in use of the term "on the front" to refer to places closer to the outside world, especially towns along Bayou Lafourche. The floating chapel of Father Toups no longer exists; improved transportation allows most to come to the actual church.

Bayou du Large, Buffalo Bayou, and Lake Mechant, all mentioned in Christopher Hallowell's account of oystering, are located in the marsh country southwest of Houma. Louisiana 315 (partly unimproved road) is the only road that goes into this area. Oysters were eaten by Louisiana Indians, who possibly smoked and traded them before the arrival of the Europeans. Europeans began to harvest them initially near New Orleans; Slavonians began to play a key role in the industry from the 1830s, and oystering expanded, artificial introduction of oysters dating from the 1880s. They were first hand-gathered, but special tongs later came into use. Dredges are used by larger boats in deeper waters and are the predominant means for harvesting today. Oystering is an important part of the Louisiana seafood business (as well as an important aspect of the local diet), though far fewer oysters are brought in than are shrimp (the oyster harvest in the 1980s ranged from around 12 to 13 million pounds annually, whereas in recent years the shrimp fleet has brought in around 48 million pounds annually of brown shrimp alone). Oyster luggers can be seen in various locations, including Empire on the Mississippi in

Plaquemines Parish and along the bay side of Grand Isle. Today there is more oystering east of the Mississippi than west. Oystermen customarily hold leases that allow them to cultivate and harvest certain sections.

The scenic rivers and streams of Louisiana number 49. They are listed with a map in Lockwood's *Discovering Louisiana* (Baton Rouge, 1986). Canoes can be rented in a number of places (near the Jean Lafitte Barataria unit, for example). Those interested in canoeing are advised to consult Dr. and Mrs. Richard Williams, *Canoeing in Louisiana* (3rd ed.; Lafayette, 1985), which includes information (and maps) on a number of streams in most regions of the state; Dean Cryar, *Scenic Streams of Louisiana* (DeRidder, La., 1995), gives details on selected streams. John Seveanair, ed., *Trail Guide to the Delta Country* (New Orleans, 1992), is an excellent guide for hiking and cycling.

Oakley, a plantation house where Audubon worked briefly as a tutor, is part of the Audubon State Commemorative Area near St. Francisville. In itself an interesting and atypical "West Indian" house with steep wooden steps and prominent jalousies, the building also houses a display of Audubon prints, and the tiny room he is believed to have occupied is furnished as it might have looked when he was in residence. The surrounding woods offer a latter-day approximation of the wilderness he knew and loved so much. The nuclear power plant noted by Michael Harwood and Mary Durant—Riverbend— was completed. But Louisiana is still a paradise for birdwatchers, particularly in the coastal marshes, where several of the refuges are legendary. For current information, visitors should consult the Louisiana Audubon Society, although the Office of State Parks can provide some information and publishes birding checklists for some state facilities.

In addition to the various books listed in this section on Louisiana flora and fauna, Percy Viosca's *Louisiana Out-of-Doors: A Handbook and Guide* (New Orleans, 1933) remains a minor classic, out of date but still containing much interesting information.

10

Cowboy's Shangri-La: Festivals, Feasts, and Other Diversions

Many Louisianians will swear that their state has more festivals and celebrations than any other, although this assertion is based on no known comparative survey. Though this could well be true, the belief that the state holds the greatest number of festivals probably stems from a local ethic that highly values partying (local lore also insists that the students of Louisiana State University were finally disqualified from the annual *Playboy* magazine rankings of top "party schools" because they were deemed too "professional" for the competition). And it stems from the signal importance of Mardi Gras (more properly called Carnival, actually a celebratory season that lasts from Twelfth Night—January 6—to the beginning of Lent. *Mardi Gras* means *Fat Tuesday*, referring to the last day of the season, the day before Ash Wednesday). Louisianians regard Mardi Gras as the *ur*-festival, and indeed it interrelates with the very social structure of Louisiana society and influences the shape of other celebrations. (During the "streaking" craze of the 1970s, even the nude young men who took part in this ephemeral form of riot mimicked Mardi Gras parades by riding in vehicles and tossing throws—beads and trinkets—to gathering crowds of spectators.) It is hardly surprising that visitors to the Bayou State should be impressed by the local devotion to Mardi Gras and other celebrations.

Louisiana Mardi Gras, of course, is one branch of European pre-Lenten carnival, a time of extreme feasting and celebrating before the Christian penitential season that precedes Easter. In New Orleans some form of Carnival goes back to French colonial times, but the present form of the celebration— elaborate parades and lavish balls—stems from the 1850s and was shaped by *américains* from Mobile, who fashioned it after that city's New Year festivities. They sought to impose a certain order on a festival that had become increasingly disruptive and sporadic. Mardi Gras began to attract visitors at an early date—the first book devoted to Mardi Gras, published in 1882, was commissioned by a railroad hoping to stimulate tourist traffic[1]—and it still draws countless numbers of people from all over.

Mardi Gras has been called a "cowboy's Shangri-la," suggesting that the festival is a paradise for those who would engage in wildness. And there is wildness, especially on Mardi Gras itself, the culmination of festivity. Thousands fill the French Quarter's narrow streets, and there is drunkenness and sexual license (though far more of the former than the latter). Costumes appear in profusion, sometimes sensual, sometimes mocking. The annual gay beauty contest attracts great crowds to its flaunting of supposed decadence. But New Orleans Mardi Gras has its family-oriented side too—children are taken to parades to catch the trinkets tossed to the crowd and to relatives' houses near parade routes. With its stately parades and time-honored balls, it is far more decorous than many European or Latin American carnivals. (Because of Carnival's formal aspect, New Orleans' Brooks Brothers store, it is said, sells more evening attire than any other American city's—more tails than New York's and Washington's combined).[2] For the city's upper class, it structures a social season, plays a role in the debutante system, and provides a venue for asserting status—in terms of what Carnival organizations one belongs to and what events one receives an invitation to. In 1992 Mardi Gras changed its shape when several upper-class Carnival groups ceased parading

1. J. Curtis Waldo, *History of the Carnival at New Orleans from 1857 to 1882* (New Orleans, 1882).

2. At least according to an informant of S. Frederick Starr, *New Orleans Unmasked: Being a Wagwit's Sketches of a Singular American City* (New Orleans, 1985), 67.

rather than conform to a new antidiscrimination ordinance that might have altered their traditional social structures.

Lyle Saxon's account of one Mardi Gras in New Orleans is a remarkably full one (though it only hints at the social divisions that mark the festival). Presented as a young boy's journey into the Crescent City and through the Mardi Gras celebration, it certainly represents the memory not of a single trip (although it is so presented to the reader) but of a number of encounters with Carnival. It is unlikely that anyone could see so much during any one Mardi Gras Day as Saxon's young traveler did—white and black, elite and working-class manifestations. Yet Saxon's semifictitious journey is a clever device for revealing so much of the festival as it existed in his day.

New Orleans' Carnival is by far the best known Louisiana celebration, but in recent years locals and visitors alike have become more aware of the other Mardi Gras in Louisiana, which has a very different shape and purpose. This is the "running Mardi Gras" *(courrir du Mardi Gras)* of the Cajuns and Afro-French Creoles in the country west of the Mississippi. Though the celebration has a variety of local forms, it involves a band of men (and sometimes women), costumed and masked, who make a round of farmsteads and other stops, where they beg for largesse—food, money, live chickens (which can be chased and are particularly desirable)—for a later communal meal. "Les Mardi Gras," as participants are called, travel on horseback or in wagons, accompanied by a band who provide music while they dance—with each other or with householders—and sing a traditional Mardi Gras song. Also in attendance is a *capitaine,* often a prominent citizen, and his assistants, who go unmasked and provide order in the midst of the chaos the celebrants work to create (needless to say, their authority is constantly tested). The precise history of the ritual is obscure, but it probably has medieval roots (as may at least one of the Mardi Gras songs). Its symbolism is multifaceted but—in some contrast to New Orleans—suggests communal solidarity while it also serves as a rite of passage for the young men of the area. When Harnett T. Kane observed a *courrir* in the 1940s, the custom was dying out, but it went through a rebirth in the fifties and sixties and in the 1990s enjoys considerable vitality in a number of places.

Beyond Carnival, there is a proliferation of festivals and ritual occasions. Like Carnival, some have deep folk roots, like the All Saints' Day vigils in places like Lacombe, Lafitte, Pierre Part, and Cane River, where residents gather to clean and decorate family graves, then plant candles on them at dusk and await the visit of the parish priest bathed in the sublime, soft light. Or like the Christmas Eve lighting of the bonfires on the Mississippi levees between New Orleans and Baton Rouge, which Hope J. Norman writes about in this section. This ceremony "to light Papa Noel" seems to go back to the nineteenth century and is quite amazing to see—miles and miles of orchestrated flames piercing the murky winter night. Or like the blessing of the Shrimp Fleet in places like Chauvin, where the procession of decorated boats—though it dates back only to the 1930s—is as colorful a spectacle as can be seen in the United States.

Other festivals involve planned presentations of Louisiana's traditions. The extremely popular New Orleans Jazz and Heritage Festival is the best known of these, but there are also (to name a few) the Louisiana Folklife Festival, which periodically changes sites; the Zydeco Festival in Plaisance, which features that Afro-French music; the Festivals Acadiens in Lafayette, which focus on Cajun music and cuisine; and the Natchitoches Folk Festival, which concentrates on the cultures of north and central Louisiana.

Individual localities also have their festivals, often created and supported by the local civic establishment and celebrating local products or ways of life. Thus there are the Yambilee of Opelousas (center of the Louisiana yam industry), the Ville Platte Cotton Festival (which includes jousting, the medieval sport revived in the antebellum South), the Crawfish Festival of Breaux Bridge, the Frog Festival in Rayne (whose name is derived from the French for *frog*), the Crowley Rice Festival (which noted photographer Russell Lee documented in 1938), the Audubon Pilgrimage in St. Francisville, and the Shrimp and Petroleum Festival in Morgan City (which proves that Louisianians can create a party out of seemingly disparate or even conflicting sources).

Of course there are other kinds of Louisiana celebrations and diversions. Harnett T. Kane wrote of one such, a traditional wedding on the prairies—replete with special paper flowers, horse-drawn carriages, and lively dancing.[3] That event's gaiety and innocence contrast with the diversion Ernst von Hesse-Wartegg discovered in New Orleans: cockfighting. Though modern readers may find such a happening distasteful (as did Mark Twain, who walked out of the one he found in New Orleans), this "sport" has not only a long but a continuing history in Louisiana, rooted in a multi-ethnic past and the rough ways of the southern frontier.

3. Harnett T. Kane, *The Bayous of Louisiana* (New York, 1944), 291–304.

Celebrations and festivals go hand-in-hand with feasting, and some Louisiana festivals are virtually synonymous with food, such as the Crawfish Festival. But feasting in Louisiana is also a celebration in its own right. Food is taken very seriously, and the state's people are extremely devoted to their cuisines, which developed historically as unique ones in America (a point acknowledged by the important Time-Life cookbook series; generally there was a volume for each country covered, but the editors divided the United States into two volumes: one for Louisiana, one for the rest of the nation). Food has been an important topic in accounts of Louisiana travel. Such writers as Julian Street and John Martin Hammond have told of their visits to fabled New Orleans restaurants (which Truman Capote claims are "the best in America"). Riding out of the Mississippi wilderness into the Felicianas in 1809, Fortescue Cuming found a gumbo nearly as quickly as he did a place to spend the night. The Tabasco Sauce factory on Avery Island (and the amazing family who produce the spicy hot concoction) has attracted such writers as the *New Yorker's* John McNulty.[4] It is central to Richard Schweid's wonderful account of his sojourn in South Louisiana and what he found there, *Hot Pepper* (excerpted earlier in this volume). Here we include a piece by Calvin Trillin, who has made several excursions to Louisiana in search of food. In this essay he tells about his quest to uncover the history of a famous recipe for roast duck and the restaurant that created it. In doing so he reveals something of the intense interest Louisiana takes in the gustatory.

4. Julian Street, *American Adventures: A Second Trip "Abroad at Home"* (New York, 1917), 663–67; John Martin Hammond, *Winter Journeys in the South: Pen and Camera Impressions of Men, Manners, Women, and Things All the Way from the Blue Gulf and New Orleans through Fashionable Florida to the Pines of Virginia* (Philadelphia, 1916), 122; Truman Capote, "New Orleans," in *A Capote Reader* (New York, 1987), 288; Fortescue Cuming, *Sketches of a Tour to the Western Country, through the States of Ohio and Kentucky; A Voyage Down the Ohio and Mississippi Rivers, and a Trip through the Mississippi Territory, and Part of West Florida* (Pittsburgh, 1810), 311; John McNulty, "Our Footloose Correspondents: A Dash of Tabasco," *New Yorker,* June 13, 1953, pp. 31–34, 36–40, 43–50, 51.

A Journey Through Mardi Gras

LYLE SAXON

> Lyle Saxon (1891–1946) wrote this travel reminis-
> cence while living in New York; though presented as a
> single, actual journey, it is certainly a composite of
> childhood and adult recollections and must be in part
> a fiction; the Zulu Carnival organization Saxon de-
> scribes, for example, did not exist when the author was
> a boy. Yet even if the piece—only a portion of which is
> reprinted here—gives us more than any Carnival spec-
> tator would be likely to see in any one day, it is a mar-
> velous trip through the Mardi Gras of Saxon's day.
> Young Lyle's grandfather has brought him to New Or-
> leans on Mardi Gras morning, and Robert, a black ser-
> vant of family friends, has been put in charge of show-
> ing the boy around. They have donned matching devil
> costumes, which obscure their respective racial identi-
> ties, and set out to see the parades. For more informa-
> tion on Saxon, see Chapter 1.

We threaded our way along, square after square, all
packed with masqueraders and those who had come to see. I wished to linger,
but Robert was firm. We would have to hurry, he told me, if we wished to be
in time for the arrival of the Zulu King.[5]

From *Fabulous New Orleans*, by Lyle Saxon. Copyright © 1928 by The Century Co., ©
1950 by Robert L. Crager & Co., © 1988 by Pelican Publishing Co. Used by permission of the
publisher, Pelican Publishing Company, Inc.

---

5. Mardi Gras organizations traditionally choose kings and queens to preside over the festivities of the season. The Zulu king is that of the principal African American parading organization.

Now the Zulu King meant no more to me than the fourth dimension, but he sounded exciting, so I demurred no longer but hurried after the devil who bounded before me. We dodged through groups of maskers, we ducked under ropes, and finally after traversing several squares, turned from Canal Street into another thoroughfare where a group of negro girls were dancing under an arcade while two negro men picked on banjos. I saw no white maskers here, but there were many negroes in costume who seemed to be holding a Mardi Gras all their own. And here I found that the crowd was moving in another direction, away from Canal Street. We went along the street with them, square after square. Past pawnshops with the three golden balls hanging outside, past cafes, where negroes sat on stools eating while other negroes served them; past saloons which smelled of stale beer and wet sawdust and from which came shouts and curses. At last we reached an open space with a large red railroad station at one side, and with a canal—or what appeared to be the end of a ship canal—directly before us. The banks of the waterway were lined with negroes, pushing and shoving about in order to gain some point of vantage. Some of them were in costume but most of them were in their everyday clothes. They were packed so tightly together that it was almost impossible to force a way between them.

Just as we found ourselves wedged into the thickest part of the crowd there came a chorus of shouts:

"Yon' he is!"

"Yon' he come!"

"Gawd a-mighty!"

"Wha' he is?"

"Da' he!"

We pushed and shoved with the rest, and in a moment actually succeeded in making our way to the water's edge, and here Robert lifted me bodily and seated the little devil on the big devil's shoulder, where I sat, legs around his neck, looking with all my eyes.

The sun shone bright on the strip of water, and there in the distance I could see a patch of purple and red which was repeated in the water below. It was the royal barge of the Zulu King approaching.[6]

6. Traditionally the Zulu king began his public appearance on Mardi Gras day by arriving by boat through the New Basin Canal. This was an imitation/parody of the arrival of white Rex, the supposed king of the entire New Orleans Carnival, who approaches the city by boat on the Mississippi.

Spectators awaiting a Mardi Gras parade, by A. G. Warren

From Edward King, "The Great South: Old and New Louisiana," *Scribner's Monthly,* November, 1873, reproduction courtesy Special Collections, LSU Libraries

Now there are a great many people who have been born in New Orleans and who have lived there all their lives, but who have never seen the arrival of the Zulu King; and I feel sorry for them, for surely there is no more characteristic sight to be seen in the South. This custom has continued for many years—a sort of burlesque of the grander Mardi Gras of the white people, and it provides the note of humor which is lacking in the great parades.

The Zulu King and his faithful henchmen were approaching slowly, the barge propelled by a tiny puffing motor-boat. The barge itself looked as if it had been rather hurriedly decorated with whatever scraps happened to be at hand. The canopy over the throne was made of sacking, and was supported by rough poles. A bunch of paper flowers adorned its top, and beneath it, in a tattered Morris chair, the king sat. He represented a savage chieftain, but whether from modesty or from fear of cold, the Zulu King wore, instead of his own black skin, a suit of black knitted underwear. There were bunches of dried grass at throat, ankles, and wrists, and a sort of grass skirt such as hula-hula dancers wear, and he wore a fuzzy black wig surmounted by a tin crown. In his hand he carried a scepter—a broomstick—upon which was mounted a stuffed white rooster. There were some tattered artificial palm-trees at the four corners of the royal barge, and a strip of red cloth was draped from palm to palm. Four henchmen, dressed almost exactly like the king—save that they wore no crowns—were capering about beside him. Some red and purple flags were stuck about here and there. And as the barge approached us, the king opened a bottle of beer and drank a toast from the bottle; while negro men and women on the bank produced flasks from their pockets and drank their own.

When they were quite near us, I saw that the king and his followers had improved upon Nature's handiwork by blackening their faces and by putting stripes of red and green paint liberally upon their cheeks and upon their black union suits. These things I noticed as the barge was tying up at the end of the canal quite near me and while flasks on shore were passing from hand to hand.

A delegation of negro men wearing evening clothes and having red and purple scarves draped from shoulder to waist, waited upon the bank, and they kept calling out greetings to His Majesty:

"Wha' de Queen?"

"Ain't yo' brought us no Queen?"

"Ain't yo' lonesome all by yo'seff?"

And to these gibes, the king answered grandly, "Ef I has a Queen she goin' tuh be a man—'cause I'm through wid wimmen!"

This was considered magnificently humorous, for a cry of joy went up from those who lined the bank.

And now came the disembarking. With difficulty the negroes in evening dress opened a way through the crowd and a wagon drawn by mules was brought close to the barge. The wagon was a large, almost square vehicle without sides; only a flat floor over the wheels. At the moment it was bare. But not for long. The king rose, picked up his Morris chair and climbed aboard. The henchmen followed, each bearing a potted palm. The bunting was stripped from the barge and was nailed into place around the edge of the wagon and the flags and flowers were distributed about. And, with the king and his four followers aboard, it moved along and another wagon took its place.

The second vehicle was much like the first, except that it had a wood-burning cooking stove in the center—a stove in which a fire burned and from the short stovepipe came a cloud of black smoke. An old negro woman stood by the stove, frying fish, and from time to time she would remove a steaming morsel from the pan and pop it into some open mouth that was eagerly upheld to receive it. The negroes crowded around the vehicle, screaming out in delight. Two negro men were seated in chairs near the stove—also aboard the wagon—cleaning fish. And there was a basketful of catfish beside them. Aside from a garland of flowers which adorned the stovepipe, the wagon was undecorated.

The men who had been waiting on the bank now mounted their steeds—mules—and sat there, making a brave show with their white shirtfronts and red and purple scarves. Two of them carried stuffed white roosters on their shoulders. Like the king's, their faces were blackened and painted with red and green stripes. And as the king's chariot moved off from the side of the canal, these outriders distributed themselves around it—a guard of honor.

Next came the fish-frying wagon, and this was followed by a motley collection of horse-drawn carriages—evidently the odds and ends from some livery stable. They were for the greater part open carriages or victorias, and they were decorated somewhat sketchily with flags and bunting. In these carriages rode various leaders of negro society; heads of lodges and fraternal organizations, wearing high silk hats; heads of negro unions, wearing badges and colored ribbons. A group of marching men followed the carriages—some in costume, some merely dressed in their best—but all highly pleased with the Zulu King and his crew.

Slowly the procession went down Rampart Street—that street which Robert and I had just traversed—and from every store, lunch-counter, billiard hall, and saloon, a crowd came out to see.

Negro women in the crowd called out invitations to the king, shaking their hips and rolling their eyes, and to these love-cries he responded with answers more amorous than delicate, while black girls exclaimed loudly to each other—and to any one else who cared to listen—"Oh, ain't he some man!" . . .

It was nearly noon before we reached Canal Street again where the great street pageants were to take place. . . .

If the street had seemed mildly insane before, it was bedlam now. A happy roar hung over the heads of the crowd, a hum of voices, punctuated with sharp cries, whistles, cat-calls. And everywhere the tinkling of tiny bells—an undercurrent of sound infinitely strange. . . .

There was a burst of music near us and a policeman rode by on horseback, clearing a narrow path through the crowd. Robert and I, crushed back against the curb, were almost under the feet of the marching men who came swinging by. It was one of the so-called "little parades" which amuse the crowds before the arrival of Rex, King of the Carnival. On a purple and gilt banner I could read the name of the organization: "The Jefferson City Buzzards"! And with a blare of cornets, they were upon us. First came twelve fat men dressed as little girls, all in white. Their huge stomachs were draped with the widest of baby-blue sashes, and they wore pale blue socks which ended half-way up their fat and hairy legs. All of them wore long flaxen curls surmounted with baby caps trimmed with blue rosettes. Nearly all of them were smoking cigars. They bowed right and left as they marched along and smiled widely, gold teeth glittering in the sunlight. Their "queen" was an unusually fat man who bulged out of a baby carriage, sucking a large stick of red and white striped candy. Another man—this one with a big mustache—was blacked up to represent a negro mammy, and pushed the carriage, perspiring copiously. The babies were followed by a group of men in white linen suits, each carrying an American flag.

They strutted with the music and kept bowing and throwing kisses to the spectators. A negro band brought up the rear—a band which played the rowdiest and bawdiest jazz that I had ever heard.

The Jefferson City Buzzards had hardly passed before another marching club followed it. This time the marchers were in Oriental costumes—men of the desert and their houris. They carried a banner bearing the name of their organization. A few minutes later another club came by, the men dressed as negro minstrels.

Suddenly I became conscious of a swelling whisper which ran through the crowd. Necks were craned. Maskers stopped their antics and stood on tiptoe, all looking in the same direction. Robert, with his hand on my shoulder, tip-toed too, shading his devil mask with white gloved hand; and then he turned to me and said—his voice muffled behind his mask—"It's de parade!" And then, almost upon us, I saw twelve blue-coated policemen on horseback rid-ing abreast. They came charging down upon the crowd and we moved back before them, falling over each other in our haste.

If the street had seemed tight-packed before, it was even worse now. Elbows came in contact with my forehead, feet smashed down upon mine; I was buffeted about, almost thrown down as the crowd became more congested around me. But Robert dragged me back to him with an effort, and in another moment I found myself seated with my legs around his neck, high over the heads of the others. And as I emerged from that undercurrent which had seemed to drag me down, I had the feeling of a swimmer rising upon the crest of a wave. And there before me, stretched out as far as I could see, was a mass of maskers, and beyond them a series of glittering mountains were moving to-ward me. . . . The Carnival King was coming.[7]

First came the mounted policemen who cleared the way, and behind them were masked courtiers riding black horses; they wore gold plumes on their hats, and their purple velvet cloaks trailed out behind them over the flanks of the horses; they wore doublet and hose, and they carried gleaming swords in their hands. There were perhaps twelve of these outriders, gaily dressed except for the fact that they wore black masks which gave a sinister effect. Behind them came a brass band tooting lustily. Two negroes carried between them a large placard emblazoned with one word, "Rex."

7. Rex, the "Carnival King," made his first appearence in 1872. Traditionally he made var-ious proclamations indicative of his taking the city under his rule on Mardi Gras day. Though selected and sponsored by a particular Carnival organization, he is generally viewed as the sym-bolic ruler of Carnival as a whole, despite the existence of various other kings chosen by other organizations.

And now the parade was actually upon us. The first float in the procession seemed to me the most wonderful thing that I had ever seen. It was a mass of blue sky and white clouds surmounted by a glittering rainbow, and under the rainbow's bridge were masked figures in fluttering silk, men and women who held uplifted golden goblets. It was the title car and upon its side was written the subject of the parade—a subject which I have wholly forgotten to-day, but which dealt with some phase of Greek mythology. The glittering float towered as high as the balconies which over-hung the street from the second stories of the houses, and as this gay-colored mountain came gliding past me I was impressed with the fact that the car was swaying and that it seemed fragile for all its monumental size. It was almost as though the whole were on springs. The car was drawn by eight horses covered in white and with cowls over their heads.

A blaring band followed the title car, then more outriders, dressed this time in green and gold and wearing purple masks; and behind them came a car which was even larger than the first. It was like a gigantic frosted wedding cake and at the top on a golden throne was seated Rex, King of the Carnival. Such a perfect king he was, with his fat legs encased in white silk tights, a round fat stomach under shimmering satin, long golden hair and a magnificent curled yellow beard! His face was covered with a simpering wax mask, benign and jovial. On his head he wore the very grandest crown I had ever seen, all gold and jewels which sparkled in the sun; and he carried a diamond scepter in his hand which he waved good-naturedly at the cheering crowd. Behind him a gold-embroidered robe swept down behind the throne, cascaded over the sloping back of the float and trailed almost to the ground, its golden fringe shaking with the movement of the car. There was gauze and tinsel everywhere and thousands of spangles glittered in the sun. At the feet of the monarch two blonde pages stood, little boys no larger than I, with long golden curls and white silk tights, which were rather wrinkly at the knees. How I envied them!

Robert and I were both screaming with delight, and I clapped my hands. And then a preposterous thing happened—a magnificent thing. The blonde monarch, so high over my head and yet so near me, leaned out and with his scepter pointed directly to me as I sat perched upon the shoulder of the big red devil. He said something to one of the pages, something which I could not hear, and the page with a bored smile tossed a string of green beads to me. It swirled through the air over the heads of the people between us and dropped almost into my outstretched hands; but my clumsy fingers missed and it fell to the ground. Immediately there was a scramble. Robert stooped, I fell from his shoulders, and I found myself lying on the pavement as though swept under a stampede of cattle. Hands and feet were all around me, but somehow in the struggle I managed to retrieve those beads, and triumphant I scrambled up again and Robert put me back on his shoulder.

This had taken only a moment, but during that time the king's car had moved on and another car was in its place. I could see glittering serpents— monstrous golden pythons which twined around white columns, and there were nymphs with green hair who held up bunches of great purple grapes as large as oranges and which glimmered in the sunshine with their iridescent coloring. The float with the serpents and grapes seemed monstrously large to me, even larger than those two which had come before, and it came to a swaying halt directly before us. I had a good opportunity to examine the serpents at close range and was somewhat relieved to find that they did not move but remained twined about the fluted columns. It was then that Robert pinched my leg to attract my attention. He was pointing toward the Carnival King, whose throne was now a short distance from us. The King's back was turned toward me now, but I could see that he was greeting some one upon a balcony opposite. I had not noticed this balcony before, oddly enough, but now as I looked I was conscious of tier after tier of seats rising from the second to the third floor of the building, the seats filled with men and women, not maskers but ordinary mortals dressed in their best. At the moment their hands were stretched out in greeting, and they were smiling. There in the first row of seats on the balcony was a beautiful girl wearing a big floppy pink hat. She stood with both hands outstretched toward Rex as he sat before her on his throne. They were separated by a distance of perhaps twenty feet, but his high throne was almost level with her, and both of them were far above the heads of the crowd in the street below. They were exchanging greetings. And then from somewhere came a man with a step-ladder which was set up in the street. Up the ladder a man ran nimbly, bearing a tray with a white napkin over it. He presented the tray to the King. Suddenly a bottle was opened with a loud pop, and I saw champagne poured out into a thin wine glass, champagne which spilled over the edge of the goblet and ran down into the street below. Rex, King of the Carnival, was toasting his queen. Years afterward, I heard the story of this, why it was done and how old the custom was, but then the small

Assembling Mardi Gras floats

From George A. Sala, *America Revisited* (London, 1883)

boy who looked upon it saw only another fantastic happening in that mad dream of Mardi Gras.[8]

The ceremony was soon over, the step-ladder was whisked away again and Rex on his swaying throne was drawn slowly down the street. I could hear the cheers which greeted him as they grew fainter in the distance, drowned in the blare of bands. One by one the gorgeously decorated floats passed before us, each telling some mythological story. There were satyrs, fawns, mermaids, centaurs, the like of which I had never seen before. Here the whole of fairy-land had become a reality before my eyes. I counted the glittering cars as they passed. There were twenty in all and almost as many bands of music. And always that strange, unreal quality, that gaudy, blatant thing which I could not define then and which I cannot define now, except that it gave to me the feeling of seeing a thousand circuses rolled into one.

By the time the last car in the parade had passed the spot in the street where Robert and I were standing, the procession had turned at some distant corner and was returning on the opposite side of Canal Street, and without moving from our position we were able to see the parade again. This time, looking with more scrutinizing eye, I noticed things which had escaped me before—that the beautiful masked women who rode upon the floats were strangely masculine in body, and that the figures of papier-mâché which had seemed so beautiful at first were not quite as realistic as I had imagined. However, I did not look upon the parade with a critical eye, but accepted it for what it was, a gay dream.

The moment that the last car had passed in the street, the crowd began to surge about again. Robert, heaving a sigh of relief, let me slide down his body to the ground, and we tried to make our way into a store where cold drinks were for sale; but every one in the crowd seemed to have the same idea, and we found it impossible to force our way inside. Accordingly we drank pink lemonade which a street vendor was dispensing at the edge of the sidewalk. It tasted only faintly of lemon and sugar, but it was cold and pink and our thirst made us grateful. . . .

[Hours later] twilight was deepening and the narrow street was filled with a moving crowd. Every one was going in the same direction, toward Canal

8. This toast took place on Canal Street at the exclusive Boston Club, where Rex's queen traditionally awaited his coming. Whereas traditional Carnival kings are prominent business and professional men, the queens are young debutantes.

Street. We were forced to fall into step and we went forward slowly. Although many wore costume, there were no false faces in evidence now—for with the first twilight the masks must be laid aside by order of the police. Robert gave me a long and rambling explanation for this in which the words "bad people" occurred over and over. I gathered that the masks had been used to shield criminals in the old days, and that the rule for unmasking with the first twilight was strictly necessary.

Canal Street presented a gay picture. There were strings of electric lights looped from corner to corner, and arches of varicolored electric bulbs crossed the streets at close intervals—yellow, green, and purple lights. From the balconies and from the tops of buildings came long streamers of yellow, green, and purple bunting, doubly noticeable now by the artificial light. Flags fluttered and the bunting billowed in the evening breeze from the river. Waves of pleasant coolness came to our grateful faces.

There were but few negroes to be seen; they had retired to their own quarter in Rampart Street, and those masqueraders who were walking about now were white men, women, and children. They seemed tired but happy, and bits of song were heard about the hum of the crowd—and everywhere the jingling of little bells, that same undercurrent of sound that had pleased me so much earlier in the day.

The balconies above the streets were filled with people and I was conscious that every one was getting into a favorable place to witness the pageant that was to come. Having seen a procession by daylight I knew—or thought I knew—what a night parade was like.

I thought that we would remain on Canal Street as we had done that morning, but Robert assured me that he knew a vantage point that was far superior, and accordingly we went up St. Charles Street for eight or more squares. All along the street men and women lined the sidewalks. Many of them had brought camp-stools or cushions and were sitting along the curb; others spread out newspapers and sat on them. In front of the stores the shopkeepers' families had gathered and were perched on boxes or tables in order that they could see above the heads of those on the sidewalk.[9] In order to walk, we had to leave the sidewalk and move along the middle of the street. There was no

9. Mardi Gras parade goers have often brought with them such objects as chairs for sitting and boxes to stand on so as to be better placed to see parades and to catch the throws tossed to the crowd. Today stepladders, often with specially made seats for children, are the most commonly seen aid.

traffic other than the moving crowd; for this was the route of the parade and it had been cleared for the coming of Comus.[10]

At last we reached Lee Circle—an open circular place where St. Charles Street widens out and becomes St. Charles Avenue, and where Howard Avenue crosses. Here the ground has been built up into a sort of round mountain, and at the top of this grass-grown mound there rises a huge fluted column of stone which in turn supports a bronze statue, of Robert E. Lee. At the base of the column is a pyramid of stone, like gigantic steps rising one above the other, each step more than a yard high. By scrambling up this giants' staircase, we reached the summit; and there, seated on the edge of the topmost step, we sat leaning back against the stone column which disappeared into the darkness above our heads. We were just in time to secure seats, for many others were there already, and within five minutes after our arrival every available inch was filled. The crowd continued to arrive and in a few minutes more the grassy slope was covered. And still they came, crowding the sidewalks until there was no more room at all.

From our perch we could see far up the avenue to where the twinkling street lights diminished in the distance. And as I grew accustomed to this god-like point of view, I saw that crowds lined both sides of the avenue as far as eye could see. And the crowd was humming like a swarm of bees. There was the feeling that comes into a theater as the lights are lowered and the footlights flash up, a feeling of joyous expectancy which is also a promise. . . .

There came a whisper which turned into a cry. The parade was coming. I looked with all my eyes up the avenue but at first could see nothing but the flickering rows of lights as they converged far away, but then, after a moment, I was conscious of a red glare in the sky—almost on the horizon it seemed, an aura which seemed to rise from the ground, or to emanate from the air itself. It was something apart from life as I knew it. It was magic itself.

As I looked, smaller lights became visible in the red glare, little twinkling lights of yellow and blue and green, bright pinpoints of flame. Then, as the endless stream of lights moved nearer I was conscious of great wreaths of black smoke which swirled upward into the darkness, smoke which held and reflected the flaring lights and which surrounded this glimmering far-off pag-

10. The Mystick Krewe of Comus is the oldest Carnival organization, its parade the original Mardi Gras parade, its king thought by many to outrank Rex himself. The Comus parade, which ceased in 1992, was the culmination of the Mardi Gras parades, moving after dark on Tuesday and creating a striking impression through lighted floats and torch bearers.

eant with a rim of fire. I heard music . . . first just a broken bar, then another, finally a melody, faint and sweet.

We were high above the parade, and it was coming directly toward us, down the avenue. Little by little objects became visible, dark shapes against the flare—men on horseback clearing the route. Then below each glowing point of flame I could discern a red figure—men holding the torches. And always the bobbing of these lights and their swirling smoke rising toward the dim stars. In the center of each of these circles of light, masses of pale color became visible—the floats, pale in the night, yet brilliant too. And they seemed to glide noiselessly and effortlessly forward; relentless, like a gigantic dragon bearing down upon the crowd.

Slowly details became clear—men on black horses, courtiers with plumed hats and black masks. The horses reared and pranced as though trying to unseat their riders. Music blared out, muffled as though various bands were trying to outdo each other, which indeed was true. And from far off I could hear cheering and rippling applause as those along the way greeted Comus, the last and most dearly loved of all the kings of Mardi Gras.

Now the torches were nearer and I could see that prancing negroes were holding the flambeaux. The torches flared, and the red-robed negroes strutted in time with the music. Possibly thirty torches were ranged around each float in the parade. And in addition there were taller, more brilliant flares of stage fire—red and green and white. These lights were reflected upon the decorated cars—cars which rose high in the air and which were shaped irregularly, mountains moving towards us, undulating as they came.

The night parade is a dream festival. Even now, twenty-five years later, I cannot look upon one of them unmoved; but to the small boy they were more real than reality.

First came the title car, shimmering with tinsel and fluttering with gauzy streamers; the torches burned yellow and blue, and the dancing lights were reflected as though from a thousand tiny mirrors. In black letters on gold I read that Comus's whim this year was "Legends of the Golden Age." Following the title car came Comus himself, riding on his swaying, glimmering throne of white and gold, and to me the king seemed suspended in the air upon his golden chair, suspended there, framed in fire. His crown and jewels sparkled with points of light. He was a blonde and jovial monarch who gestured right and left with his scepter, gestured slowly and with a superb geniality. The sheen of golden satin vied with the glistening of burnished metal. Great golden tassels quivered. And this shimmering, glittering, swaying mass passed slowly by, drawn by eight horses—horses which seemed like mysterious, unknown animals, covered with white—their eyes showing black through eyelets in the cloth. Negro men led the horses, negroes in red robes and with cowls over their heads. And everywhere the prancing negro torchbearers, and the blaring of bands. The undulation, the bobbing lights, the quivering masses of changing color, the unending rhythm, seemed to stir a similar quivering in me.

We were far enough away and high enough above the parade to feel the illusion. This was no man-made thing that came out of the darkness; it was magic.

One by one the floats passed by: Ulysses setting sail in a golden boat while his bare-armed followers pulled at long shining oars; Circe and the companions of Ulysses—great, terrible swine—built no doubt of papier-mâché, which groveled before a beautiful enchantress; Jason and the golden fleece. . . . It seemed as though all the beauty and all the riches of the world had been spilt out to make a small boy's paradise.

Many of the subjects have gone forever from my mind, but I remember one float upon which a titanic ogre stretched a threatening hand over a group of masked men who seemed unafraid, or unaware of their doom, and who danced and blew kisses to the crowd there in the shadow of those terrible clutching fingers. On another float a glittering spider trembled horribly—a spider which seemed as large as an elephant and so realistic that at any moment I expected to hear the screams of those gay maskers who had fallen into its clutches.

One after another the cars went swaying past, each one preceded by a band, and each one framed in a fiery ring of bobbing flambeaux. As the procession reached the mound upon which we sat, it turned, circled the base of the statue and continued behind us down St. Charles Street. As the last car passed, we turned to follow it with our eyes—and there, strung out along the street, we saw the gorgeous spectacle again, the backs of the floats this time—almost equally beautiful, and exhibiting another side, decorated, and sometimes filled with maskers who danced upon the swaying vehicle.

The parade moved so very slowly and stopped at such frequent intervals that Robert and I were able to keep abreast of it, and when we reached Canal Street, where the procession went first up one side of the wide street then down the other side, we were able to see it all again. And again I saw the rainbows, the bolts of lightning, the witches, the ogres, the fairies in their fluttering robes of brilliant color. The maskers on the floats were throwing trinkets to the crowd in the street—beads, tiny bags of sweetmeats, metal ornaments. And upon coming close to one car, I saw that each masker was provided with a silken bag which matched his costume—and it was from these bags that the bagatelles were produced and flung toward the outstretched hands below.

At last the parade left Canal Street and entered Bourbon Street, a narrow thoroughfare which led toward the French Opera House. So narrow was the street that the great decorated cars covered it from sidewalk to sidewalk, and the maskers who rode high on top of the cars were almost level with the balconies of wrought iron which overhung the street. Men and women on those balconies were almost able to touch those masqueraders on the floats. It was here that I realized the hugeness of these moving cars—for filling the street as they did, and lumbering over the rough pavement, the great glittering masses seemed as incredible as though the very houses were gliding past.

Here the throng upon the sidewalk was massed so tightly that it was impossible to make progress through it, and Robert and I stood jammed back into a doorway while the pageant rumbled past us. And as the last car went by the crowd began to move with the parade—moving solidly—and we were borne along willy-nilly, to the very door of the French Opera House. At the entrance to this beautiful old building each car stopped for a moment and the maskers were helped down—and the empty float continued down the street, while the silk-clad masqueraders climbed the steps and disappeared into the wide doors. In Toulouse Street at the side of the Opera House there was a long line of carriages, and gorgeously dressed ladies and gentlemen were descending from them and entering a side door. The number seemed endless. Gems flashed, there was the scent of perfume in the air. Horses plunged and their shoes struck fire from the cobblestones. And tight-packed everywhere stood people, watching the world of society as it went, laughing, to the Comus Ball.

Looking down the street, I saw the great floats lose their fairy-like quality—for as they passed beyond the door of the Opera House the negroes extinguished their torches, and with the light out, the floats became only dead things—their life and beauty gone. One after another they disappeared into the darkness, gone as utterly as a snuffed-out flame.

Country Mardi Gras

HARNETT T. KANE

Harnett Kane, a New Orleans–born journalist, was a prolific popular writer on Louisiana, the South, and the Civil War. He was apparently a frequent visitor to Acadiana. Here he writes of the "running" Mardi Gras of the country, so different from the urban New Orleans celebration described by Saxon. Country Mardi Gras must have existed in Louisiana from early times, but it was little noted by either local writers or visiting ones until recent years. The celebration was in a period of decline when Kane saw it, but has since come back into popularity.

The world has heard much of the New Orleans Mardi Gras, with its tall floats of papier-mâché, kings riding high above the populace, and costume balls with tableaux. For generations the prairies have had their rural version, less formalized, less costly, and in one instance, as I know, at least as much fun.

"Courir Mardi Gras" (running Mardi Gras) is the name of the observance. This Fat Tuesday is almost a race, and a day-long one. A thing primarily for men and horses, it consists of impromptu hell-raising that has no place for the girls; no queens on balconies, no costume ball with court of honor, although there is a happy fais-do-do in the evening.

I had talked over the subject with some of the old-timers and others who knew only the Mardi Gras of their later day. All said that the custom, unfortunately, was slipping away. Once it had started early and gone on for days; now it was reduced to a single day. Some of the localities that had continued it were giving it up, one by one. Be that as it may, a country friend remembered me a

Horsemen from the Cajun *courrir du Mardi Gras,* by Joe Deffes

Reproduced with permission from Christopher Hallowell, *People of the Bayou: Cajun Life in Lost America* (New York, 1979)

week in advance, and I arrived in his section for the occasion of man's final fling before the forty days of Lent.

Down the road that morning came the runners on their mounts, ten to fifteen of them, masked and in clown's attire, in stripes and dots and other raffish garments of reds and yellows. One fat man had donned two potato sacks, which did not quite encompass his poundage; another wore what was clearly a borrowed, well-pinned set of curtains. Several sported about in women's clothes, with toy parasols and dolls; and these had donned wigs, bustles, stuffed brassieres, and other added attractions. All were "acting the macaque" (monkey). They stopped at a store, waltzed together, sang, and asked for contributions from the grocer for their coming ball. On the road, when they met a lone man or woman, he or she was the object of fulsome attention. One of the clowns requested the honor of the dance. The lady might decline, but she was danced with whether she liked it or not. If the man rejected the offer of a waltz with one of those in female attire, he was paddled, or lost his pants for a few moments.

With the roving band went a fiddler, blowers of cowhorns, and wielders of other noise-making devices. As they moved about, their calls drew families from their houses to the road. One man was in charge of the runners, and he went forward in each case to inquire if the household were willing to receive them. The answer was almost always "Oui," and the Mardi Gras men dismounted and surrounded the family and the farm. They danced about the yard, sang, frightened some children, delighted others, and guyed the adolescents. "Eh there, Ti' Jean, when you going' ask that lil' brown-hair girl to marry you?" At the house of the girl, one of the maskers would inform her that Ti' Jean had announced himself as bored of waiting for her, and was looking for a blonde.

Soon, as everybody expected, the party approached the important matter of "the request." A traditional song, a series of doggerels that has been used for generations, was offered. In it the Mardi Gras was asked whence he came. Why, he came from Angleterre (England), and in midwinter. He went on to tell of his prowess as a drinker, of his various feats; and the singers declared themselves "good gentlemen" and made a formal petition for a "little fat hen"—always a fat one by tradition. If the farmer agreed, the men scrambled after the fowl, and it went into a large bag that one of the young members carried. A drink was in order at each stop; when the host had none to offer, he was invited to take a mouthful or two from the bottles of the runners. The visit ended with musical merci's to the mesdames et messieurs, and a request to be with the revelers that night to dance and "manger le gros gumbo."

Several times, I noted, the stop was at the home of a member of the party; and here he was at his gayest, disguising his voice and manner with special care. Invariably, Maman and the rest knew him from the first moment or two; to please his vanity, they pretended that he was, in truth, a stranger from England or some other weird place. Finally, in most cases one of the bébés murmured, "Allo, Papa," and the spell was broken. Everybody had the laugh on Papa, who said that he knew they knew all the time.

The spoils had been gathered by late afternoon, and the wives of the runners went to work upon them. Iron washpots were brought forth, fires were built under them, and gumbo was started. Hours of preparation, salting, tasting, exclamations when feathers were found in the thick soup; and then the women went home to dress before serving the meal. All the runners boasted of their powers of gumbo consumption. I saw one tired and soggy Mardi Gras consume seven heavy dishfuls and move on to the rest of the evening without visible mishap. Later I found that he stayed in bed for a week afterward.

One prairie man who was a great runner of Mardi Gras decided a few years ago to take a trip to New Orleans for the much-touted day. He came back in disappointment. He thought it a dull affair—"no spice."

A Cockfight

Ernst von Hesse-Wartegg

From *Travels on the Lower Mississippi, 1879–1880,* ed. and trans. Frederick Trautmann. For information on Hesse-Wartegg, see Chapter 3.

America's southern states—Louisiana, the Carolinas, Alabama, and others—have not outlawed cockfights. They occur in broad daylight and so often that thousands of cocks may die every year. . . .

During the famous Carnival I saw in the papers the announcement of an interstate cockfight to be held on several successive days at the big Spanish "cockpit" at the corner of Dumaine and Roman Streets in the French quarter.[11] Georgia on the one hand, Kentucky and Tennessee on the other, had sent many of their best fighting cocks. In addition, thousands of people had streamed in from southern and western states to attend Carnival. They so filled the city to overflowing that you could count on crowds at the fights.

The way to the arena led through a chaos of narrow, dirty, abandoned alleys in the quarter, once the center of Louisiana Creoles. Mean, dilapidated, empty houses. Unpaved streets, or at best with potholes and torn-up surfaces. No lights.

A circuslike, brightly lit pile took impressive shape at the corner of Dumaine: the cockpit. About a dozen people loitered about the door. Two dollars, cash, at the window. No ticket in return. I went into a spacious and bare outer hall. Big cages for the cocks lined the walls to the ceiling. On one side, the Georgians; on the other, the Kentuckians. A narrow passage went at last into the amphitheater.

From *Travels on the Lower Mississippi, 1879–1880: A Memoir by Ernst von Hesse-Wartegg,* ed. and trans. Frederic Trautmann. Copyright © 1990 by the Curators of the University of Missouri. Reprinted by permission of the University of Missouri Press.

---

11. This intersection is not in the French Quarter.

Initially I could think of nothing but a seat at a window, so stupefying was the tobacco smoke, the reek of every sort of liquor, and the crush of people. I climbed the benches one by one to the highest and the only one not taken. From there I could survey with utter clarity the whole wild scene. A thinly sanded track circled a ring at the center. Benches provided seats for about 500. Perhaps another 500 filled the entranceway, the gallery, and the rest of the place. Still they poured in. A few gas jets barely lighted these broad spaces. Fighting had not begun.

Spectators—not a woman among them—consisted, in the lesser half, of curious tourists; in the greater, of vagabonds of the saloon, the casino, and the streets. Unemployed, without steady income, often unsure even of a place to sleep, the vagabonds live from hand to mouth by gambling during the day and spending nights at cards, roulette, or the *"cockfights."* They are the curse of normal society and the enemy of the law, the rowdiest and most dangerous of the Crescent City's diverse elements. Though uniform of character, they vary in appearance. Here: Negroes and Yankees from poorer neighborhoods along the river, unkempt, in threadbare clothes. There: mulattoes in urban finery, with monocle, patent-leather shoes, and walking stick. Here: shipping-company agents. There: rich planters in suits of cool linen and broad-brimmed hats. Finally: French Creoles. *They* look *so* stylish, presences fit for the boulevards of Paris, descendants of the old French planter aristocracy, as good as destroyed as a class now. These last scions, knowledgable as masters but ignorant of work, spend their lives (so the example of the majority would lead us to believe) doing nothing during the day and gambling at night. Seeming to enjoy a privileged position at the fights, they join none less than the owners and promoters in the best seats in the house, and disport themselves like rich English lords on Derby Day. On benches opposite them a few Mexican and Texas caballeros lie stretched out. They wear traditional dress: wide-brimmed hat, jacket with intricate trim, leather chaps, and in the belt the inevitable and only-too-often-used revolver. Below them the likes of Cubans, West Indians, and other Latin Americans mingle and contrast with stocky, red-cheeked farmers from Tennessee or Kansas. Farmers have come to New Orleans to deliver grain or cotton, and to the fights to sample a bit of the city's exotic life. A motley crowd, colorful yet placid. That is, its multitudinous members converse with the calm reserve so characteristic of Americans. Not the unfailing shouts, not the commotion of such events in other countries, but quiet prevails: what might be called an *eerie* quiet.

At about 8:00 P.M., two men appeared from the outer hall. They entered the ring. Each carried a big bird in his hands. In Europe we have been accustomed to the presence of authorities such as referees and policemen, and ushers to clear the ring. Nothing of the sort here. Yet the event unfolded with order and in calm. Tourists and insiders alike left the ring of their own accord. The ring no sooner emptied than the two *"backers"* put the antagonists on the ground. Each wore another set of spurs attached by small leather straps to its own: a pair of three-inch steel bayonets. These *"gaffs"* do resemble the bayonet in form, except the upward curve that ends in a honed needlepoint. The Georgian, black and of the best breeding, also weighed the most: a five-and-a-half-pound, so-called *"shawl neck."* The Kentuckian, red, weighed a little less.

No sooner had they come into view than the Kentucky side asked odds at seven to five. Georgians responded for theirs at eight to five. As a rule the American carries his banknotes in a roll in his vest pocket. Rolls changed

New Orleans cockfight, by A. R. Waud

From *Harper's Weekly,* July 21, 1866, reproduction courtesy Special Collections, LSU Libraries

hands now, sometimes passed to a third party, always as if not a word ought be lost in the process.

The antagonists took one another's measure for a few seconds, Georgia Black versus Kentucky Red, then each hurled himself at the other. The first round or *"pass"* had begun. Black struck for Red's comb, neck, and head. Red ducked and attacked Black's wings and legs. In a moment their gaffs tangled. The backers must disentangle and separate the birds, both unhurt. No sooner back on their feet than they flung themselves at each other in a rage. This time Red gave Black a stab in the thigh that floored him. Red pecked and hacked like mad at him for a while, then stood beside his bloody foe and regarded him lying there as if dead. Red's head sank after this quiet moment. He turned to the ground and began to peck about [as if in search of food]. Black sprang up at the instant, seized Red's cobb, and jerked him down. The onlooker could not see what hold each had on the other as they rolled like two balls of feathers on the ground. Red got the better of it at last, pinning Black between his legs.

So ended the second pass. The backers picked up their birds, smoothed their feathers, and again put them on the ground about three feet apart. Georgia Black, unable to stand, collapsed. He did not get up. At each of the enemy's thrusts he struck back with his beak. If Kentucky were a *"fighter,"* the sportsmen were saying, he would exploit the advantage and finish off that Georgian. But Kentucky hesitated, wavered, shilly-shallied, obviously badly hurt himself. After a few minutes the backers returned their birds to the position of attack.

Thus, no fewer than twenty passes, with alternating luck for the pair. Bettors at ringside accordingly preferred one, then the other. "Ten to five for the red!"—"A hundred to ten for the black!"—"A hundred to fifty." Back and forth, back and forth, one bets and the other accepts by extending his hand to seal it. Neither thinks of welshing. It astonishes newcomers that bettors can remember so many different bets.

Battle had lasted over thirty minutes yet not been decided. At first they tore into one another as soon as put down. Engagements shortened, pauses for rest lengthened, until at last each round consisted of two or three rushes and a bit of a tussle. Everybody could see it plain. The end was near. The backers could still pull and pat their birds erect but the birds could scarcely stand when put down. They staggered about like drunks or they collapsed. So proud, so handsome only a half hour ago, miserable looking now: disheveled, spurs and legs

bloody, combs practically gone, heads and necks plucked clean. Yet the out-
come remained uncertain. Kentucky, the early favorite, had lost the advantage. Odds about fifty-fifty now.

In the twenty-sixth pass, he sank again. Georgia Black reeled on splayed
legs for a while; then, ignoring his own bloody head, attacked and seized the
comb. It was Black's last effort. He collapsed in front of Red, a bit of Red's
comb in his beak. Red, sitting, stabbed Black with enough force that his gaffs
had to be pulled out. Red had delivered the *coup de grace.* For, put down for
the twenty-seventh pass, Black staggered forward a few steps and fell dead.
Red outlived him—by a few seconds.

During the last pass, excitement swelled among the spectators. Betting
quickened. The nearer the end, the more the Creole heart pounded behind a
cool Yankee facade. The original, feigned indifference gave way to a paroxysm
of gesticulation, shrieks, cheers, and curses. Only genuine Yankees stayed
calm and put winnings into vest pockets without turning a hair, or met losses
with equal indifference.

The Kentucky/Georgia bout, the only *"main"* this evening, would thus be
the only one to count in the interstate competition. Twenty-six had been announced for the following evening and fourteen for the day after. Tonight a
number of *"hackfights"* followed the main: wild bouts that did not count in
the competition: random matches staged by individuals hoping to win large
bets. Pairs fought until one died. Each bout lasted anywhere from five to
thirty-five minutes.

All wagering, as I have noted, took place bettor to bettor orally—not, as at
the races, through *"bookmakers."* A rough estimate put the total at $14,000.
Tonight, after the first three or four matches, tourists left in a huff abandoning
the turf to true sportsmen. *They* stayed until dawn and spent their winnings
on whiskey or champagne.

There was gambling also at a rouge-et-noir table in the outer hall. The person who wanted to bet could lose his money more "legitimately" and more
comfortably there than at a gruesome, bloody, disgusting ringside. Stakes and
emotions ran high out there too, with bets (usually indicated by small ivory
discs) often $20 to $50. There, Creole cavaliers tried to recoup cockfight
losses. Grain, rice, and cotton merchants constituted most of the victims.

In New Orleans and many other cities, the English-language papers carried columns on the fights. Nothing about the fights amazed me more than
the length and content of the columns. Among all those words, not one, not

a hint of regret at such vulgar amusements. Here in the South, too, the American reporter restricts himself to what happened, as true an account as possible. He allows himself neither to add anything nor to reflect on what he has seen. A few days later in the same arena, English and Boston dogs engaged in a series of fights, uncommonly bloody, before equally big crowds. The paper likewise reported these "events" down to the last detail. But nobody thought it worth the trouble to speak against the abomination of making animals fight. It seems in a distant future that the Anglo-American press will wake up to its responsibilities and do what it ought to do.

Bonfires on the Levee

HOPE J. NORMAN

Norman is a journalist based in Alexandria, Louisiana, who writes here of her 1981 encounter with the festival custom of lighting bonfires along the levees of the Mississippi on Christmas Eve.

ALONG THE RIVER ROAD, ST. JAMES PARISH, LA.— On a trip to New Orleans in early November, my husband and I detoured below Baton Rouge to travel a few miles on the River Road. To our surprise, all along the route that follows the Mississippi River's torturous course were persons at work building tall wooden towers on the levee.

They were readying the Christmas bonfires.

I knew of the Louisiana river parishes' custom of lighting the way for Santa Claus on Christmas Eve by burning huge stacks of wood. Curious to learn more, I returned December 11 for an unhurried tour of the area.

On Louisiana Highway 44 below the Sunshine Bridge I spotted the first tepee-like tower. Stopping to inspect, I saw that four tall poles were lashed together around a center pole. The sides were of neatly stacked logs. Inside was more firewood.

Leroy Frederick of Union, who lives across the road, obligingly stopped his blue pickup truck when I waved at him.

"I built that for my granddaughter," he said proudly. The custom of building Christmas Eve bonfires, Frederic said, goes back to his ancestors. "I don't know how long, but I been doing it since I was nine and I'm 55 now," he said.

I drove slowly southward, noting on my right at irregular intervals bonfire towers in various stages of completion. Houses on the left varied from tumbledown deserted shanties to neat tin-roofed cottages with red poinsettias blooming out front. Occasional groves of live oaks in tangled wood suggested settings of bygone mansions.

Every few miles along the curving road a huge grain elevator or oil refinery would loom ahead, like some medieval mirage.

It was lunchtime when I rounded a bend and arrived at a seafood restaurant. Over shrimp stew I asked the waitress about the bonfires.

"There've been lots of tragedies," she said gloomily. "Last week a young man was killed when he fell off a tower. Once a girl lost her eye from a firecracker. Sometimes people get burned."

Bonfire permits are required from the St. James Parish courthouse in Convent, I learned. I stopped there for a copy.

The permits, issued "as a precaution against the possible elimination of this heritage," include the stipulation that "under no conditions are bonfires to be lit with the wind blowing from a *'southerly direction.'*" Other regulations include prohibiting the burning of tires, plastics, or creosoted lumber.

Continuing south, I spotted more and more towers on the levee. At Hester, stopping to buy freshly dug new potatoes and a splendid cauliflower from a roadside stand, I asked the farmer why no one was working on the bonfires.

"They're mostly young people. They'll be out after school," he assured me.

Sure enough, near Paulina I saw my first group of bonfire-builders meeting atop the levee to complete a tower they'd been working on "since early November," they told me.

Gathering wood from "wherever we can get it," explained Scott Poche, the workers first dug a hole for the center pole, then erected the side poles. The center, or "gut," is filled with piles of wood as the log sides are built higher and higher. Cane reeds are filled in at the last.

"You might say that's the finishing touch," Jackie Vicknair said.

The group, which included Dwayne Cantillo, Kirk Bailey, Ricky Poche, and Kurt Accorda, had also built a hut for shelter during the construction period—all of materials found at the dump, Bailey said.

The custom of lighting the bonfires "to show Santa Claus the way" goes back through the generations, the youths said. "It's our tradition."

On the night the bonfires are lit the group arrives early to tend the fire. If the wind isn't blowing in the right direction they return another night during the holidays.

The group said area roads become clogged with sightseers viewing the spectacle. "Whole busloads come from New Orleans," Poche said. Even pilots flying into New Orleans on Christmas Eve point out the levee lights to passengers.

After saying goodbye to the bonfire team, I drove on to Lutcher, where towers along the levee were so numerous that they resembled oilfield derricks. "Bonfire Capital of the World," a sign proclaimed.

On the ferry to Vacherie I met Nancy O'Connell, wife of the boat's captain, who told me that area residents start collecting bonfire wood early in the New Year.

"The bonfires are to light the way for Papa Noel," she said.

I headed north, noting that bonfires were scarcer on the west bank than the east. I stopped to talk to Brian Hymel of St. James, who was warming himself by a fire alongside a square log-cabin-type construction.

"The levee board on this side doesn't allow holes to be dug in the levee," Hymel explained. So he and a group of fifteen friends decided to build a different type from the usual tepee-shaped bonfire.

A senior at E. D. White High School in Thibodaux, Hymel said he'd learned about building bonfires "from my brother."

I asked Hymel how far north and south the bonfires are lit.

"A long way . . . all the way from Edgard to St. James at least," he replied.

I couldn't find St. James on my Louisiana map. But I'll bet Papa Noel finds it Christmas Eve.

An Attempt to Compile the Definitive History of Didee's Restaurant

CALVIN TRILLIN

Trillin, noted humorist and culinary writer, keeps traveling to Louisiana—as he tells us—for the food. On this trip he attempted to untangle the story of a famous Louisiana restaurant; in the process of recounting his efforts, he explores the pride of Louisiana chefs and the intense interest Louisianians take in food and culinary arcana. The Alice mentioned is Trillin's wife.

. . . I once went to Louisiana determined to write the definitive history of Didee's restaurant, or to eat an awful lot of baked duck and dirty rice trying. I'm quick to take up scholarly challenges in southern Louisiana. Once, I went to Mamou, Louisiana, to observe the Cajun Mardi Gras celebration because I had heard that the traditional ride of Cajun horsemen around the countryside in search of chickens for the Mardi Gras chicken gumbo often comes to a halt so that the celebrants can drink beer and eat boudin. The Cajun Mardi Gras happens to be a particularly jovial event, but I have to say that I would observe the annual conference of the society of water-treatment-plant engineers if I had reason to believe that it was interrupted every so often so that the participants could drink beer and eat boudin. At the Mamou Mardi Gras, I ate a lot of boudin while I was standing in fields chosen as rest stops—squeezing the mixture of pork and seasoning and rice out of the sausage casing with one hand and holding the wash-down can of beer in the other. It wasn't far from my normal style of boudin eating; I normally down boudin while standing in the parking lot of some Cajun grocery store that has managed to snatch me off the road by displaying in its window a hand-lettered sign that says "Hot Boudin Today." The Mamou boudin seemed particularly good, although I may have simply been in a particularly good mood because of the knowledge that even after all the boudin was gone we still had the chicken gumbo to look forward to. As I ate boudin in Mamou, it occurred to me that if sausage fanciers ever have our own annual conference I might find myself responding to a panel of experts who had concluded that there is little in common between boudin and East Coast Italian sausage by rising to remind the panel that both are normally eaten standing up.

Trying to compile the definitive history of Didee's restaurant wasn't easy. In fact, I might have given up the history game right there if it hadn't been for the baked duck and dirty rice. The event that had attracted my attention obviously qualified as what historians calling the End of an Era—the perfect moment to slip in with a definitive history. The proprietor of a tiny, family-run restaurant in a nearly abandoned section of Baton Rouge's black commercial district—Didee's, a name that had represented stupefying baked duck in Louisiana for this entire century—had sold name, duck recipe, and franchise rights to a go-go New York miniconglomerate that talked about making him "the Colonel Sanders of the duck business." All of that may strike professional historians as a simple enough tale of American commerce, but once I had arrived at Didee's and begun my research—interviewing the proprietor, Herman Perrodin, while downing a bowl of his seafood gumbo and feeling grateful for my working conditions—I realized that no tale involving Herman Perrodin was likely to be a simple tale. There was no doubt that his grandfather, Charles Adrian Lastrapes, founded the original Didee's in Opelousas, Louisiana, around the turn of the century—Perrodin's mother, Clara Lastrapes Perrodin, and her husband opened a separate Didee's in Baton Rouge in 1952—but Herman Perrodin did not fit snugly into the role of an unspoiled folk chef nurturing an old family recipe. A tall man in his fifties with a sort of lubricated manner of talking, Perrodin occasionally described himself as a "poor little old dumb boy born in a sweet-potato patch in Opelousas, Louisiana," but he also described himself as being a better chef than Paul Bocuse. "La nouvelle cuisine!" he said to me, drawing out the last word in astonishment at the sort of thing dumb folks will believe. "Don't tell *me* about la nouvelle cuisine! I've been doing la nouvelle cuisine all my goddamn life!"

The early history of Didee's restaurant, Perrodin assured me, was not all that complicated. Charles Adrian Lastrapes started serving baked duck and baked chicken and Creole gumbo and oyster loaves while running what newspaper features about Didee's usually refer to as a coffee shop and what Perrodin figured for a gambling den or a bootlegging operation. Lastrapes was always known as Didee, pronounced to rhyme with high tea—a meal, I hardly need add, that anyone fortunate enough to eat the daily fare of Opelousas would undoubtedly regard as some form of corporal punishment. Opelousas is about sixty miles west of Baton Rouge, in the section of Louisiana long dominated by the French—an area where a noted gumbo is discussed with the seriousness it deserves, and where a lot of black and white people seem to have the same last names as well as approximately the same complexions, and where attitudes toward the more enjoyable of the Seven Deadly Sins are the sort of stuff sermons are made of in Shreveport. Didee's was always a restaurant for white people, although the Lastrapes were what are sometimes called "people of color," or Creoles. There are those in Louisiana who object to the word "Creole" being used to designate people of mixed race rather than the white descendants of the Colonial French, and there are those in Louisiana who believe that people who serve the sort of baked duck that Didee Lastrapes and his second wife, Miz Anna, put out for so many years in a little restaurant just off the courthouse square in Opelousas can call themselves anything they please.

"This is edible gumbo," I said, while Perrodin paused between stories of a childhood in Didee's kitchen and stories of his wanderings around the country after he left Opelousas as a teenager ("I'm the traveling, adventurous, aggressive black sheep of the family"). He agreed that the gumbo was at least superb. In southern Louisiana, it is customary for a serious cook to assume the preeminence of his version of anything. Perrodin's son, Charles, who struck me as relatively reserved, said to me later that day, "You ever taste our shrimp etouffee? You taste our etouffee, you will throw rocks at other people's etouffee."

Didee Lastrapes died in the mid-forties, Perrodin said, but the Opelousas restaurant remained open under Miz Anna's stewardship until her death in 1970.

"Then Dee Dee's opened where Didee's had been," I said, introducing a complication I already knew about and opening what I believe the methodology specialists at the American Historical Association conferences refer to among themselves as a real bucket of worms.

Perrodin dismissed Dee Dee's with a wave of his hand.

What happened, I knew, was that Thomas and Tony Blouin, who had worked for Miz Anna for years, reopened the restaurant, choosing the name Dee Dee's for reasons Thomas Blouin once summarized pithily for a visiting reporter: "So people would know it's the same but different." I once ate at Dee Dee's. In 1972, Alice and I stopped in Opelousas on our way—well, more or less on our way—to the Breaux Bridge crawfish festival. I remember Alice speculating on the ingredients in the dirty rice, in the tone of voice a bomb-squad man might use to discuss how the terrorists rigged up something small enough to fit into a satchel but powerful enough to destroy a wing of the post office. As I remember, we had a fine meal, although I may have simply been in a particularly good mood because of the knowledge that even after the duck was gone we had the crawfish to look forward to.

"Did you think the food was any good at Dee Dee's?" I asked Perrodin.

He waved his hand again. "A lot of people can do things and a lot of people have to be directed," he said. "It went kerplop, and now they're cooking on the offshore oil rigs or something."

For most of the history we had been discussing, Perrodin was not what the historians call a primary source. The wanderings he had begun as a teenager kept him out of Louisiana until he went to Baton Rouge for a few years in the late fifties to help out his father, Arlington Perrodin, as a sort of catering manager. Perrodin told me that the jobs he had held around the country as a waiter or bartender or cook or manager would take four years to list. He could present a ten-minute declamation on what he learned along the way about which tastes are received where in what he called "the sculpture of the mouth" or on what he learned about herbs alone ("I'm like a perfumer. I mean it. I'm telling you. I studied the herbs for five years. I could tell you more about herbs than the man who wrote the book"). He could also present a declamation on the high life, and on the personal lesson he learned when he was sent to prison in Texas in 1970 as a heroin user. Perrodin talked about his drug habit the way he talked about his gumbo. One minute, while mentioning the last spice in a recipe that gives it "that zing—*respect,* I call it," he would slam his hand on the table and say, "*Voilà!* Now I got your whole mouth lit up!" A few minutes later, he would fling both hands toward the ceiling and say, "A quarter of a million dollars flowed through these arms."

When Arlington Perrodin died in 1976, a few years after Herman had come home for good, Didee's was not far from kerplop itself. It had been mentioned in national magazines; movie stars had written raves in its guestbook; the Confrerie de la Chaine des Rotisseurs (le Chapitre de Nouvelle-Orleans) had included on one of its formal menus "Canard à la Didee, Rize au Fave, Les 'Mustard Greens.'" But not many Baton Rouge people came to eat. The neighborhood was evaporating around Didee's, and Herman Perrodin could not seem to raise the capital to move or even to advertise. "You can't do anything without money," Perrodin said. "Cash money. No checks."

In 1974, a review by Richard Collin in the *New Orleans States-Item* suggesting that Didee's would flourish if it moved to New Orleans had resulted in a number of proposals, but every one of them had fallen through. During the last year of Arlington Perrodin's life, Herman took a fling at a scheme by some young Baton Rouge entrepreneurs to feature Didee's cooking in Aspen—a flop from which he acquired nothing but an interest in skiing to add to his taste for the high life. There were other offers, but Perrodin dismissed them as schemes in which he might do a lot of work without seeing any money. "I'm not waitin' for no net," he explained to me. "You can have all the net you want. Give me the gross."

After three-quarters of a century of his family's building the reputation of Didee's, the way Perrodin analyzed it, he had found himself in the position of an unappreciated and—even worse—undercompensated genius. There was Paul Bocuse, according to Perrodin's calculations, making fifteen thousand dollars for catering a meal, and there was Herman Perrodin doing all of his own cooking and ordering and bill paying and, sometimes, sweeping up—and still never taking in more than a few hundred dollars on a good day. "I got obligations and I got a life-style," Perrodin told me. "I'm not satisfied with the way I'm living. I'm not satisfied with the home I live in. I'm not satisfied with the car I drive."

Enter Omni Capital Worldwide, Ltd., go-go miniconglomerate whose name might be taken as another way of saying, "All Money Everywhere."

I had lunch at Didee's with Herb Turner, who had moved to Baton Rouge from Fort Lauderdale a couple of years before to run Omni Capital's operations in Louisiana. Turner struck me as very go-go himself. He said he had been so busy that he hadn't had time to get rid of his second Cadillac before buying his third. The previous few days had been particularly hectic, he said, because he had a guest in town—a very close personal friend who happened to be Frank Sinatra's bodyguard.

I knew I was digressing from the history of Didee's, but I couldn't resist the obvious question: "Who's watching Frank?"

"Frank's OK," Turner said, digressing himself into show business for some encouraging stories about Eddie Fisher's comeback. As it happens, Fisher once ate at Didee's, and left a rude remark about Elizabeth Taylor in the guestbook. Arlington Perrodin covered that page with clear plastic for protection.

Omni Capital, Turner told me, had been founded in New York as a tax-shelter consulting business by one investment banker who was also a CPA, and another who was also a Hollywood booking agent. In describing its history, he and another Omni executive who had joined us for lunch used the word "roll" a lot. They talked about rolling out of tax shelters into film distribution, and rolling out of timberland into housing developments. It seemed natural enough to roll out of housing developments into baked duck and dirty rice. In fact, on those rare evenings when I find myself in a place where the only alternative to sitting like a condemned man in the motel dining room is starvation, rolling into baked duck and dirty rice is something I've thought about a lot myself.

What Omni was planning, Turner said, was to build a prototype Didee's near the Baton Rouge Country Club—a Garden Room that could be adapted for private parties, an Acadian Room with beams of distressed wood, a good bar. If the prototype succeeded, Didee's Famous Restaurant. Inc., the corporation formed for the occasion, would start franchising. Turner said Omni planned to send out Didee credit cards, carrying preferential reservation privileges, to five thousand business contacts in the state. "That'll take care of that," he said. "I can't imagine the general public getting a shot at that restaurant."

"The duck is delicious," I said to Perrodin. I happen to like duck. I don't think I like it as well as Alice does. When it comes to partiality to ducks, Alice is outdone by nobody except, perhaps, other ducks. In the jockeying that goes on during the decision-making concerning what dishes are to be ordered in a Chinese restaurant, Alice always says something that has to do with duck. "You know, this place seems like the kind of place that would have great duck," she'll say, apparently having figured that out from the shade of formica on the table tops. I don't mean to complain: our friend William Edgett Smith, the man with the Naugahyde palate, always says something like, "You know, this place seems like the kind of place that would have great egg foo yung." I do like duck. I particularly liked Herman Perrodin's duck. It was by far the best thing on the plate—moist on the inside and crisp on the outside, with no fat in sight. I suppose I might have found the duck particularly satisfying because I realized that, as a member of the general public, I might be having my last shot at it.

As soon as I arrived in Opelousas, I was assured that the New York miniconglomerate had signed the wrong man. "They didn't do enough research before they closed the deal," one of the breakfast regulars at the Palace Cafe, on the courthouse square, explained to me. In Opelousas, the Perrodins' Baton Rouge version of Didee's was barely acknowledged ("I think they started some kind of catering service over in Baton Rouge"). From the way Baton Rouge was discussed at the Palace, I got the idea that anybody in Opelousas who has business in the capital waits until he gets back home to eat. Baton Rouge was described as a place where the state government and the petrochemical industry have drawn so many people from places like north Louisiana or even Mississippi that there might not be a tableful of eaters in the entire city who know the difference between splendidly prepared duck and the kind of fowl that might be considered edible by Baptists. Herman Perrodin could hardly have learned the secrets of baked-duck cooking from Didee as a boy, I was told by a man who had delivered milk to the restaurant for many years, since Didee was accustomed to sitting out on the sidewalk whittling while his wife did the cooking. The dairyman said Herman would not have been around the restaurant much anyway; even as a boy, he was apparently what people in Opelousas call "kinda sporty."

As if that were not complication enough, some lawyer in Opelousas who once had some business with Thomas Blouin, the proprietor of Dee Dee's while it lasted, informed me that Blouin had recently come off the oil rigs to take a job cooking at a restaurant between Opelousas and Lafayette, where he was prepared to cook the true Opelousas stupefying baked-duck dinner for me and most of the law firm of Sandoz, Sandoz & Schiff. At the restaurant, a place called Carroll's, near Evangeline Downs race track, I was pleased to find that Sandoz, Sandoz & Schiff lawyers are the sort of lawyers who find it easier to get down to cases if they have a pile of boiled crawfish to work on while they talk. What they talked about mainly was food. "Her oyster loaf was a knockout," one of the lawyers said, recalling how Miz Anna would scoop the middle out of a perfect French loaf and replace it with succulent fried oysters. That reminded another member of the firm about stopping in after work with a large pot he kept in his car and having Miz Anna fill it with seafood gumbo before he went home. As they talked, the lawyers deftly peeled crawfish and popped them into their mouths. It occurred to me that if a society of sausage fanciers was ever founded, the firm of Sandoz, Sandoz & Schiff might be a good bet for general counsel. "If it please the court," the firm's litigation partner would say in our defense, "I would ask that the term 'food crazy' used by this witness be stricken from the record." Conferences would be held in grocery-store parking lots, where the officers of the associaion and their attorneys could lean up against a Pontiac and chomp away at boudin. The bylaws drawn up by Sandoz, Sandoz & Schiff would make it clear that all association business would be suspended on those days when, as is sometimes said in southern Louisiana, "the crawfish are walking right across the highway."

About the time we had knocked off our first conversational bowl of crawfish, Thomas Blouin came out from the kitchen to sit down with us for a while before putting the finishing touches on the meal. He turned out to be a rather modest man, as southern Louisiana cooks go, although he did admit later in the evening that he could prepare wild duck, a notoriously difficult fowl to cook, so well that it tasted like lemon pie. As Blouin told me about his training under Miz Anna, first as a waiter and then as a cook, the lawyers said "See!" and "Listen to that!" and "He knows his onions!" When I asked who had the real Didee recipe for duck, Blouin said, "You're fixin' to eat the recipe." The duck was delicious, if not quite as crisp as Herman Perrodin's. The dirty rice—a sort of rice dressing made with chicken liver and chicken gizzard and onion and bell pepper and celery and garlic and spices and oil—was staggering, although I speak as someone who had to go to a franchise fried-chicken place to find a dirty rice he didn't like. When I accepted Blouin's kind offer of another bowl of rice, there were cheers at the table, and a couple of lawyers clapped Blouin on the back. "They signed the wrong man," one of them said. "What'd I tell you." I couldn't help but wonder whether Henry Steele Commager had ever found himself in a similar situation.

"Why, I bet he learned more about cooking on the oil rigs than he knew when Miz Anna died," Perrodin said when I reported the Opelousas theory about who knew how to cook Didee's duck. I had arrived back in Baton Rouge in time for a late lunch. Perrodin tossed off a few more disparaging remarks about Blouin, and then sat down to tell me how maquechou, a sort of stewed-corn dish the Omni executives and I had been served at Didee's with lunch, was prepared by a cook who really knew how to get your whole mouth lit up.

"But will they be able to do that sort of thing at a Didee's franchise in Alexandria or Shreveport?" I asked after Perrodin had finished a five-minute speech that included pulling his tongue out now and then to show me which part of the mouth was affected by which flavor. "Aren't you afraid they'll take shortcuts with preparation and ingredients?"

Perrodin leaned way back in his chair and stared at me, as if to make certain I had not disappeared from dumbness. "That was *canned* corn you had in the maquechou," he said. "What I was just explaining to you was the authentic way to do it. Who the hell's got time to do that?"

Thinking back on the meal, I remembered that when one of the Omni executives mentioned his company's roll into real estate, it had occurred to me that Perrodin's dinner rolls had the look of packaged hamburger buns about them. "But how about the duck?" I asked. "Doesn't that take a lot of care and experience—all that time in your grandfather's kitchen learning the secrets?"

"There are no secrets," he said. "Any idiot could do it. Why, I could stay home and tell you how to do it over the phone, and I bet *dollars* it would come out the same."

He took a fork and poked around at the duck I was eating. "Shortcuts!" he said. "This duck was cooked last night. I reconstituted it by putting it back in natural sauce just to get it warmed through. When somebody orders it, I take it out of its natural gravy and put it under the salamander and let this overhead-broiler heat come down on it, and it brings it back just like I took it out of the oven."

As Perrodin expanded on the subject, shortcuts began to sound as dramatic as spectacular gumbo or a serious heroin habit. "Why, I can take almost any kind of canned vegetable and I'll defy you to tell me if it's fresh," he said. "Shortcuts! I'm the *master* of the shortcut. I mean to tell you."

Travel Update

There are a multitude of Louisiana festivals and fairs, some of them—like the Zydeco Festival and the Festival de Musique Acadien—excellent occasions for learning about important aspects of Louisiana culture. Probably the most educational in this regard are the famous New Orleans Jazz and Heritage Festival, held the last weekend in April and the first in May; the less well known Louisiana Folk Festival, held in the fall; and the Natchitoches Folk Festival, held in July. Jazz and Heritage ("Jazz Fest"), held at the New Orleans Fairgrounds race track, has a specifically documentary section that features traditional craftspeople and includes ethnographic information on Louisiana cultures. But simply by providing a vast array of Louisiana musical entertainment, this festival educates us (by immersion, so to speak) about local musical traditions. The Louisiana Folklife Festival, originally sponsored by the state folklife program, has been located in several places but most frequently in Eunice and Monroe. It presents only traditional folk artists, craftspeople, and musicians and has a strong orientation toward providing ethnographic information through detailed signage and interviews with participants. Each July the Natchitoches Folk Festival highlights a Louisiana cultural theme (such as family traditions, cotton, oil) and primarily draws its performers from northeast and central Louisiana and the Cajun prairies.

The Pelican Guide to Louisiana lists festivals by place, and the Louisiana Almanac has a section called "Louisiana Fairs, Festivals, and Celebrations," which lists a great many by month (in the 1995–96 edition nearly ten pages of double columns). There is a Louisiana Association of Fairs and Festivals (601 Oak Lane, Thibodaux, LA 70301-6537), which publishes an annual guide, most recently called Fairs and Festivals Louisiana, that provides a listing by month, with addresses and telephone numbers for information. The Louisiana Office of Tourism publishes a quarterly calendar of events that includes information on upcoming festivals, and the Louisiana Date Book, a weekly desk calendar issued annually, prints festival and fair information. For Cajun Country, a region particularly oriented toward festivals, Acadiana Profile magazine has published a *Cajun Country Festival Guide* that lists events by month and provides more information than any of the statewide guides. The *Times of Acadiana,* a weekly newspaper, provides good coverage of area festivals. However, it is still the great traditional festival of Mardi Gras that looms so large in the local consciousness.

Mardi Gras comes in two principal and very different forms: that of urban New Orleans, which has been world-famed for over a century, and that of the Cajuns and rural Creoles, which has become known to outsiders only in recent years.

Locals like to trace New Orleans Mardi Gras back to the days of French exploration, when in 1699 Iberville's men celebrated the holiday on the banks of a little stream downriver from the present-day city. They named the stream Bayou Mardi Gras; this is said to be the first non-Indian place name in the Mississippi River Valley (a sign at Fort Jackson in Plaquemines Parish points to the bayou's location on the other side of the Mississippi). No doubt the celebration of pre-Lenten carnival took place in colonial times but probably not regularly, and the present form of the celebration dates from the middle of the nineteenth century.

The Carnival season begins on January 6, Twelfth Night. Early festivities, however, are limited to private parties and balls put on by Carnival organizations commonly called krewes. As things move closer to Mardi Gras itself (whose date varies according to the timing of Easter and Lent), these Carnival organizations sponsor parades. This activity intensifies over the weekend and Monday preceding Mardi Gras and explodes on the day itself. The parades feature elaborate floats designed according to some unified theme. Krewe members riding the floats toss throws to the watching crowds, who clamor for them. Krewe members customarily also attend a ball, often held after the parade. Before Mardi Gras Day, typically only krewe members costume, but on Tuesday large numbers of people show up for the parades "masked." Carnival is an important part of the social season for New Orleans elites, the focus for parties and debutante balls.

Lyle Saxon's description of Mardi Gras—only a portion of which is reprinted here—is a very full one for his own time (and, though the day has evolved since then, it is still similar to what he describes). Canal Street is a central locale, full of revelers (though St. Charles Avenue is too, and more popular with families and those seeking a somewhat tamer experience). Different krewes follow different parade routes, but the major parades on Mardi Gras

Day come down St. Charles and then go up and down Canal. Before the arrival of the parades, revelers show off their costumes and otherwise celebrate. Marching clubs—the Jefferson City Buzzards noted by Saxon still among them—come down the routes informally before the parades, accompanied by bands and dispensing trinkets to ladies in exchange for kisses. Then the parades roll continuously for hours, the principal one being the Rex parade. Rex, portrayed by a prominent citizen, is said to be the king of Carnival and imagined to be the ruler of the city for the day. As Saxon observed, he once stopped at the exclusive Boston Club on Canal to toast his queen—a prominent debutante. The Zulu Parade, which Saxon describes as taking place in an African-American neighborhood, used to be a very informal affair with no fixed route. In recent years it has been brought into the mainstream and precedes the Rex parade over some of the same route, though it is still African American in character.

In 1992 a city ordinance that in effect denied parade permits to organizations that discriminated on the basis of race had an important impact on the nature of Carnival. Three of the old, socially elite krewes—Momus, Proteus, and Comus—withdrew from parading rather than conform. Thus the Comus parade Saxon describes has ceased to exist. Proteus, which rolled on Monday night before Mardi Gras, was replaced by Orpheus, a krewe newly formed by musician Harry Connick, Jr., while another krewe, Bards of Bohemia, also shifted its parade to Monday night preceding Orpheus. Given Connick's background, the Orpheus parade has provided a high level of musical entertainment. It has also been notably integrated racially—though other parading groups have made at least token efforts to become more inclusive. In the 1960s, the Krewe of Bacchus set the precedent for adding new and lavish parades to the agenda. The Bacchus parade, on Sunday night preceding Mardi Gras, has been particularly spectacular and popular.

Mardi Gras has been promoted to visitors since the nineteenth century, and New Orleans fills with people for the occasion. Hotel rooms are best booked far in advance, and many hotels will make rooms available only for the entire four-day period of Saturday through Tuesday. On Mardi Gras Day many businesses are closed, and the day really is notably different from normal. The Mardi Gras balls are open to members and their guests; to attend, one would do best to have friends in the right places. If that is not possible, the Krewe of Endymion sells tickets to its Endymion Extravaganza, and the Zulu organization does the same for its ball, as do Orpheus and some others.

It is possible to get an idea of what Carnival is like without actually attending. The Louisiana State Museum has Carnival exhibits and the small Mardi Gras Museum in suburban Kenner (at the Riverfront Development Park) succeeds in conveying the flavor of the event. At Mardi Gras World in Algiers, visitors can wander around one of the great warehouses where floats are made by Blaine Kern, the largest New Orleans float maker. One can observe craftspeople at work or just mingle with the strangely disembodied float parts and endless rows of parade vehicles. Pedestrians can ride free to Algiers on the ferry at the foot of Canal Street, and Mardi Gras World provides a free bus from the ferry.

Robert Tallant, *Mardi Gras* (Garden City, N.Y., 1948), gives an idealized, popular history of New Orleans Carnival, but Reid Mitchell, *All on a Mardi Gras Day: Episodes in the History of New Orleans Carnival* (Cambridge, Mass., 1995), provides a more incisive look. Samuel Kinser, *Carnival, American Style: Mardi Gras at New Orleans and Mobile* (Chicago, 1990), provides not only an interesting historical study but also quotes from various travelers' accounts.

Rural Mardi Gras is celebrated in different ways in different localities, but the general rural Carnival pattern (as described by Harnett Kane) can be said to be the same. This form of Mardi Gras had declined by the time of World War II, but it has undergone a powerful revival in recent years, perhaps because of the general revival of Cajun ethnic pride. It is organized differently in different places—in some more formally than in others—and is most common on the Cajun prairies. It is possible to observe Cajun Mardi Gras from different perspectives. One can follow a run in one's own vehicle, but this is difficult in the case of the most popular runs and has been discouraged lest hordes of followers create traffic jams on the country roads and interfere with the participants. To facilitate public involvement in the major runs, towns like Mamou and Eunice have encouraged visitors to come to the towns and await the riders as they return and then to join in-town celebrations (one can also come to see the riders go out, though they leave at an early hour). These after-the-run celebrations are often very festive and are widely attended. In addition, visitors may participate in the well-known runs—Mamou, Eunice, Church Point—by getting there early, paying a fee, signing a release holding the run not liable for personal damages, and agreeing to abide by the rules (which include required masking). Having joined up, the visitor will be put on a wagon (unless he brings his own horse). Lesser-known, smaller runs can still be followed with some ease. The problem with these runs, however, is that a visitor is unlikely to be able to locate them without local contacts, as their starting times and places are not publicized and may vary. It is not uncommon to simply stumble across a run during the Mardi Gras season (some runs, of course, go on Mardi Gras itself, but others may go on preceding days) by driving around. Following a run is not without its dangers, however, as participants often drink heavily and may fix upon outsiders as a focus for pranks or even hostility (though followers are often welcome). A documentary film by Pat Mire (director), *Dance for a Chicken: The Cajun Mardi Gras,* 1993, provides an excellent overview of the celebration. Barry J. Ancelet, *Capitaine, Voyage Ton Flag* (Lafayette, 1987), is a cogent treatment of rural Mardi Gras.

What might be called a third form of Mardi Gras is that found in smaller Louisiana cities like Lafayette and New Roads and even in Baton Rouge, which historically was not a major Mardi Gras center. Here there are parades on the New Orleans model, but they are more low-key, informal, and accessible (both in terms of attending them as a spectator and of being a participant on a float or as a marcher). Spanish Town Mardi Gras in Baton Rouge, named after the downtown neighborhood in which it is celebrated, has gained a reputation for outrageous humor and satire. In recent years Mardi Gras has spread to other parts of the country in limited ways. The Washington, D. C., Mardi Gras is organized by the Louisiana congressional delegation and has become an important social event in the nation's capital, for example.

The bonfires described by Hope Norman constitute a festive tradition that has gained in popularity and intensified its prominence in the Louisiana Christmas season in recent years. Although found at various places along the Mississippi levees between New Orleans and Baton Rouge, the bonfires are concentrated in Gramercy and Lutcher on the east bank. Here the bonfires are regulated by town authorities, and a particularly festive but civil air prevails (gumbo is sold at the fire station). Local people erect the structures for the fires in the weeks before Christmas Eve, building most in a traditional teepee shape by layering logs and sometimes adding bamboo (which pops when ignited). At 7 P.M. on Christmas Eve the fires are lit simultaneously to provide a spectacular wall of burning light on the leeves. The reason for the fires is said to be to light the way for Papa Noel to come to Louisiana, though the origin of the custom is not entirely clear. Setting bonfires on certain days is a widespread and ancient European practice. The Louisiana custom thus might seem to be very old, but evidence suggests it was only introduced here in the nineteenth century by French priests. Though there are crowds on the levees for the fires, visitors can attend without difficulty by arriving well before 7 P.M. and parking on residential streets near the river. There are also bus and boat tours available from New Orleans. For more historical and ethnographic information, see Marcia Gaudet, "Christmas Bonfires in Louisiana: Tradition and Innovation," *Southern Folklore,* XLVII (1990), 195–206.

Cockfights such as Hesse-Wartegg saw (and Mark Twain walked out on) are, of course, no longer seen in New Orleans. Whereas historically cock-fighting was an urban or tavern phenomenon, as time went on it became a ru-ral one in the United States. Louisiana is one of a few states where this activity is still legal. In a fight, two birds, naturally aggressive but also bred as fighters, are pitted against each other. They may be equipped with specially made spurs or blades or may fight with their natural appendages only. Sometimes one bird is killed, sometimes one loses heart and simply refuses to fight on. The world of cockfighting is its own subculture. Owners may breed their own birds or employ trainers to do so. The trainers may handle the birds in the pit or there may be special handlers. Though engaged in over various parts of the state, cockfighting is certainly popular in Cajun country, where there are a number of cockpits. Macon Fry and Julie Posner list some in the *Cajun Country Guide* (Gretna, La., 1993); check the index. Indeed, for those who wish to see an ex-ample of this brutal "sport," this guidebook offers the best hope of finding a venue. Cockfighters are well aware that the fights disgust many—there have been attempts by animal rights activists to have the activity outlawed—and often the operation of cockpits is not advertised; some are in clubs open only to members.

To the regret of more than a few people, Didee's Restaurant is no longer open. Herman Perrodin's financial backing apparently did materialize. His es-tablishment had two Baton Rouge locations after the one Trillin visited, each more upscale than that colorful one, but the second closed abruptly, and no more was heard of the restaurant's fate. Baked duck has appeared with some regularity on the menus of other local eateries, though some locals feel that none can ever rival the duck at Didee's or Dee Dee's. Unlike Didee's, the Pal-ace Cafe in Opelousas, where Trillin talked food with "the breakfast regu-lars," is still in existence, on a corner across from the courthouse.

Louisiana—primarily south Louisiana—is a place where food is taken very seriously and where much delectable food is available. Local restaurant repu-tations certainly come and go and may be hotly debated. To find the best Louisiana food one can certainly ask locals for restaurant recommendations—these will at least be more carefully considered than in parts of the country—or one can try one or more of the festivals that are devoted to food or that include food concessions (often staffed by local organizations raising funds). There are, of course, various guides to restaurants in local hospitality publications and standard guidebooks. There is a *Zagat* guide for New Orleans (this series uses ratings provided by local diners, so that the end result gives some indication of local opinion). And despite its being well out of date, *The New Orleans Underground Gourmet,* by Richard Collin and Rima Collin (New Orleans, 1972), is still worth a look for the Louisiana mind set about food and restaurants. This restaurant guide (which actually covers more than the Crescent City) created something of a sensation—its meticulous and critical reviews fanned controversy in a food-mad place. On Louisiana food, consult C. Paige Gutierrez, *Cajun Foodways* (Jackson, Miss., 1992); Glen Pitre, *The Crawfish Book* (Jackson, Miss., 1993); and Peter S. Feibleman *et al., American Cooking: Creole and Acadian* (New York, 1971).

11

The World of the Spirits

Though it has been the hedonism of New Orleans—
Storyville, Bourbon Street, Carnival—that has been
most celebrated by visitors and locals alike, Louisiana
has an intense spirituality that has also attracted comment. North Louisiana shares in the revivals, the fiery
preaching, and the fundamentalist zeal of the rest of
the upland South. South Louisiana is deeply Catholic,
with a profusion of yard shrines, home altars, and public devotions. And African Americans in all parts of
the state bring their cultural heritage of worship to the
fore, engaging in joyful services, river baptisms, and a
vital tradition of gospel music.

The spiritual tradition that has most piqued the interest of visitors is voodoo—because it has seemed
darkly exotic, forbidden, and chillingly exciting. The
history of voodoo in Louisiana still awaits systematic
investigation, though it was imported by—or, if already in existence here, at least much intensified by—
the influx of both black and white refugees from Haiti
during the turmoil and violence that prevailed from
1791 to 1803 (which ultimately overthrew French co-

lonial rule and white domination there). Voodoo is one of a number of New World religions—such as Cuban Santería and Brazilian Condomble—that are "syncretic" in fusing elements of African worship with aspects of Catholicism. They are centered on spirit possession; during ceremonies worshipers enter a trance state in which spirits enter their bodies and act through them. The spirits—who may be in part associated with Catholic saints—are thought to have a close interest in the physical world, and worshipers seek favors from them and propitiate them ceremonially. Hence voodoo is closely associated with certain magical practices, including the placing and lifting of curses. Though it has been misunderstood frequently and found appalling by many, voodoo seems to have attracted numerous *sub rosa* adherents of both races in nineteenth-century Louisiana. European and American visitors were often intrigued by what they perceived as its foreignness, its intense yet close-to-the-surface supernaturalism, and its almost orgiastic vitality—so removed from the genteel Western tradition of most observers.

In New Orleans in 1885 to report on the great exposition, Charles Dudly Warner had little difficulty finding a voodoo ceremony (indeed, we should wonder whether, truly, the police did not know of it, whatever Warner thought, for the existence of such ceremonies was generally known). His approach is what might be expected from a northern literary man: undertaken with a certain sympathetic curiosity, but disapproving of the "frenzy" and the "superstition," and withal uncomprehending of the event's significance beyond a vague sense of its being a "faith-cure" session for the lower orders ("most of them in common servant attire"). Fortunately, whatever his failings and doubts, Warner was a good observer, and his description is interesting and well-drawn.

In the late 1920s Zora Neale Hurston had a harder time finding the "hoodoo" she wanted to learn about—ironic, because she, like the majority of practitioners and unlike Warner, was black. While Warner obviously wanted a quick experience for his journalistic purpose, folklorist-anthropologist Hurston sought a much deeper understanding. But the times had changed. Voodoo—at least as an organized focus for worship—had gone more underground and had declined. And Hurston's very desire for real, insider knowledge initially may have put off voodoo practitioners who were accustomed to dealing with more superficial interest. Finally she succeeded, and the accounts of her initiation into voodoo are riveting testimony to her own dedication as well as to belief in the power of "hoodoo doctors" to fix and lift curses and otherwise provide magical help. Whether voodoo has survived into late-twentieth-century Louisiana is a question of much interest to contemporary visitors, but one without an easy answer, depending on exactly what the questioner means by *voodoo* in the contemporary context.

Even with all this curiosity, exotic, intriguing voodoo has not gotten all the attention travelers have paid to the "world of the spirits." In 1819, for example, architect Benjamin Latrobe recorded in his journal an account of Holy Week devotions at St. Louis Cathedral that clearly still owed something to colonial Spanish influence. Swedish writer Fredrika Bremer, in Louisiana in the 1850s, provides a nicely drawn impression of worship in the "African Church" of New Orleans. If Bremer was unprepared for the ecstatic excitement of the service, she did view what she saw with sympathy and even fascination, as containing an "element of true African worship" despite what she saw as "irrationality and the want of good taste." And A. Oakey Hall—among many others—calls attention to the Louisiana cemeteries, whose mode of above-ground interment gives the dead such a presence in the world of the living, and to All Saints' Day, still an important Louisiana holiday, when the living honor the spirits of the dead by gathering in the cemeteries around family tombs and graves.

Holy Week

Benjamin Latrobe

For information on Latrobe, see Chapter 1.

April 8, 1819. The holy week is here celebrated with much less pomp than formerly, but still with many ceremonies that do not well accord with the simplicity of the American character, even of the Catholic religion in the old United States. . . . Every year clips off a little more of the old Spanish regime. The host is no longer carried in procession through the streets, and the public square before the Church is not any more the parade ground of the Clergy. The business is all done within the walls of the building.

The altar has been during this whole week covered with a black drapery, without ornament. On Thursday, I went into the Church about 5 o'clock in the evening. A temporary piece of scenery was erected at the end of the south aisle, which covered the side altar at that place. The side altar at the north aisle was lighted up, and a priest was officiating. The Church was excessively crowded, especially about the door & in the south aisle, & about 1,000 people were in the square fronting the Church, where, indeed, I had observed a great crowd the whole day. The decoration at the end of the south aisle consisted of a sort of gate. . . . It was made of boards, badly painted in imitation of marble. The steps were narrow & flat & not intended for use. 4 rows of candles & 5 of flower pots with very bad artificial flowers stood on the steps, and a row of candles on the ballustres, so as altogether to look like what the children would call a very pretty baby house on a large scale. Within the arch was an altar covered with drapery & tinsel, & at each side of the altar stood a wax doll, about the size of a child of 5 or 6 years old, dressed up in scarlet & a profusion of tinsel. Each held a candle in its hand. I could not make out what all this repre-

From *The Journals of Benjamin Latrobe, 1799–1820: From Philadelphia to New Orleans,* by Benjamin Latrobe, ed. Edward C. Carter II, John C. Van Horne, and Lee Formwalt. Copyright © 1980 by Yale University Press. Reprinted by permission of Yale University Press.

St. Louis Cathedral,
New Orleans, by
E. M. Law

From Will H. Coleman,
ed., *Historical Sketch Book
and Guide to New Orleans*
(New York, 1885)

sented, and nobody that I asked could inform me. On one side of the altar is a door. . . . This door was shut up, and covered with a white muslin curtain, festooned round the arch & hanging down on each side. Within the niche was an image of the virgin, about 2 feet high, dressed in black velvet; her robe was drawn out on each side & fastened to the back of the niche so as to give the whole figure a triangular shape. A silver embroidered cross extended from her chin to her feet, & at each ear she had a large silver shell. The face appeared to be of wax. This figure stood upon two steps, upon an ordinary table covered with muslin, with a little tinsel about it, & 4 candles burning before it.

Before these two altars a carpet was spread, upon the edge of which . . . lay a crucifix, with a figure about 2 feet long & two tea-waiters.

On the south side of the nave, near the principal door of the Church, was placed a common small table. Behind it was a long bench, on which sat an old grey headed man in a ordinary & rather mean dress, & upon the table stood a crucifix. The Cross was of black wood, the figure painted to represent flesh, with a grey drapery round the middle. This figure was admirably executed, but on this very account was a horrible object. The artist had represented his subject so naturally that nothing but habit could reconcile the eye to such an exhibition. The body hung as usual by nails through the palms of the hands. The sinews of the hands and arms were strained to the utmost, the fingers open, & the flesh swelled & puckered by the weight hanging to it. The body had fallen to the left side. All the pectoral muscles strained upwards; the head sinking into the cavity of the collar bones. The legs tending again to the right, & the feet, where nailed to the body of the cross, twisted upon the nails, & the wounds opening, the knees bending a little forward; in fact, so well had the artist studied his subject, & so naturally was the bloody & death-colored image painted, that nothing but habit could have reconciled the people to its use.

This was the apparatus of the ceremony that was going on the whole day. The people, of whom ¾ at least were colored, & of those a very large majority were women, in their best dresses, crowded down to the altar at the bottom of the south aisle, & after crossing themselves they kneeled down & kissed the hands, feet, & body of the crucifix which lay upon the carpet, & at the same time put a piece of money into the waiters, which when I saw them, were heaped with *bits* & *halfbits* (escalins & pikiouns—6 ¼ & 12 ½ cents) & among these many quarters & half-dollars, & some dollars.

The same ceremony of kissing the image was going on near the entrance of the Church, where there was also a waiter filled with money. The business of the old man seemed to be twofold; to guard the money & to hold the crucifix steady. On each side of the other crucifix at the altar was a soldier in uniform, with his musket & bayonet fixed. They stood on the carpet, & a large crowd were kneeling around, praying, looking about at the new comers, & occasionally laughing & conversing together upon their knees.

The earnestness & devotion with which the devotees kissed these images was very remarkable. Most of them kissed each of the hands & the feet, but many bestowed their kisses also upon the knees & breast, & repeated them several times. Several young women appeared to mix a sort of devotional passion with their kisses, & one woman, after getting near the door, turned back & kissed the image again most passionately, while tears were running down her cheeks.

As to the contribution of money, it seemed to be optional, for I observed many who gave nothing.

April 9. I went, about 12 this morning, to the Church. The scenery at the end of the south aisle was removed, & they were sweeping the building. It was full of dust, & yet a large concourse were in it, & as many on the outside. The crucifix & the old man near the door were still there, & many men & women, all colored people, were still performing the ceremony of kissing it, & the more substantial one of putting money into the waiters. Several women were there with small children, whose little mouths they put to the hands & feet of the image.

Altho' the Catholic inhabitants of this city do business on Sunday as on any other day, yet on this day, Good Friday, even the notaries have (to my great injury) shut up their offices, & the police officer has summoned one of my carters, & threatened him with a fine of 50 dollars for hauling lime on this day.

Cities of the Dead

A. Oakey Hall

From *The Manhattaner in New Orleans; or, Phases of "Crescent City" Life* (1851); for more information on Hall, see Chapter 1.

Various poets have called cemeteries Cities of the Dead; and the expression is forcible applied to those of New Orleans, of which the St. Louis is a representative specimen. Cities of the dead; because from the peculiar moisture of the soil interments are in tombs and oven-like vaults, constructed above ground; the latter in tiers of three and four along the cemetery walls, built of brick and faced with marble, upon which to inscribe the words with which affection consecrates entombed dust. In the area are private tombs constructed with granite or marble, and varied in form and finish by taste and worldly circumstance. To some, this idea of burial above ground, where each body has, as it were, a mansion to itself, and which in most cases is just large enough to hold the coffin, is revolting. I have heard many a sojourner say, "Oh, if I die, send me for burial to my northern home,—don't shut me up in those horrid cells." But to others, the idea that they stood by the side of one loved well, and conscious that but a foot of brick and mortar separated a friend's mortality . . . from their own, was gratifying. Many of the private tombs of the St. Louis Cemetery are very costly, but for the most part more curious in design and execution than artistic. Some with recesses where private masses for the dead may be celebrated; with statues and figures of the saints and decorated altars. Many are old and crumbling, and dyed green with moisture.

When the first day of November comes in, and the religious index points to it on the calendar as "All Saints' Day," the St. Louis Cemetery is thronged with pious devotees of all ages and sexes—principally females—coming to offer up prayers. At the burial altars of departed relatives, bringing tapers, and incense, and flowers, to put before them. It is not a little startling to jostle

All Saints' Day devotions, by Mircea Vasiliu

among the crowds (for I have seen at least three thousand people in attendance when the day was sunny,) walking through avenues of tombs where the dead were laid in rows above each other. To many a tender frame has issued upon such occasions from the damp alleys and causeways, a death warrant which was sealed, delivered, and executed before the expiration of another month. Of the crowd the largest number were mere idle spectators—many, the butterflies of New Orleans, who gaped, wondered, chatted, and talked, as though it were a gala day, and they invited or privileged guests at some great fête. But the humble kneelers heeded them not, and absorbed in their private griefs, thought little of the flippant laugh or stare of curiosity around them. As after such a day I have turned down Toulouse-street, leaving a hum of voices behind me in this "city of the dead," I have thought here is but another witness to the force of the old aphorism, "all men think all men mortal but themselves."

The Element of True African Worship

FREDRIKA BREMER

From *The Homes of the New World: Impressions of America* (1854), trans. Mary Howitt. Here the anti-slavery Bremer (see also Chapter 4) writes of visiting a black church in New Orleans, reporting on the "African" exuberance of the service.

I must now tell you about a real African tornado which Anne W. and I witnessed last Sunday afternoon. It was in the African Church, for even here, in this gay, light-hearted city of New Orleans, has Christianity commenced its work of renovated life; and they have Sunday-schools for negro children, where they receive instruction about the Savior; and the negro slaves are able to serve God in their own church.

We came too late to hear the sermon in this African Church, whither we had betaken ourselves. But at the close of the service, a so-called class-meeting was held. I do not know whether I have already said that the Methodists form, within their community, certain divisions or classes, which elect their own leaders or exhorters. These exhorters go round at the class-meeting to such of the members of their class as they deem to stand in need of consolation or en-couragement, talk to them, aloud or in an under voice, receive their confes-sions, impart advice to them, and so on. I had seen such a class-meeting at Washington, and knew, therefore, what was the kind of scene which we might expect. But my expectations were quite exceeded here. Here we were nearer the tropical sun than at Washington.

The exhorters went round, and began to converse here and there with the people who sat on the benches. Scarcely, however, had they talked for a min-ute before the person addressed came into a state of exaltation, and began to speak and to perorate more loudly and more vehemently than the exhorter himself, and so to overpower him. There was one exhorter in particular, whose black, good-natured countenance was illumined by so great a degree of

Life and death in a New Orleans cemetery, one of the woodcuts Lafcadio Hearn executed originally in the 1880s to illustrate his articles in the New Orleans *Item,* for which he wrote during his lengthy Louisiana sojourn

From Lafcadio Hearn, *Creole Sketches,* ed. Charles Woodward Hutson (Boston, 1924)

the inward light, by so much good-humor and joy, that it was a pleasure to see him, and to hear him too; for, although his phrases were pretty much the same, and the same over again, yet they were words full of Christian pith and marrow, and they were uttered with so much cordiality, that they could not do other than go straight to the heart with enlivening power. Sometimes his ideas seemed to come to an end, and he stood, as it were, seeking for a moment; but then he would begin again with what he had just now said and his words always brought with them the same warmth and faithfulness, and he looked like a life-infusing sunbeam. And it was only as the messenger of the joy in Christ that he preached. . . .

By degrees the noise increased in the church, and became a storm of voices and cries. The words were heard "Yes, come Lord Jesus! Come, oh come, oh glory!" and they who thus cried aloud began to leap—leaped aloft with a motion as of a cork flying out of a bottle, while they waved their arms and their handkerchiefs in the air, as if they were endeavoring to bring something down, and all the while crying aloud, "Come, oh come!" And as they leaped, they twisted their bodies round in a sort of corkscrew fashion, and were evidently in a state of convulsion; sometimes they fell down and rolled in the aisle, amid loud, lamenting cries and groans. I saw our tropical exhorter, the man with the sun-bright countenance, talking to a young negro with a crooked nose and eyes that squinted, and he too very soon began to talk and to preach, as he sprung high into the air, leaping up and down with incredible elasticity. Whichever way we looked in the church, we saw somebody leaping up and fanning the air; the whole church seemed transformed into a regular Bedlam, and the noise and the tumult was horrible. Still, however, the exhorters made their rounds with beaming countenances, as if they were in their right element, and as if every thing were going on as it ought to do. Presently we saw our hearty exhorter address a few words to a tall, handsome mulatto woman, who sat before us, and while he was preaching to her she began to preach to him; both talked for some time with evident enchantment, till she also got into motion, and sprang aloft with such vehemence, that three other women took hold of her by the skirts, as if to hold her still on the earth. Two of these laughed quietly, while they continued to hold her down, and she to leap up and throw her arms around. At length she fell and rolled about amid convulsive groans. After that she rose up and began to walk about, up and down the church, with outspread arms, ejaculating every now and then, "Halleluiah!" Her appearance was now calm, earnest and really beautiful. Amid all the wild tumult of crying and leaping, on the right hand and the left, she continued to walk up and down the church, in all directions, with outspread arms, eyes cast upward, exclaiming in a low voice, "Halleluiah! Halleluiah!" At length she sank down upon her knees on the platform by the altar, and there she became still.

After the crying and the leaping had continued for a good quarter of an hour longer, several negroes raised the mulatto woman, who was lying prostrate by the altar. She was now quite rigid. They bore her to a bench in front of us, and laid her down upon it.

"What has happened to her?" inquired Anne W. from a young negro girl whom she knew.

"Converted!" said she laconically, and joined those who were softly rubbing the pulses of the converted.

I laid my hand upon her brow. It was quite cold, so also were her hands.

When, by degrees, she had recovered consciousness, her glance was still fixed, but it seemed to me that it was directed rather inwardly than outwardly; she talked to herself in a low voice, and such a beautiful, blissful expression was portrayed in her countenance, that I would willingly experience that which she then experienced, saw, or perceived. It was no ordinary, no earthly scene. Her countenance was as it were transfigured. As soon as, after deep sighs, she had returned to her usual state, her appearance became usual also. But her demeanor was changed; she wept much, but calmly and silently.

The tornado gradually subsided in the church; shrieking and leaping, admonishing and preaching all became hushed; and now people shook hands with each other, talked, laughed, congratulated one another so heartily, so cheerfully, with such cordial warmth and good-will, that it was a pleasure to behold. Of the whole raging, exciting scene there remained merely a feeling of satisfaction and pleasure, as if they had been together at some joyful feast.

I confess . . . to having been thoroughly amused by the frolic. Not so Anne W., who regarded that disorderly, wild worship with a feeling of astonishment, almost of indignation. . . .

[In] spite of all the irrationality and the want of good taste which may be felt in such scenes, I am certain that there is in them, although as yet in a chaotic state, the element of true African worship. Give only intelligence, order, system to this outbreak of the warm emotions, longings, and presentiments of life, and then that which now appears hideous will become beautiful, that which is discordant will become harmonious. The children of Africa may yet give us a form of divine worship in which invocation, supplication, and songs of praise may respond to the inner life of the fervent soul!

A Voodoo Dance

CHARLES DUDLEY WARNER

Warner (1829–1900), eminent writer and coauthor of *The Gilded Age* with Mark Twain, came to New Orleans for the Exposition of 1885, stayed for a month, and later toured the Acadian country. From *Studies in the South and West, with Comments on Canada* (1889).

There was nothing mysterious about it. The ceremony took place in broad day, at noon in the upper chambers of a small frame house in a street just beyond Congo Square and the old Parish prison in New Orleans. It was an incantation rather than a dance—a curious mingling of African Voudoo rites with modern "spiritualism" and faith-cure. . . .

Although very few white people in New Orleans have ever seen the performance I shall try to describe, and it is said that the police would break it up if they knew of it, it takes place every Wednesday at noon at the house where I saw it; and there are three or four other places in the city where the rites are celebrated sometimes at night. Our admission was procured through a friend who had, I suppose, vouched for our good intentions.

We were received in the living-rooms of the house on the ground floor by the "doctor," a good-looking mulatto of middle age, clad in a white shirt with gold studs, linen pantaloons, and list slippers. He had the simple-minded shrewd look of a "healing medium." The interior was neat, though in some confusion; among the rude attempts at art on the walls was the worst chromo print of General Grant that was probably ever made. There were several negroes about the door, many in the rooms and in the backyard, and all had an air of expectation and mild excitement. After we had satisfied the scruples of the doctor, and signed our names in his register, we were invited to ascend by a narrow, crooked stairway in the rear. This led to a small landing where a dozen people might stand, and from this a door opened into a chamber perhaps fifteen feet by ten, where the rites were to take place; beyond this was a small bedroom. Around the sides of these rooms were benches and chairs, and the close quarters were already well filled.

The assembly was perfectly orderly, but a motley one, and the women largely outnumbered the men. There were coal-black negroes, porters, and stevedores, fat cooks, slender chamber-maids, all shades of complexion, yellow girls and comely quadroons, most of them in common servant attire, but some neatly dressed. And among them were, to my surprise, several white people.

On one side of the middle room where we sat was constructed a sort of buffet or bureau, used as an altar. On it stood an image of the Virgin Mary in painted plaster, about two feet high, flanked by lighted candles and a couple of cruets, with some other small objects. On a shelf below were two other candles, and on this shelf and the floor in front were various offerings to be used in the rites—plates of apples, grapes, bananas, oranges; dishes of sugar, of sugar-plums; a dish of powdered orris root, packages of candles, bottles of brandy and of water. Two other lighted candles stood on the floor, and in front an earthen bowl. The clear space in front for the dancer was not more than four or five feet square.

Some time was consumed in preparations, or in waiting for the worshippers to assemble. From conversation with those near me, I found that the doctor had a reputation for healing the diseased by virtue of his incantations, of removing "spells," of finding lost articles, of ministering to the troubles of lovers, and, in short, of doing very much what clairvoyants and healing mediums claim to do in what are called civilized communities. But failing to get a very intelligent account of the expected performance from the negro woman next me, I moved to the side of the altar and took a chair next a girl of perhaps twenty years old, whose complexion and features gave evidence that she was white. Still, finding her in that company, and there as a participant in the Voudoo rites, I concluded that I must be mistaken, and that she must have colored blood in her veins. Assuming the privilege of an inquirer, I asked her questions about the coming performance, and in doing so carried the impression that she was kin to the colored race. But I was soon convinced, from her manner and her replies, that she was pure white. She was a pretty, modest girl, very reticent, well-bred, polite, and civil. None of the colored people seemed to know who she was, but she said she had been there before. She told me, in course of the conversation, the name of the street where she lived (in the American part of the town), the private school at which she had been educated (one of the best in the city), and that she and her parents were Episcopalians. Whatever her trouble was, mental or physical, she was evidently infatuated with the notion that this Voudoo doctor could conjure it away, and said that she thought he had already been of service to her. She did not communicate her difficulties to him or speak to him, but she evidently had faith that he could discern what every one present needed, and minister to them. When I asked her if, with her education, she did not think that more good would come to her by confiding in known friends or in regular practitioners, she wearily said that she did not know. After the performance began, her intense interest in it, and the light in her eyes, were evidence of the deep hold the superstition had upon her nature. In coming to this place she had gone a step beyond the young ladies of her class who make a novena at St. Roch.

While we still waited, the doctor and two other colored men called me into the next chamber, and wanted to be assured that it was my own name I had written on the register, and that I had no unfriendly intentions in being present. Their doubts at rest, all was ready.

The doctor squatted on one side of the altar, and his wife, a stout woman of darker hue, on the other.

"Commençons," said the woman, in a low voice. All the colored people spoke French, and French only, to each other and in the ceremony.

The doctor nodded, bent over, and gave three sharp raps on the floor with a bit of wood. (This is the usual opening of Voudoo rites.) All the others rapped three times on the floor with their knuckles. Any one coming in to join the circle afterwards, stooped and rapped three times. After a moment's silence, all kneeled and repeated in French the Apostles' Creed, and still on their knees, they said two prayers to the Virgin Mary.

The colored woman at the side of the altar began a chant in a low, melodious voice. It was the weird and strange "Dansé Calinda."[1] A tall negress, with

---

1. The term *calinda* refers to a complex of dances originating in Africa. In parts of the Caribbean, where the dance still exists, it is most likely to be a stick-fighting dance. In Louisiana the term has been applied to a dance associated with voodoo ceremonies that is said to have seemed licentious and was banned for periods of time. It seems to have died out in the nineteenth century. Today the term is probably best known from its appearance in a Cajun folksong, "Allons Danser Colinda"; here Colinda has become a girl's name, though the song probably has some historical connection with the dance. See Shane Bernard and Julia Girouard, "'Colinda': Mysterious Origins of a Cajun Folksong," *Journal of Folklore Research*, XXIX (1992), 37–52.

a bright, good-natured face, entered the circle with the air of a chief performer, knelt, rapped the floor, laid an offering of candles before the altar, with a small bottle of brandy, seated herself beside the singer, and took up in a strong, sweet voice the bizarre rhythm of the song. Nearly all those who came in had laid some little offering before the altar. The chant grew, the single line was enunciated in stronger pulsations, and other voices joined in the wild refrain,

"Dansé Calinda, boudoum, boudoum!
"Dansé Calinda, boudoum, boudoum!"

bodies swayed, the hands kept time in soft patpatting, and the feet in muffled accentuation. The Voudoo arose, removed his slippers, seized a bottle of brandy, dashed some of the liquid on the floor on each side of the brown bowl as a libation, threw back his head and took a long pull at the bottle, and then began in the open space a slow measured dance, a rhythmical shuffle, with more movement of the hips than of the feet, backward and forward, round and round, but accelerating his movement as the time of the song quickened and the excitement rose in the room. The singing became wilder and more impassioned, a strange minor strain, full of savage pathos and longing, that made it almost impossible for the spectator not to join in the swing of its influence, while the dancer wrought himself up into the wild passion of a Cairene dervish. Without a moment ceasing his rhythmical steps and his extravagant gesticulation, he poured liquid into the basin, and dashing in brandy, ignited the fluid with a match. The liquid flamed up before the altar. He seized then a bunch of candies, plunged them into the bowl, held them up all flaming with the burning brandy, and, keeping his step to the maddening "Calinda," distributed them lighted to the devotees. In the same way he snatched up dishes of apples, grapes, bananas, oranges, deluged them with burning brandy, and tossed them about the room to the eager and excited crowd. His hands were aflame, his clothes seemed to be on fire; he held the burning dishes close to his breast, apparently inhaling the flame, closing his eyes and swaying his head backward and forward in an ecstasy, the hips advancing and receding, the feet still shuffling to the barbaric measure.

Every moment his own excitement and that of the audience increased. The floor was covered with the debris of the sacrifice—broken candy, crushed sugar-plums, scattered grapes—and all more or less in flame. The wild dancer was dancing in fire! In the height of his frenzy he grasped a large plate filled with lump-sugar. That was set on fire. He held the burning mass to his breast, he swung it round, and finally, with his hand extended under the bottom of the plate (the plate only adhering to his hand by the rapidity of his circular motion), he spun around like a dancing dervish, his eyes shut, the perspiration pouring in streams from his face, in a frenzy. The flaming sugar scattered about the floor, and the devotees scrambled for it. In intervals of the dance, though the singing went on, the various offerings which had been conjured were passed around—bits of sugar and fruit and orris powder. That which fell to my share I gave to the young girl next me, whose eyes were blazing with excitement. She put the conjured fruit in her pocket, and seemed grateful to me for relinquishing it to her.

Before this point had been reached the chant had been changed for the wild *canga,* more rapid in movement than the *chanson africaine:*

> "Eh! eh! Bomba, hen! hen!
> Canga bafio té
> Canga moune dé lé
> Canga do ki la
> Canga li."

At intervals during the performance, when the charm had begun to work, the believers came forward into the open space, and knelt for "treatment." The singing, the dance, the wild incantation, went on uninterruptedly; but amid all his antics the dancer had an eye to business. The first group that knelt were four stalwart men, three of them white laborers. All of them, I presume, had some disease which they had faith the incantation would drive away. Each held a lighted candle in each hand. The doctor successively extinguished each candle by putting it in his mouth, and performed a number of antics of a saltatory sort. During his dancing and whirling he frequently filled his mouth with liquid, and discharged it in spray, exactly as a Chinese laundryman sprinkles his clothes, into the faces and on the heads of any man or woman within reach. Those so treated considered themselves specially favored. Having extinguished the candles of the suppliants, he scooped the liquid from the bowl, flaming or not as it might be, and with his hands vigorously scrubbed their faces and heads, as if he were shampooing them. While the victim was still sputtering and choking he seized him by the right hand, lifted him up, spun him round half a dozen times, and then sent him whirling.

This was substantially the treatment that all received who knelt in the circle, though sometimes it was more violent. Some of them were slapped smartly upon the back and the breast, and much knocked about. Occasionally a woman was whirled till she was dizzy, and perhaps swung about in his arms as if she had been a bundle of clothes. They all took it meekly and gratefully. One little girl of twelve, who had rickets, was banged about till it seemed as if every bone in her body would be broken. But the doctor had discrimination, even in his wildest moods. Some of the women were gently whirled, and the conjurer forbore either to spray them from his mouth or to shampoo them.

Nearly all those present knelt, and were whirled and shaken, and those who did not take this "cure" I suppose got the benefit of the incantations by carrying away some of the consecrated offerings. Occasionally a woman in the whirl would whisper something in the doctor's ear, and receive from him doubtless the counsel she needed. But generally the doctor made no inquiries of his patients, and they said nothing to him.

While the wild chanting, the rhythmic movement of hands and feet, the barbarous dance, and the fierce incantations were at their height, it was difficult to believe that we were in a civilized city of an enlightened republic. Nothing indecent occurred in word or gesture, but it was so wild and bizarre that one might easily imagine he was in Africa or in hell.

As I said, all the participants were colored people; but in the height of the frenzy one white woman knelt and was sprayed and whirled with the others. She was a respectable married woman from the other side of Canal Street. I waited with some anxiety to see what my modest little neighbor would do. She had told me that she should look on and take no part. I hoped that the senseless antics, the mummery, the rough treatment, would disgust her. Towards the close of the seance, when the spells were all woven and the flames had subsided, the tall, good-natured negress motioned to me that it was my turn to advance into the circle and kneel. I excused myself. But the young girl was unable to resist longer. She went forward and knelt, with a candle in her hand. The conjurer was either touched by her youth and race, or he had spent his force. He gently lifted her by one hand, and gave her one turn around, and she came back to her seat.

The singing ceased. The doctor's wife passed round the hat for contributions, and the ceremony, which had lasted nearly an hour and a half, was over. The doctor retired exhausted with the violent exertions. As for the patients, I trust they were well cured of rheumatism, of fever, or whatever ill they had, and that the young ladies have either got husbands to their minds or have escaped faithless lovers. In the breaking up I had no opportunity to speak further to the interesting young white neophyte; but as I saw her resuming her hat and cloak in the adjoining room there was a strange excitement in her face, and in her eyes a light of triumph and faith. We came out by the back way, and through an alley made our escape into the sunny street and the air of the nineteenth century.

A Voodoo Initiation

Zora Neale Hurston

When Hurston died in 1960, this prominent member of the Harlem Renaissance group of writers, artists, and intellectuals had been practically forgotten; in the 1970s she was rediscovered and has come to be considered a major American literary figure, and her novels and other books are widely read. In 1927, working on an advanced degree at Columbia University, she set out to collect folklore. After recording folktales in her native Florida, she came to New Orleans to research voodoo.

Winter passed and caterpillars began to cross the road again. I had spent a year in gathering and culling over folk-tales. I loved it, but I had to bear in mind that there was a limit to the money to be spent on the project, and as yet, I had done nothing about hoodoo.[2]

So I slept a night, and the next morning I headed my toe-nails toward Louisiana and New Orleans in particular.

New Orleans is now and has ever been the hoodoo capital of America. . . .

Now I was in New Orleans and I asked. They told me Algiers, the part of New Orleans that is across the river to the west. I went there and lived for four months and asked. I found women reading cards and doing mail order business in names and insinuations of well known factors in conjure. Nothing worth putting on paper. But they all claimed some knowledge and link with

2. The word *hoodoo* probably derives from *voodoo* and is commonly used by African Americans to refer to magical practices.

Marie Leveau. From so much of hearing the name I asked everywhere for this Leveau and everybody told me differently. But from what they said I was eager to know to the end of the talk. It carried me back across the river into the Vieux Carré. All agreed that she had lived and died in the French quarter of New Orleans. So I went there to ask.

I found an oil painting of the queen of conjure on the walls of the Cabildo, and mention of her in the guide books of New Orleans, but I did a lot of stumbling and asking before I heard of Luke Turner, himself a hoodoo doctor, who says that he is her nephew.

When I found out about Turner, I had already studied under five two-headed doctors and had gone thru an initiation ceremony with each.[3] So I asked Turner to take me as a pupil. He was very cold. In fact he showed no eagerness even to talk with me. He feels sure of his powers and seeks no one. He refused to take me as a pupil and in addition to his habitual indifference I could see he had no faith in my sincerity. I could see him searching my face for whatever was behind what I said. The City of New Orleans has a law against fortune tellers, hoodoo doctors and the like, and Turner did not know me. He asked me to excuse him as he was waiting upon someone in the inner room. I let him go but I sat right there and waited. When he returned, he tried to shoo me away by being rude. I stayed on. Finally he named an impossible price for tuition. I stayed and dickered. He all but threw me out, but I stayed and urged him.

I made three more trips before he would talk to me in any way that I could feel encouraged. He talked about Marie Leveau because I asked. I wanted to know if she was really as great as they told me. So he enlightened my ignorance and taught me. We sat before the soft coal fire in his grate.

"Time went around pointing out what God had already made. Moses had seen the Burning Bush. Solomon by magic knowed all wisdom.[4] And Marie Leveau was a woman in New Orleans.

"She was born February 2, 1827. Anybody don't believed I tell the truth

---

3. A two-head in African American parlance is someone with magical powers; the term probably derives from the idea that such a person can look two ways, into both the physical and the spiritual worlds. The term *doctor* is sometimes used by itself to refer to magical practitioners.

4. There is a long-standing tradition that views the biblical Solomon as a magician. In African American tradition, Moses has also been so regarded.

can go look at the book in St. Louis Cathedral. Her mama and her papa, they wasn't married and his name was Christophe Glapion.

"She was very pretty, one of the Creole Quadroons and many people said she would never be a hoodoo doctor like her mama and her grandma before her. She liked to go to the balls very much where all the young men fell in love with her. But Alexander, the great two-headed doctor felt the power in her and so he tell her she must come to study with him. Marie, she rather dance and make love, but one day a rattlesnake come to her in her bedroom and spoke to her. So she went to Alexander and studied. But soon she could teach her teacher and the snake stayed with her always.

"She has her house on St. Anne Street and people come from the ends of America to get help from her. Even Queen Victoria ask her help and send her a cashmere shawl with money also.

"Now, some white people say she hold hoodoo dance on Congo Square every week. But Marie Leveau never hold no hoodoo dance. That was a pleasure dance. They beat the drum with the shin bone of a donkey and everybody dance like they do in Hayti. Hoodoo is private. She give the dance the first Friday night in each month and they have crab gumbo and rice to eat and the people dance. The white people come look on, and think they see all, when they only see a dance.

"The police hear so much about Marie Leveau that they come to her house in St. Anne Street to put her in jail. First one come, she stretch out her left hand and he turn round and round and never stop until some one come lead him away. Then two come together—she put them to running and barking like dogs. Four come and she put them to beating each other with night sticks. The whole station force come. They knock at her door. She know who they are before she ever look. She did work at her altar and they all went to sleep on her steps.

"Out on Lake Pontchartrain at Bayou St. John she hold a great feast every year on the Eve of St. John's, June 24th. It is Midsummer Eve, and the Sun give special benefits then and need great honor.[5] The special drum be played then. It is a cowhide stretched over a half-barrel. Beat with a jaw-bone. Some say a man but I think they do not know. I think the jawbone of an ass or a

---

5. In European tradition, Midsummer Eve (June 23) has long been associated with magic and pre-Christian ritual.

A Voodoo Woman,
fancifully and stereo-
typically re-created

From Charles Dudley
Warner, "New Orleans,"
Harper's Monthly,
January, 1887

cow. She hold the feast of St. John's partly because she is a Catholic and partly because of hoodoo.

"The ones around her altar fix everything for the feast. Nobody see Marie Leveau for nine days before the feast. But when the great crowd of people at the feast call upon her, she would rise out of the waters of the lake with a great communion candle burning upon her head and another in each one of her hands. She walked upon the waters to the shore. As a little boy I saw her my-self. When the feast was over, she went back into the lake, and nobody saw her for nine days again.

"On the feast that I saw her open the waters, she looked hard at me and nodded her head so that her tignon shook. Then I knew I was called to take up her work. She was very old and I was a lad of seventeen. Soon I went to wait upon her Altar, both on St. Anne Street and her house on Bayou St. John's.

"The rattlesnake that had come to her a little one when she was also young was very huge. He piled great upon his altar and took nothing from the food set before him. One night he sang and Marie Leveau called me from my sleep to look at him and see. 'Look well, Turner,' she told me. 'No one shall hear and see such as this for many centuries.'

"She went to her Great Altar and made great ceremony. The snake finished his song and seemed to sleep. She drove me back to my bed and went again to her Altar.

"The next morning, the great snake was not at his altar. His hide was before the Great Altar stuffed with spices and things of power. Never did I know what become of his flesh. It is said that the snake went off to the woods alone after the death of Marie Leveau, but they don't know. This is his skin that I wear about my shoulders whenever I reach for power.

"Three days Marie, she set at the Altar with the great sun candle burning and shining in her face. She set the water upon the Altar and turned to the window, and looked upon the lake. The sky grew dark. The lightning raced to the seventeen quarters of the heavens and the lake heaved like a mighty herd of cattle rolling in a pasture. The house shook with the earth.

"She told me, 'You are afraid. That is right, you should fear. Go to your own house and build an altar. Power will come.' So I hurried to my mother's house and told them.

"Some who loved her hurried out to Bayou St. John and tried to enter the house but she try hard to send them off. They beat upon the door, but she will not open. The terrible strong wind at last tore the house away and set it in the lake. The thunder and lightning grow greater. Then the loving ones find a boat and went out to where her house floats on one side and break a window to bring her out, but she begs, 'NO! Please no,' she tell them. 'I want to die here in the lake,' but they would not permit her. She did not wish their destruction, so she let herself be drawn away from her altar in the lake. And the wind, the thunder and lightning, and the water all ceased the moment she set foot on dry land.

"That night she also sing a song and is dead, yes. So I have the snake skin and do works with the power she leave me."

. . . The next day he began to prepare me for my initiation ceremony, for rest assured that no one may approach the Altar without the crown, and none may wear the crown of power without preparation. *It must be earned.*

And what is this crown of power? Nothing definite in material. Turner crowned me with a consecrated snake skin. I have been crowned in other places with flowers, with ornamental paper, with cloth, with sycamore bark, with egg-shells. It is the meaning, not the material that counts. The crown without the preparation means no more than a college diploma without the four years' work.

This preparation period is akin to that of all mystics. Clean living, even to clean thoughts. A sort of going to the wilderness in the spirit. The details do not matter. My nine days being up, and possessed of the three snake skins and the new underwear required, I entered Turner's house as an inmate to finish the last three days of my novitiate. Turner had become so sure of my fitness as a hoodoo doctor that he would accept no money from me except what was necessary to defray the actual cost of the ceremony.

So I ate my final meal before six o'clock of the evening before and went to bed for the last time with my right stocking on and my left leg bare.

I entered the old pink stucco house in the Vieux Carré at nine o'clock in the morning with the parcel of needed things. Turner placed the new underwear on the big Altar; prepared the couch with the snake-skin cover upon which I was to lie for three days. With the help of other members of the college of hoodoo doctors called together to initiate me, the snake skins I had brought were made into garments for me to wear. One was coiled into a high head-piece—the crown. One had loops attached to slip on my arms so that it could be worn as a shawl, and the other was made into a girdle for my loins. All places have significance. These garments were placed on the small altar in the corner. The throne of the snake. The Great One was called upon to enter the garments and dwell there.

I was made ready and at three o'clock in the afternoon, naked as I came into the world, I was stretched, face downwards, my navel to the snake skin cover, and began my three day search for the spirit that he might accept me or reject me according to his will. Three days my body must lie silent and fasting while my spirit went wherever spirits must go that seek answers never given to men as men.

I could have no food, but a pitcher of water was placed on a small table at the head of the couch, that my spirit might not waste time in search of water which should be spent in search of the Power-Giver. The spirit must have water, and if none had been provided it would wander in search of it. And evil spirits might attack it as it wandered about dangerous places. If it should be seriously injured, it might never return to me.

For sixty-nine hours I lay there. I had five psychic experiences and awoke at last with no feeling of hunger, only one of exaltation.

I opened my eyes because Turner called me. He stood before the Great Altar dressed ceremoniously. Five others were with him.

"Seeker, come," Turner called.

I made to rise and go to him. Another laid his hand upon me lightly, restraining me from rising.

"How must I come?" he asked in my behalf.

"You must come to the spirit across running water," Turner answered in a sort of chant.

So a tub was placed beside the bed. I was assisted to my feet and led to the tub. Two men poured water into the tub while I stepped into it and out again on the other side.

"She has crossed the dangerous stream in search of the spirit," the one who spoke for me chanted.

"The spirit does not know her name. What is she called?"

"She has no name but what the spirit gives."

"I see her conquering and accomplishing with the lightning and making her road with thunder. She shall be called the Rain-Bringer."

I was stretched again upon the couch. Turner approached me with two brothers, one on either side of him. One held a small paint brush dipped in yellow, the other bore one dipped in red. With ceremony Turner painted the lightning symbol down my back from my right shoulder to my left hip. This was to be my sign forever. The Great One was to speak to me in storms.

I was now dressed in the new underwear and a white veil was placed over my head, covering my face, and I was seated in a chair.

After I was dressed, a pair of eyes was painted on my cheeks as a sign that I could see in more ways than one. The sun was painted on my forehead. Many came into the room and performed ceremonial acts, but none spoke to me. Nor could I speak to them while the veil covered my face. Turner cut the little finger of my right hand and caught the gushing blood in a wine cup. He added wine and mixed it with the blood. Then he and all the other five leaders let blood from themselves also and mixed it with wine in another glass. I was led to drink from the cup containing their mingled bloods, and each of them in turn beginning with Turner drank mine. At high noon I was seated at the splendid altar. It was dressed in the center with a huge communion candle with my name upon it set in sand, five large iced cakes in different colors, a plate of honeyed St. Joseph's bread,[6] a plate of serpent-shaped breads, spinach and egg cakes fried in olive oil, breaded Chinese okra fried in olive oil, roast veal and wine, two huge yellow bouquets, two red bouquets and two white bouquets and thirty-six yellow tapers and a bottle of holy water.

Turner seated me and stood behind me with his ceremonial hat upon his head, and the crown of power in his hand. "Spirit! I ask you to take her. Do you hear me, Spirit? Will you take her? Spirit, I want you to take her, she is worthy!" He held the crown poised above my head for a full minute. A profound silence held the room. Then he lifted the veil from my face and let it fall behind my head and crowned me with power. He lit my candle for me. But from then on I might be a candle-lighter myself. All the candles were reverently lit. We all sat down and ate the feast. First a glass of blessed oil was handed me by Turner. "Drink this without tasting it." I gulped it down and he took the glass from my hand, took a sip of the little that remained. Then he handed it to the brother at his right who did the same, until it went around the table.

"Eat first the spinach cakes," Turner exhorted, and we did. Then the meal began. It was full of joy and laughter, even though we knew that the final ceremony waited only for the good hour of twelve midnight.

About ten o'clock we all piled into an old Studebaker sedan—all but Turner who led us on a truck. Out Road No. 61 we rattled until a certain spot was reached. The truck was unloaded beside the road and sent back to town. It was a little after eleven. The swamp was dismal and damp, but after some stumbly walking we came to a little glade deep in the wood, near the lake. A candle was burning at each of the four corners of the clearing, representing the four corners of the world and the four winds. I could hear the occasional slap-slap of the water. With a whispered chant some twigs were gathered and tied into a broom. Some pine straw was collected. The sheets of typing paper I had been urged to bring were brought out and nine sheets were blessed and my petition written nine times on each sheet by the light from a shaded lan-

6. Italian Americans bake specially shaped breads for the Feast of St. Joseph (March 19), which is especially popular in New Orleans. Probably because Italians often owned stores in black neighborhoods, St. Joseph's Day came to have religious significance for those African Americans in the Spiritual churches and, evidently, for hoodoo practitioners.

tern. The crate containing the black sheep was opened and the sheep led forward into the center of the circle. He stood there dazedly while the chant of strange syllables rose. I asked Turner the words, but he replied that in good time I would know what to say. It was not to be taught. If nothing came, to be silent. The head and withers of the sheep were stroked as the chanting went on. Turner became more and more voluble. At last he seized the straw and stuffed some into the sheep's nostrils. The animal struggled. A knife flashed and the sheep dropped to its knees, then fell prone with its mouth open in a weak cry. My petition was thrust into its throat that he might cry it to the Great One. The broom was seized and dipped in the blood from the slit throat and the ground swept vigorously—back and forth, back and forth—the length of the dying sheep. It was swept from the four winds toward the center. The sweeping went on as long as the blood gushed. Earth, the mother of the Great One and us all, has been appeased. With a sharp stick Turner traced the outline of the sheep and the digging commenced. The sheep was never touched. The ground was dug from under him so that his body dropped down into the hole. He was covered with nine sheets of paper bearing the petition and the earth heaped upon him. A white candle was set upon the grave and we straggled back to the road and the Studebaker.

I studied under Turner five months and learned all of the Leveau routines; but in this book all of the works of any doctor cannot be given. However, we performed several of Turner's own routines.

Once a woman, an excited, angry woman wanted something done to keep her husband true. So she came and paid Turner gladly for his services.

Turner took a piece of string that had been "treated" at the altar and gave it to the woman.

"Measure the man where I tell you. But he must never know. Measure him in his sleep then fetch back the string to me."

The next day the woman came at ten o'clock instead of nine as Turner had told her, so he made her wait until twelve o'clock, that being a good hour. Twelve is one of the benign hours of the day while ten is a malignant hour. Then Turner took the string and tied nine knots in it and tied it to a larger piece of string which he tied about her waist. She was completely undressed for the ceremony and Turner cut some hair from under her left armpit and some from the right side of the the groin and put it together. Then he cut some from the right arm-pit and a tuft from the left groin and it was all placed on the altar, and burned in a votive light with the wish for her husband to love her and forget all others. She went away quite happy. She was so satisfied with the work that she returned with a friend a few days later.

Turner, with his toothless mouth, his Berber-looking face, said to the new caller:

"I can see you got trouble." He shivered. "It is all in the room. I feel the pain of it; Anger, Malice. Tell me who is this man you so fight with?"

"My husband's brother. He hate me and make all the trouble he can," the woman said in a tone so even and dull that it was hard to believe she meant what she said. "He must leave this town or die. Yes, it is much better if he is dead." Then she burst out, "Yeah, he should be dead long time ago. Long before he spy upon me, before he tell lies, lies, lies. I should be very happy for his funeral."

"Oh I can feel the great hate around you," Turner said. "It follow you everywhere, but I kill nobody, I send him away if you want so he never come back. I put guards along the road in the spirit world, and these he cannot pass, no. When he go, never will he come back to New Orleans. You see him no more. He will be forgotten and all his works."

"Then I am satisfied, yes," the woman said. "When will you send him off?"

"I ask the spirit, you will know."

She paid him and he sent her off and Turner went to his snake altar and sat in silence for a long time. When he arose, he sent me out to buy nine black chickens, and some Four Thieves Vinegar. He himself went out and got nine small sticks upon which he had me write the troublesome brother-in-law's name—one time on each stick. At ten that night we went out into the small interior court so prevalent in New Orleans and drove nine stakes into the ground. The left leg of a chicken was tied to each stake. Then a fire was built with the nine sticks on which the name had been written. The ground was sprinkled all over with the Four Thieves Vinegar and Turner began his dance. From the fire to the circle of fluttering chickens and back again to the fire. The feathers were picked from the heads of the chickens in the frenzy of the dance and scattered to the four winds. He called the victim's name each time as he whirled three times with the chicken's head-feathers in his hand, then he flung them far.

The terrified chickens flopped and fluttered frantically in the dim firelight. I had been told to keep up the chant of the victim's name in rhythm and to beat the ground with a stick. This I did with fervor and Turner danced on. One by one the chickens were seized and killed by having their heads pulled off. But Turner was in such a condition with his whirling and dancing that he seemed in a hypnotic state. When the last fowl was dead, Turner drank a great draught of wine and sank before the altar. When he arose, we gathered some ashes from the fire and sprinkled the bodies of the dead chickens and I was told to get out the car. We drove out one of the main highways for a mile and threw one of the chickens away. Then another mile and another chicken until the nine dead chickens had been disposed of. The spirits of the dead chickens had been instructed never to let the trouble-maker pass inward to New Orleans again after he had passed them going out.

One day Turner told me that he had taught me all that he could and he was quite satisfied with me. He wanted me to stay and work with him as a partner. He said that soon I would be in possession of the entire business, for the spirit had spoken to him and told him that I was the last doctor that he would make; that one year and seventy-nine days from then he would die. He wanted me to stay with him to the end. It has been a great sorrow to me that I could not say yes.

Travel Update

Though Charles Dudley Warner found a voodoo ceremony he could drop in on (apparently he could have seen others as well), and though Zora Neale Hurston found hoodoo doctors to initiate her, the present-day visitor probably will have to be content with a few sites with past voodoo connections and the popular Historic Voodoo Museum on Dumaine Street. The museum is a mishmash of pictures, dolls (for "doll magic"), a rather large python, Catholic statues, an altar, and a variety of gris-gris (charms—ranging from animal bones to dried bats to holy cards to alligator and raccoon penises). The shop at the museum sells candles and voodoo kits and will make up a gris-gris bag to order. A voodoo walking tour also leaves daily from the museum. How the visitor chooses to view all this is a matter of individual taste and perspective.

New Orleans voodoo certainly is in need of historical investigation, its development still unclear. No doubt magical practices related to voodoo are still common in Louisiana. But whether voodoo has survived as an organized religious practice is another question. There is some indication that it has, in isolated ways, and certainly there has been a revival of interest in it, particularly among African Americans who see it as an aspect of African culture. However, whatever survivals there may be have remained generally very private and not open to public view.

In the popular mind voodoo is inextricably associated with the woman reputed to have been its chief practitioner in the nineteenth century, Marie Laveau. The portrait of Laveau noted by Hurston can be seen at the Louisiana State Museum, which occupies the Cabildo on Jackson Square (as well as the Presbytere and other historically significant buildings). The supposed tomb of Marie Laveau is indicative of the survival of magical practices related to voodoo; located in St. Louis Cemetery Number 1 on Rampart Street, it is generally covered by marks—most commonly X's—made with chalk or other substances, put there to bring favors or luck. Several other tombs in the cemetery are associated with famous voodoo practitioners, including Malvina Latour and Sanité Dédé, and these too may have markings or offerings—rang-

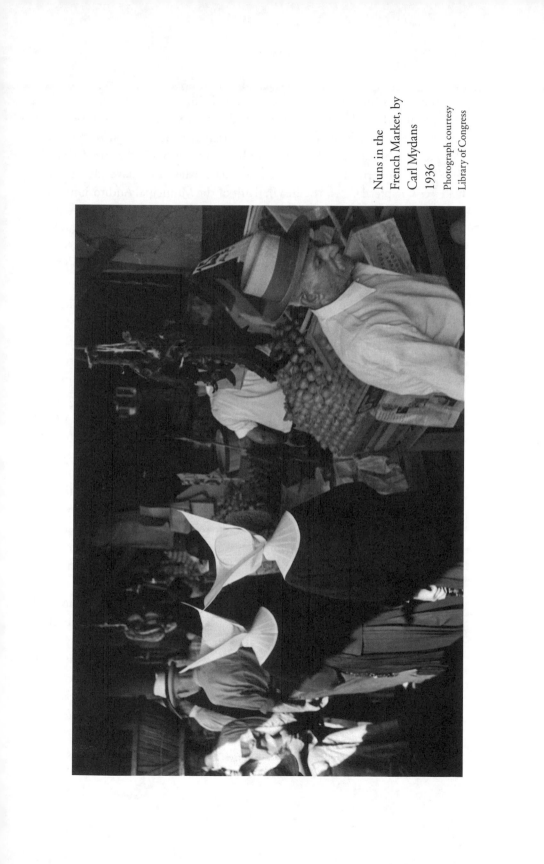

Nuns in the
French Market, by
Carl Mydans
1936
Photograph courtesy
Library of Congress

ing from shells and loose change to bottles of liquor and cane syrup—left at them. Stores that sell supplies for magical practices include F & F Botanica Supply at 801 North Broad Street (the Pharmacy Museum on Royal Street also has a case displaying voodoo supplies). Rumor has it that from time to time voodoo offerings pop up in Congo Square, where the "slave" dances were held (see Chapter 1), now the area in front of the Municipal Auditorium. And we can only speculate as to why Ernest "Dutch" Morial, the first African American mayor of New Orleans, was buried in a newly constructed tomb— itself a rarity—right next to Marie Laveau's last resting place. Highway 61, which Hurston followed for her nighttime outdoor ritual, is the Airline Highway, for many years the main road from New Orleans to Baton Rouge.

Voodoo notwithstanding, Louisiana today has no dearth of intriguing and dramatic manifestations of the spiritual. One religious movement in which "the churches' belief and ritual are traceable to Louisiana voodoo" is that of the Spiritual churches of the New Orleans area.[7] There are fifty or more such churches in the city, most of them very small, all of them almost exclusively African American. Spirit possession and spirit guides are central to their worship; their services are highly emotional and dramatic (and no doubt would shock Mrs. Bremer's companion). Church members vociferously deny any voodoo connection, tracing their origins to a woman named Leafy Anderson, who came to New Orleans from Chicago in the 1920s (there are Spiritual churches outside New Orleans, though those of the Crescent City are distinctive). They mean, of course, to reject voodoo's negative reputation for evil and magic, which certainly play no part in their religion. However, in their emphasis on spirit possession and in their syncretism (the Spiritual churches blend elements of Protestantism, Catholicism, American spiritualism, and African belief systems), they can be compared to voodoo and similar Caribbean and Brazilian religions like Santería. The Spiritual churches are not and should not be treated as tourist attractions, but like many other churches they will welcome visitors sincerely interested in learning about Spiritual beliefs and practices. In recent years Spiritual ministers have appeared at the New Orleans Jazz and Heritage Festival to discuss their beliefs and practices with the public. For excellent photodocumentation of the Spiritual churches, consult Michael P. Smith's *Spirit World: Pattern in the Expressive Folk Culture of*

---

7. Claude F. Jacobs, "Spirit Guides and Possession in the New Orleans Black Spiritual Churches," *Journal of American Folklore,* CII (1989), 49.

A New Orleans nun

From Charles Dudley
Warner, "New Orleans,"
Harper's Monthly,
January, 1887

Afro-American New Orleans (New Orleans, 1984), and for a study of the churches, see Claude F. Jacobs and Andrew Kaslow, *The Spiritual Churches of New Orleans: Origins, Belief, and Rituals of an African-American Religion* (Knoxville, Tenn., 1991). For voodoo itself, see Jessie Gaston Mulira, "The Case of Voodoo in New Orleans," in *Africanisms in American Culture*, ed. Joseph E. Holloway (Bloomington, Ind., 1990), 34–68. In the 1930s an Episcopal priest named Harry Middleton Hyatt did an extensive series of interviews with African American practioners of magic throughout the South. He published transcripts of these interviews as *Hoodoo, Conjuration, Witchcraft, Rootwork* (4 vols.; n.p., 1970–72); the texts from Louisiana provide an interesting window into the magical practices locally associated with voodoo. Like Hurston, Hyatt found Algiers to be a center for practitioners. Algiers is located across the Mississippi from New Orleans proper and can be easily reached by the Canal Street ferry. Though it no longer has the reputation of being a locality for voodoo, it is an interesting older section little visited by tourists. *Geopsychic Wonders of New Orleans,* with photographs by D. Eric Bookhardt and text by Jon Newlin (New Orleans, 1978), presents a hip, tongue-in-cheek view of the odd spirituality of the Crescent City.

What Fredrika Bremer meant by "the African Church" is not clear; there was more than one African American congregation in New Orleans at that time.

In the northeastern corner of Louisiana (in such towns as Winnsboro), some African American churches still perform the Easter Rock ritual, which clearly comes out of African cultural retentions (such as Bremer and her companion witnessed in New Orleans, though of a different variety). This ceremony takes place just after midnight on Easter morning. A procession comes into the church led by a woman who pulls on a banner (with the name of the church), causing the banner to rock with the rhythm of the people shuffling along in the procession. She is followed by twelve women in white carrying lighted lamps, and they all march—in effect, dance—around a table. As the ceremony progresses, they shuffle and sway more vigorously, receive symbolic objects, choose partners, sing, and partake of food before all proceed to the sunrise Easter service conducted by the minister of the church. Information on churches holding the service needs to be obtained locally. For historical and cultural background, consult Harry Oster, "Easter Rock Revisited: A Study in Acculturation," *Louisiana Folklore Miscellany,* I, no. 3 (1958), 21–43.

The New Orleans jazz funeral is a quasi-religious rite that has become world-famous. An African American tradition, it involves a funeral progression from church or funeral parlor to the cemetery. A brass band accompanies the body and mourners and plays solemnly on the way to the cemetery but erupts into joyous music after the body is left at the grave. Crowds of people gather to follow the band, swaying and dancing as they go (a second-line in New Orleans parlance). Brass bands and parades have a long tradition in New Orleans, and the use of bands at funerals for whites was not unknown. Today the rites are popularly associated with the funerals of jazz musicians, but various benevolent and burial societies in the black community provide funerals for members, and the funeral may include a brass band. Obviously, jazz funerals only take place when a death has occurred, so there is no way to schedule attending one much in advance. News of a funeral tends to travel through an underground network of jazz enthusiasts, so visitors to the city have no easy way of hearing about one unless they have the right local contacts. Places to inquire are Preservation Hall, the Palm Court Cafe on Decatur Street, radio station WWOZ, the William Ransom Hogan Jazz Archive at Tulane University, or Donna's Bar and Grill on Rampart, a hangout for brass band players.

In many ways New Orleans remains the intensely Catholic city Latrobe observed, a result of its French and Spanish past. Mardi Gras, though hardly a religious occasion in itself, stems from the need to celebrate before the coming of the penitential season of Lent. Attempts are still made to bring the celebration to a close by the midnight coming of Ash Wednesday. The next morning finds many Orleanians showing up at church to receive ashes on their foreheads. The religious occasion noted by A. Oakey Hall, All Saints' Day—whereby the dead are honored and commemorated—still has a particular vitality in the Crescent City and elsewhere in Louisiana that goes beyond the day's being a nationally observed Catholic holy day of obligation. An account of the November 1 occasion in the 1930s describes hordes of people coming to the cemeteries, and gumbo and "Creole beer" being sold at the gates.[8] Today the activity in such cemeteries as St. Roch's is more muted, but large numbers of people still come, bringing flowers to decorate graves and tombs. Traditionally this was a social as well as a religious occasion, a time for family members and friends to visit with each other (and, symbolically, with the departed ancestors).

The New Orleans cemeteries, with their ornate tombs and communal wall "ovens" (this local term refers to groups of small, one-person vaults set in the cemetery walls) for providing the above-ground burial precipitated by the high water table and local custom, have themselves been prominent attractions for many years. They suggest a small city where the dead remain among the living and are certainly prominent features of the cultural landscape. St. Louis Cemetery Number 1 is near the French Quarter and attracts some visitors, though it is near a high-crime neighborhood. St. Louis Number 2 is a few blocks away and visited less because of the perceived crime problem. St. Louis

8. Lyle Saxon, Edward Dreyer, and Robert Tallant, comps., *Gumbo Ya-Ya: A Collection of Louisiana Folk Tales* (Boston, 1945), 356–65.

Cemetery Number 3 is out Esplanade Avenue near Bayou St. John. Lafayette Cemetery is in the Garden District across the street from Commander's Palace Restaurant and has been undergoing restoration; as a result it is not currently open to the public. Some bus tours include a cemetery visit, and the Jean Lafitte National Park has offered cemetery tours as part of its programs. The custom of above-ground burial seems to have started during the Spanish colonial period because it so suited local conditions.

Even more dramatic All Saints' Day activities take place outside New Orleans. Several communities maintain traditional nighttime vigils in the cemeteries, which are cleaned and decorated in the days preceding. In Lacombe, for example, across Lake Pontchartrain from New Orleans, members of the community begin to gather in a number of small cemeteries at dusk and begin lighting candles on graves. By the time darkness falls, the cemeteries light up the night with a soft glow. People socialize, and a parish priest makes the rounds to bless the graves. The scene might sound like an eerie one—masses of long white candles flickering on white tombs out in the woods—but it is actually cheerfully pretty. The main cemeteries are the LaFontaine, just off Highway 190 near the post office; the Williams, back in the woods down the street from the parish church (groups of people going to the cemetery can be followed to the path leading to it); and the Osay Ordogne on Fish Hatchery Road near a shrine to Our Lady of Lourdes. Candlelight vigils (which at one time lasted all night) also take place in and around Lafitte on Bayou Barataria (the Fleming Cemetery, built on an Indian mound on the edge of the water, is especially interesting), in the parish cemetery at Pierre Part, and at St. Augustine's Church on Cane River (see also Chapter 4).

A Catholic feast day that brings about public devotion of another sort is St. Joseph's Day (March 19), important to south Louisiana's Italian community (St. Joseph is a saint of central importance in Italy). For a number of years, the St. Joseph's altar tradition has been carried out particularly by people of Sicilian ancestry. Several legends account for the origin of the tradition, including one that tells of a famine in Sicily ended by the intercession of the saint; altars were erected to give thanks. In Louisiana the altars traditionally have been erected in private homes by individuals or families who have promised to make the altar in return for some spiritual favor from St. Joseph, though in recent years altars made by Catholic organizations in public places have become more common. The altars may be small or big and elaborate but customarily consist of rows and rows of vegetarian food items, including specially baked breads. Preparation may take weeks or months. The maker of the altar may sit by it in prayer on the eve of March 19. A priest will bless the altar, and rosaries and other prayers may be said, in English or Italian. On the day of the feast itself, a skit is performed, usually by children, in which the actors pretend to be members of the Holy Family looking for lodging. They are rejected at first but then let into the house with the altar, where they are sat down and fed a feast. Often the givers of the altar will next serve a feast to all who come, sometimes great multitudes of people. The altars, which are known in other places but have particular vitality in Louisiana, are held in various communities. In larger cities like New Orleans and Baton Rouge, the givers of altars invite visitors by classified newspaper advertisements; there is a special section for them in the classifieds. Those who come can expect at least a few cookies and the all-important dried fava bean, thought to bring luck and prosperity and carried by many as a talisman all year. (The Spiritual churches may also erect St. Joseph's altars, a custom they have borrowed from their Sicilian neighbors.) For more information, see Ethelyn Orso, *The St. Joseph Altar Traditions of South Louisiana* (Lafayette, 1990).

St. Roch's cemetery (in the New Orleans neighborhood known as the Ninth Ward, at St. Roch and Derbigny Streets) is active on All Saints' Day, but its chapel is also indicative of other aspects of Louisiana's Catholicism. In a small, gated side room can be seen numerous objects presented to the chapel and St. Roch to mark the granting of curative miracles: crutches, leg braces, and the like, as well as small stone plaques with "Thanks" or "Merci" for favors received from the saint. The shrine of St. Anne, located at 2101 Ursulines at North Johnson (a shrine with a street address!) is another landmark to devotion in the Crescent City. It looks almost like someone's yard—a little corner plot surrounded by chain link with various garden decorations sprinkled around the property—that just happens to have a massive, faux rock grotto at one end. A religious-articles shop hidden in the rock sells statues and rosaries, holy water is dispensed, and the faithful seeking spiritual favors—especially women seeking a husband—climb a flight of stairs to a crucifixion scene at the top of the grotto on their knees, reciting a prayer on each step. In the past the shrine was especially busy during lunch time, though recently the saint has been forced to keep more limited hours, being open mostly in the mornings.

South Louisiana's countryside is full of signs of Catholic devotion, from the profusion of yard shrines to what is reputedly the world's smallest chapel:

a tiny, privately maintained frame structure just about big enough for a priest, his servers, and a congregation of one or two during mass (on Louisiana 405, just across from the Mississippi levee in a community called Point Pleasant). On the same River Road between Donaldsonville and Vacherie, the annual St. Amico Procession takes place. The saint is no longer recognized by the Catholic Church, but the procession has always been family-organized, not church-sponsored. It commemorates a miracle experienced by a local Italian family, whose gravely ill child was cured by a mysterious stranger thought to have been St. Amico; a statue of the saint is carried along the River Road to a private chapel. On Good Friday not far from St. Martinville, the parish priest from Catahoula leads local people in making a series of outdoor stations of the cross along Louisiana 96. The stations are posted on trees (including one at the famous and well-marked alley of trees that once extended to the Durand Plantation and that legend says was decorated for a wedding by sprinkling gold and silver dust among specially spun spider webs; the alley is itself lovely and peaceful, the little station adding to its natural cathedral-like quality).

One of the most amazing spiritual sites in Louisiana is located near Tickfaw in Tangipahoa Parish. Here is a small swath of land—a Catholic outpost surrounded by little country Baptist churches in this non-Catholic part of Louisiana—where believers hold that the Virgin Mary has been appearing since 1989. In that year a pipe fitter named Alfredo Raimundo began having visions of the Virgin, and before long others were flocking to his property, many of them claiming to see her also and to have experienced curing and other spiritual favors. Though the initial fervor died down, people still come, and Raimundo's property, a former landfill, has been developed by many hands into a strange conglomeration of outdoor shrines, chapels, and decorative features. There are statues under cupolas, wrought-iron halos, miniature model churches, garden benches, circles of rose bushes, arbors, pedestals, designs made in cinder block, and structures of indeterminate use. There is a spigot where holy water is dispensed because the Virgin directed one should be installed; there are outdoor ovens because she directed Raimundo to bake bread for all who come. Visitors leave Polaroid photographs that they believe show miraculous designs and images and deposit such messages as "Holy Father, please help me find a good job" in a particular chapel. This assemblage of the sacred can be reached by exiting Interstate 55 at Louisiana 442 and following signage to the religious-articles store run by Mrs. Raimundo.

As remote as Tickfaw, though firmly set in the midst of Catholic Cajun country, is the burial place of Charlene Richard, a folk saint whose grave has become a pilgrimage site. Charlene died of leukemia at the age of twelve in 1959. She is said to have been a pious young girl and to have offered up her final sufferings as a sacrifice to God. The Lafayette hospital room in which she died became associated with miraculous cures, as did she herself. Large numbers of people—sometimes busloads—now make their way to her grave to ask for favors, though her status has been viewed skeptically by the Catholic Church (as have the Tickfaw apparitions). The grave is located in the church cemetery of the hamlet of Richard on Louisiana 370 in Acadia Parish and can easily be found—the attentions paid to it (flowers, photographs, and petitions placed on its slab) give it an obvious prominence. Petitions to Charlene can also be found in the nearby church.

There is also a Louisiana site that has been officially recognized by the Catholic Church as a place where a miracle took place. This is the shrine to St. John Berchmans at the Academy of the Sacred Heart in Grand Coteau. Today it is a small chapel with a wooden Gothic-revival altar with a statue of the saint flanked by paintings depicting the miracle. Formerly it was an infirmary, and in 1866 a young novice nun lay dying there. John Berchmans, a Jesuit who had died in 1621 and had been beatified in 1865, appeared to her in a vision; she was well by morning. This miracle was instrumental in Berchmans' canonization in 1888. The faithful come to the shrine, sometimes in large groups, and often leave petitions on small pieces of paper in a basket provided. The shrine is in the school, which has been continuously operated—even during the Civil War—by the same order of nuns since it was founded in 1821. The school itself is very interesting, a great rambling structure, a graceful institutional version of antebellum architecture that suddenly looms up in the Louisiana countryside. Its atmosphere is sylvan and peaceful, the sounds of happy schoolchildren drifting up to the shrine. On the ground floor is a lovely chapel dating from the 1850s, a combination of Gothic-revival touches with a striking, modern, back-lit risen Christ over the altar and a simplicity of form reminiscent of New England meeting houses.

Traveler writers haven't had much to say about the mostly Protestant religious traditions of central and north Louisiana, so no selections on the subject have been included in this chapter. However, these traditions are colorful in their own right, and it is worth pointing out some notable sites. Though it is but a shadow of its former self, the vast complex of buildings that made up the religious empire of Jimmy Swaggart stand in Baton Rouge on Bluebonnet Lane (Bluebonnet exit from Interstate 10). Swaggart enjoyed wide popularity as a television evangelist, and his operation boomed in the late 1980s until he was caught in the midst of sex scandals when accused of patronizing prostitutes. He was a colorful and controversial figure—a showman who had much in common with the two Louisiana performers who were cousins he grew up with, rockabilly star Jerry Lee Lewis and country singer Micky Gilley—and some would see something distinctly Louisianian in his highly publicized rise and downfall.

A more decorous monument to the Protestantism of north Louisiana can be found in the Emy-Lou Biedenharn Bible Museum in Monroe. Endowed by Ms. Biedenharn, an opera singer whose family fortune came from bottling Coca-Cola, the museum (2006 Riverside Drive) occupies part of her former residence and displays various notable editions of the Bible and related religious literature and art.

In general, north Louisiana shares in the religious culture of the rest of the South, and the landscape is dotted with places for camp meetings, tents for religious revivals, and tiny country churches.

Index